Monuments
and Historic Places
of America

MACMILLAN
PROFILES

Monuments
and Historic Places
of America

WITHDRAWN

MACMILLAN LIBRARY REFERENCE USA
New York

Cover design by Berrian Design

Macmillan Library Reference USA
1633 Broadway, 7th Floor
New York, NY 10019

Manufactured in the United States of America

Printing number
1 2 3 4 5 6 7 8 9 10

ISBN: 0-02-865374-2

Library of Congress Cataloging-in-Publication Data

Monuments and historic places of America.
p. cm.—(Macmillan profiles)
Includes bibliographical references and index.
Summary: More than ninety articles describe monuments and memorials that commemorate people and events from our nation's history as well as battlefields, forts, factories, homes, churches, cemeteries, and laboratories.
ISBN 0-02-865374-2 (alk. paper)
1. Historic sites—United States—Encyclopedias, Juvenile. 2. Monuments—United States—Encyclopedias, Juvenile. 3. United States—History, Local—Encyclopedias, Juvenile. [1. Historic sites—Encyclopedias. 2. Monuments—Encyclopedias. 3. United States—History, Local—Encyclopedias.] I. Macmillan Library Reference USA. II. Series.

E159.M65 1999
973'.03—dc21

99–051559

Front cover clockwise from top: Mount Rushmore (copyright ©1999 PhotoDisc, Inc.); USS *Arizona* Memorial (CORBIS/Wolfgang Kaehler); The Alamo (CORBIS); Statue of Liberty (copyright ©1999 PhotoDisc, Inc.)

This paper meets the requirements of ANSI/NISO Z39.48-1992 (Permanence of Paper).

Contents

Preface ix

The Alamo 1
Alfred P. Murrah Federal Building 5
    WACO SIEGE 8
Amoskeag Mills 10
Angel Island Immigration Station 14
Appomattox Court House 19
    UNCONDITIONAL SURRENDER GRANT 22
Arlington National Cemetery 23

Belle of Louisville Steamboat 29
Benjamin Franklin National Memorial 34
The Bering Land Bridge 38

Camp David 45
Castillo de San Marcos 50
Charles W. Morgan Whaling Ship 54
Cumberland Gap 58

Daniel Freeman Homestead 65
    TIMBER CULTURE ACT OF 1873 70
Dealey Plaza 71
Dinosaur Ridge 76
Donner Pass 81

Edison Laboratories 87
Effigy Mounds 92
El Morro Fortress 98
Ellis Island 102
Ethan Allen Homestead 108

Ford's Theatre 113
Fort Clatsop 119
Fort Delaware 125
Fort Laramie 129
Fort Larned 132
Fort Mandan 136

SACAGAWEA 139
Fort McHenry 141
Fort Raleigh 147
Fort Sumter 150
Franklin Delano Roosevelt Memorial 154

Gateway Arch 159
Gettysburg Battlefield 162
Golden Spike National Historic Site 165

Harpers Ferry 171
Haymarket Square 176
Hearst Castle 181
Highland Park Ford Plant 187
Hoover Dam 191

Independence Hall 197
Iolani Palace 201

Jamestown 207
Jefferson Memorial 211
John F. Kennedy Space Center 217

Kettle Moraine 222
Kitty Hawk 226
Korean War Veterans Memorial 231

Lexington Green 237
Lincoln Memorial 241
Little Bighorn Battlefield 246
Little Rock Central High School 250
Lorraine Motel 255
Los Alamos National Laboratory 259

Manzanar War Relocation Center 265
Mayo Clinic 271
Melrose Estate 275
Mesa Verde 281
    NATIONAL PARK SERVICE 284
Monticello 286
Mount Rushmore 290
    THE BADLANDS 293
Mount Vernon 295

O.K. Corral 299

Plymouth Rock 305
Pony Express Stables 310
Portland Head Lighthouse 314

Rankin House 319
    UNCLE TOM'S CABIN 322
Rhea County Courthouse 325
Russell Cave 330

Salem Witch Trials Memorial 335
    A TWENTIETH-CENTURY WITCH-HUNT 338
San Carlos Borromeo Mission 340
Spanish Cabildo 344
    NATIONAL TRUST FOR HISTORIC PRESERVATION 348
Statue of Liberty 349
Stone Mountain Memorial 354
Sutter's Mill 358

Teapot Dome Oil Reserve 365
    OREGON TRAIL LANDMARKS 368
Tippecanoe Battlefield 368
    "TIPPECANOE AND TYLER TOO!" 372
Trinity Church 374
    NATIONAL REGISTER OF HISTORIC PLACES 377
Tuskegee Institute 378

USS *Arizona* Memorial 385
    FIFTIETH ANNIVERSARY OF PEARL HARBOR 389

Valley Forge 391
Vanderbilt Mansion 396
Vietnam Veterans Memorial 401

Washington Monument 407
Watergate Complex 410
    SCANDAL–GATE 413
Weedpatch Camp 415
Wesleyan Chapel 419
White Bird Canyon 425
The White House 430
    DOLLEY MADISON 433
Whitman Mission 435
Wounded Knee 438

Yorktown 443

Suggested Reading 449
Glossary 473
Photo Credits 497
Article Sources 501
Index 503

Preface

Macmillan Profiles: *Monuments and Historic Places of America* is a unique reference featuring over ninety articles describing monuments and memorials that commemorate important people and events from our nation's history, as well as battlefields, forts, factories, homes, churches, cemeteries, laboratories, and other places where American history happened. Macmillan Library Reference recognizes the need for reliable, accurate, and accessible reference works covering important aspects of the social studies and history curriculum. The Macmillan Profiles series can help meet that need by providing new collections of articles that were carefully selected to complement middle and high school history curricula.

Each article in *Monuments and Historic Places of America* was chosen to represent an important topic in the history of North America from the Mesozoic Era to the late twentieth century. At least one site from every American state plus Puerto Rico has been included, and every major historical period is covered. Each article focuses on a single historical site, then uses the site as a springboard for a broader discussion of the history that surrounds it or the history that it symbolizes as well as the people involved in that history.

The article list was based on the following criteria: relevance to the social studies and history curriculum of American high schools and middle schools and representation of as broad a cultural, geographic, and chronological range as possible. The article list was refined and expanded in response to advice from a lively and generous team of librarians from school and public libraries across the United States.

FEATURES

Monuments and Historical Places of America is part of Macmillan's **Profiles Series.** To add visual appeal and enhance the usefulness of the volume, the page format was designed to include the following helpful features:

■ **Time Lines:** Found throughout the text in the margins, time lines provide a quick reference source for dates and important events in the history of these historical sites.

- **Definitions and Glossary:** Brief definitions of important terms in the main text can be found in the margins. A glossary at the end of the book provides students with an even broader list of definitions.

- **Sidebars:** Appearing in shaded boxes throughout the volume, these provocative asides relate to and amplify topics.

- **Pull Quotes:** Found throughout the text in the margins, pull quotes highlight essential facts.

- **Suggested Reading:** An extensive list of books, articles, and Web sites about the monuments and historic places covered in the volume will help students who want to do further research.

- **Index:** A thorough index provides thousands of additional points of entry into the work.

ACKNOWLEDGMENTS

We thank our colleagues who publish the Merriam Webster *Collegiate© Dictionary*. Definitions in the margins and many of the glossary terms come from the distinguished *Webster's Collegiate© Dictionary*, Tenth Edition, 1996.

Monuments and Historic Places of America contains 130 photographs. Acknowledgments of sources for the illustrations can be found on page 497.

This work would not have been possible without the hard work and creativity of our staff. We offer our sincere thanks to all who helped create this marvelous work.

Macmillan Library Reference

The Alamo

The Alamo, a former Spanish mission built in the 1740s, is most famous as the site of a battle fought between a small band of Texas soldiers, led by James Bowie and William Barrett Travis, and the Mexican Army commanded by Antonio López de Santa Anna, from February 23 to March 6, 1836. With about three million visitors per year, the Alamo is the most frequently visited historic site in Texas.

Authorized by the viceroy of New Spain (Mexico) in 1716, the Mission San Antonio de Valero was established in the new city of San Antonio, Texas, by the Franciscan priest Antonio de San Buenaventura Olivares and a company of Indian converts from the Mission San Francisco Solano on the Rio Grande. Named in honor of St. Anthony of Padua and the duke of Valero, viceroy of Mexico, the San Antonio mission was a complex of structures built around a small stone tower and devoted to the agricultural and religious education of the Indians. When the tower collapsed in a severe storm around 1724, the modern site was selected, but a permanent chapel was not built until about 1744. The stone structure collapsed about 1756, and construction of a second chapel, its floor plan shaped as a cross, was begun. Never completed, it was a part of a four-acre walled complex that included priests' quarters, Indian quarters, a **granary**, storehouses, and workshops. After epidemics depopulated the San Antonio missions in 1778, the San Antonio de Valero was converted to a parish church in 1793.

Ignored by the church in the early nineteenth century, the structure became a barracks for a company of Spanish cavalry.

> *"These, and other grievances, were patiently borne by the people of Texas, until they reached that point at which forbearance ceases to be a virtue. We then took up arms in defence of the national constitution."*
> Texas Declaration of Independence, March 1836

granary: a storehouse for threshed grain.

The Alamo in San Antonio, Texas.

"Remember the Alamo" became the battle cry of the Texas army in its final victory over Santa Anna.

The cavalry used the mission from about 1801 to 1812 and gave the structure the name by which it became known to history: the Alamo. Spanish for "cottonwood," the name referred to a landmark cottonwood tree on a ranch near the town of San José y Santiago del Alamo de Parras (today called Viesca) where the cavalry company was organized. The Mexican army occupied the Alamo from 1821 until 1835, when it fell into the hands of rebellious Texans at the outbreak of their war for independence from Mexico.

After three hundred years of Spanish rule, Mexico had won independence in 1821, but was shaken by political instability that hampered its efforts to keep a firm hold on the Texas territory, where Americans were settling in alarming numbers. By 1830 the Americans in Texas outnumbered Mexicans by three to one. The Texas Revolution broke out in Gonzales in 1835 when Mexican forces tried to disarm the Americans; the Mexicans were routed and driven out of the territory. At a convention called at Washington-on-the-Brazos, Texans declared their independence from Mexico on March 2, 1836.

The month before that, however, Mexican president General Santa Anna marched on San Antonio with a force of about 2,000 to 4,000 men, intent on wresting Texas from American control forever. Mexican general Martín Perfecto Cos had used the Alamo as his headquarters before the fall of San Antonio on December 9, 1835, and built up the structure as a fortification. In the face of the advance of Santa Anna's army into Texas, a group of about 145 Texans commanded by colonels Travis and Bowie entered the Alamo on February 23, 1836. The thirteen days of siege that followed became legendary.

Travis and Bowie could have retreated in time to escape harm by Santa Anna, but chose instead to take shelter in the Alamo and prepare for battle. Travis sent a courier for reinforcements. His message read: "I have sustained a continual Bombardment and a cannonade for 24 hours and have not lost a man. . . . Our flag still proudly waves from the wall. I shall never surrender or retreat. . . . VICTORY OR DEATH." Despite Travis's requests for aid, only thirty-two men in a detachment from Goliad, Texas, joined him, breaking through Mexican lines into the fort on March 1. Travis had approximately 183 men and at least eighteen pieces of artillery to defend the fort against Santa Anna's thousands. The Alamo's defenders, coming from some eighteen of the United States and several European countries, were, for the most part, relatively new to Texas, although they were joined by a number of native Texans of Hispanic descent.

On the morning of March 6 the Mexican army advanced to end the siege. Thrown back in their first attempt, Santa Anna's men succeeded in entering the fort on their second charge and overwhelmed the defenders. Among the rebels was the former Tennessee congressman David (Davy) Crockett. According to some accounts, Crockett and five or six others survived the battle but were executed on Santa Anna's command. Because they were cut off, the defenders of the Alamo did not know that Texas had declared its independence on March 2. In fact, the flag flown over the Alamo was the Mexican flag with the date 1824 written on it, a date commemorating the signing of the first constitution of the Mexican Republic after Mexico had won its independence from Spain. It was the Mexican Republic that the Texans claimed to be defending against the **tyranny** of Santa Anna before declaring their own independence.

Nevertheless, the defenders of the Alamo, all of whom were killed, became martyrs to the Texas cause. In a misguided attempt

> "We, therefore, the delegates, with plenary powers, of the people of Texas, in solemn convention assembled, appealing to a candid world for the necessities of our condition, do hereby resolve and declare, that our political connection with the Mexican nation has forever ended, and that the people of Texas do now constitute a free, sovereign, and independent republic."
>
> Texas Declaration of Independence, March 1836

tyranny: cruel use of power.

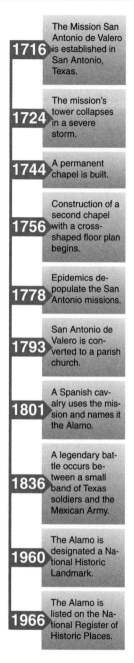

1716 The Mission San Antonio de Valero is established in San Antonio, Texas.

1724 The mission's tower collapses in a severe storm.

1744 A permanent chapel is built.

1756 Construction of a second chapel with a cross-shaped floor plan begins.

1778 Epidemics depopulate the San Antonio missions.

1793 San Antonio de Valero is converted to a parish church.

1801 A Spanish cavalry uses the mission and names it the Alamo.

1836 A legendary battle occurs between a small band of Texas soldiers and the Mexican Army.

1960 The Alamo is designated a National Historic Landmark.

1966 The Alamo is listed on the National Register of Historic Places.

annexation: the incorporation of a state or country.

to strike fear among the rebels, Santa Anna ordered fifteen noncombatants—women, children, and slaves—released so that they could carry the news of the fate of the Alamo defenders to all Texans. "Remember the Alamo" became the battle cry of the Texas army in its final victory over Santa Anna at San Jacinto on April 21, 1836.

After Santa Anna was compelled to recognize Texas's independence, Texans sought admission to the United States, but antislavery forces were opposed to the admission of another slave state, and Texas had to wait almost ten years. During that time, the independent Lone Star State was officially the Republic of Texas (1836–45). Mexico was furious when President John Tyler narrowly pushed the **annexation** of Texas through Congress. When American ambassador John Slidell was sent to Mexico to smooth relations and to negotiate the purchase of New Mexico (part of which was claimed by Texas) and California, Mexico declined to negotiate. The United States then prepared to take by force what it could not obtain by diplomacy and money. The Mexican War, also called the Mexican-American War, raged from 1846 to 1848. In the Treaty of Guadalupe Hidalgo (February 2, 1848), Mexico gave up two-fifths of its territory and received $15 million. The United States got New Mexico, present-day Arizona, and California.

Following the defeat of Santa Anna at San Jacinto, Texas granted the ruined Alamo to the Roman Catholic church in 1841, but the church did not use the mission. In 1848, after Texas had joined the Union, the Alamo became a supply depot for the U.S. Army. It was the U.S. Army that added the arched façade in 1850; the buildings were simpler at the time of the battle. Gradually, the city of San Antonio grew around the old mission and fort, and developers encroached on the mission grounds. In 1878, after the army relocated to a new supply facility at Fort Sam Houston, the property was purchased by Hugo Grenet, who used the convent as a retail store and the chapel as a warehouse. After Grenet's death in 1882, the convent remained in private hands, and the chapel reverted to the Roman Catholic church, which sold the property to the state of Texas in 1883.

That year, Adina de Zavala, granddaughter of the Mexican-born first vice president of the Republic of Texas, Lorenzo de Zavala, initiated a campaign to raise seventy-five thousand dollars to purchase the convent. After the drive stalled, Clara Driscoll of San Antonio, one of the Daughters of the Republic of Texas, advanced a no-interest loan of twenty-five thousand dollars to hold the convent until the Texas legislature could appropriate the remaining funds, which it did in 1905. The legislature turned the administration and operation of the Alamo complex over to the Daughters of the Republic of Texas, who continue to maintain it. In 1911, after a controversy was settled between Driscoll, who wanted to tear down the convent, and de Zavala, who wanted to save both convent and chapel, the Alamo—including both structures—became a museum and "The Shrine of Texas Liberty."

Since 1905 the Alamo has been cared for by the Daughters of the Republic of Texas. It was designated a National Historic Landmark in 1960 and was listed on the National Register of Historic Places in 1966. The convent was restored and dedicated as the Long Barrack Museum in 1968, and in 1985 an exhibit tracing the Alamo's history was installed in the museum. Visitors can also see the Wall of History, a permanent exhibit illustrating the history of Texas and the Alamo that was installed in 1997, and can view a film on the history of the Alamo.

The Alamo is a powerful symbol in the history of Texas and the American west. The old mission stirs strong emotions: for many, it is the cornerstone of Texas's fight for independence and statehood, and a key to the identity of modern Anglo Texas, while for many Mexicans and Mexican Americans, it is a symbol of imperial expansion and **disfranchisement**. The Alamo remains a point of tension between Mexican-American and Anglo populations in San Antonio and Texas, but it is also the most popular historic tourist attraction in the state. ◆

> *"I leave this rule for others when I'm dead, Be always sure you're right—then go ahead."*
> Davy Crockett, *Narrative of the Life of Colonel Crockett*, 1834

disfranchisement: the loss of a right or power.

Alfred P. Murrah Federal Building

OKLAHOMA CITY, OKLAHOMA

On October 25, 1998, United States vice president Al Gore stood on a flattened three acres where the Alfred P. Murrah Federal Building stood three and a half years earlier before a terrorist's bomb brought it down, killing 168 people—nineteen small children among them—and injuring 500. Gore turned the first shovel of earth for the construction of

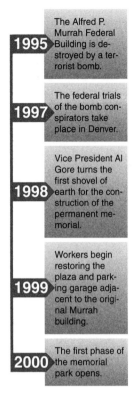

1995 The Alfred P. Murrah Federal Building is destroyed by a terrorist bomb.

1997 The federal trials of the bomb conspirators take place in Denver.

1998 Vice President Al Gore turns the first shovel of earth for the construction of the permanent memorial.

1999 Workers begin restoring the plaza and parking garage adjacent to the original Murrah building.

2000 The first phase of the memorial park opens.

a memorial that the people of Oklahoma City hoped would help rebuild their city both physically and spiritually from the worst act of terrorism in United States history.

April 19, 1995, had begun as an ordinary day for the nearly 500 employees in the Murrah building. At 9 A.M., mothers deposited their children in the second floor day care while on the other eight floors workers drank their morning coffee and greeted each other. Suddenly, at 9:02 A.M., their world exploded. First there was a blinding flash, then a noise so loud it numbed the ears. A harmless looking Ryder rental truck that had been parked at the curb had in fact been filled with a deadly combination of fuel oil and fertilizer. The explosion it created ripped a hole through the building to the top floor. Within seconds, the front of the nine-story building collapsed, each floor crashing through the other. Many people at the bottom died immediately under the cascade of cement beams. Others slid down with the collapsing floors, some dying and some surviving. Some employees on upper floors suddenly found themselves on ragged ledges, in danger of falling to their deaths. They choked on smoke and dust as they struggled to find stairwells.

Oklahoma City's rescue workers are always prepared for major disasters because Oklahoma sits in "Tornado Alley." But none were prepared for the horror they saw that morning. Firemen and police officers struggled to pull victims out from under concrete slabs, often unsuccessfully. By the end of the day, they had found their last live victim. The entire nation fixed its attention on Oklahoma City, shocked, sickened, and grieving.

Even as rescuers dug through the rubble, they and others began making personal memorials. Some scrawled comments on cement slabs. Saddened residents laid flowers at the site. From around the nation came cards, flowers, and toys. Within a few days, a chain-link fence surrounding the site became a spontaneous memorial. Visitors hung handwritten messages, stuffed animals, and photographs of loved ones on the fence. Four years after the explosion occurred, the fence still stood adorned with teddy bears, rosaries, hair ribbons, bracelets, poems, baseball caps, name badges, and T-shirts. Volunteers regularly collected the offerings and placed them among the nearly 40,000 archived items.

Soon an organization called the Oklahoma City National Memorial Foundation was formed. Families of victims worked together and decided they wanted the memorial to be a quiet place where visitors could rest and reflect on the senselessness of

terrorism and violence. In 1997 they held a design competition for a permanent memorial. The creation of a German-American design partnership won out over 623 other entries. The designers aimed to show the atrocity of what happened but also the hope for peace. The centerpiece would be 168 empty granite chairs on glass pedestals, each inscribed with the name of a victim and set in nine rows to represent the nine floors of the building. At night, light would illuminate the glass pedestals. Nineteen of the chairs would be smaller, to represent the children. An orchard of apple and pear trees would represent rescue workers, and a reflecting pool would offer calm. The memorial also included the "Survivor's Tree," an elm that had lived through the blast and became a beloved symbol to survivors. The memorial park was to open in phases, starting in late 2000. It would also include a museum and offices for the Memorial Institute for the Prevention of Terrorism.

The north side of the Alfred P. Murrah Federal Building in Oklahoma City, photographed on April 20, 1995, one day after the bomb blast.

Many survivors of that horrific day found that the emotional pain that started on April 19, 1995, did not vanish easily. In the city of 480,000, grief became a communal event. Therapists, counselors, and clergy made themselves available to Oklahoma City residents, especially those closely touched by the

Waco Siege

The deaths of four federal agents and seventy-eight members of the Branch Davidian religious group during a fifty-one-day siege of their commune headquarters outside Waco, Texas, provoked widespread controversy over the use of force in dealing with dissident sects. A botched and bloody attempt on February 28, 1993, to arrest the group's leader, David Koresh, on a weapons charge went badly awry. The cult had apparently been tipped off to the raid and ten people were killed in the ensuing gun battle, including four agents from the Bureau of Alcohol, Tobacco, and Firearms (ATF).

The action led to a fifty-one-day stalemate until U.S. attorney general Janet Reno ordered the use of force on April 19 to end the standoff. Tear gas and battering rams were used to enter the Branch Davidian compound. A raging fire engulfed "Ranch Apocalypse," killing about eighty people, including Koresh and seventeen children. Although some surviving members of the sect were tried for manslaughter and found not guilty, they were convicted of lesser charges and received extremely harsh sentences. Federal authorities believe that the Oklahoma City bombing, which took place exactly two years after Waco, was, in part, an act of vengeance for the destruction of the Branch Davidian cult.

event. However, many survivors, such as paramedics and police officers, found themselves haunted by guilt that they had lived while victims they could not save had died. These memories destroyed marriages, ruined careers, or caused nightmares and dependence on drugs or alcohol.

The pain of these survivors was compounded when, within four years of the bombing, at least half a dozen people closely linked to the disaster committed suicide. Army captain Laurence Martin had survived the blast but lost seven of his army colleagues. Martin's army career soon ended, and he had a failed love relationship. In October 1999, Martin, age forty-one, flew a single-engine Cessna plane up over Oklahoma City then dove the plane nose-first into a pasture. Two rescue workers, a federal prosecutor, a bomb-blast survivor, and the husband of one of the victims also killed themselves. At least twice as many attempted suicide, and many more report that they considered it. Mike Lenz, whose pregnant wife, Carrie, died in the bombing, broke down as he testified at the bombing suspect's trial about his own near-suicide. "There is nothing, nothing, more dangerous than a man who has no reason to live," he said.

He could have easily been speaking of the bomber himself. It did not take investigators long after the bombing to follow the chain of evidence leading to paranoid loner Timothy McVeigh, the bomber, and his friend Terry Nichols, who knew of the plan. The 1997 federal trials of the bomb conspirators took place in Denver, where defense lawyers hoped they could find an unbiased jury. Timothy McVeigh received a death sentence and Terry Nichols received life imprisonment. Prosecutors made the case that McVeigh had bombed the federal building in order to retaliate against the government for the federal raid on the Branch Davidian compound near Waco, Texas. McVeigh's bombing fell on the second anniversary of the raid, which had ended in the deaths of about eighty people. A third man, Michael Fortier, received a twelve-year prison sentence after he pleaded guilty to failing to alert authorities of McVeigh's bomb plot.

In May 1999 the Oklahoma legislature voted to redirect funds set aside for another trial of Terry Nichols. They instead marked the funds to help victims of deadly tornadoes that struck Oklahoma that month. Nichols, who was not in Oklahoma City the day of the blast, had been convicted in the federal trial of conspiring to bomb the building and of involuntary manslaughter in the deaths of eight federal agents in the blast. The state of Oklahoma intended to try Nichols for the deaths of the 160 other victims, and to seek the death penalty. Some of the victims' family members stated that Nichols's death would end their grief and bring closure to their sad story. But others, including the father of slain twenty-three-year-old Julie Marie Welch, opposed the death penalty.

In 1999 workers began restoring a half-block plaza area and an 800-space parking garage that were attached to the original Murrah building. Before the blast, many federal employees ate their lunches on the plaza and children played on swing sets there. The remnants of the blown-out building had been torn down, and the three-acre lawn that Gore stood on had been planted to cover the scars until the permanent memorial could take its place.

President Bill Clinton signed the Oklahoma City National Memorial Act of 1997 to establish the Oklahoma City National Memorial as a unit of the National Park System. The Act established the Oklahoma City Memorial Trust to manage the memorial. The Trust, a federal government corporation, would operate within the Department of the Interior in cooperation with the National Park Service. ◆

"The defendants herein, did knowingly, intentionally, willfully and maliciously conspire, combine and agree together and with others unknown to the Grand Jury to use a weapon of mass destruction . . . against persons within the United States and against property that was owned and used by the United States . . . resulting in death, grievous bodily injury and destruction of the building." Grand jury indictment against McVeigh and Nichols, U.S. District Court, August 10, 1995

Amoskeag Mills

paternalistic: controlling in a manner suggesting a father's relationship with his children.

shuttle: an instrument used in weaving to carry the thread back and forth.

spinning jenny: a spinning machine with several spindles to spin more than one thread.

spindle: a slender rod or pin used in spinning.

The textile mill complex at Manchester, New Hampshire, founded in 1838 by the Amoskeag Manufacturing Company, was part of a planned, **paternalistic** community in which employees' needs would be cared for in exchange for complete loyalty for the company. Operating until 1935, the complex was by 1915 the world's largest textile center.

The Industrial Revolution began in Britain's textile industry during the last half of the eighteenth century. It was sparked by a string of inventions that increased production by mechanizing work tasks previously performed by human labor. Among the many improvements devised by British and American mechanics were the flying **shuttle** of John Kay (1733), which speeded up weaving; the **spinning jenny** of James Hargreaves (1769) to mechanize spinning; the mechanical loom of Samuel Cartwright (1785) for mechanized weaving; the cotton gin of Eli Whitney (1794) for the mechanical removal of cottonseeds; the self-acting temple of Ira Draper (1816), which assured a constant cloth width; and ring spinning by John Thorp (1828) for increasing **spindle** speed. The construction of canal and railroad systems in the first half of the nineteenth century were crucial, since they created larger markets for the increased wool and cotton production made possible by these machines.

The mechanization of textile production changed the organization of labor. Previously, textiles had been a cottage industry, with workers operating out of their homes. The new machines made this arrangement impossible. The expensive new machines could not be distributed to each worker; furthermore they had to be grouped together at a nonhuman source of power (along a body of water), thus beginning the factory system.

In the United States, the textile industry emerged between the Revolutionary War and the War of 1812, when British mechanics who moved to America applied their skilled knowledge in their adopted homeland. The industry began in New England, where prosperous merchants were looking for ways to invest their large profits. In the 1790s Samuel Slater started up a number of small factories in the region's southern tier. A new phase began during the War of 1812 when a group of Boston merchants, with more resources than Slater, began establishing larger textile complexes. During the 1820s they started up a

Some of the buildings comprising Amoskeag's vast mill and manufacturing complex in Manchester, New Hampshire.

highly profitable textile factory, or mill, at Lowell, Massachusetts, on the Merrimack River. Employing young, single women from the New England countryside, Lowell became internationally famous as a planned, paternalistic community in which the "mill girls" lived in company boardinghouses under close supervision.

In 1837 the same group of Boston investors and entrepreneurs, organized as the Amoskeag Manufacturing Company, purchased 15,000 acres of land along the Merrimack River in New Hampshire, at Amoskeag Falls. There they began establishing a complex of mills and mill housing incorporated as the town of Manchester. Mill production began in 1838. Like Lowell, it was a totally planned community in which the workforce consisted of young unmarried women from rural areas who lived in company boardinghouses. Their lives were carefully regulated. They had to be in the boardinghouses by 10:00 P.M., when the buildings closed; they were required to go to church and were forbidden to drink alcohol.

Not long before the Civil War, the company began replacing the mill girls with Irish immigrant families who were willing

1839 Amoskeag Mills is founded as part of a paternalistic community.

1885 Amoskeag Mills becomes the largest textile operation in the U.S.

1910 French Canadians constitute 35 percent of the workforce at Amoskeag Mills.

1915 Amoskeag Mills becomes the largest textile center in the world.

1919 A five-day strike led by the United Textile Workers reduces production by 50 percent.

1922 Mill workers strike for nine months.

1934 Mill workers participate in a national strike of textile workers.

1935 The company shuts down the mill.

2000 The Massachusetts Historical Association opens an exhibit in mill building number 3.

to work cheaper. The types of strict controls imposed on the young women were not applied to the immigrants. Still, however, the paternalism of the company remained an important force, with workers receiving many benefits and living much of their social life under company auspices; the price was low wages and strict, uncomplaining compliance with company policies. In the 1870s French Canadians began leaving Quebec and coming to New England's cities, including Manchester. The Amoskeag Manufacturing Company, finding that they were especially docile workers, sent agents to Quebec to recruit more. By 1910 they constituted 35 percent of the workforce. Later immigrants, including Greeks and Poles, made up smaller proportions of the labor force.

By 1885 the Amoskeag Mills had become the largest textile operation in the country. In 1915, when the mills were at their peak in terms of size, production, and workforce, they were the world's biggest textile center. Its thirty major mills and related buildings contained eight million feet of floor space. Its 17,000 employees produced fifty miles of cloth an hour. There were seventy-four cloth-making departments, three dye houses, twenty-four mechanical and electrical departments, and a hydroelectric power station.

The physical appearance of the mill complex was at least as imposing as these numbers. The red brick mill buildings lined the gracefully curving Merrimack for half a mile on the west bank for over a mile on the east bank; they were built to curve along with the river. To the east of the Merrimack were two tree-lined canals paralleling the curves of the river, and in the area between the river and the easternmost canal were mills, related buildings, and railroad tracks. Beyond the easternmost canal lay the workers' three-to-five-story attached company houses, red brick like the mills, with high ceilings and hardwood floors. They were originally built as boardinghouses for the mill girls. Later some were redesigned as family tenements while others remained boardinghouses for unmarried workers.

The housing was built along cobblestone streets with white granite curbstone that ran from the center of Manchester westward to the mill yard. Walking to work along these streets in the morning, the laborers reached the eastern canal. Facing them across it was the front wall of the mill complex. Imbedded in the wall was the highly visible bay window of the agent, who managed the mill on behalf of the Boston investors. To get across the canal the workers crossed company bridges, then passed through wrought-iron gates and archways. This imposing physical arrangement reflected the philosophy behind the Amoskeag Mills, which saw the worker as subordinate to the dominating but benevolent authority of the company.

At the mill's peak early in the twentieth century, the company provided many benefits to employees. The most important one was low-cost housing. At one dollar per room per month, the cost fell well below the market rate in Manchester; by 1910, though, only 15 to 20 percent of the mill workers lived there. Other benefits included dental service, a visiting nurses service, a limited pension plan, a cooking school for women, a variety of clubs and sports teams, picnics, and parties.

Workers, however, had to take care to accept the status quo. Employees who did not were fired, and dismissed workers would not be able to find work in Manchester. For one thing, the company owned the land on which Manchester stood, and it made sure that there was no major competing employer. There were small shoe and cigar factories and other businesses in town, but the company's political grip on Manchester made it impossible for those enterprises to hire workers who had been discharged at the mills.

Employer–employee relations changed drastically after World War I. When war-related orders ended, Amoskeag and other northern textile mills found themselves in trouble. The newer mills of the south, employing cheaper labor and using more up-to-date machinery, were taking business away from them. Changes in consumer tastes also hurt the mills: postwar skirts were shorter; silk dresses became the fashion among well-to-do women; and paper towels and napkins began displacing the cotton variety. In 1939 the amount of cotton purchased per person was the same as in 1920.

As a consequence, Amoskeag began laying off workers, speeding up machines, and cutting wages. As paternalism and security disappeared for the workers, so did labor peace for the company. In 1919 a five-day strike led by the United Textile Workers reduced production by 50 percent. The year 1922 saw a bitter, nine-month strike. Eleven years later another strike led to violence, and the state militia was called in. In 1934 Amoskeag workers participated in a national strike of textile workers. Subsequently, wildcat sit-down strikes broke out in various departments. But unions and strikes could not be of help to workers in a sharply declining business. In September 1935 the company shut down the mill, and it was **liquidated** the following year.

"From the years 1770 to 1788 a complete change had gradually been effected in the spinning of yarns—that of wool had disappeared altogether, and that of linen was also nearly gone—cotton, cotton, cotton, was become the almost universal material for employment, the hand wheels, with the exception of one establishment were all thrown into lumber-rooms, the yarn was all spun on common jennies."
William Radcliffe,
Origin of the New System of Manufacture, Commonly
Called Power Loom Weaving, 1828

liquidated: sold off or converted as result of debt.

When war-related orders ended, Amoskeag and other northern textile mills found themselves in trouble.

At the end of the twentieth century, half of the mill buildings have been torn down. Many of the surviving buildings are used for an array of retail and other businesses, and the old mill yard area has been designated a city of Manchester historic district. The former company housing now consists of rental apartments and condominiums.

The Massachusetts Historical Association is planning an exhibit in mill building number three, built in 1870, where denim and flannel were manufactured. There will be a rotating display of various themes pertaining to the mills, and a permanent display on the growth of the Amoskeag complex and on the various immigrant groups represented at the mills. In mill number three are two open penstocks, or tubes, that brought water from the canals, that will be used to illustrate how water power was used to run the mills. Looms will also be part of the display. The entire exhibit is expected to be in operation by the end of the year 2000.

Along the Merrimack, the city of Manchester has placed ten stops that provide information about Amoskeag. The Manchester Historical Association has added the Amoskeag Millyard Scenic and Cultural Byway Visitor Information Center along the Merrimack, offering additional information. ◆

Angel Island Immigration Station

SAN FRANCISCO BAY, CALIFORNIA

quarantine: isolation imposed to keep contagious diseases from spreading.

Angel Island Immigration Station, located on the largest island in San Francisco Bay, served as the main processing center for thousands of immigrants, mostly from Asia, during the first half of the twentieth century. Through the years, the island also served as a military embarkation center, a **quarantine** station, and, until 1962, one of five Nike missile bases in the Bay Area. Angel Island was designated a National Historic Landmark in December 1997 by Interior Secretary Bruce Babbitt in recognition of its history as an immigration station and as a reminder of discriminatory practices that occurred there.

The detention center at Angel Island Immigration Station in San Francisco Bay, California.

Today Angel Island is a favored camping and hiking spot for people around the Bay Area and is visited regularly by ferry-boats bringing passengers from San Francisco and nearby Tiburon. Angel Island was quite different thousands of years ago when the Miwok Indians began hunting and fishing there. The Miwok, who lived on the north side of the bay, were still in the area in 1775 when Lieutenant Juan Manuel de Ayala steered his ship, the *San Carlos*, into San Francisco Bay on a mission to draw maps and make accurate descriptions that later Spanish explorers could use in settling the area.

The discovery of what came to be called San Francisco Bay was almost accidental, and was missed by several European ex-plorers sailing along the Pacific coast—including Sir Francis Drake—because the Golden Gate, the narrow entrance to the bay, is often obscured by fog. The Portuguese explorer João Cabrilho missed it in 1542, and Drake did not see it when he passed by in 1579. Two hundred years passed before San Francisco Bay was accidentally discovered by Gaspar de Portolá in 1769 after he mistakenly sailed about a hundred miles north of his destination of Monterey Bay.

In 1775 Lieutenant de Ayala anchored in a cove on Angel Island that has since been named Ayala Cove. From this safe harbor, Ayala's captain, Don José de Canizares, set out to explore the great bay and to make a map, the first ever drawn of San Francisco Bay. Ayala named the island Isla de los Angeles, in keeping with explorers' custom of naming sites for the religious feast days nearest the time of discovery.

During this time, Angel Island was uninhabited, but Russian sea otter hunters established a storehouse there in 1808. In 1814 the damaged British ship H.M.S. *Raccoon* limped from the coast of Oregon and took shelter in San Francisco Bay. The twenty-six-gun sloop-of-war was repaired in Ayala Cove from March 13 to 19, 1814. This is the origin of the name of the deep-water channel between Angel Island and the port of Tiburon, Raccoon Strait.

The island was used as a cattle ranch in the 1830s and '40s by Antonio Maria Osio, who had obtained permission from the Mexican governor of California. General Vallejo, the military commandant of Alta California, agreed to the request as long as some of the island was reserved for a harbor defense.

In the early 1850s, while thousands were pouring into San Francisco Bay to hunt for gold up near Sacramento, a sandstone quarry was established on the east shore of Angel Island, now called Quarry Point. The quarry operated until the 1920s, and later became the parade ground at Fort McDowell (also known as the East Garrison).

fumigated: treated chemically to disinfect or kill.

A quarantine station was opened at Ayala Cove in 1892, where ships could be **fumigated** and immigrants suspected of carrying diseases could be kept in isolation. The first ship quarantined (shortly before the opening of the station) was the steamship *China*, in April 1891, because some of the passengers were sick with smallpox. Passengers were checked by a doctor, then bathed with **carbolic** soap and kept in barracks for fourteen days. The island's quarantine station soon developed into Angel Island's more extensive immigration facility.

carbolic: used as an antiseptic or disinfectant.

Angel Island was a busy center of U.S. Army activity during the Spanish-American War (1898) and the Philippine Insurrection that followed. The army facilities, officially named Fort McDowell in 1900 in honor of Major General Irwin McDowell, processed soldiers going to and returning from the Philippines, and housed troops returning from the Philippines with contagious diseases.

During the Great War (World War I), which began in 1914 but which the United States did not enter until 1917, about

4,000 men per month passed through Fort McDowell, where they were issued uniforms and equipment, and shipped to units in Hawaii, the Philippines, and the western United States. By 1926 the fort was the largest troop staging facility on the west coast, handling about 40,000 men per year.

The busiest period in Fort McDowell's history was during World War II, when it was part of the San Francisco Port of Embarkation, along with nearby Fort Mason, the Oakland Army Terminal, and Camp Stoneman. The United States was fighting on two fronts, in the Pacific, against Japan, and in Europe, against Germany and Italy. More than 300,000 men were shipped through the fort to the Pacific Theater of Operations. Japan surrendered on August 14, 1945, and the troops returning from the Pacific swarmed through Fort McDowell. In December 1945, the center's busiest month, 23,632 men were processed. A reorganization of the San Francisco Port of Embarkation did not include Fort McDowell, and the base was closed. The flag was lowered for the last time on August 28, 1946.

Meanwhile, following its use as a quarantine station, Angel Island was used as an immigration processing center for over thirty years. About a mile east of the quarantine station at Ayala Cove, construction was begun in 1905 of an immigration facility that came to be known as China Cove. Modeled to some extent on the construction of Ellis Island in New York Harbor (first built in 1892), the Angel Island center was designed to be and promoted as the "Ellis Island of the West"; it opened in 1910. World War I soon interrupted the anticipated influx of European immigrants; the majority came from Asia.

But Angel Island was not Ellis Island. The east coast facility usually processed immigrants in three to five hours (as long as they passed medical and legal checks), and did not try to obstruct their passage into the United States. Officials on Angel Island, however, seemed to create barriers designed to prevent immigrants from entering the United States, especially Chinese immigrants.

Chinese immigrants first came to California in 1848, as word spread around the world about the discovery of gold in the area. Discriminatory legislation soon forced the Chinese out of the gold fields, and they found low-paying jobs laying tracks for the Central Pacific Railroad, reclaiming swampland in the Sacramento delta, and doing other types of menial labor. An economic recession in the 1870s made jobs scarce, and many Californians cried out that the Chinese were taking all the jobs.

1775 Explorer Juan Manuel de Ayala anchors in a cove on Angel Island.

1808 Russian hunters establish a storehouse on Angel Island.

1830 Antonio Maria Osio begins using Angel Island as a cattle ranch.

1851 A sandstone quarry is established on the island's east shore.

1892 A quarantine station is opened on Angel Island.

1898 Angel Island becomes a center of military activity during the Spanish-American War.

1945 In December, Fort McDowell's busiest month, 23,632 men are processed to fight in World War II.

1958 Angel Island becomes a state park.

1997 The immigration station is designated a National Historic Landmark.

"There is hereby levied on each person, male and female, of the Mongolian race, of the age of eighteen years and upwards, residing in this State, except such as shall, under laws now existing, or which may hereafter be enacted, take out licenses to work in the mines, or to prosecute some kind of business, a monthly capitation tax of two dollars and fifty cents, which tax shall be known as the Chinese Police Tax."

California Anti-Coolie Act of 1862

Many Chinese were deported, and restrictive immigration laws were enacted that allowed entry only to those with family already in the United States. The Chinese Exclusion Act of 1882 was the most famous of such laws.

A loophole in the exclusion law stipulated that any Chinese person who could "prove" that his or her father was already in the United States could be admitted. Not surprisingly, many "paper sons" and "paper daughters" bought falsified documents linking them with a supposed father in America. Also, Chinese immigrants already residing in the United States would list numerous fictional children back home in China in order to provide blanks for applicants to fill. American immigration officials were often at a loss to distinguish fact from fiction after the great 1906 earthquake and fire destroyed many original records. It was in an effort to thwart the illegal schemes of entry that the immigration officials at Angel Island devised a rigorous interrogation process.

The immigration and detention facility at Angel Island opened in 1910, and for thirty years it was the point of entry for approximately 175,000 Chinese immigrants (and the turnaround point for countless others). Most applicants were detained on Angel Island for two weeks to six months. Some, however, were detained for as long as two years. The detainees were kept in crowded communal quarters; one hundred persons would sleep in bunk beds stacked three high in a room of about 1,000 square feet. Some detainees lost hope and committed suicide. Others worked out their anguish by writing, brushing, or carving poetry into the walls.

One poem, written by an immigrant from Heungshan, read in part:

> *There are tens of thousands of poems on these walls*
> *They are all cries of suffering and sadness*
> *The day I am rid of this prison and become successful*
> *I must remember that this chapter once existed . . .*

The U.S. government closed the immigration facility in 1940, an action prompted by a fire that destroyed the administration building in August of that year. The last of the Chinese exclusion laws were repealed by federal action in 1943, replaced by a quota of 105 persons per year. Immigration from China was closed following the communist takeover by Mao Zedong's forces in 1949, but in 1965 the Immigration and Nationality

Act set forth guidelines making immigration to the United States much less burdensome for Chinese.

The detention barracks were scheduled for demolition in 1970, but when inspecting the abandoned site with his flashlight a park ranger named Alexander Weiss happened to notice vast expanses of Chinese calligraphy carved and brushed on the walls. Through the efforts of ranger Weiss and the Angel Island Immigration Station Historical Advisory Committee, the barracks were saved from demolition, and legislation was passed granting $250,000 to preserve and restore the barracks. The Immigration Museum on Angel Island, supported by the Angel Island Immigration Station Foundation, has the long-term goal of becoming the west coast's premier center for the study of Asian immigration. Angel Island became a state park in 1958, and the Immigration Station was designated a National Historic Landmark in 1997. ◆

Appomattox Court House

CENTRAL VIRGINIA

Appomattox Court House was a small village in central Virginia near the town of Appomattox. First designated as a National Historical Park in 1954, this area comprises about 1,700 acres in rural Virginia, and includes within its boundaries the McLean House, where Confederate general Robert E. Lee tendered his surrender to Union general Ulysses S. Grant, bringing the Civil War to an end on April 9, 1865. The two generals met for this momentous occasion at the home of Wilmer and Virginia McLean, in Appomattox Court House. Appomattox Court House National Historic Park offers visitors walking tours, audiovisual presentations, interpretive displays, museum exhibits, and other activities designed to preserve the history of the Civil War and its final battles.

Without supplies to feed his starving troops, General Lee knew that the war had nearly reached its end.

The final weeks of the Civil War were anticlimactic in many ways. By September of 1864, Union forces had decisively broken the back of the Army of the Confederacy with General William Tecumseh Sherman's deadly and unstoppable "March to the Sea" and his capture of Atlanta. Still, the South fought on for months, until late in March of 1865. By that time, the Union army was rapidly taking the final Confederate stronghold, Virginia. Rebel

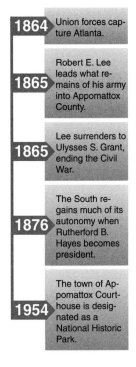

1864 Union forces capture Atlanta.

1865 Robert E. Lee leads what remains of his army into Appomattox County.

1865 Lee surrenders to Ulysses S. Grant, ending the Civil War.

1876 The South regains much of its autonomy when Rutherford B. Hayes becomes president.

1954 The town of Appomattox Courthouse is designated as a National Historic Park.

troops had been pushed out of Petersburg, Virginia, and the capital of the Confederacy, Richmond, Virginia, was captured. General Lee and his army were in retreat, but they were rapidly running out of places to run to.

At the end of the nine-month battle for Petersburg, the Army of Northern Virginia, led by General Lee, had been reduced to but 44,000 men. On the other side of the battlefield was General Grant with a force of 128,000 troops, and Major General Philip H. Sheridan, who had with him some 70,000 additional men. The long-running battle had depleted supplies, and morale among the troops was terrible. Meanwhile, just 128 miles away, in North Carolina, General Joseph Johnston and his Army of Tennessee still fought on against General Sherman.

General Lee had no choice but to concentrate on the defense of the last major stronghold of the Confederacy—the city of Richmond. Lee ordered Major General John Gordon to attack nearby Fort Stedman, but though the rebel forces occupied the fort, they lost it almost immediately in a massive counterattack. Still, Grant perceived the danger that Lee presented. A resupplied and refitted Army of Northern Virginia, were it to join up with the Army of Tennessee, could present a dangerous force. Grant ordered Major General Philip H. Sheridan to take 50,000 troops and occupy a strategic position just south of Lee's embattled forces, at a place called Five Forks.

Two of Lee's trusted officers, major generals George Pickett and Fitzhugh Lee, held onto Five Forks through the first assault, but a second one caught them by surprise, scattering the rebel forces. General Lee called for support troops to be sent from Richmond, but there was little hope that help would arrive in time. Grant was launching strong attacks at several points along the Confederate line of defense, and by April 2 his troops had broken through and were advancing upon Lee's own position in Richmond.

It was impossible to hold the city against the determined assault of General Grant and his Union forces. As defense works fell one by one—first Fort Gregg, then Fort Baldwin, the tattered Confederate forces were forced to desert the Confederate capital and retreat across the Appomattox River.

On April 8, 1865, General Lee led what was left of his Army of Northern Virginia into Appomattox County; his goal: Appomattox Station, where advance troops led by Confederate general R. Lindsay Walker were guarding the supply trains waiting at the South Side Railroad depot. But that goal was not to be

The courthouse in Appomattox Court House, Virginia.

realized—before Lee and his men could get there, General Philip Sheridan and a contingent of Union cavalry successfully attacked and dislodged Walker's encampment, taking the much needed supplies into Union control.

When word of the Union action reached Lee, he and his men were encamped just north, near the town of Appomattox Court House. Without supplies to feed his starving troops, Lee knew that the war had nearly reached its end. But he was not about to give up hope just yet. After all, by Lee's own reckoning, he had marched his troops well ahead of their pursuers and had finally joined up with the forces of generals Gordon, Longstreet, and Fitzhugh Lee. He felt that their combined strength might be enough to take on Sheridan's men and reclaim the lost supplies.

Unfortunately, General Lee did not realize just how great a force he would be confronting. Believing that the enemy comprised only Sheridan's cavalry, Lee felt certain that he could carry the day with an infantry assault. What he did not realize was that Union general George Crook had also set up a position ahead of the advancing Confederate troops. He set two cavalry units in Lee's path, and although some of the Confederate troops managed to break through this barrier, it was only the beginning.

Unconditional Surrender Grant

"Unconditional Surrender" was the most popular of several nicknames bestowed on Union general Ulysses S. Grant during the Civil War. Grant earned the nickname after Union forces captured Fort Donelson in Tennessee in 1862. During surrender negotiations, the fort's Confederate commander, Simon B. Buckner, proposed an armistice to discuss terms. Grant replied that no armistice would be accepted, but only "unconditional surrender." The words were carried north and often replaced Grant's Christian name, Ulysses Simpson.

"I would say that, peace being my great desire, there is but one condition I would insist upon, namely, that the men and officers surrendered shall be disqualified for taking up arms against the Government of the United States until properly exchanged."

Grant, letter to Lee, April 8, 1865

In their dogged march to the South Side Railroad, Lee's forces soon saw that their western escape route was blocked by an overwhelming force of Union soldiers, as the Army of the James, commanded by Union general Edward Ord, advanced upon Confederate lines. The encounter did not last long—at 11:00 A.M., Lee ordered a truce flag be flown. Surrounded on three sides, with no hope of getting supplies to feed and rearm his troops, Lee recognized that he had no choice. He sent word to General Grant that he was prepared to surrender.

The two great opposing generals met in the home of Wilmer and Virginia McLean early in the afternoon of April 9, 1865. General Grant's terms of surrender, presented in the form of a letter addressed to General Lee, were duly signed and with Lee's signature, the Civil War was effectively over. Two weeks later, on April 26, General Joseph Johnston would follow suit, surrendering to General William Tecumseh Sherman; with Confederate generals Richard Taylor, Edmund Kirby Smith, and Canby doing the same over the course of the next few weeks. The last of the southern generals to surrender was General Stand Watie, whose Cherokee forces in Oklahoma surrendered on June 23, 1865. But before the final surrenders had been tendered, President Abraham Lincoln was assassinated by John Wilkes Booth.

With the fall of the Confederacy, the South faced the long and difficult challenge of rebuilding. Its slavery-based economy was in ruins, the war had claimed the lives of vast numbers of its young men, and the states were subject to military rule, imposed by Lincoln's successor, President Andrew Johnson. Resentments ran high, and powerful secret organizations, among them the Pale Faces and the better-known Ku Klux Klan, sprang up throughout the South in reaction to the imposition of the Fifteenth Amendment, which guaranteed African-American men the right to vote, and to the presence of Yankee occupiers of southern territory, who were referred to as Carpetbaggers.

The South was determined to regain its autonomy from northern "interference," and gained a good measure of it as a result of the presidential election of 1876. The results of that election gave the popular vote to Democratic contender Samuel J. Tilden, but there were some irregularities that placed the electoral college votes of three southern states in dispute. The votes—enough to swing the election to Tilden's opponent, Rutherford B. Hayes—were won with a promise that the northern military presence would be withdrawn, that funds would be allocated to rebuild the devastated infrastructure of the southern states, and that the South would regain control of its political process and patronage systems. This compromise permitted the southern states to reshape themselves into the segregated and racially oppressive societies that persisted until the success of the civil rights movement of the 1960s.

Civil War buffs view Appomattox as but one of many exciting chapters in the era's history. Others view it as the site of the defeat of the South. Still others see it as a symbol of southern courage against all odds. While all these interpretations may be legitimate, it must be recognized that Appomattox symbolizes the final knitting together of all the fractious states into a single, united nation.

When the southern states seceded from the Union, President Abraham Lincoln feared that the young nation over which he presided had been placed in terrible jeopardy. His reason for entering into the war was simple: to preserve the Union at all costs. And in this goal he was successful, for while individual states might continue to challenge policy or legislation, never again would the threat of secession challenge the territorial integrity of the United States. The National Historical Park at Appomattox Court House, Virginia, celebrates that heritage. ◆

> *"The terms upon which peace can be had are well understood. By the South laying down their arms, they would hasten that most desirable event, save thousands of human lives, and hundreds of millions of property not yet destroyed."*
>
> Grant, note to Lee, April 9, 1865

Arlington National Cemetery

NORTHEASTERN VIRGINIA

Called "America's most sacred ground," Arlington National Cemetery in northeastern Virginia possesses the remains of over 250,000 of America's presidents, political leaders, war heroes, and civilians. The 612-acre plot of serene, rolling hills dotted by thousands of white headstones is one of the most striking sites around Washington, D.C. Arlington is one of

Union soldiers stand in front of Arlington House, former home of Confederate general Robert E. Lee, in 1864. The estate later became Arlington National Cemetery.

only two national cemeteries administered by the army (the other is that of the Soldiers' and Airmen's Home in Washington, D.C.). It is not America's largest national cemetery, but it is indisputably its most famous.

However, Arlington did not start out as a national cemetery to honor America's war dead. It was once part of a 1,100-acre plantation built by George Washington's adopted grandson George Washington Parke Custis, and was originally intended as a living memorial to the first president. In 1831 Mary Anna Randolph Custis, who had inherited the property, married Robert E. Lee, her childhood sweetheart and distant cousin. For thirty years, the couple lived in the imposing Greek revival-style mansion overlooking Washington, D.C., and the Potomac River. However, shortly after Lee resigned from military service rather than fight against Virginia in the Civil War in 1861, Federal troops confiscated the estate and turned the plantation into the headquarters for the Army of the Potomac.

Brigadier General Montgomery C. Meigs immediately set aside two hundred acres of the plantation as a national military cemetery. A memorial with the remains of victims of the Battle of Bull Run stood among its first monuments. By June 15, 1864, sixty-five soldiers were buried at Arlington, and by the end of the Civil War, more than 16,000 lay in peace there. In 1863 a section of the former estate was set aside as a Freedman's Village, a camp providing temporary refuge for freed slaves from

A funeral procession at Arlington National Cemetery in 1991.

the South. There they were provided with food and shelter until they resettled to other areas. By the time the Freedman's Village shut down in the late 1880s, more than 3,800 former slaves had been buried at Arlington with headstones reading simply "Civilian" or "Citizen."

General Lee and Mary Anna Randolph Custis never returned to their former home at Arlington. However, their eldest son, Custis Lee, successfully challenged the confiscation of his parents' property in the U.S. Supreme Court during the 1880s. Congress then rightfully purchased the property from Lee for $150,000 in 1883. By that time Arlington was already a well-established national cemetery.

Prominent military officers and war heroes from every conflict in which the United States has fought are buried in Arlington National Cemetery. Fallen soldiers from battles prior to the Civil War were reinterred at Arlington after 1900. Just a few of the military burials include George Scratchley Brown, former chairman of the Joint Chiefs of Staff; George Crook, who captured the Native American chief Geronimo; Daniel "Chappie" James Jr., the country's first African-American four-star general; and Ernest Wrentmore, who, at twelve years old, was the youngest soldier to serve in World War I.

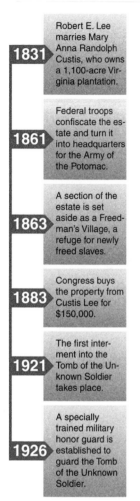

1831 Robert E. Lee marries Mary Anna Randolph Custis, who owns a 1,100-acre Virginia plantation.

1861 Federal troops confiscate the estate and turn it into headquarters for the Army of the Potomac.

1863 A section of the estate is set aside as a Freedman's Village, a refuge for newly freed slaves.

1883 Congress buys the property from Custis Lee for $150,000.

1921 The first interment into the Tomb of the Unknown Soldier takes place.

1926 A specially trained military honor guard is established to guard the Tomb of the Unknown Soldier.

In addition to military heroes, Arlington National Cemetery contains the remains of people who served the country in other ways. In 1998 U.S. Capitol police officers John Michael Gibson and Jacob Joseph Chestnutt, who were killed in the line of duty, were buried honorably at Arlington. United States Supreme Court Justices interred there include Hugo Black, William J. Brennan, Warren Burger, and William Douglas. Astronauts include Roger Chaffee, who was killed in an accident during a 1967 mission; and Donn Eisele, who successfully flew the first manned flight of the Apollo spacecraft in 1968. Senators and congressmen include William Gibbs McAdoo and Daniel Sickles. Only two U.S. presidents are buried at Arlington National Cemetery: John F. Kennedy and William Howard Taft. A few illustrious civilians are buried at Arlington, including famed boxer Joe Louis, actor Lee Marvin, and explorer Charles Wilkes, who discovered Antarctica.

Women are also well represented at Arlington National Cemetery. Most performed remarkable military service to their country, including Lillian Harris, an early career army officer who retired in 1968. Rear Admiral Grace Murray Hopper was a pioneer in data processing, the inventor of the COBOL computer language, and the oldest officer on active duty when she retired at age eighty in 1986. Juliet Hopkins, a Confederate heroine known as the "Florence Nightingale of the South," was interred at Arlington in 1890. Anita McGee was the first female army surgeon and founder of the U.S. Army Nurse Corps. Barbara Rainey was the first U.S. navy aviator. Arlington National Cemetery also houses the remains of Marguerite Higgins, a Pulitzer Prize-winning journalist and the only female correspondent during the Korean conflict. Vinnie Ream was the first woman artist to be commissioned by the government when she sculpted a portrait of Abraham Lincoln for the Capitol; she was interred at Arlington in 1914. Finally, famous wives interred alongside their husbands at Arlington include First Lady Jacqueline Kennedy Onassis, who was laid to rest alongside John F. Kennedy in 1994 under an eternal flame.

Monuments throughout the cemetery commemorate particular battles and groups of people. The Battle of the Bulge Memorial commemorates those who lost their lives in the famous World War II battle of the same name. The Pan American Bombing Memorial honors the victims of the terrorist bombing of a Pan Am aircraft over Lockerbie, Scotland. The Space Shut-

The Tomb of the Unknowns at Arlington National Cemetery.

tle Challenger Memorial remembers those killed in the ill-fated mission on January 28, 1986, including civilian Christa McAuliffe, the first "teacher in space." The Marine Corps War Memorial—better known as the Iwo Jima Memorial—represents the raising of the American flag on Mount Suribachi during World War II, and memorializes all U.S. marines killed in the line of duty since 1775. The soldiers depicted in the cast bronze sculpture are buried at Arlington. The newest large-scale monument at Arlington National Cemetery is the Women in Military Service for America Memorial.

Perhaps the most famous burial at Arlington is the Tomb of the Unknowns. The tradition of symbolizing all the unidentified victims of a conflict with the remains of a single soldier began after World War I, when Allied officials found that they could not identify the remains of many war victims. The United States, as well as France, Britain, Belgium, Italy, and other countries set up national memorials to these unnamed servicemen who sacrificed their lives for their countries. The first interment into the Tomb of the Unknowns at Arlington took place on November 11, 1921, after the remains of a chosen unknown soldier had traversed the Atlantic ceremoniously from French shores aboard the U.S. naval ship *Olympia.*

By 1926 a specially trained military honor guard had been established to guard the Tomb of the Unknowns. Since 1936 these sentinels have held a twenty-four-hour vigil at the tomb in the heart of the cemetery. A fifty-ton piece of Colorado marble sculpted by Thomas Hudson Jones marks the tomb, and an inscription reads "Here Rests in Honored Glory an American Soldier Known But to God." The changing of the guard takes place every hour in the fall and winter, and every half hour in spring and summer. During this solemn ceremony, sentinels take twenty-one steps, then face the tomb for twenty-one seconds, symbolizing the twenty-one-gun salute, the military's highest honor.

In recent history, two controversies have surrounded Arlington National Cemetery. The first concerns the Tomb of the Unknowns, which until recently housed the remains of four unidentified soldiers, one each from World Wars I and II, the Korean conflict, and the Vietnam War. On May 14, 1998, the remains of the Vietnam Unknown were disinterred and identified through DNA analysis as those of air force first lieutenant Michael J. Blassie, who was shot down near An Loc, Vietnam, in 1972. The officer's family successfully lobbied the government to have the remains moved near their home in St. Louis, Missouri, and the tomb at Arlington currently remains empty pending a decision about its disposition.

The second issue concerns how to determine who is allowed to be buried in Arlington National Cemetery as demand increases and the cemetery's rolling green hills begin to reach capacity. In response to public pressure to outline more specific rules about burial and to eliminate favoritism, the government now issues specific guidelines that dictate who may be buried at Arlington National Cemetery, limited to certain categories of honorably discharged U.S. servicemen and -women. In addition to in-ground burial, Arlington National Cemetery contains a recently expanded columbarium with a capacity of up to 100,000 cremated remains. Approximately twenty funerals currently take place at Arlington National Cemetery every day.

Arlington National Cemetery attracts nearly four million visitors a year. Many also tour Arlington House, the former mansion of Mary Anna Randolph Custis and Robert E. Lee, which contains many original furnishings and George Washington memorabilia. ◆

Belle of Louisville Steamboat

The *Belle of Louisville*, a stern-wheel river steamboat on the Ohio River based at Louisville, Kentucky, is one of only two steam-powered stern-wheel river passenger boats and is the only day packet boat still operating on the Ohio, Missouri, and Mississippi rivers. This handsome steamboat is one of the prides of Louisville—along with the Kentucky Derby, Fort Knox, and its well-respected theological seminaries and whiskey distilleries. In the early years of steamboat travel in the nineteenth century, Louisville was one of the major ports of embarkation and destination, and it is fitting that this historic city should have a grand steamboat to commemorate its role in the settling of the west. Today, *Belle* carries excursion charters, educational tours, and promotional tours on the Ohio River.

Mark Twain writes in *Life on the Mississippi* (1883) that when he was a boy, there was but one "permanent ambition" among his comrades in Hannibal, Missouri, on the west bank of the Mississippi River: "That was, to become a steamboat man." The *Belle of Louisville*, although of more recent manufacture than the steamboats Twain grew up to pilot, is an excellent example of the kind of riverboat that changed the cultural and commercial life of the United States in countless ways since its invention in the 1810s. *Belle* was built as the *Idlewild* in 1914 at Pittsburgh, Pennsylvania, and worked on the Ohio and Mississippi rivers primarily as a ferry, but also as a day packet carrying freight and passengers and occasionally as an excursion boat. She was reconditioned and rechristened the *Belle of Louisville* on October 14, 1962, before a crowd of 3,000, and has been admired by the people of Louisville and visitors ever since.

Steamboats allowed transportation of settlers from east to west and bound the nation closer together in the nineteenth century.

29

The historic paddle steamer *Belle of Louisville* on the Ohio River in Louisville, Kentucky.

keelboat: a large, shallow freight boat with a timber or steel piece at the bottom that supports the frame.

Following the Revolutionary War (1775–83) and the War of 1812, vast numbers of Americans moved westward from the towns and cities along the Atlantic coast. In the late 1700s many immigrants moving westward would go overland across Pennsylvania to Pittsburgh, Wheeling, or Redstone, and then board a boat on the Ohio River. The roads were improving but still poor, and the twisting and often shallow conditions of rivers did not permit sailing vessels. In every river, navigators had to contend with shallows, sandbars, shifting channels, and submerged, invisible snags such as trees that could tear a boat apart. Barges, flatboats and **keelboats** were used to transport people and cargo, but they moved slowly, and returns upriver were arduous or impossible. The voyage upriver from New Orleans to Louisville by keelboat or barge took from three to four months. Flatboats, the cheapest form of river transportation, were usually intended for one-way travel—downriver—and were broken up for lumber once they reached their destination. American inland navigators had long fashioned combinations of Native Americans' pirogues (enlarged dugouts) and bateaus (plank-on-frame construction) because these shallow-bottomed craft operated well on the western rivers, especially when a keel was added to help steer the boat. Keelboats were usually forty to eighty feet long and about seven to ten feet across, and could travel about fifteen miles per day, either by oars at the bow or by poles pushed by the crew standing along the side. Engineers had been working on applying steam power to navigation since the 1780s.

In 1787 a steamboat built by James Rumsey of Maryland chugged along the Potomac River at four miles per hour, and in 1790 John Fitch built a steamboat that traveled twice as fast. Robert Fulton launched the *Clermont* in 1807, a 150-foot-long boat that ran up the Hudson River from New York City to Albany in thirty-two hours, and made the return trip in thirty hours. This is generally regarded as the beginning of commercial steamboat navigation. Fulton built the *New Orleans* (371 tons) at Pittsburgh in 1811, which steamed along the Ohio River to the Mississippi and down to New Orleans, a distance of 2,000 miles. Fulton is often credited with inventing the steamboat, and indeed his contributions were substantial, but his deep-draft Fulton steamers carried the engine belowdecks, and worked best in deeper waters, while a different design was needed on the shallower, trickier western rivers.

Captain Henry Miller Shreve in 1816 put the **boilers** on deck and designed a new type of engine that distributed the machinery over a wider area of the hull; having the engine above deck allowed the boat to move in shallower waters. Shreve's design used a high-pressure engine that drove the paddlewheel propeller. Shreve and Daniel French built the *Comet* (25 tons, 1813), the *Despatch* (25 tons, 1814), the *Enterprise* (75 tons, 1814), and the *Washington* (403 tons, 1816). In 1815 Shreve took the *Enterprise* to New Orleans, disregarding the fact that Fulton and his partner Robert Livingston (one of the negotiators of the Louisiana Purchase) had a **monopoly** on steamboat sailing privileges in Louisiana waters. Legal fights ensued, but the competition was on, the cargo-carrying profits were obvious, and soon many steamboats other than Fulton's were cruising the western rivers. In 1817 fourteen steamboats were reported on the rivers, and two years later there were twice as many, mainly between the principal ports of Louisville and New Orleans. In 1817 Shreve's *Washington* made the trip from New Orleans to Louisville in twenty-five days. Henry M'Murtrie wrote in *Sketches of Louisville and Its Environs* (1819), "This was the trip that convinced the despairing public that steamboat navigation

> *"But after a while the steamboats so increased in number and in speed that they were able to absorb the entire commerce; and then keelboating died a permanent death."*
> Mark Twain, *Life on the Mississippi*, 1883

boilers: the part of a steam generator in which water is converted into steam.

monopoly: exclusive control of a commodity in an economic market.

would succeed on the western waters." By the mid-1850s, steamboats were making the same upriver trip in five and a half to six days, at average speeds of ten miles per hour.

Captain Shreve introduced several innovations, but one of the most characteristic of the way steamboats look was his addition of a second deck. Later engineers added more decks. By the time Mark Twain became a riverboat pilot in the late 1850s, steamboats were equipped with ornate, palatial cabins and private staterooms, bars and barber shops, orchestras, and **calliopes**, the steam-driven pipe organs that for many people are as integral to the steamboat as the paddlewheel.

calliope: an instrument like an organ, having a series of steam whistles.

The historical consequences of steamboat travel cannot be exaggerated. The nineteenth-century superhighways allowed transportation of settlers from east to west, greatly reduced the western farmers' reliance on east coast shipping firms, sped communications between parts of the country, and generally bound the nation closer together than had ever been imagined possible. Alexis de Tocqueville, the author of *Democracy in America*, wrote in his journal on a trip down the Mississippi in 1831: "There isn't anyone who does not recognize that the discovery of steam has added unbelievably to the strength and prosperity of the Union, and has done so by facilitating rapid communications between the diverse parts of this vast body. . . . Of all the countries in the world America is the one where the movement of human thought and industry is the most continuous and swift."

The advent of railroad travel around the nation only hastened the spread of people and the movement of goods to all corners of the growing nation—particularly after 1869 when the transcontinental railroad joined Atlantic with Pacific—but in doing so, the "Iron Horse" displaced the steamboat as the primary means of transportation. Steamboats continued to be used as ferries and excursion craft on the rivers, however, and steamboats were still being constructed, though fewer orders were coming in to the shipyards.

In 1914 the West Memphis Packet Company ordered a new steamboat from the Pittsburgh yard of James Rees and Sons, on the Allegheny River. On October 18, 1914, the new steamboat was christened *Idlewild*, and in January 1915 she set out for her first home port in Memphis, Tennessee, on the Mississippi River. The *Idlewild* worked mainly as a ferry between Memphis and Hopefield Point, Arkansas. *Idlewild* was sold to the Tri-State

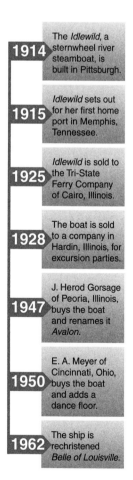

1914 The *Idlewild*, a sternwheel river steamboat, is built in Pittsburgh.

1915 *Idlewild* sets out for her first home port in Memphis, Tennessee.

1925 *Idlewild* is sold to the Tri-State Ferry Company of Cairo, Illinois.

1928 The boat is sold to a company in Hardin, Illinois, for excursion parties.

1947 J. Herod Gorsage of Peoria, Illinois, buys the boat and renames it *Avalon*.

1950 E. A. Meyer of Cincinnati, Ohio, buys the boat and adds a dance floor.

1962 The ship is rechristened *Belle of Louisville*.

Ferry Company of Cairo, Illinois, in 1925, and again she ferried cars and passengers back and forth across the Mississippi. In 1928 the boat was sold again to a company in Hardin, Illinois. The New St. Louis and Calhoun Packet Company ran *Idlewild* mainly on the Ohio River, carrying excursion parties. During the hard times of the Great Depression in the early 1930s, *Idlewild* towed barges in between excursion trips.

In 1947 *Idlewild* was sold to J. Herod Gorsage of Peoria, Illinois, who renamed the ship *Avalon*. As *Avalon*, the steamboat "tramped" for excursion business in Omaha; New Orleans; Stillwater, Minnesota; Joliet, Illinois; Charleston, West Virginia; and Knoxville, Tennessee. *Avalon* was sold in 1950 to E. A. Meyer of Cincinnati, who operated the boat on the same kinds of tramping excursions as Gorsage had done. Meyer made several improvements to *Avalon*, including adding a 33 × 96–foot maple dance floor and enclosing the main and boiler decks, which would allow a longer operating season by protecting passengers from the rain and cold. To allow the boat to pass under bridges and thereby extend her reach on the rivers, Meyer shortened the stacks (exhaust pipes) by ten feet and removed the pilothouse dome. E. A. Meyer's company went bankrupt in 1962, and *Avalon* was sold at auction.

It was over the objections of some Louisville taxpayers that Judge Marlo Cook of the Jefferson County Fiscal Court bought the steamboat. The boat needed work, but the city of Louisville contributed to the repairs, made between August and October 1962. On October 14, 1962, the boat was rechristened *Belle of Louisville*. One of *Belle*'s first assignments was to race the *Delta Queen* during the celebrations around the Kentucky Derby. The Derby is America's most famous horse race, run since 1875 at Churchill Downs, Louisville, on the first Saturday of May. Since that first steamboat race it has been an annual tradition that *Belle* and the *Delta Queen* race, and the winner receives a crown of golden elkhorns. In the thirty-five-odd years since the races began, the two boats' win–loss record is about even.

When she is not racing the *Delta Queen*, the *Belle of Louisville* is busy as a "goodwill ambassador" for the city that adopted her. *Belle* carries excursion charters and school and promotional tour groups along the Ohio River, pleasing and thrilling her passengers who may have flown in jets and sped along the interstate, but had never traveled in a grand and stately style until they stepped onboard a steamboat. ◆

"We pass mile after mile, and it is nothing but trees standing up to their branches in water. A water-turkey now and again rises and flies ahead into the long avenue of silence. A pirogue sometimes flits from the bushes and crosses the Red River on its way out to the Mississippi, but the sad-faced paddlers never turn their heads to look at our boat."
Mark Twain, *Life on the Mississippi*, 1883

Benjamin Franklin National Memorial

PHILADELPHIA, PENNSYLVANIA

> *"I grew convinc'd that truth, sincerity and integrity in dealings between man and man were of the utmost importance to the felicity of life; and I form'd written resolutions, which still remain in my journal book, to practice them ever while I lived."*
>
> Benjamin Franklin, *Autobiography*, 1789

odometer: an instrument used for measuring distance.

chandlery: the business of making and selling candles.

The Benjamin Franklin Memorial Hall, in Philadelphia, Pennsylvania, first opened its doors to the public in 1938. Designed by architect John T. Windrim, the Hall features a 1600-ton rotunda, reminiscent of the Roman Pantheon. Its centerpiece is a twenty-foot-high marble statue of the great man for whom the hall is named. Created by sculptor James Earle Fraser, the statue is an impressive tribute to Franklin the philosopher, the statesman, and the scholar. In 1976 the United States Congress dedicated the hall as the Benjamin Franklin National Memorial. Today the hall forms a part of the Franklin Institute Science Museum. The memorial is also an educational center, sponsoring historical scholarship on Franklin's personal legacy and inquiry into issues of national and international scope.

Within the memorial, visitors can see a variety of Franklin's possessions, ranging from his printing table to the equipment he used when performing his scientific experiments. Other Franklin memorabilia on display include such homely items as a tea set he received as a gift when serving as ambassador to Paris and the **odometer** he used as a postal worker.

Born into a large working-class family in Boston on January 17, 1706, Benjamin Franklin's early childhood education was limited at best—he had only two years of formal schooling before becoming apprenticed to his father's **chandlery** shop. Quickly learning to detest the monotonous routine of his labors, he chose instead to follow his brother into the printing business, where he remained until the age of fifteen. Such workaday beginnings could not begin to suggest that this young boy would someday achieve a level of greatness rivaled by few others in the history of America.

It was during his apprenticeship at the print shop that young Franklin's self-education began in earnest. A voracious reader, by the age of twelve he had begun trying his own hand at writing—a vocation that he would continue nearly up to the time of his death. But Boston could not hold the adventurous

BENJAMIN FRANKLIN

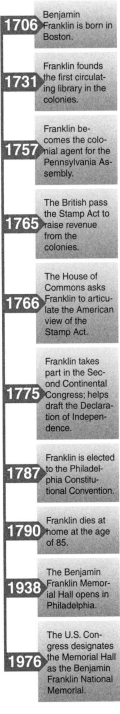

1706 Benjamin Franklin is born in Boston.

1731 Franklin founds the first circulating library in the colonies.

1757 Franklin becomes the colonial agent for the Pennsylvania Assembly.

1765 The British pass the Stamp Act to raise revenue from the colonies.

1766 The House of Commons asks Franklin to articulate the American view of the Stamp Act.

1775 Franklin takes part in the Second Continental Congress; helps draft the Declaration of Independence.

1787 Franklin is elected to the Philadelphia Constitutional Convention.

1790 Franklin dies at home at the age of 85.

1938 The Benjamin Franklin Memorial Hall opens in Philadelphia.

1976 The U.S. Congress designates the Memorial Hall as the Benjamin Franklin National Memorial.

young Ben Franklin for long, and when he was seventeen he traveled to Philadelphia where he put his printer's skills to use in the shop of one Samuel Keimer. Here he enjoyed enough success to save for a protracted visit to England in the mid 1720s, after which he returned to Philadelphia to assume ownership of the *Philadelphia Gazette* at the age of twenty-four.

Already an accomplished printer, a writer, and a publisher, Franklin still needed other interests to engage his always active mind. He threw himself into civic enterprises, founding the Philadelphia city police and firefighters company. In 1731 he founded the first circulating library in the colonies. Five years later, Franklin's many philanthropic and civic contributions earned him political recognition—he was selected to serve as clerk to the Pennsylvania Assembly.

Meanwhile, Franklin's lack of formal education proved no hindrance to the exercise of his intellect. His fascination with the workings of the natural world induced him to perform his own investigations and experiments, out of which some remarkable inventions were born, including bifocal lenses, the wood-burning stove that even today bears his name, and the lightning rod. His inquiries and results were significant enough to impress the learned men of his day, and he received honorary degrees from most of the prestigious institutions of higher learning in England and America.

With so many successful accomplishments under his hand, Franklin was able to retire at the age of forty-two to devote himself to an enterprise that had grown to occupy his attention: politics and diplomacy. He ran for a seat in the Pennsylvania Assembly, where he became embroiled in the political issues of the day. By 1757 he had become the colonial agent for the Assembly, in which capacity he traveled to England to lobby for causes important to the Pennsylvania colony's interests. His stay in London, which with only minor interruptions would last until 1775, earned him great social and political success. He ultimately came to serve as something of a spokesman for all the American colonies.

But by 1765 trouble had begun to brew between the colonies and their English masters. The British passed the Stamp Act in an attempt to raise revenue from the colonies. Back in America, the Act was universally reviled, and in 1766 the House of Commons called upon Franklin to answer questions concerning the American view of the issue. Franklin spoke resoundingly against the act, earning him a reputation as a defender of colonists' rights. When, nearly ten years later, Franklin became embroiled in a political scandal that cost him his post, he became embittered against his British colleagues and became an outspoken proponent of American independence from the British crown.

With the loss of his political appointments in London, Franklin returned to Philadelphia on March 20, 1775. Upon his arrival, he was immediately selected to attend the Second Continental Congress. With fellow members Thomas Jefferson and John Adams, he became involved in the drafting of the Declaration of Independence.

After the promulgation of the Declaration of Independence, the colonies were at war with Great Britain. Now Franklin's consummate diplomatic skills would be of signal importance. His first efforts—to recruit the support of the Canadian colonies—met with failure, but his next attempts would be far more successful. He traveled to France in the company of Silas Deane and Arthur Lee to negotiate an alliance. This posting, which lasted a total of nine years, kept him out of the battlefields in the Americas, but his contribution to the war effort should not go unrecognized. Through his diplomatic skills he negotiated a treaty of alliance with France, which secured much needed military and trade support and may well have marked the turning point in the war.

The Benjamin Franklin Memorial in Philadelphia.

After serving on the commission that negotiated the end of the Revolutionary War, the seventy-seven-year-old Franklin was by no means prepared to retire, but he had grown tired of his diplomatic duties and was ready to try something new. Two years later he returned to Philadelphia, where he was elected chief executive of the Commonwealth of Pennsylvania. When, in 1787, the Philadelphia Constitutional Convention was called, Franklin was elected to that as well. There he called for an end to the contentiousness that at times threatened to derail the drafting of a constitution for the newly independent nation, and led the attendees to a unanimous acceptance of the final document.

In his last years, Benjamin Franklin's life was as rich as it had ever been. As a renowned statesman, philanthropist, philosopher, and scientist, he entertained or corresponded with many important people until the pain of his physical ailments (**gout** and gallstones) made such activity too difficult. He died at home on April 17, 1790, at the age of eighty-five. His funeral was held at Christ Church, near his home, and he lies buried there on the church grounds. ◆

gout: a form of arthritis that affects the joints of the feet and hands.

The Bering Land Bridge

ALASKA

nomadic: describing a type of people that roamed around territory without a fixed residence.

"We tend to think it 'normal' that the seas should occupy the center of Beringia and intriguing or unusual that the floors of those seas have been exposed as dry land in the past. In fact, the Bering Land Bridge has been dry land more often than not for the past two million years or more."

Richard E. Morlan, Canadian Museum of Civilization, 1996

The Bering Land Bridge, now submerged under hundreds of feet of ocean, once connected the continents of Asia and North America and provided the gateway for the migration of the first humans into the Americas. Most scientists today agree that these first Americans were **nomadic** hunter-gatherers, a Mongolian people from northeast Asia who crossed the Land Bridge at various times during the Ice Age. But beyond this general agreement, a lively debate exists among and between geologists, archaeologists, geographers, anthropologists, and other scientists, and each year, new discoveries advance or discredit answers to the following questions: When did the first humans cross the Land Bridge? 50,000 years ago? 25,000 years? 13,000 years? What were their migration routes south and east? How, for example, did they reach the southern tip of South America? By land? By sea? How long did their journey take? Hundreds of generations? Thousands? Amid these questions, though, there is near consensus about one thing: before the Bering Land Bridge was exposed by falling ocean waters, no human beings had ever before occupied the western hemisphere of the earth.

The Bering Land Bridge was once a continuous landmass that extended between what is now northwest Alaska and eastern Siberia, and it separated the northern Pacific Ocean from the Arctic Ocean. This "bridge" was more than 1,000 miles wide, and scientists refer to the area once encompassed by this vast land bridge as *Beringia*, named after the Danish explorer Vitus Bering, a Russian naval commander who was one of the first Europeans to explore water routes in the region. The Land Bridge now lies beneath the Bering Sea of the Pacific Ocean and the Chukchi Sea of the Arctic Ocean, and, at the narrowest point, a mere fifty-five miles of ocean separate Siberia from Alaska.

The Bering Land Bridge was first exposed during the Ice Age, also known as the Pleistocene epoch, a division of geologic time during the quaternary period of the Cenozoic era. Geologists dispute the dates corresponding to the Ice Age. Some say it began as early as 2.6 million years ago; others claim it began as recently as 1.5 million years ago. Most scientists, though, believe that the Ice Age ended approximately 10,000 years ago,

when the recent epoch (or Holocene) began, a time that extends up to the present day.

The distinguishing feature of the Ice Age was the spread of glacier ice over more than one quarter of the land surface of the earth. Up to two miles thick, these vast ice sheets covered much of the northern half of North America. At various times during the Ice Age, for scientific reasons still largely unknown, the climate of the globe cooled dramatically, freezing much of the earth's oceans near its poles, and this polar ice "flowed" over land into temperate areas. Because the volume of the earth's **hydrosphere** never changes, once the oceans turned to ice and began moving, the sea levels of the earth fell correspondingly. All over the globe, between the islands of Indonesia, between the continent of Europe and the United Kingdom, and between Asia and North America, sea levels dropped as much as 500 feet, and landmasses were revealed where before there was only sea. These landmasses, known as continental shelves, were underwater plains extending out from continents into the ocean. Where these continental shelves were shallow, land "bridges" formed.

Like the term "bridge," the term "Ice Age" is misleading, for the movements of glacial ice occurred not during any one "age,"

Seward Peninsula, just south of the Arctic Circle, where an unsubmerged remnant of the Bering Land Bridge has been set aside as a natural preserve.

hydrosphere: the aqueous vapor of the atmosphere.

A watery tundra at the Bering Land Bridge Natural Preserve in Alaska.

but during hundreds of ages, or cycles, periods of cooling and warming that probably lasted between 100,000 and 130,000 years. Perhaps as many as twenty-five cycles occurred during the last two million years. It is during one of the final cycles, known as the Wisconsinan glacial period, that many scientists believe the first humans migrated across the Bering Land Bridge.

These first "Americans" were a Stone Age people, who likely lived in skin tents for shelter and followed migrating herds of bison, mammoths, and other large game across the Land Bridge into the Americas. They probably traveled in bands of no more than one hundred, and their migration was spread out over geologic time, corresponding to the rising and falling ocean waters of the Ice Age. During the warming periods of the glacial cycles, when the ice sheets melted, the rising sea levels would isolate neighboring peoples, who would then over time form distinctive cultures.

The rising sea level would isolate neighboring peoples, who would then form distinctive cultures.

Insufficient evidence exists today to explain any other migration into the Americas prior to the Norse arrivals in Greenland and Newfoundland around C.E. 1000, and so these prehistoric people who crossed the Land Bridge were most certainly the ancestors of the hundreds of tribes of Native Americans in North, Central, and South America of the present day. The dif-

Circular lakes called maars, formed by underwater volcanic explosions, at Bering Land Bridge Natural Preserve.

ferences between these now widely diverse, indigenous Americans can be explained in at least three ways: (1) the genetic variability among their initial Asian ancestors; (2) their adaptation over thousands of years; and (3) their intermixing with Europeans and other groups after the time of Columbus.

The archaeological evidence for the existence of humans in America 12,000 to 13,000 years ago is now well established and accepted. Stone tools and other artifacts **radiocarbon-dated** to this time period have been gathered at multiple sites in the American southwest and in South America. But evidence of human presence at times *prior* to this is scarce and inconclusive, and so just when the Bering migration *first* took place is the subject of great dispute. Still, there have been noteworthy discoveries that suggest a more long-standing presence. In the Yukon, bone tools have been radiocarbon-dated to 22,000 B.C.E. In the Valley of Mexico, campfire remains have been radiocarbon-dated to 21,000 B.C.E., and in the Andes Mountains of Peru, stone tools and butchered animal bones have been dated to 18,000 B.C.E. Archaeological finds such as these, which point to an earlier migration, are slowly gaining acceptance.

Great speculation also surrounds the migration of Paleo-Indians down and across North and South America. Many

radiocarbon-dated: determining age of old material by means of the content of carbon-14.

Ancient volcanic rock formations called tors at Bering Land Bridge Natural Preserve.

The Bering Land Bridge National Preserve is home to some of the largest volcanic craters of their kind.

scientists believe that the early Americans traveled by foot, first across the Land Bridge and then south between the Laurentide and Cordilleran ice sheets, before finally reaching the unglaciated lands to the south. Other scientists contend that a coastal migration by a sea-adapted people took place. Among these theorists, some believe that this coastal migration occurred in addition to a land migration, while others claim that once across the Land Bridge, the first Americans, blocked by glacial ice, had no other alternative than to travel down the Pacific coast. Proving this theory is difficult, though, and will remain so, for as glacial warming cycles occurred, ancient shorelines and possible human settlements were covered by the rising oceans. Still, artifacts uncovered in both Peru and Chile around the time of 12,500 B.C.E. reveal the presence of a lively maritime culture. In Peru, particularly, where the continental shelf drops steeply to the ocean floor, little of the ancient shoreline was lost, and stone cutting tools and great quantities of seabird and fish bones have been discovered. Though this does not provide direct evidence for coastal migration (a sea culture could have evolved later, after a land migration), it does strongly suggest its possibility.

Though the Bering Land Bridge is mostly underwater today, an unsubmerged remnant of the Bridge, just south of the Arctic Circle on Alaska's Seward Peninsula, has been made into a National Preserve by the United States Park Service. The Bering Land Bridge National Preserve commemorates the journey of the first humans into America. The preserve comprises 2.7 million acres, and is a vast landscape ranging from **alpine** to wet tundra. The preserve is extremely remote; no roads lead there, and it can be reached only by bush plane or boat. In winter, the preserve can only be accessed by planes on skis, by snow machine, or by dogsled. The preserve is home to some of the largest volcanic craters of their kind on the planet, called explosion craters, which have formed volcanic lakes called maars, and these lakes, and the nearby coastline, host more than 170 species of birds. The preserve is home also to a wide range of animal life including musk ox, grizzly bears, polar bears, wolves, wolverines, foxes, moose, and reindeer; seal, walrus, and whales are found in the waters offshore.

alpine: mountainous; above the timberline.

Though remote, the preserve is a destination for fishing, backpacking, nature observation and photography, and in winter, cross-country skiing and snow-mobiling. Visitors to the preserve can also learn about the **subsistence** lifestyle still practiced by many Alaskan natives living in villages nearby. These Inupiaq and Upik peoples, still commonly referred to by many as Eskimos, are of Inuit descent, and were probably the last peoples to migrate across the Land Bridge somewhere between 2,000 and 4,000 years ago. Some groups still speak a dialect of Inuit also spoken by groups in Siberia, who refer to their language as *Yuit*. These native Alaskans have more ancestry in common with these people of Siberia than they do with many indigenous peoples in the Americas. ◆

subsistence: the barest means in terms of food, clothing, and shelter to sustain life.

Camp David

Catoctin Mountain, Maryland

Hidden in the thick oak forest of a mountainous region in Maryland lies a guarded compound where American presidents have forged crucial events of world history. This compound, called Camp David, was designed to provide the president of the United States with a private, secluded place for recreation, contemplation, rest, and relaxation. Located about sixty miles by air from Washington, D.C., in Maryland's Catoctin Mountain Park, Camp David has seen the private lives of many presidents and their families and has also served as the setting for international peace talks and other meetings with foreign dignitaries and guests.

President Franklin D. Roosevelt was the first to use the camp. The federal government had purchased the land in 1936 in order to develop a recreational facility. The project, begun under the Works Progress Administration (WPA), was meant to demonstrate how rough terrain and eroded soil could be turned into productive land. Roosevelt set up the WPA in 1934 to give work to Americans who were unemployed due to the Great Depression (1929–42). The government's Civilian Conservation Corps (CCC) joined the Catoctin project in 1939. The CCC provided work for unemployed unmarried young men, who lived in camps managed by army officers. In addition to food and shelter, workers received $30 per month, of which $25 had to go to relatives or dependents. Camp Misty Mount became the first working camp of the development, and a third camp, Camp Hi-Catoctin, completed in the winter of 1938–39, became a family camp for federal employees.

"The people of the Middle East yearn for peace so that the vast human and natural resources of the region can be turned to the pursuits of peace and so that this area can become a model for coexistence and cooperation among nations."

Camp David Accords, preamble, 1978

President Richard Nixon and Britain's prime minister Edward Heath take a stroll at Camp David in 1973.

But the president himself needed a place to escape the heat and stress of Washington. Roosevelt had been accustomed to relaxing aboard the presidential yacht, the *Potomac*, or at his family estate in Hyde Park, New York. But in 1942 the U.S. Secret Service became concerned about the president's safety in the *Potomac*. World War II had brought an attack on Pearl Harbor in 1941, and German U-boats lurked close in Atlantic waters. The president's health was also a concern. The humid climate of Washington affected his sinuses, so aides sought a new retreat for Roosevelt. They wanted a place within a 100-mile radius of Washington in cool mountain air. They selected Camp Hi-Catoctin, where the temperature was almost 10 degrees cooler than Washington, and Roosevelt first visited the site on April 22, 1942. A main building called the Bear's Den became the presidential lodge. Roosevelt renamed the camp *Shangri-La* from James Hilton's 1933 novel, *Lost Horizon*, about an ideal mountain kingdom.

In its early days the camp featured simple food, rustic cabins, and furniture salvaged from the attic of the White House. Roosevelt made good use of the retreat, finding refuge while still managing his duties as leader of a nation at war. In the midst of the war, Roosevelt hosted Prime Minister Winston Churchill of

Great Britain at Shangri-La, where the two men discussed the Normandy invasion. The two leaders took time to fish in Hunting Creek, two miles away, and Churchill went for a beer at the Cozy Restaurant in the nearby small town of Thurmont.

Harry S Truman, who took office following Roosevelt's death in 1945, designated Shangri-La as the official presidential retreat. The camp became a year-round getaway, so the cabins were winterized, and heat was installed. Truman, a Missouri native, only visited the camp nine times in his nearly eight years of office, though he often made it available to his aides.

When Dwight D. Eisenhower became president, he shunned presidential luxuries but was persuaded to hang on to the retreat in the Catoctins. He renamed the camp after his grandson, David Eisenhower, in 1953. He and his wife, Mamie, also supervised various additions to the camp, including barracks and recreational facilities for the camp staff as well as a three-hole golf green.

Premier Nikita S. Krushchev became the first leader of the Soviet Union to visit the United States when he came, at Eisenhower's invitation, to meet the president at Camp David in September 1959. Their meeting created hope of a thaw in the Cold War between the communist and noncommunist nations of the world. Krushchev's friendliness at Camp David caused observers to refer to the "spirit of Camp David," and he invited Eisenhower to visit the Soviet Union. However, in May 1960 the Soviets shot down a U.S. spy plane over their nation, and Krushchev demanded an apology from the United States for the plane's presence in their air space. Eisenhower refused to apologize, so Krushchev withdrew his invitation.

Each president used Camp David in different ways. John F. Kennedy and his wife, Jackie, made plans to build their own summer home and did not show immediate interest in Camp David. However, Kennedy suddenly found the camp handy in an emergency. When Cuba had become openly communist in 1960, tensions between the United States and the Soviet Union became aggravated. Kennedy oversaw a badly botched invasion of Cuba by way of the Bay of Pigs in April 1961. This event brought the United States to the brink of war, and Kennedy summoned Eisenhower to Camp David to seek his advice. The meeting was Kennedy's first visit to Camp David. Later, he and Jackie stayed there with their son and daughter, John Jr. and Caroline, while their summer home was under construction. To their surprise, they liked Camp David and had their horses brought up from Virginia.

1936 The federal government buys land in Maryland for use as a recreational facility.

1939 The government's Civilian Conservation Corps joins the Cacotin project.

1939 Camp Hi-Cacotin becomes a family camp for federal employees.

1942 Franklin D. Roosevelt first visits Camp Hi-Cacotin and renames it Shangri-La.

1945 Harry S Truman designates Shangri-La as the official presidential retreat.

1953 Dwight D. Eisenhower renames the camp after his grandson, David.

1959 Nikita S. Krushchev accepts Eisenhower's invitation to Camp David.

1961 John F. Kennedy summons Eisenhower to Camp David for advice after the Bay of Pigs.

1978 Israeli prime minister Menachem Begin and Egyptian president Anwar Sadat sign a peace agreement called the Camp David Accords.

After the tragic death of Kennedy, his successor, Lyndon B. Johnson, met at Camp David with his secretaries of state and defense and other top advisors to confer about the Vietnam War. Although he may have preferred his own Texas ranch, Johnson grew to appreciate the sanctuary of Camp David. His wife, Lady Bird, once said, "To me Camp David is more a psychological journey than a physical one. I leave my troubles outside the gate."

Escaping the heat in Washington has often meant more than fleeing hot temperatures. President Richard Nixon and his family would sometimes travel to Camp David twice a week, with visits becoming longer and more frequent as Nixon's political troubles deepened. Americans later learned that Nixon taped every conversation that took place in his presence in the White House and at Camp David for nearly two and a half years. He had constructed an elaborate system of hidden microphones and tape recorders. In the spring of 1973 Nixon sweated from heat generated by the Watergate scandal. It had become known that he and his top aides had knowledge of an illegal break-in at Democratic headquarters in the Watergate Hotel in Washington that had taken place on June 17, 1972. Nixon huddled with his aides at Camp David. In July the courts requested that Nixon turn over tapes of conversations from the White House. Nixon refused at first, but eventually he released tapes that showed his direct involvement in the Watergate break-in. Congressional leaders warned of their intent to remove Nixon from office, but Nixon officially resigned on August 9, 1974.

Following the secrecy of Nixon, President Gerald Ford opened Camp David to the press. Ford hosted some journalists at the compound, but efforts to keep details of Camp David private were maintained for security reasons.

By far the most important event to take place at Camp David was the signing of a peace agreement between Prime Minister Menachem Begin of Israel and President Anwar Sadat of Egypt in 1978. The agreement became known as the Camp David Accords, and Jimmy Carter was the president who invited the two leaders for the summit. Carter and his aides had their hands full encouraging communication and comprise between the two enemies, who did not warm up to each other at Camp David. The conflict between Israel and Egypt had grown following the war of 1967, when Israel seized the Sinai Peninsula and Gaza Strip from Egypt, the Golan Heights from Syria, and the West Bank from Jordan. In 1973 Egypt and Syria attacked Israel, but Israel won. In the Camp David Accords, Israel

> *"After a peace treaty is signed, and after the interim withdrawal is complete, normal relations will be established between Egypt and Israel, including full recognition, including diplomatic, economic and cultural relations; termination of economic boycotts and barriers to the free movement of goods and people; and mutual protection of citizens by the due process of law."*
>
> Camp David Accords, 1978

agreed to pull out of the Sinai Peninsula. Israel and Egypt also agreed to work on self-rule for the Palestinians of the West Bank and the Gaza Strip. The group spent nearly two weeks at Camp David, but the peace agreement they hammered out had yet to be fully realized by the end of the century.

Ronald Reagan, far from his beloved California ranch, visited Camp David more than any of his predecessors, logging 571 visits. He mainly used it to spend time with his family and friends. He did not offer it to his staff to use when he was gone, and he did not entertain foreign guests or hold high-level meetings at Camp David as often as other presidents had. Reagan's successor, George Bush, met with several high-level people at Camp David, including Soviet president Mikhail Gorbachev and British prime minister Margaret Thatcher.

President Bill Clinton spent occasional holidays at Camp David with his wife, Hillary, and their daughter, Chelsea. When Clinton became mired in scandal surrounding his extramarital affairs, he retreated to Camp David several times. He usually spent his time reading or golfing with guests at the Maple Run Golf Course, about ten minutes from Camp David. Clinton spent less time at Camp David than previous presidents did. Some observers suggested that Clinton preferred the excitement of Washington.

Today, the cluster of mountain cabins where Roosevelt found refuge has grown into a large, well-guarded compound of many buildings and facilities. A security fence surrounds the camp, and a gatehouse on the entrance drive guards the compound. Not far inside the entrance is a helicopter landing pad where visitors often arrive. Near the pad is a skeet-shooting range. Other sports facilities on the grounds include two swimming pools, tennis courts, the small golf course, and a bowling alley. A nature trail forms a semicircle around the compound, and many visitors use it for walking or jogging.

The camp has an office for the president from which regular business can be conducted. Living quarters for the first family, formerly Roosevelt's Bear's Den, are now called the Aspen Lodge. The Laurel Lodge is a large building that features a staff dining hall. There are numerous smaller guesthouses on the compound as well as barracks for military personnel and quarters for household staff. In the midst of the anxious atmosphere created by the Cold War, the captain in charge of Camp David oversaw the construction of a bomb shelter for the president. In 1991 a chapel was dedicated at Camp David.

Following the secrecy of Nixon throughout his presidency, President Gerald Ford opened Camp David to the press.

The military office of the White House administers Camp David, while the U.S. Navy operates the camp. The camp is officially a navy base, and sailors and marines guard and patrol the premises. Near Camp David is Catoctin Mountain Park, which features public camping facilities and over twenty-five miles of hiking trails. Also nearby is the Cunningham Falls State Park, with camping, fishing, hiking, and swimming. ◆

Castillo de San Marcos

SAINT AUGUSTINE, FLORIDA

"On 17 June 1527, Governor Pámfilo de Narváez left the port of San Lúcar de Barrameda authorized and commanded by Your Majesty to conquer and govern the provinces which should be encountered from the River of Palms to the cape of Florida."
Álvar Núñez Cabeza de Vaca, *Adventures in the Unknown Interior of America*, 1542

exoskeletons: the hard and external supporting of shellfish, oysters, etc.

The Castillo de San Marcos National Monument in Saint Augustine, Florida, is the oldest extant European fortification in the United States. The Spanish began construction on the castillo, Spanish for "castle," in 1672 to protect the Spanish colonial settlement of Saint Augustine. Established as a military base by the general Don Pedro Menendez de Aviles in 1565, the Presidio of San Agustin is itself the oldest continually occupied European settlement in the continental United States. The Castillo de San Marcos and the surrounding city commemorate the history of Spain's exploration and colonization of North America, which began in 1513 when the explorer Ponce de Léon claimed *La Florida* for Spain.

The Castillo de San Marcos was built at the command of the Spanish queen regent Mariana, who ordered its construction in response to a pirate attack on Saint Augustine in 1668. Nine other forts, each built of wood, had already stood on the site. The Spanish made their new fort out of the local stone "coquina," so named for the "little shells" of long dead shellfish whose **exoskeletons** bonded together to form material. The coquina was quarried from Anastasia Island, across the bay from the castillo, and ferried to a construction site that serves today as the fort's parking lot. The Spanish crown sent stonemasons from Cuba to produce the stone blocks, which were bonded together on the construction site using lime made by baking oyster shells in kilns until they crumbled into a fine white powder. The lime was mixed with sand and fresh water to produce the mortar that still holds the castillo together. Under construction for twenty-three years, the castillo was finally completed in 1695.

The Castillo de San Marcos National Monument embraces two neighboring forts on the coastline near Saint Augustine. The masonry Fort Matanzas stands fourteen miles south of the city, overlooking the Matanzas River. It was built by the Spanish from 1740 to 1742 as a perch from which soldiers could observe enemy vessels approaching Saint Augustine from the south. The protection of Saint Augustine from such encroachments was vital, since the town was an important stronghold for Spain's defense of the primary trade route to Europe through the Gulf Stream, and as a territorial capital marking the northern reaches of the Spanish empire in the New World. Fort Matanzas quartered at least six Spanish soldiers who took turns climbing a wooden watchtower to scan the horizon for ships. Since Fort Matanzas lacked armament of its own, if a potential enemy was sighted, the soldiers would send a warning north to Saint Augustine by runner or log canoe.

Two miles north of Saint Augustine lies Fort Mose, established in 1738 as another vital defense outpost for the Spanish. Although the original Fort Mose was destroyed by a British attack in 1743, a second fort constructed in 1752 still stands. Fort Mose is best known as the site of the first legally sanctioned free

Castillo de San Marcos, the oldest masonry fort in the continental United States, in Saint Augustine, Florida.

1565 Don Pedro Menendez de Aviles establishes the presidio of San Augustin as a military base.

1668 Spanish queen regent Mariana orders construction of the Castillo de San Marcos to protect against pirate attacks.

1672 The Spanish begin building the castillo.

1695 The castillo is finally completed.

1738 Fort Mose is established as a legally sanctioned free black settlement.

1763 The British gain possession of Saint Augustine; most local subjects of Spain move to Cuba.

1861 The Americans change the name of the Castillo de San Marcos to Fort Marion.

1898 Fort Marion is used to imprison deserters from the army.

1900 Fort Marion is removed from the registry of active bases.

1924 Castillo de San Marcos becomes a national monument.

black settlement in North America. Florida governor Manuel Montiano established the settlement in 1738 as a place of sanctuary and freedom for Africans formerly enslaved in English colonies. Fort Mose remained a free black settlement until 1763, when the British gained possession of Saint Augustine, and most local subjects of the Spanish Crown relocated to Cuba.

Castillo de San Marcos and the city of Saint Augustine witnessed a historical tapestry of colonial occupation in the Americas. A succession of Spanish, British, United States, and Confederate flags flew there over the centuries. Although the fort was built for military defense, all of the changes in occupation were the result of military agreements or political treaties. The Castillo de San Marcos was never taken by force.

The first Spanish period, lasting nearly two hundred years, from 1565 to 1763, witnessed many challenges to Spain's hold on the territory. The first occurred in early November 1702, when British forces laid siege to Saint Augustine. Over 1,200 citizens of the city sought refuge within the walls of the castillo for almost two months, until the siege was broken by a relief fleet from Havana, Cuba, which trapped the British ship in Saint Augustine's harbor. The British burned their ships and the city as they withdrew, to prevent their capture by the Spanish. After the 1702 siege, the Spanish inhabitants initiated construction work to improve the castillo and Saint Augustine itself. The interior rooms of the fort were pulled into the courtyard to provide space for the construction of vaulted arch ceilings. The walls of the fort were raised from their original twenty-six feet to their present thirty-three-foot height. The renovations also included the placement of heavy garrison guns around the perimeter of the gundeck, to augment those already standing in the corner bastions. Additionally, the Spanish built walls around Saint Augustine to further fortify the city against enemy encroachment.

James Edward Oglethorpe, an Englishman, launched a second British siege on Saint Augustine in 1743. After taking forts San Diego, Picolatta, and Mose, Oglethorpe's blockade of Saint Augustine's city harbor placed troops and cannon batteries on Anastasia Island to sustain constant fire at the city and the castillo, in hopes that the governor of Florida would surrender both to the English. After thirty-eight days of siege, the British withdrew.

The British finally gained possession of Saint Augustine in 1763, when the Treaty of Paris ended the Seven Years' War with a provision that Britain would gain the Florida Territory with

the return of Havana to Spain. The British divided Florida into East and West Florida, making Saint Augustine the capital of East Florida. During the American Revolution, East Florida remained loyal to King George and England, and the castillo became a regimental headquarters for the area. It also served as a prison for captured American patriots. The British period ended in 1784, when Spain formed an alliance with the rebelling American colonies and declared war on Britain, with the specific hope of regaining Florida for Spain. The war ended before Spanish troops could battle their way eastward from New Orleans, but Spain regained Saint Augustine in the treaty settlement after the Revolution.

Park rangers fire a cannon at Castillo de San Marcos.

The second Spanish period lasted from 1784 to 1821, during which Florida faced numerous problems. The area's native Seminole population welcomed runaway African slaves across the borders, causing disputes with neighboring territories. In addition, an increasing number of pirates, ruffians, and other scoundrels maintained a base in Florida. These problems, combined with unrest in Spain's South American colonies and heavy pressure from the U.S. government, caused Spain to cede Florida to the United States.

The first American period lasted from 1821 to 1861, at which point the Americans changed the name of the Castillo de San Marcos to Fort Marion in honor of the Revolutionary War hero General Francis Marion. For many years, the fort's converted storerooms served as jails for **recalcitrant** Seminole Indians, including Seminole chief Osceola, who was imprisoned there in 1837. The state of Florida joined the Union in 1845; in 1860 Florida seceded from the Union and joined the Confederacy. However, Fort Marion remained in Union hands during most of the Civil War after a Union gunboat took the city and fort in 1862 after Confederate forces abandoned the area. Thereafter, the fort was under the control of the United States government, which used it as a prison for Kiowa, Cheyenne, Comanche, Arapahoe, and Apache Indians captured during America's westward expansion. During the Spanish-American War in 1898, the fort imprisoned court-martialed deserters from the American Army. In 1900 Castillo de San Marcos was removed from the registry of active bases; it became a national monument in 1924. ◆

recalcitrant: refusing to obey authority.

Charles W. Morgan Whaling Ship

MYSTIC SEAPORT, CONNECTICUT

The *Charles W. Morgan*, the last survivor of the thousands of wooden whaling ships that once sailed proudly out of New England's harbors, was constructed in the New Bedford, Massachusetts, shipyard of Jethro and Zachariah Hillman in 1841. New Bedford, still a lively fishing community, was one of the most important whaling communities of the eastern seaboard from the mid 1700s to the mid 1800s. So, too, was Mystic, Connecticut, which today is home to the *Morgan*. The grand old ship, preserved as a museum commemorating the seagoing culture of the past, served eighty years at sea before being retired in 1921.

The *Morgan*, 113 feet in length, was one of the giants of the sea. Her **beam** runs 27 1/2 feet, and she sits deep in the water, drawing at 17 1/2 feet. For most of her career she was rigged as a

beam: heavy, horizontal crosspiece of a ship.

double-topsail bark—a ship that could run fast before wind when hunting her prey.

After long and distinguished service as a whaler, in 1921 the *Morgan* was taken into the care of an organization called Whaling Enshrined, Inc., which is dedicated to preserving the maritime legacy of Atlantic coastal communities. The organization first moored the ship at South Dartmouth, Massachusetts, on the estate of Colonel Edward H. R. Green. There she languished until 1941, when she was acquired by the Marine Historical Association, operating out of Mystic, Connecticut.

The industry that is embodied in the *Charles W. Morgan* has deep roots in Europe—there is convincing historical evidence for the claim that the Basques hunted whales from land as early as the tenth century. But the oceangoing, large-scale pursuit of these behemoths of the sea is believed to have originated with the Dutch in the early 1600s. In the Americas, the first whaling ships set sail from Nantucket, Massachusetts, during the early 1600s, and other Atlantic coastal cities soon followed suit. Nantucket may have been the first home to whaling, but it soon ceded pride of place to New Bedford, which became the preeminent center for whaling in the American colonies and, later, the United States.

Perhaps the single most important event in the history of this young industry was the capture of a sperm whale in 1712 by a whaling ship sailing out of Nantucket. The oil of this particular species was found to be particularly useful as a fuel for lamps, and the profits that could be realized from a single specimen inspired a huge increase in the number of fishermen who were willing to risk the perils of the sea for the fortunes that could be made.

Soon, ships were sailing deep into the Atlantic, and even carried the hunt around Cape Horn and up into the waters of the Pacific. By the early 1800s many of the eastern seaboard's coastal communities had joined New Bedford in building and servicing the great whaling ships. But as quickly as the industry began, it met its doom, at least in the United States. By the 1850s the costs of pursuing the great oceangoing mammals became too great to support. The numbers of whales declined, so that the expense of mounting a whaling expedition often went unrewarded. A further blow to the industry was struck with the development of kerosene. This new fuel burned more cleanly and was far cheaper to produce, seriously cutting into the demand for sperm oil. With the advent of the Civil War and the

"Now, the grand distinction drawn between officer and man at sea, is this—the first lives aft, the last forward. Hence, in whale-ships and merchantmen alike, the mates have their quarters with the captain; and so, too, in most of the American whalers the harpooneers are lodged in the after part of the ship."
Herman Melville, *Moby-Dick*, 1851

The famous whaling ship *Charles W. Morgan* in full sail in 1925.

disruption of trade that it occasioned, the industry suffered a final blow from which it never recovered.

Whaling continues today, but today's whaling ships are huge, high-tech factories on which the carcass of a captured whale can be completely processed, permitting major economies of scale. But the ecologically conscious late twentieth century has dealt another blow to the industry, with the recognition that many whale species have been seriously depleted—some close to extinction. In 1985 an international **moratorium** on commercial whaling was passed, but several nations, notably Japan, Russia, Norway, and Iceland, have continued the practice. In the United States, many of the communities that led the industry in the eighteenth and nineteenth centuries are now host to "whale watch" cruises and other events that bolster awareness of the need to protect the whales, and activist groups such as Greenpeace have even gone so far as to directly challenge the big industrial whalers on the open seas.

moratorium: an authorized delay or stopping of a specified activity.

Ships like the *Morgan* provided the inspiration for one of America's premiere literary figures, Herman Melville (1819–91). He had sailed to the South Seas on a whaler, the *Acushnet*, and was so appalled by the conditions aboard that he fled the ship in the Polynesian Islands where he spent some time as a captive of a native tribe. Another whaler, passing through the region, provided him with his opportunity for escape, but once again the conditions on board inspired him to take drastic action and he joined the crew in mutinying. His adventures at sea provided him with the material from which he fashioned the novels that would earn him immortality, among them *Typee, Omoo*, and most famously, *Moby-Dick*.

Moby-Dick has been rightly viewed as an extraordinarily rich, symbolic tale of quest and obsession, and of the struggle between good and evil. But it is equally important as a chronicle of the conditions of life aboard the whaling ships of Melville's day, and as such it is an invaluable record of a way of life now long past.

Though the technology of the industry was less complex than that employed by the whalers of today, ships like the *Morgan* were still designed to do more than hunt whales. The vast bulk of these sea mammals meant that the whalers had to be capable of handling the preliminary processing of their haul. For this, the comforts of the crew had to be sacrificed in order to make space for the huge try-pots, or kettles, in which the whale blubber was rendered ("tried") to convert it into oil.

Below the deck, the quarters for the ship's officers took up much of the remaining available space, and crew was housed in tiny, dark, overcrowded quarters. The contract for a single voyage might run for several years at one go, and much of that time could easily be spent without a glimpse of dry land. The sailors who worked under such conditions were, of necessity, a very special breed.

Mystic Seaport, current home of the *Morgan*, is today a museum complex dedicated to the preservation of America's maritime history. The town, and the Mystic River for which it is named, has long been associated with shipbuilding—since as long ago as the 1600s. In the earliest years, shipbuilders were often farmers as well, who built ships to trade along the coast to the south and with the islands of the Caribbean. But with the advent of the whaling industry, such shipbuilding communities became much more significant. Mystic itself is known to have sent up to four whalers out each year.

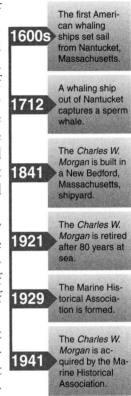

1600s The first American whaling ships set sail from Nantucket, Massachusetts.

1712 A whaling ship out of Nantucket captures a sperm whale.

1841 The *Charles W. Morgan* is built in a New Bedford, Massachusetts, shipyard.

1921 The *Charles W. Morgan* is retired after 80 years at sea.

1929 The Marine Historical Association is formed.

1941 The *Charles W. Morgan* is acquired by the Marine Historical Association.

In 1838 the Greenman family—George, Clark, and Thomas—built a shipyard—George Greenman & Co.—on the shores of the Mystic River. Over the next forty years, their shipyard constructed nearly 100 vessels, including the clipper ship *David Crockett* (today also on display at Mystic Seaport), and a part of the Union fleet for the Civil War. But at the end of the Civil War, whaling went into a decline, and the shipbuilders of maritime communities like New Bedford and Mystic turned to servicing the fishing fleets and private vessels.

Mystic's maritime industry suffered over the years, and for a time the community became a manufacturing center, but the town, and a few of its farsighted citizens, kept the seagoing heritage alive. In 1929, less than a decade after the last shipwright closed up shop, three residents got together to form the Marine Historical Association, dedicated to the preservation of New England's maritime legacy. They ultimately made their headquarters on a part of the property once held by George Greenman & Company.

In the early days of the Historical Association, there were few exhibits and only one boat on view for the public. But in 1941 the Association took over the restoration and safekeeping of the *Charles W. Morgan,* which had by that time outlived all other wooden whalers. While World War II hindered the expansion of the association, once the war was over the association quickly grew and took on the task of preserving the historic buildings of the community and acquiring a vast collection of maritime artifacts.

To care for the ships that came under its purview, the association established a restoration shipyard on the site of the Charles Mallory shipyard, erstwhile competitors to the Greenman outfit. The museum facility now sees to the preservation not only of the *Morgan,* but also of the 1882 square-rigger the *Joseph Conrad;* the *L. A. Dunton,* a 1921 fishing schooner; and the *Sabino,* a fully operating steamboat that was built in 1908. ◆

> *"Concerning all this, it is much to be deplored that the mast-heads of a southern whale ship are unprovided with those enviable little tents or pulpits, called crow's-nests, in which the lookouts of a Greenland whaler are protected from the inclement weather of the frozen seas."*
>
> Herman Melville, *Moby-Dick,* 1851

Cumberland Gap

KENTUCKY, VIRGINIA, AND TENNESSEE

The Cumberland Gap, a route through the Appalachian Mountains leading into Kentucky Territory, was discovered for European settlers by English physician Thomas

Walker in 1750. He named the passage for William Augustus, the duke of Cumberland. Today it is the site of the Cumberland Gap National Historical Park, which commemorates the first great westward migration (1815–20), when large numbers of settlers made the move from Virginia and the eastern states into the newly opened American interior.

The park straddles the borders of three states: Kentucky, Virginia, and Tennessee, and maintains headquarters in Middlesboro, Kentucky. It comprises fifty-five miles of hiking trails, camping facilities, and restored early settlements. The park sponsors performances and exhibits about the early settlers to pass through the Gap. Interested visitors can retrace a part of the journey that the early settlers made, tour the Hensley settlement (which includes one of the original dwellings, now restored by the Park Service), and attend performances of the music of the early settlers. Featured prominently are memorabilia and exhibits of perhaps the most famous historical figure associated with the region: Daniel Boone.

Long before the Cumberland Mountain was formed, the region was relatively flat. At that time, the Yellow Creek cross-cut the area as it flowed south to join the Powell River. As geologic pressures forced the land upward during the formation of the Appalachian Mountain Range, the creek's bed formed a notch in the upthrusting rock. This notch or gap opens out into the Middlesboro Basin, leading to a second gap, which pioneers called "The Narrows," and which cuts through nearby Pine Mountain, finally opening out into the Bluegrass territory of Kentucky.

The Appalachians formed a natural geologic barrier to population expansion to the west, effectively keeping the whole western expanse of the continent out of the reach of settlers from the east. There had long been Europeans exploring the interior, notably the Spanish (traveling up from the south) and the French (entering the interior from points north in Canada), but their numbers were relatively few. It was not until Dr. Walker's discovery of the Cumberland Gap that passage from east to west was made relatively easy, and large numbers of would-be settlers could consider making the trip.

With the discovery of the Cumberland Gap, the once impassable barrier of the Appalachians was finally broached, but it would be a decade and a half before American settlers made regular use of the passage. Travel through the Gap was by no means easy—the terrain was rugged, over mountains and through deep forest. But it was more than the physical hardship of the trip

"These mountains are in the wilderness, as we pass from the old settlements in Virginia to Kentucky, are ranged in a S.W. and N.E. direction, are of a great length and breadth, and not far distant from each other. Over these, nature hath formed passes that are less difficult than might be expected from a view of such huge piles. The aspect of these cliffs is so wild and horrid, that it is impossible to behold them without terror."
Daniel Boone, *The Adventures of Col. Daniel Boone*, 1784

The Pinnacle overlooking Kentucky's Cumberland Gap.

that held westward migration at bay for so long. Political considerations of the time prompted England's King George to issue a decree forbidding travel into the contested lands beyond the mountains. In addition, on the western side of the gap were Cherokee, Delaware, and Shawnee settlements, and these groups had no intention of surrendering their lands to white interlopers. Nonetheless, in 1767 a thirty-three-year-old veteran of the French and Indian War made the trip through the rugged terrain on one of his many extended hunting treks. This trailblazer, Daniel Boone, got his first glimpse of the rich woods and fields of Kentucky and resolved to return someday.

Boone was greatly impressed by the beauty and wealth of the lands of "Kentucke" and would no doubt have made the trip on his own one day. But the decision was soon to be made for him. A wealthy Virginian, retired judge Richard Henderson, had long nursed the hope of founding a settlement in the territory beyond the Appalachians, ever since it was proved possible to make the trek through the mountains. But as long as the Indians on the western side of the gap were hostile, Henderson could find few souls hardy enough to risk the crossing. When, in the early 1770s, an uneasy peace was established between the Virginia settlers and some of the Indians of the west, Henderson felt the time was ripe to set his plan in motion.

In 1774 Henderson organized a group of backers to form the Transylvania Company, through which he negotiated the purchase of a vast tract of land bounded by the Ohio and Cumberland rivers—in Kentucky territory—from the Cherokee. It mattered little to Henderson that neither he nor the Cherokee had the legal standing required to make the purchase official—he was convinced that once the British authorities were confronted with the fact of an actual, established settlement, they'd easily be persuaded to grant him legal title.

Henderson, however, was not a frontiersman. In order to convince others to join in his plans, he needed someone with extensive backwoods experience to safely lead his first settlements over the mountains, through the Cumberland Gap, and into the rich territory of Kentucky. He knew Daniel Boone had made the trip just seven years earlier, and was well aware of the frontiersman's reputation as an accomplished hunter, tracker, and Indian fighter, so he hired Boone to lead an initial party of thirty men through the Gap, cutting a road as they went. The route they cleared came to be called the Wilderness Road, and for the next forty-five years this would be the principal route taken by settlers hoping to make their fortunes in the untamed American interior.

It took Boone and his original party a little more than a month to break through into Henderson's questionably purchased Kentucky real estate. In April of 1775 they arrived in central Kentucky and set to building the fort that would be needed to protect the settlement that was to come. With Fort Boone in place, Henderson felt his planned settlement would be secure enough, so he set out with a party of eighty, all of whom intended to build homes in the new territory. Along the way, his group was joined by some 200 more would-be western settlers, and in short order they established the community of Boonesboro. By the end of the year, the Transylvania Company settlers numbered more than 900, and they had laid claim to more than a half a million acres of land.

With this first community, the westward expansion of settlers across the American continent was well and truly begun. Once independence had been won, the newly formed United States actively encouraged western settlements, motivated in

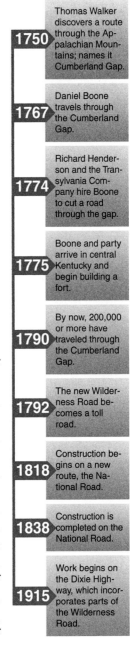

1750 Thomas Walker discovers a route through the Appalachian Mountains; names it Cumberland Gap.

1767 Daniel Boone travels through the Cumberland Gap.

1774 Richard Henderson and the Transylvania Company hire Boone to cut a road through the gap.

1775 Boone and party arrive in central Kentucky and begin building a fort.

1790 By now, 200,000 or more have traveled through the Cumberland Gap.

1792 The new Wilderness Road becomes a toll road.

1818 Construction begins on a new route, the National Road.

1838 Construction is completed on the National Road.

1915 Work begins on the Dixie Highway, which incorporates parts of the Wilderness Road.

part by the need to secure control of territory that would otherwise be taken by Spanish, English, and French settlers. By 1790 200,000 or more had traveled through the Cumberland Gap to seek their fortunes in the lands of the American interior, and 5 percent of the total population of the United States lived west of the Appalachian mountain range. Just thirty years later, that figure would exceed 20 percent.

With all this traffic, it was not long before the road that Boone and his fellow trailblazers had cut had to be widened. While early groups of travelers through the gap were relatively small, by 1792 the route had to accommodate the wagonloads of hopeful pioneer families who succumbed to dreams of wealth and opportunity in the "land of milk and honey," as Boone had once described his beloved Kentucky. The new, widened Wilderness Road was contracted to private operators, who charged a toll on all traffic.

Soon enough, the pressure of increasing traffic meant that other routes into the west would be found and in 1818 construction was begun on a new route, called the National Road, which would ultimately run from Cumberland, Maryland, to Vandalia, Illinois. When this new, more convenient road was completed in 1838, it spelled the end of the trail for the Wilderness Road through the Cumberland Gap, which soon fell into disuse. The Wilderness Road, including the point where it crosses the Cumberland Gap, received a new lease on life with the invention and early popularity of the automobile. Parts of the route were incorporated into the great early-twentieth-century highway project known as the Dixie Highway, constructed from 1915 to 1927, which ultimately extended from Ontario to Florida.

Although the Wilderness Road did not long retain its unique status as the gateway to the American interior, its historical and symbolic significance should not be minimized. It was the very first of America's doorways into the western territories, giving birth to a generation of dreamers, adventurers, and explorers, and settlers who ultimately claimed the continent from east to west. At the time that Lewis and Clark made their famed explorations with the Corps of Discovery, Boonesboro was America's westernmost settlement, beyond which lay virgin territory and, at the time, unknown wonders.

The traffic through the gap also increased the tempo of the conflicts that arose as white settlers arrived in ever increasing numbers to claim ever expanded tracts of land from the Indian groups who occupied the territory. The opening of the gap to settler travel marked the beginning of the end to any hopes that white usurpation of tribal lands would cease. It set into motion the inexorable western expansion that would ultimately displace all the original peoples of the American interior and push the borders of the nation all the way to the Pacific coast. ◆

Daniel Freeman Homestead

BEATRICE, NEBRASKA

The Daniel Freeman homestead is officially listed as the first claim filed under the Homestead Act, passed by the United States Congress in 1862. This legislation was enacted with the goal of hastening the settlement of America's western territories. According to the terms of the act, beginning on January 1, 1863, a single man over the age of twenty-one, a married man under twenty-one, or a widowed female head of household who did not already own more than 160 acres of land anywhere else in the country was eligible to file a homestead claim on surveyed land that was as yet unoccupied by other white settlers.

Daniel Freeman's claim to fame as first homesteader was earned through a combination of his fortuitous military service, impatience, and the complicity of a land office clerk in Brownville, Nebraska. While Freeman was stationed at Fort Leavenworth, he learned of the passage of the act. He found a prime stretch of acreage along the Cub Creek. Afraid of missing out on his claim, he convinced the land office registrar to open for business at 12:01 A.M. on January 1, the earliest possible legal moment to file. Although his certificate of claim is not the only one designated "number 1" (the numbering sequences were unique only to individual districts), his is believed to have been filed at the earliest time on opening day.

But filing was not the only qualification required to gain title to homesteaded land. In addition to the initial filing, claimants had six months to "prove up" (make basic improvements to) their land and then had to live on it for five years.

Freeman's property was established to commemorate the importance of the Homestead Act and the lives of the pioneers.

This cabin built by George Washington Palmer in 1867 on his homestead along Bear Creek northeast of Beatrice, Nebraska, was moved to Homestead National Monument of America in 1950.

The southern states felt threatened by new settlements in the west because many settlers came from the antislavery northern states.

Freeman had to complete his tour of military duty before he was able to take up residence, which he did in 1865, along with his wife, Agnes Suiter Freeman, their children, and his three children from his first marriage (to Elizabeth Wilbur, who died in 1861). Daniel Freeman never abandoned his claim, remaining there until his death on December 31, 1908. His wife remained in residence on the property until she died in 1931.

In 1839 Daniel Freeman's property was designated Homestead National Monument of America, established to commemorate importance of the Homestead Act and the lives of the pioneers who settled land under its provisions. The monument includes Freeman's original homestead foundations and grounds, as well as the Freeman School, a one-room red brick schoolhouse built in the early 1870s. The park also includes the Palmer–Epard cabin, built by George Washington Palmer in 1867 on his homestead along Bear Creek, northeast of the Freeman property. The cabin was moved to the grounds of Homestead National Monument in 1950. The Palmer–Epard cabin is typical of those built by homesteaders and other pioneers who settled in the tall-grass prairie regions of the central United States during the 1800s. In addition, the Homestead National Monument comprises nearly 100 acres of restored tall-grass prairie.

By the middle of the nineteenth century, the United States territories had been extended from the original Atlantic colonies all the way to the Pacific coast. The population was growing rapidly, settlements had been established throughout most of the continent, and a transportation system comprising railways, river and canal systems, and roadways had made most of the country's lands accessible for settlement. The indigenous peoples—the Indians—had been displaced and tucked out of the way on reservation lands, and European claimants for American territories had been dislodged.

The older settlements of the northeast and the south were thriving, to be sure, but only in the west were there still vast tracts of unsettled lands to inspire dreams of pioneering. And for a young nation, western settlement was important—by bringing hitherto unsettled lands into production, the national wealth would be increased; and as settlements grew they would comprise new markets for goods produced in the east and south.

Thus, as the population of the United States grew, demands grew as well—for the government to make free land available for settlement. But any hopes of an easy resolution of these demands were stymied by political issues—particularly the growing controversy over slavery. An uneasy balance had been achieved between the slave states of the south and free states of the north. As new western lands were settled, the issue of statehood would arise, which might upset this fragile balance. The southern states felt particularly threatened by the prospect of encouraging new settlements in the west, for the majority of settlers seemed to be coming from the antislavery northern states. The settlers, therefore, would most likely opt against establishing proslavery constitutions.

Throughout the 1850s, southern states managed to block free land legislation in Congress even against the heavy lobbying of such powerful northern interests as Horace Greeley, publisher of the *New York Tribune*. But the pressure for population expansion into the western territories could not be forever ignored, and by the time of Lincoln's election to the presidency in 1860 it became clear that some sort of homesteader policy would have to be developed. Still, it would take another year and the secession of the south from the Union before any formal legislation could be passed.

On May 20, 1862, President Abraham Lincoln signed the Homestead Act into law, effectively opening the floodgates for the full settlement of the lands of the American west. According to the Act, any head of household (male or female) who was over the age of twenty-one and who was a citizen or prospective

"Be it enacted, That any person who is the head of a family, or who has arrived at the age of twenty-one years, and is a citizen of the United States . . . shall . . . from and after the first of January, eighteen hundred and sixty-three, be entitled to enter one quarter-section or a less quantity of unappropriated public lands, upon which said person may have filed a pre-emption claim."

Homestead Act of 1862

The Freeman School, a
one-room schoolhouse,
was built in 1872.

citizen of the United States was entitled to stake a claim of 160 acres of surveyed public domain land. The land was essentially free—the only cost was the payment of a nominal registration fee. The claimant was obligated to make certain improvements on the land, and to maintain five years of continuous residence, after which legal title would go to the homesteader automatically.

The provisions of the Act seemed heaven-sent to would-be settlers. The requirements seemed reasonable, and the price certainly could not be better. But although there were many who, like Daniel Freeman, wanted nothing more than to secure their own homestead claim, quite a few failed to prove up their claims and moved on, no better off than when they had started out.

Would-be settlers fueled their homesteading hopes on the dream of making a comfortable life on a productive farm out in the fabled territory of the Great Plains, but their dreams were frequently based on unrealistic expectations. How could emigrants from the northeast imagine the foreign landscape of the plains? The treeless expanses meant there would be no local wood for building, the land itself proved difficult to plow, and the scarcity of water made it difficult to irrigate crops once they were planted.

The harsh realities of life on the plains defeated all but the hardiest, most determined of homesteaders, and gave rise to a way of life peculiarly suited to the difficult conditions. Since conventional building materials such as wood were prohibitively expensive in most of the territory, settlers learned to improvise. While Daniel Freeman managed to build a log cabin, most settlers had to settle for building houses from piled strips of sod. These were often leaky, drafty affairs, uncomfortable and difficult to heat. And the lack of wood for fuel made even heating and cooking a problem. The resourceful homesteader learned to use a combination of buffalo dung and hay for a slow-burning, if odiferous, source of fuel.

The lack of water, too, required ingenuity if a homesteader were to supply his or her home and farm with this necessary commodity. Since there were few homestead claims graced with a creek, river, or stream, the settlers needed to find a good spot in which to sink a deep well. The dry climate did not make things any easier—while rain barrels were set out to capture any moisture the weather might make available, the scarcity of rain in the region made this an unreliable source. Indeed, the reliance on barrel-stored water gave rise to a particular scourge of the region—prairie fever, or typhoid, which spread like wildfire across the plains and arose from the fact that humans and cattle alike drank from the storage barrels.

Even if the weather cooperated with the homesteader, and a relatively snug and dry sod house could be built, it was still a requirement of proving the claim that some land be placed in cultivation. This, too, proved difficult. Prior to the arrival of the homesteaders, the Great Plains had never been cultivated, and the natural ground cover was a tough, matted form of grass. Standard plows such as those used on farms back east simply couldn't cut through the sod, and it was a backbreaking chore to do it by hand.

Because of the great hardships of proving up a homesteader claim, pioneer families on the plains learned to be extraordinarily self-sufficient, and to set great store on hard work. But they also learned the need for community and cooperative effort. A group of farmers, each of whom might be unable to afford the tools for sodbusting to clear a field could join together to hire the services of professional ploughmen. Neighbors worked together to help one another cope with sickness or

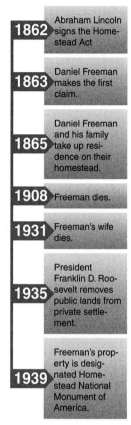

1862 Abraham Lincoln signs the Homestead Act

1863 Daniel Freeman makes the first claim.

1865 Daniel Freeman and his family take up residence on their homestead.

1908 Freeman dies.

1931 Freeman's wife dies.

1935 President Franklin D. Roosevelt removes public lands from private settlement.

1939 Freeman's property is designated Homestead National Monument of America.

Timber Culture Act of 1873

Like the Homestead Act, which granted up to 160 acres of land to settlers like Daniel Freeman, the Timber Culture Act of 1873 was part of the federal government's effort to settle the west with individual farmers. The Timber Culture Act granted a further 160 acres to any head of a family who planted and maintained forty acres of trees for ten years. Pre-industrial farmers were dependent on wood for much of their material culture. Many believed that forests brought rain, and planting trees on the plains provided the basis for increased settlement. The act also allowed people who homesteaded marginal land to acquire more than the 160 acres they could claim under the Homestead Act. The Desert Land Act of 1877 encouraged settlement and development of the arid lands farther west by offering claimants allotments of 640 acres for only $1.25 an acre, with the understanding that the land would be irrigated within three years.

disasters. Slowly, small towns began to spring up to service the scattered, isolated farms, and to provide a community center where people could come together. Still, the life of a homesteader was exceptionally difficult, and a full two thirds of all the original homesteaders gave up before qualifying for title to their lands.

The initial Homestead Act was but the first of many offerings of free public lands for settlements. In the 1890s, an economic depression destroyed the fortunes of many families, and there was a great hunger for the chance to make a fresh start. When rumors began to fly that the Cherokee Territory—west of the Kansas and Oklahoma Territories—would be declared open for settlement, it touched off the last and biggest land run ever held in the United States. All participants had to register in advance, and were prohibited from entering the territory until the official opening of the territory, scheduled for noon of September 16, 1893.

Would-be claimants hung from the ladders along the sides of trains, clutching their claim-stakes and ready to leap off the train to the land of their dreams.

The frenzy for land was incredible. Would-be claimants hung from the ladders along the sides of trains, clutching their claim-stakes and ready to leap off at the site of the land of their dreams. People came from all over the world to participate, though only a relative few would ultimately gain the free land they hoped for. Many lost their lands to claim jumpers, who took advantage of the briefest of absences from the staked territory. And most could not endure the five-year residency requirement, chased off their lands by natural disasters like drought or by the simple hardship of homesteader life.

The land run of 1893 was the last of the major land give-aways, but not the end of the Homestead Act. Public lands continued to be made available through its provisions until 1935, although the rules underwent some amendment. The residency requirement was reduced from five years to three in 1912, and it was extended to cover forestlands and pasturage as time went on. In 1935, when President Franklin D. Roosevelt removed public lands from private settlement, over 285 million acres had been given away under the provisions of the act. ◆

Dealey Plaza

DALLAS, TEXAS

For Americans old enough to remember, November 22, 1963, remains imprinted on their minds in vivid detail. On that day, President John F. Kennedy was shot and killed as he rode through the streets of Dallas, Texas, sending the nation into a state of shock. For many decades afterwards, people would examine and reexamine the events of that day, trying to answer the questions of why and how it happened. The Sixth Floor Museum at Dealey Plaza offers visitors a place to study the tragic assassination and perhaps settle some of their own questions about the terrible event. The museum is located on the sixth floor of the former Texas School Book Depository building in downtown Dallas, the site from which the assassin aimed his rifle.

John Fitzgerald Kennedy was born May 29, 1917, the second son of Joseph Patrick Kennedy and Rose Fitzgerald Kennedy, both of politically active Irish Catholic families in Boston. John Kennedy was born in Brookline, a Boston suburb; the large affluent Kennedy family later moved to the upscale suburbs of New York City. Kennedy graduated from Harvard University in 1940, and later enlisted as a seaman in the U.S. Navy. He became a war hero after a Japanese destroyer demolished his PT boat in the South Pacific and he helped rescue his men. Kennedy won a seat in the U.S. House of Representatives in 1946. He was reelected to the House in 1948 and 1950. In 1952 Kennedy won the election for U.S. senator from Massachusetts; he won reelection to that seat in 1958.

Kennedy married Jacqueline "Jackie" Lee Bouvier (b. July 28, 1929), the daughter of a wealthy Wall Street broker, on

"And so, my fellow Americans: ask not what your country can do for you—ask what you can do for your country. My fellow citizens of the world: ask not what America will do for you, but what together we can do for the freedom of man."
John F. Kennedy, inaugural address, January 20, 1961

Dealey Plaza in Dallas, Texas, c. 1967. Lee Harvey Oswald shot John F. Kennedy from the sixth floor of the Texas School Book Depository (the large building on the top left).

September 12, 1953. The couple had a daughter, Caroline, born in 1957, and a son, John F. Jr., born in 1960. Another son, Patrick Bouvier, died fewer than forty-eight hours after his birth in 1963.

In 1960 Kennedy ran a tough race against Republican vice president Richard M. Nixon for the U.S. presidency. Kennedy won and was inaugurated as the thirty-fifth American president on January 20, 1961.

Police found the sniper's perch in a corner of the sixth floor where the shooter had hidden behind boxes piled near a window.

In November 1963 Kennedy made what was to be a three-day trip to Texas to enlarge his political support before the 1964 presidential campaign, in which he planned to run for a second term. The presidential plane, Air Force One, left Washington, D.C., on Thursday, November 21, and traveled to San Antonio, Houston, and Fort Worth. On Friday the plane arrived at Dallas's Love Field at 11:37 A.M. The president, Mrs. Kennedy, Vice President and Mrs. Lyndon B. Johnson, and others would travel in a motorcade through the streets to the Dallas Trade Mart, where Kennedy was to speak at a luncheon. The president sat in the rear seat of an open limousine on the right side, with Jacqueline on his left. Texas governor John B. Connally sat in a seat in front of the president, and Mrs. Connally sat to her husband's left. Two Secret Service agents, one driving, rode in the front seat.

Well-armed Secret Service agents filled a limousine behind the president's car. Vice President and Mrs. Johnson rode in a third car, also accompanied by Secret Service men. Although Dallas had many people opposed to Kennedy, cheering crowds lined the route as the motorcade moved down Main Street. Leaving Main Street for the last leg of the trip, the procession needed to make a sharp turn onto Houston Street and then onto Elm Street, which bordered Dealey Plaza, a small, odd-shaped, sloped park with grass, benches, and a statue. The seven-story tan brick Texas School Book Depository warehouse lay on the corner of Houston and Elm. Some employees from the building had gathered at the building entrance to watch the parade.

At 12:30 P.M., the motorcade turned on to Elm Street moving at about eleven miles per hour. They were five minutes from the Trade Mart. Suddenly, a shot rang out and a bullet hit the curb near the president's car. A second shot followed, ripping through the president's back and out his throat. Connally was also hit in the back. The president's confused driver slowed the car, and a third shot shattered the president's skull. A panicking Mrs. Kennedy attempted to crawl off the back of the car, but a Secret Service agent from the car behind thrust her back into her seat. The limousine rushed to nearby Parkland Memorial Hospital as Mrs. Kennedy held her dying husband in her lap. Doctors made desperate efforts to save the president, but he died at 1:00 P.M., never having regained consciousness. The seriously wounded Connally survived.

Vice President Johnson remained at the hospital until Kennedy died, then went to the airport. Mrs. Kennedy arrived shortly with the coffin holding her husband's body. Onboard Air Force One, at 2:39 P.M., U.S. District Judge Sarah T. Hughes administered the oath of office to Johnson, who became the thirty-sixth president of the United States. Uncertain of who was behind the assassination, the new president hastened to leave Dallas, and the plane took off for Washington carrying the new president, his wife, Mrs. Kennedy, and the body of the late president.

Police rushed into the Texas School Book Depository building after witnesses said the shots had come from a sixth-floor window. They found the sniper's perch in a corner of the sixth floor where the shooter had hidden behind boxes piled near a window. The killer had fled, and police began searching for a warehouse employee who had taken off a few minutes after the

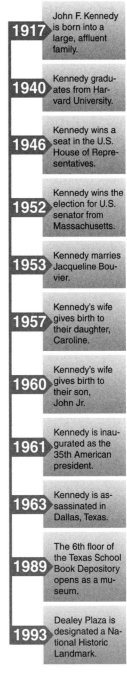

1917 John F. Kennedy is born into a large, affluent family.

1940 Kennedy graduates from Harvard University.

1946 Kennedy wins a seat in the U.S. House of Representatives.

1952 Kennedy wins the election for U.S. senator from Massachusetts.

1953 Kennedy marries Jacqueline Bouvier.

1957 Kennedy's wife gives birth to their daughter, Caroline.

1960 Kennedy's wife gives birth to their son, John Jr.

1961 Kennedy is inaugurated as the 35th American president.

1963 Kennedy is assassinated in Dallas, Texas.

1989 The 6th floor of the Texas School Book Depository opens as a museum.

1993 Dealey Plaza is designated a National Historic Landmark.

shooting. At 1:15 P.M., a Dallas policeman, J. D. Tippet, saw the suspect walking along a local street and attempted to detain him. Lee Harvey Oswald drew a revolver and shot Tippet dead.

Dallas police arrested the twenty-four-year-old Oswald in a theater a short time later. After searching his wife's home, police compiled a large amount of evidence. They found the murder weapon, an Italian rifle with a telescopic sight, hidden in the School Book Depository. Oswald had purchased the rifle from a mail-order firm, and his palm prints covered it. Police soon charged Oswald with the murders of Kennedy and Tippit. Oswald was a former U.S. marine who had visited the Soviet Union and tried to become a Soviet citizen. Rejected by the Soviet government, he moved to Texas with his Soviet wife and worked various low-wage jobs. In Texas, Oswald became involved with supporters of Cuba's communist dictator Fidel Castro.

The sudden death of the American president shocked the world. On Sunday, November 24, his coffin lay in state in the Capitol Rotunda where hundreds of thousands of people filed past it. Kennedy was buried with full military honors at Arlington National Cemetery across the Potomac River from Washington, D.C. The nation grieved with Kennedy's brave widow, clad in black and clasping the hands of her two children. That same day, two police officers handcuffed to Oswald led him through a corridor of the police station on their way to the county jail. Suddenly, out of the crowd, a Dallas nightclub owner, Jack Ruby, stepped forward and shot Oswald as television viewers watched nationwide. Oswald died at Parkland Hospital.

Johnson appointed Chief Justice Earl Warren to head what became known as the Warren Commission to investigate the assassination. In September 1964 the commission issued an 888-page report that concluded that Oswald had acted alone. But many Americans disagreed with the Warren Commission report and theories that Kennedy died as a result of a conspiracy abounded. Some theories have connected Oswald with the Mafia, and others have speculated that he was a spy for the Soviet Union. Some theorists have tied him to the U.S. Central Intelligence Agency (CIA) or the FBI. One question that lingered in many people's minds is that a second gunman may have been involved. Some witnesses thought they heard shots from a grassy **knoll** in Dealey Plaza, or saw suspicious activity near there, though the Warren Report discounted their stories. During the 1970s a special committee of the U.S. House of Repre-

"Let every nation know, whether it wishes us well or ill, that we shall pay any price, bear any burden, meet any hardship, support any friend, oppose any foe, in order to assure the survival and the success of liberty."

John F. Kennedy, inaugural address, January 20, 1961

knoll: a small rounded hill.

sentatives reexamined the evidence. Experts testified to the committee that shots had been fired from two locations near Dealey Plaza. The committee concluded in 1978 that Kennedy "was probably assassinated as a result of a conspiracy." Others challenged the committee's conclusion. In 1982 the National Research Council, a scientific organization, issued a report disputing the House committee's finding. In 1991 filmmaker Oliver Stone released a movie, *JFK*, that stirred up many of the conspiracy issues.

The only known film of the entire assassination is a silent 8mm color home movie of the Kennedy motorcade immediately before, during, and after the shooting made by Abraham Zapruder, a Dallas dress manufacturer. The Warren Commission and the House Select Committee on Assassinations relied on it to answer questions about how the shooting transpired.

Due to its significance in American history, Dealey Plaza has been officially designated as the Dealey Plaza National Historic Landmark District. The Dallas County Historical Foundation operates the Sixth Floor Museum, which opened on Presidents' Day 1989. The museum maintains a variety of exhibits to help visitors from around the world understand the historic event. A section on the early 1960s gives background on political events, lifestyles, fashions, and the international setting of the era. A short film on the Kennedy presidency records his life and career.

Visitors can look down at Dealey Plaza from the south-facing windows of the sixth floor, and see the view Oswald would have had in 1963. A film, composed only of historic footage and audio broadcasts, summarizes the events surrounding the assassination. Another film analyzes national and world reaction to the assassination, including material about prayer vigils in India and torchlight parades in Germany. A special section of the museum explores the official investigations of the assassination. Other displays examine the acoustical evidence, photographs, **forensic** and **ballistics** tests, and other evidence examined during each major investigation. Alleged conspirators and their motives are discussed in this section as well as criticisms of the various investigations. The museum also includes an audiocassette tour with excerpts from historic radio broadcasts and the voices of reporters, police officers, and eyewitnesses. Historians and assassination buffs can use the museum's Public Research Center, which holds more than 14,000 items relating to the assassination, including

Many Americans disagreed with the Warren Commission report, and theories that Kennedy died as a result of a conspiracy abounded connecting Oswald with the Mafia, the CIA, or the FBI.

forensic: dealing with the application of scientific knowledge to legal problems.

ballistics: the study of the processes within a firearm as it is fired.

newspapers, photographs, books and magazines, video- and audiotapes, and other documentary materials. ◆

Dinosaur Ridge

Morristown, Colorado

I n 1877 professor Arthur Lakes and a friend, Captain Beckwith, were out exploring for leaf fossils near the town of Morristown, Colorado, when they stumbled upon what appeared to them at first to be the fossil impression of a large tree branch. Further inspection lead them to fragments of fossil bone and then to a huge vertebra thirty-three inches in diameter. This was no tree branch. What they had found would become one of the richest sites of dinosaur bones and fossils ever discovered. Their finds at Dinosaur Ridge were the first documented discoveries of dinosaurs in the western United States, and many of the dinosaurs uncovered there were the first discoveries of their kind in the world. Now well known, *Stegosaurus armatus*, *Allosaurus*, and *Apatasaurus Ajax* (*Brontosaurus*) were all first discovered at Dinosaur Ridge. By the end of 1877 ten quarries had opened along Dinosaur Ridge, and over the proceeding years a "gold rush" of paleontologists and other scientists would descend on the region. Similar sites were discovered at Cañon City, Colorado, Corno Bluff, Wyoming, and in 1908, near Vernal, Utah, discoveries would lead to what is now Dinosaur National Monument.

Dinosaur Ridge was formed approximately sixty-six million years ago when the whole region was tilted sharply by the rising of the Rocky Mountains to the west.

Dinosaur Ridge is located fifteen miles west of downtown Denver, Colorado, along the front range of the Rocky Mountains. The site has become famous not only for its wealth of dinosaur bones and fossils of bones, but also for hundreds of distinct dinosaur tracks, or footprints, called trace fossils. Dinosaur Ridge has so many sets of tracks that paleontologists refer to the site as the "Dinosaur Freeway." The discoveries at Dinosaur Ridge provide significant clues to the ongoing understanding of the earth's history. By knowing what kinds of dinosaurs lived where and when, scientists can better understand the causes behind the dinosaurs' extinction, as well as the geological and climatic changes that affected the evolutionary history of both extinct and living organisms.

Paleontology is the study of prehistoric animal and plant life through the analysis of fossil remains, and paleontologists study these remains as they appear in different layers of the earth, called strata. The Law of Superposition states that a given stratum must be older than any stratum on top of it, and it follows from this, generally, that older fossils appear in lower levels of the earth's strata. The bones, fossils, and trace fossils found at Dinosaur Ridge date back to the Mesozoic era, which is also referred to as the Age of Reptiles, for dinosaurs were dominant on land throughout the entire age. The Mesozoic era began approximately 225 million years ago, and it ended approximately 65 million years ago.

Paleontologists divide the last 570 million years into eras, periods, and epochs. The Mesozoic era (*meso* meaning *middle*) comes after the Paleozoic era (*paleo* meaning *ancient*), and before the Cenozoic era (*ceno* meaning *recent*). The Mesozoic era is divided into three distinct periods, the Triassic, the Jurassic, and the Cretaceous.

Dinosaurs first evolved during the Triassic period (225 million to 195 million years ago). Dinosaurs, then, were not nearly

Visitors can see fossils of dinosaur bones on the west side of Dinosaur Ridge in Morristown, Colorado.

bipedal: two-footed.

carnivorous: flesh-eating.

alluvial: found in or made up of sand or clay gradually deposited by moving water.

conifer: cone-shaped trees or shrubs like evergreens.

as large as our common conception of them today, for even the largest species rarely exceeded fifteen feet in length. Most were **bipedal**, running on their hind-feet. The marine reptiles, *Ichthyosaurs*, and the flying reptiles, *Pterosaurs*, evolved during this time also.

During the Jurassic period (195 million to 136 million years ago), dinosaurs continued to evolve into a wide array of sizes, with some weighing as much as eighty tons. This is the age of the four-footed *Sauropods*, like *Ankylosaurus* and *Stegosaurus*, as well as the two-footed, **carnivorous** *Tyrannosaurus*, and the winged *Pterodactyl*.

During the Cretaceous period (136 million to 65 million years ago), sea levels rose across the globe, submerging one third of the earth's land mass, and most of western North America at this time lay beneath a vast swamp. By the end of this period, all the dinosaurs had become extinct from the earth. The cause of this extinction is not definitively known, but one theory postulates that 65 million years ago, a comet, or asteroid, collided with the earth, and the resulting dust and debris in the earth's atmosphere blocked or filtered the sun's radiation, leading to the death of plants and animals upon which the dinosaurs depended for food.

The earth and its atmosphere were far different during the Mesozoic era. Days were several minutes shorter, because the sun then was not as powerful. (Scientists believe the sun has been slowly brightening over time.) Carbon dioxide, a gas that retains the sun's heat, was more prevalent, and so the surface of the earth was appreciably warmer. The earth's landmass was entirely united, a supercontinent scientists call Pangaea, meaning "all land." Correspondingly, the earth's oceans were united also, a vast sea referred to as Panthalassa, or "all seas." About 200 million years ago, near the end of the Triassic period, the earth's continents slowly began to separate. As a result, less land occupied the equatorial regions of the earth, and this led to more diverse climates and more diverse species of plants and animals.

In the middle of the Jurassic period, the region now comprised by Dinosaur Ridge was not a ridge at all, but a low-lying, **alluvial** plain of large rivers, streams, lush ferns and mosses, and a canopy of tall **conifer** trees. This habitat was home to *Apatasaurus* (commonly known as *Brontosaurus*), *Diplodocus*, *Stegosaurus*, and other herbivorous dinosaurs, and it was home also to many carnivores, like *Allosaurus*, that preyed on them. All of the bones discovered at Dinosaur Ridge date back to this Jurassic period. Dinosaur carcasses that washed onto Jurassic

sandbars were preserved over geologic time as thousands of layers of sediment gradually accumulated atop them and a sea advanced, covering everything.

The footprints of various types of dinosaurs line the rocks on the east side of Dinosaur Ridge.

Dinosaur Ridge was formed approximately 66 million years ago when the whole region was tilted sharply by the rising of the Rocky Mountains to the west. This massive upheaval revealed thousands and thousands of long-buried layers of earth, a stratigraphy dating back to Pre-Cambrian time. In certain places, Jurassic sandstone riverbeds were exposed, and it was in these Jurassic riverbeds that most of the bones and fossils at Dinosaur Ridge were discovered. Similar sedimentary layers of hardened sand and silt, first deposited during the Jurassic period, have yielded rich dinosaur discoveries all over the Rocky Mountain west. These deposits have come to be known as the Morristown Formation, named after the town of Morristown, Colorado, near Dinosaur Ridge.

Bones from these deposits provide paleontologists with a variety of clues regarding dinosaur interaction, body form, weight, posture, and muscle orientation. Rings within bones indicate growth rates, and broken or brittle bones suggest disease and other hardships associated with dinosaurs' lives.

While most of the bone and fossil discoveries at Dinosaur Ridge were found in Jurassic sedimentary rock, the dinosaur footprints were discovered in sandstone beds of the more recent Cretaceous period, and these footprints date back roughly 100 million years. The first footprints were uncovered by accident in the 1930s during dynamite blasting for a roadcut that was to pass over Dinosaur Ridge. Subsequent digs by paleontologists revealed several hundred more footprints.

Fossil footprints are classified by paleontologists as trace fossils. Trace fossils provide indirect evidence of ancient life and reflect some aspect of behavior. Examples of trace fossils include footprints, trails, burrows, gnawings, nests, and dung. The trace fossils at Dinosaur Ridge began as footprints in soft mud or clay that gradually hardened under the hot sun. Over geologic time, the hardened tracks were overlaid with layers upon layers of mud and clay during floods. At Dinosaur Ridge, footprints reveal the presence of two kinds of dinosaurs: therapods and ornithopods. Therapods were carnivores who stood erect on their two hind legs and left bipedal tracks. Ornithopods were **herbivores** that left either bipedal or **quadrupedal** tracks. Most tracks at Dinosaur Ridge reveal both manus (front foot) and pes (back foot) impressions. The manus impressions are three-toed with a circular or oval outline, while the pes impressions, also three-toed, are more narrow. Ornithopod tracks are often wider than therapod tracks, while therapod tracks are often deeper than ornithopod tracks, suggesting a horizontal walking posture.

herbivore: animals that chiefly eat grass or other plants.

quadrupedal: four-footed.

The tracks at Dinosaur Ridge are preserved in the Cretaceous sandstone in two main ways: (1) as impressions, or molds, of the original foot; and (2) as casts formed by sediment filling and overlying the original impression. Some dinosaurs were so heavy that their weight displaced layers of sediment beneath the surface, and these deformations are called undertracks. Though these tracks can be attributed to general classifications, and they do provide paleontologists with clues as to dinosaurs' movement, speed, and walking habits, no tracks provide enough detail to ascertain the exact **genus** or species of the track maker. Still, had dinosaurs bones never been discovered, conclusive evidence of dinosaurs would still exist in the form of these trace fossils.

genus: a category of biological classification ranking between the family and the species.

Visitors today to Dinosaur Ridge can participate in guided or self-guided interpretive tours of more than 300 dinosaur footprints. At both the Morristown Natural History Museum and the Dinosaur Ridge Visitor Center, visitors can view exhibits of dinosaur bones and fossils and trace fossils, as well as practice paleontological excavation techniques of dinosaur bones, including fossil extraction of a *Stegosaurus* discovered on Dinosaur Ridge in 1877. Students and teachers can also attend educational lectures, workshops, and Science Day camps. Evidence of an ancient, Cretaceous sea can be seen in the "ripple-marked" sandstone that marks the upper layers of Dinosaur Ridge, and all round them, onlookers can witness the multicolored, pastel shades of shale, sandstone, and siltstone that make up the thousands of rock layers of Dinosaur Ridge, some of which date back more than one billion years. ◆

Donner Pass

EASTERN CALIFORNIA

The gruesome fate of the Donner Party has a unique place in the legends of westward travelers; what happened to this group of emigrants in the 1840s is both horrifying and heartbreaking, particularly considering that they were tantalizingly close to their destination, San Francisco, when about half the party perished near the border of California and Nevada, near present-day Lake Tahoe. The chilling tale is redeemed, however, by the courage of the pioneers, the heroic self-sacrifice of the men in the rescue parties, and the fact that some of the Donner Party did survive.

Today the Donner Party and other pioneers who crossed the Sierra Nevada are remembered and rediscovered by about a quarter million visitors each year at Donner Memorial State Park. The park, west of Truckee, California, offers camping (150 sites), picnicking, boating, fishing, and hiking at altitudes of about six thousand feet.

During the winter of 1845—during a decade of westward migration that came to be called the "fabulous forties" even before the discovery of gold in California in 1848—James Frazier Reed and Jacob and George Donner decided to leave their homes in Illinois and move to California after reading *The Emigrants' Guide to Oregon and California* by Lansford Warren Hastings. The book touted California as a place "where perennial spring and never failing autumn stand side by side" and recommended

"Death would have been preferable to that awful meal, had relentless fate not said: 'Take, eat that ye may live. Eat, lest ye go mad and leave your work undone!'"
Eliza Poor Donner,
The Expedition of the Donner Party and Its Tragic Fate,
1911

1845 James Frazier Reed and Jacob and George Donner decide to leave Illinois and move to California.

1846 A caravan of 72 wagons sets out westward from Illinois.

1846 Stranded in snowdrifts, the party resorts to eating bark, twigs, mice, and eventually human flesh.

1847 Seven surviving members of the Forlorn Hope party reach an Indian village.

a route to California beginning in Independence, Missouri. Hastings advised travelers to proceed northwestward to the Kansas-Nebraska region, move on to the north fork of the Platte River to Fort Laramie in present-day Wyoming, cross the Continental Divide, and then proceed southwestward to Fort Bridger, also in Wyoming. From there, the author recommended a route that would cut two or three hundred miles from the journey: southwest to the Salt Lake Desert, west to the Humboldt River, and down to San Francisco Bay.

On April 15, 1846, emigrants gathered at Springfield, Illinois, to begin their westward trek. Among the travelers were George and Tamsen Donner and five children from his previous marriages; Jacob and Elizabeth Donner and their seven children; and James and Margaret Reed, their three children, and James Reed's mother, known as Grandma Keyes. Other families included the Eddys, Breens, Murphys, Pikeses, Kesebergs, Wolfingers, Graves, and McCutchens. Seventy-two wagons set out from Springfield. By the time the caravan reached Independence, it included almost three hundred wagons. Once the group crossed the Sandy River and arrived at Fort Laramie, George Donner was elected captain of a caravan of about forty wagons.

It was customary for a caravan to elect a captain as the central authority, and usually several lieutenants would be appointed to sections of the wagon train to keep order in the ranks, to ensure that the captain's commands were carried out, and to organize the wagons into position when the caravan stopped for the night. The captain was the one to select where the train would camp out for the night, usually based on the recommendations of guides or reports from scouts sent ahead to survey the terrain. Wagons were usually drawn together in a circle or square, end to end, to form a corral to hold the horses, mules, and cattle, as well as to form a defense for the passengers from Indian attack, buffalo herds, or storms that might make the animals stampede. In general, the ox-drawn trains averaged about ten miles per day, and horse- or mule-drawn wagons could travel about ten to fifteen miles in a day.

The group traveled on across Wyoming to Fort Bridger, where the travelers paused to discuss the shortcut recommended by Hastings's guidebook, the so-called Hastings Cutoff. While some of the group opted for the trail to Fort Hall—a longer route, but proven—George and Jacob Donner, the Reeds, and others decided to proceed to the shortcut, partly on the strength of a letter from Lansford Hastings, the guidebook author and "daredevil mountaineer," who had promised to meet them. Hastings did not show, and the shortcut turned out to be dead end for half the group, and even for the survivors it was a trail of horror and despair. The Donner and Reed group found the trail through the Wasatch Mountains in Utah to be nearly impassable; the canyons were choked with thickets, and the travelers could only progress a few feet at a time. This might have been an opportune moment to admit they had made a mistake and turn back to take the trail to Fort Hall chosen by the others.

The trek across the Salt Lake Desert would have been grueling enough even if the emigrants had had water. The eighty-nine travelers began quarreling; one man was murdered, and his killer was banished from the group. Indians preyed on their livestock. By the time the group reached the green meadows along the Truckee River on the other side of the desert, they were exhausted, the animals were dying, and the group decided they must stop and rest awhile. Weary as they were, had they known what was coming, they would have marched onward. On October 23, they prepared to enter the steep eastern face of the Sierra Nevada mountain range. Toward the end of October, the advance party reached Truckee Lake (now called Donner Lake), while the remainder stayed behind at Prosser Creek to repair a broken wagon. On October 28, about a month earlier than usual, a storm blew in, dumping six inches of snow on the ground and drifts three to five feet deep on the passes.

The faint trail was now obscured by snow. The travelers pressed ahead but were driven back by sleet. After another storm blew in that night, they knew they were trapped in the mountains. Winter had arrived. November ended with four straight days and nights of snow, and December brought in wind, sleet, and rain. At both Donner Lake and Prosser Creek, the party built shelters and huddled close as the snows continued to fall and their food supplies dwindled. They could neither continue forward nor return. The snow was twenty feet deep in some places near the camps at Alder Creek and Donner Lake. Most of the cattle that hadn't already wandered off and become buried in the snowdrifts had to be killed for food. By December 10, Jacob Donner and three others in the Donner huts along Alder Creek had died. The emigrants were eating bark and twigs, and the lucky ones caught a few mice.

A group of fifteen, later known as the "Forlorn Hope," set out on December 16 to try to reach California by foot. The ten

"There was no food in Starved Camp. There was nothing to eat save a few seeds, tied in bits of cloth, that had been brought along by some one, and the precious lump of sugar. There were also a few teaspoonfuls of tea. They sat and lay by the fire most of the day, with what heavy hearts, who shall know!"

C. F. McGlashan, *History of the Donner Party,* 1879

"Like fated trains of other epochs whose privations, sufferings, and self-sacrifices have added renown to colonization movements and served as danger signals to later wayfarers, that party began its journey with song of hope, and within the first milestone of the promised land ended it with a prayer for help."
Eliza Poor Donner, *The Expedition of the Donner Party and Its Tragic Fate*, 1911

men and five women had barely enough rations to last six days. By Christmas Day, the Forlorn Hope travelers had been without food for four days, and they knew that if any of them were to reach civilization, one of them must die. A new snowstorm blew in, and the Forlorn Hope group was snowbound, huddling around a campfire. They drew lots, but then could not carry through with the plan to kill one of their members. Two days later, after another snowstorm had blanketed them, they found that four of their members had died. The survivors then stripped, roasted, and ate the flesh of the dead and tried to regain their strength. As they pressed on, their stores of flesh were exhausted; when the two Indian guides with them collapsed on the trail—they had refused to eat the human meat—the survivors shot and ate them. The survivors then turned to eating moccasins, the strings of their snowshoes, and an old pair of boots. On January 10, 1847, thirty-two days after they had set out from the main party, the seven remaining members of Forlorn Hope—five women and two men—at last reached an Indian village. The Indians carried or dragged them to the Johnson Ranch at Wheatland, leaving a trail of bloody footprints in the snow.

The first relief party, of seven men on foot, reached the group camped at Donner Lake on February 19. There, survivors had eaten boiled hides and bones, and they too had resorted to cannibalism. The rescuers started back with a group of twenty-one survivors, three of whom died on the way out. They were met by a second relief party, which reached the camp at Donner Lake on March 1. Seventeen more survivors started back with the second rescue expedition, but they were met by a blizzard that stalled them in the snow for a week. This group's hands and feet froze, and the three who died were eaten. A third relief party found nine people still alive at Donner Lake, though three were too weak to travel. The third relief party started back with five survivors, including two daughters of George and Tamsen Donner. George Donner was dying, and once she was confident that her daughters would survive, Tamsen Donner chose to stay with her husband in hopes of nursing him back to health. By the time the fourth relief party arrived, only one man was still living—just barely—in squalor amid the bones of his former companions, including, presumably, Tamsen and George Donner. Eighty-one people had pitched camp at Alder Lake and Donner Lake in November 1846; forty-five of them made it across the mountains.

Given the history of the Donner Party, this particular state park can be excused from depicting in too much detail the "activities" for which those pioneers are remembered, and for offering instead a Pioneer Monument and the Murphy family cabin site. The Emigrant Trail Museum shows the natural and human history of the area, with particular attention to the geologic upheavals that formed the Sierra Nevada and made so formidable a barrier to the travelers from "back East." With Donner Lake and Creek at the park, and Lake Tahoe National Forest nearby, visitors to Donner Memorial State Park can see some of the best of California's "perennial spring and never failing autumn" that Lansford Hastings described so seductively in the 1840s. ◆

Edison Laboratories

WEST ORANGE, NEW JERSEY

Built on the site of Thomas Alva Edison's laboratories and home in West Orange, New Jersey, the Edison National Historic Site and its exhibits first came under the stewardship of the National Park Service during the late 1950s and early 1960s as a donation from the inventor's heirs.

Edison's West Orange laboratory was devoted to research and development—what Edison called "the business of inventing." The first of the buildings in the complex were constructed in 1887, to Edison's personal specifications. In 1888 further structures were added as his research and design facilities expanded. Here he and his "muckers" dreamed up all sorts of new gadgets, from the electric light bulb to the motion picture camera.

The buildings that make up Edison's laboratory look little different from New Jersey's many other abandoned factory enclaves. Thus, it is difficult to recognize how this collection of buildings could have had such an impact on the development of industry and technology in the nation. The six oldest brick buildings housed Edison's physics, chemistry, and **metallurgy** labs, his machine and pattern shop, his research library, and his experimental labs. The buildings constructed a year later were dedicated to the manufacture of articles invented in the research complex. In addition to all the inventions credited to Edison, he also invented a method of merging research and design with production and distribution—an integration of tasks that was unheard of before Edison began working in his West Orange laboratories.

Thomas Edison was born on February 11, 1847, in Milan, Ohio, to Samuel Ogden Edison Jr. and Nancy (Elliott) Edison.

"We are striking it big in the electric light, better than my vivid imagination first conceived. Where this thing is going to stop Lord only knows."
Thomas Edison, in a letter, 1879

metallurgy: the science of metals.

87

Thomas Edison's laboratory in West Orange, New Jersey, where Edison worked from 1887 to 1931.

His father was a successful businessman at the time of young Thomas's birth, but the family suffered financial reverses in 1854 and they relocated to Port Huron, Michigan, to make a fresh start. There Thomas attended a school taught by the Reverend G. B. Engle, but his first experience of formal education lasted only a few short months. The Reverend and his wife found Thomas so impatient and distracted that they deemed him mentally impaired—a judgment that so outraged Mrs. Edison that she promptly pulled Thomas out of the school and decided to personally oversee his education.

Mrs. Edison's approach to educating her son proved to be ideally suited to his gifted mind and wide-ranging curiosity. She taught him basic reading, writing, and math, but she also introduced him to the subjects that would become the passion of his later life: physics and chemistry. Young Thomas took to his mother's prescribed course of study with determination, and by the age of ten had begun the kind of original experimenting that would characterize the rest of his life.

But however important his mother's approach to his education may have been to the development of his mind, he still was only, in his words, "playing" at his makeshift laboratory in the

family cellar. The turning point, when Edison ceased playing and began experimenting and inventing in earnest, was his loss of hearing, which occurred when he was still a youth. Rendered shy by his infirmity, he redoubled his devotion to his studies, and began to explore the newest scientific and technological developments of his day. One of these, the telegraph, provided the foundation upon which Edison's later life as an inventor would be built.

Edison's chemistry laboratory in West Orange.

At the age of fifteen Edison attached himself to a local mentor, J. U. MacKenzie, to learn how to operate the telegraph. By the time he was sixteen he was proficient enough to seek employment and traveled around the midwest working as a telegraph operator. In 1867 he decided to try his luck out east, and took a position with Western Union, in Boston, Massachusetts, where he worked until 1869. Because the work entailed long periods with nothing to do, Edison used his spare time to read science books. When, in the course of his reading, he discovered the work of English scientist Michael Faraday, Edison became inspired to try inventing full-time.

Edison and his crew returned to West Orange to invent the motion picture camera and develop improvements to existing sound technology.

With his first patent under his belt, for an electric recording device, Edison left Boston for New York City, where he found

Edison's desk, preserved as he left it, at his laboratory in West Orange.

work in a firm called Law's Gold Indicator Company. But Edison was not about to give up his plans to become a full-time inventor, and within a few months he found two other like-minded men—Franklin L. Pope and James N. Ashland—with whom he formed the firm of Pope, Edison, and Company. The men intended to design and build instruments for use in the telegraph industry, as well other experimental items. The company enjoyed near overnight success, and the partners sold it to the Gold and Stock Telegraphic Company for a good profit. At the age of twenty-three, Thomas Edison found himself financially successful enough to strike out on his own.

Edison took his profits from the sale of his company and invested it in the first of what he came to call his "invention factories," this one in Newark, New Jersey. Here, where he worked for six years, he concentrated on producing refinements on stock-market **tickers** and telegraph equipment, but also carried on original, unrelated research as well. His time in Newark was very productive—it yielded approximately 200 patents.

ticker: a telegraphic device for recording stock market quotations.

By 1876, however, Edison was ready to expand operations, and he relocated to Menlo Park, New Jersey, where he had had a plant constructed to his own specifications. For ten years, he and his colleagues worked in a fever of invention and experimentation, and some of his most famous innovations were produced at the Menlo Park facility, including the phonograph and the incandescent light bulb. With the success of this latter invention, he became the operator of the first electrical power sta-

tion in the world, located in New York City. (A reconstruction of the Menlo Park facility is now housed in the Henry Ford Museum in Dearborn, Michigan.)

Glenmont, where Edison and his family lived from 1886 to 1931, in West Orange, New Jersey.

By 1886 Edison had once more outgrown his surroundings, and the following year found him in West Orange, New Jersey, overseeing the construction of his next, and last, invention factory. Ten times the size of the Menlo Park complex, this would become so extraordinarily productive a research facility that Edison and his crew soon averaged a new patent every five days. It was here that he and his team would invent the motion picture camera, and where they would develop improvements to existing sound technology, among many, many other innovations and inventions.

Edison's innovation went further than simply integrating the inventing process with production and distribution. He also was among the first to build a highly dedicated research team, his "muckers." It was their task to build, test, and refine Edison's inventions. He drew on talent from all over the country and Europe. Among them were Jonas Aylsworth, a chemist who worked closely in the development of materials with which to make phonograph recordings.

Another of Edison's muckers was John Ott, who became Edison's chief model maker and supervised the machine shop. A third was William Kennedy Laurie Dickson, whose work focused on development of the motion picture camera and studio; there is some dispute as to whose contribution—Edison's or Dickson's—was ultimately more important to the nascent film industry. Edison could be difficult to work with at any time, but it appears that these two had a stormier relationship than most in the lab, and Dickson ultimately left to work for Edison's competitors.

The laboratory complex of Thomas Edison's final invention factory houses the largest collection of Edisoniana in the world, with as many as 400,000 individual artifacts, and the extraordinary archives of this creative genius—over five million documents. From sketches of prototypes to masters of early sound recordings, and models of inventions, the collection housed here is unique in the world.

Edison's home, Glenmont, a 15.67-acre estate that was built in 1880, is also part of the Edison National Historic Site. Today, the house contains the Edison family's original furnishings. It has twenty-nine rooms, a greenhouse, a garage, a barn, and the family gardens. Thomas Edison and his second wife, Mina, are buried at Glenmont. ◆

Effigy Mounds

NORTHEASTERN IOWA

In northeastern Iowa, along the high bluffs of the Upper Mississippi River, mysterious earthen mounds, built by the ancestors of today's Native Americans, cover the landscape in the shape of bears, birds, bison, deer, turtles, snakes, and other animals. In 1949 these "effigies," or animal "likenesses," were preserved for future generations as a part of the Effigy Mounds National Monument.

Earthen mounds were once common along the shores of the great rivers of America's east and midwest, and from the Mississippi River to the Atlantic coast, thousands upon thousands were built over the last two millenniums. Yet at no other known place but the upper Mississippi River valley were earthen mounds built to resemble animals. The exact purpose of these

effigy mounds is shrouded in mystery, and archaeologists and anthropologists offer many theories regarding their significance. The investigation of this mystery can only lead us to a better understanding of the culture and beliefs of one of America's first peoples.

An aerial photograph of the Marching Bear Group of effigy mounds in Iowa. The mounds were outlined with lime for this photograph.

The Mound Builders that flourished along the Mississippi River were farmers who lived in permanent village settlements, and anthropologists and archaeologists refer to these agricultural civilizations as *Mississippian*. The soil there was rich and fertile, rejuvenated by annual flooding, and the Mound Builders tilled the land by hand and by hoe, cultivating maize, squash, beans, and other domesticated crops. They hunted deer, elk, duck, and fur-bearing beaver and otter and muskrat, and they fished the rivers and sloughs for food. Because of the abundance all around them, these Mississippian peoples could move beyond the mere concern for survival, and so theirs was far more than a subsistence economy. The Mound Builders were traders and travelers who used the great rivers and their tributaries to conduct commerce in a chain that extended hundreds of miles in every direction. From mounds in Iowa and Illinois, archaeologists

One of the bear mounds that make up the Marching Bear Group.

obsidian: dark-colored or black volcanic glass.

mica: a group of minerals that crystallize in thin, translucent or colored layers.

cremation: the burning of a dead body into ashes.

have excavated copper from Michigan's Upper Peninsula, seashells from the Gulf Coast, volcanic glass from the Rocky Mountains, **obsidian** from the Yellowstone plateau, and **mica** from Appalachia.

At Effigy Mounds National Monument, 191 mounds have been preserved, twenty-six in the shape of animals. Of these twenty-six, effigies of bears and birds are the most common. The largest effigy mound found there, Great Bear Mound, is 137 feet long, 70 feet across, and roughly 3 1/2 feet high. At another site within the monument, ten bear mounds and three bird mounds lay clustered together. Near Peebles, Ohio, an effigy mound called Serpent Mound snakes its way a remarkable distance of 1,350 feet. The cultural significance of these animal effigies is not well understood. Some sites clearly performed a burial function, for human bones have been excavated from them. Circular fireplaces placed near the head of many effigy mounds may perhaps have been used as altars during funeral rites. At other mound sites in other areas, the excavation of charred skeletal remains suggests evidence of **cremation**.

Some speculate that burial mounds performed a practical function, for if a death occurred in winter, the Mound Builders lacked the tools necessary to dig deeply into the frozen ground. Others believe the animal effigies were sacred spiritual sites, places of ritual, where ceremonies occurred that extended a deep gratitude and respect to the animals upon whom the people depended for their food supply. In these ceremonies, a pact was made with the animals, and a harmony with them was established. Aside from these speculations, it seems clear also that some mounds performed a far less dramatic purpose. Excavation from these mounds has revealed thousands of corncobs, squash rinds and seeds, and other kinds of agricultural debris.

Farther south, in the central Mississippi valley, the Mound Builders gathered together in far greater numbers, and archaeologists and anthropologists believe that the mounds there served still another function. At one site in particular, near present-day St. Louis, evidence suggests that a Mississippian city existed that may have been populated by as many as 40,000 people. This site, called Cahokia, is believed to be the largest city in North America prior to the arrival of Columbus, and hundreds of mounds existed there, some rising as high as fifty feet in the air. It is speculated that a hierarchical government, or chiefdom, was centralized there, and that mounds played both ceremonial and civic functions. Clusters of mounds gathered around a central plaza, and the higher mounds may have served as platforms for the residences of important officials, chiefs or priests. The varying size of these mounds, and their locations in the community, may have been outward signs of the class and prestige of those who lived near or atop them. Also, burial excavations in the area have revealed exotic artifacts and jewelry, and a comparison of such sites with other, more simple burial mounds, further suggests the presence of a stratified, status-based civilization. In the valley surrounding Cahokia, evidence of smaller hamlets and villages has been discovered, and in many of these villages, only one mound exists, which may indicate the village's relative importance and lesser relation to the central capital. Other capitals with outlying settlements, like Cahokia, existed at varying distances along the Mississippi all the way south to the Gulf Coast.

In addition to this great diversity of purpose, mounds took on many different sizes and shapes, including flat-topped or terraced pyramids, cones, ovals, and simple, linear constructions. The mounds were probably made by carrying baskets of earth, each possibly weighing up to sixty pounds, and by the stamping of feet. Because of the massive size of some of the

Burial excavations in the Effigy Mounds area have revealed exotic artifacts and jewelry.

One of numerous conical mounds (round domes of earth, 2 to 10 feet high and 10 to 20 feet in diameter) at Effigy Mounds National Monument.

mounds, construction must have taken a small army of manual laborers. Some of the largest mounds may have been added to and added to, taking generations to reach their final dimensions. Archaeological evidence of Paleo-Indian civilization in the region dates back to 12,000 B.C.E., and scientists believe the oldest mounds may have been built as early as 4000 B.C.E.. The Mound Builder society was the culmination of more than 8,000 years of cultural development, and they most certainly were the ancestors of the Choctaw, Dakota Sioux, Kickapoo, Winnebago, Otoe, and Iowa peoples, to name only a few of the Native American groups living in the region today.

The ancestors of today's Native Americans were not always thought to have been the great Mound Builders of North America. For self-serving, prejudiced reasons, many European settlers in nineteenth-century America were tremendously reluctant to attribute the mounds' construction to a people they perceived as heathen. They believed that such complex earthworks, such obvious evidence of "civilization," could not possibly be the work of a people they believed inferior to themselves. They believed that, instead, the sophisticated Mound Builders must have been a "vanished race," most likely of white, European origin, who for some unknown reason had disappeared or were wiped out by "savage" Indians, who came later. With this ironic rationalization, European settlers could portray the Indians they encountered as **interlopers**, with no true claim to the land. This false belief was finally exposed for what it was in the late nineteenth century by the scientist Cyrus Thomas of the Smithsonian Institution. Beginning in 1890, for four years he excavated mounds in the Mississippi River Valley, and his findings decisively concluded that many of the mounds had been constructed both *during* and *after* the time of first European contact, thus putting to rest the question of the true ancestral identity of the Mound Builders.

interloper: intruder.

The last effigy mounds are believed to have been built around 1300 C.E., and just as the effigy mounds' purpose is mysterious, so too is the cause of decline for their builders. In other mound building communities, the cause of decline is far clearer. Mound Building communities in Florida and Mississippi were thriving when the Spanish explorer Hernando de Soto encountered them in the 1540s, and the demise of the Mound Builders in these southeastern communities is directly related to the European invasion of the Americas. Mound Building peoples were decimated by disease, sold into slavery by European slave traders, and murdered by the thousands. The last of the Mound Builder civilization hung on in small pockets in the Mississippi delta, before disappearing forever sometime in the 1700s.

Mound Building peoples were decimated by disease, sold into slavery by European slave traders, and murdered by the thousands.

Visitors to the Effigy Mounds National Monument today can explore eleven miles of self-guided trails winding among and around the effigy mounds. The Monument sponsors lectures and archaeological presentations, as well as Native American storytelling and dance and drum ceremonies. Visitors witness pottery-making, basket-making, pipe-making, and bead-working demonstrations by Native American artists living in the region. The Monument is habitat also for hundreds of species of migratory birds, including bald eagles, great blue herons, egrets, and cormorants, and bird-watching hikes are popular.

Today, archaeologists estimate that less than 10 percent of the estimated 10,000 mounds that once covered northeastern Iowa still exist. Since the turn of the twentieth century, these mounds have been plowed under for farms, built over by developers, and eroded by weather. The primary goal of the Effigy Mounds National Monument is not archaeological excavation, but preservation. No excavations are planned for the foreseeable future. ◆

El Morro Fortress

SAN JUAN, PUERTO RICO

The complex of fortifications in and around San Juan is an extraordinary tribute to the defensive planning and engineering skills of a number of individuals, from Field Marshall Alejandro O'Reilly, who conducted the research on which the design of the defenses was based, to the team of architects and engineers led by Lieutenant Colonel Thomas O'Daly who designed and executed the plans. Today they form part of the San Juan National Historic Site, centered on the capital of Puerto Rico.

The El Morro Fortress (full name: San Felipe del Morro Fortress) forms the centerpiece of this defensive installation— one so well designed that it indeed lived up to the terms of the royal decree that approved its construction: "San Juan in Puerto Rico shall be a city of the first order of support for the island, bulwark of the Antilles, [and] safeguard of the Gulf of Mexico." Today the fortress is part of the National Park Service, which maintains the facility as a historic site.

Spain was the first European nation to colonize the Americas, but the Spanish could not hope to maintain their monopoly on the new lands for long unless they established and maintained a strong defense. The first rival to try to take Puerto Rico from Spain was the French, in 1528. This attack spurred Spain to build a defensive structure, *La Fortaleza,* in San Juan. Completed in 1533, it remains in use today as the Governor's Residence.

To consolidate and expand the defense of the settlement of San Juan, El Morro fortress was constructed beginning in 1539, and its value was clearly underscored when the city came under attack by Sir Francis Drake in 1595. Unfortunately, it proved inadequate to the task of defense just three years later, when the settlement was briefly captured by a second British attack.

The Dutch, another of Spain's early rivals for empire, made their opening moves to challenge Spanish supremacy in the New World by attacking the island of Puerto Rico in 1625. Spain succeeded in repelling the attack, but only after the city was partially destroyed by the invaders. Spain quickly recognized the need to strengthen the defenses of the island. The early fortifications at San Juan were among the first sites slated for upgrade. City walls were built, and they were later extended

1528 The French try to take Puerto Rico from Spain.

1533 Spain builds the defensive structure La Fortaleza in San Juan.

1539 Work begins on the construction of El Morro fortress.

1595 El Morro fortress protects San Juan during an attack by Sir Francis Drake.

1625 The Dutch attack San Juan; Spain later upgrades fortifications.

1897 Spain grants Puerto Ricans the right to self-rule.

1900 Spain cedes Puerto Rico to the United States.

1933 The United Nations declares El Morro fortress a world heritage elite.

El Morro Fortress in San
Juan, Puerto Rico.

northward from San Juan to connect the city to the two primary forts nearby: El Morro and San Cristobal.

A protracted period of peace lasting well into the eighteenth century, however, led the Spanish to neglect the island's physical defenses, and the fortifications soon fell into disrepair. But when the British began to aggressively challenge Spain's Caribbean holdings at the end of the 1750s, it became clear that neglect could no longer be tolerated. The British campaign had early successes, including the 1762 conquest of Havana, so Spain's King Charles III ordered the defenses of the Puerto Rican capital to be repaired and improved.

Accordingly, King Charles III decreed that Field Marshall Alejandro O'Reilly undertake an initial assessment of Puerto Rico's vulnerabilities and strengths. O'Reilly spent two months in 1765 gathering the information he required for a comprehensive analysis of the defensive needs of the island. The results of his fact-finding tour formed the basis of his "General Program of Military Reform" with an appended "Project of Fortifications."

Charles III considered San Juan to be of utmost importance to the maintenance of Spain's New World colonies, and he was therefore quick to see the value of O'Reilly's recommendations.

From O'Daly's design arose one of the most sophisticated defensive installations to be established in the Americas.

He immediately ordered that they be put into effect. Lieutenant Colonel Thomas O'Daly was appointed to supervise the repairs and new construction, supported in this enterprise by three engineers and two architects. Work on the fortifications commenced on January 1, 1766.

O'Daly and his fellow engineers aimed to make Puerto Rico's defenses "active"—that is, they sought to do more than simply provide thick walls to repel invasion. Instead, they intended to use the fortification's defenses to make enemy approach to the capital daunting, if not impossible. They noted that El Morro Fortress, northwest of San Juan at the entrance to the bay, was perfectly situated to prevent enemy ships from entering San Juan harbor. Fort El Canuelo, located across the bay from El Morro, was equally well placed. It could support El Morro in the defense of the bay, and it could block the passage of enemy ships to the Isla de Cabras. The Castle of San Cristobal, which had been built northeast of the city of San Juan, provided coverage of the shoreline, should enemy forces attempt to land and attack from that direction.

O'Daly's design for the defensive emplacements in and around San Juan called for multiple installations, including a defensive ditch, batteries of artillery, and the construction of an additional fort, Fort Abanico. From his design arose one of the most sophisticated defensive installations to be established in the Americas.

At the end of the nineteenth century, the United States had finally achieved a position of secure sovereignty within its borders and was beginning to look beyond its borders at establishing itself as a world power. Given the nation's revolutionary heritage, it is not hard to understand that one important ideological element of American foreign policy would be to foster independence movements in neighboring lands. This, combined with the expansionist drive that had led to the settlement of the continent from the Atlantic to the Pacific shores, gave birth to a dawning interest in establishing an overseas presence for the United States similar to that which was enjoyed by the British, Germans, and French.

In the Western Hemisphere, there were two tempting possibilities for U.S. acquisition: Cuba and Puerto Rico. These were all that were left of Spain's once-vast holdings in the Americas, and Cuba was actively seeking to free itself from colonial status. From 1868 to 1878 Cuban revolutionaries had engaged in a bloody war for independence that only ended when Spain

> From 1868 to 1878 Cuban revolutionaries had engaged in a bloody war for independence that ended when Spain promised to institute political reforms that would cede more autonomy to Cuban citizens.

promised to institute political reforms that would cede more autonomy to the island's citizens and end the corruption and oppression that had hitherto marked Spanish rule there.

But Spain reneged on its promises of reform, and in 1895 Cubans once again rebelled, hoping to wrest independence from the Spanish. While guerrilla battles raged in the jungles, the insurrectionists could not hope to take the garrisoned cities on their own, and tales of Spanish brutality soon made headlines in newspapers throughout the United States led by the Hearst flagship paper, the *New York Journal*. Hearst's editorial line strongly supported the cause of U.S. interventionism on behalf of the Cuban rebels, and soon brought the Congress over to his way of thinking.

While President Grover Cleveland resisted the pressure to commit American forces to the Cuban cause, his successor, President William McKinley, was ultimately moved to act. The event that triggered U.S. intervention was the sinking of the U.S. battleship *Maine*, which had been anchored in Havana Harbor. Although the cause of the explosion that claimed the lives of the ship's 260-man crew has never been determined, the incident provided the final impetus to force President McKinley into requesting Congress to declare war. On April 11, 1898, that declaration was made official.

While revolutionary fervor had been going on in Cuba, Puerto Rico was also straining at Spain's colonial leash, and as early as 1812 its people had gained recognition as full citizens of Spain rather than colonial subjects. By the middle of the century, a reformist movement had gained strength, and a Puerto Rico secessionist movement was born. Spain responded to increasingly vociferous calls for Puerto Rican independence by granting ever broader reforms. In 1873 slavery was abolished and political autonomy was increased. But none of these reforms was adequate to fulfill Puerto Rican aspirations for full independence.

When the prospect of the United States officially entering the Spanish-Cuban conflict began to look inescapable, Spain attempted to short-circuit further agitation in Puerto Rico that might hamper the larger war effort against the United States and Cuba. In 1897 it essentially granted to the Puerto Rican people the right to self-rule, and approved local political elections. However, these steps to autonomy would never be fulfilled: almost immediately after the first locally elected representative government took office in San Juan, Spain ceded

Spain ceded Puerto Rico to the United States in the Treaty of Paris, which brought the Spanish-American War to an end.

Puerto Rico to the United States in the Treaty of Paris, which brought the Spanish-American War to an end. The great fortifications of El Morro and San Juan, which could no doubt have withstood a military assault, could not prevent the negotiations of diplomats. The United States immediately imposed military rule, which lasted until 1900. When a civilian government was once again permitted, it had only limited authority, with the majority of control held by the U.S. federal government. ◆

Ellis Island

New York Harbor

> "Our family left England shortly after I was born and sailed to America. What a glorious sight as all the little Hopes clambered up on deck as the ship steamed into New York Harbor."
> Bob Hope, speech upon receiving the Ellis Island Medal of Honor, 1986

ordnance: cannon or artillery.

Long before Ellis Island became famous around the world as "America's front door" through which millions of immigrants entered the United States, it was a sandy island of only 3.3 square acres that was barely visible at high tide. Today the island is home to the Ellis Island Immigration Museum (part of the Statue of Liberty National Monument), which receives about two million visitors each year. Because of its role as an entryway for about twelve million (from whom about 40 percent of the U.S. population is descended) and as the place where they officially left the old country behind, Ellis Island is one of the most emotionally compelling national monuments. It is not unusual to see old people (and sometimes their grandchildren) weeping as the ferryboat approaches the island, especially with the sight of the Statue of Liberty towering nearby, lifting her lamp "beside the golden door."

Situated one mile southwest of Manhattan near the New Jersey shore and called Kioshk, or Gull Island, by the local Indian tribes, the island had plentiful oyster beds and was known as Oyster Island for many generations during the Dutch and English colonial periods. In addition to Kioshk and Oyster, its various names have included Dyre, Bucking, and Anderson's island. The island's last private owner, one Samuel Ellis, purchased it in the 1770s, and the United States bought it from New York State in 1808. Before becoming an immigration station, the island served as a hanging site for pirates, a harbor fort, and an ammunition and **ordnance** depot called Fort Gibson (named for an officer killed during the War of 1812).

After the Revolutionary War (1775–83), the United States government decided that it was critical to build coastal fortifications in New York Harbor, for early in the war the British had been able to sail straight into the harbor without a fight, and they occupied the city till the end of the war. The United States bought the island and included it in a series of fortifications built around the city shortly before the War of 1812. The harbor defense system included two earthworks forts at the entrance to New York Harbor at the Verrazano Narrows, Fort Wood on Bedloe's Island (now Liberty Island, home of the statue), Castle Williams on Governor's Island, and Castle Clinton at the Battery (now called Castle Garden, the fort near where the ferries dock to take visitors out to Ellis Island and the Statue of Liberty). The fortifications on Ellis Island included a parapet for three tiers of circular guns.

In America's early days, of course, there was no national "immigration policy" as such; for about the first 150 years, settlers simply arrived in boats, established settlements, or joined existing settlements, and were on their own. For a century after the Revolutionary War and the establishment of the United States of America, each state was responsible for its own immigration. The movement of peoples to the new nation was steady for many decades, and mainly limited to western European nationalities, but began to diversify and increase dramatically around the middle of the nineteenth century. Because of political instability in Europe, famines, deteriorating economic conditions, political or religious repression, and the increasing availability of ships to carry people, the stream of immigrants became noticeably more populous, particularly after the American Civil War (1861–65).

Because New York was America's largest city and the destination of many shipping lines, most immigrants entered through New York's reception depot at Castle Garden at the Battery, which opened in 1855. But that station was too small to accommodate the large numbers of immigrants, and many people complained that the officials were corrupt and were either causing or allowing unsuspecting newcomers to be exploited or otherwise abused by immigration officers or opportunists who bribed the officials.

In 1890 Congress transferred responsibility for the processing of immigrants from the states to the federal government, and in 1892 the station was moved from Castle Garden to a new building on Ellis Island. The immigration center opened on January 1, 1892, and the first immigrant to be processed at Ellis

1770 Samuel Ellis buys the island.

1808 The United States buys Ellis Island from New York State.

1890 Congress transfers responsibility for the processing of immigrants from the states to the federal government.

1892 The immigration station is moved from Castle Garden to Ellis Island.

1897 The immigration building is destroyed in a fire.

1900 The new fireproof Main Building opens.

1954 Ellis Island is officially closed.

1965 President Lyndon Johnson makes Ellis Island part of the Statue of Liberty National Monument.

1976 Ellis Island opens to the public.

1984 A $165 million renovation of Ellis Island begins.

The Main Building at Ellis Island immigration station in New York Harbor, where millions of immigrants were processed before their entrance into America.

Island was a fifteen-year-old Irish girl named Annie Moore, accompanied by her two brothers.

The new immigration building had been constructed of Georgia pine and a slate roof, and served well for five and a half years, until it somehow caught fire on the night of July 14, 1897, and burned to the ground. Fortunately no one was killed in the blaze, but it was an irretrievable loss to historians and genealogists that the fire consumed federal and state immigration records dating back to 1855. The United States Treasury, the federal department responsible for immigration, ordered that a new facility be established, and required that all future immigration structures on Ellis Island be fireproof. The new Main Building—the one that houses the present Immigration Museum—was opened on December 17, 1900, and 2,251 immigrants were processed on that day.

The little island was gradually expanded by landfill, some of which may have come from the tunnels being dug around this time for the New York City subway system, whose first line opened in 1904. Gradually the island grew to accommodate thirty-five new buildings and processing centers until it reached its present size of twenty-seven and a half acres. The big steamship companies around the turn of the century included Cunard, White Star, Red Star, and Hamburg-America. First- and second-class passengers on these ships did not have to go through the inspection procedures at Ellis Island, but were given a quick inspection onboard the ship. The government reasoned that anyone who could afford the more expensive berths on the liners would likely be affluent enough not to become a burden because of illness or legal complications. The passengers in third class or steerage traveled in less sanitary conditions in cramped quarters near the bottom of the steamships on the two-week voyage across the Atlantic from Europe. When the ship docked in New York City at the Hudson or East River piers, the first- and second-class passengers would disembark first, go through the customs line at the piers, and enter freely into the New World. The steerage and third-class passengers were transported to Ellis Island by ferry or barge.

The inspection process at Ellis Island—which often included about 5,000 immigrants per day—would take about three to five hours, if all went well. The examinations were conducted by officials of the United States Public Health Service and the U.S. Bureau of Immigration (now known as the Immigration and Naturalization Service). The inspections were performed in the Reception Room, or Great Hall. The doctors would quickly check for various diseases, and soon grew adept at giving "six-second physicals"; it was said that through experience the physicians became able to identify many common ailments (such as anemia, trachoma, goiters, or varicose veins) simply by glancing at an immigrant. If a physician diagnosed that the immigrant had a contagious disease, or if a legal examiner determined that he or she was likely to become a public charge or an illegal contract laborer, then the applicant would be sent back to the port of origin. A special building had been constructed to house the excluded applicants with contagious diseases until they could be sent back to the mother country.

Before the ship had left its port of origin, each immigrant's name had been entered on the ship's manifest log (a register of all people on board), along with his or her answers to twenty-nine standardized questions. At Ellis Island, the newcomer's answers were scrutinized by the legal examiners to check the person's personal history (for example, did he have a police record back home?). Each immigrant would be asked a rapid-fire list of questions, such as name, birthplace, and destination. What is your trade? Do you have a job? How much money do you have?

"It was the stir and bustle of trade, together with the tremendous immigration that followed upon the war of 1812 that dislodged them. In thirty-five years the city of less than a hundred thousand came to harbor half a million souls, for whom homes had to be found."
Jacob A. Riis, *How the Other Half Lives: Studies Among the Tenements of New York*, 1890

The Great Hall at Ellis Island immigration station, restored to appear as it did in 1918.

About 20 percent of the arrivals were detained for one reason or another. Immigrants who had no money, or who appeared to have an incurable disease, disability, or other defect that would diminish their ability to work, were held back for further examination and a hearing before a Board of Special Inquiry. In addition, women and children traveling alone were held until officials could make sure they would be looked after (as by a family member) after they left Ellis Island. While waiting, the detainees were housed in dormitories and ate meals in a large dining hall that seated 1,200. Most of those detained were eventually allowed to enter; only 2 percent of the applicants were denied entry.

Immigration to the United States decreased as Europe was engulfed in the Great War, later called World War I, beginning in 1914. Suspected "enemy aliens" were brought to Ellis Island and detained, but between 1918 and 1919 these suspects were transferred to other locations so that the U.S. Navy and the Army Medical Department could use the island. After the war, during the "Red Scare" (fear of communists after Russia's 1917 Bolshevik Revolution), thousands of suspected radicals were interned at Ellis Island, and some were deported.

Ellis Island's uses as an immigration portal began to decline in the early 1920s, as many Americans began to complain that the nation could not take any more immigrants. The Quota Laws of 1921 and the National Origins Act of 1924 restricted the numbers and places of origin for immigrants, in favor of western and northern Europeans, and to the disadvantage of would-be immigrants from southern and eastern Europe.

During World War II, Ellis Island's baggage and dormitory buildings were a holding pen for captured enemy merchant seamen, and the U.S. Coast Guard trained about 60,000 servicemen there. In 1954 the last detainee was released—a Norwegian merchant marine named Arne Peterssen—and Ellis Island was officially closed.

In 1965 President Lyndon Johnson made Ellis Island part of the Statue of Liberty National Monument. From 1976 to 1984 Ellis Island was open to the public on a limited basis. In 1984 began a major, $165-million renovation—the largest restoration of a historic site in the nation's history—organized by the Statue of Liberty–Ellis Island Foundation in partnership with the National Park Service. After extensive cleaning, painting, structural reinforcements, and installation of museum exhibits, the Main Building was opened to the public on September 10, 1990.

The Ellis Island Immigration Museum's exhibits are spread over 40,000 square feet on three floors of the Main Building, which itself was restored to look as it did around the years 1918 to 1924. The exhibits include museum objects (such as documents, ships' manifests, passports, children's toys, clothing, and luggage), photographs, oral histories, interactive displays, and videos. Through enlarged photographs, videos, and tape recordings, and physical objects left behind or donated by immigrants, the museum conveys vividly the experiences of the millions of newcomers as they passed through these halls generations ago. The Ellis Island Oral History Project has collected over 1,500 interviews in a long-term effort to preserve the firsthand recollections of immigrants' experiences during the years 1892 through 1954, and is still taking applications. The interviews are being transcribed and added to a computer database that can be accessed in the Immigration Museum's library.

No visitor to Ellis Island can help but sense the presence of ghosts, and feel a strong sweep of emotions, from wonder and pride to sorrow and sympathy for the millions of individual lives that passed through here, transforming forever their own destinies and that of the new world they came to discover. ◆

"The poorest immigrant comes here with the purpose and ambition to better himself and, given half a chance, might be reasonably expected to make the most of it. To the false plea that he prefers the squalid houses in which his kind are housed there could be no better answer. The truth is, his half chance has too long been wanting, and for the bad result he has been unjustly blamed."
Jacob A. Riis, *How the Other Half Lives: Studies Among the Tenements of New York*, 1890

Ethan Allen Homestead

BURLINGTON, VERMONT

E
than Allen's farm sits high on a bluff in Burlington, surrounded by the forests and mountains of Vermont. The little farmhouse was the home of Vermont's most colorful hero. When he and his family moved to the Burlington area in 1787, it was the very edge of the American frontier. Allen's homestead is a lone survivor of the many small, isolated farms that eighteenth-century settlers carved out of the American wilderness. These farms symbolized the dreams of pioneers who sought a piece of land of their own to live on, to farm, and to raise their families in freedom.

Why would Ethan Allen or anyone else leave the relative safety of colonial towns and set out into the back country? Some pioneers simply sought adventure, excitement, and freedom. Most Vermont settlers came from New England colonies like Massachusetts and Connecticut, where local governments dictated almost every aspect of the colonists' lives, right down to the kinds of clothes they could wear and the church they could attend.

Other pioneers struck out into the wilderness in search of inexpensive land. Litchfield, Connecticut, where Ethan Allen was born in 1738, had become overpopulated and land had become expensive. Owning land was very important in the 1700s because people who were not landowners could not vote or hold elected office. Land was also the main source of wealth. Timber, cleared lots, fish, and animals were natural resources the owner could sell, and crops could support a family well.

For all these reasons, Ethan Allen chose to leave his Connecticut home. He knew that he would only be able to prosper if he owned land, and Vermont was full of rich land. A farmer in Vermont could buy large pieces of land cheaply and develop it over the years. Allen loved exploring and adventure, and had traveled up and down northern Vermont's lonely mountains as a youth, hunting and fishing alone for weeks at a time. For several years, he lived in the town of Bennington in southern Vermont, but he was drawn to the northern Vermont frontier. Tremendously tall and strong, he was outspoken on local matters, disagreed with church teachings, and often fought with his neighbors. As a result, he never managed to fit into the communities of Bennington or Litchfield, and occasionally got thrown out of town. The Vermont frontier was eventually settled by independent-minded people like Allen, sometimes misfits and troublemakers, who wanted to live in a new land, away from old ideas.

In Bennington in the 1760s Allen founded the Green Mountain Boys, a group of Vermont settlers who fought for the rights of individuals to own the land they farmed. As their leader, Ethan Allen inspired the Green Mountain Boys to defend their land grants against New York, whose government claimed to own Vermont. Because Ethan and his brothers owned thousands of acres of Vermont land, it was in their best interest to make sure that New Yorkers did not get a foothold in Vermont. Allen ordered harassment and humiliation to be used against Yorkers, but he forbade killing anyone. The Green Mountain Boys often attacked at night. They burned down Yorker barns, turned cattle loose, and surrounded Yorker farms and made frightening noises. They once gave a New York official the "high chair treatment"—tied him to his chair and suspended it high in the air for hours. Ethan Allen himself grabbed two surveyors by their hair, lifted them off the ground, and knocked their heads together until they agreed to leave for good. Not surprisingly, some colonists considered Allen immature and irresponsible.

Despite their unconventional and controversial tactics, Allen and the Green Mountain Boys proved indispensable at a crucial point in the fight for American freedom. Allen's love of independence led him to support the cause of the Revolution and to detest the British. At the start of the Revolutionary War in 1775 the British occupied Fort Ticonderoga in New York, which sat right across Lake Champlain from Vermont. From the fort, the British controlled transportation on this crucial waterway through the continent. In May 1775, with Benedict Arnold, who had not yet betrayed the colonists' cause, Allen and the Green Mountain Boys captured the fort in a daring nighttime attack, one of the first victories of the Revolution. When they approached the fort's commander's room, some say that Allen demanded he surrender "in the name of the Great Jehovah and the Continental Congress." Others say that Allen ordered him to "come out of there, you rat, or I'll smoke you out." In either case, the commander did indeed give up the fort and was sent off to Connecticut as a prisoner. Always impulsive and independent, Allen then decided, without authority from General George

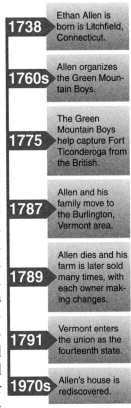

1738 Ethan Allen is born is Litchfield, Connecticut.

1760s Allen organizes the Green Mountain Boys.

1775 The Green Mountain Boys help capture Fort Ticonderoga from the British.

1787 Allen and his family move to the Burlington, Vermont area.

1789 Allen dies and his farm is later sold many times, with each owner making changes.

1791 Vermont enters the union as the fourteenth state.

1970s Allen's house is rediscovered.

Ethan Allen (center) meeting Captain de la Place at Fort Ticonderoga.

Washington, to try to capture Montreal from the British. He was soundly defeated and spent much of the rest of the war as a prisoner of the British.

After the war, Ethan Allen and the Green Mountain Boys began to build homes and farm their land in Vermont. During the late 1700s life on the Vermont frontier was rife with hardship. Roads were little more than paths through the mountains and woods, so even reaching the homestead could be difficult. Many settlers could only reach their land on foot, carrying all their belongings in rough oxcarts. Towns and houses were few and far between, but an occasional tavern would give them a place to stay for the night. Settlers might be injured or killed by wild animals, snow, rushing rivers, or illness.

Once pioneers arrived on their new land, much work had to be done. Ethan Allen worked on his farm with his second wife, Fanny, until his death in 1789. He and Fanny raised their children and the children of Ethan's first wife, Mary, who had died many years earlier. At the Allen homestead, there were eleven people living under one roof. There were no stores, so a family like the Allens had to be self-sufficient. Ethan and a few hired helpers cleared land and planted crops like rye and corn. Fanny was responsible for clothing and feeding the entire household. She grew the family's food in her kitchen garden. There were no doctors on the frontier, and women also grew herbs to treat illness and injury. Fanny and her children made linen clothes from flax they had grown, spinning the flax by a long, laborious process into thread, then weaving the thread into cloth, which was finally made into a garment. The family also made its own candles. They had to use the sun's rays to spark a flame. Sometimes, if the fire in the family fireplace went out, one of the children was sent to a neighbor's home to bring back live coals. Itinerant blacksmiths and shoemakers traveled from village to village doing the few jobs that settlers were not equipped to handle themselves.

Children on the frontier also worked hard. They carried water, cooked, sewed, hunted, and cleared land. Children learned to read if their parents taught them. The Allen children were lucky, for their parents were well educated. Fanny was a botanist who was consulted by farmers about their crops. Ethan wrote several books, and often signed his letters "The Philosopher."

Meanwhile, the thirteen colonies became the United States. Vermont, with its land carved out from New York and New Hampshire, was not one of them. It was a small, independent country, denied admission as a state because New York still claimed that it owned Vermont. Stubborn Vermonters continued to seek statehood. By 1789 Kentucky also wanted to join the Union. To maintain the balance of slave and free states, New York reluctantly withdrew its claim and Vermont entered the union as the fourteenth state in 1791, followed by Kentucky as the fifteenth.

After Allen's death in 1789, his farm was sold and during the years the property changed hands many times. Each owner added rooms, moved windows, and built new barns until Allen's little brown farmhouse became hidden beneath additions and layers of siding and paint. People eventually forgot that an eighteenth-century house lurked inside. The site served as a dairy farm during the first half of the twentieth century. In the 1970s Ethan Allen's house was rediscovered. Vermonters bought the property and almost 300 acres of Allen's original farmland. Later construction was peeled away, revealing the remains of the house Ethan Allen had built two centuries earlier. Much of the original building had decayed, and historians had to speculate as

"Princes may make laws and repeal them, but they can neither make nor destroy virtue, and how indeed should they be able to do what is impossible to the Deity himself? Virtue being as immutable in its nature as the divine will which is the ground of it."
Ethan Allen, *Reason, the Only Oracle of Man*, 1854

The restored home of Ethan Allen in Burlington, Vermont.

to what it looked like during Ethan Allen's life. They restored the house using lumber that would have been available to Ethan Allen, and filled it with furnishings appropriate to Allen's time.

Today, the Ethan Allen Homestead is a museum open to the public. Archaeological digs on the site have uncovered more than 10,000 artifacts that tell the story of Vermont's eighteenth-century settlers. Hundreds of acres of forest around the homestead preserve the landscape just as it was when Ethan Allen first arrived. The building that served as a barn for the twentieth-century dairy farm has become an education center, housing exhibitions on life in Ethan Allen's Vermont. ◆

Ford's Theatre

WASHINGTON, D.C.

Ford's Theatre, at 511 10th Street NW in Washington, D.C., is the site of President Abraham Lincoln's assassination in 1865. Commemorating one of the most tragic events in U.S. history, Ford's Theatre National Historic Site consists of this three-story, red brick structure and the house across the street in which Lincoln died. Plays, musicals, and other theatrical productions are staged as a living memorial to the sixteenth U.S. president. Historic objects associated with the story of the assassination are exhibited in a basement museum.

Abraham Lincoln ironically had struggled through four turbulent years to bring an end to the American Civil War only to die of violence spawned by the conflict. On April 14, 1865, five days after Confederate general Robert E. Lee surrendered to Union general Ulysses S. Grant at Appomattox, Lincoln was shot by John Wilkes Booth, a Southern sympathizer.

Lincoln, his wife, Mary Todd, Major Henry Reed Rathbone, and Rathbone's fiancée, Clara Harris, had arrived at Ford's Theatre at 8:30 P.M. to watch a performance of *Our American Cousin* from the presidential box on the second floor.

Booth, a well-known Shakespearean actor, was familiar with the theater and with the play. At about 10:15 P.M., while only one actor was on stage and the audience was laughing loudly, Booth entered the box, shot Lincoln in the back of his head and stabbed Rathbone in the left arm. As he jumped to the stage, Booth broke a bone in his left leg but made his way to an alley behind the theater. He mounted a horse and escaped before the 1,675 theatergoers realized what had happened.

"I mourned and yet shall mourn with ever-returning spring."
Walt Whitman, "When Lilacs Last in the Dooryard Bloom'd," 1866

Ford's Theatre in
Washington, D.C.,
c. 1865, site of Lincoln's
assassination.

Charles A. Leale, a twenty-three-year-old who had just completed his medical studies, and Dr. Charles S. Taft rushed to the unconscious president. They had Lincoln carried across the street to a narrow back bedroom in the home of William Petersen, a tailor. Leale, Taft, and about another dozen doctors knew that the president was mortally wounded, but they tried to make him comfortable throughout the night. Lincoln died at 7:22 A.M. the next day.

Booth, meanwhile, picked up other weapons he had left at the Surratt Tavern and fled with a coconspirator, David Herold, on horses into southern Maryland. They stopped at the home of Dr. Samuel Mudd, who set Booth's broken leg. They continued south toward the Potomac River, hid in the woods for a few days, and crossed the Potomac into Virginia. On April 26, Union troops surrounded them in a tobacco barn on Richard Garrett's farm near Port Royal, Virginia. Herold surrendered. Soldiers set the barn on fire hoping to force Booth out. He refused to budge and was shot and killed by Sergeant Boston Corbett.

Booth had hatched his plot in late 1864, but his first attempt to kidnap Lincoln failed. Meeting mostly in Mary Surratt's boardinghouse tavern, the conspirators finally drew up a scheme in which Booth would kill Lincoln, Lewis (Paine) Powell would kill Secretary of State William Henry Seward, and George Atzerodt would kill Vice President Andrew Johnson. Only Booth succeeded. Powell wounded Seward. Atzerodt got drunk and lost his nerve to pursue Johnson.

Besides Herold, the other conspirators were soon arrested and put on trial by a military commission. Herold, Atzerodt, Powell, and Surratt were hanged on July 7. Samuel Arnold and Michael O'Laughlin, who were involved in the initial plot, and Mudd were given life sentences. Edman Spangler, who held Booth's horse behind Ford's Theatre, was given six years of hard labor. O'Laughlin died in prison, and the other three were later pardoned by Andrew Johnson. Mary Surratt's son John, who had been involved in the initial plot, fled the United States but eventually was returned, tried, and acquitted.

Lincoln's assassination shocked a nation already saturated with the death and destruction of the Civil War. A funeral was held April 19 in the White House, and long lines of mourners filed past his body as it lay in state there and at the Capitol. On April 21 Lincoln's body and the body of his son Willie, who had died in 1862, left Washington by train for Springfield, Illinois, where the family had lived for nearly twenty-five years. With stops for services in Baltimore, Philadelphia, New York City, Chicago, and other major cities, the memorial procession took nearly two weeks.

Lincoln had risen to the presidency from humble rural beginnings. He was born in a one-room log cabin on February 12, 1809, near Hodgenville, Kentucky, to Thomas and Nancy Hanks Lincoln. His father was a carpenter and farmer. When Abraham was only seven, the family moved to southern Indiana. He spent much of his time helping with chores about the farmstead and received very little formal schooling. His mother died in 1818, and the next year his father married a widow, Sarah Bush Johnston, who raised Abraham and his sister.

The Lincolns moved to central Illinois in 1830, and, at twenty-one, Abraham headed off to make a living on his own. He worked on a flatboat heading to New Orleans, clerked in a store, failed at running a store with a partner, served as a village postmaster, assisted a surveyor, split rails for fences, and did a variety of other jobs. During the Black Hawk War he served in

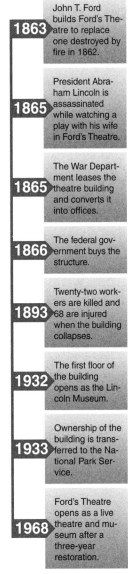

1863 John T. Ford builds Ford's Theatre to replace one destroyed by fire in 1862.

1865 President Abraham Lincoln is assassinated while watching a play with his wife in Ford's Theatre.

1865 The War Department leases the theatre building and converts it into offices.

1866 The federal government buys the structure.

1893 Twenty-two workers are killed and 68 are injured when the building collapses.

1932 The first floor of the building opens as the Lincoln Museum.

1933 Ownership of the building is transferred to the National Park Service.

1968 Ford's Theatre opens as a live theatre and museum after a three-year restoration.

John Wilkes Booth.

the militia for ninety days and was elected captain, but he did not see military action.

After running unsuccessfully in 1832 for the Illinois legislature, Lincoln was elected to the General Assembly four times. During this period, he also studied law. He was admitted to the bar in 1837 and moved to Springfield, the state capital. He married Mary Todd on November 4, 1842, and they had four sons. On his third try as a Whig, he was nominated and elected to the U.S. House of Representatives. Because of his opposition to the Mexican War, he was defeated for reelection and returned to his law practice in Springfield.

He stayed out of politics for five years, then lost an election for the U.S. Senate. Lincoln then joined the newly formed Republican party. He again lost a U.S. Senate race but gained national attention in a series of debates with Stephen A. Douglas for advocating a halt to the expansion of slavery into new states.

In 1860 he won the Republican nomination for president. The nation was deeply divided into sections, and Lincoln faced three other candidates in the general election. The split vote helped him defeat Douglas, a northern Democrat; John C. Breckinridge, a proslavery southern Democrat; and John Bell, a Constitutional Unionist. South Carolina soon seceded from the Union, and by the time Lincoln was inaugurated in March 1861 six other southern states had left, too. By mid-April the country was entangled in a bitter war.

The Civil War consumed Lincoln both as president and commander in chief. He took an active role in selecting and replacing generals and in deciding the Union's broad military goals. At the same time, he faced opposition from Democrats to many of his policies concerning civil liberties and differences and infighting among Republicans and within his cabinet. But overall, he governed with an even hand and won reelection in 1864 against Democrat George B. McClellan, a Union general Lincoln had relieved of command in 1862.

Lee surrendered on April 9, 1865, and five days later Lincoln decided to spend an evening relaxing at a theater. At the time, John T. Ford's playhouse was one of the most elegant and popular theaters in Washington. Ford had built the theater in 1863 to replace one destroyed by fire on December 30, 1862. The new theater opened eight months later, and 495 performances were staged until it was closed by the assassination. Ford was allowed to reopen the theater after the trials and hangings, but he received threats that it would be burned down. The War Department leased the building in August 1865 and converted it into offices. The federal government purchased the structure the next year.

Tragedy continued to plague the place: twenty-two workers were killed and sixty-eight were injured on June 9, 1893, when all three floors collapsed. The building then was used for storage until February 12, 1932, when the Lincoln Museum opened on the first floor to display Osborn Oldroyd's collection of Lincoln objects that the government had purchased. The building was transferred to the National Park Service in 1933.

"Much is said about the 'sovereignty' of the States, but the word even is not in the National Constitution, nor, as is believed, in any of the State constitutions. What is a 'sovereignty' in the political sense of the term? Would it be far wrong to define it 'a political community without a political superior'?"

Abraham Lincoln, July 4, 1861

Lincoln's box in Ford's Theatre, where he was sitting when he was shot.

Lincoln's assassination shocked a nation already saturated with the death and destruction of the Civil War.

Ford's Theatre was fully restored between 1965 and 1968, when it was reopened as a live theater and a museum. Furnishings are similar to those in the theater in 1865; those in the presidential box are reproductions except for the red damask sofa on which Rathbone was sitting. The numerous objects on display in the museum include the .44 calibre Deringer pistol Booth used to kill Lincoln, clothing Lincoln was wearing at the time, knives and other weapons carried by the accused, and White House china used by the Lincolns. Many of the artifacts come from the Oldroyd collection.

Ford's Theatre National Historic Site is open from 9 A.M. to 5 P.M. daily except for December 25. The National Park Service gives interpretive talks about the assassination in the theater when it is not in use for rehearsals or matinees. The first floor of the house where Lincoln died, which is also known as the Petersen House, is open for tours. The rooms include the front parlor, where Mary Todd Lincoln spent the night of April 14–15; the back parlor, where Secretary of War Edwin M. Stanton questioned eyewitnesses as he began his investigation of the assassination; and the bedroom where Lincoln died. The furnishings are not original but are representative of the period. ◆

Fort Clatsop

I n 1805–06 Meriwether Lewis and William Clark wintered at Fort Clatsop after their trailblazing journey from the Mississippi River to the Pacific Ocean. Their expedition across the North American continent between the Spanish colonies on the south and British Canada to the north provided the first detailed knowledge of the American northwest. It also awakened an interest that lured a procession of trappers and settlers into the region and helped make Oregon U.S. territory. Fort Clatsop National Memorial, a unit of the National Park Service, commemorates the winter campsite of the Lewis and Clark expedition and honors the Native American people who befriended them. The site is located near the extreme northwest corner of Oregon and tells the story of the Lewis and Clark expedition.

Fort Clatsop fosters a sense of stepping back in time to the early 1800s. Nestled in a lush, forested environment, the rustic log replica of the original fort, built by the local community in 1955, allows visitors to develop an appreciation for the struggles and hardships experienced by the thirty-three-member Corps of Discovery. The wetland habitat and associated wildlife of the area also played a significant role in Lewis and Clark's Fort Clatsop experience. Approximately fifteen miles south of the park, the Salt Works replica commemorates the site where members of the Lewis and Clark expedition extracted salt by boiling seawater.

In the early 1800s the U.S. government knew little about the North American continent. Before this expedition, the region between the Mandan Indian villages in present-day North Dakota and the Pacific Ocean was known only to the Native Americans who inhabited the region. Thomas Jefferson had been curious about this part of North America for many years and had tried several times without success to mount an expedition. When he became president in 1801, he hired Meriwether Lewis as his secretary and planned another expedition to

"We having fixed on this situation as the one best calculated for our winter quarters, I determined to go as direct a course as I could to the seacoast."
William Clark, journal, December 8, 1805

A reconstruction of Fort Clatsop as it looked during the 1805/1806 winter, when the party of Lewis and Clark encamped there.

explore the west. Jefferson and Lewis spent countless hours researching and consulting with experts on medicine, navigation, science and the lower Missouri River. Jefferson wrote a long letter to Lewis with instructions for the trip and it was then that Lewis invited his former army commander and friend William Clark to join the expedition as cocaptain. In addition to these instructions, Jefferson made sure the expedition was well supplied with presidential peace medals to be presented to chiefs of the tribes as symbols of peace and friendship.

President Thomas Jefferson had instructed Lewis and Clark to explore the Missouri River to its source, establish the most direct land route to the Pacific, and make scientific and geographic observations. They carried with them the destiny as well as the flag of the young nation westward across thousands of miles of land known previously only to the American Indian tribes who lived there, and fired the imagination of the American people, linking them across the continent on which they lived. However, the expedition represented more than a geographic exploration, as Jefferson charged Lewis and Clark with a quest for knowledge of the historic inhabitants and resources of the country through which they passed.

Lewis and Clark set out on their monumental journey on May 14, 1804, from the mouth of the Missouri River near St. Louis, in Wood River, Illinois. Their three objectives were to find, if possible, and map the fabled Northwest Passage; to learn about the people living in the west and to tell them about the United States; and to learn about the soil, land formations, plants, animals, fossils, geology, and climate of the areas they traveled through. With them was Clark's slave, a man named York, who would become the first black person to cross the North American continent.

After a tedious journey of five months, the Lewis and Clark party spent the first winter at Fort Mandan, North Dakota, 1,600 miles up the Missouri River, in a fort that they built among the Mandan Indian villages. Here they acquired the services of Toussaint Charbonneau, an interpreter of mixed heritage, who joined the expedition with his young wife, Sacagawea, and their infant son.

On April 7, 1805, the party left Fort Mandan and followed the Missouri and its upper branches into an unknown world. After traversing the Rocky and Bitterroot mountains, the expedition traveled some 600 miles by water down the Snake and Columbia rivers, reaching the Pacific Ocean—their western terminus and goal—on November 14, 1805. Finding themselves on the storm-bound north side of the Columbia, at a place called Station Camp, near present-day McGowan, Washington, the explorers had to decide where to spend the winter. They desired a more sheltered area, with an abundance of elk and where fresh water was available. Members of the Chinook tribe told them of the area along the southern side of the river, and with much discussion each member was given the opportunity to share an opinion, including York and Sacagawea. The expedition truly represented a diversity and collaboration unheard of 200 years ago, and together they determined their winter would be across the river.

When the decision had been made to relocate, Lewis, with a small party, scouted ahead and found a suitable location for their winter quarters. The site was three miles up the Netul River, which was later renamed the Lewis and Clark River. On December 7, 1805, the expedition members began to build a fort on the west bank of the waterway. By Christmas Eve they were under shelter. They named their temporary structure Fort

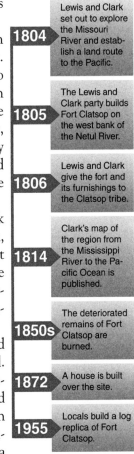

1804 Lewis and Clark set out to explore the Missouri River and establish a land route to the Pacific.

1805 The Lewis and Clark party builds Fort Clatsop on the west bank of the Netul River.

1806 Lewis and Clark give the fort and its furnishings to the Clatsop tribe.

1814 Clark's map of the region from the Mississippi River to the Pacific Ocean is published.

1850s The deteriorated remains of Fort Clatsop are burned.

1872 A house is built over the site.

1955 Locals build a log replica of Fort Clatsop.

Costumed volunteers at Fort Clatsop demonstrate an early 19th-century method of stretching and scraping hide.

The Lewis and Clark expedition would not have survived the winter for their return trip home if it had not been for the Clatsop people.

Clatsop after the friendly American Indians living in the area. It was to be their home for the next three and a half months and here the explorers, including Sacagawea and her infant son, spent the winter.

The nearest neighbors to Fort Clatsop were members of the Clatsop Indian band of the Chinook Nation. The Clatsops lived in plank houses in small fishing villages along the south shore of the Lower Columbia River and the Pacific Ocean. Their diet included salmon, other fish, deer, elk, roots, and berries. They were also very capable traders who had been trading historically for many hundreds of years. In addition they, along with their Chinook neighbors north of the Columbia, had much experience dealing with the earlier white explorers who had come to the area by ship and also traded. The Clatsop people also assisted the Lewis and Clark party in obtaining food, locating a suitable fort site, building and obtaining canoes, learning the region's topographic features and local flora and fauna, understanding the local traditions and languages, and obtaining needed supplies and equipment through trade. The Lewis and Clark expedition would not have survived the winter for their return trip home if it had not been for the Clatsop people.

Life at the fort was far from pleasant. It rained every day but twelve of the 106 days at Fort Clatsop. Clothing rotted and fleas infested the furs and hides of the bedding. The dampness gave nearly everyone some illness, which Lewis treated vigorously.

With all this adversity, the members of the expedition continued to prepare for their return trip. Perhaps the most important activity undertaken during the Corps of Discovery's winter stay at Fort Clatsop was the reworking of the journals by the leaders and the preparation of organized accounts of the scientific data gathered thus far during the journey. While at Fort Clatsop, Clark prepared many of the maps that were among the most significant contributions of the expedition. Thus there were two reasons the Lewis and Clark expedition survived the winter of 1805–06 and had a successful journey home: the assistance and knowledge provided to them by the Clatsop people, and their ability to take invaluable information they had gathered along the way and contribute to history some of the most important journals and maps ever created.

On March 23, 1806, Lewis and Clark presented the fort and its furnishings to Chief Comowool (Coboway) of the Clatsops, and began their return trip to St. Louis. Some returned to family and friends; others remained in the "wilderness," and all have gained a place in history among the greatest of explorers. Within a few years the fort fell into ruin, but the site quickly became an object of great interest to explorers and travelers, beginning with the arrival of the Astorians in 1811. Fur trappers, fisherman, farmers, and loggers also moved into the area shortly after the expedition left. Since the nearby city of Astoria, Oregon, was the first American settlement west of the Rockies, the fertile forest and farmlands of the region were the first public lands claimed, and transferred to, private American ownership. Many changes were made to the landscape as the region was developed for personal and commercial use. One change occurred in the early 1850s when the deteriorated remains of Fort Clatsop were burned and the land partially cleared for farming. A house was built over the site of the fort in 1872 but fortunately, in preparation for the centennial celebration of the Lewis and Clark expedition, the Oregon Historical Society purchased the site in the early 1900s. To commemorate the 150th anniversary of the expedition, the fort replica was built by local community organizations based upon the few remaining descriptions of the original fort and Clark's original floor plan sketched on the cover of his journal.

After the expedition, Clark produced a map of the region from the Mississippi River to the Pacific Ocean. This map was published in 1814 and was the first fairly accurate map of the west. With their discovery of the extensive Rocky Mountains,

The fort fell into ruin, but the site quickly became an object of great interest to explorers and travelers, beginning with the arrival of the Astorians in 1811.

A costumed volunteer at Fort Clatsop sews a buckskin moccasin.

estuary: an inlet of the sea where the tide meets the freshwater current.

the Corps of Discovery finally put to rest the rumor of the existence of a northwest passage across the continent. Jefferson's other objectives were also met. The explorers wrote extensively about the American Indians they encountered. They learned and recorded as much as they could about the politics, languages, occupations, food, clothing, health, customs, and beliefs of the people they met. These descriptions are, in many cases, the only information we have of long-established cultures that in a matter of years were either permanently altered or disappeared altogether. They also wrote scientific descriptions of 122 new kinds of animals and 178 new kinds of plants. The descriptions of the ancient forests, pristine wetlands and **estuaries**, and wildlife species and their abundance that were written in their journals have proved to be extremely valuable today.

Today Fort Clatsop National Memorial is administered as a unit of the National Park Service, ensuring that this rich history is treasured and preserved, and that this place and landscape that tell the story of our nation's diverse culture is protected for future generations. An archaeological research project is currently being undertaken to locate scientific evidence of the original fort. Facilities include a visitor center, the fort replica, historic spring and canoe landing site, a picnic area, water and hiking trails and a bookstore managed by the fort Clatsop Historical Association. The salt works site is also administered by the park. ◆

Fort Delaware

PEA PATCH ISLAND, DELAWARE

Colonial era legends hold that a boat carrying a cargo of peas upended in the Delaware River, spilling its freight onto a sandy islet, where the peas promptly took root and sprouted. Whether the legend has any basis in fact matters little—it is enough that it gave the name to Pea Patch Island, the site of Fort Delaware.

The precursor for the fort was a simple temporary earthwork, built in 1813 to provide defense for the city of Philadelphia during the War of 1812. A more permanent structure was erected in 1819, but it succumbed to fire twelve years later, and the present fort was designed to replace the damaged masonry structure. It would take nearly twenty-four years before the work could be completed, however, due to a dispute between Delaware and New Jersey as to just who had claim to the island.

From these embattled beginnings, it might have begun to appear that no permanent fort would ever be erected on little Pea Patch Island, but in 1847 Congress quickly made up for all these false starts by appropriating a million dollars to finance the construction of the largest and most modern fort in the nation (the original appropriation was later increased by another million dollars). Work commenced in 1849, and the final structure was completed ten years later, just in time for the start of the Civil War.

During the Civil War the fort saw no military action, but rather served as a prisoner-of-war camp. At war's end, it was

During the Civil War the fort saw no military action, but rather served as a prisoner-of-war camp.

Fort Delaware on Pea
Patch Island in Delaware.

decommissioned: re-
moved from service.

staffed only with enough personnel to maintain it in readiness
condition, and in 1896 it received new gun installations, in
anticipation of attacks on Philadelphia during the Spanish-
American War. The fort saw no action however, and in 1903
the force garrisoned at the fort was reduced to a token staff. It
would be fully manned twice more, during World War I, and
World War II, but at no time during its entire history were the
guns of the fort ever fired for anything but ceremonial reasons.
In 1944 Fort Delaware was **decommissioned**, and ultimately its
control and maintenance was transferred to the state of
Delaware. In 1950 the Fort Delaware Society was charged with
the site's preservation and interpretation.

In 1847 Fort Delaware was designed to be a state-of-the-art
defensive structure. The outer line of defense was a thirty-foot-
wide moat that is spanned by a drawbridge on the Delaware side
of the island. The fort proper was made up of a pentagon-shaped
enclosure constructed of thirty-two-foot-high walls of brickwork and granite blocks. At points along the perimeter, the
walls attained a thickness of thirty feet. Within the fort's walls,
a two-acre parade ground was bordered on the east and west by
barracks—the western barracks containing the fort's mess hall.

To the north of the parade ground were the administrative offices and the officers' quarters. The original design underwent some alterations over the years. In 1898, for example, concrete gun emplacements were built into the southern part of the fort, intruding on a portion of the original parade grounds, and necessitating the removal of the east barracks.

Fort Delaware has seen little use as a true defensive fort—its greatest claim to fame comes from its use as a prisoner-of-war camp during the Civil War. At the war's beginning, a company of artillery was garrisoned in Fort Delaware, soon to be joined by the Commonwealth Artillery of Pennsylvania, a volunteer unit. But the fort was well outside the combat arena from the very earliest days of the war, so its use as a defensive structure was limited. Instead, it became one of several forts that were pressed into service to house captured enemy soldiers and political prisoners. It was to become known to Confederate prisoners as "Fort Delaware Death Pen" and earned the reputation of being the most foul of all the Civil War prisoner camps on either side of the battlefield.

Fort Delaware received its first sizeable contingent of Confederate prisoners in 1862, with the Union defeat of Stonewall Jackson's troops at the battle of Kernstown. Two hundred and fifty captured Confederate troops were transported to Fort Delaware and crowded into barracks that were clearly inadequate to their task.

Knowing that this group represented just the first wave of prisoners to be accommodated within the fort, Captain A. A. Gibson, commanding officer, ordered the construction of wooden barracks capable of accommodating 2,000 prisoners at a time. Unfortunately, Captain Gibson seriously underestimated his future needs—in just a year, Fort Delaware would be housing more than 8,000 prisoners, and by August of 1863 the prisoner population exceeded 12,500. Gibson ordered further structures to be erected, but never succeeded in outpacing his rapidly growing population. At its peak, facilities had been built to accommodate no more than 10,000 prisoners, and the prison compound had spread beyond the fort itself to occupy nearly all the available land on the island.

The makeshift barracks constructed to house the great numbers of prisoners incarcerated in the fort were crude affairs. Rough-hewn planks were thrown together to form pens in which as many as ten rows of barracks were constructed. Three tiers of bunks lined the barracks walls, and prisoners were permitted either a single blanket or an overcoat for covering. The

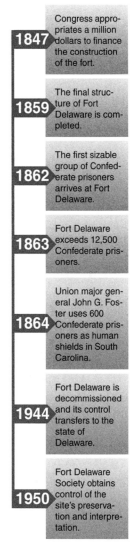

1847 Congress appropriates a million dollars to finance the construction of the fort.

1859 The final structure of Fort Delaware is completed.

1862 The first sizable group of Confederate prisoners arrives at Fort Delaware.

1863 Fort Delaware exceeds 12,500 Confederate prisoners.

1864 Union major general John G. Foster uses 600 Confederate prisoners as human shields in South Carolina.

1944 Fort Delaware is decommissioned and its control transfers to the state of Delaware.

1950 Fort Delaware Society obtains control of the site's preservation and interpretation.

brackish water of the Delaware was undrinkable, but no other provision had been made to supply the prisoners need, so they were reduced to collecting rainwater runoff from the roofs. Food was tightly rationed—often limited to a few hard crackers and a tiny portion of bacon, when meat was available at all.

The island was plagued with mosquitoes, supplies and medical services were never adequate to meet the needs of the often wounded or ailing prisoners, and the structures were dark, dank, and airless. Conditions were universally appalling, for the lowliest of privates and the mightiest of captured generals, such as General James J. Archer, taken at the Battle of Gettysburg, and for political prisoners such as Burton H. Harrison, the private secretary to Jefferson Davis. In the conditions that prevailed at the prison, illness frequently meant death—some 2,700 prisoners died during their stay. Most of these casualties are buried just a few miles away, in the National Cemetery at Finn's Point, on the New Jersey side of the Delaware River.

The appalling conditions in which Fort Delaware's prisoners were kept are but one aspect of the structure's history that has earned it a degree of infamy. More terrible still is the tale of "the immortal 600," the shameful treatment of whom must rank high in any enumeration of the evils of war.

In 1864 Union major general John G. Foster learned of a plan by Confederate officials to transfer 600 prisoners of war from Georgia's overcrowded Andersonville prison to a new location in the city of Charleston, South Carolina. This move caused some difficulty for Foster's military command, as he was actively shelling the South Carolina city, but since he knew the location of the Union prisoners he was able to avoid firing on his own captured troops. But the Confederate prisoner transfer gave Foster an idea of his own. He, too, would transfer some prisoners, but he would make far more effective tactical use of the action than the Confederates had done.

Foster's plan was simple, though it violated every accepted standard for the proper rules of engagement in war. He would take 600 imprisoned Confederate officers from their confinement in Fort Delaware and place them as human shields before his own artillery batteries. The hope was that the Confederate counter-artillery would not return fire, for fear of killing their fellow officers. He would justify this action by claiming it to be simple retaliation for the imprisonment of Union troops in Charleston. Upon receiving authorization from Washington, Foster was quick to put his plan into motion.

Conditions at the island were universally appalling, for the lowliest of privates and the mightiest of captured generals.

At Fort Delaware, the news filtered into the prisoners' barracks—600 men were soon to be sent south. Speculation ran high, mostly centered on the supposition that the men would be part of a prisoner exchange. On August 20 the men were put aboard a ship heading for South Carolina. They arrived at their destination on September 1, where they remained aboard ship as final preparations were made on Morris Island, where Foster's artillery was emplaced. On September 7, the prisoners were disembarked and placed within a stockade that had been built in front of Foster's guns. Insisting that the men would remain in harm's way unless the Confederates moved their Union prisoners—an impossible demand, given that all routes out of the city were blocked by Union forces—Foster kept the "600" in the line of fire, even though the southern forces chose not to desist in counterfiring against his artillery. Even after the Confederate forces succeeded in relocating their own prisoners from Charleston to Columbia, South Carolina, Foster continued to employ his human shields.

Although Foster's gambit ultimately failed, the fate of the "600" was sealed. When Union general William Tecumseh Sherman looked likely to succeed in taking Charleston, the utility of these hostages became nonexistent. Foster shipped them to Fort Pulaski, in Georgia, where they endured conditions even more deplorable than those they recalled from Fort Delaware. By the time that they should have been released, their numbers had declined to less than half, and the survivors were in such poor shape that their own deaths appeared imminent. Before they could be sent home they had to be returned to Fort Delaware to recuperate from their terrible experiences. ◆

> Foster kept the "600" in the line of fire, even though the southern forces chose not to stop in counterfiring against his artillery.

Fort Laramie

WYOMING

From 1834 to 1890 Fort Laramie, Wyoming, lay at a crossroads in the American west and witnessed a parade of settlement—the boisterous era of the fur traders, the cavalcade of overland travelers, the signing of significant Indian treaties and their resultant wars, and the coming of cattlemen and homesteaders. Founded in the summer of 1834 as a fur-trading post and initially named Fort William, the modest cottonwood

The signing of the Fort Laramie Treaty in 1868.

stockade was also called Fort Laramie, after a Frenchman killed on the Laramie River a decade earlier. The fort was founded to serve the Rocky Mountain fur trade, but it also quickly captured trade with the Oglala and Brule Sioux Indians as well.

Pierre Choteau Jr. and Company acquired the fort in 1836 and rebuilt it five years later. The company named the enlarged adobe-walled post Fort John, although it remained better known as Fort Laramie. Fur trading along the Laramie River was steady, but it never equaled the much larger harvests in the upper Missouri country or on the southern Great Plains.

The passing of a few Oregon-bound missionaries in the 1830s presaged an emigrant cavalcade traveling dirt trails in the 1840s and 1850s. The numbers were unparalleled, swelling from one thousand people through Fort Laramie in 1843, to three thousand in 1845, and eight thousand in 1847. In 1852 nearly sixty thousand individuals headed west, most lusting for California gold. To one and all, Fort Laramie was a haven offering touches of civilization and opportunities to refit before continuing the arduous road ahead.

Emigrants soon cried out for protection, which the politicians willingly provided. In the summer of 1851, the regiment of Mounted Riflemen arrived at the fort with an offer to buy Fort John for four thousand dollars. The acquisition was approved, and the post was rechristened Fort Laramie.

In 1851 and again in 1868 Fort Laramie hosted extraordinary delegations from the Sioux, Cheyenne, Arapaho, Crow, and other tribes of the Great Plains, first to negotiate unfettered emigrant passage on the trails and then to transform the Indians from nomadic hunters into Christianized farmers. In 1851 as many as ten thousand Indians attended the Fort Laramie or Horse Creek Treaty negotiations, during which the Indians agreed to allow traffic to pass unmolested through their country in return for annual payments of fifty thousand dollars.

Seventeen years later, the Fort Laramie Treaty of 1868 represented an honest attempt to end hostilities on the central and northern Great Plains—hostilities that had boiled continuously since 1854 when John L. Grattan's command was killed near the fort. By the 1860s the Sioux and their allies fiercely contested white traffic on the overland road and the newer Bozeman Trail to the Montana gold fields. Peace overtures, however, included demands that the Sioux move to a permanent reservation and give up long-held traditions. Neither the 1851 treaty nor the 1868 treaty brought about intended results.

The decades of the 1860s and 1870s were particularly chaotic at Fort Laramie, as its enlarged garrisons protected the Pony Express, the overland telegraph, and trail traffic and engaged in repeated campaigns against the Indian tribes. These were heady times for the warriors of both races, and events like the Great Sioux War of 1876 to 1877 brought unparalleled excitement and intensity to the work at Fort Laramie.

With the end of the war, however, much larger posts were constructed to guard the Great Sioux Reservation in South Dakota, and the coming of the transcontinental railroads ended emigrant travel by foot and wagon. Cattlemen and homesteaders spread across Indian country in the 1880s making the old treaties and war fort obsolete. The army abandoned Fort Laramie in the spring of 1890. It was designated a National Monument on July 16, 1938; in 1960 the fort became a National Historic Site, and today Fort Laramie's considerable remains are preserved as a unit of the National Park Service. Eleven of the Fort's original buildings have been restored and refurnished to

"From this day forward all war between the parties to this agreement shall for ever cease. The government of the United States desires peace, and its honor is hereby pledged to keep it. The Indians desire peace, and they now pledge their honor to maintain it."

Fort Laramie
Treaty, 1868

look as they did during the mid 1800s. The foundations of lime grout shells of other buildings are also preserved. ◆

Fort Larned

LARNED, KANSAS

> "The troops at this post will be prepared for inspection tomorrow at 4:30 P.M. in light marching order. All enlisted men except the guard, sick, one hospital attendant, one cook to each company, one baker, and one man in charge of the corral, will appear under arms. The staff at this post will report at 15 minutes past 4:00."
>
> Fort Larned records, 1868

In the mid-nineteenth century, the central plains region of the United States was still a wild and dangerous place. The Plains Indians were hostile to white settlements. Having had long experience with the dubious concept of "treaties" and recognizing that a few traders and travelers today inevitably meant wagonloads of settlers were soon to come, they were not disposed to welcome intruders into the region. In addition, the climate could be harsh and unforgiving, and the terrain difficult, for westbound travelers. The Santa Fe Trail provided a well-marked route for the early adventurers, hunters, and traders, as well as for the wagonloads of pioneering families who came later. It offered two options to the traveler: a wet route, well-watered and with plenty of grazing for cattle; and a dry route, which was significantly shorter, but which had few watering holes, creeks, or streams.

To provide a base for the military effort to cope with hostile confrontations between the Indians who occupied the region and the whites passing through to points south and west, Fort Larned was established in 1859 in southwestern Kansas. The second largest military operation on the Santa Fe Trail (after Fort Union, New Mexico), it remained in active military operation until 1878.

The Fort Larned National Historic Site commemorates the history of the Santa Fe Trail and the period known as the Indian Wars of the late 1800s. The fort itself still contains nine of its original buildings, including the barracks, commissary, blacksmith shop, hospital, blockhouse, and officers quarters, all of which have been restored and refurnished for visitors to view. A tenth structure was reconstructed in 1988 and modified to house the administrative offices, museum, and visitor's center for the site.

The park extends beyond the walls of the fort itself, and includes a portion of the original Santa Fe Trail. Among the trail features included within the park's boundaries are Pawnee Forks Crossing, where both the wet and dry routes converged, and

The parade ground and officer's quarters at Fort Larned in Kansas, with an 1867-era U.S. flag.

Ash Creek Crossing and Pawnee Rock, familiar landmarks to travelers on the wet route of the trail. A detached additional portion of the park, called the Santa Fe Trail Ruts Area, is located a little over four miles south of the fort. Here visitors can see preserved the gouges that westbound wagons once carved deep into the earth as they made their way along the trail.

In 1540 Don Francesco Vasques de Coronado was a man with a dream. He had heard tell of a fabulous city of gold, called Cibola, lying somewhere north of Spain's conquered territories in Mexico and he meant to make his fortune by finding and claiming them for the Spanish crown. He set forth with an army of soldiers, guides, and slaves to conquer the great legendary city, but when his party arrived at their destination they found only a multistoried adobe community of Zuni Indians, with no gold in sight. He named the region the "Kingdom of New Mexico," claimed it in the name of the Spanish crown, and moved on in his quest for treasure.

With new lands to administer, in 1598 the Spanish king got around to appointing Don Juan de Onate as first governor-general of the New Mexico Territory. Onate established the original capital of the province at San Juan Pueblo. When Onate retired in 1609, he was succeeded by Don Pedro de Peralta, who soon moved the capital to the site of present-day Santa Fe. But the **indigenous** peoples were not pleased with their new neighbors, and in 1680 they rebelled. After sacking and burning the city, they reclaimed the area for themselves, only to be reconquered in 1692 by a force led by Don Diego de Vargas. For the next 120 years, Spain would retain her hold on the region.

Spain was not interested in permitting free trade between her New Mexico holdings and the expansionist Americans to the north. Travel through the region was severely restricted, and trade was tightly controlled. But in the early 1800s interests in the United States were looking more and more covetously at the Spanish-held territories of Florida, California, New Mexico, and Texas. For reasons that remain unclear today, the governor of the Louisiana Territory, General James Wilkinson, commissioned Zebulon Pike to lead a party of exploration whose itinerary was to include discovering a route into the Spanish-held region around Santa Fe. Pike's party set out from St. Louis in 1806 and, after much travel, ultimately crossed over into Spanish territory.

In February of 1607 a Spanish force caught up with Pike and arrested him, taking him under guard to explain his presence to the governor of the province. Pike feigned ignorance, claiming to have taken a wrong turn at the Red River, which at the time formed the boundary between American territory and New Mexico. He was ultimately released, and brought back to the United States valuable geographical information, including several possible routes into and through New Mexico.

In 1821 Mexico—which at the time included the territories of present-day Texas and New Mexico—achieved independence from Spain. Suddenly, the trade restrictions imposed by Spain were no longer in force, and trappers and traders from the United States territories quickly moved in, hoping to acquire the goods, particularly silver, that could be found in the Santa Fe region. Now Zebulon Pike's maps and proposed travel routes became extremely useful to explorers who hoped to blaze a convenient trade route between Santa Fe and St. Louis—then the westernmost American city to which transportation had been fully established.

William Becknell was one of those early explorers and would-be traders. Almost immediately upon hearing that trade

indigenous: native.

1598 The Spanish king appoints Don Juan de Onate as first governor of the New Mexico Territory.

1609 Don Pedro de Peralta succeeds Onate and moves the capital to what is now Santa Fe.

1806 Zebulon Pike and party set out from St. Louis and cross over into Spanish territory.

1821 Mexico wins independence from Spain; U.S. trappers and traders move quickly into the Santa Fe region.

1823 William Becknell blazes what becomes the Santa Fe Trail.

1859 Funds are appropriated to build Fort Larned to protect caravans from Indian raids.

1861 Fort Larned becomes an Indian agency, from which the army administers the Central Plains Indians.

1878 Fort Larned is removed from active service.

restrictions with Santa Fe had been lifted, he set out from Missouri with a small party carrying manufactured trade goods in exchange for which he acquired furs and silver. His success inspired others—including Jacob Fowler and Hugh Glenn, who realized similar profits from their enterprise. In 1823 Becknell once again made the trip, this time with three wagons full of merchandise. With wagons, Becknell knew he would have to find a less difficult route, and he blazed what would soon become famous as the Santa Fe Trail.

Once the Santa Fe trade was well established, the United States was faced with several conflicting needs. It had entered into treaty agreements with the Plains Indians through whose territory the Santa Fe Trail ran, and wished at first to avoid confrontations between those peoples and the traders who were flocking south to New Mexico. The government renegotiated treaty boundaries to carve one route on which safe passage would be guaranteed, but it was less convenient than Beckworth's trail, and was therefore little used. As traders insisted on traveling across Indian territory, hostilities increased, and trading parties came under increasing attack.

Along the Kansas leg of the trail, which passed through present-day Larned, the Osage and Kaw (Kansas) peoples were particularly angered by the ever-increasing traffic of traders and, eventually, settlers, and attacks on travelers increased in number and ferocity. By the 1840s, with the U.S. annexation of Texas, the traffic only increased. As with the treaties of the more eastern tribes, the agreements once reached between the United States and the Osage, Kaw, and other indigenous groups would not be honored at the expense of the U.S. expansionist impulse, and the demand for military protection could no longer be ignored in Congress. This situation was only exacerbated when, in 1854, the Kansas Territory was formally opened up to settlers, abrogating all the earlier treaties with the Indians of the region. Funds had to be found to cover the costs of building military installations in the territory and along the Santa Fe Trail—among them, Fort Larned.

Becknell's route to Santa Fe brought travelers to a fork in the Pawnee River where there were three separate places to cross. Because the river ran high at times, at one of these crossing points a campsite was established where travelers could rest up before facing the challenge of fording the waters. Where there were travelers, there would be entrepreneurs who saw profits to be made, and here was no exception—Boyd's Ranch,

"The United States agrees that the following district of country, to wit: commencing at the point where the Arkansas River crosses the 37th parallel of north latitude, thence west on said parallel the said line being the southern boundary of the State of Kansas to the Cimarone River . . . shall be and the same is hereby set apart for the absolute and undisturbed use and occupation of the Indians herein named."

Treaty with the Cheyenne and Arapaho, 1867

near the crossing, offered liquor, gambling, and prostitutes to military men stationed nearby as well as to the traders, trappers, and travelers who were passing through.

With the 1854 opening of the Kansas territory to settlers, all prior restrictions on whites entering the region were lifted. By 1859 traffic through the area was so well established that the original camping ground became the site of a stagecoach station. Indian raids on trade caravans and the stage's coaches soon reached levels that the U.S. Congress found intolerable, and funds were quickly appropriated for the erection of Fort Larned to provide protection and maintain a constant military presence. In 1861 it became an Indian Agency, from which the military administered the increasingly restricted Indian peoples of the Central Plains. In 1867–68 it served as a major staging area for troops assigned to fight in the Indian wars that led to the final conquest of the native peoples. By 1878 the indigenous peoples had been so completely brought under U.S. control that the need for an active military presence no longer existed, and Fort Larned was removed from active service. ◆

> As traders insisted on traveling across Indian territory, trading parties came under increasing attack.

Fort Mandan

CENTRAL NORTH DAKOTA

F ort Mandan, on the east bank of the upper Missouri River in central North Dakota, marks the site where the members of the Lewis and Clark expedition quartered from November 1804 to April 1805, before continuing their journey west. Lewis and Clark passed through the Mandan area again on their return east in 1806.

The Lewis and Clark expedition was the first scientific expedition sponsored by the United States government. From May 1804 to September 1806, Meriwether Lewis, William Clark, and their Corps of Discovery became the first U.S. citizens to cross the North American continent. The geographical achievement, and the American claim of sovereignty in the Pacific northwest, captured the popular imagination, but the principal sponsor, President Thomas Jefferson, intended the expedition to be much more than a romantic adventure. Jefferson charged Lewis and Clark with a complex task. They were instructed to make a complete scientific survey of the regions

> "Visited the Mandans with all the men that could be spared from the fort. Talked with the Chief and several of the older men of the tribe."
>
> William Clark, journal, March 20, 1805

along their route up the Missouri River, across the Rocky Mountains, and down the Columbia River to the Pacific and to determine the latitude and longitude of important sites. Jefferson asked them to describe plant and animal life and the cultures of the native people they encountered. In addition, they were to evaluate the possibilities of the different areas for trade and agriculture and even try to establish peace with and among the native tribes they met.

A reconstruction of North Dakota's Fort Mandan on the site of the original fort.

Lewis, Jefferson's private secretary, was appointed to command the expedition along with Jefferson's friend William Clark. After leaving Pittsburgh in a specially constructed **keelboat** on August 31, 1803, Lewis sailed down the Ohio to pick up Clark at his home in Clarksville, Indiana. As they journeyed down the Ohio and up the Mississippi to St. Louis, they began to pick up recruits for their party. The explorers spent the winter of 1803 to 1804 at Camp Dubois or Camp Wood River, on the Illinois side of the Mississippi, waiting for the ice of the Missouri to melt and for the official transfer of Louisiana to the United States.

keelboat: a large, shallow freight boat with a timber or steel piece at the bottom that supports the frame.

By May 14, 1804, the party was ready to set out up the Missouri in the galley-like keelboat and two smaller boats, or **pirogues**. The first stage of the journey, on the lower Missouri,

pirogue: canoe-shaped boat.

was through country relatively well known, at least to the French traders and trappers who had extracted its wealth in furs and established business relations with the Indians over the previous decades. The explorers had maps of the river from northeastern Nebraska to the villages of the Mandan Indian tribes in North Dakota—maps drawn in the previous decade by the trader John Evans, who had traveled under Spanish auspices. The explorers met with the Oto and Missouri Indian chiefs at the Council Bluff in eastern Nebraska and established official relations between these tribes and the United States for the first time.

The party stayed a few days with the Arikara Indians in South Dakota. During their visit, the explorers participated in ceremonies to name chiefs (really a confirmation of the status quo), to give peace medals, and to establish a nominal sovereignty over the tribe. Taking an Arikara chief with them to make peace with the Mandans, they continued up river. At the Mandan and Hidatsa villages in North Dakota, near present-day Washburn, they established Fort Mandan, their winter quarters from November 1804 to April 1805.

Construction on the fort began on November 3, under the direction of Sergeant Patrick Gass, a skilled carpenter. The men worked for about four weeks, using lumber from a cottonwood grove near the site. The fort was simple, with a roughly rectangular main building flanked by two rows of smaller huts, which were surrounded by a triangular wall made from upright cottonwood logs. Clark's diary records that he and Lewis moved into their cabins on November 20, although construction continued until just before Christmas. The expedition's blacksmiths set up a forge to make tools and other implements that they could trade with the Indians for food during the winter. While at Fort Mandan, Lewis and Clark met the Canadian trader Toussaint Charbonneau and his Shoshone wife, Sacagawea, whom the expedition hired to serve as interpreters and intermediaries with Indians they would meet farther west. The couple's son, Jean Baptiste Charbonneau, born in February 1805 at Fort Mandan, also became a member of the party.

In April 1805 the explorers left Fort Mandan and continued up the river in the two pirogues and several dugout canoes. After a month-long portage of the Great Falls of the Missouri, they passed the Three Forks of the Missouri and continued up the westernmost fork, which they named the Jefferson, to reach the Continental Divide in August. There they saw more moun-

> *"We looked for a winter camp, but could not find anything suitable at first. At last, we decided to camp a point below where we were and build a fort for the winter. Wood and game are scarce, the men hear, thus they want to camp as close to those things as possible. The Mandans say that they will help with food this winter if the men stay nearby."*
> Meriwether Lewis, journal, November 1, 1804

Sacagawea

Sacagawea was a Shoshone Indian woman who became a guide and translator for the Lewis and Clark expedition from 1804 to 1805. Kidnapped as a child by the Hidatsa Indians, Sacagawea was taken from her home in Idaho to Mandan Indian country and eventually sold to French-Canadian fur trader Toussaint Charbonneau. It was through Charbonneau that Sacagawea became associated with Lewis and Clark. During their travels through the midwest, Lewis and Clark decided to spend the winter of 1804 with the Mandans in present-day North Dakota. They built a shelter, which they named Fort Mandan, and waited out the snowy months. Realizing they would need a guide, the group leaders hired Charbonneau, insisting he bring his wife, Sacagawea, as a translator, along with their infant son. Her knowledge of both Shoshone and Hidatsa, combined with Charbonneau's ability to translate Hidatsa into French, made Sacagawea a valuable asset. Using her language skills, she was able to secure food and horses from native tribes along the way that allowed the explorers to advance to the Pacific Ocean. Her mere presence, along with that of her young son, provided safety for the party, as a native woman and child traveling with white men indicated peaceful intentions.

As the expedition moved through Shoshone territory, Sacagawea met her brother, who was now the chief of the tribe. Through him she was able to gather valuable information about the lands across the Continental Divide. With Sacagawea's help, the Lewis and Clark expedition became the first to reach the Pacific Ocean over land. There is a monument erected at the site where she is said to be buried and the numerous other monuments, landmarks, and memorials that bear her name speak volumes of Sacagawea's life and contributions to the Lewis and Clark expedition.

tains stretching out to the west and realized that the portage to the headwaters of the Columbia would not be as easy as they had hoped. Fortunately, they also met the Shoshones, Sacagawea's people, and obtained not only horses but a guide who could lead them across the tangled mountain to navigable waters heading to the Pacific.

The Shoshone guide, whom they called "Old Toby," took them on a tortuous trek across the Bitterroot Mountains, down the Bitterroot River in western Montana, and again across the Bitterroot Range at its widest part. As the first snows began to fall, the explorers survived on horsemeat and condensed soup until they reached the country of the Nez Percé on the Clearwater River in western Idaho. They made canoes and, leaving their horses with the Nez Percé, continued once more by water down the Clearwater, the Snake, and the Columbia. Coming out of the mountains, they entered the barren Great Columbia

Plain and then the thick rain forest near the coast. Clark's "Ocean in view! O! the Joy," written on November 7, 1805, was just a little premature, but a few days later they did indeed stand on the shore and watch the waves of the Pacific roll in.

The explorers spent the winter of 1805 to 1806 at Fort Clatsop, named for the nearest Indian tribe in Oregon, south of the Columbia **estuary**. On March 23, 1806, they began their journey up the Columbia. They had delayed until then because they knew the interior country would be impassable from winter snows. They secured horses from tribes near the mouth of the Snake and continued overland to the Nez Percé country. Finding the Bitterroots still under several feet of snow, they stayed among the friendly Nez Percé for more than a month. Finally, some local guides enabled them to find the trail over the mountains despite the remaining snows.

Once over the Bitterroots, the explorers made a radical departure from their previous methods. Confident in their ability to survive, they split the party into two detachments in order to see more new territory. Traveling northeast across the Continental Divide to the Great Falls of the Missouri, Lewis intended to explore the Marias River. Clark went southeast to explore the Yellowstone. His trip was relatively uneventful, but Lewis's resulted in the only violent encounters with Indians of the entire expedition when he and three of his men had a skirmish with some young Blackfoot Indians who tried to steal their guns and horses. Traveling down the Missouri by canoe, Lewis encountered further misfortune when he was accidentally shot by one of his own men, the nearsighted Pierre Cruzatte, who mistook him for an elk.

The two parties reunited in North Dakota, revisited the Mandans, and persuaded the Mandan chief to accompany them to see the president. At the Mandan villages, they also left Sacagawea and Charbonneau. After visiting the Arikaras, the explorers raced downstream. On September 23, 1806, after being gone twenty-eight months, they reached St. Louis, where the citizens, who had long given them up for lost, gave them a noisy welcome.

Lewis reached Washington near the end of 1806 and turned the expedition journals over to Jefferson. The president intended for Lewis to write the history of the expedition, but he also appointed Lewis governor of Upper Louisiana (and Clark as superintendent of Indian Affairs for the territory). The appointment not only kept Lewis from working on the history but also

estuary: an inlet of the sea where the tide meets the freshwater current.

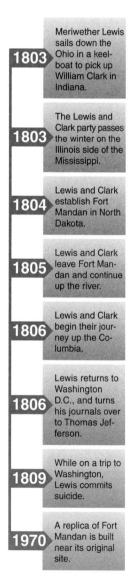

1803 Meriwether Lewis sails down the Ohio in a keelboat to pick up William Clark in Indiana.

1803 The Lewis and Clark party passes the winter on the Illinois side of the Mississippi.

1804 Lewis and Clark establish Fort Mandan in North Dakota.

1805 Lewis and Clark leave Fort Mandan and continue up the river.

1806 Lewis and Clark begin their journey up the Columbia.

1806 Lewis returns to Washington D.C., and turns his journals over to Thomas Jefferson.

1809 While on a trip to Washington, Lewis commits suicide.

1970 A replica of Fort Mandan is built near its original site.

led to personal disaster. The pressures and frustrations of office and a long-standing tendency to depression finally led Lewis to commit suicide in 1809 while on a trip to Washington. Clark then collaborated with Nicholas Biddle in producing an account of the great journey. Unfortunately, the scientific volume that was intended to accompany the narrative was never written. The scientific accomplishments of the Corps of Discovery were not fully appreciated until many years later.

Fort Mandan was destroyed in a fire shortly after the expedition's visit. During the twentieth century, archaeologists undertook a search for the remains of the fort, and designated a site in a wooded area on the banks of the Missouri River where they believe Fort Mandan once stood. A full-scale replica of Fort Mandan was constructed during the 1970s. The North Dakota Lewis and Clark Interpretive Center in Washburn provides an overview of the Lewis and Clark expedition, with special emphasis on the time spent at Fort Mandan. The town of Washburn also hosts an annual "Lewis & Clark Days" on the first weekend in June. ◆

Fort McHenry

BALTIMORE, MARYLAND

In Baltimore harbor, on Whetstone Point, one of the most historically and symbolically significant defensive structures of the United States was first built in 1776. Then called Fort Whetstone, it was strategically situated to prevent the invasion of Baltimore by the British during the Revolutionary War, but the simple fact of its presence seems to have been enough protection for the city. The British Navy never attacked Baltimore, but that happy circumstance did not diminish the vigilance of the military authorities of the newly independent United States. Secretary of War James McHenry succeeded in getting approval for the design and construction of a new, improved fortification on the original Fort Whetstone site. Jean Foncin, a French engineer, was given the commission, and the new fort was named for its principle supporter.

Fort McHenry has had a long, impressive history, but perhaps the most famous event associated with the site is the twenty-five-hour shelling the fort withstood during the War of

"Then, in that hour of deliverance, my heart spoke. Does not such a country, and such defenders of their country, deserve a song?"

Francis Scott Key, 1814

Fort McHenry, near
Baltimore, Maryland.

autonomy: independ-
ence.

1812. Every schoolchild knows the history of America's Revolutionary War, but few realize that this conflict did not definitively establish the independence of the newly formed United
States. In fact, less than forty years after having fought so hard
to win its autonomy, America very nearly returned to England's
colonial fold. The conflict that so jeopardized the fledgling nation's **autonomy** was the War of 1812.

   At the start of the nineteenth century, the United States
was expanding rapidly. Settlers were pouring through the Cumberland Gap to settle new lands in Kentucky and beyond, and
when, in 1803, the Louisiana Territory was purchased from
France, the opportunities for expansion seemed very nearly limitless. But the new nation faced challenges, nonetheless, as
France, Spain, and Great Britain each sought to hold onto
territories—or at least income from trade—in the New World.

   These challenges came to a head in 1807, when France and
England went to war over control of trade coming from the
American continent. The two European powers threw up
blockades around American ports, and the British were not
above confiscating American ships or kidnapping American
sailors and impressing them into the Royal Navy. This practice

had already, in 1807, caused confrontation between the United States and Great Britain. After an incident in which the USS *Chesapeake* was boarded by British seamen, President Thomas Jefferson was outraged. He retaliated with an embargo on shipments trying to leave American ports and banning British ships from U.S. waters.

The disruption of trade caused by the French and British blockades had a devastating impact on the American economy, and continuing British excesses on the high seas constituted an intolerable affront to U.S. sovereignty. As a result, war fever ran high, particularly among the "War Hawks," an anti-British political party that originated in the western territories. They became increasingly vocal in their calls for military action.

Of course, there were motivations beyond patriotic fervor behind the westerners' anti-British sentiments. It was believed that the British were secretly supporting the Indians of the northwest territories in their resistance to the encroachment of American settlers. Perhaps more important was the hope that a war with Britain would provide an excuse to appropriate the Floridas, Mexico, and far western holdings of Britain's ally Spain. The War Hawks lobby ultimately succeeded in pushing forward its agenda in the nation's capitol: in 1812 the U.S. Congress passed a bill declaring war on England, and President James Monroe signed it into law.

War Hawk fever notwithstanding, the War of 1812 was nearly disastrous for the United States, which was unprepared militarily and economically to take on so powerful a foe as England. On land, early U.S. initiatives met with discouraging defeat, although the relatively tiny American Navy did manage to achieve unexpected success in isolated confrontations with the British Fleet. Nonetheless, by 1814 it was beginning to look highly likely that the United States would lose and become, once again, a British possession.

In August of that year, things were looking particularly bleak. The British scored a powerful blow against the United States when its troops occupied Washington, D.C., and burned the nation's capitol to the ground. With the American government in flight, the British moved quickly to consolidate their victory by attacking the nearby city of Baltimore, touching off the engagement that provided the moral turning point of the war.

Baltimore's defenses were formidable. No British ship could enter the harbor without passing before the guns of Fort

> *"Be it enacted by the Senate and House of Representatives of the United States of America in Congress assembled, That war be and the same is hereby declared to exist between the United Kingdom of Great Britain and Ireland and the dependencies thereof, and the United States of America and their territories."*
> U.S. Declaration of War, June 18, 1812

Soldiers wearing 1812-era military uniforms stand in formation at Fort McHenry.

McHenry—to take the city, the fort's guns would have to be silenced. The British Navy sailed up to the challenge, and on September 13, 1814, subjected the fort to twenty-five hours of continuous shelling. The battle was witnessed by a thirty-five-year-old Washington lawyer, detained on a British truce ship that lay anchored eight miles from the action. The witness's name was Francis Scott Key.

Key had been involved in negotiating a prisoner release from the British, but had not been able to return to U.S. territory before the bombardment of the fort got under way. Watching from the deck of the British ship, Key saw the shelling finally end at 7 A.M. on September 14. That's when the young lawyer spotted the U.S. flag that still flew proudly over the fort. The sight so moved him that he took pen in hand to compose the first lines of the best known patriotic poem in American literature: "Oh, say, can you see/by the dawn's early light/o'er the ramparts we watched. . . . ." His poem, "The Star-Spangled Banner," eventually became the U.S. national anthem.

With the inspiring example of Baltimore before them, the U.S. forces redoubled their efforts and successfully halted British efforts to take Plattsburg, New York. In December of

1814, negotiators for the two belligerants signed the Treaty of Ghent, marking the official end of the war and reaffirming American sovereignty. But it wasn't until January of 1815 that the final battle was fought, when Andrew Jackson soundly trounced British forces at the Battle of New Orleans.

With the outbreak of the Civil War, Fort McHenry once again had a significant role to play in the nation's defense. Many of Maryland's citizens sympathized with the rebel cause, making it necessary for Union troops to be stationed there to prevent the state from going over to join the Southern rebellion. Fort McHenry's guns, originally intended to protect Baltimore from invasion, were now turned inward upon the city itself, so that they could be used to quell any armed insurrection that might arise.

But the fort served an additional purpose as well—for which it has been nicknamed the "Baltimore Bastille." Beginning in 1861, the fort was used as a prison for Maryland residents who were arrested on suspicion of being Southern sympathizers. Among those so detained were the leaders of the Baltimore police force and several prominent politicians. Although some of these detainees were released upon swearing a loyalty oath to the Union, others were held without trial for the duration of the war.

Prisoners of war were also temporarily detained within McHenry's fortified walls, pending their transfer to the established prisons of Point Lookout, Fort Delaware, and Johnson's Island. It remained in active service long after the end of the Civil War, until July 20, 1912. Even though the fort served only as a temporary transfer station, at times the inmate population reached extraordinary heights—nearly 7,000 were incarcerated there at the end of the Battle of Gettysburg.

At the close of the Civil War, Fort McHenry remained an active military installation, but never again served a defensive function. It briefly fell into civilian use, from 1912 to 1917; for the last half of that period it was designated a city park and public beach. But in 1917 the fort was once again pressed into the country's service, when it was reactivated as U.S. Army General Hospital No. 2 to serve the needs of wounded veterans returning from the trenches of World War I.

Fort McHenry continued to be used as a hospital installation for the next eight years, ultimately growing to become the largest military hospital in the nation. In addition, a portion of the present day park complex functioned as a U.S. Coast Guard training center. The fort remained in national service until 1923, when the hospital facility was closed down.

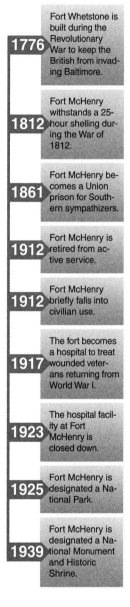

1776 Fort Whetstone is built during the Revolutionary War to keep the British from invading Baltimore.

1812 Fort McHenry withstands a 25-hour shelling during the War of 1812.

1861 Fort McHenry becomes a Union prison for Southern sympathizers.

1912 Fort McHenry is retired from active service.

1912 Fort McHenry briefly falls into civilian use.

1917 The fort becomes a hospital to treat wounded veterans returning from World War I.

1923 The hospital facility at Fort McHenry is closed down.

1925 Fort McHenry is designated a National Park.

1939 Fort McHenry is designated a National Monument and Historic Shrine.

The U.S. flag as it looked in 1812, flying at the entrance to Fort McHenry.

Fort McHenry received National Park designation in 1925. Responsibility for maintaining the site was transferred from the control of the War Department and fell under the administration of the National Park Service in 1933. In 1939 it received the designation of National Monument and Historic Shrine— it is the only designated Historic Shrine in the nation. Even with these designations, Fort McHenry still saw active service during World War II, when it served as a Coast Guard training center.

Today the park offers a variety of visitor activities, from films to walking tours. The site consists of Star Fort and forty-five acres of surrounding land and emplacements. Visitors can see historical and military memorabilia, the restored barracks, and the flagpole from which the flag that inspired Francis Scott Key once flew. There are, of course, important events scheduled around Flag Day, and in the summer a group called the Fort McHenry Guard conducts activities that commemorate the successful 1814 defense of Baltimore from British attack. In addition, the site is a popular destination for participants in Civil War reenactments, which are conducted annually on the grounds during the month of April. ◆

Fort Raleigh

ROANOKE ISLAND, NORTH CAROLINA

Fort Raleigh was the site of England's first attempt in 1585 and 1587 to settle a colony in North America. The fort was built on Roanoke Island off the coast of present-day North Carolina. The colony was inspired and funded by Sir Walter Raleigh, with Queen Elizabeth's blessing, and also involved Sir Richard Grenville and Sir Francis Drake, among the greatest names in England's age of exploration. The settlement failed, however, and by 1590, its last settlers had mysteriously vanished. Fort Raleigh is sometimes called the Lost Colony, because no one has ever known what became of the inhabitants. Though short-lived, the Roanoke settlement was of lasting importance because it established England's claim to the land of Virginia and was the first step in England's eventual ownership of the Atlantic coast of what is now the United States. Settlements at Jamestown would follow in 1607, and at Plymouth in 1620.

Roanoke Island is a twelve-mile-long, three-mile-wide isle off the coast of North Carolina, between Albemarle Sound and the Outer Banks. Today, Fort Raleigh National Historic Site commemorates the place where, more than four hundred years ago, the English first attempted to found a colony in the New World. Fort Raleigh has a museum and buildings that re-create what the settlement would have looked like around 1587, and is the site of ongoing excavations to uncover artifacts and possible clues to the fate of the Lost Colony.

In the 1570s England was in an increasingly tense "cold war" with Spain, only years from open war with the dreaded Spanish Armada. Sir Humphrey Gilbert, an accomplished soldier and explorer, and half brother of Sir Walter Raleigh, persuaded Queen Elizabeth that England should enlarge its overseas territories to protect the national interest and prevent Spain from becoming too powerful. In 1578 Elizabeth granted Gilbert a patent to start and govern a colony in "remote, heathen, and barbarous lands not actually possessed of any Christian prince, nor inhabited by Christian people." The queen promised that the inhabitants would be treated equally as Englishmen. Gilbert died before establishing a colony, however, so Elizabeth transferred the patent to Gilbert's Sir Walter Raleigh. Raleigh was one of the lights of the Elizabethan age—a dashing

"Knowe yee . . . we give and graunt to our trustie and welbeloved servant Walter Ralegh, Esquire, and to his heires assignee for ever, free libertie and licence from time to time, and at all times for ever hereafter, to discover, search, finde out, and view such remote, heathen and barbarous lands, countries, and territories, not actually possessed of any Christian Prince, nor inhabited by Christian People."

Queen Elizabeth I, charter to Sir Walter Raleigh, 1584

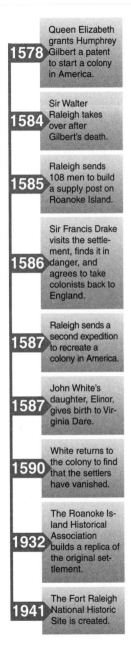

1578 Queen Elizabeth grants Humphrey Gilbert a patent to start a colony in America.

1584 Sir Walter Raleigh takes over after Gilbert's death.

1585 Raleigh sends 108 men to build a supply post on Roanoke Island.

1586 Sir Francis Drake visits the settlement, finds it in danger, and agrees to take colonists back to England.

1587 Raleigh sends a second expedition to recreate a colony in America.

1587 John White's daughter, Elinor, gives birth to Virginia Dare.

1590 White returns to the colony to find that the settlers have vanished.

1932 The Roanoke Island Historical Association builds a replica of the original settlement.

1941 The Fort Raleigh National Historic Site is created.

courtier, explorer, and man of letters—and one of the queen's favorites.

In 1584 he sent a scouting expedition to explore the North American coast and find a good site for a settlement. Raleigh's scouts spent several weeks with the friendly Indians of Roanoke Island and returned to England praising the "plentiful, sweete, fruitfull and wholsome" soil of the region. Elizabeth, known as the Virgin Queen because she was not married, agreed to let the area be called Virginia in her honor. In 1585 Raleigh sent 108 men to build a supply post on Roanoke Island for the English privateers who were attacking Spain's ships in the Caribbean.

Things might have gone better for this first group of colonists had they built houses and planted crops instead of spending all their time searching for gold. It seems they forgot that they had been sent to build a supply post that London could depend on. The gentlemen who might have been organizers and leaders were unwilling to work, and had few practical skills anyway, so they set a poor example. The local Indians, who had been friendly with Raleigh's scouts the previous year, soon grew tired of feeding the indolent colonists, and turned hostile. When Sir Francis Drake visited with his fleet in 1586, he found the settlement in danger and agreed to take colonists back to England. Sir Richard Grenville, the leader of that ill-fated colony, left only fifteen men to secure England's claim to the region until a new group of colonists could arrive to join them.

In 1587 Raleigh sent a second expedition, a group of more than a hundred men, women, and children. The settlers' goal was to re-create a typical rural English community in the American wilderness. Two leading members of the group had taken part in the earlier attempt to colonize Roanoke: John White, a skilled mapmaker and artist, appointed by Raleigh to serve as governor of the second expedition; and Thomas Harriot, a scholar and mapmaker who later published an illustrated account of the expedition that was translated into four languages.

Governor John White had explored part of the Chesapeake Bay during his first visit to the Atlantic coast, and wanted to set up the colony there. But the expedition's pilot refused to take the ships beyond Roanoke Island, which was where Sir Walter Raleigh expected them. Upon reaching the island that Grenville had left only the year before, the colonists of 1587 found nothing of the fifteen men but bones and signs that the settlement had been attacked.

Amid these ill omens, the group unloaded and began to settle on Roanoke Island. Soon after they landed, Governor White's daughter, Ellinor (or Elyoner) White Dare, gave birth to Virginia Dare, the first English child born in the Americas. About a month after the colonists' arrival, White sailed back to England to gather reinforcements and additional supplies, but once in London he was compelled to stay. England and Spain were on the brink of war. King Philip II of Spain had built up a massive **armada** of 130 warships and was threatening to invade England; Queen Elizabeth could not spare a single ship for the distant colony.

armada: a fleet of warships.

Governor White could not return to his colony until 1590. Instead of finding a flourishing colony, he discovered that the settlement had been abandoned. The only clue to the settlers' fate was the word "CROATOAN" carved into a doorpost. White believed that this referred to an Indian tribe about fifty miles south of the island, for its chieftain, Manteo, had been friendly, and White naturally assumed that the colonists had fled to Manteo for shelter when other Indians attacked. But White could not persuade the captains of his ship to go in search of the missing settlers, so he had to return to England not knowing what had become of the colonists of Roanoke. Modern historians have surmised that the settlers of the Lost Colony probably moved north to live among the Chesapeake Indians, who were killed in 1606 by the Powhatan tribe of Virginia under Chief Powhatan. It is also possible that a great drought sometime during White's three-year absence may have doomed the settlers.

Upon reaching the island, the colonists of 1587 found nothing of the fifteen men but bones and signs that the settlement had been attacked.

John White and Thomas Harriot saved some of their drawings and notes from the first expedition. Harriot wrote a book about Virginia, and in 1590 he published an illustrated edition with reproductions of White's drawings. Published in four languages, this volume gave many Europeans their first images and descriptions of the landscapes, plants and animals, and native inhabitants of North America.

On April 30, 1894, the Roanoke Colony Memorial Association purchased the fort and ten acres of surrounding land to set aside for a memorial. Two years later the association extended the tract to 16.45 acres and erected the Virginia Dare memorial. The Roanoke Island Historical Association was formed in 1932, and with federal aid the association constructed an open-air theater and a series of buildings that show how the original settlement probably appeared. The theater is the site of performances of Paul Green's symphonic drama *The Lost Colony*, first performed in 1937 to commemorate the 350th anniversary of the colony's founding.

Fort Raleigh National Historic Site is located on Roanoke Island, near the Outer Banks, about ten miles south of Kitty Hawk, where the Wright brothers experimented with gliders and early airplanes around 1900. The historic site was created in 1941, and enlarged in 1990 to include exhibits of Native American culture, the Civil War, and a freedmen's colony. A museum in the Lindsay Warren visitor center exhibits the history of the expeditions and colonies. In 1947 archaeologists working for the U.S. government announced that they had uncovered artifacts from the settlement, and excavations have been ongoing in the 1990s, searching for clues in a mystery that few expect can ever be solved. ◆

Fort Sumter

CHARLESTON HARBOR, SOUTH CAROLINA

Davis and his cabinet decided not to wait for the arrival of Lincoln's expedition, but to risk the onus of firing the first shot.

Fort Sumter, located on an artificial island inside the entrance to Charleston Harbor, was the scene of the opening battle of the American Civil War. A pentagon, with brick walls about three hundred feet long, forty feet high, and eight to twelve feet thick, the fort was still under construction in 1860. To it, on the night of December 26, U.S. army major Robert Anderson moved his garrison of troops from Fort Moultrie at the edge of the harbor entrance, where he and his men had been exposed to the threat of attack by rebelling South Carolinians.

Having declared their state an independent republic, the South Carolinians resented the presence of what was to them a foreign flag, and they looked upon Anderson's move to Fort Sumter as an act of aggression. They considered it another hostile act when, in January 1861, U.S. president James Buchanan sent the unarmed merchant ship *Star of the West* with reinforcements for the fort. As the ship approached Charleston Harbor, South Carolina shore batteries opened fire and compelled it to turn back.

The Confederate government early established its policy with regard to the two principal forts remaining under federal control in the seceded states. On February 15, 1861, the Provisional Congress of the Confederacy in Montgomery, Alabama, secretly resolved that "immediate steps should be taken to obtain possession of Forts Sumter and Pickens . . . either by negotiation or force." Confederate president Jefferson David thereupon sent to Washington three commissioners—Matin J. Crawford, John Forsyth, and A. B. Roman—to try negotiation. He also ordered Confederate general P. G. T. Beauregard to Charleston to take command of the harbor and make preparations for the use of force.

In Washington, the Confederate commissioners failed to get an audience with any member of the Lincoln administration, but Secretary of State William H. Seward communicated with them through a go-between. The commissioners thought it a great diplomatic victory for the Confederacy when Seward pledged that his government would not, without notice, undertake to change the situation at Sumter. As Commissioner Crawford reported, the Confederate States "were not bound in any way whatever to observe the same course," but were left free to continue their preparations for attack. "We think, then, that the policy of 'masterly inactivity,' on our part, was wise in every particular."

Fort Sumter in Charleston Harbor is shown here in 1861 under a Confederate flag.

1860 U.S. Army major Robert Anderson moves his troops to Fort Sumter.

1861 South Carolinians fire on a ship carrying reinforcements to Fort Sumter; Anderson surrenders the fort.

1863 Union forces make two unsuccessful attempts to retake and capture Charleston.

1865 The U.S. flag is raised over the fort for the first time in several years.

1876 The fort begins service as a lighthouse.

1948 Fort Sumter becomes a National Monument.

Such inactivity displeased Governor Francis W. Pickens and his fellow South Carolinians, who demanded immediate action. "The President shares the feeling expressed by you that Fort Sumter should be in our possession at the earliest possible moment," Secretary of War Elroy P. Walker assured Governor Pickens on March 1, but cautioned: "Thorough preparations must be made before an attack is attempted, for the first blow must be successful."

General Beauregard proceeded to extend and enlarge the batteries surrounding and targeting the fort. His preparations practically complete, he advised the Davis government on March 27 that the expulsion of Anderson from Sumter "ought now to be decided on in a few days." Davis gave Beauregard the following instructions on April 2: he should be ready to strike whenever the commissioners withdrew from Washington, and meanwhile he should cease to allow Anderson the privilege of buying groceries in Charleston.

On April 8 the Davis government heard from the commissioners that they had met a final "refusal" and considered their mission at an end. This news alone would have been sufficient to trigger an assault on Sumter, but even more ominous news arrived on Montgomery on the same day. A telegram from Beauregard said Governor Pickens had just received a massage from President Abraham Lincoln to the effect that "provisions would be sent to Sumter peaceably, otherwise by force." Secretary Walker immediately replied to Beauregard: "Under no circumstances are you to allow provisions to be sent to Fort Sumter."

Davis and his cabinet decided not to wait for the arrival of Lincoln's expedition but, instead, to risk the onus of firing the first shot. On April 10 Walker on behalf of Davis ordered Beauregard to demand immediate evacuation of the fort and, if refused, to "reduce" it. The next day Anderson rejected the demand but said he and his men would be "starved out in a few days." Walker then authorized Beauregard to "avoid the effusion of blood" if Anderson would state a time for his withdrawal and would agree meanwhile not to fire unless fired upon. Beauregard sent James Chesnut, Roger A. Pryor, and two aides by boat to present this offer to Anderson after midnight. Anderson promised to hold his fire and to evacuate in three days—unless he should receive "controlling instructions" or "additional supplies." Chesnut and Pryor told him his reply was unsatisfactory and a bombardment would begin in an hour.

The bombardment began at 4:30 on the morning of April 12, 1861. Anderson was unable to make much of a response, completely outgunned as he was. He received no assistance from Lincoln's expedition, which proved a fiasco. The leading warship, *Powhatan*, had been misdirected to Fort Pickens, other vessels had been delayed by a storm, and the rest stood helplessly offshore. Cannon balls battered the brick walls of the fort, while hot shot set fire to the wooden buildings inside. Anderson surrendered at noon on April 14. All his eighty-four soldiers and forty-three laborers had survived, but two men died as a result of a gun explosion during the surrender ceremonies.

Among Confederate leaders it had been an axiom that a clash at Sumter would induce Virginia and other states of the upper south and the border to secede. None of these states did so immediately, but Virginia, Tennessee, Arkansas, and North Carolina seceded in consequence of Lincoln's call for troops on April 15. Southerners generally rallied to the support of the Davis government. Northerners did the same with respect to the Lincoln administration. Most of them believed the Confederates had convicted themselves of war guilt, but the Confederates accused Lincoln of having deliberately provoked the attack.

In 1863 Union forces made two unsuccessful attempts to retake and capture Charleston. The U.S. flag was not again raised over the fort until April 14, 1865, exactly four years after the surrender.

The remains of Fort Sumter at the end of the Civil War bore little resemblance to the impressive structure that had marked the April 1861 engagement. The U.S. Army attempted to restore the fort during the decade following the war in order to maintain it as a military installation. They had to level or rebuild jagged portions of the destroyed walls, cut a new sally port through the left flank, and rebuild storage magazines, cisterns, and gun placements. From 1876 to 1897 the fort was not **garrisoned**, and served instead as a lighthouse station. For many years, maintenance of the site was so poor that the gun platforms rotted, the guns rusted, and the island itself suffered from erosion. Fort Sumter's brief witness to the Spanish-American War resulted in minor renovations and maintenance. However, no further improvements were made until World War II, and in 1948 Fort Sumter became a National Monument. It is now a major tourist attraction, and every year thousands of people travel by boat from Charleston to visit the fort. ◆

"I am ordered by the Government of the Confederate States to demand the evacuation of Fort Sumter. The flag which you have upheld so long and with so much fortitude, under the most trying circumstances, may be saluted by you on taking it down."
General Pierre Beauregard, note to Major Robert Anderson, April 11, 1861

garrison: fortified place with troops and guns.

Franklin Delano Roosevelt Memorial

WASHINGTON, D.C.

T he Franklin Delano Roosevelt Memorial is a tribute to the thirty-second president of the United States, who guided the nation through the Great Depression and World War II. The memorial, which opened to the public on May 2, 1997, became the fourth monument to an American president on the National Mall, joining the Washington Monument, the Lincoln Memorial, and the Jefferson Memorial.

Franklin Delano Roosevelt was born on January 30, 1882, on a large family estate in Hyde Park, New York, into a family of established wealth. His parents, members of New York State's enclosed social elite, knew little of the problems of ordinary Americans. Franklin graduated from Harvard University in 1904. In 1905 he married Anna Eleanor Roosevelt, a distant cousin and a niece of President Theodore Roosevelt. Two years later, after attending Columbia Law School in New York City, Roosevelt gained admission to the New York State bar.

"I pledge you, I pledge myself, to a New Deal for the American People."
Franklin D. Roosevelt, 1932

A Democrat, Roosevelt served in the New York State Senate from 1911 to 1913, until President Woodrow Wilson asked him to come to Washington as assistant secretary of the navy. Roosevelt served in that position to 1920. That year he was the vice-presidential running mate of James Cox on the unsuccessful Democratic national ticket. After his defeat, he worked as an attorney in private practice and headed the New York office of the Fidelity and Deposit Company of Maryland.

poliomyelitis: polio, an acute infectious disease found especially in children.

In August 1921 Roosevelt was stricken with **poliomyelitis**. Never again would he be able to walk unaided. With the help of a cooperative press, he was able to keep his disability from public knowledge. He learned to walk with leg braces and a cane and was hardly ever photographed in his wheelchair.

Making a political comeback in 1928, Roosevelt won a two-year term as governor of New York in 1928 and was reelected in 1930. In the progressive tradition of New York Democrats, he supported a liberal program including minimum wage legislation, expanded workmen's compensation, greater workplace safety, a fairer deal for small farmers, and stronger regulatory power for the state government over business. But since the Re-

THEY (WHO) SEEK TO ESTABLISH
SYSTEMS OF GOVERNMENT BASED ON
THE REGIMENTATION OF ALL HUMAN
BEINGS BY A HANDFUL OF INDIVIDUAL
RULERS... CALL THIS A NEW ORDER.
IT IS NOT NEW AND IT IS NOT ORDER.

A statue of Franklin D. Roosevelt and his dog Fala at the FDR Memorial in Washington, D.C.

publicans controlled both houses of the legislature, he enacted only a small fraction of his agenda.

In 1932 Roosevelt won the Democratic nomination for president and easily defeated incumbent Herbert Hoover, who was presiding over the worst depression in American history. Utilizing solid Democrat majorities in both houses of Congress, his great communication skills, demonstrated most vividly in his radio talks or "fireside chats," and a buoyant, optimistic personality that renewed the hopes of Americans, Roosevelt was able to use the nation's crisis to revolutionize the role of the federal government in American life. Previously, providing direct assistance to poor and working Americans had been a function of state and local authorities that usually lacked the resources to be of great help. During the Depression, Roosevelt—or FDR, as he now became known—transferred much of the responsibility to the federal government as part of what he called his New Deal.

Through the Federal Emergency Relief Act of 1933, the federal government for the first time gave grants to state and

"I see one-third of a nation ill-housed, ill-clad, and ill-nourished. The test of our progress is not whether we add more to the abundance of those who have much; it is whether we provide enough for those who have too little."
Franklin D. Roosevelt, 1937

local authorities for emergency assistance to the poor. (Hoover had given loans.) Thanks to massive public works projects supervised by such agencies as the Public Works Administration, the Works Progress Administration, and the Civilian Conservation Corps, millions of the unemployed were able to earn at least a small living. Other key New Deal legislation assisted America's workers. The National Industrial Relations Act of 1933 and the National Labor Relations Act of 1935 gave workers the right to be represented by unions if they so chose. The Fair Labor Standards Act of 1938 established federal minimum wage and maximum hour standards.

The Agricultural Adjustment Acts of 1933 and 1938 attempted to help struggling farmers by reducing production in order to raise prices. The Resettlement Administration, created in 1935, assisted the rural population with relocation assistance and loans to small farmers, tenant farmers, sharecroppers, and farm laborers for buying land and equipment. Longer-term legislation to protect ordinary Americans from economic devastation included the Banking Act of 1933. It created a Federal Deposit Insurance Company to guarantee bank accounts under $5,000. Even more fundamental was the Social Security Act of 1935. It guaranteed American workers and their immediate survivors a lifetime retirement pension.

Eleanor Roosevelt, the president's outspoken wife, was an independent political voice who sometimes backed liberal causes that FDR felt were too controversial for him to support. An example is the area of civil rights. Close to the National Association for the Advancement of Colored People (NAACP), Mrs. Roosevelt spoke out forcibly for federal antilynching legislation. FDR himself did not risk endorsing it because he depended on southern representatives and senators to pass his New Deal legislation.

As the threat of a European war grew in the late 1930s, the New Deal receded in importance. Once World War II began in Europe in 1939, FDR did a masterful job of gently steering an **isolationist** public toward supporting the Allies, led by Britain and later the Soviet Union, who were fighting the German Nazis, Italian Fascists, and Japanese warlords. In 1940 he negotiated an arrangement that traded fifty old American destroyers to Britain in exchange for leases on British bases in the western hemisphere; it was, in reality, a disguised form of aid to Britain. After he had been safely reelected for an unprecedented third term in November 1940, Roosevelt initiated a larger-scale assis-

isolationist: one who opposes the involvement of a country in international alliances.

tance program, called Lend-Lease. Enacted in March 1941, it was a way of providing massive help to the Allies without providing direct credits or direct financial aid.

Once the United States entered the war in December 1941 following the Japanese bombing of Pearl Harbor in Hawaii, Roosevelt provided the same strong leadership at home as he had during the New Deal. Through fireside chats, speeches, press conferences, and visits to military sites and factories, he conveyed the same confidence and optimism as during the 1930s. Some of his military decisions were questioned. Critics criticized his demand for unconditional Axis surrender on the grounds that it would discourage anti-Hitler resistance within Germany and lengthen the war. But given the highly obnoxious political program of the enemy, his demand seems justified. Others opposed his delay of a European landing until June 1944. However, the huge number of landing craft and airplanes required for the invasion was not in place until then, according to many historians.

Roosevelt died on April 12, 1945, just months after his fourth-term inauguration and months before the successful end of the war. Many Americans wept at the loss of a man who, they believed, had been a great leader both in the crisis of economic collapse and the crisis of war.

Unlike the massive Lincoln and Jefferson Memorials and the soaring Washington Monument, the FDR Memorial is spread out widely over a 7.5-acre landscape. Designed by Lawrence Halprin and costing $48 million, it is divided into four connected, open-air rooms with walls of red granite, each room representing one of Roosevelt's terms as president. Throughout are shade trees, shrubbery, waterfalls, calm pools, and quiet alcoves that give visitors a feeling of being in a secluded park or garden rather than in an imposing structure.

In the rooms are a total of twenty-one Roosevelt quotations, carved into the granite by master stone carver John Benson. Each room also features statues and bronze bas-reliefs commissioned from sculptors Leonard Baskin, Neil Estern, Robert Graham, Tom Hardy, and George Segal. In the first room, a life-size bas-relief depicts FDR waving from an open car during his first inaugural parade. The second room displays a group of statues that express both the suffering and hope of the Depression: a weary looking rural couple, life-sized figures in a bread line, and a figure listening intently to a fireside chat. New Deal programs are represented by a wall-sized bas-relief that faces five freestanding columns.

1882 Franklin Delano Roosevelt is born in Hyde Park, New York.

1911 Roosevelt begins a term in the state senate.

1913 Roosevelt becomes assistant secretary of the navy.

1920 Roosevelt is vice presidential candidate on the unsuccessful Democratic ticket.

1921 Roosevelt is struck with polio.

1928 Roosevelt wins a two-year term as governor of New York State.

1932 Roosevelt wins the Democratic nomination for president; defeats Herbert Hoover.

1945 Roosevelt dies months after his fourth term inauguration.

1997 Roosevelt Memorial opens in Washington, D.C.

1998 The National Park Service announces it will add a sculpture of Roosevelt in a wheelchair to the memorial.

"The only thing we have to fear is fear itself."
Franklin D. Roosevelt, 1933

bas relief: sculptures in which figures are carved in a flat surface so that they project only a little from the background.

boa: a woman's long fur or feather scarf worn around the neck or shoulders.

In the third room, the granite wall is reduced to rubble, symbolizing the devastation of World War II. The dominant presence is a nine-foot-high statue of FDR seated, a cape draped over him with his dog Fala at his feet. An inscription in this room reads: "We have faith that future generations will know that here, in the middle of the twentieth century, there came a time when men of good will found a way to unite, and produce, and fight to destroy the forces of ignorance, and intolerance, and slavery, and war."

In the fourth room, a dramatic waterfall cascades into a series of sparkling pools, creating a water garden alongside a dramatic plaza. A statue of Eleanor Roosevelt stands in front of the United Nations symbol. A thirty-foot-long **bas relief** depicts Roosevelt's funeral cortege. A quotation for a speech that FDR was to deliver days after his death reads: "The only limit to our realization of tomorrow will be our doubts of today. Let us move forward with strong and active faith."

The completion of the FDR Memorial was delayed for some forty years by issues related to financing and design. Political issues also intruded. A fox-fur **boa** was removed from the statue of Eleanor Roosevelt because of protests from animal rights activists. Because of pressures from antitobacco forces, Roosevelt is not depicted with his trademark cigarette holder. Groups representing the disabled called for a depiction of Roosevelt in a wheelchair, although FDR took great pains to disguise the fact that he used one. At first this lobby was unsuccessful, but in July 1998, only fourteen months after the memorial's opening, the National Park Service announced that it was commissioning a sculpture of Roosevelt in a wheelchair, to be placed at the entrance to the memorial. ◆

Gateway Arch

SAINT LOUIS, MISSOURI

The Gateway Arch, on the banks of the Mississippi River in St. Louis, Missouri, is the centerpiece of the Jefferson National Expansion Memorial. The arch was commissioned to commemorate the Louisiana Purchase of 1803, and the pioneers who opened up America's western territories. Finnish-born Architect Eero Saarinen won the national competition in 1948 with his winning design, which became the tallest man-made monument in the United States.

Saarinen won the competition with his proposal for a 630-foot arch built of stainless steel, standing as a symbolic doorway to the American West. But it would be another fifteen years before construction was begun, and two more until its completion on October 28, 1965, at a cost of approximately $15 million. Below the arch is the Museum of Westward Expansion, which houses a variety of displays from animal specimens to a Native American tipi, as well as an exhibit that details the journey of Lewis and Clark and the Corps of Discovery. The arch itself stands well rooted on sixty-foot-deep foundations so that it can stand sturdily in the face of strong winds and earth tremors. A twenty-mile-per-hour wind will cause the top of the arch to sway one inch; the structure is designed to sway a total of eighteen inches. Visitors can ride a specially constructed tramway to the summit of the arch, where they can enjoy a panoramic view out across the territory that once lured explorers, adventurers, and pioneers ever deeper into the American west.

The Gateway Arch represents the spirit of expansion that gripped the nation in the early years of the nineteenth century.

> *"Neither an obelisk nor a rectangular box nor a dome seemed right on this site or for this purpose. But here, at the edge of the Mississippi River, a great arch did seem right."*
>
> Eero Saarinen, 1948

The Gateway Arch in St. Louis, Missouri.

By that time, settlers had pushed as far west as they could before running into the French-owned Louisiana Territory. This region had originally been claimed by the Spanish, who first entered the territory in the 1500s but failed to establish an effective occupational force. Approximately one hundred years later, Robert Cavelier, Sieur de la Salle, explored the territory for France and, emboldened by the meager Spanish presence, claimed it for his king, Louis XIV. Thus did the territory receive its name: Louisiana.

Spain, however, did not appreciate the summary **appropriation** of a region that it still considered its own. When, in the late 1750s, France called upon Spain to help fight the English in the Seven Years' War, the question of ownership was raised. The price for Spain's alliance with France would be the return of the Louisiana Territory to its original claimants, the Spanish throne. This was particularly important because, in the course of aiding France in its cause, Spain lost its Florida colonies.

But France was not completely happy with the loss of the territory. The vast reaches of the region and its potential wealth made it an attractive piece of real estate with which to expand

appropriation: the act of taking for one's own or exclusive use.

the French colonial presence in the New World. In the late 1790s, French diplomats reopened a dialog with Spain about the possibility of regaining the territory. On October 1, 1800, Spain ceded the territory back to France as part of the terms of the secret Treaty of San Il de Fonso.

Back in the United States, President Jefferson viewed the transfer of ownership back and forth between Spain and France with alarm. France was ruled by Napoleon—no stranger to the urge for empire—and Jefferson feared that with France in possession of the territory, national security would be threatened. After all, whoever controlled the territory also controlled the mouth of the Mississippi River and therefore controlled access to the Gulf of Mexico. The potential for serious disruption of U.S. trade was high.

Jefferson decided upon a plan of action—he would send an **emissary** to France to try to determine just who, in fact, owned Louisiana and the Floridas, and to determine what it would take for the United States to acquire ownership. This emissary, Robert R. Livingston, was able to ascertain that France held Louisiana and the port city of New Orleans, but that Spain retained control of the Florida territories.

Unfortunately, Spain did not honor its own cession of the territory to France, and on October 16, 1802, it shut down the New Orleans port to U.S. traffic. This had an immediate potential for disaster for the U.S. economy. Settlers in the west and midwest depended upon access to New Orleans—they shipped their goods down the Mississippi River to the port city where the merchandise was then transferred to oceangoing vessels and shipped on to the settlements along the Atlantic coast. Without the rights to transfer in New Orleans, all trade between the American inland and the coastal cities was effectively halted.

The Jefferson administration could not let this situation stand. Given that the French were the legal holders of the territory, President Jefferson sent James Monroe to Paris to negotiate for the purchase of the port of New Orleans. Monroe was instructed to try for the Florida territories as well, if they were up for grabs.

Jefferson's negotiations were aided by Napoleon's own problems and ambitions. The French ruler was facing serious disruptions in his West Indian possessions, where slave revolts led by Toussaint L'Ouverture were threatening the plantations of Santo Domingo. Unable to wrest back control of the islands

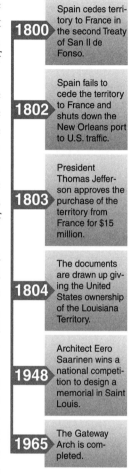

1800 Spain cedes territory to France in the second Treaty of San Il de Fonso.

1802 Spain fails to cede the territory to France and shuts down the New Orleans port to U.S. traffic.

1803 President Thomas Jefferson approves the purchase of the territory from France for $15 million.

1804 The documents are drawn up giving the United States ownership of the Louisiana Territory.

1948 Architect Eero Saarinen wins a national competition to design a memorial in Saint Louis.

1965 The Gateway Arch is completed.

emissary: a person or secret agent sent on a specific mission.

and faced with grave financial and military losses, Napoleon determined to turn his imperial ambitions toward Europe and England. He abandoned his island possessions and prepared to go to war with Great Britain. Since wars are always costly affairs, Napoleon was open to the prospect of turning a profit on the sale of Louisiana, to fund his English adventuring.

The arch itself stands well rooted on sixty-foot-deep foundations so that it can stand sturdily in the face of strong winds and earth tremors.

Livingston and Monroe were understandably surprised when they opened negotiations for the purchase of New Orleans and Florida and found that the whole of the Louisiana Territory was on offer as well. Although the additional territory went far beyond their original brief, they were not averse to a little sharp horse-trading, and ultimately settled on a price that the French found acceptable—$15,000,000. President Jefferson swallowed a few qualms he had about the constitutionality of the purchase and approved the deal, and the Senate ratified it into law on October 20, 1803. It would be another few months before the territory was actually transferred to U.S. possession—Jefferson had to wait until France took formal possession from Spain (of the lower territory on November 30, of Upper Louisiana on March 9, 1804) before the documents transferring ownership to the United States could be drawn up.

But the U.S. acquisition of the Louisiana Territory was well worth the wait. With it, the land area comprising U.S. territory was doubled almost overnight. There would, for a time at least, be more than enough "elbow-room" into which the new American republic could expand. ◆

Gettysburg Battlefield

SOUTHERN PENNSYLVANIA

The July 1863 Battle of Gettysburg marked the turning point of the American Civil War. The Battle of Gettysburg did not end the war, which continued for another two years, nor did it attain any major war aim for either the North or the South. However, it has been considered the great battle of the Civil War, where more men fought and died than in any other battle before or since on North American soil. Today the Gettysburg Battlefield in Gettysburg National Military Park, located in south central Pennsylvania, an hour from Lancaster's Dutch County, remains a shrine to the Union

Union and Confederate dead lie together on the Gettysburg battlefield in this photo taken shortly after the 1863 battle.

and Confederate soldiers who fought there. Over a thousand monuments and cannons covering over forty miles of roads commemorate such historic events as Lincoln's Gettysburg Address and Picket's Charge, and sites where significant turns in the battle occurred, such as Bloody Run, Little Round Top, and Devil's Den.

The story of the Gettysburg Battlefield began on July 1, 1863, when a Confederate brigade in Confederate general Robert E. Lee's 75,000-man Army of Northern Virginia observed by chance a forward column of the cavalry in Union general George G. Meade's 90,000-man Army of the Potomac. In June General Lee had decided to push the war northward by first destroying an important railroad bridge at Harrisburg, Pennsylvania. Lee then intended to move his troops up into Philadelphia, Baltimore, or Washington. While Confederate troops under the command of J. Johnston Pettigrew were exploring the town of Gettysburg for supplies, they spotted Meade's advance cavalry led by General John Buford. Pettigrew's brigade attacked the Union Cavalry on McPherson Ridge, west of town. At first the Union troops were outnumbered, but upon receiving reinforcements from Union commander John Reynolds's Infantry division, they were able to drive the Confederates back until they were overpowered by the Confederates' own reinforcements and driven back through

"Now we are engaged in a great civil war, testing whether that nation, or any nation so conceived and so dedicated, can long endure. We are met on a great battlefield of that war. We have come to dedicate a portion of that field as a final resting-place for those who here gave their lives that that nation might live."
Abraham Lincoln, Gettysburg Address, 1863

Memorials line Rickett's Union Battery at Gettysburg National Historic Battlefield.

town. The bulk of General Meade's army arrived overnight, and took their positions to fight.

The second day of battle continued with partial successes for the Confederate forces, and General Lee's order to attack Union flanks might have successfully taken Little Round Top if General G. K. Warren had not saved it for the Union by observing that the strategic hill was unmanned. Two lines of battle swept up in parallel arcs nearly a mile apart, with Union forces on Cemetery Ridge, facing Confederate forces on Seminary Ridge to the west. The Confederate attack against the entrenched Union Right on East Cemetery Hill ultimately proved futile, and the next day, July 3, 1863, Lee attacked the Union Center, engaging the massed guns of both sides in thunderous open fire.

The climax of the Battle of Gettysburg occurred when Confederate general George E. Pickett massed a relentless infantry assault of 15,000 soldiers to charge across a mile-long stretch of open field toward the Union center on Cemetery Ridge while Union artillery and rifles fired at the advancing Confederate troops. The attack became known as "Pickett's Charge." However, the charge ended disastrously, for when the Confederate troops reached the Union line, they were unable to break it. In less than an hour, more than 4,000 Confederates and 3,000 Union troops were dead, the battle ended, and Lee was forced to retreat. In all, the Battle of Gettysburg left behind a total of approximately 50,000 Confederate and Union casualties, 5,000 dead horses, and utter devastation in the town and surrounding land of Gettysburg.

Four months after the Battle of Gettysburg, the Commonwealth of Pennsylvania dedicated seventeen acres of land on Cemetery Hill to the Gettysburg National Cemetery. The Honorable Edward Everett of Massachusetts, the most celebrated orator of the day, was scheduled to present a two hour oratory describing the three days of the Battle of Gettysburg, speaking on the purpose of war, and reviewing the funeral practices of ancient Greece. Since the cemetery was not the property of the federal government, no one expected President Lincoln to attend the ceremony. However, when he accepted an invitation, officials asked him to participate in the program. The speech he gave there was the Gettysburg Address, which lasted only two minutes, but is one of the most famous orations in American history. ◆

> *"It was now too evident to be questioned, that the thunder-cloud, so long gathering blackness, would soon burst on some part of the devoted vicinity of Gettysburg."*
> Edward Everett, Gettysburg oration, November 19, 1863

Golden Spike National Historic Site

PROMONTORY SUMMIT, UTAH

Located at Promontory Summit, Utah, Golden Spike National Historic Site commemorates the May 10, 1869, completion of the first transcontinental railroad. This historic achievement was commemorated with a golden spike that was presented and symbolically tapped into a special railroad tie. Watching this event, a telegrapher transmitted dot . . . dot . . . dot . . . "Done," and across the nation guns fired, bells tolled, and whistles blew in jubilation as the final spike was driven in the first railroad that spanned the continent. The achievement of a railroad across the country linked the nation physically and economically, and brought about great changes to the American west.

The idea of transcontinental rail travel originated in the 1830s, shortly after railroads began operating in America. By

"Railroad iron is a magician's rod, in its power to evoke the sleeping energies of land and water."

Ralph Waldo Emerson, *Essays, First Series*, 1841

terminus: a boundary or limit.

the beginning of the Civil War, America's eastern states were linked by 31,000 miles of rail. However, virtually none of this network went beyond the Missouri River. Thus, the idea of having a transcontinental railroad was conceived with the purpose of spanning the "Great American Desert." It would boost trade, shorten the emigrant's journey, and help the army control Indians hostile to white settlement. Also, there was a strong interest in linking the eastern states with a growing population in California.

Surveys of various cross-country rail routes were identified in the 1850s. By 1862 one of the most earnest evangelizers of the project was a Californian named Theodore Judah, who had his own plan for a transcontinental railroad. The young engineer had surveyed a route over the Sierra Nevada and persuaded wealthy Sacramento merchants to form the Central Pacific Railroad. That year, Congress authorized the Central Pacific to build a railroad eastward from Sacramento, and in the same act chartered the Union Pacific Railroad. After the beginning of the Civil War removed southern senators from the debate over the location of the railroad, the central route near the Mormon Trail was chosen, with Omaha as the eastern **terminus**. Each railroad received loan subsidies of $16,000 to $48,000 per mile, depending on the difficulty of the terrain, and ten land sections for each mile of track lain.

Both railroad companies broke ground in 1863, but neither made much progress while the country's attention was diverted by the Civil War. A second Railroad Act of 1864 doubled the land subsidies, but little track was laid until labor and supplies were freed up at the war's end in 1865.

Most railroad construction was completed during a four-year period between 1865 and 1869, and both companies faced tremendous obstacles. Central Pacific crews came up against the rugged Sierras almost immediately. Union Pacific started with easier terrain, but their work parties were harassed by Indians. With eight flatcars of material needed for each mile of track, supplies were a logistical nightmare for both railroads, especially Central Pacific, which had to ship every rail, spike, and locomotive 15,000 miles around Cape Horn. Both companies pushed ahead faster than anyone had expected. The work teams, often headed by ex-army officers, were drilled until they could lay two to five miles of track a day on flat land.

The building of the transcontinental railroad involved people with diverse values and ethnic backgrounds who came together for a common purpose. Union Pacific drew on the vast pool of America's unemployed: Irish, German, and Italian immigrants, Civil War veterans from both sides, and ex-slaves— 8,000 to 10,000 workers in all. It was a volatile mixture, and drunken bloodshed was common at the "Hell-on-wheels" towns thrown up near the base camps. Because California's labor pool had been drained by the rush for gold, Central Pacific imported 10,000 Chinese, the backbone of the railroad's workforce.

By mid-1868 Central Pacific crews had crossed the Sierras and laid 200 miles of track, and the Union Pacific had laid 700 miles over the plains. As the two workforces neared each other in Utah, they raced to grade more miles and claim more land subsidies. Before a meeting point could be decided, the grading crews for both companies pushed beyond each other. Competing graders advanced over 100 miles in opposite directions on parallel grades in northern Utah. The competition between the two railroad companies was intense, perhaps culminating in April, 1869, when the Central Pacific Railroad won a bet by laying ten miles of track in one day, a record that has never been surpassed.

Congress finally declared the meeting place between the two railroad companies to be Promontory Summit, where on May 10, 1869, two locomotives pulled up to the one-rail gap left in the track. The final rails were put down, and after a prayer and a series of speeches, the golden spike was presented and symbolically driven into a special tie. Subsequently, the final iron spike was driven. Amid cheers and general enthusiasm, the two engines, No. 119 and the Jupiter, moved up until they almost touched. Construction superintendents for each railroad, Grenville Dodge and his counterpart, Samuel Montague, shook hands as they posed for the famous "East meets West" Champagne Photograph. In total, the Central Pacific laid 690 miles of track; the Union Pacific laid 1,086.

Following the golden spike ceremony at Promontory Summit, the western United States was wrought by two rails 4 feet 81/2 inches apart, snaking across hundreds of miles of wilderness. They joined two oceans and cemented the political union of states with a physical link. But they were also a wedge through the frontier. The west belonged to the Indians and the enormous herds of buffalo on which they depended. Many Indians fought white settlement of their land, but as the railroads brought in car after car of troops and supplies, the warriors could no longer resist the army. Settlers flowed in behind and put the

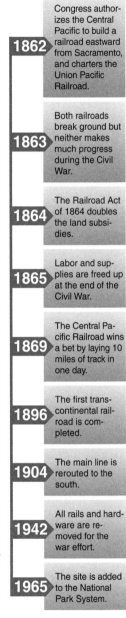

1862 Congress authorizes the Central Pacific to build a railroad eastward from Sacramento, and charters the Union Pacific Railroad.

1863 Both railroads break ground but neither makes much progress during the Civil War.

1864 The Railroad Act of 1864 doubles the land subsidies.

1865 Labor and supplies are freed up at the end of the Civil War.

1869 The Central Pacific Railroad wins a bet by laying 10 miles of track in one day.

1896 The first transcontinental railroad is completed.

1904 The main line is rerouted to the south.

1942 All rails and hardware are removed for the war effort.

1965 The site is added to the National Park System.

land to plow, while millions of buffalo were killed. For these late emigrants, the railroad changed what it meant to be a pioneer. The railroad companies built railroad stations along the way, and settlements grew up around them. Twenty years after the railroad was completed, the frontier was history. The life of American Indians was forever changed.

A major anticipated benefit of the railroad—increased trade with the Far East—never materialized. The **Suez Canal** was completed the same year as the railroad, and Far East goods could now be shipped to Europe faster by way of the canal than across America. But that loss was compensated for by the rapidly growing western rail trade, out of which a vigorous, interlocking economy developed. The western mountains were rich with low-grade silver, lead, and copper **ores**, made profitable by long trains of ore cars. They were used by industries in the east, whose products found a growing market in the west. Western agriculture made great advances as new farming techniques, livestock strains, and machinery moved in by rail. Cash, generated by the produce shipped east, poured into the region, and budding western financiers learned how to raise money to capitalize new industry. Factories were built, and the growing industrial population provided a new market for western farm produce.

More than economically, the railroads tied the west to the eastern states. They altered the very pace of life, putting people on a schedule rather than gearing their activities to natural rhythms. National politics came west, as candidates made whistle stop tours of small towns in search of votes. As railroads made travel into the west safe and comfortable, visitors from the eastern states and Europe toured the "New America." Their sometimes exaggerated accounts of the region engendered the Old West myths that helped shape American culture. With the coming of the railroads, the west, for so long the vast, forbidding "out there," was brought into the national life.

Travel times were significantly reduced following the completion of the transcontinental railroad. In an age when we can now cross the country by air in five hours, it requires imagination to appreciate the significance of the transcontinental railroad that made it possible to travel from New York to San Francisco by train in about seven days. Previously, the journey would have taken up to six months by wagon. The change in travel times after the continent was linked by rail in 1869 is compara-

Suez Canal: an artificial water passage in Egypt that joins the Mediterranean Sea and the Red Sea.

ore: a mineral containing a valuable metal for which it is mined and worked.

"Let us complete the grand design of Columbus by putting Europe and Asia into communication, and that to our advantage, through the heart of our country . . . . Let us make the iron road, and make it from sea to sea."
Thomas Hart Benton, 1849

ble in significance to the first person walking on the moon, a hundred years later in 1969.

Today, the National Park Service is responsible for administering Golden Spike National Historic Site. After 1869 Promontory continued to exist as a town site along the main rail line. After 1904, the main line was rerouted to the south, and the rail line north of the Salt Lake was then called the Promontory Branch. Rail operation continued up until 1942, after which all rails and hardware were removed for the war effort. The site was added to the National Park System in 1965. The historic site includes 2,735 acres, much of which is along fifteen miles of the old railroad grades. Visitors can see stretches of parallel grade, **trestles, culverts**, and constructions camps used by railroad workers. A visitor center has been built and offers an array of exhibits, films, and history talks. The last spike site closely resembles the historic scene when the last spike was driven over 130 years ago. Tracks have been relaid, and replica locomotives face together with their cowcatchers almost touching. The golden spike ceremony is reenacted throughout the year for visitors to see and appreciate how the transcontinental railroad was completed. ◆

trestle: a braced framework of timbers, piles, or steelwork for carrying a railroad over a dip in the land.

culvert: a pipelike duct that passes under a railroad track.

Harpers Ferry

WEST VIRGINIA

On October 16, 1859, white abolitionist John Brown and a small band of black followers and white followers attacked the federal musket factory and arsenal buildings at Harpers Ferry, Virginia (now West Virginia), in an effort to start a slave uprising. Although the attackers were quickly defeated, the assault was one of the events that sparked the Civil War.

During the 1850s the northern and southern states became increasingly polarized over the issue of slavery. Northerners believed that the federal government was coming increasingly under the control of the slaveholding states. They could point to a number of developments. In 1850 Congress passed the Fugitive Slave Act, which made it easier for southern slaveholders to recapture slaves who had escaped to the northern free states. The Missouri Compromise of 1820 had barred slavery from most of the Louisiana Purchase. But the Kansas–Nebraska Act overrode the ban, stating that the territorial legislatures of Kansas and Nebraska would decide whether slavery would be allowed. Then the U.S. Supreme Court, in *Dred Scott* v. *Sanford* (1857), ruled that the Missouri Compromise was unconstitutional, and that slaves and their descendants were not U.S. citizens. The decision outraged many in the north and led them to believe that the Court, as well as Congress, was doing the slaveholders' bidding. They also regarded presidents Franklin Pierce (1853–57) and James Buchanan (1857–61), elected on the Democratic ticket, as prisoners of a southern-dominated party.

Meanwhile, slave owners felt increasingly threatened during the 1850s. Abolitionists openly defied the Fugitive Slave

"I wish to say furthermore, that you had better— all you people at the South— prepare yourselves for a settlement of that question that must come up for settlement sooner than you are prepared for it."
John Brown, 1859

171

Harpers Ferry, at the confluence of the Shenandoah and Potomac rivers, as it looked in 1865.

Act, hiding fugitives and in some cases even seizing them after they were in the hands of northern authorities. Abolitionist propaganda became increasingly militant, and some abolitionists (albeit a minority) reversed their previous opposition to the use of force against slavery. Most ominous for slaveholding interests was the rapid growth of the new Republican party in the north and west. It was the first major party to oppose the extension of slavery into the territories.

In 1859 John Brown set fire to the tinderbox of antagonism between north and south. Brown, from Connecticut, failed in a number of business enterprises. Motivated by a morally and religiously based hatred of human bondage, he joined the abolitionist cause in 1849 and two years later began working in the Underground Railroad, which helped fugitive slaves to reach the north.

Absolutely certain of the righteousness of the antislavery cause, he was among the minority of abolitionists who supported the use of violence. After the Kansas–Nebraska Act of

1854, pro- and antislavery forces rushed into Kansas, both seeking to dominate the territory. Civil war broke out. In 1855 Brown joined five of his sons at Osawatomie, Kansas. The following year, he and six others, including four of his sons, massacred five supporters of slavery there.

By the end of 1857 the antislavery forces had won the day in the Kansas Territory, and Brown turned to a plan that had been evolving in his mind for some time. At a meeting in Chatham, Canada, in May 1858, he told a group of followers of his plan to invade western Virginia and establish a "free state" in the Appalachian Mountains. He believed that slaves would flock to his mountain base, which would enable him to march south and enlarge his state. Brown even brought to Chatham a constitution for the state. Some followers objected, but Brown, an intelligent, articulate, and charismatic man, carried the day. From the same wealthy and influential group of New Englanders who had funded his activities in Kansas Territory, Brown obtained money for his new project, although the backers did not know (and, for their own protection, did not want to know) the details.

By 1859 Brown had added a new component to his plan: he would begin his campaign by attacking the federal musket factory and armory at Harpers Ferry, located in the Blue Ridge Mountains in what was then western Virginia. His goal was not to seize arms, as is often assumed; he already had more than enough weapons. Rather, his goal was to create a storm of publicity that would inform the slaves of what he was doing, causing them to rebel and join his band; then he would leave Harpers Ferry and establish his state.

Harpers Ferry was located on a small, V-shaped spit of land created by the merging of the Potomac River, moving southeastward, and the Shenandoah River, flowing northeastward, the merged Potomac then flowing eastward through a gap in the mountains. At its tip, just where the rivers merged, Harpers Ferry was linked to Maryland by the Potomac River Bridge. Upstream along the Shenandoah River, lay the Shenandoah Bridge. The U.S. musket factory and armory, enclosed by a brick wall, lay up the Potomac just 200 yards from the Potomac River Bridge. Two U.S. arsenal buildings, where some of the weaponry produced at Harpers Ferry was stored, lay about the same distance from the bridge along the Shenandoah River. Less than half a mile further upstream was Hall's Rifle Works, a private factory producing high-quality guns with grooved or "rifled"

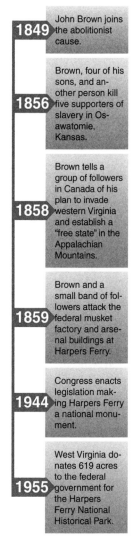

1849 John Brown joins the abolitionist cause.

1856 Brown, four of his sons, and another person kill five supporters of slavery in Osawatomie, Kansas.

1858 Brown tells a group of followers in Canada of his plan to invade western Virginia and establish a "free state" in the Appalachian Mountains.

1859 Brown and a small band of followers attack the federal musket factory and arsenal buildings at Harpers Ferry.

1944 Congress enacts legislation making Harpers Ferry a national monument.

1955 West Virginia donates 619 acres to the federal government for the Harpers Ferry National Historical Park.

barrels for the federal government. These rifles were highly accurate guns for their time.

In July 1859 Brown rented a small farm on the Maryland side of the Potomac, some five miles upriver from the Potomac River Bridge. Inconspicuously, Brown brought in arms that had been stored at Chambersburg, Pennsylvania. Twenty-one volunteers, five black and sixteen white, joined him there in the summer and fall. To make the household seem a normal one, Brown had a daughter and daughter-in-law join them. On Sundays, Brown, operating under the pseudonym Smith, preached at a local church. As the time of the raid approach, Brown told his supporters about his plan to begin with an attack on Harpers Ferry. A number of them feared it would be a suicide mission, but the forceful Brown managed to quell although not remove their doubts.

> "The true question is, Did John Brown draw his sword against slavery and thereby lose his life in vain? And to this I answer ten thousand times, No! No man fails, or can fail, who so grandly gives himself and all he has to a righteous cause."
>
> Frederick Douglass, 1881

On the evening of Sunday, October 16, Brown and seventeen of his men left the farmhouse and marched toward the Potomac River Bridge. (Three were left behind to bring supplies and weapons later.) Crossing the bridge, they captured the night watchman and left guards of their own. The men then walked the some 200 yards to the entrance of the brick-walled musket and armory compound, taking the guard prisoner as well. Having seized the compound, some of them moved along the Shenandoah, taking over the arsenal, the Shenandoah Bridge, and Hall's Rifle Works. Meanwhile, on Sunday evening and Monday morning they took more than sixty hostages and locked them in the firehouse that was on the premises of the musket factory.

Brown wanted the news of his raid to spread. So when a train pulled in at the Harpers Ferry station, Brown let it continue on with the news of the attack, which the train conductor spread by telegraph. Soon the secretary of war asked Colonel Robert E. Lee of Virginia to lead federal forces to Harpers Ferry. Lee agreed, but did not reach Harpers Ferry with his soldiers until 11:00 P.M. Monday. Before then Virginia **militiamen** began counterattacking between noon and 1:00 P.M. on Monday, and many townspeople joined them. The combined forces quickly captured the two bridges and Hall's Rifle Works.

militiamen: members of an army composed of citizens rather than professional soldiers called up in times of emergencies.

Meanwhile, Brown waited for slaves to join his ranks, but only a few did. By 2:00 P.M. it was too late to retreat: Brown had waited too long. He was trapped in the firehouse with a few of his men and the hostages. He sent out several men to ask for a truce, but they were shot one by one. At sunset, militiamen were still flocking into town. During the evening Colonel Lee arrived. On Tuesday morning after sunrise, his marines made their way into the firehouse and Brown's forces were quickly subdued. Brown was wounded. Ten of his followers had been killed, some had fled. No slave uprising had occurred.

Brown's trial began on October 25, just a week after his capture. The jury brought in a guilty verdict on October 31. On November 2 the judge sentenced him to death by hanging for murder and treason against the state of Virginia. Given a chance to speak, Brown—who had been calm and articulate since his capture—made an eloquent defense of the struggle against slavery. At his hanging on December 2, 1859, he remained dignified and calm.

Brown felt that although he had not achieved his goals, his raid had at least riveted the nation's attention on the question of slavery. In that he was correct. Slaveholders, always terrified at the prospect of slave rebellion, reacted with shock to the raid. They were also infuriated that many nonviolent opponents of slavery expressed their admiration for Brown; these abolitionists saw him as a man who had acted decisively against an evil institution that, they feared, was gaining a stranglehold over the national government. The raid and its aftermath strengthened the political position of southern extremists, who claimed that northerners were hell-bent on destroying slavery and were willing to use any means to do so. Therefore, it can be regarded as a step toward secession and Civil War.

> John Brown felt that although he had not achieved his goals, his raid had at least riveted the nation's attention on the question of slavery.

In 1944 Congress enacted legislation making Harpers Ferry a National Monument. Eleven years later West Virginia, in which Harpers Ferry had been located since the state's creation in 1861, donated 619 acres to the federal government for the Harpers Ferry National Historical Park operated by the National Park Service. Land was also obtained from Maryland and Virginia, so that the highlands surrounding the town are also part of the park.

Harpers Ferry changed hands several times during the Civil War. In the fighting, the arsenal buildings, Hall's Rifle Works, and the musket factory—except for the firehouse—were destroyed. The firehouse, now known as John Brown's Fort, was disassembled and moved several times after the Civil War. Beginning in 1909 it resided on the campus of Storer College, a traditionally black school in Harpers Ferry. The National Park Service obtained the building in 1960. But the site of the former musket factory, where the building was originally located, is mostly covered by railroad track embankments, so in 1968 the Park Service placed the firehouse fort some 150 feet east of its original location. It is a one-story brick structure covered with slate, with copper gutters and downspouts, measuring 35.5 feet by 24 feet.

At first, the focus of the National Historical Park was on the years 1859 to 1865. After 1980 the scope of attention was broadened to cover the entire nineteenth century. Still, a number of the homes and stores existing at the time of Brown's raid have been or are in the process of being restored both externally and internally. One of the most prominent is the Harper House, completed in 1782 and the oldest surviving structure in town. ◆

Haymarket Square

CHICAGO, ILLINOIS

anarchist: one who rebels against any authority or ruling power.

Just off Chicago's Haymarket Square on May 4, 1886, a still-unidentified person threw a bomb at policemen attempting to break up an **anarchist** meeting. The systematically unfair trial of eight anarchists for the death of a policeman created a national and international sensation.

The emergence of big corporations after the Civil War spurred the development of the modern labor movement. The depression from 1873 to 1877 was the immediate spark for widespread trade union agitation. Nationwide railroad strikes erupted in 1877, leading to bloody clashes between strikers,

militia: a body of citizens organized for military service.

state **militias**, and federal troops. The Knights of Labor, the first important national trade union in U.S. history, became a powerful force as a result of the labor struggles of these years.

Another, although milder, depression began in 1883 and lasted until 1886. Again, labor agitation, often led by radicals, sprang up. Railroad strikes broke out again in 1884 and 1885. Businessmen feared a repeat of 1877 and many of them believed that the trade unions, or at least the more radical ones, should be crushed. Radicals foresaw a final clash between workers and capitalists that would end private property and leave workers in control of the economy

It was in this atmosphere of strife, tension, and expectation that a national eight-hour-workday movement played itself out. The Federation of Organized Trades and Labor Unions, an organization of national unions that would become the American

Haymarket Square in
Chicago, c. 1935.

Federation of Labor, was founded in 1881. In 1884 its national
convention called for a movement to win the eight-hour day by
May 1, 1886. Hundreds of thousands of laborers became involved in the struggle through organizations such as Chicago's
Eight-Hour Association, and at many businesses they achieved
their goal. Those not succeeding by the May 1 target date were
to go on strike. As that date approached, worker support swelled
while businessmen lived in dread of the violence they feared
would break out.

   In 1883 the anarchist-oriented International Working People's Association (IWPA) was formed. In 1886 it had less than
one thousand members, mostly immigrants from Germany, Bo-
hemia, and Britain. Its strongest base was Chicago, where the

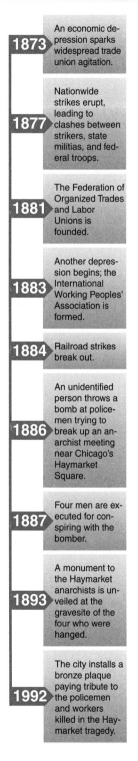

1873 An economic depression sparks widespread trade union agitation.

1877 Nationwide strikes erupt, leading to clashes between strikers, state militias, and federal troops.

1881 The Federation of Organized Trades and Labor Unions is founded.

1883 Another depression begins; the International Working Peoples' Association is formed.

1884 Railroad strikes break out.

1886 An unidentified person throws a bomb at policemen trying to break up an anarchist meeting near Chicago's Haymarket Square.

1887 Four men are executed for conspiring with the bomber.

1893 A monument to the Haymarket anarchists is unveiled at the gravesite of the four who were hanged.

1992 The city installs a bronze plaque paying tribute to the policemen and workers killed in the Haymarket tragedy.

IPWA had several hundred members; its foremost leaders there were Alabama-born Albert Parsons and German-born August Spies. The IPWA favored the overthrow of capitalism by the workers, and advocated violent means to achieve that end. At first the anarchists shunned the eight-hour movement; reform of capitalism would do no good, they believed, since the root of the workers' problem lay in the system of private property. But as the movement grew, most IPWA members, including Parsons and Spies in Chicago, changed their minds. The eight-hour struggle, they decided, could be turned toward social revolution, or at least could be used as a vehicle for spreading anarchist views. Because of their speaking and organizational skills, the anarchists reached the top ranks of the eight-hour campaign's leadership in Chicago.

On Saturday, May 1, over 300,000 workers went on strike against 13,000 business establishments across the nation. The largest number of strikers was in Chicago, where 40,000 laborers walked out of work. Despite all of the fearful anticipation, violence was avoided, in Chicago and elsewhere. But trouble came, unexpectedly, on Monday, May 3, when Chicago policemen used clubs and pistols against strikers at the McCormick Reaper Works on Blue Island Avenue. At least two strikers were killed and a large number were injured.

Spies, who witnessed the mayhem, issued a leaflet calling on workers to arm themselves. On the evening of May 3, IWPA anarchists gathered at Grief's Tavern on West Lake Avenue. They decided to call a protest meeting for the following night at Haymarket Square. The square was a widening of Randolph Street, running east to west, between Desplaines Street on the east and Halsted Street on the west, a two-block stretch. It could accommodate some 20,000 people. It was one of the city's five designated market areas, where farmers sold directly to the city's poorer workers, who were looking for cheap food. On market days it was crowded with people, horses, and wagons. The site was chosen because of its size and its location near several working-class neighborhoods.

When August Spies arrived at Haymarket Square on May 4 at 8:15 P.M., he found a disappointingly small crowd of 2,000 to 3,000 people. Since the gathering was dwarfed by the square, he shifted the meeting around the corner to Desplaines Street, just north of the Haymarket, in front of Crain's Alley, on the east side of Desplaines. The alley was a driveway that came to a dead end at the factory of Crain's Plumbing Company.

At 8:30 P.M. Spies began speaking, standing on a wagon just six or eight feet north of the mouth of the alley. Parsons arrived and took over at 9:00 P.M.; he spoke for an hour. Their speeches advocated violence in general, but made no call for violence at the moment; their rhetoric, in fact, was a bit milder than usual. At 10:00 P.M. Parsons was relieved by Samuel Fielden, who spoke in the same vein.

Meanwhile, the authorities were prepared to shut down the meeting should violence seem imminent. The mayor of Chicago was present at the beginning of the rally and stayed awhile; he left believing there was no threat to order. However, some 200 policemen were gathered at the Desplaines Street Station just south of Haymarket Square. Detectives had been placed at the meeting with instructions to rush back to the station house if disorder seemed likely.

At about 10:10 P.M. dark clouds gathered and gusty winds came up and people began to scatter. Fielden began winding up his remarks, saying that workers could not rely on the law; he urged them to "Keep your eye upon it, throttle it, stab it." His tone, witnesses later said, did not suggest that he was trying to instigate violence then and there, but two detectives immediately rushed back to the police station to report that he was inciting the crowd to violence against the police. Quickly, almost 200 policemen left the station and marched, curb to curb, north up Desplaines toward the gathering, which now numbered just 200 or 300. A police captain ordered the crowd to disperse. Fielden protested but then agreed to cooperate. He was stepping down from the wagon when a number of people saw something fly above the audience. It landed among the policemen, who were across Desplaines Street from the mouth of Crain's Alley. When the bomb landed, it made a huge sound and shattered windows for blocks. It wounded many policemen. But only one of the seven eventual police deaths—that of Mathias Degan—can be attributed exclusively to the bomb, because the enraged police then began firing their guns wildly, even shooting each other inadvertently. Their two-to-three-minute spree ended with seven or eight civilian deaths and from thirty to forty wounded.

On May 27 ten men were indicted for conspiring with the bomb thrower in the murder of Degan. One turned state's evidence and the other successfully fled. The remaining eight were Albert Parsons, August Spies, Michael Schwab, Samuel Fielden, George Engel, Adolph Fischer, Oscar Neebe, and Louis Lingg, all affiliated with the IWPA. Meanwhile, the press convicted the

"The day will come when our silence will be more powerful than the voices you are throttling today."
August Spies, 1887

men before the trial and created an atmosphere of hysteria against the anarchists, not just because they had committed the crime but because all except Parsons were foreigners and so could not possibly be "true Americans."

Awaited with intense expectation, the trial of the Haymarket defendants was the most famous in late-nineteenth-century America. It began June 1896, some seven weeks after the Haymarket tragedy, with Judge Joseph E. Gary presiding. Gary was thoroughly biased against the defendants. He allowed the seating of jurors who acknowledged that they had already decided on the defendants' guilt, gave the prosecution more leeway in questioning than he gave the defense, ruled in favor of the prosecution on every matter of dispute, and spoke of the defendants with open hostility.

The prosecution did not produce credible evidence that the accused had conspired with the bomb thrower, a difficult task since the identity of the thrower was (and remains) unknown. There was also no persuasive evidence that the speakers' words incited the criminal act. Six of the eight defendants could demonstrate that they were not even at the meeting when the bomb was thrown, and the other two were plainly visible on the speakers' platform. Nevertheless, in August the jury came back with guilty verdicts that meant death by hanging for seven of the accused and a fifteen-year jail sentence for the eighth, Oscar Neebe. Sympathy demonstrations by labor and radical organizations across the United States and Europe were held. The eight made legal appeals, which were rejected. On November 10, 1887, the day before the scheduled executions, Governor Richard Oglesby commuted the sentences of Schwab and Fielden to life imprisonment. On that day Lingg committed suicide. The death sentences of the remaining four were carried out on November 11.

> *"The police followed the retreating anarchists and sent deadly volleys into their midst."*
> John J. Flinn, *History of the Chicago Police from the Settlement of Community to the Present Time*, 1887

By 1889 the fear of anarchists had eased somewhat in Chicago. Also that year, two of the policemen who had played key roles in the pursuit and arrest of the Haymarket defendants were discharged from the police department for bribery and trafficking in stolen goods. These developments changed the political climate enough so that a committee to free the three survivors—Neebe, Schwab, and Fielden—could be formed with the support of prominent citizens. In 1892 John P. Altgeld, admired as a man of high integrity, was elected the first Democratic governor of Illinois since the Civil War. Taking office in January 1893, he studied the trial record for months. On June

26 he signed pardons for the three. In a statement accompanying the pardons, he made it clear that the reason for his decision was not mercy, but a belief that the trial had been a **travesty** of justice for reasons that he detailed at some length.

On June 25, 1893, the day before Altgeld's pardon, a monument to the Haymarket anarchists was unveiled at the gravesite of the four who had been hanged (and which would eventually become the resting place of seven of the eight defendants). It is located in what was then Waldheim Cemetery (and is now Forest Home Cemetery), ten miles west of Chicago along the Desplaines River in Forest Park, Illinois. It was designed by sculptor Albert Weinert for a committee headed by Albert Parsons's widow. In front of a granite shaft are two bronze figures, a woman as Justice placing a crown of laurels on the head of a fallen worker while about to unsheath a sword. On the base of the statue are engraved August Spies's last words on the scaffold: "The day will come when our silence will be more powerful than the voices you are throttling today." Every year on the Sunday closest to May 4 and on November 11, labor organizations hold a ceremony at the memorial in tribute to the Haymarket victims. The deed to the monument is held by the Illinois Labor History Society.

> The jury came back with guilty verdicts that meant death by hanging for seven of the accused and a fifteen-year jail sentence for the eighth.

Over a century went by before any commemoration of the Haymarket Square tragedy was installed at the scene of its occurrence. Finally, in March 1992 a bronze plaque was installed by the City of Chicago on the east side of Desplaines Avenue a few steps north of Randolph Street, at Crain's Alley. The plaque, embedded in the sidewalk, pays tribute to the policemen and the workers who were killed. The only surviving building is the one forming the south side of the alley. The bomb, it is believed, was thrown from the vestibule of this building. ◆

Hearst Castle

SAN SIMEON, CALIFORNIA

Better known as Hearst Castle, the Hearst San Simeon State Historical Monument is a historic house museum that was given to the state of California in 1957 by the Hearst Corporation. Located near San Luis Obispo in California's Santa Lucia Mountains overlooking the Pacific Ocean, the

An aerial view of Hearst Castle at San Simeon, California.

> *"I am convinced that I could run a newspaper successfully. Now, if you should make over to me the Examiner—with enough money to carry out my schemes—I'll tell you what I would do!"*
>
> William Randolph Hearst, letter to his father, 1885

opulent castle boasts a Mediterranean-revival architectural style, which complements its Spanish and Italian art collections from the sixteenth and seventeenth centuries. The main building looks like a Spanish cathedral, while the guest houses, gardens, and pools arranged around it create the impression of a hilltop village.

Hearst Castle was built by noted American newspaperman William Randolph Hearst, who was born in San Francisco in 1863, the only son of mining magnate and politician George Hearst and noted philanthropist and educator Phoebe Apperson Hearst. Beginning in 1873, ten-year-old William Randolph Hearst toured Europe for twenty-one months. On the trip he became well versed in art and antiquities and developed a lifelong passion for collecting. In 1879 he enrolled at St. Paul's preparatory school in New Hampshire, but after two years he was asked to leave. After another European trip in 1881, he entered Harvard University; his lack of discipline precipitated his expulsion in the spring of 1885.

In 1887 Hearst persuaded his father to make him proprietor and editor of the *San Francisco Examiner*. Hearst thus began a fabled career as a newspaperman. He immediately revolutionized west coast journalism by adopting techniques successfully employed by Joseph Pulitzer in New York City. In 1894 and 1895 he bought two New York newspapers, which he named the *Morning* and *Evening Journal*. In competition with Pulitzer's *World*, Hearst pushed sensationalism to its limits by playing to the lowest tastes of his readership and exploiting acts of human weakness. He also provided entertainment through serial novels, political cartoons, advice to the lovelorn, and the first comic-strip character, the "Yellow Kid." (From that comic strip character's name comes the term *yellow journalism*.) The rivalry between Hearst and Pulitzer helped bring about the Spanish-American War; in fact, Hearst believed that he was the major contributor in forcing the government's hand in the conflict. Another result of the rivalry and sensationalism was that the *Journal* had the largest circulation of any newspaper in the world; more than 1.25 million copies were sold daily beginning in 1898.

Hearst Castle's grand facade.

Hearst was not nearly as successful in politics as he was in the newspaper business. In the presidential campaigns of 1896 and 1900 he wholeheartedly supported Democratic nominee William Jennings Bryan. In 1902 he ran for, and won, a congressional seat from Manhattan. He then tried, unsuccessfully, to become the Democratic presidential nominee in 1904. The following year, he and Judge Samuel Seabury helped create a Municipal Ownership League in a third-party effort to win the mayor's seat in New York City. He became the league's nominee but lost narrowly to incumbent George B. McClellan. In 1906 he was defeated in a race for governor of New York by Republican Charles Evans Hughes. By 1908 somewhat disenchanted with the major political parties, he launched a third party named the Independent League. The following year, he ran somewhat reluctantly for mayor of New York City and finished third in the race. He was never again a threat as a political candidate.

Hearst pushed sensationalism to its limits by playing to the lowest tastes of his readership.

In the meantime, Hearst began amassing a communications empire. He acquired eighteen newspapers in twelve cities including Boston, Baltimore, Chicago, Detroit, Los Angeles,

The Guest Library at Hearst Castle.

Milwaukee, New York, and San Francisco. He supplied news and features through King Features Syndicate, International News Service, and International News Photos. He owned nine magazines, including *Cosmopolitan, Good Housekeeping, Harper's Bazaar, House Beautiful,* and *Town and Country.*

After 1910 Hearst increasingly moved to the political right. Often a critic of President Woodrow Wilson, he so strongly opposed the administration's pro-Allied leanings that the British and French barred his news empire from using their cable and mails after October 1916; Canada likewise banned all Hearst newspapers. Although softening his stance with America's entry into World War I, Hearst bitterly denounced the League of Nations and the World Court.

When George Hearst died in 1895, his wife, Pheobe, inherited the family's 250,000 acres of ranchland, which included Piedra Blanca, San Simeon, and Santa Rosa. When Phoebe died in 1919, her son took possession of the property. Soon after his mother's death, Hearst began building a residence on the

San Simeon property, which the family had previously used for camping excursions. Tired of sleeping in tents and cabins, Hearst intended to build a modest, but more comfortable, summer retreat at San Simeon. He hired San Francisco architect Julia Morgan, telling her "I would like to build a little something." The project escalated, however, and by 1947, when construction finally ended, the San Simeon estate comprised 165 rooms surrounded by 127 acres of gardens, terraces, pools, and walkways.

The first structures to be completed were three guest houses, later named Casa del Mar (House of the Sea), Casa del Monte (House of the Mountain), and Casa del Sol (House of the Sun). In 1922 construction began on what became the estate's main building, a magnificent 137-foot high mansion called Casa Grande. Casa Grande was ready for occupancy in 1927, but construction on the structure continued for the next twenty years until the building had 115 rooms, including a theater, a wine cellar, and a library with over 4,000 books. The rooms were decorated with Hearst's vast collection of priceless artworks, which included antique furniture, mantels, doors, paintings, sculptures, and tapestries.

The Refectory at Hearst Castle.

Because of his personal extravagance, Hearst was forced to surrender control of his properties.

neoclassical: revival of the Classical in art, literature, music, and architecture.

liquidated: settled business accounts by dispersing assets and debts.

"*He is the greatest menace to the freedom of the press that exists in this country, because instead of using the great chain of newspapers he owns, and the magazines, and the news—disseminating agencies of the country that he controls to disseminate the truth to the people, he prostitutes them to the propaganda that pursues the policy he dictates.*"
Senator Sherman Minton, 1936, describing Hearst's tactics

Hearst Castle's 127-acre grounds include two large swimming pools. The outdoor Neptune Pool, which is faced with marble and lined with **neoclassical** statues and columns, lies in front of a Greco-Roman temple façade. Seventeen colorfully painted dressing rooms are located nearby. The smaller indoor Roman Pool was large enough for Hearst to build two tennis courts on its roof.

Hearst lived at San Simeon on and off during the 1920s and 1930s. However, by 1937 his empire had become financially hard pressed. Because of his personal extravagance, he was forced to surrender control of his properties to legal adviser Clarence Shearn, who promptly began to retrench economically by closing or selling Hearst newspapers, magazines, radio stations, and supplementary news wires. Shearn also **liquidated** real-estate holdings, auctioned off many valuable art objects, and temporarily halted construction on the castle at San Simeon. Despite these measures, the Hearst empire did not begin to stabilize until after World War II. And although Hearst resumed control over the largest publishing conglomerate in the United States, his power was somewhat diminished.

Throughout his adulthood, Hearst led a social life that was quite bizarre, if not scandalous, to most Americans. As a young man, he kept a mistress until his mother ended the arrangement. He was especially fascinated by women in show business. In New York City during 1897, he escorted the Willson sisters, Broadway dancers, about town; on April 28, 1903, he married the younger sister, Millicent. Fourteen years and five sons later, he met Marion Davies, a Ziegfeld Follies showgirl thirty years his junior. After his wife refused to divorce him, he lived with Davies, mainly at San Simeon, while his wife resided in New York.

In 1947 Hearst suffered a heart attack that partially incapacitated him. He halted construction on the San Simeon estate for good, and took up permanent residence at Davies's Villa in Beverly Hills. He died in 1951 at the age of eighty-eight.

After Hearst's death, his corporation maintained ownership of the San Simeon estate. In 1957 the Hearst Corporation gave Hearst Castle as a gift to the state of California in commemoration of the lives and accomplishments of William Randolph Hearst and his mother, Phoebe. The next year, the estate was opened to the public for tours. Hearst Castle was named a National Historic Landmark in 1976. ◆

Highland Park Ford Plant

HIGHLAND PARK, MICHIGAN

H enry Ford revolutionized the automobile industry and the entire industrial world when he initiated assembly line production of the Model T car in 1913. The assembly line was first deployed at the Highland Park Ford plant in Highland Park, Michigan.

Born in 1863, Ford became an apprentice machinist in 1879. After three years of apprenticeship, he worked setting up and repairing Westinghouse steam engines. Becoming an engineer at the Edison Illuminating Company in Detroit in 1891, he was promoted to chief engineer two years later. Fascinated by the new self-propelled vehicles appropriately known as "automobiles," Ford built a gasoline-driven car in 1896. Called the Quadricycle, the driver steered with a **tiller**; it had two forward speeds and no reverse.

tiller: a bar or handle used for steering.

In 1899 Ford founded the Detroit Automobile Company, which failed in less than two years. He then decided to race cars as a way of drawing attention to his vehicles. Beginning in 1901 his successes with his racers, especially the 999 and the Arrow, gained him the publicity he sought. He founded the Ford Motor Company in 1903. Ford's biggest financial backer, Andrew Y. Malcolmson, wanted to build expensive cars but Ford wanted to create a car for the average individual. Initially, the company produced the Model N car, following it with the slightly modified R and S models.

But Ford's greatest success—a world-famous success—came with the production of the Model T, first produced in October 1908 at the company's Piquette Avenue Plant in Detroit. Previously, automobiles were the property of the elite. The Model T, which sold at $850 for the touring car, made them available to the ordinary man and woman.

"No work with interest is ever hard. I am always certain of results. They always come if you work hard enough."
Henry Ford, *My Life and Work*, 1922

The most famous car in history, the Model T was appreciated by the public immediately for its sturdiness, dependability, and power. It had a four-cylinder, 22-horsepower motor and it reached speeds of from 40 to 45 miles per hour. The ten-gallon gas tank was under the front seat. It had a planetary transmission

Workers assemble a Model T in 1913 at the Highland Park Ford plant in Michigan.

operated by foot pedals rather than the usual hand levers; since it could be shifted quickly from forward to reverse, drivers found it easier to get out of potholes. The electrical system produced sparks for the cylinders, eliminating the need for expensive and heavy dry batteries, the first time this had been accomplished in a low-priced car. Its unique, removable cylinder top made servicing easier. The extensive use of vanadium steel made the car both lighter and more rugged. Offered in several colors during the first few years of production, it later came in black only.

Public demand for the car was insatiable, rising dramatically year after year. This gave Ford the incentive to speed up production and also to cut costs to further increase demand. He constantly sought to do both. Interchangeable parts were a key to the Industrial Revolution. He was always looking for better machine tools in order to create perfect interchangeability, so that the workers assembling the cars would not need to take time to file, grind, saw, or hammer parts in order to make them fit. At Piquette Street he attained an absolute interchangeability that eliminated the need for handwork. Ford and his engineers also developed many smaller efficiencies. For example, they developed the single cylinder block for all four cylinders; previously, each cylinder had been separately enclosed.

To increase output further, Ford asked pioneering architect Albert Kahn to construct a huge new plant for the production of the Model T, replacing the Piquette Street structure. It was located on a former racetrack near the outskirts of Detroit in Highland Park, Michigan. The sixty-two-acre Highland Park Ford plant was one-sixth of a mile long (over three city blocks) and four stories high, with one million square feet of floor space, the largest building in Michigan at the time. Using the new technique of reinforced concrete, Kahn was able to create wide, unobstructed work areas in a nearly fireproof building. Reinforced concrete also made it possible to create building walls that were mostly window, opening the factory to daylight. That and the fact that the building was well ventilated made the Highland Park plant a welcome change from the typical factory of the day.

Officially opened in December, the new plant began producing Model Ts early the following year. During fiscal year 1911–12, 35,000 of them were produced at the plant by 6,800 workers. In 1912–13 production more than doubled, but so did the workforce, to 14,300. Yet in 1913–14, production nearly doubled once more while the workforce actually declined to 12,900 employees. It was the introduction in 1913 of the assembly line at Highland Park that so dramatically raised the number of cars produced per worker.

Before the assembly line, work teams gathered around stationary cradles on which were placed all of the parts needed to make one component of a car, such as an engine or transmission. Each worker, sitting on a bench, would then proceed to make complete components. The finished components would then be carried to another workstation, where an additional component was put together and added to the previous assemblage.

All of that changed with the assembly line. Workers now stood along a conveyor belt, waiting to perform their job as the assemblage moved past them. This system made it possible to break down the assembling process into many small, simple tasks, with each worker responsible for just one step. For example, one worker might put a nut on a bolt, with the next worker

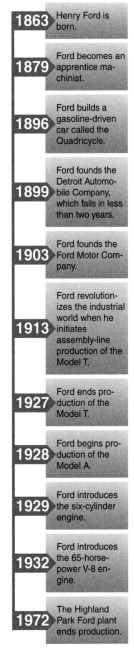

1863 Henry Ford is born.

1879 Ford becomes an apprentice machinist.

1896 Ford builds a gasoline-driven car called the Quadricycle.

1899 Ford founds the Detroit Automobile Company, which fails in less than two years.

1903 Ford founds the Ford Motor Company.

1913 Ford revolutionizes the industrial world when he initiates assembly-line production of the Model T.

1927 Ford ends production of the Model T.

1928 Ford begins production of the Model A.

1929 Ford introduces the six-cylinder engine.

1932 Ford introduces the 65-horsepower V-8 engine.

1972 The Highland Park Ford plant ends production.

fastening it. Ford, influenced by the time-and-motion studies of Frederick Taylor, had the conveyor belt run at waist level to minimize the workers' movements. This was the system that not only increased output, but reduced the need for skilled workers. Ford commented that under his new system, the need for the worker to think was minimized.

The assembly line was introduced at the Highland Park plant in the spring of 1913, first to magneto assemblies, where each worker now had to perform only one or two tasks instead of the twenty-nine operations they once had to do. By the end of the summer, every stage of the process up to chassis assembly was being done on the assembly line. Increased production meant that the chassis assembly department was being flooded with work, so that final stage of assembly was put on the assembly line. In 1910 the Highland Park plant produced 100 Model Ts a day; in 1917 daily output was 2,000.

In 1914 Ford announced that he would share his vastly increased profits with his workers. Wages were increased to five dollars a day, about double the previous average, and daily hours were cut from nine to eight. Yet the workers paid a big price for these gains. Their work was mindless and they had to repeat the same motions all day. They no longer sat, but stood. So although the assembly line, when applied throughout the industrial sector of the economy, made possible a much higher material standard of living, many social critics argued that it degraded work and the worker. Ford placed special burdens on his assembly line workers. He sent representatives to workers' homes to make sure that they were leading moral lives and had the "right" opinions—"moral" and "right" by Ford's standards. This type of intrusion did not last for long, but the basic issues raised by social critics persisted.

In the early 1920s Ford built the Rouge plant on the River Rouge in Dearborn, Michigan, which surpassed the Highland Park plant in size and sophistication. The vast complex of factories, forges, and assembly lines represented an effort to perform as many of the processes as possible required for making a car. For example, it included steel and glass factories so the company did not have to buy those materials from outside; this strategy is known as vertical integration.

Nevertheless, by the mid-1920s Ford's company was no longer the unchallenged leader of the automotive industry. General Motors had become a serious competitor, and Chrysler would soon be a major player. At the same time, the public was tiring of

> *"I will build a motor car for the great multitude . . . constructed of the best materials, by the best men to be hired, after the simplest designs that modern engineering can devise . . . so low in price that no man making a good salary will be unable to own one and enjoy with his family the blessing of hours of pleasure in God's great open spaces."*
>
> Henry Ford, 1903

the Model T as issues of style and comfort became increasingly important. General Motors responded by offering a wide variety of models. So Ford ended Model T production in 1927 and the following year began producing the Model A. The consumer had a choice of four colors and seventeen body styles. It had a windshield of safety glass, four-wheel brakes, and hydraulic shock absorbers. But the Model A was soon surpassed by other models with more important innovations, such as the six-cylinder engine in 1929 and the 65-horsepower V-8 engine in 1932.

Whatever the future brought, the Model T—of which 15 million were produced between 1908 and 1917—remains the most famous car ever. Known also as the Tin Lizzy and the flivver, it is renowned in song and story. Even its shortcomings, such as the need to drive it backward up steep hills, are recalled tenderly.

The Highland Park Ford plant, which still stands at Woodward Avenue and Manchester Street in Highland Park, continued to manufacture Ford automobiles after the Model-T era until it was closed for production in 1972. It has since been used to store cars of discontinued models and crashed cars that are the subjects of lawsuits against Ford. The building, however, has been allowed to decay considerably. ◆

By the mid-1920s, Ford's company was no longer the unchallenged leader of the automotive industry.

Hoover Dam

ARIZONA/NEVADA BORDER

The stunningly massive Hoover Dam, rising 726 feet above the bed of the Colorado River, sits on the border of Arizona and Nevada, thirty miles southeast of Las Vegas. The dam was the largest in the world at its completion in 1935, having harnessed one of the west's most extensive and wild rivers.

In April 1902 President Theodore Roosevelt signed the Reclamation Act to stimulate the development of sixteen sparsely populated western states by irrigating the desert. The Act created the Reclamation Service, later called the Bureau of Reclamation. This agency, under the Department of the Interior, was charged with the mission of reclaiming the desert for the needs of a growing country. *Reclamation* referred to improvements in usage of water and land resources for agricultural

An aerial photograph of Hoover Dam and Lake Mead, on the border between Arizona and Nevada.

and other purposes. Reclamation Service engineers were sent to investigate the possibility of controlling and tapping the power of the Colorado River.

The Colorado River Basin begins in Wyoming and fans south into Utah and Colorado. The Colorado River itself, which starts in the Rocky Mountains of Colorado, flows through the Grand Canyon in Arizona, borders the southern tip of Nevada and a stretch of California, then crosses the Mexican border to empty into the Gulf of California. The river drains a total area of about 250,000 square miles.

In 1905 the Colorado River flooded the Imperial Valley of southeastern California, leading to further investigations concerning how to control the river. In 1922 a report was submitted to the U.S. Congress recommending construction of a dam at or near Boulder Canyon. In November, representatives of the seven Colorado River Basin states met in Santa Fe, New Mexico, to sign a compact. In 1931 the Bureau of Reclamation accepted bids for construction of the dam and power plant. The contract was awarded to a construction and engineering firm named Six Companies, made up of some of the west's most successful builders and designers of dams, bridges, roads, and tunnels. They bid $48,890,995.

Construction on the dam began that year. More than 16,000 people worked on its construction, with more then 3,000 workers on a single shift. Wages started at 50 cents an hour, which was considered good pay during the Great Depression. It was good enough to draw 5,000 men and their families to settle in the Nevada desert during the project. For two years, workers poured concrete twenty-four hours a day seven days a week. Much work on the dam took place at great heights and with large machinery; consequently it was very dangerous. Ninety-six workers died building the dam.

The first step in building the dam was to stop the river, and the method used remains a marvel of engineering. Workers built four diversion tunnels running through the canyon walls parallel to the river, two on each side. Fifty feet in diameter, with a three-foot thick concrete lining, each tunnel averaged 4,000 feet in length. It took nearly two years to construct the four tunnels. To force the river into the tunnels, two temporary dams were built, one upriver and downriver from the construction site. Thus the river was forced around the site though the canyon walls.

At the time of its completion, Boulder Dam, as it was originally named, was the largest structure of its kind in the world. Finished in 1935, it was two years ahead of schedule. The dam was renamed for President Herbert Hoover in 1947.

The primary function of Hoover Dam is to regulate the flow of the river, thereby providing flood control, irrigation, and drinking water to cities and towns in southern California. The dam creates a reservoir to store water during wet times so that it can be used in dry times. Irrigation water from the Hoover Dam has made the Imperial Valley one of the world's greatest farming areas. And due in part to the massive water supply created by the Hoover Dam, the cities of Los Angeles and San Diego have grown to huge proportions. Hoover Dam also kicked off a building boom in the west and helped cement the marriage of private enterprise and federal financing that came to characterize the western economy after World War II.

The generation of electricity, or hydroelectric power, is a secondary function of the dam. The Hoover Dam hydroelectric power plant has two wings, one on each side of the river. Each

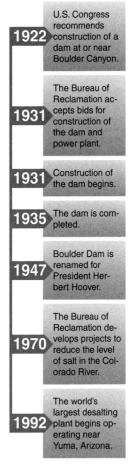

1922 U.S. Congress recommends construction of a dam at or near Boulder Canyon.

1931 The Bureau of Reclamation accepts bids for construction of the dam and power plant.

1931 Construction of the dam begins.

1935 The dam is completed.

1947 Boulder Dam is renamed for President Herbert Hoover.

1970 The Bureau of Reclamation develops projects to reduce the level of salt in the Colorado River.

1992 The world's largest desalting plant begins operating near Yuma, Arizona.

Water rushes through jet flow gates at Hoover Dam.

wing is 650 feet long and eight stories high. The tunnels constructed to divert the river now hold pipes that carry water from the reservoir to turbines, engines that turn generators that produce electric power. There are three miles of the water pipes, each thirty feet in diameter. There are nine generators on the Arizona side and eight in Nevada. The generator units are seventy feet tall and weigh more then 2,000 tons. Each one produces 133,000 kilowatts of electricity, enough to power 100,000 homes at a rate of 1000 kilowatt-hours per month. The whole plant serves about 1.3 million people per year, with more than half of the electricity going to California, and the remainder going to Nevada and Arizona. Las Vegas receives less then 5 percent of its power from Hoover Dam.

The gleaming monumental dam, a leading symbol of twentieth-century technology and the "triumph" of human beings over nature, immediately became a major tourist attraction. In addition, Lake Mead, the reservoir created by the dam, became the site of many water sports activities, especially fishing, swimming, water skiing, and boating. Lake Mead is 115 miles long, with a total area of 233 square miles. The Lake Mead National Recreation Area is administered by the National Park Service.

Over a million people a year visit Hoover Dam, which is a National Historic Landmark. Visitors can take guided tours of the dam and power plant. A regular tour begins by descending in an elevator 520 feet down into the canyon wall. After the descent, visitors walk through a tunnel into the power plant. Wheelchairs are available for those who need them. The tour is half a mile in distance and lasts for about thirty to thirty-five minutes.

While exploring the dam's depths, tour guides enthrall visitors with facts of the massive proportions of the dam. Visitors learn that Hoover Dam is the tallest all-concrete dam in the country, 726.4 feet from top to bottom, as tall as a sixty- or seventy-story building. The top, which accommodates a section of highway, is 45 feet thick and the dam's base is 660 feet thick. The dam weighs 6.6 million tons, containing 3.25 million cubic yards of concrete. This roughly equals enough concrete to build a two-lane highway from San Francisco to New York City or a sidewalk around the equator.

On a special "hard hat" tour of the dam and power plant, visitors receive a more in-depth view of the dam's inner workings. These special tours, which require participants to wear hard hats, explore areas like the generator shaft gallery, the needle valve house, the seepage gallery and sump room, and other behind the scenes areas. The Hoover Dam visitor's center also includes a multimedia presentation about water use, early exploration of the region, and the construction of the dam. A video monitor shows various short films about the dam.

Although it is undeniably one of America's Seven Modern Civil Engineering Wonders, as designated by the American Society of Civil Engineers, some critics blame Hoover Dam for destruction of the natural environment. By redirecting water to the desert, the dam spawned a commercial culture hungry for development at any cost, leading eventually to extensive urban sprawl in the southwestern United States. In addition, the use

"After Mr. Hoover left office, the Interior Department . . . avoided the use of the name 'Hoover Dam' where possible, and used the names 'Boulder Canyon Dam' or 'Boulder Dam.' After hearing testimony relative to the need for clarifying the present situation with regard to the name of this dam, it is apparent to this committee that affirmative legislative action by Congress is desirable."

Congressional Resolution, March 6, 1947

Irrigation water from the Hoover Dam has made the Imperial Valley one of the world's greatest farming areas.

of fertilizers and other chemicals on irrigated land increased the salt content of the water returning to the river. By 1970 salt in the Colorado River had reached an unacceptable level. The Bureau of Reclamation developed projects to reduce the salt in the river basin by 1 million tons per year by 2010. This program includes the world's largest desalting plant, designed to treat seventy-five million gallons of water per day, which began operating in 1992 near Yuma, Arizona.

Ecology groups, such as the Sierra Club, point to studies indicating that dams devastate fish runs and destroy fragile ecosystems. Defenders of dams point to the benefits of hydropower, arguing that dams help reduce air pollution because hydropower is the most plentiful and most efficient renewable energy resource available. But ecologists claim that of the nearly 75,000 dams on U.S. rivers, only a fraction of them produce power. They also claim that hydropower accounts for only about 10 percent of the electricity generated in the United States. In response to these concerns, modern engineers and planners now take ecological issues into consideration when designing dams. ◆

Independence Hall

PHILADELPHIA, PENNSYLVANIA

Independence Hall in Philadelphia, Pennsylvania, has been called the "birthplace of the United States of America." Some of the most pivotal events in early American history took place in Independence Hall's Assembly Room. From the Declaration of Independence to the Articles of the Confederation and the U.S. Constitution, the documents drafted in that room shaped the new nation and still form the basis of American government. The Founding Fathers convened there under the aegis of the Continental Congress, discussing everything from who should run the country to what would be an appropriate design for the American flag.

The building that came to be called Independence Hall was constructed between 1732 and 1756, and was originally intended to be the State House for the colony of Pennsylvania. Based on a design by Andrew Hamilton and Edmund Woolley, Independence Hall is an example of colonial **Georgian** architecture, a harmonious brick structure complete with white trim and classically inspired details such as a **Palladian** window on its south façade. Inside, Independence Hall is composed of meeting rooms, galleries, and chambers for conducting official business of the state.

The architects planned an understated, well-proportioned brick structure topped by a great white tower meant to house a 2,080-pound bell, which has come to be known as the "Liberty Bell." The Liberty Bell was rung during important events, as on July 8, 1776, when the bell summoned people to the yard behind Independence Hall to hear the first public reading of the

"We hold these truths to be self-evident, that all men are created equal, that they are endowed by their Creator with certain unalienable Rights, that among these are Life, Liberty, and the pursuit of Happiness."
The Declaration of Independence, 1776

Georgian: artistic style during the period the first four Georges were kings of England (1714-1830).

Palladian: revived classical style in architecture based on the works of Andrea Palladio.

Independence Hall in Philadelphia.

epicenter: a focal or central point.

Declaration of Independence. Cast in London, the original bell arrived in Philadelphia in August 1752, but it cracked during initial testing. Philadelphia craftsmen melted it down and refashioned a second bell. When the second bell also cracked, a third was created and hung in the tower of Independence Hall. The bell was inscribed with a biblical passage: "Proclaim Liberty throughout all the Land unto All the Inhabitants Thereof." During the British occupation of Philadelphia in 1777, the bell was dismounted and sent to Allentown, Pennsylvania, for protection. The third bell cracked in the 1830s, reputedly as it was rung at the death of Chief Justice John Marshall.

The image of the Liberty Bell is more important today symbolically rather than historically, for it has come to stand for American liberty and independence. In the 1830s New England abolitionists chose the bell as a symbol of the antislavery movement in their pamphlets, since its inscription refers to *all* inhabitants of the land. The bell was exhibited widely at national fairs and exhibitions across the country in the late nineteenth and early twentieth centuries. During the 1926 World's Fair in Philadelphia, the Liberty Bell was the symbol of the exhibition as the nation celebrated its 150th birthday. An enormous eighty-foot replica with 26,000 light bulbs formed part of an elaborate gateway to the World's Fair exhibition halls, and fair souvenirs like pins and flags featured the image of the famous cracked Liberty Bell.

Independence Hall and the sites that surround it—including Congress Hall, the Old City Hall, the Carpenter's Hall, the Philadelphia Merchants Exchange, Christ Church, and the First and Second Banks of the United States—formed the backdrop for some of early America's most dramatic events. In the mid-eighteenth century, even though the city was only a few decades old, with unpaved streets, a thriving port, and a small downtown, Philadelphia served as the **epicenter** of the growing nation.

The First Continental Congress, a group of delegates from the thirteen original colonies, first convened in Philadelphia for seven weeks in 1774 to address the problems caused by British rule. Normally, the group would have gathered in Independence Hall, but at that time the building was perceived to be teeming with royalist sympathizers, also known as Tories. They convened instead in the nearby Carpenter's Hall, headquarters for the nation's most important trade guild of builders. The group included George Washington, John Adams, Samuel Adams, and Patrick Henry. The Congress appealed to King George III of England to bring peace between Britain and the colonies, and launched a boycott against trade with Britain. In a rousing speech inspiring unity among the colonies, Patrick Henry proclaimed, "I am not a Virginian, but an American."

The following year, the Second Continental Congress reconvened on May 10 in the Assembly Room of Independence Hall. There they laid the groundwork for a new independent federal government by forming an army, issuing currency, and selecting diplomats. At that meeting, the Congress appointed George Washington as commander in chief of the Continental Army. Meanwhile, the colonies began forming their own state governments. When the group assembled at Independence Hall again on July 4, 1776, they adopted the Declaration of Independence. Over the following few years, the Founding Fathers worked out all the details of the new government in the rooms of Independence Hall. In 1777 they detailed the procedures and powers of the new government by signing the Articles of Confederation, and they agreed on a design for the American flag. During the same year, British troops briefly occupied Independence Hall, converting its rooms and halls into hospital wards for wounded soldiers. In 1781 the Founding Fathers ratified the Articles of the Confederation, which united the thirteen colonies.

Finally, in 1787, the Founding Fathers drafted the U.S. Constitution, which laid down the basic laws that prevail in the land today. The Constitution resulted from a series of orderly yet contentious meetings from May to September 1787 of the so-called Constitutional Convention. This remarkable group was made up of James Madison, Benjamin Franklin, Alexander Hamilton, Roger Sherman, and other delegates from the colonies. George Washington presided over the convention. Reputedly, though the summer of 1787 was hot, the windows of

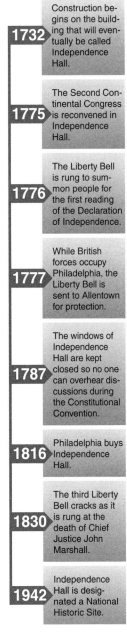

1732 Construction begins on the building that will eventually be called Independence Hall.

1775 The Second Continental Congress is reconvened in Independence Hall.

1776 The Liberty Bell is rung to summon people for the first reading of the Declaration of Independence.

1777 While British forces occupy Philadelphia, the Liberty Bell is sent to Allentown for protection.

1787 The windows of Independence Hall are kept closed so no one can overhear discussions during the Constitutional Convention.

1816 Philadelphia buys Independence Hall.

1830 The third Liberty Bell cracks as it is rung at the death of Chief Justice John Marshall.

1942 Independence Hall is designated a National Historic Site.

Independence Hall were kept closed so that no one would overhear the important discussions.

From 1790 to 1800 Philadelphia served as the nation's temporary capital while Washington, D.C., was being prepared as the official federal home. Independence Hall and the buildings immediately surrounding it once again witnessed a series of important events, including the election of President Washington to a second term, the drafting of the Bill of Rights, and the admission of Vermont, Kentucky, and Tennessee to the new Union. The Old City Hall, adjacent to Independence Hall, served as the home of the nation's Supreme Court.

Only after the Revolution did the building come to be called Independence Hall, in recognition of the important events there that had culminated in America's independence. However, the history of Independence Hall did not end in the late eighteenth century. After the Pennsylvania capital was moved temporarily from Philadelphia to Lancaster in 1799, the building stood empty for several years. The artist Charles Wilson Peale then used Independence Hall to display his eclectic collection of paintings and natural history exhibits. In 1816 the city of Philadelphia purchased the building.

By the nineteenth century Independence Hall had become a symbol of American independence and patriotism. In 1861 President Abraham Lincoln traveled to Independence Hall to raise the American flag, which had just added a thirty-fourth star to welcome the state of Kansas to the Union. Beginning in 1860, Philadelphia schoolchildren collected pennies to pay for a statue of George Washington, which still stands before the entrance to Independence Hall. Throughout the century Independence Hall was used for official parties, drawing presidents Jackson, Van Buren, Harrison, Tyler, Polk, Fillmore, Pierce, and Buchanan from Washington, D.C.

Already in the early nineteenth century the public regarded Independence Hall as a pivotal historical monument that deserved to be restored and opened to the public. By the 1876 centennial celebrations, historians and local officials had attempted to restore the building to its late-eighteenth-century appearance. In 1942 it was designated a National Historic Site, and in the same year the Independence Hall Association was created to protect the building and establish the Independence National Historical Park.

Since America's bicentennial celebration in 1976, the Liberty Bell has stood in a special exhibition pavilion, and a replica

"We the people of the United States, in order to form a more perfect union, establish justice, insure domestic tranquility, provide for the common defense, promote the general welfare, and secure the blessings of liberty to ourselves and our posterity, do ordain and establish this Constitution for the United States of America."

Preamble to the Constitution of the United States of America, 1787

stands in its original place. Currently there are plans to create a more appropriate setting for the Liberty Bell that will accommodate the 1.6 million visitors that flock to visit it annually, and to place the bell alongside Independence Hall, its original home.

Today, Independence Hall looks much the same way that it did in the late eighteenth century. The Assembly Room includes the original silver inkstand used to sign the Declaration of Independence and the Constitution. Another treasure is the chair George Washington sat in as he presided over the Constitutional Convention, carved with the image of the rising sun. Independence Hall is operated under the National Park Service as part of Independence National Historical Park, which includes not only Independence Hall but twenty-four adjacent sites. The area has been called the most historic square mile in the nation. ◆

> "We must, indeed, all hang together, or most assuredly we shall all hang separately."
>
> Benjamin Franklin, 1776

Iolani Palace

HONOLULU, HAWAII

On the island of Oahu, in the Hawaiian capital city of Honolulu, the only two royal palaces in the United States stand facing one another. One of these never truly saw service as a palace. It had been commissioned by King David Kalakaua, but he was displeased with the results and rejected the building. It serves today as the Hawaii Judiciary Building.

King Kalakaua was not to be deterred in fulfilling his desire for a fine royal residence, however. He succeeded on his second try with a building he called Iolani, which means "heavenly bird." Built in 1882 for a total cost of $360,000, Iolani Palace originally served as home to King Kalakaua, and as the headquarters of the Hawaiian government.

When Kalakaua commissioned the construction of the palace, his aim was to impress the world beyond Hawaii's borders with his stature as a ruler of equal importance as any other king or president. He spared no expense, commissioning furniture and installations to rival those being built for the U.S. presidential residence, the White House. He even installed full electricity in the palace in 1887, well before the White House

> "The right to grant a constitution to the nation has been, since the very first one was granted, a prerogative of the Hawaiian sovereigns."
>
> Queen Liliuokalani, *Hawaii's Story by Hawaii's Queen*, 1898

Iolani Palace, the residence of Hawaii's last monarchs, in Honolulu.

gilded: covered with a thin layer of gold.

cabal: a small group of persons joined in a secret, often political, conspiracy.

was electrified, at an expense that exceeded the cost of the construction of the palace itself. The throne room, **gilded** and richly appointed, occupied half of the ground floor of the building, with a reception area and dining room taking up the remainder of the space. The royal residence took up the whole of the second floor.

With the death of Kalakaua in January of 1891, his sister, Liliuokalani, took the Hawaiian throne and assumed residence in Iolani Palace. Her stay there would be brief and tragic: with the successful 1893 coup by a **cabal** of U.S. businessmen and marines, Iolani Palace became the seat of the illegally declared "Republic of Hawaii," and ultimately served as the prison of Hawaii's last legitimate monarch. When Hawaii was annexed to the United States in 1898, administration of the territory was centered at the palace, as was the early state government. Space considerations eventually forced the government offices to be transferred to a newly built capitol building in 1969, whereupon the palace became a museum.

By the time of King David Kalakaua's reign, the Hawaiian royal family had been in decline for some time. The kingdom, founded as a result of the unifying efforts of King Kamehameha I in 1758, had only twenty years of relatively peaceful isolation before it came to the attention of the wider world. Although the islands had been visited by a Spanish ship as early as 1555, they were quickly forgotten until 1778, when Captain Cook made his first visit. Cook's visit would ultimately prove disastrous for both the Hawaiians and himself. With his arrival, he set the stage for the influx of traders, missionaries, and settlers that would ultimately destroy the monarchy. And only one year after first arriving at Hawaii, Cook himself was killed in a dispute between his crew and the local inhabitants.

The Hawaiian Islands (then known as the Sandwich Islands) were situated on the Pacific route to China. They made a convenient stopover point for provisioning the ships that plied the European trade in sandalwood and furs with China. This being so, Hawaii could not hope to maintain its isolation from U.S. and other foreign interests for long after Cook's visit. At first, the trade benefited both the seagoing Europeans and the Hawaiians, but this happy circumstance of mutual profitability was not to last.

With trading ships came European businessmen, some of whom stayed to settle on the islands. Soon, the lure of China trade profits were augmented by the attraction of money to be made in the cultivation of plantation crops, and later, in supporting the Pacific whaling industry. Still, Kamehameha I succeeded in keeping his islands peaceful and prosperous until the end of his rule in 1819. The real trouble did not begin until the following year when his successor, Kamehameha II, permitted a contingency of missionaries to establish a foothold on Hawaii Island.

The missionaries established a school and church and soon had the ear of several members of the royal family—most notably Queen Kaahumanu, mother of the king. She encouraged missionizing and supported the establishment of mission-run schools. The influx of foreigners meant the introduction of diseases hitherto unknown on the Islands, and mortality among the indigenous population ran high. In addition, the monopoly of education by the mission schools meant the systematic destruction of Hawaiian culture and traditional practice. As the foreign business interests became more and more entrenched on the islands, they began to exert undue influence on the Hawaiian political process.

By the time of King Kalakaua's reign, the Hawaiian monarchy was overwhelmingly bent to the service of American business interests. As long as King Kalakaua was happy to devote

1882 King Kalakaua builds Iolani Palace for his residence and as the seat of Hawaii's government.

1887 Full electricity is installed in the palace.

1891 King Kalakaua dies and his sister, Liliuokalani, assumes residency at the palace.

1893 U.S. businessmen take control of Hawaii; the palace becomes the seat of the Republic of Hawaii.

1898 Hawaii is annexed to the United States and administration of the territory is centered at the palace.

1969 Space constraints cause the government offices to be moved to a new capitol building.

1978 After nine years of restoration, Iolani Palace is officially opened to the public as a museum.

"Now, to avoid any collision of armed forces and perhaps loss of life, I do, under this protest, and impelled by said forces, yield my authority until such time as the Government of the United States shall, upon the facts being presented to it, undo the action of its representative and reinstate me in the authority which I claim as the constitutional sovereign of the Hawaiian Islands."

Queen Liliuokalani, upon yielding her throne, January 17, 1893

bayonet: a knife attached to the end of a rifle.

himself to an extravagant, playboy lifestyle, there was little cause for conflict. But in 1881 Kalakaua set out to take a grand world tour, leaving his sister in charge of the kingdom's affairs. Unlike her brother, Liliuokalani was not blind to the dangers presented by the foreign economic interests, and did not cater to them. This caused no little outrage among the wealthy foreign settlers, and began the ill will that would ultimately result in her deposition.

Still, perhaps it was Liliuokalani's strength that caused King Kalakaua to assume, on returning from his world tour, a more assertive role for the monarchy. He attempted to establish diplomatic relations with the Japanese in an effort to break the largely American stranglehold on his trade options. He attempted to replace the Hawaiian constitution, which greatly favored foreign interests, with one more responsive to and representative of indigenous Hawaiians. And he commissioned a royal residence as the outward symbol of the power of the Hawaiian monarchy.

But symbols would not be enough to overcome the entrenched American economic interests. Throughout the 1880s, overt pressures from the business community continued to mount. A cabal of wealthy white planters, businessmen, and professionals had been formed in the late 1870s by a lawyer named Lorrin Thurston, dedicated to the annexation of the islands. In 1887, this group—called the Hawaiian League—forced King Kalakaua at gunpoint to sign a new constitution of their own devising. Their document, known to Hawaiians as the "**bayonet** constitution," stripped the king of his autonomy, granted U.S. warships full rights to a permanent port at Pearl Harbor, and withdrew from most indigenous Hawaiians the right to vote. Three years later, an ailing King Kalakaua died of kidney disease.

With her brother's death, Liliuokalani became queen of the Hawaiian Islands, but she was unwilling to accept the figurehead role allotted her by the American business interests. Meanwhile, those business interests—by now largely centering on the sugar plantation economy—were themselves feeling threatened by outside pressures. The U.S. domestic sugar industry was in trouble, and to shore it up the government decided to cut its imports. The only way that growers in Hawaii could hope to maintain their huge profits in trade with the United States would be through annexation. The last thing they needed was a Hawaiian monarch who was determined to regain national sovereignty.

Lorrin Thurston and his colleagues from the Hawaiian League took steps to sound out the U.S. government's position on the annexation of Hawaii just as Queen Liliuokalani was meeting with Hawaiian leaders to draft a new constitution that would restore full power to the monarchy. It was to be promulgated from the balcony of Iolani Palace on January 14, 1893, and throngs of people came in anticipation of the announcement. But within the throne room, foreign diplomats and members of the business community had turned out in force to dissuade her of this action. Seeing that she had no support even among her own ministers, Queen Liliuokalani stopped short of her original plans, announcing only that a constitution would be established at some future date.

The queen's discretion was inadequate to spare her from retaliation by the business community. On that same evening, leaders of this group met and drafted plans to overthrow the monarchy. Two days later, they called upon a contingent of marines to come ashore at Oahu, claiming the need to protect American holdings on the island. These forces, armed with Gatling guns and cannon, marched on the palace. By the following day, faced with the overwhelming military force arrayed before the palace doors, Queen Liliuokalani was forced to surrender her rule. She was ordered to vacate the palace, and to submit to house arrest in her husband's family home, Washington Place.

Iolani Palace became the seat of the illegal provisional government installed by the Lorrin Thurston cabal. Sanford Dole, a judge and the son of a missionary, was named president of the new administration. Martial law was declared, and enforced by the intimidating presence of American marines. On February 1, 1893, the American flag was raised over the palace.

The deposition of Queen Liliuokalani aroused the patriotism of many Hawaiians. There was great hope at first that the U.S. government, back in Washington, would disavow the actions of the provisional government and reinstate the queen. But while the U.S. president, Grover Cleveland, condemned the actions of his countrymen, he ultimately refused to take the firm steps that were required to dislodge the usurpers of the Hawaiian throne.

Once it became clear that there would be no help from the American government, a group of Hawaiian royalists began to meet in secret, making plans to restore Liliuokalani to power. They imported guns from San Francisco, hoping to raise a rebel

"... if a feeble but friendly state is in danger of being robbed of its independence and its sovereignty by a misuse of the name and power of the United States, the United States cannot fail to vindicate its honor and its sense of justice by an earnest effort to make all possible reparation."
President Grover Cleveland, speech to Congress, December 18, 1893

army sufficient to challenge the illegal government. But somehow the group was betrayed, and the group found themselves facing armed police. All hope of organized rebellion was dashed, and instead the insurrectionists were forced into hiding. After days of fighting, the core members of the royalist rebels were taken into custody.

When the last of the rebel leaders had been taken into custody, the sheriff appeared at the door of Washington Palace, where he arrested Liliuokalani for complicity in the plot. He brought her back to Iolani Palace, where she was imprisoned and—in her own throne room—tried as a traitor. There were to be no last minute reprieves for the former queen. In the presence of a crowd of onlookers, Liliuokalani was found guilty and sentenced to five years imprisonment in a small room on the second floor of the palace. There, under the threat that her supporters would be executed if she refused to comply, she signed her name to a document formally dissolving the Hawaiian monarchy for all time.

> In the presence of a crowd of onlookers, Liliuokalani was found guilty and sentenced to five years' imprisonment.

Liliuokalani would not ultimately serve her full term—she was paroled after eight months—but she never again ascended to the throne. When her rights to the lands of the monarchy were finally restored she donated most of them to the Hawaiian people, including Iolani Palace, which served as Hawaii's capital until 1969.

When Hawaii's new capitol building was completed in 1969, the palace was turned over to an organization called Friends of Iolani Palace, whose task was to restore the building to its original splendor. The organization initiated a worldwide search for the opulent late-nineteenth-century furnishings with which the palace was originally decorated, and eventually recovered more than 1,000 pieces. Missing items that were not found were replaced with period and **facsimile** furnishings. In 1978, after nine years of restoration, Iolani Palace was officially opened to the public as a museum. Visitors can tour the magnificent throne room (which contains the original gilded thrones), the reception area, and the dining room on the first floor, as well as the royal living quarters on the second floor. The queen's bedroom has been furnished to look as it did while Liliuokalani was imprisoned, and contains a quilt she began stitching during the long days of her imprisonment. Many of palace's original furnishings remain unaccounted for, and Friends of Iolani Palace maintains an ongoing search to recover them. ◆

facsimile: an exact reproduction or copy.

Jamestown

Jamestown, a settlement founded in 1607 on the James River between present-day Norfolk and Richmond, Virginia, is famous for many firsts in American history. By most accounts Jamestown was the first permanent English settlement—a distinction also claimed by Plymouth in New England (1620)—though it was largely abandoned after 1698 following a series of devastating fires and other misfortunes. It was in Jamestown that European farmers cultivated their first tobacco fields in 1612, but of more lasting significance was the July 30, 1619, meeting of the first representative government set up by European settlers, the assembly known as the Virginia House of Burgesses. Jamestown was also the site of the first landing of African slaves in North America in 1619, though many years would pass before the slave trade developed into a large-scale operation.

Today Jamestown is a national historic site, and excavations begun in the 1930s are underway to uncover artifacts and remains of the Jamestown fort and some of the settlement's shops. The site is part of a historical reservation triangle that also includes Cape Henry and Yorktown on the peninsula between the James and York rivers, and Williamsburg, the beautiful town that in 1699 became the capital of Virginia after Jamestown proved impossible to maintain.

In 1585, twenty years before the founding of Jamestown, Queen Elizabeth and her prized adventurer Sir Walter Raleigh had tried to establish a settlement on Roanoke Island, off the coast of present-day North Carolina. That attempt met failure several

> *"The land we see around us is overgrown with trees and woods, being a plain wilderness, as God first ordained it."*
> William Strachey, secretary of the Jamestown colony, 1607

Reconstructed ruins of some of the buildings that once formed Jamestown, in present-day Virginia.

years later with the mysterious disappearance of the settlers, temporarily discouraging the English from launching another colony.

Two events in the early 1600s led England to take a new interest in the Americas. First, James I became king in 1603 and made peace with Spain, ending a conflict that had drained English energy and resources for years. Second, France began making plans to colonize North America. Not wanting to be outdone by the French, a group of British merchants organized the Virginia Company of London, chartered by King James I in 1606, to establish a colony in the New World.

The Virginia Company was a business venture, and the people who invested in it expected to make a profit. At the same time, the colonization of North America became a national mission that would bring glory to England. It was also, to some extent, a religious mission. Captain John Smith, the military officer for the colony of Jamestown, wrote that one purpose of colonization was to bring the Indians "the true knowledge of God and his holy Gospell."

In the spring of 1606 King James gave the Virginia Company a charter to found a colony in the region of Virginia along the Atlantic coast of North America. (The land called Virginia, which included present-day North Carolina, had been named after Queen Elizabeth, the "virgin Queen.") In December 1606, under the command of Captain Christopher Newport, the ships *Susan Constant, Discovery,* and *Godspeed* set sail from England, carrying 144 colonists bound for Virginia.

Even before reaching North America, the colonists ran into trouble. During the voyage thirty-nine people died from illness. Quarrels arose among the survivors and grew so heated that Captain Smith was charged with mutiny and arrested. When the ships reached the coast of Virginia in April 1607, Captain Newport opened a sealed box containing instructions for governing the colony. The instructions named seven leading colonists to form a ruling council. One of those listed was John Smith, but the other six members promptly voted him off the council.

The mood of discord continued as the colonists searched up and down the coast for a good place to build a settlement. On May 14, 1607, they finally chose a point of land near the mouth of a large river that flowed into Chesapeake Bay. They began building a fort and settlement, which they called Jamestown after the king. The river, too, was given the king's name.

The low-lying, marshy site where the colonists settled proved unhealthy. It not only lacked a good source of drinking water but also turned out to be a breeding ground for the mosquitoes that carry the disease malaria. Illness took a high toll on the colony. By the end of 1607 all but forty of the Jamestown settlers had died of either hunger, dysentery, malaria, or yellow fever.

Disagreements among the council members continued. Three of them returned to England in June 1607, two months after their first landing, when Captain Newport went back for more settlers and supplies. Lacking strong leadership, the colonists who remained would not work together for the good of the community. As with the Roanoke settlement twenty years before, many of the colonists were aristocrats who regarded physical labor as beneath them, and possessed no practical skills. Instead of hunting, fishing, and planting crops, most colonists spent their days searching for gold, playing games, and generally lazing around. Without meat and corn from the nearby Powhatan Indians, the Jamestown settlement might not have survived.

Captain Newport returned to Jamestown with supplies and 120 new settlers in January 1608, which must have been a great relief after the many deaths by the end of 1607. Soon afterward, however, a fire swept through the fort and storehouse, destroying the much-needed supplies and housing. At this difficult

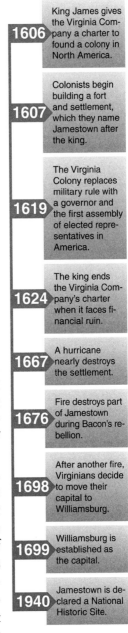

1606 King James gives the Virginia Company a charter to found a colony in North America.

1607 Colonists begin building a fort and settlement, which they name Jamestown after the king.

1619 The Virginia Colony replaces military rule with a governor and the first assembly of elected representatives in America.

1624 The king ends the Virginia Company's charter when it faces financial ruin.

1667 A hurricane nearly destroys the settlement.

1676 Fire destroys part of Jamestown during Bacon's rebellion.

1698 After another fire, Virginians decide to move their capital to Williamsburg.

1699 Williamsburg is established as the capital.

1940 Jamestown is declared a National Historic Site.

time, John Smith stepped forward as the colony's leader. He visited the Powhatan Indians to restore good relations with them and obtain some food. He also forced each colonist to spend a certain number of hours each day planting and tending crops or repairing buildings: "He that will not work shall not eate," Smith insisted. His efforts enabled the colony to survive. But when he left for England to tend an injury in the fall of 1609, the colonists once again fell into bickering and laziness. They suffered horribly during the winter of 1609–10, which came to be known as the "starving time." Only sixty-five colonists out of about 180 survived those terrible winter months.

In 1610 the Virginia Company sent a military governor to Jamestown to continue the more structured policies of Captain John Smith. Under military rule, the colony became much more stable. Colonists dug wells and planted gardens and field crops. They also began to grow tobacco. Although the Virginia Company made no profit, some individual colonists prospered by raising and selling tobacco.

To attract more settlers, the Virginia Company introduced a new system of land distribution, which promised grants of land to colonists and indentured servants. The population increased steadily. Between 1619 and 1622 more than three thousand new colonists arrived in Jamestown, including the settlement's first women, a shipload of ninety "younge, handsome and honestly educated maydes" sent in 1619 by the Virginia Company as wives for the settlers. At the same time, however, the disease rate remained very high, for the colony had not moved from the swampy, mosquito-infested land. Three-quarters of the newcomers died within their first three years in North America.

In 1619 the Virginia Company replaced military rule with a governor, and the first assembly of elected representatives in America—the Virginia House of Burgesses—met on July 30 in Jamestown. That same year, a Dutch ship and an English ship called *Treasurer* brought the first African slaves to Virginia. The Dutch and English ships were privateers, and the slaves had been stolen from a Spanish slave ship. The slaves' arrival laid the foundation for a prosperity based on tobacco plantations and slave labor. Until about 1680, however, indentured servants outnumbered slaves as the colony's main laborers; white men from London were less expensive.

As Jamestown grew, colonists began to settle outside the original town. New settlements sprang up along the James and other rivers, turning Virginia from a wilderness into an English

> "When it shall please God to send you on the coast of Virginia, you shall do your best endeavour to find out a safe port in the entrance of some navigable river, making choice of such a one as runneth farthest into the land, and if you happen to discover divers portable rivers . . . make choice of that which bendeth most toward the North-West for that way you shall soonest find the other sea."
>
> King James's instructions for the Virginia Colony, 1606

community. An Indian uprising in 1622 reversed that pattern somewhat, as colonists in outlying farms and settlements sought refuge in Jamestown.

Meanwhile, the Virginia Company faced financial ruin. The king ended the company's charter in 1624, making Virginia a royal colony (another first) under the direct control of the English crown. Jamestown became the capital of Virginia. Colonial leaders continued to hope that the town would prosper, but its unhealthy location remained a disadvantage. A terrible hurricane with twelve-foot waves nearly destroyed the settlement on August 27, 1667. Fire destroyed part of Jamestown in 1676 during Bacon's rebellion (a power struggle between a young planter, Nathaniel Bacon Jr., and the aged governor of Virginia, Sir William Berkeley, over how to respond to Indian attacks). After another fire in 1698, Virginians decided to move their capital to Williamsburg, which had a better location. Williamsburg was established as the capital in 1699. Jamestown slowly shrank and died as colonists abandoned it for healthier terrain and more fertile lands.

Excavations around the original fort during the 1930s uncovered traces of the settlement. The island (since carved by the James River from its former position along the mainland) was incorporated into the Colonial National Historical Park, and, later, into the U.S. National Park Service in the 1930s. Jamestown was declared a National Historic Site in 1940, and excavations were renewed for a while in the 1950s. The park is a popular tourist attraction, particularly among the many who visit nearby Williamsburg each year. Ongoing excavations by the Jamestown Archaeological Assessment, supported by the National Park Service, are uncovering artifacts and new data about the original settlement, including the remains of a gunsmith's shop and an earthen fort constructed between 1665 and 1667 to protect the settlers against raids by the Dutch. ◆

> *"Heaven and earth never agreed better to frame a place for man's habitations."*
> John Smith, describing the Jamestown territory, 1607

Jefferson Memorial

WASHINGTON, D.C.

The memorial to Thomas Jefferson, America's third president, stands opposite the White House at the south end of Washington, D.C.'s, Tidal Basin. The neoclassical structure, officially called the Thomas Jefferson Memorial, was designed by John Russell Pope, a noted American architect who also designed the West Building of the National Gallery of Art, Constitution Hall, the National Archives building, and the building occupied by the Federal Reserve Board. Pope died in 1937, shortly before construction began on the Jefferson Memorial, and his design was later modified by architects Otto R. Eggers and Daniel P. Higgins.

Plans for a memorial to Thomas Jefferson had been under discussion for decades before Congress finally authorized the project in 1934, allocating $3 million for construction. The Thomas Jefferson Memorial Committee was subsequently formed and met for the first time in April 1935. The committee was made up of twelve commissioners and headed by Fiske Kimball, director of the Philadelphia Museum of Art and author of two groundbreaking works on Jefferson: *Thomas Jefferson and the First Monument of the Classical Revival in America* and *Thomas Jefferson: Architect*. The committee considered four different Washington, D.C., locations for the memorial, and Pope was directed to prepare four site-specific designs. A circular domed monument for the Tidal Basin, modeled after the Pantheon in Rome, was finally chosen.

Pope originally designed a memorial with a 220-foot diameter and a height of 144 feet, to be built at a cost of $9 million. Franklin Delano Roosevelt, who was president at the time, requested that the project be scaled back to the $3 million originally allocated, and Pope revised his design to decrease the monument's size. When pictures of the proposed monument and details of its site and cost were published in the newspapers, however, a storm of protest arose. People objected that Pope's design lacked originality and vitality—its **neoclassical** style had become unfashionable and the design seemed outmoded. One critic scoffed at the memorial, calling it "Jefferson's muffin." Famed American architect Frank Lloyd Wright pronounced it "Pope's arrogant insult to the memory of Thomas Jefferson." Others objected to the chosen site because the design required the sacrifice of 171 of the 2,700 flowering cherry trees (a gift to the United States from Japan in 1912) that lined the Tidal Basin. Many also objected to the public expense, since the country was still suffering the effects of the Great Depression. Indeed, on August 23, 1937, the House Appropriations Committee withdrew the $3 million allocated for the memorial. Only four days later John Russell Pope died of abdominal cancer.

> *"If there be any among us who would wish to dissolve this Union or to change its republican form, let them stand undisturbed as monuments of the safety with which error of opinion may be tolerated where reason is left free to combat it."*
>
> Thomas Jefferson, first inaugural address, 1801

neoclassical: revival of classic style and form in art, literature, and music in England (c.1660–c.1740).

The Jefferson Memorial in Washington, D.C.

However, Congress reauthorized the project and the funding. Pope's widow, Sadie, and Otto R. Eggers and Daniel P. Higgins of his firm carried on with Pope's plans, slightly modified after his death. A groundbreaking ceremony was held on December 15, 1938, with President Roosevelt turning over the first shovelful of soil. Roosevelt laid the memorial's cornerstone on November 15, 1939. Most objections to chopping down the cherry trees ceased after Japan bombed Pearl Harbor in 1941 and the United States entered World War II. The memorial was completed and dedicated on the 200th anniversary of Jefferson's birth on April 13, 1943. An audience of five thousand gathered at the dedication ceremony, where Roosevelt praised Jefferson as an "Apostle of Freedom."

The monument's architectural style reflects the ancient Greek and Roman models Jefferson admired and emulated in his own buildings. Pope's design recalls Jefferson's designs for his Monticello home and the University of Virginia. The memorial's dome is surrounded by fifty-four **Ionic** columns and fronted by a classical **portico** and **pediment** on the side facing the Mall. The dome, with its interior diameter of 86.3 feet, rises 96 feet above the ground, the entire memorial matching the Lincoln Memorial in height. The overall dimension of the stylobate on

Ionic: ancient Greek architecture style marked by columns topped by spiral-shaped ornaments.

portico: a covered entrance with a roof supported by columns.

pediment: a triangular decorative feature over a door or window.

> *"I shall often go wrong through defect of judgment. When right, I shall often be thought wrong by those whose positions will not command a view of the whole ground. I ask your indulgence for my own errors, which will never be intentional, and your support against the errors of others, who may condemn what they would not if seen in all its parts."*
>
> Thomas Jefferson, first inaugural address, 1801

epigrammatic: witty; clever.

which the memorial stands is 182.9 feet. Each column in the Jefferson Memorial is 41 feet high and weighs 45 tons. The weight of these columns necessitated a special foundation of concrete-filled steel cylinders sunk into bedrock.

The interior walls of the memorial are made of white Georgia marble; its floors are of pink and gray veined Tennessee marble, while the exterior walls and dome are made from Vermont Imperial Danby marble. The interior of the coffered dome is white Indiana limestone. Above the entrance to the monument is a sculptured bas relief by A. A. Weinman depicting the signers of the Declaration of Independence; Jefferson is seen standing on the left with Benjamin Franklin, while John Adams, Roger Sherman, and Robert Livingston are seated at the right.

Inside the memorial stands a bronze statue of Thomas Jefferson by sculptor Rudolph Evans. This stands nineteen feet high—the same height as the seated Lincoln in his memorial at the other end of the Tidal Basin. Jefferson wears a fur-collared coat like the one given him by Thaddeus Kosciuszko, a Polish general who had fought for America during the Revolutionary War.

The inner dome and walls of the memorial are inscribed with writings by Jefferson. The quotations were chosen to demonstrate different aspects of his multifaceted mind as well as his gift for **epigrammatic** expression. The dome is encircled with this statement from a letter Jefferson wrote to Dr. Benjamin Rush in 1800: "I have sworn upon the altar of God eternal hostility against every form of tyranny over the mind of man."

One wall bears resounding lines drawn from the Declaration of Independence, which Jefferson drafted:

> We hold these truths to be self-evident, that all men are created equal, that they are endowed by their Creator with certain inalienable Rights, that among these are Life, Liberty, and the pursuit of Happiness. That to secure these rights, Governments are instituted among Men. . . . We . . . solemnly publish and declare, that these . . . colonies are and of Right ought to be free and independent states. . . . And for the support of this declaration, with a firm reliance on the protection of divine Providence, we mutually pledge our Lives, our Fortunes and our sacred Honor.

Another wall is inscribed with a passage from the Bill for Establishing Religious Freedom, drafted by Jefferson and passed by the Virginia Assembly in 1786:

> Almighty God hath created the mind free. All attempts to influence it by temporal punishments or burthens . . . are a departure

from the plan of the Holy Author of our religion. . . . No man shall be compelled to frequent or support any religious worship or ministry or shall otherwise suffer on account of his religious opinions or relief, but all men shall be free to profess and by argument to maintain, their opinions in matter of religion. I know but one code of morality for men whether acting singly or collectively.

A further inscription is drawn from Jefferson's *Notes on the State of Virginia*, written in 1785:

God who gave us life gave us liberty. Can the liberties of a nation be secure when we have removed a conviction that these liberties are the gift of God? Indeed I tremble for my country when I reflect that God is just, that his justice cannot sleep forever. Commerce between master and slave is despotism. Nothing is more certainly written in the book of fate than that these people are to be free. Establish the law for educating the common people. This it is the business of the state to effect and on a general plan.

The Jefferson Memorial also includes a forward-looking quotation from a letter Jefferson wrote to Samuel Kercheval in July 1816:

I am not an advocate for frequent changes in laws and constitutions, but laws and institutions must go hand in hand with the progress of the human mind. As that becomes more developed, more enlightened, as new discoveries are made, new truths discovered and manners and opinions change, with the change of circumstances, institutions must advance also to keep pace with the times. We might as well require a man to wear still the coat that fitted him when a boy as civilized society to remain ever under the regimen of their barbarous ancestors. ◆

1934 Congress authorizes a memorial for Thomas Jefferson and allocates $3 million for construction.

1935 The Thomas Jefferson Memorial Committee meets for the first time.

1937 The House Appropriations Committee withdraws the $3 million allocated for the memorial.

1938 Franklin D. Roosevelt turns over the first shovelful of soil at a groundbreaking ceremony.

1939 Roosevelt places the memorial's cornerstone.

1941 Most objections to chopping down the cherry trees cease after Japan bombs Pearl Harbor.

1943 The memorial is dedicated on the 200th anniversary of Jefferson's birth.

John F. Kennedy Space Center

CAPE CANAVERAL, FLORIDA

The John F. Kennedy Space Center (KSC) is located adjacent to Cape Canaveral on northern Merritt Island, a barrier island complex on Florida's Atlantic coast midway between Jacksonville and Miami. This strip of marsh and sandy scrub thirty-four miles long and between five and ten miles wide houses the United States' only launch complex for manned space operations. The Space Center is one of several installations operated by the National Aeronautics and Space Administration (NASA), the federal civilian agency responsible for the U.S. space program. In 1961 Congress authorized NASA to develop federal lands near Cape Canaveral into a launch and operations facility for the Apollo moon shot program. Since then, KSC has served as NASA's launch and payload processing base for hundreds of spaceflights, including the Skylab space station, the Space Shuttle program, and robotic spacecraft that have explored the solar system and beyond.

The primary facilities on KSC are located in Launch Complex 39. Besides the two Space Shuttle launch pads, Complex 39 includes the Launch Control Center, which houses the computers and personnel that initiate and monitor launches; the Orbiter Processing Facility, where the Shuttle orbiters are refurbished after each mission; a 15,000-foot runway for Shuttle landings; and the Vehicle Assembly Building, one of the largest buildings in the world, where the Shuttle orbiter is teamed with its external rockets in preparation for launch. The majority of

"It's a great honor and privilege for us to be here, representing not only the United States but men of peace of all nations, and with interest and a curiosity and a vision for the future."

Neil Armstrong,
from the moon,
July 20, 1969

217

The Kennedy Space
Center in Florida.

northern Merritt Island is unused by KSC, and its lands and waters are protected as a National Wildlife Refuge.

The U.S. space program was made possible by advances in rocket technology developed for the second World War. By 1949, under the guidance of Wernher von Braun and others, V-2 rockets were being tested at the air force's newly activated Long Range Proving Ground at Cape Canaveral. These soon gave way to the more powerful Redstone and Atlas rockets, which safely blasted payloads of plants and animals hundreds of miles into space, thus establishing the feasibility of human space flight.

After the USSR successfully launched the first artificial satellite (*Sputnik* I) into space in October, 1957, President Eisenhower called for an immediate response, proposing legislation to advance the United States into the Space Age. Only three months later, Congress passed the National Aeronautics and Space Act of 1958, creating NASA and initiating implementation of a national manned spaceflight project.

The objectives of Project Mercury, which culminated in six manned spaceflights from 1961 to 1963, were specific: to orbit a manned spacecraft around earth; to investigate man's ability to function in space; and to recover both man and spacecraft safely. With the exception of the second Mercury flight, when astronaut Virgil (Gus) Grissom's capsule sank in the ocean after splashdown, all of the goals were successfully met. On May 5, 1961, Alan B. Shepherd became the first American in space when a Redstone 3 rocket carrying his *Freedom* 7 capsule was launched from Cape Canaveral. Shepherd attained a **suborbital** flight of fifteen minutes before achieving successful splashdown and recovery. The third manned Mercury mission in February 1962 sent an American into orbit for the first time when John H. Glenn completed three earth orbits in his four-hour flight aboard *Friendship* 7. The Mercury team's successful completion of its goals over a short period of time provided the encouragement necessary for the continued growth of the space program.

In 1961 President Kennedy announced plans to fly American astronauts to the moon, and shortly afterward NASA began acquiring land adjacent to Cape Canaveral to develop as a launch and operations complex for the resultant Apollo program. By 1967 Complex 39 was operational, and the new space center was known as Cape Kennedy.

The second U.S. manned space program was announced in January 1962. The Gemini program, named for its two-man crew, was conceived after it became evident to NASA officials that an intermediate step was required between Project Mercury and the Apollo program. In twelve flights, the Gemini program accomplished its goals of subjecting humans and equipment to spaceflight up to two weeks in duration and performing rendezvous, docking, and propulsion with orbiting vehicles.

In October of 1968 the first manned flight of the Apollo project, Apollo 7, blasted off from Complex 39 on the new Saturn rocket and completed 163 earth orbits in eleven days. Apollo flights 8–10 sent the spacecraft into **lunar** orbit and performed tests in preparation for the historic Apollo 11 mission, during which, on July 20, 1969, Neil Armstrong became the first man to walk on the moon. Five more Apollo crews successfully landed on the moon, collecting geological samples and performing successively longer Extra-Vehicular Activities (EVAs) on the moon's surface. Apollo mission 13 was aborted after an oxygen tank rupture, but the crew survived and was safely returned to earth.

suborbital: a flight in which a spacecraft follows a curved path of less than one orbit.

"Be it enacted by the Senate and House of Representatives of the United States of America in Congress assembled . . . the Congress hereby declares that it is the policy of the United States that activities in space should be devoted to peaceful purposes for the benefit of all mankind."
National Aeronautics and Space Act of 1958

lunar: of or on the moon.

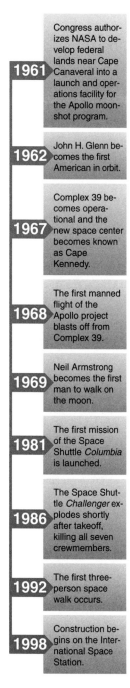

1961 Congress authorizes NASA to develop federal lands near Cape Canaveral into a launch and operations facility for the Apollo moonshot program.

1962 John H. Glenn becomes the first American in orbit.

1967 Complex 39 becomes operational and the new space center becomes known as Cape Kennedy.

1968 The first manned flight of the Apollo project blasts off from Complex 39.

1969 Neil Armstrong becomes the first man to walk on the moon.

1981 The first mission of the Space Shuttle *Columbia* is launched.

1986 The Space Shuttle *Challenger* explodes shortly after takeoff, killing all seven crewmembers.

1992 The first three-person space walk occurs.

1998 Construction begins on the International Space Station.

In all, twelve manned and unmanned Saturn V/Apollo missions were launched from Cape Kennedy between 1967 and 1972. In 1973 America's first experimental space station, Skylab, was placed into earth orbit, followed by three-member crews aboard Saturns later that year. Designed for long duration missions, the Skylab program objectives were twofold: to prove that humans could live and work in space for extended periods, and to expand our knowledge of solar astronomy well beyond earth-based observations. The Saturn/Apollo era ended in 1975 with the launch of a Saturn IV/Apollo crew on a joint manned mission with a Soyuz spacecraft crew from the former Soviet Union.

Shortly after the first moon landing, NASA's recommendations for the future of the space program included establishing a space station for planetary exploration and servicing it with a reusable space vehicle. After much investigation and debate, the Nixon administration eventually endorsed the development of the Space Transportation System (STS), commonly known as the Space Shuttle, the first reusable spacecraft. STS consists of an orbiter, usable for up to 100 missions, and a partially recoverable external tank booster system for launch. Designed for routine use of space, the Shuttle operates in low earth orbit. In space, it is a base to deploy payloads; it is also used to repair and service satellites, and to serve as a platform for scientific research. It is launched in the conventional manner, and in orbit, operates like a spacecraft. When returning to earth, upon entry into the atmosphere, the orbiter sails back like a glider and lands at a designated ground location.

At Cape Kennedy, now called the Kennedy Space Center, the Apollo launchpads were modified for STS, and the necessary support facilities were built. After a rigorous test program, on April 12, 1981, the first mission of the Space Shuttle *Columbia* was launched. Since then, NASA's fleet of four Shuttles has completed nearly 100 missions, carrying more than 1.5 million pounds of cargo and over 600 major payloads into orbit, and performing hundreds of microgravity and life sciences experiments.

The twenty-fifth Shuttle flight ended in disaster on January 28, 1986, when Space Shuttle *Challenger* exploded shortly after liftoff, killing all seven crewmembers. Shuttle flights were suspended until September 1988 and then resumed on a more conservative schedule.

The Shuttle program has resulted in several notable achievements, including the rescue and repair of disabled satellites (including the Hubble Space Telescope in 1993) and the first three-person space walk (1992). Starting in 1995, shuttles began docking with the Russian space station *Mir*, in the first phase of a joint U.S.–Russian program that has culminated in the construction, beginning in 1998, of the International Space Station (ISS).

ISS is the end result of a much-delayed U.S. space station program. Unable to convince Congress to allocate the necessary funds, NASA turned to space agencies around the world to establish a partnership. The ISS draws upon the resources and scientific expertise of sixteen cooperating nations, including the United States, Canada, Japan, Russia, and the eleven participating member nations of the European Space Agency. A total of forty-four Space Shuttle and Russian Proton rocket launches will be required to assemble the facility on-orbit by 2004. It will be livable and permanently manned with international astronaut crews beginning in early 2000. The ISS is designed as a permanent orbiting science institute in space, doing research in the materials and life sciences that are intended not only to benefit people and technologies on earth, but to continue the NASA mission of enabling our long-term exploration of space.

Concurrent with ISS construction, NASA's systematic exploration of Mars will continue with Mars Orbiter/Surveyor and Lander/Rover robotic spacecraft set for launch every twenty-six months. Currently, NASA's plans, which may change depending on technological breakthoughs, are to operate the ISS for at least the first decade of the next century, and to send astronauts back to the moon or on to Mars during the second decade of the new century.

Visitors to KSC are welcome at the Visitor's Complex (formerly Spaceport USA). The complex features a wide variety of exhibits and activities related to the space program, including guided bus tours of KSC and Cape Canaveral Air Station; IMAX movies incorporating footage shot by Shuttle astronauts; moon rocks and other historical human spaceflight exhibits; and a full-scale model of the International Space Station. The Rocket Garden features authentic rockets and spacecraft displays, such as the Ambassador, a full-scale, walk-through model of a Space Shuttle. A limited number of car and bus pass tickets are available for public viewing of Shuttle launches on the KSC grounds. ◆

"We choose to go to the moon in this decade and do the other things, not because they are easy, but because they are hard, because that goal will serve to organize and measure the best of our energies and skills, because that challenge is one that we are willing to accept, one we are unwilling to postpone, and one which we intend to win."

John F. Kennedy, 1962

Kettle Moraine

EASTERN WISCONSIN

bog: a small marsh or swamp.

Scientists who postulate a continuing Ice Age believe that today we may live amid an interglacial warming period between glacial advances.

The Kettle Moraine region of eastern Wisconsin, startlingly unique in its geological diversity, is a one-hundred-mile rolling upland of hills and ridges and valleys, of lakes and **bogs** and marshes. The landscape itself is a kind of classroom for those interested in the impact and effect of the continental glaciers that once dominated much of North America.

The Kettle Moraine region was formed by the movement of massive ice sheets during the last Ice Age, or Pleistocene epoch, a division of geologic time during the Quaternary period of the Cenozoic era. Geologists dispute the dates corresponding to the Ice Age. Some say it began as early as 2.6 million years ago; others claim it began as recently as 1.5 million years ago. Most scientists believe the Ice Age ended approximately 10,000 years ago, but even this is disputed by some who claim the Ice Age has not yet ended, and in the geologic future, the colossal glaciers may return again.

The distinguishing feature of the Ice Age was the spread of glacier ice over more than one quarter of the land surface of the earth. Up to two miles thick, glaciers covered much of the northern half of North America. At various times during the Ice Age, for scientific reasons still largely unknown, the climate of the globe cooled dramatically, freezing much of the earth's oceans near its poles, and this polar ice "flowed" over land into temperate areas.

The term "Ice Age" is misleading, though, for the movements of glacial ice occurred not during any one "age," but during hundreds of ages, or cycles, periods of cooling and warming that probably lasted between 100,000 and 130,000 years. Those scientists who postulate a continuing Ice Age believe that today we may live amid an interglacial warming period between glacial advances. (Indeed, a change of only 9°F [5°C] of our annual global temperature would result in a return to the Ice Age.) Perhaps as many as twenty-five glacial cycles have occurred during the last two million years. It is during the final (or most recent) cycle, known as the Wisconsinan glacial period, that the rugged, scenic Kettle Moraine region was formed. The glacial sculpting of the earth's surface that occurred then marks the most recent major episode in the earth's geological history.

Kettle Moraine region in Wisconsin.

The theory of continental glaciation is relatively new to the science of geology. The Swiss-American naturalist Louis Agassiz introduced the theory in the mid-nineteenth century, and it is universally accepted as accurate today. No other explanation can account for the consistent, repeated pattern of ridges and depressions except for the carving action of the glaciers.

Near the end of the Wisconsinan period, around 25,000 years ago, the Laurentide Ice Sheet, a continental glacier that ranged from the Rocky Mountains to the Atlantic coast, flowed south into Wisconsin and covered roughly two thirds of the state. The glacier flowed easily into lowland river valleys now occupied by Lake Superior and Lake Michigan, Green Bay, and the Fox River, but its progress was slowed or redirected by existing uplands. (Despite such obstacles, glacial ice often sheared off hills and bluffs down to their very bedrock.) As a result of redirection, the ice sheet in Wisconsin divided into six major sections, or lobes; the distinct landscape of the Kettle Moraine region was formed along the intersection of two of these lobes, the Lake Michigan lobe and the Green Bay lobe. These glacial lobes fluctuated between advance and retreat and **stasis** for roughly 15,000 years before finally receding as global temperatures warmed.

stasis: a state of balance or equilibrium.

As the glaciers advanced slowly over land, their undersides froze around grains of sand, silt, pebbles, and boulders, picking them up and carrying them. This frozen material in the glacier's base gouged the landscape, leaving scratches and scars in bedrock, called *striations*. The power and magnitude of these continental glaciers is difficult to comprehend. Glaciers ground bedrock into fine powder. They **abraded**, crushed, and fractured the earth. They transported trillions of tons of rock southward, incorporating nearly everything into their accumulating mass.

abraded: scraped or rubbed off.

As temperatures warmed and the glaciers retreated, they deposited this material, called *till*, in numerous ways. Boulders that traveled great distances, called *erratics*, were abandoned thousands of miles from their place of origin. When the ice melted, boulders, pebbles, silt and sand were released, which then formed ridges, called *moraines*. These moraines grew increasingly in size, as melting ice brought a continual supply of glacial debris to the lobe's edges.

Moraines took on several forms. *End moraines*, **perpendicular** to the ice flow, were formed by till deposited at the leading edge of the advancing glacier. *Ground moraines* were deposited beneath the moving ice itself. *Terminal moraines* were those end moraines formed at the outermost edges of the glacier's advance, a band of ridges that marked the farthest progress south. *Recessional moraines* formed as the glacier retreated northward, and *interlobate moraines* formed between the distinct glacial lobes. These interlobate moraines are found all over the Kettle Moraine country. Some of these moraines rise no more than thirty feet above the surrounding landscape; others, especially those in the Kettle Moraine region, rise as high as 250 or 300 feet.

perpendicular: exactly upright; vertical.

Depressions in the earth, known as *kettles*, formed when massive blocks of ice detached from glaciers and were subsequently buried in debris. As the ice melted, and the debris subsided, depressions of incredible variety resulted in gigantic lakes, marshes, fens, and bogs. Over time, torrents from glacial meltwater and draining kettle lakes cut the spectacular gorge known today as the Dalles of the St. Croix River, and less dramatic meltwater distributed fine layers of sand and silt all over the region, leaving rich, fertile soil for future farmers.

One kind of glacial deposit is still not well understood by geologists. *Drumlins* are elongated hills shaped somewhat like teardrops, and they usually occur in groups behind end moraines, sometimes in groups of hundreds. These drumlins run

parallel to the glaciers advance and retreat, and their striations and long axis indicate the ice sheet's direction of flow.

As glaciers advanced, retreated, then readvanced and reretreated, they picked up and erased earlier deposits, or pushed still more material onto existing moraines. But the glaciers were not always in a state of continual movement. Often, a state of equilibrium existed between advance and retreat, when melting matched momentum. The result was stagnant, static ice. At such times, cracks formed in the ice, and conical hills, called *kames*, rose up where streams carrying glacial debris poured down these cracks. Streams flowed beneath the ice as well, and as stream tunnels filled with debris, *eskers* formed. These eskers today wind like narrow snakes all over the Kettle Moraine region.

Visitors to the Kettle Moraine region today can visit three distinct units of the Kettle Moraine State Forest. Taken together, the Northern, Central, and Lapham Peak units cover more than 46,000 acres. This area includes more than sixty miles of hiking trails, including sections of the 1,000-mile Ice Age National Scenic Trail, which extends nearly the length of the entire state and follows the end moraines of the most recent glaciation. State Forest Visitor Centers sponsor naturalist-guided hikes and self-guided interpretive trails, as well as lectures,

Bikers and hikers can view distinctive land formations as they follow the Ice Age Trail through Wisconsin's Kettle Moraine.

The Antarctic Ice Sheet is still more than two miles thick.

exhibits, and films featuring glacial history. The Kettle Moraine's list of year-round recreational opportunities is considerable. Backpacking, camping, mountain-bike riding, and horseback riding are common. Forest lakes and streams offer swimming, canoeing, boating, camping, and fishing. In the autumn months, hunters find small game, waterfowl, and deer. In the winter months, the State Forest grooms more than fifty miles of cross-country skiing trails, and snowshoeing, snowmobiling, and ice fishing are also popular.

Though the last glaciers retreated from the region some 10,000 years ago, thousands of kettle lakes and moraines still dot the countryside. In other areas farther south, where glaciers retreated much earlier, erosion has reduced the **topography** to plains and gently rolling hills, and the effect of glaciation is almost imperceptible. In such places, **sediment** and organic debris has filled in kettle depressions, and kames and eskers have worn away. Continental glaciers are not altogether gone, though. Two still exist today: the Antarctic and the Greenland. The Antarctic Ice Sheet is still more than two miles thick, and its ice holds more than two thirds of all the freshwater on the earth. ◆

topography: the surface features of the land.

sediment: matter deposited by water or wind.

Kitty Hawk

NORTH CAROLINA

Wilbur's idea was to warp the glider's wings, modeling them after his observation of birds' flight.

Kitty Hawk, North Carolina, called "Chickahauk" in the local Indian phrase for "good hunting grounds," is the historically recognized site of Orville Wright's first successful power-driven airplane flight on December 17, 1903. Although the groundbreaking twelve-second flight actually took place four miles away, at Kill Devil Hills, Wright's exultant telegraph home was dispatched from Kitty Hawk. Combined with the unusual names of the places, and their remote geographies, the confusion between the two locations caused newspaper datelines to publicize the flight itself as an event that took place in Kitty Hawk, and as a result historic records have preserved a slight inaccuracy. And although Kitty Hawk was the reported location of the Wright brothers' first successful flight, their research and early experiments began in their native town of Dayton, Ohio, as early as 1899. In spite of these slight inaccuracies

in the historical legend of Kitty Hawk, the high dunes, strong winds, and sand-softened landings on the isolated stretch of beach near the Kill Devil Hills bore witness to more than a thousand of the Wright brothers' experiments with gliders in the period 1900–1905. Kitty Hawk is currently a unit in the Wright Brothers National Memorial, which contains a recently refurbished replica of the original Wright Flyer, various historical markers and reconstructions, as well as other memorabilia of the First Flight.

The Wright brothers make their historic flight on the sands of Kill Devil Hills, North Carolina, in 1903.

Orville Wright (born August 19, 1871, in Dayton, Ohio) and Wilbur Wright (born April 16, 1867, in Millville, Indiana) began as small business proprietors of a prosperous bicycle shop in Dayton, Ohio. In 1896 two events catalyzed their transformation from small businessmen to aeronautic adventurers. Otto Lilienthal, a famous experimenter with gliders, died in a flying accident, in the same year that Samuel Langley launched the first successful powered glider models. Orville and Wilbur decided to put their mechanical and analytical ability to work at a task that had seen the failure of many fine minds. Their serious work began in 1899, when Wilbur initiated the project by writing

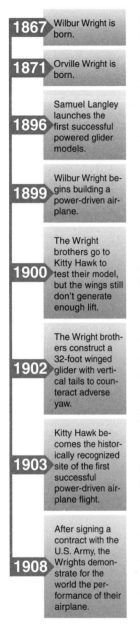

1867 Wilbur Wright is born.

1871 Orville Wright is born.

1896 Samuel Langley launches the first successful powered glider models.

1899 Wilbur Wright begins building a power-driven airplane.

1900 The Wright brothers go to Kitty Hawk to test their model, but the wings still don't generate enough lift.

1902 The Wright brothers construct a 32-foot winged glider with vertical tails to counteract adverse yaw.

1903 Kitty Hawk becomes the historically recognized site of the first successful power-driven airplane flight.

1908 After signing a contract with the U.S. Army, the Wrights demonstrate for the world the performance of their airplane.

lateral: sideways.

warp: twist or bend.

camber: a slight curve of the surface of an aircraft.

to the Smithsonian for literature. They spent the next four years trying old strategies and developing new ones with the goal of developing some form of mechanized human flight.

The Wright brothers began their invention process with what they called "Design and Test Strategy." Their method involved building a glider design and then testing it, but this strategy proved ineffective because the inevitability of various uncontrolled human errors and unpredictable weather conditions made it impossible to tell if the glider failed because of a design flaw, because of a discrete error on the part of the pilot, or because of some other testing condition. After approaching their project through this strategy, the Wright brothers discarded it in favor of the more analytically powered technique that would eventually prove successful. They began to carefully study the research, mistakes, and limitations of previous work by previous inventors. They were particularly interested in Octave Chanute's *Process in Flying Machines* and old volumes of the *Aeronautical Annual*.

When the Wrights began their research, inventors had already nearly perfected methods of lift and propulsion. Orville and Wilbur knew that their work would consist of finding a way to achieve **lateral** control, the aspect of flying gliders that had met with the least success thus far. Conventional wisdom of the past assumed that lateral control respected the principle of inherent stability, but one of the brothers' first innovations in 1899 was to reject this theory, and instead construct a glider in which lateral control would depend on the pilot. Wilbur's idea was to **warp** the glider's wings, modeling them after his observation of birds' flight, so that the pilot would be able to rotate them and stabilize his flight. The Wrights first tested wing-warping on a five-foot biplane kite, and when they were confident in their design, they built a seventeen-foot glider. In 1900 they went to Kitty Hawk in order to test their model, but the wings still didn't generate enough lift. They had to fly the glider as a kite, and Wilbur's free-flight time totaled only ten seconds.

In 1901 the Wrights continued to work, sharply focused on the lift problem. They increased the **camber** of the 1901 model glider, and lengthened its wing span to twenty-two feet, the largest glider anyone had yet attempted to fly. The brothers returned to a new camp at Kill Devil Hills this time, but their machine was unpredictable and tended to pitch wildly and climb into stalls. Attempts to place more control in the hands of the pilot failed, and the Wrights finally realized that their work had depended upon the false data of other inventors.

A memorial to honor the Wright brothers at Kitty Hawk, North Carolina.

Highly discouraged, and on the verge of giving up, the Wrights instead built a wind tunnel so they could produce their own data. The product of this new research was the 1902 thirty-two-foot winged glider with vertical tails to counteract adverse yaw (the machine's tendency, when the pilot raised the left wing to initiate a right turn, to instead slip to the left). Now the pilot could move a hip cradle to warp the glider's wings. However, the design was still flawed. Sometimes when the pilot tried to raise the lowered wing to come out of a turn, the machine would instead slide sideways toward the lowered wing, and spin into the ground. Orville suggested a moveable tail to counteract this tendency, and Wilbur perfected the design by linking the tail movement to the warping mechanism, so that the plane could turn and stabilize smoothly. Again, the Wrights' innovation rejected conventional wisdom, which was modeled on a marine methodology, and impracticably dictated steering by rudder. Instead, the Wrights saw that, unlike a boat, a plane turned by rolling. After six hundred test glides, the Wrights were satisfied that their 1902 design was in fact the first working airplane.

In the year preceding the successful December 1903 flight, the Wrights powered their aircraft with their own design of a lightweight gasoline-powered commercial engine. More im-portant, however, the Wrights' most scientifically original achievement was to design the first effective airplane propeller. They needed very efficient propeller and lifting surfaces that would function with the flight power of their light new engine model, and before the Wrights' important innovation, no such propellers existed and current marine propeller theory was insuf-ficient for the task of designing them. Equipped with their newly designed engine, the Wright Brothers returned to their camp at Kill Devil Hills and mounted it to a new 40-foot, 605-pound *Flyer* with double tails and elevators. On December 14 the brothers flipped a coin, and Wilbur won the toss. However, he oversteered after leaving the launching rail, and after three and a half seconds in the air, he stalled and plummeted into the sand.

Three days later, the *Flyer* was repaired and ready for flight. At twenty-seven mph, the winds were heavier than the Wrights would have liked, since they had predicted the *Flyer*'s cruising speed at 30–35 mph, and since it would slow their groundspeed considerably. In spite of these setbacks, at 10:35 Orville posi-tioned himself, tested the controls, and released the restraining wire. The new aircraft left the ground, with Wilbur running along beside it. Orville was aloft for twelve seconds, flying 120 feet from the guardrail at a total airspeed of 34 mph. The Wrights continued to take turns flying three more times that day; by the fourth and final flight of the day, Wilbur took the *Flyer* 852 feet in fifty-nine seconds. In 1904–05 the Wright Broth-ers continued to refine their flying skills over a field in Ohio; by 1905 their average flight length was thirty-eight minutes.

In spite of their historical achievement in 1903, a dubious U.S. Army refused to meet with the Wright brothers when they offered their flyer to the national institution. After this, the Wrights did not fly for another three years. When they finally signed a contract with the U.S. Army in 1908, the brothers (Orville in America and Wilbur in France) demonstrated for the world the performance of their airplane. After Wilbur demonstrated the flyer's reliability and his skill as a pilot internationally, there was no doubt that the Wrights had truly achieved mastery in human flight. Until 1910, when the French began to rapidly improve the Wrights' basic control system design, there remained a significant gap between the progress of the Wrights and European aviators.

Contemporary visitors to Kitty Hawk, North Carolina, can find the Wright Brothers National Memorial on the Outer Banks of North Carolina in the town of Kill Devil Hills, midway between Kitty Hawk and Nags Head. At the Visitor Center, exhibits and reproductions of the 1902 glider and 1903 flying machine tell the story of the Wright brothers' quest for flight. Other monuments include a large granite boulder at the first flight area to mark the spot where the first airplane left the ground, near reconstructions of the Wrights' 1903 camp buildings. One of the camp buildings is a replica of the hangar for the 1903 *Flyer*; the other is a replica of the one used as a workshop and living quarters that year. The site also includes a Wright Memorial Shaft crowning Big Kill Devil Hill. The monument is a gray granite **pylon**, standing atop what was once a ninety-foot-high dune that has been stabilized with grass. It honors the Wright brothers and marks the site of the hundreds of early glider flights they took leading up to the first powered flight. ◆

pylon: a post marking a prescribed flight course of an airplane.

Korean War Veterans Memorial

WASHINGTON, D.C.

Honoring the 1.5 million U.S. men and women who served in Korea under trying circumstances, the Korean War Memorial lies at the west end of the Mall in Washington, D.C., just across the reflecting pool from the Vietnam Veterans Memorial. Dedicated on July 27, 1995, the memorial commemorates those who left home and homeland to aid in an international struggle against aggression—a conflict that helped determine the course of the cold war, the global political and diplomatic struggle between communist and noncommunist systems following World War II (1939–45).

Begun when the United States was trying to put the hardships of a world war behind it, waged in a distant land, and concluded not with the enemy's surrender but with a negotiated truce, the Korean War (1950–53) has often been referred to as "the forgotten war" by historians. What was anticipated as a short, decisive repelling of the enemy became a prolonged and frustrating fight that threatened to spread beyond Korean borders. Americans served not only as soldiers but also as nurses, doctors, clerks, and chaplains and in other combat and support roles.

The Korean War Memorial is a triangular-shaped stone and steel construction featuring nineteen statues that depict a squadron of U.S. combat troops wearing ponchos, the wind blowing at their backs. Visitors to the memorial come first to this triangular "field of service," which is intended to evoke the experience of American ground troops on patrol in Korea. Strips of granite and scrubby juniper bushes suggest the rugged Korean terrain; the windblown ponchos on the nineteen steel statues that World War II veteran Frank Gaylord created recall the harsh weather endured by American soldiers. This symbolic patrol brings together members of the air force, the army, the marines, and the navy and portrays servicemen from a variety of ethnic backgrounds.

A granite curb on the north side of the statues lists the member countries of the United Nations that sent troops or gave medical support in defense of South Korea. On the south side stands a wall of black granite, intermingling on its polished surface the reflections of the statues with the etched images of more than 2,400 unnamed servicemen and women. Louis Nelson Associates composed this mural using period photographs; a computer-generated stencil then guided the sandblasting that carved the images in stone. These images reveal the determination of the U.S. forces and the countless ways in which they answered the call to duty.

The adjacent "pool of remembrance," encircled by a grove of linden trees, provides a setting for quiet reflection. The numbers of those who were killed, wounded, declared missing in action, or made prisoners of war are etched into the curb. Opposite this counting of the war's toll, a granite wall bears a message inlaid in silver: "Freedom Is Not Free."

Begun as a war between South Korea and North Korea after the north's invasion of the south, the conflict swiftly developed into a limited international war involving the United States and nineteen other nations. At the end of World War II, Korea was divided at the 38th parallel into Soviet (North Korean) and U.S. (South Korean) zones of occupation. In 1948 rival govern-

> *"The invasion of the territory of the Republic of Korea by the armed forces of the North Korean authorities, which began on June 25, 1950, was an act of aggression initiated without warning and without provocation, in execution of a carefully prepared plan."*
>
> Report of the United Nation's Commission on Korea, 1950

The Korean War
Veterans Memorial in
Washington, D.C.

ments were established: the Republic of Korea in the south, led by President Syngman Rhee, and the Democratic People's Republic of Korea in the north, led by Kim Il Sung. Relations between these governments were increasingly strained, and on June 25, 1950, the North Korean Army, substantially equipped by the Soviet Union, crossed the 38th parallel and invaded South Korea, thus beginning the conflict.

The United States immediately responded by sending supplies to Korea, quickly broadening its commitment. On June 27 the U.N. Security Council, with the Soviet Union voluntarily absent, passed a U.S.-sponsored resolution calling for military sanctions against North Korea. Three days later, President Harry S Truman ordered combat forces stationed in Japan to be sent to Korea. American and South Korean forces and eventually combat units from nineteen other nations were placed under a unified U.N. command headed by the U.S. commander in chief in the Far East, General Douglas MacArthur. All forces were grouped in the U.S. Eighth Army. The action was unique because neither the United Nations nor its predecessor, the League of Nations, had ever used military measures to repel an aggressor.

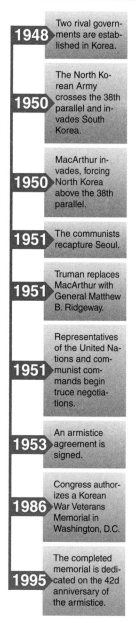

1948 Two rival governments are established in Korea.

1950 The North Korean Army crosses the 38th parallel and invades South Korea.

1950 MacArthur invades, forcing North Korea above the 38th parallel.

1951 The communists recapture Seoul.

1951 Truman replaces MacArthur with General Matthew B. Ridgeway.

1951 Representatives of the United Nations and communist commands begin truce negotiations.

1953 An armistice agreement is signed.

1986 Congress authorizes a Korean War Veterans Memorial in Washington, D.C.

1995 The completed memorial is dedicated on the 42d anniversary of the armistice.

Even after President Truman committed American ground forces to Korea, the war went badly for the U.N.-backed forces. Before the North Koreans were stopped in August, they had captured Seoul, the capital of South Korea, and the Americans and South Koreans had been pushed back to a small perimeter around the southern port city of Pusan. American reinforcements were able to hold this small area, however, and on September 15, 1950, General MacArthur launched an amphibious invasion at a port city behind enemy lines. In a coordinated move, U.N. forces broke out of the Pusan perimeter. Very quickly the North Koreans were routed and forced above the 38th parallel.

Seeing an opportunity to curtail communist expansion, President Truman approved orders for U.N. forces to cross the 38th parallel and push the enemy above the Yalu River, which separated North Korea from China. Despite repeated warnings from the Chinese that they would enter the war if the Americans came near the Yalu, U.N. forces crossed into North Korea on October 7 and later captured its capital city, thus adding China to the enemy forces. After hard fighting in which General MacArthur's units had to fall back, the Chinese retired, and General MacArthur continued his offensive.

Shortly after this overture, the Chinese struck again in massive numbers. U.N. troops—tired, outnumbered, and not equipped to fight a fresh enemy in the bitter Korean winter—were soon in retreat. The communists reoccupied the capital city on December 5 and, sweeping into South Korea, recaptured Seoul on January 4, 1951. The communist offensive was halted by January 15 along a front far south of Seoul. The U.S. Eighth Army took the offensive on January 25, and the Chinese slowly withdrew from South Korea. Seoul fell to the United Nations again on March 14. By April 22 U.N. forces had occupied positions slightly north of the 38th parallel.

Unwilling to engage in an all-out war with China, President Truman abandoned as his objective the military reunification of Korea and returned to his original goal of stopping communist aggression in Korea. When General MacArthur persisted in publicly criticizing U.S. policy, President Truman, on the recommendation of the Joint Chiefs of Staff, removed him from his command in April 1951 and installed General Matthew B. Ridgway as commander in chief; General James Van Fleet then took command of the Eighth Army. U.S. troop strength remained at around 260,000. Forces from other U.N. nations stayed at about 35,000, while Republic of Korea forces grew from some 280,000 to about 340,000. The communist forces increased from approximately 500,000 to 865,000. Some of the most desperate battles took place on hills that Americans called Old Baldy, Capital, Pork Chop, T-Bone, and Heartbreak Ridge.

On July 10, 1951, following preparatory talks, representatives of the United Nations and communist commands began truce negotiations. General Ridgway was the chief U.N. negotiator with the North Koreans and Chinese. Even while the talks were under way, however, small unit actions, bitter and decisive, continued to take place. The war's unpopularity played an important role in the 1952 presidential victory of Dwight D. Eisenhower, who had pledged to go to Korea to end the war. Negotiations between the United Nations and communist commands broke down four different times, but after much difficulty and nuclear threats by President Eisenhower, an armistice agreement was signed on July 27, 1953. United States losses were placed at over 54,000 dead and 103,000 wounded. South Korean deaths numbered 415,004 and those of the U.N. allies totaled 3,094. Estimated communist casualties were two million.

Prisoners received inadequate food, clothing, and shelter and poor medical treatment, which often resulted in loss of lives.

During truce negotiations, a new problem arose in regard to **repatriation** of prisoners. Because of the apparent unwillingness of communist soldiers who had been made prisoners of war (POWs) to return to their homelands, the U.N. Command posited the principle of "voluntary repatriation," stating that prisoners of war should not be returned against their will. Although the Geneva Convention does not specifically authorize voluntary repatriation, the U.N. Command held that the humanitarian spirit of the convention would be violated if the prisoners were forcibly repatriated. Following a yearlong deadlock, the new principle was finally incorporated into the armistice agreement, and the belligerents were granted the right to speak with prisoners who were opposed to repatriation.

repatriation: the return to the country of one's birth or citizenship.

The Korean War was distinctive among wars throughout history for the extensive and effective use of psychological warfare, or "brainwashing" of prisoners, by North Korea. The communist forces were responsible for numerous violations of the Geneva Convention: prisoners received inadequate food, clothing, and shelter and poor medical treatment, which often resulted in loss of lives. The experience created long-lasting emotional hardships for many American veterans who had been POWs.

In October 1986 Congress authorized a Korean War Veterans Memorial in Washington, D.C., to be directed by a twelve-member board of Korean War veterans appointed by the president. In 1989 the board selected a design created by a team from State College, Pennsylvania. There was intense debate, however, about how to implement the design, which almost derailed the project. It took three years before a revised plan, developed by Cooper-Lecky Architects, received full approval. The completed memorial was dedicated on July 27, 1995, the forty-second anniversary of the armistice that ended the Korean War. ◆

Lexington Green

LEXINGTON, MASSACHUSETTS

The first shots fired in the Revolutionary War in America were exchanged on the Lexington Green, a grassy triangle at the center of the small Massachusetts town twenty miles west of Boston. At this site just before dawn on April 19, 1775, some seven hundred British soldiers on their way to Concord to seize a stockpile of weapons were met by about seventy-seven American minutemen, led by Captain John Parker. His command to his band of farmers, as recollected by one of the veterans, is now carved on a boulder near the spot where the men formed a line: "Stand your ground. Don't fire unless fired upon, but if they mean to have a war, let it begin here!"

Each side accused the other of opening fire, and the conflicting accounts have never been resolved. At the end of the brief engagement, in which the British suffered no casualties, eight Americans lay dead, ten wounded. The American Revolution had begun.

The years preceding the Battle of Lexington were a time of political ferment throughout the thirteen colonies. Increasing numbers of Americans moved from resistance to rebellion against the authority of the British Parliament over issues of trade, taxes, and the quartering of British soldiers in American cities. Boston was a center of radical activity, where leaders like the fiery orator Samuel Adams constantly reminded their fellow citizens that their liberties were in danger. On the night of December 16, 1773, a group of radicals took matters into their own hands. Adams, Paul Revere, and others boarded three British ships in Boston Harbor and dumped 340 chests of tea into the sea to protest the British tax on tea.

> *"The revolution was effected before the war commenced. The revolution was in the hearts and minds of the people."*
> John Adams, 1818

237

A statue of a minuteman stands on Lexington Green to honor the men who fought in the Battle of Lexington in 1775.

The harsh British response to the Boston Tea Party aroused the indignation of colonists everywhere. Monies and supplies were collected in many colonies in support of Boston when the British closed its harbor. The inhabitants of Brooklyn, New York, sent 125 sheep to the citizens of the beleaguered city, "hoping thereby you may be enabled to stand more firm (if possible) in the glorious cause in which you are embarked," as Israel Putnam wrote on behalf of the Committee of Correspondence for the Parish of Brooklyn.

Every colony except Georgia sent delegates to the First Continental Congress, which assembled at Philadelphia on September 5, 1774. Delegates discussed their grievances against England and passed a Declaration of Rights, listing the ways their rights to "life, liberty, and property" had been violated. The Congress advised colonists to stop buying goods from England and to form armed militias.

The Massachusetts provincial congress responded to the call for a patriot militia. In September 1774 it had organized the first minutemen, armed citizens who agreed to turn out for military duty at a minute's notice. Some of these men had been trained fighting in the French and Indian War, but many were farmers, artisans, and tradesmen with little military experience. In addition to forming militias, Massachusetts colonists began to stockpile weapons and ammunition. One cache of military supplies—cannon and gunpowder, musket balls and flints, dried beef and other foodstuffs—was stored in Concord, a small town a few miles from Lexington.

In the early months of 1775 the British government was preparing for military action against the colonies. General Thomas Gage, newly appointed as royal governor of Massachusetts, received orders from London to suppress the rebellious colonists. He directed his troops to seize the store of munitions at Concord. American spies learned of his plan, and when the British redcoats left Boston Common on the night of April 18, 1775, Paul Revere was ready to spread the alarm through the countryside.

Born in Boston in 1735, Paul Revere was one of New England's leading silversmiths and a dedicated American patriot. His midnight ride of April 18 was not his first mission. In May 1774 he rode to Philadelphia with the news that the British had closed Boston Harbor. On the night of April 18, Revere wanted to call out the minutemen. He also wanted to warn his friends Samuel Adams and John Hancock that the British were coming. Adams and Hancock were staying in Lexington while attending meetings of the provincial congress at Concord. The British held a warrant for the arrest of these two men, whom they regarded as dangerous troublemakers.

Before starting out on his ride, Revere wanted to know whether the British would take the longer land route from Boston or the shorter route over the water to Charlestown and then on foot to Concord. He sent someone to spy on the British, and then signal with lanterns from the high bell tower of North Church—one if by land, two if by sea. The British chose the route over the water, but Revere was ahead of them, warning the countryside.

"Paul Revere's Ride," the poem by Henry Wadsworth Longfellow, made Paul Revere famous, but he was not the only one riding that night. William Dawes set out from Boston along a different route and joined Revere at Lexington. There Revere was detained by a British patrol, but Dr. Samuel Prescott, who was riding home after a visit to his fiancée, escaped the British and brought the news to Concord. Revere was released an hour and a half later and hurried to help Adams and Hancock leave Lexington.

The Lexington minutemen mustered about midnight in response to Revere's alarm. They waited through the night at Buckman Tavern, which faces the Green. When a scout rushed in to report that the British were only half a mile away, Captain Parker ordered William Diamond to beat a drum, and the men formed a line on the Green. The British marched up in formation, and their commander, Major Pitcairn, shouted, "Lay down your arms, you damned rebels, and disperse!" Someone fired a shot, and the British soldiers, in defiance of their orders, fired volley after volley, then leveled their bayonets and charged the minutemen. Among the eight American dead was Jonathan Harrington Jr., who died on the steps of his house on the Green. The British did not suffer any casualties and continued on their march to Concord.

Most of the American military supplies had been hidden or destroyed before the British reached Concord at about 7 A.M.

1773 Samuel Adams, Paul Revere, and others board three British ships in Boston Harbor and dump 340 chests of tea to protest the British tax on tea.

1774 Every colony except Georgia sends delegates to the First Continental Congress; the Massachusetts congress organizes the first minutemen.

1775 The Second Continental Congress opens in Philadelphia at Independence Hall, where delegates appoint George Washington commander in chief of a new Continental Army.

1776 The Declaration of Independence is formally approved on July 4.

1799 America's first Revolutionary War monument, an obelisk, is erected at the western end of Lexington Green.

When the troops could not find the munitions, they began setting fire to houses. Some 400 Concord minutemen, led by Captain Isaac Davis, confronted a party of British at the North Bridge. Shots rang out and the British were forced to retreat. These patriots were the "embattled farmers" of Ralph Waldo Emerson's famous poem, who "fired the shot heard round the world."

The alarm was spread throughout eastern New England by booming cannons and pealing church bells, signals for which the colonial militia had been waiting. Men left their farms and towns, taking up their muskets and marching toward Lexington. Many did not arrive in time to fight in the battles of Lexington or Concord, but they were on hand for the running battle that took place along the British march of retreat to Boston.

The daylong fight on the route to Boston claimed many more casualties than the engagements at Lexington and Concord. Some seventy British were killed and 200 wounded, while fewer than 100 Americans were killed or wounded. Although the British had been reinforced by a thousand men under the command of Lord Percy, they were unable to defend themselves from the Americans, who shot at them from behind houses and barns, trees and stone walls. This was the first use of guerrilla warfare, the colonists' best defense strategy against the British.

News of the battles of Lexington and Concord exploded throughout the colonies, and almost immediately afterward minutemen left for Massachusetts from Connecticut, New Hampshire, and other nearby states. The Massachusetts Committee of Safety sent out an appeal for help on April 28, 1775, urging patriots to "give all assistance possible in forming the army. Our all is at stake." Sixteen thousand New Englanders joined forces and began the Siege of Boston, which forced the evacuation of the British troops the following March.

The Second Continental Congress opened in Philadelphia at Independence Hall in May 1775. Delegates appointed George Washington as the commander in chief of a new Continental Army, formed from the local militias and minutemen. They also appointed Thomas Jefferson and others to a committee that drafted the Declaration of Independence. Formally approved on July 4, 1776, this historic declaration was not a call to arms. The Declaration of Independence was the result of the arms taken up on that fateful April morning, when the shots the minutemen fired were indeed heard round the world.

> *"Can it be said with any color of truth and justice, that this continent of three thousand miles in length, and of a breadth as yet unexplored, in which, however, it is supposed there are five millions of people, has the least voice, vote, or influence in the British Parliament?"*
>
> Samuel Adams,
> *The Rights of Colonists*, 1772

Visitors to Lexington Green today can see the grassy triangle surrounded by frame houses dating from the time when the battle was fought. At the eastern point is Henry Hudson Kitson's statue *The Minute Man*, dedicated in 1900. The figure, holding a musket, stands upon boulders taken from the stone walls that gave cover to the militia as they fired on the British in retreat.

Facing the Green is Buckman Tavern, where the minutemen awaited the arrival of the British. Inside the tavern a door is still scarred with a bullet hole from the morning's battle. There are also exhibits of eighteenth-century muskets, cooking equipment, and furniture. A newly renovated Visitor's Center on the Green presents a twenty-five-minute multimedia show, "Road to Revolution."

The alarm was spread by booming cannons and pealing church bells, signals for which the colonial militia had been waiting.

The Old Burying Ground, just west of the Green, contains the graves of Captain Parker and a British soldier who died at Buckman Tavern from wounds he received during the retreat from Concord. Overlooking the Green from a hill is a replica of the Old Belfry, with the bell that pealed the midnight alarm. At the western end of the Green is America's first Revolutionary War monument, an obelisk erected in 1799. A plaque on the base bears an inscription that begins: "Sacred to the Liberty & the Rights of Mankind!!!/ The Freedom & Independence of America,/ Sealed & defended with the blood of her sons." Each year on Patriot's Day (the third Monday in April), the Battle of Lexington is reenacted by uniformed minutemen and redcoats. ◆

Lincoln Memorial

WASHINGTON, D.C.

The Lincoln Memorial in Washington, D.C., honors the sixteenth U.S. president's enduring legacy. In leading the nation through four years of the Civil War, Abraham Lincoln preserved the Union, freed the slaves, and brought hope to generations of oppressed people throughout the world. The monument, in the shape of a classic Greek temple, sits prominently in West Potomac Park at the end of the National Mall.

The Lincoln Memorial in Washington, D.C.

The site is rooted in symbolism. It is located next to the Potomac River, a dividing line between the North and the South during the Civil War. On a hill directly across the river stands Arlington House, the home and memorial of one of Lincoln's chief foes, Confederate general Robert E. Lee. There, too, is Arlington Cemetery, initially established for Union soldiers killed in the war. From the Lincoln Memorial's west side, Memorial Bridge crosses the Potomac linking, both physically and symbolically, these shrines and the north with the south.

The memorial building has even deeper historical roots. Henry Bacon's design is based on the Parthenon honoring Athena, the ancient goddess of wisdom, in Athens, Greece. Bacon turned the temple, however, so the entrance would be on a side instead of on one end and so the longer dimension would more fittingly define the west end of the mall. The thirty-six exterior Doric columns represent the states in the Union at the time of Lincoln's death. Their names are cut into the **frieze** above the columns; the states subsequently added to the Union are inscribed elsewhere in the building. Two other forty-four-foot Doric columns are positioned in the entrance, and eight fifty-foot Ionic columns are inside.

frieze: a horizontal decorated band around a room or building.

The effort to build a major monument in Washington to commemorate Lincoln began in 1867, two years after the assassination, when Congress approved the incorporation of the Lincoln Monument Association. Proposals for the memorial's form and site were debated for many years, and attempts to raise funds were not successful. Other efforts to honor Lincoln in the city were underway. A statue of Lincoln by Vinnie Ream, now in the U.S. Capitol's Statuary Hall, was completed and dedicated in 1871. Another, *The Freedman's Monument* by Thomas Ball, was dedicated in 1876 in Lincoln Park east of the Capitol. Many members of Congress desired a more substantial monument, but they could not agree on what it should be. One proposal called for a memorial highway between Washington and Gettysburg, Pennsylvania, where Lincoln gave his short but eloquent Gettysburg Address dedicating a national cemetery on the Civil War battlefield.

Finally, Congress passed legislation in February 1911 to build a memorial. An appointed commission decided on the location in West Potomac Park and invited architects Henry Bacon and John Russell Pope to submit designs for the structure. Bacon was chosen to develop a final design, which Congress approved on January 29, 1913.

Ground was broken in 1914 on February 12, Lincoln's 105th birthday. Work on the foundations took a little more than a year, because the memorial was being built on wetlands near the Potomac that had been drained and filled. A sub-foundation consisting of 122 concrete piers with steel reinforcing rods was anchored to the bedrock. A second foundation of piers was laid on top. Those piers were linked together to form the floor, which was covered with marble. The cornerstone was laid in 1915, and over the next seven years the building itself was constructed out of Colorado yule marble and Indiana limestone.

Though the building's classical appearance is well known, it is Daniel Chester French's statue of a pensive, seated Lincoln that becomes inscribed in the memories of the more than four million people who visit the memorial each year. French's portrayal of Lincoln the War President is massive, but its powerful impact stems from the simplicity of the solitary, solemn figure.

French was selected to do the sculpture in December 1914 after the building itself was underway. He was known as the leading American sculptor and had worked on other projects with Bacon. Throughout the whole process, the two men conferred often to refine plans. As called for in his contract, French

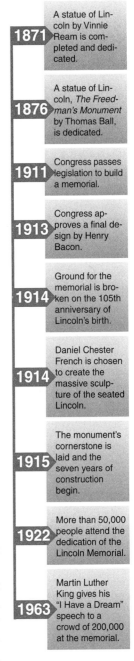

1871 A statue of Lincoln by Vinnie Ream is completed and dedicated.

1876 A statue of Lincoln, *The Freedman's Monument* by Thomas Ball, is dedicated.

1911 Congress passes legislation to build a memorial.

1913 Congress approves a final design by Henry Bacon.

1914 Ground for the memorial is broken on the 105th anniversary of Lincoln's birth.

1914 Daniel Chester French is chosen to create the massive sculpture of the seated Lincoln.

1915 The monument's cornerstone is laid and the seven years of construction begin.

1922 More than 50,000 people attend the dedication of the Lincoln Memorial.

1963 Martin Luther King gives his "I Have a Dream" speech to a crowd of 200,000 at the memorial.

designed and produced a model for a ten-foot statue, but he increased the dimensions to 19 feet high by 19 feet wide in 1918 when it became evident that the statue would be too small in the 60-by-70-foot hall.

Under French's direction and assistance, Piccirilli Brothers, Inc., carved the statue over a four-year period in the firm's New York studio. It consists of twenty-eight blocks of white Georgia marble and sits on a pedestal of Tennessee marble. The statue is centered near the back of the great hall and faces the Reflecting Pool, the Washington Monument, and the Capitol two miles to the east. Lincoln's Gettysburg Address is inscribed on the interior south wall and his second inaugural address is on the north wall. Murals painted by Jules Guerin depict principles representative of Lincoln's beliefs and actions. The mural on the south wall shows an angel of truth freeing a slave plus figures representing justice and immortality. The mural on the north wall interprets the unity of the north and south with figures symbolizing fraternity and charity. The murals are sixty feet long and twelve feet high.

More than 50,000 people attended the dedication of Lincoln Memorial on May 30, 1922, and the proceedings were broadcast nationwide by radio. Among the 3,500 distinguished guests and officials was former secretary of war Robert Todd Lincoln, the only surviving son of the sixteenth president. Dr. Robert Moton, president of Tuskegee Institute, gave the main address. Ironically he was not allowed to sit on the speakers' platform and instead was seated in a separate section for black Americans. Blacks had gained their freedom but were still struggling for equality. As president of the Lincoln Memorial Commission, Chief Justice and former president William Howard Taft presented the memorial to President Warren G. Harding, who received it on behalf of all Americans, "those of us today, and for those who follow after."

Harding's words reflected Secretary of War Edwin M. Stanton's statement "Now he belongs to the ages" when Lincoln died on the morning of April 15, 1865, after being shot by John Wilkes Booth the night before at Ford's Theatre. Lincoln had not been a particularly popular president. His reputation as a leader had risen gradually from the beginning of the Civil War to the Confederacy's surrender on April 9, but it soared—except in the south—immediately after his death.

In the north, he became a martyr to the preservation of the nation and to the freeing of the slaves. Writers and orators re-

"Our popular Government has often been called an experiment. Two points in it our people have already settled—the successful establishing and the successful administering of it. One still remains—its successful maintenance against a formidable internal attempt to overthrow it.

Abraham Lincoln,
special session
message, July 4,
1861

ferred to him as the Savior of the Union and the Great Emancipator. He was mourned in European countries where it was uncommon for such a common man to attain the highest governmental office. His honesty, his sense of humor, his humility became legendary. He was admired for both his patience and his determination. In time, he was recognized for strengthening the link between two American democratic ideals: individual freedom and the common good.

On Lincoln's birthday the current U.S. president or a representative visits the Lincoln Memorial and lays a wreath at the statue, as do many foreign dignitaries when they are in the U.S. capital. But more significantly, Americans of all ages and tourists from around the world climb the memorial steps to pay their respects and read the inscription of his Gettysburg Address: ". . . that this nation under God shall have a new birth of freedom—and that government of the people, by the people, for the people shall not perish from the earth."

The memorial has become a symbolic rallying point, or forum, for various causes, especially civil rights. In 1939 the Daughters of the American Revolution prohibited Marian Anderson, an internationally known black **contralto**, from presenting a concert at Constitution Hall in Washington. As a result, Eleanor Roosevelt, wife of President Franklin D. Roosevelt, resigned her membership in the organization. With the Roosevelts' endorsement, Secretary of the Interior Harold Ickes then gave Anderson permission to sing at the Lincoln Memorial. The concert attracted a crowd of 75,000 at the memorial and Reflection Pool on April 9, Easter Sunday.

The Rev. Martin Luther King Jr. gave his "I Have a Dream" speech before a crowd of 200,000 at the memorial on August 28, 1963. Referring to Lincoln's Emancipation Proclamation as "a great beacon of hope to millions of Negro slaves," King said, "I have a dream that one day this nation will rise up and live out the true meaning of its creed: We hold these truths to be self-evident that all men are created equal." The speech helped elevate King as a national leader and galvanized the civil rights movement in the 1960s.

The Lincoln Memorial, on 23rd Street NW at the end of the National Mall, is administered by the National Park Service. Rangers are on duty from 8 A.M. to midnight every day except December 25 to answer questions and to give interpretive talks. ◆

"With malice toward none, with charity for all, with firmness in the right as God gives us to see the right, let us strive on to finish the work we are in, to bind up the nation's wounds, to care for him who shall have borne the battle and for his widow and his orphan, to do all which may achieve and cherish a just and lasting peace among ourselves and with all nations."
Abraham Lincoln, second inaugural address, March 4, 1865

contralto: a singer with a voice that ranges between mezzo-soprano and tenor.

Little Bighorn Battlefield

SOUTHEASTERN MONTANA

The Little Bighorn Battlefield National Monument in southeastern Montana marks the location of one of the most famous defeats in U.S. military history, the Battle of Little Bighorn. Often called Custer's Last Stand, the battle occurred June 25 and 26, 1876, when troops of the 7th U.S. Cavalry fought against Sioux and Northern Cheyenne Indians on the Little Bighorn River. Lieutenant Colonel George Armstrong Custer had split his regiment, numbering about 600, to attack an Indian village from two directions. Custer was unprepared for the presence of about 2,000 Indian warriors—under the leadership of Sitting Bull, Crazy Horse, and other chiefs—who annihilated Custer and all of the men under his immediate command. The warriors also besieged the other seven companies for two days. About 260 soldiers lost their lives, while Indian deaths probably did not exceed forty or fifty.

The Battle of Little Bighorn became the most significant event of the Sioux War of 1876. The U.S. government waged the war to force buffalo-hunting bands of the Sioux and Cheyenne tribes to give up their lifestyle and settle on the Great Sioux Reservation (present-day South Dakota west of the Missouri River), where other bands already lived under the terms of the Treaty of 1868. However, the Indians who chose not to accept reservation life had good cause to distrust the treaties of the U.S. government, since treaties were routinely broken as white settlers poured into the west. The Indian hunting bands, the U.S. government charged, had raided friendly Indians and committed scattered thefts against white settlers in western Montana. These tensions came to a head with the discovery of gold in the Black Hills, which were part of the Great Sioux Reservation guaranteed to the Indians by the treaty. White miners overran the hills, which the Lakota Sioux considered sacred. The U.S. government wanted to

General George
Armstrong Custer.

buy the Black Hills, but the Sioux refused to sell. By forcing the hunting bands onto the reservation and destroying their independence, the government hoped to weaken their ability to obstruct the sale of the Black Hills.

In June 1876 the army organized an offensive against the hunting bands in the Yellowstone River basin of Montana, approaching from three directions. General George Crook advanced from the south; Colonel John Oliver Gibbon from the west; and General Alfred Howe Terry from the east. Custer and the 7th Cavalry rode with Terry. Custer had already gained fame as a merciless Indian fighter, especially for a cruel surprise attack on a Cheyenne village on the Washita River several years earlier. Of the 103 Indians killed in that raid, 92 of them had been women, children, and elderly people.

On June 22 Terry detached Custer and his regiment to march up Rosebud Creek and seek out the Indians, thought to be in the Little Bighorn Valley. Terry would accompany Gibbon up the Yellowstone and Bighorn rivers and cut off the northward flight of the Indians as Custer struck from the south. Custer located the Sioux village early on June 25. He intended to defer his attack until the next day, but the Indians discovered him, and, fearing they would scatter, Custer advanced at once to attack. He divided the regiment into three battalions led by Captain Frederick W. Benteen, Major Marcus A. Reno, and himself. Benteen departed on a mission aimed at ensuring that no Indians camped in the Little Bighorn Valley above the main village. Custer and Reno approached the village itself.

Sioux leader Tatonka-I-Yatanka, better known as Sitting Bull.

Although Custer's plan remains speculative and controversial, apparently he intended to strike from two directions. He sent Reno to cross the Little Bighorn and charge the southern end of the encampment, while he turned north to hit the other end. Reno, however, was repulsed and driven from the valley. When he took up a defensive position on the high bluffs lining the east side of the river, the warriors were free to concentrate on Custer at the northern end of their village. They kept him

A pile of bones memorializes the Little Bighorn battle in this photo taken at the battlefield in 1877.

out of the village and confined to rough country east of the river. Within an hour, they wiped out his entire command of 210 men. Joined by Benteen, Reno dug in on his hilltop four miles to the south and held out until the next day, when the approach of Terry and Gibbon from the north caused the Indians to withdraw to the south.

For the Sioux and Cheyennes, the Battle of Little Bighorn was a great triumph. For the United States, it was a major military disaster. The death of Custer, a flamboyant popular hero, and his entire immediate command stunned the American people and led to greatly intensified military activity. The U.S. Army sent one-third of its total forces to the Great Plains, and the soldiers did not hesitate to wreak revenge, often burning Indian villages to the ground. By the spring of 1877, most of the Sioux and Cheyennes had surrendered and settled on the reservation. The government decreased the size of the Sioux reservation and took possession of the Black Hills.

Headstones in the fields of Little Bighorn National Monument mark the graves of U.S. Army soldiers who died there.

Controversy immediately surrounded the battle and has raged ever since. Custer, Reno, Benteen, Terry, and even President Ulysses S. Grant—all had their critics and supporters. Whether he was a reckless fool or a victim of the failures of others, however, Custer won immortality, and the Battle of Little Bighorn became firmly embedded in the history and folklore of America. The spectacle of Custer and his little band of troopers dying on their Montana hilltop is one of the most vivid and enduring images in the popular imagination.

One reason for the controversy over Custer's last battle lies in the fact that no soldiers lived to tell their tale. Indians who claimed to be eyewitnesses gave several reports to U.S. agents on the Indian reservations, which then appeared in newspapers and journals. Many of the accounts contradicted each other, and none has been considered accurate. However, some archeological findings have supported certain details. In 1985 the National Park Service sent its own archeologists to the area. Using metal detectors and digging tools, the team examined the battlefield and ultimately uncovered more than 4,000 artifacts.

By examining the positions of such items as cartridge shells, the team could recreate the locations of the combatants. They determined that Custer and his men had stood their ground in

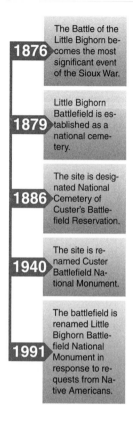

1876 The Battle of the Little Bighorn becomes the most significant event of the Sioux War.

1879 Little Bighorn Battlefield is established as a national cemetery.

1886 The site is designated National Cemetery of Custer's Battlefield Reservation.

1940 The site is renamed Custer Battlefield National Monument.

1991 The battlefield is renamed Little Bighorn Battlefield National Monument in response to requests from Native Americans.

a V-shaped pattern on a location called Last Stand Hill, but they were surrounded and overrun by Indians bearing heavy firearms. As the battle came down to hand-to-hand combat, the Indians finished off their enemies with hatchets and clubs. Interesting archeological remnants include such items as a finger bone with a wedding ring still on it, cavalry boots, and a human vertebra with an arrowhead in it.

Little Bighorn Battlefield National Monument receives thousands of visitors each year. Indians visit the site as a monument to the only time they successfully defended their homeland against white settlers. Other Americans visit the site as a reminder of brave men who died in the line of duty. Visitors can view remnants of the battle in a museum. A large stone monument stands in the park, and white markers show where soldiers' bodies were found on the battlefield. The Custer National Cemetery, containing nearly 5,000 dead, lies within the park.

The area was established as a national cemetery by the secretary of war in 1879, to protect the graves of 7th Cavalry troopers buried there. In 1886, the site was proclaimed National Cemetery of Custer's Battlefield Reservation to include burials from other campaigns and wars. The site was turned over by the secretary of war in 1940 and designated Custer Battlefield National Monument. On December 10, 1991, the battlefield was renamed Little Bighorn Battlefield National Monument, in response to the requests of the Lakota, Cheyenne, Arapaho, Arikara and Crow tribes whose ancestors had witnessed or participated in the Battle of the Little Bighorn. The U.S. Congress also voted to install a memorial to honor the American Indians who fought and died in the battle. ◆

Little Rock Central High School

Little Rock, Arkansas

I n September 1957 Central High School in Little Rock, Arkansas, was the site of a dramatic federal–state confrontation over racial desegregation. Provoked by Governor Orval Faubus, mobs of white Arkansans attempted to

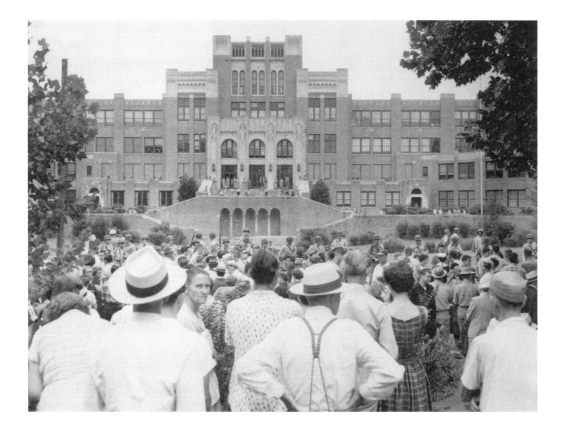

block black students from entering the school, leading President Dwight D. Eisenhower to send federal troops to protect the students.

From 1938 through 1950, the U.S. Supreme Court issued a series of rulings that barred racial segregation in the professional and graduate schools of America's universities. But the Court's next important decision on school segregation was the most important of all. On May 17, 1954, the Justices announced their ruling in *Brown* v. *Board of Education of Topeka, Kansas* (1954), a suit by the National Association for the Advancement of Colored People against segregated public schools. The judges unanimously declared that "separate educational facilities are inherently unequal" and were therefore unconstitutional. This reversed the Court's *Plessy* v. *Ferguson* ruling of 1896, which had upheld "separate but equal" accommodations for blacks and whites. The *Brown* decision spelled the eventual end of racial segregation not only in schools but in general. It also sparked the civil rights movement of the 1950s and 1960s.

A crowd gathers outside Central High School in Little Rock, Arkansas, as Arkansas National Guard troops prevent African-American students from entering to register in September 1957.

"We come then to the question presented: Does segregation of children in public schools solely on the basis of race, even though the physical facilities and other 'tangible' factors may be equal, deprive the children of the minority group of equal educational opportunities? We believe that it does."

Chief Justice Earl Warren, Supreme Court ruling in *Brown v. Board of Education of Topeka, Kansas*, 1954

In May 1955, a year after the *Brown* ruling, the Supreme Court issued guidelines for carrying out its decision. The integration of formerly segregated schools, the justices said, should proceed "with all deliberate speed." Since "deliberate" and "speed" are almost opposites, the ruling left a great deal of room for interpretation. Many segregationists were pleased with the 1955 ruling, believing that it opened the possibility for an indefinite delay of integration. Little Rock, however, seemed an unlikely place for serious resistance. Little Rock mayor Woodrow Mann, school superintendent Virgil Blossom, and the area's U.S. representative, Brooks Hays, were all racial moderates prepared to accept gradual integration. On May 22, 1954, just five days after the *Brown* ruling, the Little Rock school board announced that it would comply with the Supreme Court's ruling. A year later, the board unanimously adopted a plan proposed by Superintendent Blossom to begin at the high-school level and add the lower grades over the following six years. The only strong local opponent of the plan was the NAACP, which argued that it was too gradual.

In the spring of 1957, just over 500 black students lived in the Central High district. The eighty or so who were interested in pioneering the desegregation process were interviewed by the superintendent and staff, who selected seventeen of them to enter the high school in September. Of these, eight changed their minds, leaving nine students. On August 30 a federal district court judge turned aside legal efforts to block integration, which now seemed set to occur on September 3, 1957, the first day of school.

Suddenly, however, Governor Orval Faubus stepped in to block integration. His last-minute troublemaking can be explained by the racial and political climate in the south at the time, and by Faubus's own political situation. In 1956 resistance to desegregation began running strong. A number of southern states vowed that they would not integrate their schools, and 101 of the 128 southerners in Congress signed a manifesto vowing to resist integration. Ku Klux Klan organizations sprang up, and chapters of the newly formed, pro-segregationist White Citizens Councils sprang up throughout the south. Meanwhile, Faubus, facing a difficult reelection bid, hoped that a hard-line segregationist position would win him votes. And he could reasonably hope to succeed, since the previous year President Eisenhower had failed to act when Governor Allen Shivers of Texas had defied a court order for school integration.

So on September 2, the day before schools were to open, Faubus, not previously known for racial demagoguery, announced that he anticipated violence at Central High—although no one else did—and therefore would send a National Guard contingent to the school the next day. On September 3 the Guard blocked the African-American students from entering the school; that was clearly the real reason for the Guard's presence. A federal court immediately ordered that integration proceed on September 4. This time an angry mob of white racists, provoked by Faubus's actions, was at the school, and again the guardsmen turned away the black students.

Faubus had defied a federal court order, and it was now President Eisenhower's responsibility to enforce it. A believer in states rights who never endorsed the *Brown* decision (although he said it should be obeyed), Eisenhower was reluctant to intervene. In a press conference during the Little Rock crisis he stated that "you cannot change people's hearts merely by laws." But events forced him to act. For one thing, Little Rock had become the focus of national and international attention. For another, the situation on the ground got worse. On Friday, September 20, a federal court ordered Faubus to end his obstructionism. Instead of using the guardsmen to enforce the court order, the governor simply withdrew them; in that way he could claim to be obeying the court order when in fact he was leaving the African-American students vulnerable to violence. Meanwhile, some of his aides spent the weekend stirring up the very mob violence that Faubus had claimed to fear when he first sent in the Guard. On Monday, September 23, over 1,000 furious and sometimes hysterical racists were at the school. When they learned that the black students had been brought into the school, the mob attacked black reporters and broke school windows. Policemen led the African-American students out a side door.

On the evening of September 23, the president went on television to denounce the "disgraceful occurrence" at the school and demanded an end to defiance of the federal courts. When a still larger mob formed the next day, roaming free without hindrance from the governor, Eisenhower federalized the Arkansas National Guard and sent in the 101st Airborne Division. On September 25 the black schoolchildren returned to Central High. Throughout the year they were taunted by white students and their parents. But in May 1958 Ernest Green, the sole black student in the senior class, became the first African American to graduate from Central High.

1954 U.S. Supreme Court rules segregated schools unconstitutional in *Brown v. Board of Education.*

1955 U.S. Supreme Court issues guidelines for carrying out its decision in *Brown.*

1956 Resistance to Supreme Court ruling grows; 101 southern congressmen sign a manifesto vowing to resist integration.

1957 The National Guard prohibits nine black students from entering Little Rock Central High School.

1958 Ernest Green becomes the first African American to graduate from Central High; Governor Faubus tries to close public schools to avoid integration.

1959 A federal court declares the state's school-closing law unconstitutional and reopens all schools.

The story did not end there, however. Faubus succeeded in changing the political climate in Arkansas. The use of federal troops made him a hero to many whites; he easily won reelection and remained governor until 1967. Moderate congressman Brooks Hays was replaced by a hard-line segregationist. In August 1958 Governor Faubus called a special session of the state legislature, which passed a law allowing him to close public schools to avoid integration and to lease the schools to private school corporations. The following month, he ordered Little Rock's three high schools closed for the 1958–59 school year.

In June 1959 a federal court declared the state's school-closing law unconstitutional, and the city's high schools opened in August 1959. However, desegregation progressed slowly. In 1964 only 123 out of almost 7,000 registered African-American schoolchildren in Little Rock were attending desegregated schools in the city. Not until 1972 were all of Little Rock's public schools integrated.

The construction of Little Rock Central High, which remains a functioning high school, was completed in 1927. Constructed at a cost of $1.5 million, it is 564 feet long and 365 feet wide and located at 14th and Park Streets. It has a capacity for 3,000 students. Since 1927, other buildings have been added, such as a field house in 1951. In 1977 the U.S. Department of the Interior accepted Central High's main building for listing on the National Register of Historic Places. Five years afterward the department was designated to be a National Historic Landmark. In November 1998 President Bill Clinton, a former Arkansas governor, signed a bill making Central High a National Historic Site.

In September 1997 Little Rock held a fortieth anniversary commemoration of the historic events at the school. On the steps of Central High, President Clinton met the nine black students who desegregated the school in 1957–58. During that month a former gas station across the street from the school, restored to its 1950s appearance, opened as the Central High School Visitors Center and Museum. The Visitors Center offers photographs related to the desegregation crisis and audiovisual segments detailing the events before and during the crisis, along with its aftermath. The museum, yet to be built, will include not just exhibits about the events at Little Rock, but the part that those events played in the larger story of public school desegregation and the civil rights movement as a whole. The Visitors Center and Museum is part of the Central High National Historic Site. ◆

"If those nine children could walk up those steps 40 years ago, all alone, if their parents could send them into the storm armed only with school books and the righteousness of their cause, then surely together we can build one America — an America that makes sure no future generation of our children will have to pay for our mistakes with the loss of their innocence."
Bill Clinton, 1997

Lorraine Motel

MEMPHIS, TENNESSEE

On April 4 1968, civil rights leader Dr. Martin Luther King Jr., winner of the Nobel Peace Prize, was killed by an assassin's bullet while standing on a balcony of the Lorraine Motel in Memphis, Tennessee. Twenty-three years later the restored building was opened as the National Civil Rights Museum, a tribute to King and to the civil rights movement of the 1950s and 1960s in which King played the leading role.

Born in Atlanta in 1929, King was the son of a Baptist pastor who was one of the most prominent leaders of the local black community. King entered Atlanta's Morehouse College, a traditionally African-American school, at the age of fifteen and graduated in 1948. King earned a bachelor of divinity degree from Crozer Theological Seminary in 1951; there, he first became aware of Indian leader Mohandas K. Gandhi's nonviolent social protest philosophy. In 1955 he received a Ph.D. in theology at Boston University.

Meanwhile, in 1954 King had become pastor of the Dexter Avenue Church in Montgomery, Alabama. Late the following year Rosa Parks, a local NAACP activist, refused to move to the back of one of the city's segregated buses. That sparked the Montgomery Bus Boycott, beginning in December 1955, in which the city's African Americans refused to use the municipal bus system.

King reluctantly accepted a call of local black leaders to head the Montgomery Improvement Association, which ran the boycott. At that point, King did not fully understand Gandhi's views. For example, King believed that nonviolence did not prohibit self-defense, and he had a gun in his house at the beginning of the boycott. With the help of Bayard Rustin, a northern black and student of Gandhi who came to Montgomery to advise King during the boycott, he learned that nonviolence was an absolute for Gandhi. He also learned that nonviolence was not simply a passive refusal to use force, but an active method for confronting evil. The highly effective bus boycott ended in victory when a U.S. Supreme Court ruling in November 1956 ordered the end of segregated seating.

By the end of the boycott, the initially hesitant King was prepared to lead a southwide crusade against segregation. In

"I have a dream that my four children will one day live in a nation where they will not be judged by the color of their skin but by the content of their character. I have a dream today."
Martin Luther
King Jr., 1963

The Lorraine Motel in Memphis, Tennessee, where Martin Luther King Jr. was assassinated as he stood on the balcony in the spot now marked by a wreath.

1957 King and other southern ministers formed the Southern Christian Leadership Conference to guide the struggle; King was elected its president. In February 1960 black college students initiated sit-ins at lunch counters and other public accommodations in the south that practiced segregation. Two months later King helped form the Student Nonviolent Coordinating Committee (SNCC), which would become a major voice in the civil rights struggle.

In 1961 and 1962 King led a civil rights campaign in Albany, Georgia. The effort failed because the media-savvy sheriff carefully avoided using violence against the demonstrators, so as not to take the chance of them becoming martyrs. But the deep hatred that underpinned racism, hatred that nonviolent confrontation sought to expose, was bound to produce violence. Next, King moved his campaign to Birmingham, Alabama. There, Sheriff Eugene "Bull" Connor's abhorrence of African Americans and short temper made him a perfect foil for King. Civil rights demonstrations began in April 1963, and before long Connor was using fire hoses and police dogs against peacefully demonstrating children. Northern public opinion was outraged, and this anger provided the political support for the his-

toric Civil Rights Act of 1964, which outlawed racial segregation in public life, banned employment discrimination, and
barred the granting of federal funds to organizations or programs
that discriminated by race.

During the Birmingham campaign, King was arrested. His
"Letter from a Birmingham Jail," a powerful defense of his strategy of nonviolent confrontation, increased his already high
stature. His reputation as a powerful orator was strengthened by
his "I Have a Dream" speech at the March on Washington in
August 1963, the most famous of a series of dramatic, riveting
speeches that he gave over the years as a civil rights leader. King
received international recognition for his work in 1964, when
he was awarded the Nobel Peace Prize.

In 1964 King's protests against voting discrimination in
Selma, Alabama, generated a violent reaction from Sheriff Jim
Clark. Again, as with Birmingham, public reaction led to major
civil rights legislation. In this case it was the Voting Rights Act
of 1965, the first effective voting rights legislation since Reconstruction. Within a few years blacks, for the first time in the
twentieth century, were voting in large numbers throughout the
south.

The Montgomery bus
boycott is commemorated
with this exhibit at the
National Civil Rights
Museum in Memphis.

1929 Martin Luther King Jr. is born.

1951 King earns a bachelor of divinity degree from Crozier Theological Seminary.

1954 King becomes pastor of the Dexter Avenue Church in Montgomery, Alabama.

1955 King receives a Ph.D. in theology at Boston University.

1956 Montgomery's bus boycott ends when the U.S. Supreme Court orders the end of segregated seating.

1957 King helps form and becomes leader of the Southern Christian Leadership Conference.

1960 King helps form the Student Non-violent Coordinating Committee.

1968 King is shot while standing on the balcony of the Lorraine Motel.

1991 The National Civil Rights Museum opens.

The Civil Rights Act and Voting Rights Act spelled the end of the south's system of legalized discrimination. King then turned his movement northward, and led protests against unofficially segregated housing in Chicago. The campaign failed. King underestimated the amount of racism in the north and misunderstood northern politicians like Chicago mayor Richard Daley who, unlike Connor and Clark, were too liberal to create martyrs for the movement but not liberal enough to have a real commitment to change. King then altered his focus to economic issues, while also becoming an outspoken opponent of the war in Vietnam. Late in 1967 he began organizing a Poor People's Campaign to be held in the nation's capital in the spring of 1968. Early that spring he went to Memphis, Tennessee, to support black sanitation workers striking for union representation.

On April 4, 1968, during his second visit to Memphis, King was standing on a balcony of the local Lorraine Motel when he was killed by a single bullet fired from a nearby rooming house. A drifter and petty criminal named James Earl Ray pleaded guilty to the slaying and received a ninety-nine-year sentence.

In the years following King's death, the thirty-two-room, L-shaped Lorraine Motel went through a period of decline, becoming a haven for drug addicts, drug dealers, and pimps. Still, many people from around the world came to visit the historic site. In 1982 the motel was bought at a foreclosure auction for $144,000 by citizens interested in restoring the building and creating a memorial for King. With state, county, city, and private funds totaling $9.2 million, the 10,000-square-foot National Civil Rights Museum was created as a nonprofit enterprise. It opened on September 28, 1991, a tribute not just to King but to the entire civil rights movement of the 1950s and 1960s.

Rooms 306 and 307, where King and his followers stayed, have been re-created exactly as they were when King was assassinated. On the balcony lies a wreath where King fell. The rest of the museum is devoted to audiovisual, interactive exhibits representing events from the U.S. Supreme Court's school desegregation decision of 1954 to the Memphis sanitation workers' strike of 1968. For example, the exhibit for the Montgomery Bus Boycott of 1955–56 features a Montgomery city bus of 1955 vintage. If a visitor sits up in front, the mechanical "driver" turns his head and orders the rider to "move to the back of the bus." Visitors can sit at a 1960s-type lunch counter and see a videotape of student sit-ins. Moving on, museum guests find themselves in Birmingham, Alabama, in the middle of a skirmish between demonstrators and Bull Connor's police. At the March on Washington display, the visitor stands amid placard holders and hears King's "I Have a Dream" speech. Near the end of the museum tour is an orange garbage truck and a group of plaster marchers, representing black sanitation workers, who hold signs that read "I Am a Man." A video presentation about the Memphis sanitation strike of 1968 is played.

There are many other exhibits. They include vivid depictions of the desegregation crisis of 1957 at Central High School in Little Rock, Arkansas; the Freedom Rides of 1961; Freedom Summer of 1964, when young blacks and whites from around the country came to Mississippi to register black voters; and a biographical exhibit about Martin Luther King. ◆

> *"We must come to see, with one of our distinguished jurists, that 'justice too long delayed is justice denied.'"*
> Martin Luther King Jr., April 1963

Los Alamos National Laboratory

LOS ALAMOS, NEW MEXICO

The Los Alamos National Laboratory occupies forty-three square miles of canyons and mesas in northern New Mexico, about thirty-five miles northeast of Santa Fe. It was founded in 1943 as the research and test facility for the Manhattan Project, which developed the first nuclear weapon during World War II under the guidance of Dr. J. Robert Oppenheimer. Today, the lab's staff of scientists and support personnel continues to apply their technical expertise toward issues of national security, as well as to a large and diverse range of programs in energy, nuclear safeguards, biomedical science, environmental protection, computer science, and materials science.

The Los Alamos National Laboratory is divided into fifty technical areas situated according to **topography**, functional relationships, and historical developments at the site. Half of the lab's employees and floor space is located in TA-3, the main technical area. What is arguably the greatest concentration of scientific computing power in the world is housed here, in the

topography: the surface features of the land.

Visitors to the Bradbury Science Museum in Los Alamos, New Mexico, can see bomb cases identical to those dropped over Hiroshima and Nagasaki in 1945.

cryogenics: the science that deals with the production of low temperatures and their effect on the properties of matter.

Central Computing Facility and Advanced Computing Laboratory. TA-3 also includes the materials science, earth and space, chemistry, physics, and **cryogenics** laboratories, a Van de Graaff particle accelerator, the director's office, administrative offices, and the main library.

When Dr. Oppenheimer first arrived in Los Alamos with a select group of scientists, they were housed in the school buildings of the former Los Alamos Ranch School for Boys. Today, only the Fuller Lodge and the buildings comprising "bathtub row" remain from the original TA-1 complex. The Los Alamos Historical Museum is also located here. At the Health Research Lab (TA-43), scientists study long-term health and environmental effects of energy and defense technologies, and research new techniques for diagnosis and treatment of disease. Other facilities at Los Alamos include an explosives research and testing facility, a Weapons Engineering facility, the Pajarito Site where the fundamental behavior of nuclear chain reactions is studied, and the Plutonium Facility, which performs most of the lab's nuclear materials activities.

The roots of Los Alamos lie in Nazi Germany's discovery of nuclear fission in 1939. Renowned nuclear physicist Werner Heisenberg experimentally performed the procedure, in which a slow neutron splits a heavy atom into two atoms of approximately half the weight of the original, releasing tremendous amounts of energy. German refugee scientists in America were concerned about the uses Adolf Hitler might make of the discovery, and persuaded Albert Einstein to write a letter to President Franklin Roosevelt warning him of the danger. The result was a U.S. commitment to nuclear research, with the goal of producing an atomic weapon before the Germans.

By the time the United States entered World War II in December 1941, several projects investigating the feasibility of nuclear weapons were under way. Theoretical physicist J. Robert Oppenheimer of the University of California Berkeley convened a summer study in June 1942 to review the current research. Theorists Hans Bethe, John Van Vleck, Edward Teller, Felix Bloch, Richard Tolman, and Emil Konopinski concluded that a fission bomb was feasible. After the conference, Oppenheimer's Berkeley team oversaw a number of experimental studies at scattered sites around the country. Given the difficulties of coordinating these studies, it soon became clear that the project needed a remote laboratory that could bring the scientists together as a team while ensuring military security.

In late summer 1942 Brigadier General Leslie Groves was selected to head the nuclear weapons effort, soon christened "The Manhattan District," after the Corps of Engineers' practice of naming projects after its headquarters city. Groves had previously successfully overseen the Army Corps of Engineers' Pentagon construction project. In the first week on board, Groves secured top military priority for the project, created a new government department to oversee it (the precursor to the Department of Energy) and acquired a site in Tennessee for a plutonium production plant. His next task was to name a director for the proposed weapon design lab. Groves selected Dr. Oppenheimer, who had previously built strong theoretical physics departments at Cal Tech and UC Berkeley.

In November 1942 a site was acquired that satisfied the project's terrain, security and access requirements. The Los Alamos Ranch School for boys in northern New Mexico also offered fifty-four school buildings that could be used as immediate lodging for the staff. Because the school buildings were the only houses in Los Alamos with bathtubs during the war, these residences were nicknamed "Bathtub Row." An additional 62,000 acres of land surrounding the school was also acquired by the army. To the existing buildings were added soldiers' barracks, a

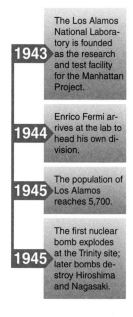

1943 The Los Alamos National Laboratory is founded as the research and test facility for the Manhattan Project.

1944 Enrico Fermi arrives at the lab to head his own division.

1945 The population of Los Alamos reaches 5,700.

1945 The first nuclear bomb explodes at the Trinity site; later bombs destroy Hiroshima and Nagasaki.

mess hall, officers' quarters, an administration building, a theater, an infirmary, apartments, a bachelor dormitory, and laboratory technical buildings. These were built with great urgency, though the remote location of the site would prove to be a hindrance in the construction effort.

The teams that had been working on the theoretical calculations at scattered university sites under Oppenheimer's direction would form the nucleus of the new laboratory. But of the thirty-three scientists Oppenheimer originally recruited from across the country, only fifteen eventually came to Los Alamos. Edward Condon, who had directed the Westinghouse Research Laboratory, agreed to serve as Oppenheimer's assistant. Others on the new team included experimental physicist Robert Bacher and theorist Hans Bethe of Cornell, Berkeley physics professor Edwin McMillan, John Manley and Robert Serber of the University of Illinois, Washington University theorist Edward Teller, and University of Chicago experimentalist Samuel Allison. Enrico Fermi, who successfully triggered the first nuclear chain reaction in December 1942, arrived in 1944 to head his own division.

Soon Oppenheimer's original estimates of a scientific and technical staff of 100 and a total population of 650 proved to be much too conservative for the huge problem at hand, which involved inventing a brand new technology from purely experimental discoveries in nuclear physics, metallurgy, chemistry, and ordnance. By 1943 the population of Los Alamos, including civilian and military staff, support personnel, and their families had soared to 1,500. By January 1945 it had reached 5,700.

The first year of the lab was spent designing a nuclear gun-type weapon that worked by firing one part of a mass of fissionable material (critical mass) into another, but this technique was found to be impossible using plutonium. Since so much had already been invested in the plutonium manufacturing plants in Tennessee and Washington, the gun device was scrapped. In the second year of its existence, therefore, the laboratory was reorganized to solve the much more difficult problem of an implosion-type bomb that detonated a high explosive around a hollow sphere of uranium, thereby crushing it into a critical mass. Because of the uncertainties surrounding the new weapon, it was decided that, unlike the gun, the implosion bomb would have to be tested. The Trinity test site, named by Oppenheimer after a John Donne poem, was selected in the central New Mexico desert.

"An experiment in the New Mexican desert was startling—to put it mildly. Thirteen pounds of the explosive caused the complete disintegration of a steel tower sixty feet high, created a crater six feet deep and twelve hundred feet in diameter, knocked over a steel tower a half mile away, and knocked men down ten thousand yards away."

Harry Truman, diary, July 25, 1945

Robert Christy of the Theoretical Physics Division at the lab produced a conservative design for what was called, for security reasons, "the gadget." The design was ordered fixed by General Groves in February 1945 so that the device could be ready for a test by July. Though detonators, fuses, and high-explosive lenses required by the design had yet to be perfected, Los Alamos scientists and technicians succeeded in producing all of the components by July 13.

At 5:29 A.M. on July 16, 1945, the first nuclear bomb exploded at the Trinity site with a force of 21,000 tons of TNT, vaporizing the tower it stood on. It released four times the heat of the interior of the sun, created a pressure of 100 billion atmospheres and was seen 250 miles away. Los Alamos had succeeded in producing a nuclear weapon only two years, three months, and sixteen days after the inception of its lab.

By this time, Germany had surrendered, but the war in the Pacific against Japan was still on, and despite the protests of some scientists against using the new super weapon on civilian targets, a nuclear bomb was dropped on Hiroshima, Japan, on August 6, 1945. Three days later another bomb destroyed Nagasaki, the Japanese surrendered, and the nuclear age had begun. In the future, the technology pioneered at Los Alamos would be used not only for weapons but for nuclear reactors producing energy for consumers and for propulsion. The team's theoretical findings would provide the basis for many scientific discoveries regarding the physical nature of the universe.

During the U.S.–USSR nuclear standoff, the so-called cold war of the 1960s through the 1980s, Los Alamos was charged with overseeing the development, construction, transportation, and maintenance of the United States' $13.5 trillion nuclear weapons stockpile. Since the end of the cold war, the defense mission of the lab has shifted toward developing environmentally sound nuclear technologies and reducing the danger caused by the spread of nuclear weapons.

The tradition of a multidisciplinary approach to complex scientific problems that began with the Manhattan Project continues at the lab today with a scientific, technical, and support staff approaching 10,000 people. Current and future programs include environmental research related to energy, waste disposal, air pollution, and global warming; life sciences studies in genetics and biomagnetism, helping scientists understand and treat diseases of the brain; developing lasers as a tool in applications ranging from medical technology to defense; and the use

"In both Hiroshima and Nagasaki the tremendous scale of the disaster largely destroyed the cities as entities. Even the worst of all other previous bombing attacks on Germany and Japan, such as the incendiary raids on Hamburg in 1943 and on Tokyo in 1945, were not comparable to the paralyzing effect of the atomic bombs."
Report of the Manhattan Project Atomic Bomb Investigating Group, June 1946

of particle accelerators to investigate the basic components of matter.

Since World War II, when Los Alamos scientists pioneered the use of the first electronic computer, the lab's unique, computing intensive requirements have stimulated computer science research, including the development of supercomputer technology.

The laboratory offers a number of offerings of interest to the curious visitor. The Bradbury Science Museum presents a history of the lab from the Manhattan Project to the present, and includes interactive exhibits, demonstrations, and films that explore the development of the first atomic bomb and related scientific topics. A twenty-five-mile driving tour through the lab grounds stops at historical sites such as the original Bathtub Row, as well as many of the modern facilities. Los Alamos also contains the remains of prehistoric Native American settlements, including cliff dwellings and a pueblo at the Tsirege Ruins and the Bandelier National Monument. ◆

Manzanar War Relocation Center

CENTRAL CALIFORNIA

Manzanar War Relocation Center in California's Owens Valley, west of Death Valley, was one of ten internment camps established to confine about 110,000 Japanese Americans during World War II. The internment of Japanese-American citizens between 1942 and 1945 is now widely regarded as a regrettable and unnecessary overreaction to war hysteria. Thousands of survivors of the internment camps received a monetary award and a presidential apology in 1990, but the dishonor still stings many Japanese Americans. Not a single act of disloyalty or sabotage preceded the incarceration.

The historic site, about halfway between Los Angeles (to the south) and Reno, Nevada, was designated a National Historic Site in 1992, and, as the best-preserved of the ten former internment camps, is the only one to have received this designation. Little remains of the barracks from the early 1940s, but the auditorium is still standing, as are two stone police buildings at the entrance, and the cemetery at the back of the 813-acre site holds a memorial to the internees. The Eastern California Museum in Independence, about five miles to the north, holds an extensive collection of exhibits, photographs, drawings, paintings, and artifacts about Manzanar, and guides conduct tours of the site twice daily.

There had long been a strong intolerance of Asians on the west coast, particularly in California. Japanese and Chinese

> *"An American citizen, after all, is an American citizen."*
> General John DeWitt, December 26, 1941

Manzanar War Relocation Center, near Independence, California, photographed by Dorothea Lange during a dust storm, July 3, 1942.

immigrants were specifically excluded or at least severely limited by state laws and by such federal legislation as the Chinese Exclusion Act of 1882 and the Immigration Act of 1924, which limited Japanese immigration. Other discriminatory laws prevented immigrants from becoming citizens, thereby enforcing an alien status on people who would gladly have sought citizenship. After Japan's surprise air assault on Pearl Harbor on December 7, 1941, war passions and old prejudices were aroused against the Japanese, even those who had lived their entire lives in the United States.

After Pearl Harbor, many military officials saw Japanese Americans as a security risk.

At the time, only 1 percent of the California population was Issei (first-generation Japanese Americans) or Nisei (children of Issei). The morning after Pearl Harbor, California governor Culbert L. Olson and Attorney General Earl Warren (later Chief Justice of the United States Supreme Court) worked with sheriffs and district attorneys to dismiss all Issei and Nisei from civil service positions. Licenses to practice law and medicine were revoked.

After Pearl Harbor, many military officials saw Japanese Americans as a security risk. Secretary of the Navy Frank Knox and several army and navy officers insisted that Japanese Americans in Hawaii had participated in the attack at Pearl Harbor, and they argued that Japanese Americans on the Pacific coast would probably engage in sabotage or assist Japan in an invasion of the west coast. In support of the military's claims, and often

exaggerating them, west coast newspapers published articles that emphasized the dangers of allowing Japanese immigrants and their children to remain in California, Washington, and Oregon. Strident or paranoid voices within the military persuaded President Roosevelt to sanction the removal of all Japanese Americans from the Pacific coast. On February 19, 1942, Roosevelt issued Executive Order 9066, which gave the military the power to designate "military areas" from which it could exclude "any and all persons."

Between March and June 1942, the army ordered all Japanese Americans in most of California, Oregon, and Washington to leave their homes and report to civil control stations—frequently Christian and Buddhist churches. Military authorities allowed the Japanese to bring only as much luggage as they could carry. The army gave the residents of Terminal Island in Los Angeles Harbor less than three days to store or sell their personal possessions and arrange to rent homes, farms, and businesses; Japanese Americans in other areas had as much as ten days.

Japanese Americans from San Pedro, California, arrive at the Santa Anita Assembly Center in 1942 before being deported to Manzanar and other internment camps.

A monument marks the site of Manzanar War Relocation Center.

Unscrupulous people took advantage of some Japanese Americans by buying their furniture and automobiles for a fraction of their value. Other Japanese Americans stored their belongings in churches or community organization buildings, many of which were looted during the war.

Buses and trucks took Japanese Americans and their baggage from the churches to assembly centers. These temporary concentration camps were usually located at county fairgrounds and horse-racing tracks. In the summer and fall, they were shipped to more permanent relocation centers.

To administer the relocation centers, Roosevelt created the War Relocation Authority (WRA) in March 1942, a month after Executive Order 9066. The WRA operated ten camps: Manzanar in Owens Valley and Tule Lake in northern California's remote Siskiyou County; Poston and Gila River in Arizona; Jerome and Rohwer in Arkansas; Granada (also known as Amache) in Colorado; Topaz in Utah; Minidoka in Idaho; and Heart Mountain in Wyoming.

Manzanar, Spanish for "apple orchard," was for many years a farming and ranching area in the Owens Valley, on the east side of the high Sierra Nevada mountain range, after first being explored by the Spanish in the seventeenth century. For thousands of years the area was inhabited by Paiute Indians, but in the mid 1800s they were marched away to Fort Tejon to make room for European immigrant farmers and ranchers. Early in the 1900s Manzanar was a thriving agricultural community with a population of about 200. In 1919 Manzanar was bought by the government and the water from the Owens River was diverted to the Los Angeles Aqueduct. The farmlands turned to desert.

On March 21, 1942, busloads of Japanese Americans from California, Oregon, Washington, and Hawaii began arriving at Manazanar, a desolate camp of barracks hastily constructed on infertile land in the shadow of the Sierra Nevada. Within six months, over 10,000 people were relocated to Manzanar. The 504 barracks measured 120 by 20 feet and were divided into six one-room apartments that ranged in size from 320 to 480 square feet. The rooms were furnished with army cots, straw mattresses, and electricity. Each block of fifteen barracks shared bath, latrine, mess ("dining"), and laundry buildings. Temperatures in the Owens Valley varied between extremes: even in late spring the temperature could dip below freezing, and in summer the heat would rise to over 110 degrees.

Amid these unpromising surroundings, surrounded by barbed wire and watchtowers with armed guards, the Japanese Americans did their best to carry on with something like normal life. Girls could join a choir, boys could play in a basketball league and in physical education programs, and there were churches—Buddhist (the largest congregation), Catholic, and Protestant. In the ten relocation camps, there were 2,120 marriages, 5,981 christenings, and 1,862 funerals.

Camp life strained family relationships. Most families lived in one-room apartments and were thus deprived of privacy. Parents complained that they could not discipline their children. Older women found themselves with more leisure time than they had had before the war. Working women received the same amount of pay as men, and the traditional patterns of arranged marriages disintegrated.

The camp experience upset the social order within the community. Although at first the WRA deprived the older men of power within the community—a move that embittered many internees—the traditional community leaders were later allowed to participate in camp "self-government." In December 1942 angry inmates at Manzanar attacked other prisoners whom they accused of collaborating with the WRA. Military police moved in to stop the riot and fired tear gas and bullets into the crowd. Two people died.

1924 The Immigration Act limits immigration of Japanese to the U.S.

1941 War passions are aroused against Japanese Americans after Japan's attack on Pearl Harbor.

1942 Franklin D. Roosevelt gives the military the power to designate areas from which it can exclude people.

1942 The army orders all Japanese Americans in most of California, Oregon, and Washington to report to civil control stations.

1948 Congress passes the Evacuee Claims Act, allowing Japanese Americans to receive monetary compensation.

1976 Gerald Ford issues a formal apology to Japanese Americans.

1988 Congress passes a bill issuing an apology and $20,000 to each survivor of the camps.

1992 The Manzanar War Relocation Center is designated a National Historic Site.

Many government actions exacerbated fear and despair within the camps. In 1943 the WRA separated "loyal" from "disloyal" Japanese Americans and placed the "disloyals" in a segregation center at Tule Lake. In 1944 the army began drafting men from the camps for active military service, a move that sparked a considerable resistance movement. Both the draft and the segregation of "disloyals" further split already divided families and communities.

Throughout World War II, U.S. courts upheld the legality of internment. In late 1944, however, the U.S. Supreme Court ruled that the government could not continue to impound people without proof of disloyalty. The army rescinded the exclusion order on January 1, 1945, and Japanese Americans were allowed to return to the coastal areas of California, Washington, and Oregon.

> *"If Japan wins this war we have the most to lose. We hope America wins and quickly. We voluntarily evacuated as the only means by which we could demonstrate our loyalty."*
> Chiye Mori, editor of the *Manzanar Free Press*, April 21, 1942

After internment, many Japanese Americans sought restitution from the federal government. In 1948 Congress passed the Evacuee Claims Act, which allowed Japanese Americans to receive monetary compensation. Claimants generally received one-tenth of the value of their losses. A redress movement resurfaced in the late 1960s and early 1970s and, over the course of two decades, achieved many of its goals. President Gerald Ford rescinded Executive Order 9066 in 1976 and issued a formal apology to Japanese Americans. Federal courts vacated opinions that had upheld the constitutionality of the internment. In 1988 Congress passed a bill issuing an apology and a tax-free payment of twenty thousand dollars to each survivor of the camps.

A letter of apology on White House stationery conveys the nation's sense of guilt and awkwardness many years after the war's end:

A monetary sum and words alone cannot restore lost years or erase painful memories; neither can they fully convey our Nation's resolve to rectify injustice and to uphold the rights of individuals. We can never fully right the wrongs of the past. But we can take a clear stand for justice and recognize that serious injustices were done to Japanese Americans during World War II. In enacting a law calling for restitution and offering a sincere apology, your fellow Americans have, in a very real sense, renewed their traditional commitment to the ideals of freedom, equality, and justice. You and your family have our best wishes for the future.

Sincerely,

George Bush
President of the United States

Manzanar National Historic Site is maintained by the National Park Service and is represented by exhibits at the Eastern California Museum, but the site itself has largely returned to the arid flatland it was between the diversion from the Owens River and the building of the barracks. In addition to the auditorium and the stone sentry posts at the entrance, the cemetery is still there with its memorial obelisk inscribed with Japanese characters. Every year on the last Saturday in April, a pilgrimage group (open to the public) gathers at the gates and visits the site of the internment of ten thousand Japanese Americans. Those who come to remember and pay their respects may also see performances of taiko drumming, ondo dance, a roll call of the internees, and readings of poetry. The final event of the day is a religious ceremony conducted at the cemetery in honor of the dead and the descendants of those imprisoned in the valley under the Sierra Nevada where the apple orchards used to grow. ◆

President Gerald Ford rescinded Executive Order 9066 in 1976 and issued a formal apology to Japanese Americans.

Mayo Clinic

ROCHESTER, MINNESOTA

The Mayo Clinic in Rochester, Minnesota, is a world-famous institution known for its many contributions to medicine. The clinic has long attracted people from far and wide, both famous and unknown, who come to be cured of serious illnesses or to learn how to cure others.

Two brothers whose love of medicine began as children founded the clinic. William James Mayo, born in 1861, and Charles Horace Mayo, born in 1865, learned medicine from their father, pioneer doctor William Worrall Mayo. Dr. Mayo was born in England and came to the United States in 1845 when he was twenty-six. He graduated from the University of Missouri Medical School in 1854 and married Louise Abigail Wright. The couple had three girls and two boys and settled in a pioneer village, Le Sueur, Minnesota, and later in Rochester.

The Mayos were a studious family. Mrs. Mayo had a telescope set up on the roof where she taught the children about the stars. She also gave them botany lessons in the garden. The couple borrowed money against their house to pay for Dr. Mayo to travel to New York City to spend much of 1872 studying at Bellevue Hospital. They also invested in a microscope from

The Mayo Clinic in Rochester, Minnesota, in 1959.

Germany, making Dr. Mayo one of the first doctors in the country to use a microscope in his practice.

The Mayo boys helped their father in his office, rolling bandages and mixing salves. They even helped their father, also the county **coroner**, with postmortem examinations. Also called autopsies, such examinations are carried out on bodies to discover the cause of death if there is doubt about what happened, such as an undiagnosed disease or a possible suicide or murder. Charlie and Bill learned a great deal from the autopsies as well as from watching other surgeries their father performed.

coroner: a public officer whose chief duty is to determine the causes of an individual's death.

Surgery in the mid-1800s was very primitive. It often failed because doctors did not know how to prevent or stop infections and shock, both of which killed many patients. Two European doctors, Sir Joseph Lister and Louis Pasteur, had just begun to make some progress against infection. The British surgeon Lister discovered antiseptics in 1865, greatly reducing deaths due to infection by sterilizing operating rooms. Lister's work was supported by that of the French bacteriologist Pasteur, who developed the germ theory of disease. As the young Mayo brothers were growing up, physicians and scientists around the world passionately debated the ideas of Lister and Pasteur.

The Mayo brothers grew into medicine naturally. "It never occurred to us that we could be anything but doctors," William Mayo once wrote. In 1880 William went to the University of

Michigan Medical School, where he impressed professors with his practical knowledge. He graduated in 1883. Charles graduated from Chicago Medical School (now Northwestern University Medical School) in 1888. Both brothers returned to Rochester and practiced medicine with their father.

One evening in 1883 a tornado struck the Rochester area, killing twenty-two people and injuring more than a hundred. Dr. Mayo and his two sons cared for the injured at a hotel, at their office, and at a convent. Soon they turned a dance hall into a makeshift hospital. The Sisters of St. Francis, who helped through the crisis, approached Dr. Mayo later and said, "Rochester needs a hospital." Concerned with the expense, Dr. Mayo protested, but the nuns offered to raise the money. In 1889 they opened St. Mary's Hospital with forty beds and three doctors—Dr. William W. Mayo and his two sons. The Mayos' offices stood across the street from St. Mary's.

Visiting Europe to recover from whooping cough, Charlie attended a lecture by Pasteur in Paris, where he learned about bacteria. He went on to Germany, where he saw completely sterile operating rooms. Back home, Charlie shared his knowledge with his father and Bill, who had also been studying antisepsis. The Mayos made St. Mary's into an exceptionally clean hospital and performed surgeries in sterile rooms.

The hospital's reputation grew. The Mayos only charged patients what they could afford and often charged nothing. People came from neighboring states to Rochester for treatment. In 1890 Edith Graham, a graduate of a Chicago nursing school, joined the staff to teach nursing skills. In 1893 she and Charlie married. Bill had married Hattie May Damon in 1884. The curiosity that the brothers had grown up with inspired them to travel all over the country to hospitals and medical schools to watch surgeons work. In order to keep their commitment at home, they made a pact that one of them would always be present in Rochester. The brothers accepted their first partner in 1892.

Charlie once saved a man's leg and wrote a detailed report on his technique for the *Annals of Surgery*, the most prestigious surgery journal at the time. The man had an infected knee joint, and to avoid amputating the leg, Charlie made a deep incision and drained the infection. Will wrote articles about abdominal surgery for publication and by 1905 he was considered the leading authority on abdominal surgery in America. Over their entire careers, the two brothers published more than 1,000 articles in medical journals. Their devoted mother read every article.

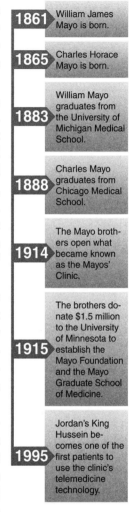

1861 William James Mayo is born.

1865 Charles Horace Mayo is born.

1883 William Mayo graduates from the University of Michigan Medical School.

1888 Charles Mayo graduates from Chicago Medical School.

1914 The Mayo brothers open what became known as the Mayos' Clinic.

1915 The brothers donate $1.5 million to the University of Minnesota to establish the Mayo Foundation and the Mayo Graduate School of Medicine.

1995 Jordan's King Hussein becomes one of the first patients to use the clinic's telemedicine technology.

After the senior Doctor Mayo died in 1911 at the age of ninety-two, the sons carried on. In 1914 the brothers opened a building big enough to house all of their offices and laboratories. The names of five partners were on the building, but everyone called it Mayos' Clinic. Soon the clinic was too small. The brothers donated $1.5 million dollars to the University of Minnesota in 1915 to establish the Mayo Foundation and the Mayo Graduate School of Medicine. The school became one of the world's leading graduate medical centers.

Doctors from around the world came to observe the Mayos. They gave speeches to packed auditoriums, and they each developed a warm speaking style. Charlie became known for his skill in **thyroid** surgery. He taught surgery at the University of Minnesota Medical School from 1915 to 1936. He served as president of the American Medical Association in 1917 and the American College of Surgeons in 1925. Bill served as president of the American Medical Association in 1906 and the American Surgical Association in 1914. Both brothers served in the armed forces during World War I (1914–18) and became brigadier generals in the medical reserve in 1921. In 1929, within two months of each other, the two brothers died of natural causes.

thyroid: a large gland lying in front and on either side of the trachea.

By the end of the 1990s, the Mayo Clinic had become one of the world's largest medical centers, with nearly 900 physicians, surgeons, and medical scientists on its staff. St. Mary's Hospital and Rochester Methodist Hospital had merged with the Mayo Clinic in 1986. Mayo's staff physicians care for patients through a group practice style of medicine, pioneered by the Mayo brothers. The Mayo Clinic's reputation for developing new medical technology and procedures draws people from around the world, including a number of famous people. United States Supreme Court Justice Harry Blackmun, a native of Rochester and the clinic's first in-house lawyer, returned each year to Mayo, where he was long remembered as a brilliant lawyer.

While the Mayo Clinic may treat up to 40,000 patients a month, 1.5 million people visit its Internet site each month.

King Hussein I of Jordan became a patient of the Mayo Clinic in 1992 when he had a kidney and a ureter removed in cancer surgery. In 1995 Hussein became one of the first patients to use the clinic's telemedicine technology. Doctors in Jordan used cameras to transmit live images to doctors at Mayo, who viewed them on a screen. In addition to examining Hussein, Jordanian doctors showed Mayo doctors images of other patients' blood vessels, a chest X-ray, and an electronic scan of a brain cyst. The Mayo doctors planned further international links with Greece, Argentina, Chile, and Colombia.

The Mayo Clinic provides health information to the public in the form of books, newsletters, and CD-ROM's. Their periodical, *Mayo Clinic Health Letter*, provides medical information written for the consumer. In the late 1990s the clinic put medical information on an Internet Web site (www.mayohealth.org). A dozen full-time editorial workers publish medical news on the site daily; each story is reviewed by at least three physicians. While the Mayo Clinic may treat up to 40,000 patients a month, 1.5 million people visit its Internet site each month. The Mayo brothers would probably be delighted that people share medical knowledge through the Internet. William Mayo once described their great success as coming from "the desire to aid those who are suffering; the desire to advance in medical education by research, by diligent observation, and by the application of knowledge gained from others; and most important of all, the desire to pass onto others the scientific candle this spirit has lighted." ◆

Melrose Estate

NATCHEZ, MISSISSIPPI

Melrose is one of the finest antebellum homes in Natchez, Mississippi, a city famously rich with palatial dwellings. The estate is the keystone property of the Natchez National Historical Park, established in 1988 by an act of Congress to preserve and interpret the history of Natchez and its people. Melrose is extraordinary not only for its external beauty, but also for its good fortune in having been owned by families who preserved and restored but never renovated the house. As a result, Melrose has remained virtually unchanged since it was first built in the 1840s for John and Mary Louisa McMurran. In addition to the preservation of the Melrose mansion, the dependencies (external residences) in back are also well preserved, along with slave quarters, a kitchen, privy, a carriage house and stable, and a smokehouse.

Melrose was built fifteen years before the Civil War (*antebellum* is Latin for "before the war") during the glory years of King Cotton, when that crop made planters in the Mississippi

Melrose was built during the glory years of King Cotton.

The antebellum mansion at the center of Melrose estate in Natchez, Mississippi.

Delta wealthy in the same way that the oil and computer industries have generated fortunes in more recent times. Around the 1850s Natchez had more millionaires than any other city in the United States, with the possible exception of New York. It was an economy based on slave labor, and with that morally unsustainable foundation it could not last, but even after the Civil War (1861–65) and the Emancipation Proclamation (1863), cotton was still planted and harvested by black laborers, many of whom, though legally free, were still bound to the land and their employers as securely as they had ever been.

Natchez, built on a bluff two hundred feet above the Mississippi River, is named for the sun-worshiping, mound-building Indian tribe that occupied this ground for hundreds of years before the Europeans began exploring the Mississippi River. In 1714 the French established an outpost on the bluff overlooking the wide river and the forests of Louisiana on the west bank. In 1716 Fort Rosalie (*Fort Rosalie des Natchez*) was built on this strategic location by Jean-Baptiste Le Moyne, Sieur de Bienville, two years before he established New Orleans (*La Nouvelle-Orléans*) 270 miles downriver, near the mouth of the Mississippi. The French soldiers and settlers infuriated the Natchez by abusing their women and taking over their fields and homes. The Natchez warriors attacked Fort Rosalie on November 28, 1729; they massacred about 250 whites, captured others, and freed the slaves. The French, in an alliance with Choctaw Indians, waged a merciless campaign against the Natchez for the next two years, and by 1732 the tribe had been annihilated. Fort Rosalie was rebuilt, but the surviving French farmers left the area. No buildings survive from the French period.

Between the 1760s and the early part of the next century, Natchez passed back and forth from French possession to Spanish to British, back to Spanish, then to American, because, in addition to the American Revolution (1775–83), several wars were being fought between the European powers in the Old World and the New. The population of Natchez grew during the

Revolution, particularly with settlements by loyalists to the British crown, as this land was then part of British West Florida.

After difficulties in growing tobacco and **indigo**, local planters turned to cotton. Eli Whitney's invention of the cotton gin in 1793 (a device that mechanically removed the seed from the boll) made large-scale production of cotton much easier and more profitable. Natchez's local crop grew from 36,351 pounds in 1794 to 1.2 million pounds four years later. Between the 1790s and the 1820s, cotton planters around Natchez made astonishing fortunes, and built homes to match.

indigo: a blue dye obtained from plants.

One of the new immigrants lured to the profitable Mississippi Delta was John McMurran. John Thompson McMurran was born in Pennsylvania in 1801. Before 1823 McMurran moved to Port Gibson, Mississippi, about forty miles north of Natchez, where he taught school and studied for the state supreme court examination. By late 1825 McMurran was handling cases in Natchez, and the next year he joined the growing law firm of his friends John Quitman and William B. Griffith. On January 11, 1831, McMurran married Mary Louisa Turner, the seventeen-year-old daughter of Edward Turner, a former state attorney general, speaker of the Mississippi House of Representatives, and a justice of the state supreme court. McMurran, from a middle-class northern family, now found himself at a higher level of society than he had ever known before. The year after their marriage, around the time McMurran was appointed as Secretary of the Bar of Natchez, Mary Louisa's father deeded to her and her husband a house and lot in town known as Holly Hedges. Then, in 1833, Edward Turner gave his daughter and son-in-law a plantation in Adams County called Hope Farm, with 645 acres and twenty-four slaves. In 1835 McMurran was elected to the Mississippi House of Representatives, and the following year he was elected to the board of directors of the new Commercial Bank of Natchez.

Between the 1790s and the 1820s, cotton planters around Natchez made astonishing fortunes, and built homes to match.

John and Mary Louisa McMurran had three children, though only two survived childhood: Mary Elizabeth, who died in 1833 before her third birthday; John Thompson, born in 1833; and a second daughter, also named Mary Elizabeth, born in 1835. In December 1841 the McMurrans purchased 132 acres several miles east of town, where several other prominent planter families had begun building homes on spacious tracts of land. Many of these houses still stand today, and are among the grandest residences in Natchez, including Auburn (owned by

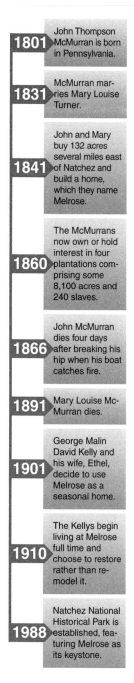

1801 John Thompson McMurran is born in Pennsylvania.

1831 McMurran marries Mary Louise Turner.

1841 John and Mary buy 132 acres several miles east of Natchez and build a home, which they name Melrose.

1860 The McMurrans now own or hold interest in four plantations comprising some 8,100 acres and 240 slaves.

1866 John McMurran dies four days after breaking his hip when his boat catches fire.

1891 Mary Louise McMurran dies.

1901 George Malin David Kelly and his wife, Ethel, decide to use Melrose as a seasonal home.

1910 The Kellys begin living at Melrose full time and choose to restore rather than remodel it.

1988 Natchez National Historical Park is established, featuring Melrose as its keystone.

the Duncans, built in 1812), Monmouth (Quitmans, 1818), Woodlands (Turners), and Linden (Kers, c. 1800).

On their new property the McMurrans built their new home, named Melrose, after the Scottish abbey celebrated in Sir Walter Scott's novel *Lay of the Last Minstrel*. Melrose was designed and built by Jacob Byers, a Natchez architect, and completed around 1845–47. An entry dated August 23, 1859, from the diary of T. K. Wharton, a visiting architect, gives an idea of what Melrose looked like soon after it was built: ". . . but surpassing all, that of Mr. McMurran, looking for all the world like an English park, ample mansion of solid design in brick with portico and pediment flanked by grand forest trees stretching away on either side, and half embracing a vast lawn in front of emerald green comprising at least 200 acres through which winds the carriage drive—the place is English all over."

"English all over," but technically speaking, the mansion is in the architectural style called Greek Revival, which was the dominant look in the United States from about 1820 to 1860. In their elegant book *Classic Natchez*, architectural historians Randolph Delehanty and Van Jones Martin write that Melrose was "the first grand-scale Natchez villa to be built in the Greek Revival style with no Federal admixtures and no Italianate foreshadowings. . . . The proportions of the two-story house are massive and restful—more horizontal than vertical—though the plan is a variation of the Rosalie prototype. The wide, two-story, pedimented entrance portico is supported by two pairs of unfluted Doric columns and shades the stuccoed three-bay center of the brick façade. . . . The complex provides a priceless view into the defining conceit of cotton-era Natchez—the suburban villa estate."

The McMurrans kept an average of nineteen slaves on the property to work in the house and maintain the grounds. The work ranged from cooking and washing to tending the estate's vast grounds and maintaining the horses and carriages. In each room in Melrose was a pull-cord or lever that rang a bell to summon a servant when needed. The fall and spring court sessions kept McMurran busy in town, but in the summers the family would often go back east or to Europe to escape the intense Mississippi heat. Winters are relatively mild in Natchez, and the cold months were a time of much socializing and visiting among neighbors.

By 1860, on the eve of the Civil War, the McMurrans owned or held interest in four plantations comprising some

8,100 acres and 240 slaves, with an approximate value of $275,000—which in those days was a fortune high enough to put the family in the top one percent of southern society. But although the McMurrans owned plantations in Mississippi and Louisiana, they lived at Melrose, and Melrose was a villa, or country estate, not a plantation.

The Civil War brought an end to the McMurrans' good fortune. Soon after South Carolina seceded from the Union, Mississippi joined the other Deep South states in January 1861 in also withdrawing from the United States. New Orleans and Memphis fell to the Union forces in the spring of 1862. Natchez, without a railroad link to the rest of the Confederacy, was deemed militarily insignificant and was left undefended. The Union forces concentrated on Vicksburg, upriver, for it did have railroad lines, connecting with Jackson and other cities. The siege of Vicksburg lasted from May 19 until July 4, 1863; the Union gunboats' bombardment of that city on a bluff drove some people to dig caves in the hillsides, while others hid in the basements of their destroyed houses. Vicksburg's surrender was a crushing loss for the Confederacy. In the same week that Vicksburg surrendered, General Robert E. Lee was losing the three-day battle of Gettysburg in Pennsylvania.

> The McMurrans named their new home Melrose, after the Scottish abbey celebrated in Sir Walter Scott's novel *Lay of the Last Minstrel.*

In March 1864 Mary Elizabeth McMurran Conner died at the Turners' (her grandparents') home, Woodlands, to which she had been carried after a physician was forbidden from crossing Federal lines to attend her at Melrose. Within a year, two of her children died at Melrose. John McMurran was shot in the face by a Union soldier as he attempted to cross the Federal lines on his way to Melrose, but he survived. The McMurrans decided to sell Melrose in late 1865 or January 1866, about a half year after the war ended. The house and most of its furnishings were sold to Elizabeth Davis, the wife of George Malin Davis, a Natchez attorney and planter, and the family moved to Woodlands. About a year after selling Melrose, John McMurran was on a steamboat bound for New Orleans when, just above Baton Rouge, the boat caught fire and was run aground. McMurran escaped the flames, but his hip was broken and his back injured, and he lay for hours on the cold muddy riverbank until help came. He died four days later, around December 30, 1866. Mary Louisa McMurran lived at her family home, Woodlands, until her death in 1891.

From 1866 until 1901, under the ownership of Elizabeth and George Malin Davis, Melrose was practically unoccupied, except occasionally by Julia Davis, their daughter, who inherited the house in 1877, and her husband, Dr. Stephen Kelly. In 1883, when Julia and her father died, Melrose and several other mansions and plantations passed to her six-year-old son, George Malin Davis Kelly. The boy's father, Dr. Kelly, preferred to live in New York, so Melrose was left in the care of two former Davis family slaves, Jane Johnson and Alice Sims. Johnson and Sims and their families lived in the outbuildings and cared for the property for many years; had they not been on the grounds, it is likely that looters or vandals would have invaded Melrose.

In 1901 George Malin Davis Kelly and his wife, Ethel Moore Kelly, living in New York, decided to use Melrose as a seasonal home. When they inspected the house, they found dust covers over the furniture, silver stored in a trunk, and china still in the pantry—everything just as it was left in 1883. Considering the poverty, chaos, and desperation around the south in the years after the Civil War, even among the formerly wealthy, it is a near miracle that the house was undisturbed.

Considering the poverty, chaos, and desperation around the south in the years after the Civil War, it is a near miracle that the house was undisturbed.

George and Ethel Kelly lived at Melrose full-time beginning in 1910, and chose to restore the house rather than remodel it, a decision that many architectural historians find remarkable and even enlightened. It is due in large part to the protection of Jane Johnson and Alice Sims, and then the Kellys, that Melrose looks today essentially as it did when Mississippi seceded from the Union.

George Kelly died in 1946, and Mrs. Kelly lived at Melrose until her death in 1975 at the age of ninety-seven. The following year, Mr. and Mrs. John Callon of Natchez bought the house and restored it. The Callons sold Melrose and eighty wooded acres around it to the National Park Service in 1990, at which time the house became the centerpiece of the newly created Natchez National Historical Park. In addition to Melrose, the park owns the original site of Fort Rosalie (though the French fort is no longer there) and the William Johnson House on State Street in downtown Natchez. William Johnson was a free African American, a successful barber and entrepreneur in the mid 1800s, and his diary has been published. Johnson's admirable three-story brick town house was built in 1841, a time when the city's population of 4,800 consisted of 2,994 whites, 1,599 slaves, and 207 free blacks. ◆

Mesa Verde

SOUTHWESTERN COLORADO

I
n the recesses and alcoves of precipitous canyon walls at Mesa Verde, ancient cliff dwellings look down upon the surrounding landscape. These cliff dwellings, some of which contain more than one hundred separate rooms, are the long-abandoned residences of the Anasazi, a Navajo name that means "ancient ones." What we know of the Anasazi, through both anthropological and archaeological investigation, is considerable; they lived and flourished at Mesa Verde for more than 600 years. They were sophisticated basketmakers and potters and farmers and builders, a well-adapted people in an arid, sparsely populated country. But what we do not know is equally noteworthy, for the most perplexing mysteries have yet to be solved: What compelled the Anasazi to leave their homes on the mesa tops and climb high up into the cliffs? Why did they inhabit these cliffs for so short a time—not even one hundred years—before abandoning Mesa Verde completely in a span of less than two generations? Though the Cliff Dwellers' motivations may never be understood, their spectacular architecture can be, for they left behind one of the best preserved, most notable archaeological sites in the world.

Mesa *verde* in English means green table, a description that captures well this 8,500-foot plateau that rises up from the Mancas and Montezuma valleys of southwestern Colorado. Mesa Verde is part of a vast upland of deep canyons and plateaus, of brilliantly colored cliff walls, of green junipers and piñon pines—all of which distinguish the Four Corners region, so-named because it marks the meeting place of the state boundaries of Colorado, Utah, Arizona, and New Mexico.

The first evidence of human occupation of the Mesa Verde area dates back 10,000 years, and the Paleo-Indians living then are believed to be the ancestors of the Anasazi. Archaeologists divide the Anasazi era into two historical periods, the Basketmaker Period and the Pueblo Period, and among these two categories are several subcategories.

The *Early Basketmakers* (1000–500 B.C.E. to 500 C.E.) were an Anasazi people living in the low-lying valleys of the Four Corners area. Sometime in the first century C.E., they moved

mesa: a small, high plateau or flat tableland with steep sides, especially in the southwestern United States.

What compelled the Anasazi to leave their homes on the mesa tops and climb high up into the cliffs?

Cliff dwellings at Mesa Verde in Colorado.

nomadic: traveling from place to place with no fixed home.

adobe: sun-dried brick.

from a primarily **nomadic**, hunter-gatherer society to a more agricultural society. Though they probably still lived in small communities without permanent housing, around this time they began practicing floodwater farming. They cultivated maize and squash and gathered wild seeds and plants. As the name suggests, they were accomplished basketmakers, which they wove from split willow, rabbitbrush, or skunkbush. Baskets were lined with pitch for waterproofing and used for everything from water carrying and grain storage to cooking.

Around 500 C.E. the *Modified Basketmakers* began inhabiting single-family, permanent dwellings. They built "pit-houses" with rounded, sunken floors dug two to three feet into the earth and enclosed by timbered walls and **adobe** roofs. They planted beans and pumpkins now also, and they stored their food in sunken pits, called *cists*, covered over by a stone slab. Crude pottery, shaped like gourds, was also developed.

Around 700 two remarkable shifts occurred in the lives of the Anasazi. First, they began living at a considerably higher elevation, atop the mesas of the region, which rose from 5,000 to 11,000 feet above sea level. This move coincided with a signifi-

cant architectural advancement: the construction of stone surface dwellings. Archaeologists refer to this era as the *Early
Pueblo Period*. The Anasazi of this period flourished, living in
elaborate cities made up of interconnected houses, courtyards
and thriving, outlying agricultural fields. They were experienced builders, constructing tall, straight walls of carefully
placed sandstone bricks and a mix of mud and water mortar.
More rain fell at this higher elevation, which meant better
farming and a longer planting season. At this time also the
turkey was domesticated, whose meat provided food and whose
feathers provided material for clothing.

Notable technological advances were made during the period as well. Pottery improved and diversified, and elaborately
decorated pots, bowls, canteens, ladles, jars, and mugs replaced
basketry almost entirely. Bow and arrow hunting superseded
spears, and wooden **spindles** facilitated weaving. The Anasazi   **spindle**: a slender rod or
constructed sophisticated water reservoirs, fed by a series of   pin used in spinning.
ditches that captured rainwater. This water was then used both
for extensive irrigation and as a community water supply.

Not only did the building materials and location of the
Anasazi's dwellings change, but so too did their interior design.
Between the Basketmaker and Pueblo periods, Anasazi houses
began to incorporate a circular, additional room, called a *kiva*.
Kiva is a Hopi word meaning "ceremonial room." Kivas in early
pit-houses often consisted only of small, shallow holes, called
sipapus, dug into the floor of the dwelling's only room. But kivas
in the later Pueblo period were set apart in separate rooms of
larger, communal, multifamily dwellings. Most of our understanding of these chambers comes from the study of modern
Pueblo peoples, for whom kivas still have spiritual significance.
Archaeologists speculate that early *sipapus* symbolized the place
where the Corn Mothers, ancient supernatural beings, emerged
from the earth and gave life to all the plants, animals, and people. During kiva ceremonies, the people gave thanks to the
Corn Mothers and prayed for rain or an abundant harvest or for
social good.

During the *Classic Pueblo Period* (1050–1300), architectural
construction advanced still more, and immense, multistoried "-
apartment-like" dwellings dominated the mesa tops. Some structures rose to as many as five stories and housed hundreds of people. Kivas in these houses were often located on above-ground
stories, reached by ladder through a smoke hole in the ceiling.
The population of the Anasazi swelled during this period, and

National Park Service

Mesa Verde, like many of America's historical sites, is administered by the National Park Service. The U.S. Congress established the National Park Service, within the Department of the Interior, in an act signed by President Woodrow Wilson on August 25, 1916. The new agency was to provide strong central administration of the loosely managed national parks and monuments. The act declared that the fundamental purpose of the parks was "to conserve the scenery and the natural and historic objects and the wildlife therein and to provide for the enjoyment of the same in such manner and by such means as will leave them unimpaired for the enjoyment of future generations."

Over the years the areas under the management of the National Park Service came to include recreational and cultural areas as well as natural wonders and historic monuments, which became known collectively as the National Park System. Since many of the areas administered by the National Park Service had been set aside as federal preserves before the establishment of the service—the first being Yellowstone National Park in 1872—Congress in 1970 designated 1872 as the date of the origin of the National Park System. Recognizing the expanded purpose of the National Park System, it declared that the areas were "preserved and managed for the benefit and inspiration of all the people."

some communities contained more than 1,000 people. Extensive trade routes developed also, and roads linked perhaps seventy distinct Anasazi communities. Archaeological excavations at Mesa Verde have revealed seashells taken from the Pacific Ocean, thousands of miles distant.

But at this point, the archaeological understanding of the Anasazi begins to unravel. After nearly 600 years of Anasazi village occupation on the plateaus of Mesa Verde, the Anasazi abandoned their multistory residences and began scaling the steep canyon walls, living in natural cave recesses in the cliffs. No satisfactory, conclusive explanations have been offered for this dramatic lifestyle change. Some speculate that the Anasazi were driven to the cliffs by attacking invaders, perhaps by another Anasazi community elsewhere, perhaps by a Native American tribe of different ancestry. While this hypothesis may be the most plausible, investigation and excavation in the area have revealed neither the presence of another tribe nor the burial evidence of violence attributable to war.

Whatever the cause, some major disruption or tension must have befallen the Anasazi, for the cliff dwellings were far less practical than their multistory homes on the ground. While more defensible, it must have been far more difficult to trans-

> **Archaeological excavations at Mesa Verde have revealed seashells taken from the Pacific Ocean, thousands of miles distant.**

port water and other supplies up the cliff walls, and access for the elderly must have taken significant ingenuity. Quarters in the cliff dwellings appear to have been very close, and some caves may have contained as many as 800 people. At such high altitudes, the caves were damp and cold in winter, and more difficult to warm by fire. (In many rooms at Mesa Verde entire walls and ceilings are blackened by smoke.)

Most of the cliff dwellings were built during a remarkably brief, ten-year period, from 1230 to 1240, and these dwellings were occupied for no more than one or two generations; by 1290 the entire area was abandoned. Again, no conclusive theory has been offered to explain the evacuation. Some argue that the Anasazi may have been forced to leave by outside raiders. Some theorize that they were drawn to recently discovered lands to the south and west that offered a milder climate and easier subsistence living. Others speculate that a severe drought struck the area, and the people left only after years and years of crop failure. Indeed, tree rings examined from this time indicate that a period of drought did accompany these years, but the Anasazi had weathered droughts of similar proportion in earlier generations, and so this explanation is still found lacking. Still others speculate that, in addition to drought, crop failure may have resulted from erosion and soil depletion, due to poor agricultural practice. But this is unlikely, for the Anasazi had farmed the area successfully for more than 600 years, and no definitive evidence to support this soil depletion theory exists. Today, the cliff dwellers remain an archaeological riddle that may never be fully solved. After hundreds of years of successful adaptation and sophistication, what possibly could have precipitated such a hastened change and abandonment?

The cliff dwellings at Mesa Verde were first discovered by whites in 1874, and in 1906 the Mesa Verde National Park was founded. It was then, and still is, the only National Park established to preserve the works and culture of a people. At such heights, the cliff dwellings at Mesa Verde have been relatively untouched by erosion, and so are extremely well preserved. Visitors today to the park can climb multiple stairs and ladders and crawl through tunnels from room to ancient room. Both ranger-guided and self-guided tours are available, and include Cliff Palace, in Cliff Canyon, with 200 rooms and twenty-three kivas; Spruce Tree House, in Spruce Tree Canyon, with 114 rooms and eight kivas; and Balcony House, in Soda Canyon, with thirty-eight rooms and two kivas.

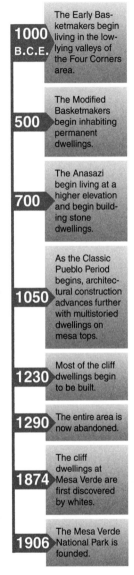

1000 B.C.E. The Early Basketmakers begin living in the low-lying valleys of the Four Corners area.

500 The Modified Basketmakers begin inhabiting permanent dwellings.

700 The Anasazi begin living at a higher elevation and begin building stone dwellings.

1050 As the Classic Pueblo Period begins, architectural construction advances further with multistoried dwellings on mesa tops.

1230 Most of the cliff dwellings begin to be built.

1290 The entire area is now abandoned.

1874 The cliff dwellings at Mesa Verde are first discovered by whites.

1906 The Mesa Verde National Park is founded.

Today, twenty-four Native American tribes trace their ancestry back to the Anasazi people. Like the Anasazi of the Classic Pueblo Period, today's Pueblo tribes living in the Four Corners area of Arizona and New Mexico are an agricultural people. Many occupy multiterraced, adobe brick structures, with upper level interiors reached by moveable ladders and by trapdoors in roofs and ceilings. Pueblo villages often contain one or more kivas, used for ceremonial purposes similar to those of their Anasazi ancestors. The Pueblo people of today are highly regarded for their traditional art, and their pottery and woven baskets are prized by museums and art collectors. ◆

Monticello

CHARLOTTESVILLE, VIRGINIA

Monticello, Italian for "little mountain," was the home of Thomas Jefferson, drafter of the Declaration of Independence and America's second president. Jefferson's home is part of a 600-acre estate situated on the summit of one of Virginia's Blue Ridge Mountains overlooking the Rivanna River near Charlottesville, Virginia. Jefferson himself designed and built Monticello, and lived there off and on for fifty-three years.

Jefferson was born in Albemarle County, not far from Monticello, on April 13, 1743. He was the eldest son of Peter Jefferson, who died when Thomas was only fourteen. Peter Jefferson had been a surveyor, and his son inherited his surveying and mapping abilities. Self-taught as an architect, Jefferson was a brilliant draughtsman and mathematician, renowned for the precision of his plans. He greatly admired classical architecture and imitated Greek and Roman models. "Architecture is my delight," he once stated, "but it is an enthusiasm of which I am not ashamed, as its object is to improve the taste of my countrymen, to increase their reputation, to reconcile them to the rest of the world. . . ."

The original Monticello was a humble brick bachelor cottage, known now as the Honeymoon Cottage or South Pavilion, on the estate's west lawn. Jefferson began construction on the cottage in 1770, and brought his bride, Martha Wayles Skelton, to live there in 1772. In 1796, after spending five years in Paris as United States minister to France, and three in Philadelphia, Jefferson returned to Monticello and completely

"Whether I retire to bed early or late, I rise with the sun."

Thomas Jefferson, 1780

altered plans for his home. His years in Paris influenced Jefferson's ideas on architecture and have left their mark on Monticello. Jefferson came to admire Greek and Roman architecture, and his design for Monticello shows the influence of Italian Renaissance architect Andrea Palladio. In addition, Jefferson was moved by the construction of Paris's Hôtel de Salm (now the Palace of the Legion of Honor) to abandon his original two-story house for one that looks as though it is a single-story high, though it is actually three, like the hotel. The windows of the bedrooms on the two upper floors of Monticello are only half the height of the ground floor rooms, in imitation of an elegant Parisian townhouse.

Many of the materials from which the house is built were found on the property. Stones were quarried from the mountain, and bricks baked in kilns on the estate. Timbers were cut from the surrounding forests; nails were made in Jefferson's own nailery. Dressed stone and window glass were imported from England, however. Much of the furniture and furnishings Jefferson acquired while abroad were brought to Monticello.

Visitors to Monticello are struck by the separation of public from private space, which not only reflects the taste of the time and place in which it was built, but also reveals the extraordinary split in Jefferson between the public and the private man. Though he was a Virginia patrician and cavalier, he was also a pragmatic pioneer. He led a very public life but was intensely private and reticent. Sternly moral, he was also an epicurean who delighted in pleasure. Authoritarian and exacting, he could also be tender and compassionate.

The public rooms of Monticello, which include a dining room and tearoom, are located to the right of the main entrance. On the left of the entrance are Jefferson's private quarters, his bedroom and his cabinet or study, the latter looking out on the library and a greenhouse on the south side. Unlike most mansions of the time, Monticello lacks a grand central staircase; staircases leading to the upper rooms are narrow, steep, and almost hidden because Jefferson thought stairs wasted space. The dome room, which Jefferson called his "sky room," probably served as storage space.

Jefferson loved to work with his hands and kept a room with a carpenter's bench in it. Among gadgets that he designed or actually made at Monticello are a seven-day calendar clock, a weathervane, a chaise longue with an attached candle for reading, a revolving coatrack, and a polygraph that made copies of

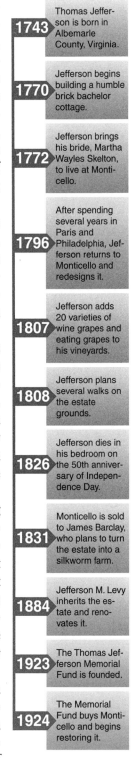

1743 Thomas Jefferson is born in Albemarle County, Virginia.

1770 Jefferson begins building a humble brick bachelor cottage.

1772 Jefferson brings his bride, Martha Wayles Skelton, to live at Monticello.

1796 After spending several years in Paris and Philadelphia, Jefferson returns to Monticello and redesigns it.

1807 Jefferson adds 20 varieties of wine grapes and eating grapes to his vineyards.

1808 Jefferson plans several walks on the estate grounds.

1826 Jefferson dies in his bedroom on the 50th anniversary of Independence Day.

1831 Monticello is sold to James Barclay, who plans to turn the estate into a silkworm farm.

1884 Jefferson M. Levy inherits the estate and renovates it.

1923 The Thomas Jefferson Memorial Fund is founded.

1924 The Memorial Fund buys Monticello and begins restoring it.

Monticello in
Charlottesville, Virginia.

original documents—long before the days of Xerox. Monticello is also crammed with objects reflecting Jefferson's interests. In the hall are mammoth bones and tusks, buffalo hides, and Indian artifacts; about 150 prints and paintings hang on the walls; and busts and statues decorate the rooms. Jefferson loved to read and nearly every room contains books.

Jefferson's enthusiasm for landscape gardening was as great as his passion for architecture. Although he came to dislike British Georgian architecture, he loved English gardens. Thus his neoclassical mansion with its white dome and columns, red brick walls and white trim is surrounded by a romantic landscape and lush gardens full of exotic plants from many parts of the world. In his orchards Jefferson planted apple, pear, peach, nectarine, fig, pomegranate, mulberry, and almond trees; he sent abroad for orange trees, olives and acacias. With the help of a friend he planted thirty vines on the south side of the house above the orchards in 1774; in 1807 he added twenty more different varieties of wine grapes and eating grapes imported from as far away as Bordeaux, Burgundy, and Champagne.

In 1808 Jefferson laid out his serpentine walk around the mansion's lawn and four roundabouts or circular walks cut around the mountain. Jefferson also devised his own "ha-ha," or cattle barrier, comprising a concealed wall and ditch for keeping livestock away from the domestic quarters.

Monticello was a plantation as well as a country house, and the estate was built and maintained largely by slave labor. From the first, its owner tried to make Monticello self-sufficient. Slaves at Monticello were trained to raise cash crops such as corn, wheat, and tobacco; nail making and metalworking were carried on as economic enterprises. When the first Monticello was built, Jefferson owned about forty slaves. In constructing his first home he was chiefly dependent on hired craftsmen. As the years went by, however, slaves played a greater role in the building of the second Monticello. It was Jefferson's practice to apprentice young male slaves to white craftsmen; as a result, some of Jefferson's slaves became good craftsmen themselves. Nowhere is the separation of private from public space or of the formal from the working parts of the estate more apparent than in the location and design of the slave quarters and outbuildings. It was customary in the south at that time to keep kitchens separate from houses for the sake of safety from fire. The "dependencies" or working quarters at Monticello, eventually numbering nineteen different buildings, were constructed in long wings stretching out on either side of the house but removed from it and built into the hillside beneath terraces. Mulberry Row, where mulberry trees were planted, was the site of the slave quarters. This part of the estate comprised barns, stables, a law office, nailery, kitchens, pantry, buttery, summer dairy, laundry, and smoke rooms.

Jefferson's father-in-law, John Wayles, had three wives; when the last one died, he took a female slave, Betty Hemings, as his mistress and had six children with her. The youngest of these children was Sally Hemings, born in 1873, the year of John Wayles's death. When Wayles died, Jefferson inherited ownership of his slaves, including the Hemings family, who came to live at Monticello. During his lifetime Jefferson's political opponents claimed that after his wife died, Sally Hemings became his mistress and eventually bore five children to him. The eldest, Tom, died in infancy; the others were three boys—Beverly, Madison, and Eston; and a girl, Harriet. Madison Hemings later testified that Jefferson was his natural father. Generations of Jefferson's legal descendants denied that their famous ancestor engaged in sexual relations with a slave. They claim instead that Jefferson's nephew Peter Carr had fathered Sally Hemings's children. More recent research, including comparisons of the DNA

> *"The letters of a person, especially one whose business has been chiefly transacted by letters, form the only full and genuine journal of his life."*
>
> Thomas Jefferson, 1823

of Jefferson's white and black descendants, appears to confirm that Sally Hemings was indeed Jefferson's mistress, and that her five children were also Jefferson's. At his death, Jefferson possessed more than eighty slaves. He set some of them free in his will, but because he was in debt, they were not liberated.

Jefferson died in his bedroom on the fiftieth anniversary of Independence Day, 1826. By this time, because Jefferson had become ill and was deeply in debt, a grandson had taken over management of the estate. In 1831 Monticello was sold to James Barclay, a Charlottesville druggist who planned to turn the estate into a silkworm farm. When this project failed, the house, its outbuildings, and 200 acres were sold for $2,500 to Uriah P. Levy. An admirer of Jefferson, Levy spent most of his time in New York, so that the estate soon fell into decay. Although Levy bequeathed Monticello to the nation as an agricultural school for children, the estate was confiscated under the Confederacy in 1864 and the property broken up. In 1884 Jefferson M. Levy, nephew of Uriah, inherited Monticello and renovated it.

At the turn of the century, noted orator and statesman William Jennings Bryan, an ardent Jeffersonian, embraced the cause of reclaiming Monticello for the nation. Some years later Maud Littleton formed the Monticello Memorial Foundation. Jefferson Levy was made several offers for Monticello, including one for a million dollars; he refused. When he finally agreed to sell the estate for half that amount, the ensuing arguments over details of sale and management shelved its actual transfer, and the estate eventually fell on the market again. Meanwhile, the Thomas Jefferson Memorial Fund had superseded the Monticello Memorial Foundation. This nonprofit corporation, founded in 1923, managed to purchase Monticello the next year and begin restoring the buildings and gardens. More than half a million people visit the estate every year. Monticello is depicted on the obverse of the Jefferson nickel coin. ◆

> *"I have compared notes with Mr. Adams on the score of progeny, and find I am ahead of him, and think I am in a fair way to keep so. I have 10 1/2 grandchildren, and 2 3/4 great-grand-children; and these fractions will ere long become units."*
>
> Thomas Jefferson, c. 1820

Mount Rushmore

Black Hills, South Dakota

Majestic portraits of four American presidents protrude from Mount Rushmore, in the Black Hills of South Dakota. Visitors marvel at this shrine to democracy

and the vision of one artist, in the form of sixty-foot-high faces standing some 500 feet above the ground.

The striking visages of presidents George Washington, Thomas Jefferson, Theodore Roosevelt, and Abraham Lincoln were the brainchild of the sculptor John Gutzon Borglum, born in Idaho in 1871, the son of Danish immigrants. A student of the famous French sculptor Auguste Rodin, Borglum established a prolific career as an artist on the east coast of the United States. The artist had executed works on a smaller scale of figures from America's past and present, including a portraits of presidents such as Woodrow Wilson, and dynamic sculptures depicting battles. His work *Mares of Diomedes* was the first sculpture by an American artist that the Metropolitan Museum of Art purchased. When invited to embark on Mount Rushmore, he was working on a giant granite **relief** sculpture—a monument to the Confederacy—on the side of Stone Mountain outside of Atlanta, Georgia.

relief: the projection of figures and forms from a flat surface, so that they stand wholly or partly free.

In 1924 Borglum answered the plea of Doane Robinson, the superintendent of the South Dakota State Historical Society, for a sculptor to create a massive stone monument in the mountains in South Dakota. Robinson worked tirelessly in 1923 and

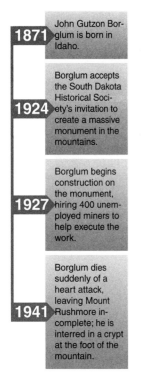

1871 John Gutzon Borglum is born in Idaho.

1924 Borglum accepts the South Dakota Historical Society's invitation to create a massive monument in the mountains.

1927 Borglum begins construction on the monument, hiring 400 unemployed miners to help execute the work.

1941 Borglum dies suddenly of a heart attack, leaving Mount Rushmore incomplete; he is interred in a crypt at the foot of the mountain.

1924, speaking before groups and writing letters to rally support for a great mountain memorial that would attract people to his home state, "colossal art, in a scale with the people whose life it expresses." When one of Robinson's letters reached Borglum in 1924 during his work at Stone Mountain—a project that had gone sour due to disagreements with local officials—the artist jumped at the opportunity to move his studio to the Black Hills of South Dakota.

Doane Robinson had conceived of depicting western heroes such as Custer, Buffalo Bill, and Lewis and Clark, in a mountainous region of South Dakota called the Needles. But Borglum had in mind something more national in scope. He wrote: "We believe the dimensions of national heartbeats are greater than village impulses, greater than city demands, greater than state dreams or ambitions. Therefore, we believe a nation's memorial should, like Washington, Jefferson, Lincoln and Roosevelt, have a serenity, a nobility, a power that reflects the gods who inspired them and suggests the gods they have become."

Borglum chose a solid granite outcropping on a cliff known as Mount Rushmore, located in Harney National Forest near the mining town of Keystone. He chose the site because of its favorable southeastern exposure, its solid granite surface perfect for sculpting, and its dramatic setting amidst a group of 7,000-foot mountains. Robinson, along with Senator Peter Norbeck and Congressman William Williamson, helped secure permission to begin the sculpture. Supporters of the project began raising money for the work. When President Calvin Coolidge took an extended summer holiday to the Black Hills in 1927, Borglum and Norbeck convinced him to formally dedicate Mount Rushmore. During his speech, Coolidge referred to the mountain as a "national shrine" and pledged federal support for the sculpture project.

The sculptor began this mammoth project in 1927 at the age of sixty. He hired 400 unemployed miners in the area to help execute the work, which continued on and off between 1927 and 1941 as funding and weather conditions permitted. In addition to working on the presidential faces themselves, the workers set out dynamite, operated pneumatic drills, and constructed buildings and roads in the desolate, uninhabited area. Borglum and his assistants removed 450,000 tons of granite from the mountainside, most of it with precise dynamite blasting that combined Borglum's experience at sculpting mountainsides with the workers' expertise in mining. Borglum executed a

The Badlands

The Badlands are a severely eroded region of steep hills, deep gulleys, and shallow canyons near Mount Rushmore in western South Dakota. The area's distinctive land formations were created in ancient times by the sudden descent of ash, sand, and earth, perhaps borne by wind, from volcanic eruptions in the far northwest that buried several hundred square miles of land. Water erosion later carved this material into many fantastic forms. The volcanic flow engulfed vast herds of Paleolithic animals where they had been feeding in the swamps, the remains of which were later exposed by erosion.

The federal government established the region as the Badlands National Monument in 1939 and built a system of highways into the more scenic regions of the park. The Badlands were discovered by fur traders early in the nineteenth century, and for more than 150 years scientific societies, museums, and educational institutions have engaged in uncovering the buried paleontological treasures so long entombed. Included in these relics are the fossils of mammoths, elephants, camels, horses, and many other mammals whose descendants still exist.

The Sioux Indians took refuge in the vastness of the Badlands when pursued by the U.S. Army in the Messiah War of 1890. The term "badlands" is now used to describe any area with a similarly eroded topography, as in North Dakota.

1:12 scale model of the sculpture, whose measurements were transferred to the actual monument. After the work was roughed out by blasting, workers executed the details with a special pneumatic drill according to Borglum's instructions.

For Borglum, the grouping of the four presidents represented the first 150 years of American history, and in his words, "the formal rendering of the philosophy of our government into granite on a mountain peak." George Washington, first president of the United States, occupies the most prominent position, followed by Thomas Jefferson, president-philosopher and author of the Declaration of Independence. Abraham Lincoln, sixteenth president and Borglum's favorite historical leader, occupies the far right edge of the cliff. Theodore Roosevelt, twenty-sixth president, may seem an unlikely choice for the fourth portrait, but Borglum was a longtime friend and supporter of the president. The artist studied famous painted and sculpted portraits of Washington, Jefferson, and Lincoln, as well as life masks (plaster casts of the presidents' faces made during their lifetime) of each man. Borglum sculpted Roosevelt's face from memory, perhaps accounting for a less idealized and more "human" rendering.

In addition to the dramatic setting, the most compelling aspect of the work is its sheer scale. Each head is fifty to seventy feet high, equivalent to a six-story building. Each of George Washington's eyes is approximately eleven feet across, his nose is twenty feet long, his mouth eighteen feet wide. If they had been sculpted in full-length, each man would stand approximately 465 feet tall.

Mount Rushmore National Memorial remains incomplete, as Borglum died suddenly of a heart attack in 1941. Originally Borglum envisioned that the colossal portraits would continue to the waistline, but the sculptor's death halted the project. Also, Borglum had planned for a Hall of Records, a huge vault in the canyon lying behind Lincoln's head, which would have housed records of the memorial, and copies of documents such as the Declaration of Independence and the Constitution. The sculptor's son, Lincoln Borglum—named for the sixteenth president—refined the sculpture for seven months after his father's death. When the project was finally abandoned, the total bill amounted to $989,992.32. Borglum was interred in a crypt at the foot of Mount Rushmore.

From the beginning, the monument proved controversial. At first, Borglum's funding fluctuated with the political and economic whims of the country, and funding was nearly squelched at the approach of World War II. For as many visitors who see the monument as a glorious symbol of democracy, at least as many critics have ridiculed the project as an egocentric artist's expensive flight of fancy. Some Native Americans of the Sioux nation, for whom the Black Hills are sacred, have voiced resentment at the appropriation of this territory for sculpting images of American presidents, and view it as a symbol of oppression rather than one of freedom. Ironically, Borglum spoke out against injustices toward native peoples, at the time of his death, had begun plans for a mountain monument to the Sioux nation nearby in South Dakota.

Today, Mount Rushmore is administered by the National Park Service, and the Mount Rushmore Society works to preserve the monument. Nearly 2.5 million visitors trek to the Black Hills of South Dakota annually to see Mount Rushmore. Visitors to Mount Rushmore can tour Borglum's mountainside studio for a glimpse of plaster models and tools he used to execute the project. They can also walk the Presidential Trail, a mountainside gallery that offers stunning views of the four faces against a natural setting of pine, aspen, spruce, and birch trees. ◆

"We, here in America, hold in our hands the hopes of the world, the fate of the coming years; and shame and disgrace will be ours if in our eyes the light of high resolve is dimmed, if we trail in the dust the golden hopes of men."
Theodore Roosevelt, 1912

Mount Vernon

VIRGINIA

Mount Vernon, the home of America's first president, occupies over 500 acres along the Potomac River a few miles south of Washington, D.C. George Washington made his mark on every inch of this historic plantation, which served as his principal residence for forty-five years. Though his military and political career drew him away often, George Washington's heart remained at Mount Vernon throughout his life.

Mount Vernon began as a small house built by George Washington's father on 8,000 acres of land. The house was passed on to Washington's older half brother, Lawrence, who named the estate after his commanding officer, Admiral Edward Vernon of the British Navy. Washington became master of Mount Vernon at the age of nineteen, after his brother succumbed to an illness.

During his residency, Washington built five complete farms and a fishery on the property, each with its own staff. Like most plantations of the era, Mount Vernon was self-sufficient and relied on slave labor for all of its operations. The farms supplied everything that was needed to live, including crops and livestock such as sheep, cows, hogs, and horses. Some slaves were trained as boatmen, carpenters, shoemakers, house servants, or millers, but approximately three-quarters worked six days a week in the vast fields of Mount Vernon. The workers made their own clothes, shoes, furniture, candles, and soap. At the time of his father's death in 1743, Washington had already inherited ten slaves along with 500 acres of land. In 1799 316 slaves worked on the estate. In accordance with Washington's will, all were emancipated at the time of his death.

The main plantation house with its large **piazza** overlooks the Potomac. The elegant residence had been constructed in 1735, but Washington enlarged it substantially between 1759 and 1787. The building takes advantage of the natural beauty of the site, with **colonnades** offering views over the river. Likewise, the piazza unites outdoor and indoor living spaces; Washington, his family, and guests spent many hours there.

Many of the furnishings and other household effects at Mount Vernon are authentic. The main dining room is the

"No estate in America is more pleasantly situated than this." George Washington, journal, 1793

piazza: a large, covered porch.

colonnade: a series of columns set at regular intervals that support a roof.

The west façade of Mount Vernon, George Washington's Virginia home.

Palladian: revived classical style in architecture based on the works of Andrea Palladio.

largest and most ornate room in the house, striking for its green walls—selected by Washington himself—as well as the unusual depictions of crops, tools, and farm animals that decorate the plaster moldings. The **Palladian** window and furniture reflect eighteenth-century taste.

Washington made many improvements to the main house. He added a study to the house, which became a private retreat from the busy activities of the plantation. There he penned letters and managed the plantation's diverse operations from a room with an austere, utilitarian décor befitting his frugal character. George and Martha Washington added a master bedroom that provided some privacy from the estate's many visitors. The room doubled as Martha's office, and there she oversaw the operation of the household, and taught her children and grandchildren to read and sew.

Washington had been trained as a surveyor, so it is no surprise that the grounds of Mount Vernon were a showplace of the time. Washington replaced all the plantation's outbuildings, landscaped expansive gardens, and created new lawns around the plantation. In the upper garden he maintained a greenhouse full of exotic plants and flowers sent to him by dignitaries and heads of state from around the world. The lower or kitchen garden, tended by two to four slaves, provided fresh produce for the main house year-round.

At Mount Vernon, Washington also demonstrated his diverse skills as an architect, builder, and experimental farmer. He applied new techniques of crop rotation that transformed the former tobacco plantation into a diverse farm of wheat, corn, and potatoes. He also designed and built a unique sixteen-sided "treading barn" in 1794, which was used to exercise horses and thresh wheat at the same time.

We know much about the history of Mount Vernon thanks to the detailed journals of George Washington himself. Born February 22, 1732, in Westmoreland County, Virginia, Washington kept regular journals as early as his teenage years. As a sixteen-year-old visiting what were then frontier lands in the Shenandoah Valley, Virginia, he describes sleeping out in the open, as well as talking with Native Americans, sharing their food, and watching their dances in the flickering firelight. At nineteen Washington joined the Virginia militia, rising through the ranks as an officer aiding a British victory in the French and Indian War. Four bullets ripped his coat during the scuffle, but he emerged from battle uninjured.

When George married Martha Dandridge Custis—a widow with two young children—on January 6, 1759, Mount Vernon became their home. The couple entertained many guests and relatives at the plantation, where Washington enjoyed fox hunting, billiards, cards, and dancing.

By the 1760s and 1770s, however, Washington was often gone from home for long periods as opposition to British rule rose and the events of the American Revolution unfolded. He often traveled to Williamsburg, then Virginia's capital, where he served in the House of Burgesses. Later he journeyed to Philadelphia, where he was elected to the Second Continental Congress and finally as commander in chief of the Continental Army in 1775. By then, resentment toward British rule had reached a height. Having fought on the side of the British two decades earlier, Washington led his revolutionary forces to a victory over British troops at Yorktown, Virginia, in 1781.

When a peace treaty was signed with the British in 1783, Washington surprised many observers by resigning his post and returning to Mount Vernon to live privately outside of the public

1732 George Washington is born in Westmoreland County, Virginia.

1735 George Washington's father builds Mount Vernon as a small house on 8,000 acres.

1743 George Washington inherits 10 slaves and 500 acres.

1759 George Washington marries Martha Dandridge Custis; they move into Mount Vernon.

1783 After the Revolutionary War, Washington resigns from the army and returns to Mount Vernon.

1789 Washington learns that he has been elected president and reluctantly leaves his home for the inauguration.

1796 Washington retires to Mount Vernon.

1799 Washington dies at Mount Vernon; in accordance with his will, all 316 slaves are freed.

1983 Mount Vernon's slave memorial is replaced with a new one designed by Howard University students.

eye. His retirement was short-lived, however. Delegates asked Washington to preside over a constitutional convention in Philadelphia, which resulted in the drafting of the American Constitution. When it was time to elect a leader for this newly formed government, Washington was chosen unanimously. Leaving home for his inauguration in 1789, the reluctant president wrote in his journal: "About 10 o'clock I bade adieu to Mount Vernon, to private life, and to domestic felicity, and with a mind oppressed with more anxious and painful sensations than I have words to express, set out for New York in company with Mr. Thompson, and Colonel Humprhies, with the best dispositions to render service to my country in obedience to its call, but with less hope of answering its expectations."

During his two terms as president, Washington orchestrated the design of a new capital named for him. Urged to continue with a third term, Washington turned the reigns over to newly elected John Adams in 1796, and finally retired to Mount Vernon, his longtime wish. However, this idyllic life lasted only three years. After riding through a winter storm, Washington fell ill and died on December 14, 1799, at Mount Vernon.

George and Martha Washington are buried in a tomb at the end of a brick path on a hill overlooking the Potomac. Two marble sarcophagi lie side by side within a brick structure enclosed by a wrought-iron gate. Washington left explicit instructions in his will about the construction of the tomb, which was to replace the original family vault, explaining: "I desire that a new one of Brick, and upon a larger Scale, may be built at the foot of what is commonly called the Vineyard Inclosure . . . ." Nearby, the slave burial ground houses the remains of 50 to 100 slaves, who were commemorated with a memorial marker in 1929, later replaced in 1983 with one designed by students from Howard University.

Many important events took place at Mount Vernon. On April 14, 1789, Washington learned that he had been officially elected president in Mount Vernon's formal dining room. Ten years later, he died at the age of sixty-seven in his bed in the master bedroom he and Martha had designed.

Mount Vernon has always been one of America's most revered and most visited places. During the Civil War, it was considered neutral ground and was never fired upon. Today, when naval ships traveling the Potomac pass Mount Vernon, their flags are lowered to half-mast and the crewmen stand at attention. ◆

> *"About 10 o'clock I bade adieu to Mount Vernon, to private life, and to domestic felicity, and with a mind oppressed with more anxious and painful sensations than I have words to express, set out for New York . . . with the best dispositions to render service to my country in obedience to its call, but with less hope of answering its expectations.*
>
> George Washington, journal, April 16, 1789

O.K. Corral

TOMBSTONE, ARIZONA

Tombstone, Arizona, calls itself "The Town Too Tough To Die." Located in the southeast of the state, close to the Mexican border, Tombstone became famous as a "Wild West" town in the 1800s, especially for the legendary shootout at the O.K. Corral. Today, visitors from far and wide come to Tombstone to experience the spirit of the old west, so deep a part of the American identity.

In the early afternoon of October 26, 1881, the three Earp Brothers—Virgil, Wyatt, and Morgan—along with John Henry (Doc) Holliday, confronted suspected cattle rustlers Joseph Isaac (Ike) Clanton, William (Billy) Claiborne, William (Billy) Clanton, Robert Finley (Frank) McLaury, and Thomas Clarke McLaury in a vacant lot facing Fremont Street in Tombstone. In the point-blank shootout that followed, an estimated thirty shots were fired in twenty to thirty seconds. Tom and Frank McLaury and Billy Clanton were killed; Ike Clanton and Billy Claiborne ran; and Virgil and Morgan Earp received leg and shoulder wounds.

In the point-blank shootout, an estimated thirty shots were fired in twenty to thirty seconds.

The gunfight at the O.K. Corral was a tragic bloodletting, later celebrated in songs, motion pictures, television shows, and documentaries as well as in books, articles, and stories beyond number. The fight did not occur in the O.K. Corral, however. Instead, it occurred in an empty lot between the home of city councilman W. A. Harwood and the boardinghouse of photographer Camillus Fly. The O.K. Corral, nearly 100 feet east, opened onto Allen Street. The question remains whether the error in naming the gunfight is attributable to faulty memories

An undated photograph of the gated entrance to the lot in Tombstone, Arizona, where the gunfight at the O.K. Corral occurred.

of old-timers and is perpetuated out of habit or whether, as biographer Paula M. Marks suggests, it is attributable to the fact that O.K. Corral "has a ring to it."

The colorful Earp brothers had a great deal of combined experience in law enforcement. Virgil Walter Earp, born in 1843 in Kentucky, was a Civil War veteran. He served several law enforcement positions in Arizona before becoming Tombstone's chief of police and city marshal, his job at the time of the shootout. Wyatt Berry Stapp Earp, born in 1848 in Illinois, had served as a lawman in Missouri and in the lawless frontier town of Dodge City, Kansas. He moved to Tombstone in 1879 and served in various law enforcement positions in his more than two years there. At the O.K. Corral gunfight, Wyatt was a stand-in deputy city marshal, appointed by his brother Virgil. Morgan S. Earp, born in Iowa in 1851, rode shotgun for Wells Fargo in the Tombstone area and was occasionally deputized by his brother Virgil. Morgan was a special policeman at the time of the O.K. Corral gunfight.

The causes of the shootout were varied. Earlier, Wyatt Earp had pistol-whipped, or "buffaloed," outlaw leader "Curly" Bill Brocius over the accidental shooting of Tombstone's first city

marshal, Fred White. Then, in an unrelated affair, Wyatt proposed to rustler Ike Clanton that he betray three outlaws who had attempted to hold up a Wells Fargo stage and had killed the driver. Wells Fargo had posted a "dead or alive" reward of $3,600 dollars. As a candidate for sheriff of the newly formed county of Cochise, Wyatt wanted the glory of capturing the bandits. He told Clanton to set the killers up. Wyatt would then see that Clanton received the reward. Clanton agreed and enlisted the aid of Frank McLaury. The plot miscarried, through no fault of Earp's, but Clanton claimed betrayal and swore revenge.

The lot now called the O.K. Corral in Tombstone.

Recent scholarship has presented more compelling causes for the shootout. Wyatt and Virgil Earp were successful businessmen in Tombstone. They owned property, held mining claims and water rights, and made money gambling. They had everything to lose by a shootout. Probably, they intended only to arrest and disarm the cowboys. But Morgan Earp and Doc Holliday were loose cannons. They owned no property or other interests in Tombstone, and they had problems with Ike Clanton and Frank McLaury. A number of witnesses testified that Morgan Earp and Doc Holliday fired the first shots. Morgan was reported to have said, "Let them have it." Wyatt and Virgil Earp were left with no choice but to fight.

1843 Virgil Wyatt Earp is born in Kentucky.

1848 Wyatt Berry Stapp Earp is born in Illinois.

1851 Morgan S. Earp is born in Iowa.

1881 The three Earp brothers confront suspected cattle rustlers in what becomes known as the gunfight at the O.K. Corral.

1882 Morgan Earp is shot in the back and killed as he plays billiards.

1905 At the time of his death, Virgil Earp is the deputy sheriff of Esmeralda County.

1934 The Bird Cage Theater reopens with everything preserved in its original state.

1959 Tombstone Courthouse State Historic Park opens.

On December 28, 1881, Virgil was ambushed and badly wounded. Wyatt was appointed a deputy United States marshal to replace his wounded brother. On the night of March 18, 1882, Morgan Earp was shot in the back as he played billiards in Hatches' Parlor on Allen Street in Tombstone. The killers escaped in the dark. The shooting and maiming of Virgil Earp and the killing of Morgan were acts of revenge for the shootout at the O.K. Corral.

After the killing of Morgan, Deputy U.S. Marshal Wyatt Earp issued warrants for the arrest of suspects Frank Stilwell, Florentino Cruz, Peter Spenser, Jacob Fries, and Hank Swilling. Warrants were not issued for rustler chiefs John Peter Ringo and "Curly" Bill Brocius, although Wyatt suspected both men. In less than a week, Wyatt and his posse killed Stilwell, Cruz, and gang member Johnny Barnes. Ringo committed suicide in July 1882. Wyatt claimed to have killed Brocius as well, but others who knew him said that Brocius had left Arizona months before the alleged killing took place.

Wyatt Earp had taken the law into his own hands. He was charged with murder, and a warrant was issued for his arrest. Now a fugitive himself, he rode to Colorado. Although his personal vendetta cannot be held as a good example of law enforcement, the disappearance of Brocius and the isolation of Ringo broke the back of organized crime in southeastern Arizona. Wyatt died in Los Angeles in 1929. Virgil, in spite of a permanently crippled arm, was elected the first city marshal of Colton, California. He returned to Arizona later, and at the time of his death in 1905, he was deputy sheriff of Esmeralda County.

Tombstone lies about seventy miles southeast of Tucson, twenty miles east of the San Pedro River, and fifteen miles southwest of the Dragoon Mountains. The town was founded in 1877 as a mining camp called Goose Flats after prospector Ed Schieffelin found silver in the nearby hills. The town was later renamed Tombstone after someone told Schiefflin that all he would ever find near the Dragoon Mountains was his own tombstone.

Today tourists can step into the past as they view the area's many sights, including reenactments of the gunfight at the O.K. Corral. They can visit Boot Hill cemetery, where the graves of many famous gunmen are located, and they can stroll the boardwalks on Allen Street, where they might stop in at some of Tombstone's best known saloons. The most famous of these is the Bird Cage Theater, a saloon and dance hall that opened in 1881. The saloon was the site of sixteen gunfights, and bullet holes riddle the walls and floors. The Bird Cage closed in 1889 when the mines that were the source of Tombstone's wealth flooded with underground streams, and Tombstone's population shrank. The theater was boarded up completely intact and stayed closed for over fifty years. When it was reopened in 1934, everything inside was preserved in its original state.

Tombstone Courthouse State Historic Park came into existence in 1959. The courthouse had been built in 1882 at a cost of nearly $50,000. But when the county seat moved from Tombstone to Bisbee in 1929, the grand old building met a doubtful future. The building stood vacant until 1955, when the Tombstone Restoration Commission acquired it. It opened in 1959 as a state park.

Other sites of interest include the historic and currently active army base of Fort Huachuca, located thirty minutes west of Tombstone. The Calvary Post Museum on the base depicts Cochise County's Indian and pioneer heritage. The surrounding mountains and communities in Cochise County also offer visitors insight into Arizona's history. Throughout the year there are several special events to commemorate Tombstone's past, such as "Territorial Days," "Helldorado Days," "Vigilante Days," and "Tombstone's Rose and Art Festival." ◆

The saloon at the Bird Cage Theater was the site of sixteen gunfights, and bullet holes riddle the walls and floors.

Plymouth Rock

PLYMOUTH, MASSACHUSETTS

The Plymouth Colony, established in 1620 in Massachusetts, has a permanent place in American history for being the first permanent English settlement in New England. Thirty-five years after England's first, and failed, attempt to establish a colony on Roanoke Island, off present-day North Carolina, the Virginia Company invested in a venture by a group of Puritans, called Pilgrims, and the ship that carried them to the New World was the *Mayflower*. The Pilgrims were unusually intense in their religious conviction, at odds with the establishment Church of England, and were comparable to a present-day religious sect or cult, breaking off and building their own village far from the mainstream. Their social instincts, however, were brotherly and rather democratic, not lending themselves to domination by a single person. As for the Virginia Company, the investors were hoping for a handsome return from the venture.

"Plymouth Rock" has become a common name for the place where the settlers are imagined to have stepped off the boat, though in fact no such rock was mentioned in any early accounts of the settlement. The first documented reference to the rock as a historic site came about two hundred years later, in James Thatcher's *History of Plymouth* in 1832. Thatcher recounts that in 1741 when the town was planning to build a new wharf in the harbor, Elder Thomas Faunce, a ninety-five-year-old *Mayflower* descendant and a third ruling elder of the Plymouth Church, identified the glacial boulder in the harbor as the spot where the Pilgrims first set foot on Plymouth land. The

"Being thus passed the vast ocean, and a sea of troubles before in their preparation (as may be remembered by that which went before), they had now no friends to welcome them nor inns to entertain or refresh their weatherbeaten bodies; no houses or much less towns to repair to, to seek for succor."
William Bradford, *History of Plymouth Plantation*, c. 1650

305

The year 1620 is inscribed on Plymouth Rock in Plymouth, Massachusetts.

large boulder is now in a prominent position in Plymouth Harbor as part of Pilgrim Memorial State Park, about thirty-five miles south of Boston, and in the harbor floats the *Mayflower II*, a replica of the ship that carried the Pilgrims to North America nearly four centuries ago.

In the early 1600s the English government gave large grants of land in North America to private companies for establishing colonies. The Virginia Company of London received an application for a patent from the Pilgrims, an extremist group of about thirty-five Puritans who disagreed with the teachings and policies of the Church of England. Most Puritans wanted to reform the Anglican Church in one way or another, but the Pilgrims believed it necessary to break away from the Anglican Church altogether. They were Separatists. Their uncompromising views had brought them into conflict with church authorities and their neighbors in Scrooby, Yorkshire, where they had attempted a settlement between 1590 and 1607. With the Dutch government's permission, the Pilgrims emigrated to the city of Leiden in the Netherlands in 1609 and stayed until 1618, but after several years they became dissatisfied with life there. Some from the Leiden group chose to move to North America to found a new community where they believed it must be easier to live according to their faith.

The Pilgrims received the patent they had requested from the Virginia Company, and decided to establish their colony on the northern part of the Virginia Company's land, far from the Anglican settlements in Virginia. To finance their voyage, they entered into an arrangement with a group of London merchants led by Thomas Weston, a Puritan. The Pilgrims agreed to farm, build houses, and fish for seven years, after which time they would share any profits from the enterprise with the merchants.

The Pilgrims left Leiden on July 31, 1620, on board an old, small ship called *Speedwell*, and sailed to Southampton, England, where they met the *Mayflower*. The *Mayflower* was a three-masted, double-decked merchant ship of 180 tons that sailed at a normal speed of about 2.5 miles per hour. The two ships set out from Southampton on August 15, 1620, but about a week later they had to pull in to port at Dartmouth, farther along the southern coast of England, because the *Speedwell* was leaking. They sailed again around September 2, but the *Speedwell*'s problems continued, so they docked again and decided to leave the smaller ship behind. One hundred and two passengers—of whom thirty-five were Pilgrims—finally set sail aboard the *Mayflower* on September 16.

The Pilgrims arrived in the harbor of what is now Provincetown, Cape Cod, Massachusetts, on November 19, 1620. They set down anchor, gathered wood and fresh water, and explored the bay and environs. When the Pilgrims first touched land at Cape Cod, they were about two hundred miles northeast of the Virginia territory where they had expected to land. Because this location was outside the areas described by their patent from

"We, whose names are underwritten, the Loyal Subjects of our dread Sovereign Lord King James, . . . enact, constitute, and frame, such just and equal Laws, Ordinances, Acts, Constitutions, and Offices, from time to time, as shall be thought most meet and convenient for the general Good of the Colony; unto which we promise all due Submission and Obedience"
The Mayflower Compact, November 1620

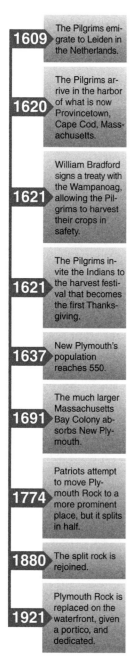

1609 The Pilgrims emigrate to Leiden in the Netherlands.

1620 The Pilgrims arrive in the harbor of what is now Provincetown, Cape Cod, Massachusetts.

1621 William Bradford signs a treaty with the Wampanoag, allowing the Pilgrims to harvest their crops in safety.

1621 The Pilgrims invite the Indians to the harvest festival that becomes the first Thanksgiving.

1637 New Plymouth's population reaches 550.

1691 The much larger Massachusetts Bay Colony absorbs New Plymouth.

1774 Patriots attempt to move Plymouth Rock to a more prominent place, but it splits in half.

1880 The split rock is rejoined.

1921 Plymouth Rock is replaced on the waterfront, given a portico, and dedicated.

the Virginia Company, some passengers asserted that the terms of the patent—including the conditions explaining how the new colony should be governed—were no longer valid. To keep order, the Pilgrims' leaders drew up an agreement known as the Mayflower Compact. They pledged allegiance to the king, but agreed to government by majority rule: they, the settlers, would choose the leaders of the colony and obey the government established by those leaders. On November 21, 1620, all forty-one free adult males on board signed the document.

The Pilgrims decided not to settle on the first land they came to, and sailed along the Massachusetts coast for about a month before they found a spot that looked suitable. The *Mayflower* sailed into Plymouth harbor on December 26, and remained at anchor until the Pilgrims could build houses in the new settlement, which they named New Plymouth. The good ship sailed back to England on April 5, 1621, and reached London safely. It is unknown what became of the Pilgrims' *Mayflower* because of confusion with several other contemporary ships also named *Mayflower*.

The site of the Plymouth colony had actually been noted in 1605 by the French explorer Samuel de Champlain as he sailed along the Massachusetts coast. The site looked ideal: it had plenty of fresh water and cleared land, and no Indians were visible in the vicinity. The settlers built a crude palisade for defense and a common warehouse for supplies, and each family constructed its own shelter. The settlement site was vacant because recent outbreaks of disease had wiped out the previous inhabitants. The Indians' misfortune turned out to be a blessing for the Pilgrims, for the epidemic had been so recent that the Indians' cornfields had not yet turned back into wilderness. Nonetheless, the first winter at New Plymouth was traumatic for the settlers, and nearly half of them died from scurvy and exposure. The stores of corn the Indians had left behind enabled the remaining settlers to survive their first winter in North America.

As the Pilgrims planted their first corn crop the following spring, two Native Americans visited the settlement. Squanto, who had learned English as the captive of an English sea captain, showed how to plant squash between the rows of corn and how to fertilize the land. He also helped the Pilgrims negotiate with the nearby tribe of Wampanoag Indians. In 1621 Governor William Bradford signed a treaty with Massasoit, chief of the Wampanoag, that allowed the Pilgrims to harvest their crops in safety, in a peace that lasted fifty years. To celebrate God's favor that had allowed them to survive in the new land, in October 1621 the Pilgrims held a harvest festival and invited the Wampanoag. This is the feast that is commemorated every November as Thanksgiving.

New Plymouth continued to be beset by difficulties. For the first nine years, the colony had no fully trained minister—a serious lack for a colony founded on religious principles. In 1622 the London Puritan merchant Thomas Weston arrived in Plymouth with a new group of settlers, but few of the newcomers shared the Pilgrims' beliefs. These settlers were persuaded to move up the coast, so they began their own settlement at Weymouth, or Wessagusset. It lasted only a year. In 1625 a group led by Thomas Morton established another settlement nearby at Mount Wollaston (now Braintree). The Morton group's drinking and dancing were an affront to the earlier settlers, and in1628 the Pilgrims forced Morton and his company to go back to England.

The Plymouth colony's biggest problem was its failure to show a profit. The investors had hoped to make money from fishing and the fur trade, but most of the Pilgrims devoted themselves to farming and praying. By 1626 most of the original investors sold their shares and split the money with the settlers. New Plymouth's prospects improved in the 1630s, when the larger and wealthier Massachusetts Bay Company established a colony to the north. Plymouth was able to sell livestock and grain to the new settlers, and the colony slowly began to grow. By 1637 its population had reached 550, and new Pilgrim settlements had been founded around Plymouth.

Although it survived and prospered to some extent, Plymouth never became very large. The colony's growth was limited by its failure to expand its community beyond Puritan Separatists or to develop any economic activity besides small farming. It was soon overshadowed by neighboring colonies, particularly Boston, thirty-five miles up the coast in a much better natural harbor, settled by the elder John Winthrop in 1630 as the main colony of the Massachusetts Bay Company. In 1691 the much larger Massachusetts Bay colony absorbed New Plymouth, which by then had about 7,500 inhabitants.

In 1774 the famous rock in the harbor was moved—that is to say, half of it was moved—when patriots inspired by the Revolutionary War attempted to move the rock to a more prominent public place in the village. A team of thirty oxen

"All this while the Indians came skulking about them, and would sometimes show themselves aloof off, but when any approached near them, they would run away; and once they stole away their tools where they had been at work and were gone to dinner. But about the 16th of March, a certain Indian came boldly amongst them and spoke to them in broken English, which they could well understand but marveled at it."
William Bradford, *History of Plymouth Plantation*, c. 1650

was yoked to the rock, but the boulder split in half. The bottom part was left at the shore, but the top half was carted to the town square and leaned against an elm tree. In 1880 the rock was rejoined and a monumental Victorian canopy was built over it. The date 1620 was carved in the rock at this time. On Plymouth's tercentenary (three-hundredth anniversary) the rock was temporarily moved to make way for renovations along the waterfront. Plymouth Rock was replaced on the waterfront and given a portico by the National Society of the Colonial Dames of America, and dedicated on November 29, 1921.

Today Pilgrim Memorial State Park is the smallest but also the most frequented park in the Massachusetts State forest and park system. A million visitors a year come to see Plymouth Rock and the *Mayflower II* docked in the harbor. For Americans, as well as for visitors from around the world, Plymouth Harbor is a little like New York's Ellis Island or the Statue of Liberty, on a more modest scale, and imbued with a density of historical and symbolic significance that seems only to grow as America matures. ◆

Pony Express Stables

ST. JOSEPH, MISSOURI

"Wanted, two hundred grey mares, from four to seven years old, not to exceed 15 hands high, well broke to the saddle, and Warranted Sound, with black hoofs, and suitable for running the 'Overland Pony Express.'"

Leavenworth Daily Times, February 10, 1860

By early evening on April 3, 1860, an excited crowd had assembled on the street in front of Pikes Peak Stables in St. Joseph, Missouri. A brass band struck up a tune while, inside the stables, a young man named Johnny Fry saddled up a spirited chestnut mare named Sylph. Mounted on a pony nearby was ten-year-old Billy Richardson, half brother of station manager Paul Coburn. Fry leaped into the saddle, gathered up the reins, and clucked softly to urge his horse into motion. As he rode out into the street, young Richardson eagerly followed—he wanted to tag along for the first part way of what was to be a historic ride.

At about 7:00 P.M., Coburn tossed a *mochila* (a specially designed saddlebag) up to the riders—young Richardson caught it just as a cannon boomed. The two young riders set off through the town to the ferry landing, where Richardson turned the bag over to Fry, its rightful carrier, then turned his pony back toward town. With a slap of the reins, Fry guided his horse onto the ferry, and thus began the inaugural run of the Pony Express.

By 1860 the nation's railway and telegraph service had reached only as far west as St. Joseph, Missouri. But the discovery of gold at Sutter's Mill had brought settlers to California in unprecedented numbers, and as the population exploded, so too did the need for better communication between the eastern states and the settlers of the westernmost territories of the nation. Something had to be done to reduce the time it took to send a letter—under the current system, a letter could take as much as six months to travel from Washington, D.C., to Sacramento, California.

The U.S. government had begun searching for answers to the problem of timely mail delivery across the continent since the establishment of the national postal service in 1847. The early decades of service were conducted by private contractors, but none could cut the delivery time to much less than four weeks. As the California population continued to grow, and especially as the threat of Civil War grew ever greater, the government's need to secure a guaranteed, rapid mail delivery system became so desperate that Congress even commissioned a $30,000 study of the practicality of a plan to use camels to carry the mail.

The freighting firm of Russell, Majors, and Waddell had a less colorful, but more likely solution. They were old hands at conveying westbound goods and passengers overland, and one of the partners, William H. Russell, thought that it might be highly profitable if his firm could be the one to solve the problem of timely delivery of the mail. His company had already entered the mail business, through a subsidiary called the Central Overland, California, and Pikes Peak Express Company, but it used the conventional stagecoaches to carry the mailbags, and it still took weeks for the mail to get through.

Another firm, the Butterfield Overland Mail, provided serious competition for the mail-carrying business. It used a longer, southern route through that linked Missouri to San Francisco via Texas and Arizona, and it had already been awarded the government contracts for the service in 1856. Russell, however, was convinced that if he could significantly cut the time it took to transport the mail across the continent, he could win those contracts away from Butterfield.

Russell had in mind a model first developed in ancient China and reported to the west by famed explorer Marco Polo:

1847 The United States establishes a national postal service.

1856 The Butterfield Overland Mail is awarded government contracts to provide postal service.

1858 George Chorpenning is able to deliver a presidential message from Missouri to Sacramento in about 17 days using relay posts with horses and riders.

1860 William H. Russell announces the launching of his Pony Express.

1959 The Pony Express National Memorial is established at the site of the original Piles Peak Stables.

relay posts strung out along the route, at each of which a horse and rider team would be stationed. Just two years earlier, in 1858, a man named George Chorpenning had tried such a scheme, and managed to deliver a presidential message from Missouri to Sacramento in just over seventeen days. With a similar arrangement, using the best riders and fastest horses he could find, Russell calculated that he could guarantee ten-day service. Without waiting for government approval or funding, he announced that his "Pony Express" would be launched from St. Joseph, Missouri, on April 3, 1860.

From the evening when Johnny Fry rode his horse Sylph down the main street of St. Joseph until November 21, 1861, when the final Pony Express run was completed, only nineteen months had elapsed. The long anticipated government contracts never came through, and by the time the service closed down, the firm of Russell, Majors, and Waddell had lost $200,000.

Still, the riders were paid, and paid handsomely, for their skill and dedication—a policy that attracted some of the most remarkable young horsemen of the day into service for the Express. One such was "Pony Bob" Haslam, who discovered that the relief rider who was to take the *mochila* from him at Buckland's Station in California had deserted his post. To keep the delivery on time, Haslam simply changed horses and rode on to the next relay stop—a distance of 190 miles in all—rested for nine hours, and then carried the westbound pouch all the way back to his starting point.

Jack Keetley was another of the legendary riders of the Pony Express. He, too, found himself with no relief at his appointed relay stop and carried the mail through, then doubled back to return to his home station, but unlike Haslam he neglected to rest. When he arrived back at his home station in Seneca, Kansas, the waiting stable hands had to remove him from the saddle—he was sound asleep.

Most famous of all the Pony Express riders must be William Cody. At fifteen years of age, he had yet to earn his nickname, "Buffalo Bill," when he rode for the Express. But he was not too young to have had perhaps the wildest ride in the history of the service. Riding from Red Buttes Station, Nevada, he discovered that the rider who was to take the *mochila* on the next leg of the relay had been killed by Indians. He took the mail on, all the way to Rocky Ridge Station, for a total of 322 miles, stopping only to change horses along the way. His epic ride, which used

"I will, under no circumstances, use profane language, that I will drink no intoxicating liquors, that I will not quarrel or fight with any other employee of the firm, and that in every respect I will conduct myself honestly, be faithful to my duties, and so direct all my acts as to win the confidence of my employers, so help me God."

Pony Express Riders' Oath, 1860

a total of twenty-one horses, took twenty-one hours and forty minutes.

The Pony Express Stables, now a museum, in St. Joseph, Missouri.

All the riders had certain attributes in common: they were young (none older than eighteen), small, tough, and wiry. And they had to be loyal—the company required that they swear an oath of sobriety, courtesy, and honesty before they mounted up for a run. Their mounts, too, were selected for endurance and speed—long-legged, but small and swift, they had to be able to achieve galloping speed of twenty-five miles per hour and handle the often rugged terrain through which the Pony Express route passed.

The site of the original Pikes Peak Stables, from which Johnny Fry departed on the inaugural run of the legendary overland mail service, now houses the Pony Express National Memorial, which was established in 1959. The original wooden structure still stands, but was covered with brick and enlarged in the early 1900s. The stone foundations of the first stables are visible inside the museum. The museum also maintains the original well from which the Pony Express horses were watered. Museum visitors can view exhibits and films that commemorate

Pony Express history and provide a glimpse into how the service operated. The Pony Express National Memorial hosts an annual reenactment of the start of the Pony Express, as well as demonstrations of horsemanship and other related activities.

Nearby is the Patee House, which served as the Pony Express headquarters for the duration of its operation, and played host to many of the legendary characters of the Old West as well. Behind Patee House is another location of importance to the history of St. Joseph and the legacy of the Old West: the Jesse James house, where the infamous outlaw lived until he was gunned down, just two blocks away, by Bob Ford on April 3, 1882. The home is now a museum, which includes an exhibit of items from Jesse James's grave, recovered in 1995 when the outlaw was exhumed for **forensic** study. A life-sized bronze statue of a galloping horse carrying a Pony Express rider stands in front of the St. Joseph Civic Center. ◆

forensic: specializing in the application of scientific knowledge in an investigation of a crime.

Portland Head Lighthouse

CAPE ELIZABETH, MAINE

I n the 1780s the maritime community of Portland, then still a part of Massachusetts, was a well established port settlement with a lucrative fishing and trading industry. As more ships plied their way in and out of the harbor—heading in large part to the Canadian settlements to the north—local merchants and businessmen perceived a need to build a lighthouse for the safety of the oceangoing traffic. In 1786 these worthies successfully petitioned the government in Boston for permission to begin construction of the first such structure to be built along the Maine coastline, and construction began in the following year. Unfortunately, funds soon ran out, and the partially completed lighthouse was not completed until 1791, after the newly elected first president of the United States—George Washington—authorized $1,500 to finish the job.

The lighthouse was completed after George Washington authorized $1,500 to finish the job.

The structure still stands, in altered form, within the boundaries of Fort Williams Park, on Cape Elizabeth, in present-day Maine. Its tower originally rose seventy-two feet, and was constructed of lime and rubblestone. Since then, the tower has been lowered (by twenty-five feet, in 1813), raised (by twenty feet, in 1864), lowered again (by twenty feet, in 1882), and finally restored to nearly its original height in 1883. The 1883 structure, which included a powerful beacon, would not suffer further changes for more than 100 years—in 1989 the old lantern was replaced with a modern revolving beacon of the type used in airports.

The Maine seacoast communities, large and small, lived off the bounty of the sea. Major cities, such as Portland, conducted a lively trade up and down the coast, and received ships from Europe as well. Smaller communities subsisted on a fishing or lobstering economy, and many member of today's coastal villages still earn their living in this way. But the 3,500-mile coastline of Maine is unforgiving of human error. A fisherman who returns to port in dark of night or in foul weather faces no gentle sandy shore, but gravelly beaches or hard, rocky outcroppings that can batter a ship to splinters.

No wonder, then, that more than sixty-five lighthouses shine forth along the coast of Maine—the beacons are absolutely necessary to protect the lives and livelihood of the fishing and shipping industries. Nearly all of them can be visited, and most have colorful histories that form a part of the Maine maritime heritage.

The town of Portsmouth, New Hampshire, was an important fishing, trading, and whaling community from its earliest days of settlement. In 1820 a lighthouse was built in Portsmouth Harbor, near Kittery, Maine, to guide the seagoing traffic in and out of the port. Unfortunately, that first structure was destroyed during its first winter of existence, as the harbor was battered by severe storms. It was only replaced in 1831, and the new structure—with a series of improvements made over time—survived some forty years.

By 1872 serious damage to the structure necessitated major repairs, and the resulting tower, which stands seventy-five feet high, remains today. It has, however, faced its share of catastrophes, including flooding through its second story windows in 1886, when a violent storm whipped up huge waves that crashed against the tower. (The windows are today boarded up.) Modernization of the light (in 1963) and modification of the foghorn (in 1991) were done to improve its effectiveness and reduce structural damage.

For years the states of New Hampshire and Maine held competing claims to Whaleback Light, but the rocky islet on which it is built has finally been determined to lie within Maine's borders.

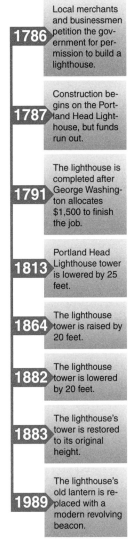

1786 Local merchants and businessmen petition the government for permission to build a lighthouse.

1787 Construction begins on the Portland Head Lighthouse, but funds run out.

1791 The lighthouse is completed after George Washington allocates $1,500 to finish the job.

1813 Portland Head Lighthouse tower is lowered by 25 feet.

1864 The lighthouse tower is raised by 20 feet.

1882 The lighthouse tower is lowered by 20 feet.

1883 The lighthouse's tower is restored to its original height.

1989 The lighthouse's old lantern is replaced with a modern revolving beacon.

In 1710 a ship called the *Nottingham Galley* crashed onto the ledges of Boon Island, stranding its crew on its inhospitable shore. With no natural resources to sustain them, and having lost all supplies when the ship was sunk, they are reported to have ultimately resorted to cannibalism. (Their story is presented in fictional form in the novel *Boon Island*, by Kenneth Roberts.)

Boon Island, which lies just six miles offshore of the city of York, Maine, received some of the harshest weather that the Atlantic can dish out, and ships passing nearby during a storm could long expect to suffer the fate of the *Galley's* crew. Because of this incident, fishermen from the mainland began to stock the island with caches of supplies for survivors of the inevitable shipwrecks to use while they awaited rescue from the mainland. But clearly, something more needed to be done.

In 1799 the people of York finally raised the funds to build the first lighthouse on the island, which survived for five years. Twice more a beacon would be placed here, and twice more the structure would fall victim to the brutal local storms, before the present granite tower was finally put in place in 1852. This tower is the tallest of all the lighthouses along the Maine coast, and is stoutly made, but it, too, has taken some serious beatings. In 1978 a violent storm tossed boulders against the structure, destroying many of the outbuildings and briefly submerging the island under heavy seas.

Built in 1879 on Nubble Island, the Cape Neddick Lighthouse protects maritime traffic passing around Cape Neddick Point. Neither the oldest of Maine's lighthouses, nor possessed of the most colorful history of other such structures, it has nonetheless a unique claim to fame. The spaceship *Voyager*, launched in 1977, had two separate missions: first, to fly by Jupiter and ship back to earth photographs of that giant planet; and second, to continue on into deepest space, in hope of encountering intelligent life somewhere out there. Among the materials it carried for the edification of any extraterrestrials it might encounter on its journey were photographs of earth structures and features that would be visible to observers from space—and among them is a picture of the Cape Neddick Lighthouse.

At the mouth of Cape Porpoise Harbor, part of the township of Kennebunkport, Maine, lies Goat Island, where a lighthouse was first erected in 1835. The location of the island provided some protection from the violence of the sea and the

In the 1960s and 1970s, the Maine Coast Guard carried out a program of installing automated lights, doing away with the need for human attendants.

weather, so the structure never suffered the severity of damage
of other lighthouse installations along Maine's coastline.
Nonetheless, in 1860 the citizens of Kennebunkport chose to
replace the original structure with a sturdier brick tower, which
stands today.

All of Maine's lighthouses were originally operated by keepers whose task was to maintain the lights and foghorn alarms,
and to render assistance should ships or boats be wrecked in
spite of their warnings. In the 1960s and 1970s, however, the
Maine Coast Guard carried out a program of installing automated lights, doing away with the need for human attendants.
But fate had other plans for the Goat Island Lighthouse: with
the election of Kennebunkport resident George W. H. Bush to
the vice presidency, the Coast Guard saw that the lighthouse
was perfectly situated to serve as a security outpost—it stands
just about a mile from the Bush family compound at Walker's
Point. It wasn't until the end of Bush's term as president, in
1990, that the light was automated and the lighthouse ceased to
have a human operator.

Before the trend to automation in the 1960s and 1970s, all
of Maine's lighthouses included a keeper's residence, a separate

structure at the base of the tower where the human operator of the light could live with his family. The life was often difficult: it was not uncommon for the frequent and brutal Atlantic storms to force the keepers into the tower for protection, while their homes were battered into splinters by the crashing waves. Lighthouse keepers were generally married—the isolation and monotony of the keeper's life was difficult to sustain alone. But even with a family, many keepers found that they could not last long in the position, and some particularly difficult postings, such as at the Boon Island Lighthouse, saw a rapid turnover in personnel.

At other locations, the keepers found ways to make their time on the job more enjoyable. At Wood Island, near Biddeford at the mouth of the Saco River, for example, the keeper posted there in the 1870s ran a distillery and a pub, guaranteeing a steady procession of visitors from the mainland. Unfortunately, one night the pub's **conviviality** got a little out of hand, and patrons somehow set the place on fire. Luckily, the lighthouse survived.

conviviality: festive activity.

The keepers of the Cape Neddick Lighthouse in the early 1900s found their own solution to their isolated existence—and a way to make a little extra cash, as well. They began to operate a ferry to the island, offering visitors a tour of the lighthouse. The success of their sideline business, however, spelled the end of their positions on the island—they were ultimately fired for neglecting their duties. One of their successors kept a cat for company. At nineteen pounds, the cat was a most impressive beast, and legend has it that he would swim the channel to visit feline friends on York Beach. ◆

Rankin House

RIPLEY, OHIO

The Rankin House stands at the crest of "Liberty Hill" in the small town of Ripley, Ohio, just north of the Kentucky border. It is one of at least sixty-four safe houses in western Ohio that formed an important segment of the Underground Railroad, a secret but vast network of havens for escaped African slaves making their way north to freedom in the 1800s. Abolitionists—people who wished to *abolish* slavery—worked together and independently in the Ripley community, risking their lives and their homes to help an estimated two thousand people flee to Canada. The secret operations were at times highly organized and labor-intensive: extra meals, beds, and horses were kept at the ready; elaborate tunnels were dug between safe houses; coded messages were memorized and passed south. At other times the assistance was quite spontaneous: runaway slaves, desperate for help, fearing that they would be turned over to slave hunters at each contact, occasionally stumbled across sympathizers willing to help.

The Underground Railroad plays a significant part of America's national history and stands as a dramatic and eloquent protest against the institution of slavery. Despite the fact that African captives had resisted enslavement since the first slave ship arrived in Virginia in 1612, by the 1800s, nearly 100 million Africans had been taken from their homes and sold into slavery—many to work in cotton plantations in the southern states. The abolitionist resistance and the Underground Railroad operated at their peak from 1830 to 1865, when slavery was abolished in the United States by the Thirteenth Amendment to the Constitution.

"A lighted candle stood as a beacon which could be seen from across the river, and like the north star was the guide to the fleeing slave."
John Parker, a Ripley abolitionist and former slave, 1865

The home of John Rankin in Ripley, Ohio, which served as a stop along the Underground Railroad.

John Rankin was one of the first abolitionists to clearly articulate the many reasons why slavery is immoral and unjust.

The Rankin House was built specifically as a station house on the Underground Railroad and soon became one of its busiest passage points due to its proximity to proslavery towns in Kentucky, just across the Ohio River. The Rankin family— John, his wife, Jean, and their thirteen children—held deep, moral convictions against slavery, devoting forty years to abolitionist causes. John Rankin, a Presbyterian minister, was one of the first abolitionists to clearly articulate the many reasons why slavery is immoral and unjust. These principles were originally outlined in several letters the Reverend wrote to his brother in Virginia after hearing the disturbing news that his sibling had purchased slaves. These "Letters on American Slavery" were published three times between 1826 and 1860 and were standard reading among abolitionists.

Early on, the abolitionists dared to defy both local laws and the U.S. Constitution. Most northern states had begun restricting the slave trade in 1804, prohibiting new sales and gradually abolishing its practice. Northerners were still constrained, however, by a law called the Fugitive Slave Act, originally passed in 1793 and redefined in 1850, that allowed slave hunters to enter and search the private properties of anyone remotely suspected of harboring runaway slaves. Since slave hunters could too easily monitor and search the Reverend's first home, located on Ripley's central Front Street, Rankin built another home "in the country" that stands as an achievement to the ingenuity of slavery opposition.

The new Rankin house was built on a high bluff that allowed the family to watch over the town, the Ohio River, and a long stretch of the Kentucky shoreline. A long staircase of one hundred steps leads up from the Ohio River, these being the "stairs of liberty" many slaves climbed on their way to safety. The house included several secret rooms and a large compartment underneath the back porch in which to hide men and women during bounty hunters' searches. No slaves were ever caught in the Rankin house, even though bounty hunters searched it—sometimes at gunpoint—over a hundred times, and even though the Rankins sometimes hid up to twelve fugitives at a time.

Despite these risks, every night, when it was determined safe, a candle was lit in the window, acting as a beacon that could be seen up to six miles away along the river. The entire Rankin family kept a vigilant watch over the river. Whenever a distressed person appeared—by boat, by foot when the river froze, or within the current itself—a family member was ready to usher him or her to safety. Food, drink, and shelter were provided, then quick transportation to the next depot. Thus, the Rankin House served as a watchtower, a lighthouse, and a fortress for those seeking freedom in the north. The word spread among southern slaves that if they followed the North Star, the star of hope, they would soon be free. Many seeking freedom followed the Mississippi River north until it joined the Ohio River, and followed that until they saw a candle burning in an Ohio safe house, like the one in John and Jean Rankin's home.

It was at such a juncture that some claim the term Underground Railroad was first coined. As the story goes, a slave hunter was pursuing an escapee from Kentucky named Tice Davids. The chase was so close that Tice decided to swim the width of the Ohio River—a fast-moving and cold two hundred yards. The slave hunter opted to make the trip by rowboat without allowing Tice's swimming figure out of his sight. Although he watched Tice's slow progression against the river's current, and saw him pull himself onto shore, when his own boat landed minutes later Tice was nowhere to be found. The slave hunter looked everywhere and finally went home frustrated, reporting to his neighbors that "Tice Davids must have escaped in an Underground Railroad." What the slave hunter did not know was that, just above the shoreline, a candle flickered in the Rankin House window, and Tice knew where to go for cover. Within a few perilous weeks of bustling from one safe house to another, Tice entered Canada a free man.

"Does not every American Christian owe to the African race some effort at reparation for the wrongs that the American nation has brought upon them? Shall the doors of churches and school-houses be shut upon them? Shall states arise and shake them out?"

Harriet Beecher Stowe, *Uncle Tom's Cabin*, 1851

Uncle Tom's Cabin

Uncle Tom's Cabin is a famous antislavery novel by Harriet Beecher Stowe, an American writer and reformer. The book was first published as a serialized novel under the title *Uncle Tom's Cabin; or Life Among the Lowly* in an antislavery paper, *National Era,* in 1851 and 1852. It was published as a bound book on March 20, 1852. *Uncle Tom's Cabin* was an immediate popular success; by the outbreak of the Civil War, a million copies had been sold.

Stowe wrote *Uncle Tom's Cabin* to draw attention to the evils of slavery. The story presented a brutal examination of slaveholding and slave life in the south. The slave-driving Simon Legree, and the patiently loyal Uncle Tom have both passed into common speech as symbols of cruel management and patient suffering. The book made thousands of Americans aware of the pain and cruelty of slavery, of slave hunting with packs of dogs, and of the real human cost of the slave system. Mrs. Stowe had included a kindly and sympathetic Kentucky plantation owner in her novel, but he was generally forgotten by those who were impressed by the drama of escaping slaves rushing toward Canada and freedom. The novel owed some of its sudden popularity to the fact that its author was sister to Henry Ward Beecher, one of the country's most effective abolitionist preachers. Without question, *Uncle Tom's Cabin* intensified the disagreement between north and south that led to the Civil War.

Thus, although there was no true rail, no train or specific trek, the metaphor of an invisible railroad, carrying passengers to a better place, captured the imaginations of many and word of it spread quickly southward. Those dedicated to helping fugitives became known as conductors, and their safe houses were called stations or depots. On southern plantations, songs about "catching the next train home" were sung and passed along with renewed hope.

Yet the more successful and organized the Underground Railroad became, the more the slave masters tried to stop it—by law, by intimidation, and by brute force. The Rankins and other abolitionists took courageous personal risks to sustain the movement. The Fugitive Slave Laws that allowed slave owners to reach into northern homes also levied steep fines and imprisonment. In addition, some individual slave owners, frustrated with the financial loss of their human properties, offered rewards for the assassination of well-known and successful abolitionists like John Rankin and John Parker, a former slave and active Ripley conductor. In one instance, a Kentucky slave owner offered a $2,500 cash reward for the "murder or abduction of John

Rankin." A Ripley newspaper quickly printed a response that speaks to the determination of the community: the editor warned, "I would remind my friends across the river that if they murder Mr. Rankin, destroy his property, or even burn the town of Ripley, they will never save one slave by it . . . . God has given us the right of hospitality and we will never surrender it but with our lives." Reverend Rankin, like many, considered himself to be following higher moral laws that outranked the laws of the United States government.

But laws were not easily changed and slavery had become a volatile political issue that plagued relations between the north and south. Many white-owned businesses were economically tied to America's leading agricultural industries—cotton and tobacco. One such businessman, a New York merchant, coldly addressed the abolitionists justifying what he acknowledged as the "great evil" of slavery as a business necessity.

"We are not such fools as not to know that slavery is a great evil. But it was consented to by the founders of the Republic. It was provided for in the Constitution. . . . There are millions upon millions of dollars due from Southerners to the merchants of this city alone, the payment of which would be jeopardized by any rupture between North and South. We cannot afford to let you or your associates succeed in your endeavors to overthrow slavery. It is not a matter of principal to us. It is a matter of business necessity. We do not mean to allow you to succeed. We mean to put you Abolitionists down—by fair means if we can, by foul means if we must." The business necessity allowed many northerners to turn a blind eye to reports of inhumane conditions and the injustice of human enslavement.

At the height of these tensions, a novel appeared in 1852 that greatly deepened the public sympathies for the slaves. Harriet Beecher Stowe, an abolitionist from the same Ohio region, based her tale mostly on firsthand accounts of runaway slaves, as well as plantation life that she had seen in Kentucky and tales from the conductors of the Underground Railroad. Living so near Ripley, she routinely visited the Rankin House and talked to fugitives about their trials to become free. On one such visit, John Rankin told Stowe the story of a woman he had seen crossing the thawing Ohio River at night, dangerously leaping from one broken ice patch to the next with a baby cradled in her arms. That account inspired the character of Eliza in Stowe's *Uncle Tom's Cabin*. Stowe's book did much to focus the nation on the critical inhumanity of slavery. Eight presses printed the

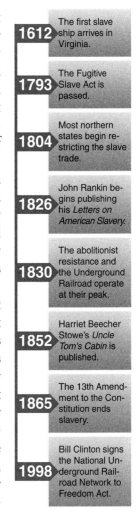

1612 The first slave ship arrives in Virginia.

1793 The Fugitive Slave Act is passed.

1804 Most northern states begin restricting the slave trade.

1826 John Rankin begins publishing his *Letters on American Slavery*.

1830 The abolitionist resistance and the Underground Railroad operate at their peak.

1852 Harriet Beecher Stowe's *Uncle Tom's Cabin* is published.

1865 The 13th Amendment to the Constitution ends slavery.

1998 Bill Clinton signs the National Underground Railroad Network to Freedom Act.

book day and night to meet the demands; it sold over one and a half million copies within the first years of its release and was translated into twenty-two languages. The book was banned in some places because its ideas were considered too dangerous, but its gritty depiction of slavery strengthened the abolitionist movement and further divided the north and south. The book was so influential that, when Stowe met President Lincoln, he reportedly commented, "So this is the little woman who started this Great War."

Although Stowe's book and firsthand accounts from Harriet Tubman, the Rankin family, William Lloyd Garrison, Sojourner Truth, and others give us memorable stories of the Underground Railroad, we will never know its full history. Because secrecy was essential to maintaining the networks and exposure meant large fines, imprisonment, or violent attacks, few records were kept. Rather the history relies largely on recollections, letters, journals, and some publications from those with the material means to publish. Historians acknowledge that this evidence is just a portion of what would have been necessary for the stunning accomplishment of such a large network. It is well known, for instance, that freed slaves and black communities from the north largely organized and funded many of the abolitionist activities and newspapers, yet because African Americans had little political power, we have few records of their heroism. The invisibility that made the Underground Railroad so effective and pervasive as a means of peaceful protest has also made it elusive to history books. The Rankin House with its secret rooms and documented significance is one monument that unveils this rich history. The house, with its "stairs to liberty" has been recently restored by the Ripley community and the National Park Service and can be visited today. Other houses in the community also have tunnels, concealed rooms, and, most important, local storytellers who continue to pass on the oral history to interested visitors.

In 1998 a National Underground Railroad Network to Freedom Act was signed by President Clinton, formally organizing and linking the hundreds of Underground Railroad sites across twenty-nine states. The financial support includes a Freedom Center in Cincinnati, Ohio, just fifty miles from Ripley, containing a museum and an educational center. The Freedom Center is dedicated to developing and preserving the vital history of America's Underground Railroad. ◆

"An atmosphere of sympathetic influence encircles every human being; and the man or woman who feels strongly, healthily, and justly, on the great interests of humanity, is a constant benefactor to the human race. See, then, to your sympathies in this matter!"

Harriet Beecher Stowe, *Uncle Tom's Cabin*, 1851

Rhea County Courthouse

DAYTON, TENNESSEE

The Rhea County courthouse in Dayton, Tennessee, became the site of one of the most famous trials in United States history in 1925. With a population of only 1,800, rural Dayton became the unlikely location for a world-famous battle between science and religion when believers in the biblical story of creation faced off with those who believe that modern humans developed through a process called evolution. The Scopes trial made little impact legally, but it had a significant impact on the philosophical and religious views of Americans. The questions tackled in the trial are still debated in schools and courts around the country.

The specific issue leading to the Scopes trial was the teaching of evolution in public schools. Many years earlier, the debate over evolution had begun after the publication of Charles Darwin's *On the Origin of the Species by Means of Natural Selection* (1859), which gave detailed evidence supporting the theory of evolution. The theory of organic evolution holds that all life currently on earth evolved from simple organisms. Darwin's work met with a high level of acceptance, and within a few short years, most scientists had incorporated his ideas into their own research.

However, many Christians rejected the concept of evolution because the first book of the Bible, Genesis, says that God created the world in six days. Many Christians understand this story as a factual, historical account. In addition, Christians objected to the suggestion that humans could have evolved from lower life forms. Scientists found so many similarities between humans and apes that they theorized a common ancestry between the two. Some Christians felt this contradicted their belief in a divine and special relationship between God and humans.

By 1920 almost all colleges and high schools in the United States and Europe taught evolution in biology classes. However, people called fundamentalists thought that belief in God was eroding and that science, especially Darwin's theory, was to blame. Fundamentalist Christians fought to uphold what they considered the fundamentals of Christianity. In a series of

> *"There is no more reason to believe that man descended from some inferior animal than there is to believe that a stately mansion was descended from a small cottage."*
> William Jennings Bryan, 1925

pamphlets called *The Fundamentals* (1910) they maintained such beliefs as the Bible being infallible and the genuineness of all miracles in the Bible.

In the 1920s fundamentalists proposed laws in twenty states to ban teaching evolution in the public schools. Several states, including Tennessee, passed such legislation. Tennessee's law, called the Butler Act, passed in 1925 and called for a fine of $100 to $500 against anyone in the public schools who taught "any theory that denies the story of the Divine Creation of man taught in the Bible." The American Civil Liberties Union (ACLU) in New York City sought to challenge the Butler Act, believing that it violated the constitutional principle of the separation of church and state. The ACLU contacted newspapers in Tennessee, offering to pay all legal expenses for anyone willing to test the law. Several Dayton residents, including two lawyers and the county superintendent of schools, decided to take up the issue. They convinced John T. Scopes, a modest twenty-four-year-old high school science teacher, to stand trial on the charge of teaching evolution. The local sheriff arrested Scopes on May 7, 1925, about six weeks after the Butler Act passed.

The first indication of the magnitude of their venture came when William Jennings Bryan, a world-renowned statesman and orator, offered to assist the prosecution in the case. The sixty-five-year-old Bryan had become famous as a politician and a leading public speaker, especially on religious issues. As a Democrat, he had run unsuccessfully for president of the United States three times. He had supported several popular causes that had earned him the loyalty of many ordinary people and the nickname "The Commoner." Bryan saw the theory of evolution as a great evil and made fighting it one of his top priorities.

But the defense soon had an equal to Bryan on its side when the most famous American lawyer, Clarence Seward Darrow, joined their cause. Darrow, born in 1857, had earned an international reputation as a brilliant criminal defense attorney, and was known for his cleverness, wit, and eloquence. Darrow had been observing the activities of the fundamentalists nationwide, and grew concerned about the spread of their message.

As Scopes's trial date, July 10, 1925, approached, the little town of Dayton took on a carnival atmosphere. People came from miles around as well as from other states. In addition, evangelists, preachers, and other Christians accumulated. Vendors provided food and merchandise. Darrow described the

> "Be it enacted by the General Assembly of the State of Tennessee, That it shall be unlawful for any teacher in any of the Universities, Normals and all other public schools of the State which are supported in whole or in part by the public school funds of the State, to teach any theory that denies the story of the Divine Creation of man as taught in the Bible, and to teach instead that man has descended from a lower order of animals."
>
> Tennessee Evolution Statute, 1925

scene in his biography: "Hot dog booths and fruit peddlers and ice cream vendors and sandwich sellers had sprung into existence like mushrooms on every corner and everywhere between. . . . Evangelist tents were propped up at vantage points around the town square."

On the morning of the trial, which became known as the Scopes Monkey Trial, the courtroom swelled with hundreds of spectators and journalists, including the famous H. L. Mencken. When Bryan approached the courtroom, the crowd cheered. The judge, John Raulston, opened the session with a prayer (to the dismay of Darrow, who had not seen such a religious display in his nearly forty years of practicing law in Chicago). The judge permitted loudspeakers to be placed outside the courthouse so the crowds could hear the trial. The case also became the first broadcast trial as it was transmitted over the airwaves by WGN radio in Chicago.

In his first speech of the trial, Darrow did not waste words. He called the Butler Act a "brazen and bold" attempt to destroy

Clarence Darrow leans on a desk at the Rhea County courthouse in Dayton, Tennessee, during the Scopes Monkey Trial in 1925. John Scopes is seated to Darrow's right.

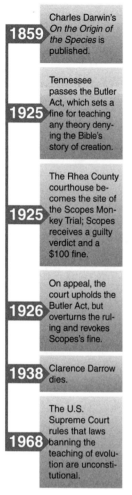

1859   Charles Darwin's *On the Origin of the Species* is published.

1925   Tennessee passes the Butler Act, which sets a fine for teaching any theory denying the Bible's story of creation.

1925   The Rhea County courthouse becomes the site of the Scopes Monkey Trial; Scopes receives a guilty verdict and a $100 fine.

1926   On appeal, the court upholds the Butler Act, but overturns the ruling and revokes Scopes's fine.

1938   Clarence Darrow dies.

1968   The U.S. Supreme Court rules that laws banning the teaching of evolution are unconstitutional.

learning and blamed Bryan for its passage. Darrow held the audience spellbound with his manner of speaking, his voice rising and falling dramatically while he paced the floor. He declared the Bible "a book primarily of religion and morals. It is not a book of science." He argued that by making it a crime to teach evolution in the public schools, soon legislators may find it a crime to teach it in Catholic schools, and soon the topic could be banned in newspapers or books. Many spectators were impressed with Darrow's speech, while others were shocked to hear him speak in what they felt was irreverence.

During the trial, the prosecution called several witnesses, including students, to prove that Scopes had taught evolution. Darrow tried to call in a zoologist to explain evolution, but Bryan successfully blocked the move. Bryan boomed in his preacher's voice that "the Bible is the word of God," and that "The Bible is the only expression of man's hope of salvation." People in the courthouse proclaimed "Amen" as if they were in church. Bryan preached about how the teaching of evolution would destroy the basic beliefs of Christianity, such as the Virgin Birth of Jesus and the resurrection of the body. At the end of Bryan's speech, the audience broke into thunderous applause.

It appeared to observers that the trial was over. Without an expert witness, Darrow had been unable to show evolution as a widely accepted doctrine. Many journalists packed their equipment and left Dayton that weekend, certain Scopes would be found guilty. But what happened next was one of the most astonishing events in courtroom history.

On Monday, July 20, Darrow's co-defense attorney announced, "The defense desires to call Mr. Bryan as a witness." The move surprised everyone, especially Bryan. By this point, the judge had moved the entire court proceedings to an outdoor stage because the floor of the courtroom had begun to crack under the strain of the crowd. Intense summer heat had caused all the men, including the lawyers, to remove their suit coats, and everyone fanned themselves continuously with handheld fans.

As Bryan willingly sat on the witness chair in front of the 5,000 spectators in the afternoon sun, Darrow bored into him. "You have given considerable study to the Bible, haven't you, Mr. Bryan?" he began. "Yes, I have," Bryan responded. Darrow then asked him if he claimed that everything in the Bible should be interpreted literally, that is, as fact. Bryan said that some things in the Bible were meant to illustrate a point. Then Darrow asked Bryan about certain biblical events such as the earth standing still and a whale swallowing Jonah. Bryan insisted he believed the Bible. Darrow asked him what he thought would happen if the earth stood still. Bryan appeared uncomfortable with such a scientific question. Darrow told Bryan that the earth would have become a "molten mass." Darrow went on to interrogate Bryan about time frames in the Bible. Bryan became flustered with such calculations as the length of time since creation. Darrow asked Bryan what he knew of ancient Chinese or Egyptian civilizations that may have begun before the date that biblical readers had deduced as the beginning of the world. Bryan admitted a lack of knowledge.

Darrow pursued the question of the world being created by God in six days. Darrow asked, "Do you think the earth was made in six days?" Bryan answered, "Not six days of twenty-four hours." The crowd gasped. Darrow pressed Bryan to explain what the Bible meant by a day. "I am simply saying it is a period," Bryan said, further saying that creation "might have continued for millions of years." Fundamentalists in the audience were shocked by what they heard Bryan saying, for they believed that all the words in the Bible were facts, not allegories or metaphors. Finally, Bryan exploded and told the judge, "The only reason Mr. Darrow has here is to slur at the Bible." Darrow burst back, "I am examining you on your fool ideas that no intelligent Christian on earth believes!" The session was soon over and crowds pressed upon Darrow to congratulate him, while a baffled Bryan walked away nearly alone. Five days later, still in Dayton, Bryan died of a stroke during his afternoon nap.

Scopes received a guilty verdict and a $100 fine. About a year later, the case came before the Tennessee Supreme Court. The Court upheld the Butler Act, but overturned Judge Raulston's ruling and revoked Scopes's fine. Scopes left teaching and became a geologist. Darrow continued to work in Chicago until his death in 1938 at the age of eighty. The movie *Inherit the Wind* (1960) is an acclaimed dramatization of the Scopes trial.

In the 1960s public schools began teaching evolution again, partly for fear that U.S. students were falling behind in science. In 1968 the U.S. Supreme Court ruled that laws banning the teaching of evolution were unconstitutional. But through the remainder of the 1900s, creationists—believers in the literal biblical version of creation—continued to exert a strong influence on school curriculums throughout the United States.

"I do not consider it an insult, but rather a compliment to be called an agnostic. I do not pretend to know where many ignorant men are sure—that is all that agnosticism means."

Clarence Darrow, 1925

Visitors to Dayton can see the Rhea County courtroom, still in use today, and visit the Scopes Trial Museum on the building's lower level. The courtroom and museum are open weekdays except holidays throughout the year. The museum is operated by Rhea County and the Rhea County Historical Society. In addition, visitors can obtain a map of nearly twenty buildings in Dayton that have historic significance concerning the trial, including the Bailey Boarding House, where Scopes lived and which is now a bed-and-breakfast.

Each year, Dayton hosts the Scopes Trial Play and Festival during the third week of July. The play, which lasts a couple of hours, is adapted directly from court transcripts and presented in the courtroom where the trial took place. Members of the audience are selected to serve on the jury. The festival offers a taste of the fun that accompanied "The World's Most Famous Court Trial." The festival features tours of historic homes with ties to the trial, vendors of handmade crafts, and performances of traditional music. The play and festival is presented by Bryan College and the Dayton Chamber of Commerce. Bryan College, in Dayton, is named after Williams Jennings Bryan. The college published the "Tennessee Evolution Case" in 1927, which contains the original transcript of the trial. ◆

> In the 1960s public schools began teaching evolution again, partly for fear that students were falling behind in science.

Russell Cave

NORTHEASTERN ALABAMA

Russell Cave, in the northeast corner of Alabama, contains artifacts dating back almost ten thousand years and is one of the most extensive archaeological records of habitation by Native Americans in the eastern United States. The cave is one of the richest archaeological sites in the southeast, and, with about seven miles of mapped, mostly horizontal passageways, it is one of the most extensive caves in Alabama. Russell Cave lies near the borders of Tennessee and Georgia; the closest city is Chattanooga, Tennessee. The cave was designated a national monument by President John F. Kennedy in 1961. Its museum was recently remodeled and enlarged to include artifacts and information on the Creek, Cherokee, and Choctaw tribes whose ancestors once inhabited Russell Cave in cold-weather months. The cave and the museum offer one of the fullest views of how the first inhabitants of North America fled, clothed, and protected themselves in the millennia before the arrival of Europeans.

In 1817 Captain John Woods, a Cherokee veteran of the Revolutionary War, received 640 acres for a reservation. Captain Woods built a stone house (still standing) on the property, and was later joined by another veteran, Major James Doran from Virginia. Doran later sold the part of the land that includes the cave to his brother-in-law, Colonel Thomas Russell of North Carolina, also a veteran of the Revolutionary War, who gave his name to the cave. The Russell family sold the property in 1928 to Oscar Ridley.

In 1953 an engineer named Paul H. Brown was surveying the area for the Tennessee Valley Authority when he was shown Russell Cave and subsequently leased it for excavations from 1953 to 1955. Brown was joined by Charles K. Peacock, LeBaron Pahmeyer, and J. B. Graham; all four were members of the Tennessee Archeological Society. Brown published a preliminary report on his findings in 1954, but realized that a thorough exploration of the site was beyond the society's ability. The group contacted the Smithsonian Institution; Carl F. Miller inspected the cave, and based on his findings, the Smithsonian arranged a cooperative agreement with the National Geographic Society to continue explorations from 1956 to 1958. In 1958, the National Geographic Society purchased 310 acres from landowner Oscar Ridley and donated the land to the National Park Service.

President Kennedy designated Russell Cave a national monument in 1961, and in July of the following year the National Park Service conducted its own excavation. This dig revealed most of the artifacts now on display at the Russell Cave museum. Carbon dating from the charcoal from the cave's campfires has enabled archaeologists to determine the approximate ages of the finds.

Nomadic bands of Native Americans happened upon the cave around nine thousand years ago. Very little is known about them, but experts think that the first group to occupy the cave probably numbered around fifteen to twenty. A handful of chipped flint points that were probably spear points was found twelve feet below the surface of the present cave floor. The Indians lived in the cave only during the fall and winter months; during the rest of the year they kept alive by hunting wild game and gathering wild plants. This was Stone Age life, before the age of agriculture.

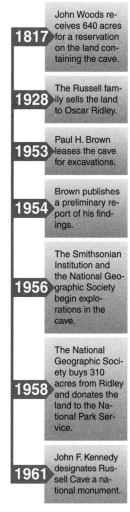

1817 John Woods receives 640 acres for a reservation on the land containing the cave.

1928 The Russell family sells the land to Oscar Ridley.

1953 Paul H. Brown leases the cave for excavations.

1954 Brown publishes a preliminary report of his findings.

1956 The Smithsonian Institution and the National Geographic Society begin explorations in the cave.

1958 The National Geographic Society buys 310 acres from Ridley and donates the land to the National Park Service.

1961 John F. Kennedy designates Russell Cave a national monument.

The entrance to Russell Cave in Alabama.

seismic: caused by an earthquake.

Geologists have determined that the cave's first inhabitants could not have lived there before 9,000 years ago because prior to that time the entire cavern was filled with water. Then, a **seismic** shift occurred that caused a great rockfall from the roof and shunted the water to one side and raised the floor of the cave above the water level. Archaeologists have measured the radioactive carbon remaining from the charcoal of the Indians' campfires to date the arrival of the cave's first inhabitants at sometime between 6550 and 6145 B.C.E.

The cave provided a convenient shelter and its stream was a source of fresh water; its relative warmth in the winter (about 56 degrees) kept the stream from freezing. In the warmer months, the people probably camped along the nearby Tennessee River and hunted wild game in the forests; in the cold months they could live off the nutrient-rich nuts gathered from the trees in the forest.

Archaeologists have divided the periods of Native American life into four periods, dated approximately: the Paleo (12,000–7500 B.C.E.), Archaic (7500–1000 B.C.E.), Woodland (1000 B.C.E.–C.E. 700), and the Mississippian (700–1540). It is generally agreed that the ancestors of Native Americans migrated to the Americas over a land bridge that once connected Siberia and Alaska between 30,000 and 10,000 years ago. This was during the Ice Age of the Pleistocene epoch, which ended about

11,000 years ago. Wandering bands of big-game hunters tended to live in extended families of about twenty to forty people; they traveled light with few possessions other than fire-making tools, spears tipped with stone or bone points, and their domesticated hunting dogs. As the Ice Age ended and many of the large mammals they had once hunted became extinct, the Paleo-Indians' culture evolved into the Archaic culture that relied on fishing, small-game hunting, and gathering wild plants and shellfish.

The Archaic Indians who lived at Russell Cave between the 6000s and 1000 B.C.E. hunted deer, turkey, squirrel, raccoon, rabbit, gray fox, bobcat, and skunk. Porcupines, too, apparently once lived this far south, for their bones have been discovered at the deepest levels of the cave. The cave dwellers roasted the game over fires, or stewed them in containers of bark or skin. They would heat the water in a skin container by heating rocks in the fire, then dropping them in the water. They hunted with short spears tipped with a stone point (many chips have been found in the cave, indicating that the spear points were fashioned there) and propelled by an atlatl, or throwing stick. The skins of the larger animals were scraped by sharpened stones and made into clothing and the stewing containers mentioned above. Archaeological digs have uncovered needles and awls that the Indians used to sew hides together, as well as fishhooks fashioned out of bone.

Deep in the Archaic-level deposits, archaeologists have found impressions of cane matting on a clay floor, so it is likely that they also wove baskets; these items, however, like anything made of wood or animal hide, have since decomposed. The Archaic period Indians also occasionally buried their dead in the cave. Several human skeletons have been found in shallow burial pits carved out of the cave floor.

Around 1000 B.C.E., near the beginning of the Woodland period, the Indians' way of life changed in many ways, primarily with the beginning of agriculture and the formation of larger, more populated settlements. The artifacts found at about this level of the digs include bone and shell and bear-tooth ornaments, smaller weapon points that suggest the use of bow and arrow instead of spear, and significant amounts of pottery used for storing and cooking food. The bone tools from this period, such as needles and fishhooks, were more finely made than in previous times.

The Woodland period was much more stable and prosperous, thanks to the steadier supply of food afforded by agriculture.

The cave provided a convenient shelter and its stream was a source of fresh water; its relative warmth in the winter kept the stream from freezing.

The women tended to the planting of corn, beans, squash, pumpkins, and other foods, while the men hunted small game and fished. Women had a high status in the society, as kinship relations were organized matrilineally (in the mother's line of descent). The presence of burial mounds from this period indicate that the Indians had grown more numerous and that their culture had become sophisticated enough for the development of political and religious institutions, and organized enough to sustain the large effort of building the mounds. The Woodland Indians paid close attention to the manner of burial, dressing the bodies carefully and providing them with food and tools for use in the afterlife.

Women had a high status in the society, as kinship relations were organized in the mother's line of descent.

Shortly after the close of the Woodland period, around 500 C.E., the Native Americans made less use of Russell Cave. They probably did not need it as much as formerly because their society had grown more organized around settlements. It was still used, however, for shelter during winter hunting parties. In later centuries, the Cherokee occupied this part of the Tennessee Valley, though the artifacts they left have been few, and close to the cave's surface. The only artifact found from the Historical Period (beginning with European explorations around 1540) is a metal fishhook, which could have been left either by a Native American or a European.

Located seven miles northwest of Bridgeport, Alabama, Russell Cave National Monument is carefully maintained to give visitors a glimpse of prehistoric life and of Native American cultures as they existed before the arrival of the Europeans after 1500. Rangers at the monument give demonstrations of prehistoric tools and weapons and lead guided walks and cave explorations. ◆

Salem Witch Trials Memorial

I n August 1992, three hundred years after more than twenty women and men were hanged for witchcraft in Massachusetts, a memorial was dedicated in Salem as a tribute to the victims and as a plea for tolerance and moderation. The so-called "Salem Witch Trials" of 1692 took place in Salem Village (since renamed Danvers), Massachusetts, and have haunted American history ever since. Today, in addition to the Witch Trials Memorial, Salem has the Salem Witch Museum, Salem Witch Village, and Witch Dungeon Museum where visitors can learn more about Puritan life in seventeenth-century Massachusetts and the social and religious conditions that led to their frenzied hunt for witches.

> *"I am no witch. I am innocent. I know nothing of it."*
> Bridget Bishop, hanged in Salem, June 10, 1692

In Europe, religious persecution of people accused of being witches or sorcerers began around the early 1400s—often as a way of accounting for plagues or crop failures—and became more common during the sixteenth and seventeenth centuries. Trials, convictions, and executions of accused **heretics** and witches reached their peak during the Spanish Inquisition, when as many as one hundred people were executed in a single day in a mass burning called an *auto da fé* (Spanish for "the delivering of sentence in matters of faith"). The Inquisition, however, was more concerned with religious heresy than with witchcraft. In some parts of Europe, people accused of being witches continued to be hanged or burned at the stake up until around 1750.

heretic: one who disagrees with an accepted belief or doctrine.

The Puritans of New England had come to North America with the dream of creating God's kingdom on earth, but the

The Witch Trials Memorial in Salem, Massachusetts.

fulfillment of this glorious project had not gone smoothly. The colonists were battered by Indian wars such as King Philip's War (1675–76) and frustrated by political developments in England that resulted in Massachusetts losing its charter—the written grant from the king that had conferred certain rights and privileges—and becoming part of the Dominion of New England. Many Puritans interpreted these difficulties as signs that Satan was attacking their community. Ministers such as Cotton Mather warned that the devil was trying to overthrow the kingdom of Christ, using witches as his servants.

Mather published a widely read book, *Memorable Providences*, which described the suspected witchcraft and execution in 1688 of Goody Glover, an Irish washerwoman in Boston. The hysteria surrounding this case closely resembled what was to come in Salem Village, though there were other executions of accused witches before the great Salem witch-hunt, and others would follow. A woman named Margaret Jones was executed for witchcraft in Boston in 1648; soon afterward, Mary Parsons of Springfield, Massachusetts, was indicted for witchcraft but was executed for having killed her child; and Ann Hibbins was hanged in Boston on June 19, 1656. It was said that the witches made a bargain with Satan and received supernatural powers to harm others, generally by causing the illness or death of people or their livestock.

Although no single factor can explain the witch-hunting hysteria that soon developed, it helps to understand that in the late 1600s Salem Village was undergoing stresses of change and uncertainty. While Salem had previously been a devout, "God-fearing" town like the others in New England, a mercantile elite was gaining influence in the town. The prominent members of the town's society were less eager than in former years to take leadership positions, and two families, or clans—the Putnams and the Porters—were competing for control of the village and its religious life. Meanwhile, Salem Village, whose economy was mainly based on agriculture, was torn between agrarian independence from the town of Salem, or closer links with Salem's sea trade. Some citizens wanted life to be simple and the society closed, while others wanted greater connection with the larger world outside. In contemporary terms, the village was feeling the stresses of traditional religious versus secular, worldly values.

In 1688 one of Salem Village's most prominent elders, John Putnam, invited a new preacher to be minister of the town's church. Samuel Parris had been a planter and merchant in Barbados, in the West Indies. Parris moved to Salem Village with his wife, Elizabeth, their six-year-old daughter, Betty, their niece Abigail Williams, and their slave, Tituba, purchased in Barbados but originally from West Africa.

In February 1692 young Betty Parris became ill and behaved in a most strange manner. She complained of fever, dashed about the house, dove under furniture, and contorted in pain. No one knew what was causing Betty's illness or fits. Then some of her playmates, including eleven-year-old Ann Putnam, seventeen-year-old Mercy Lewis, and Mary Walcott also began to behave strangely. A doctor, William Griggs, was called in to investigate. When his own remedies failed, he suggested there could be some supernatural origin to the girls' behavior. It was already "understood" that witches often practice their powers on children, so the doctor's hypothesis seemed plausible.

People began to suspect that Tituba might have influenced the girls, for she had often thrilled them with tales of magic, voodoo, rituals, and other elements of native folklore, which the children naturally found fascinating. Soon other local girls began to demonstrate the same "afflicted" behavior, including Elizabeth Hubbard, Susannah Sheldon, and Mary Warren.

1648 Margaret Jones is executed for witchcraft in Boston.

1656 Ann Hibbins is hanged in Boston for witchcraft.

1688 John Putnam invites Samuel Parrish to be minister of the town's church.

1692 A special court meets in Salem to try the witchcraft cases; by September it executes fourteen women and five men.

1750 The execution of accused witches comes to an end in Europe.

1992 Holocaust survivor Elie Wiesel dedicates the Salem Witch Trials Memorial as a tribute to the victims and a plea for tolerance.

A Twentieth-Century Witch-Hunt

The expression "witch-hunt," calling up memories of the Salem witch trials, was used to characterize the post-World War II concern with communist conspiracies. Under pressure from conservatives in and out of Congress, President Harry Truman issued Executive Order 9835 on March 12, 1947, setting up a federal loyalty program. This was followed by the establishment of similar loyalty programs at the state and local level.

The dangers posed by the real threat of Soviet power and the goading of Republicans who accused Truman and the Democrats of being "soft on communism" led to the sensational trial of the Communist Party leadership. Indicted under the Smith Act of 1940, eleven communists were charged with and convicted of attempting to organize the overthrow of the U.S. government. Of more immediate impact were Senator Joseph R. McCarthy's attempts to take over the loyalty program at all levels. Beginning in 1950 McCarthy claimed to have a list of known communists who were working in the state department. Following up the technique of naming names and figures, but producing little substantial evidence, McCarthy accused a large number of individuals of being communists or communist sympathizers. The stridency of these charges and his attack on the U.S. Army brought McCarthy a vote of censure by the U.S. Senate in 1954. The most publicized case arising from the witch-hunt of the 1950s was the confrontation between Alger Hiss and Whittaker Chambers, and Hiss's subsequent conviction on perjury charges. Another case, the trial of Ethel and Julius Rosenberg, ended with the execution of the Rosenbergs in 1953.

They would fall down in frozen postures, contort themselves into grotesque poses, and complain of biting and pinching sensations.

In late February arrest warrants were issued against Tituba and two other women, Sarah Good and Sarah Osborn. Good was a social misfit and homeless, and Osborn was old, irritable, and had not attended church in over a year. The Putnam family accused these women of practicing witchcraft against the girls, and insisted on examinations. County magistrates Jonathan Corwin and John Hathorne scheduled examinations, and villagers came forward with stories of food mysteriously gone bad and livestock born with deformities following visits by one of the accused. Tituba first denied having anything to do with witchcraft, but then changed her story and said she had been approached by a tall man from Boston who asked her to sign in his book and asked her to do his work. This man, she claimed, sometimes appeared as a hog or a dog. Tituba said that she and four other women, including Osborn and Good, had flown through the air on their poles. She had tried to seek counsel from Reverend Parris, she explained, but the devil had blocked her path. After hearing Tituba's "confession," most skeptics were silent, and the witch-hunt was on.

Soon more townspeople—mostly girls and young women— were "possessed," falling into fits before the church officials and civil magistrates who were investigating the matter. The afflicted girls began claiming that they had been pinched or bitten by the specters (invisible presences) of the accused witches; even a four-year-old girl named Dorcas Good, Sarah Good's daughter, was accused, and imprisoned for eight months. The jailed suspects began to see admission of guilt as the only way to avoid hanging. Deliverance Hobbs was the second, after Tituba, to confess to being a witch. She said she had pinched the girls because the Devil commanded her to, and she had flown on a pole to attend a witches' sabbath in a nearby field. Later, as the hysteria spread to Andover and other nearby towns, the accusations widened to include wealthy, respectable women and some men related to them. Even Lady Phips, wife of Sir William Phips, governor of Massachusetts, and George Burroughs, a former minister of Salem, were accused.

> *"I am wronged. It is a shameful thing that you should mind these folks that are out of their wits."*
> Martha Carrier, hanged August 19, 1692

A special court met in Salem in early summer 1692 to try the witchcraft cases. The first person to be sentenced to death was Bridget Bishop, who was hanged for witchcraft on June 10. By late September, the court had executed fourteen women and five men. Another elderly man was pressed to death, and several perished in prison. It is interesting that those who admitted to practicing witchcraft (whether it was true or not) were spared the death sentence; only the convicted who refused to confess were executed (such as Bridget Bishop, who said, before she was hanged, "I am no witch. I am innocent. I know nothing of it").

Even before the court began its grim task, some people in the community spoke out against accusing people on extremely flimsy evidence. Many of the charges were based on testimony that someone had been tortured or pinched by an apparition— a supernatural image—of the supposed witch. Several ministers, including Increase Mather, claimed that this kind of vision (or "spectral evidence") was insufficient proof of witchcraft, because Satan might take the shape of an innocent person. After a few months of convictions and executions, other colonists came to believe that the witch-hunt was a terrible mistake.

Governor Phips disbanded the special court in October 1692. In January of the next year, another court sentenced three more people to death, but they were not executed. In all, more than 250 people, 80 percent of them women, had faced accusations of being witches. Afterward some judges and jury members publicly confessed that they had been tragically wrong.

The Salem Witch Trials Memorial was dedicated in August 1992 by Nobel Peace Prize laureate Elie Wiesel, a survivor of the Auschwitz death camps. The memorial, winner of several national design awards, shows the victims' protests of innocence inscribed in stone but interrupted in mid-sentence by a granite boundary wall that symbolizes society's indifference to oppression. Stone benches within the memorial bear the names and execution dates of each of the twenty victims (e.g., "REBECCA NURSE, HANGED, JULY 19, 1692"). The memorial quietly honors the victims and stands as a sober reminder of what can happen when a spirit of tolerance and understanding is overriden by suspicion and hysteria. ◆

> Those who admitted to practicing witchcraft were spared the death sentence; only the convicted who refused to confess were executed.

San Carlos Borromeo Mission

CARMEL, CALIFORNIA

In 1768 King Charles III of Spain, reacting to rumors of possible English and Russian settlement along the Pacific coast of North America, ordered Jose de Galvez, the Visitor General of New Spain, to investigate at the possibility of sending a colonizing expedition from Mexico to Alta California. Galvez organized an expedition with the goal of establishing three Spanish missions, to be supported by the military. The mission sites had been chosen earlier during exploratory expeditions along the California coastline. The first mission would be built in southern California, near San Diego; the second would be located farther north near Monterey Bay; the third would be established along the Santa Barbara channel where the largest concentration of California's Native Americans lived.

The expedition was placed under the leadership of Padre Junipero Serra, a Spanish Franciscan priest and university professor. Highly talented and a skillful leader, Serra had earlier established a chain of mission in the Sierra Gorda region of Mexico. Serra regarded his appointment as president of the Alta California missions as a gift from his God. The main goal of Serra and other Spanish missionaries was to convert the Native Americans to Christianity, then train them to become productive citizens of Spain. Once the Spanish considered the native peoples to be properly trained, the Franciscans were to turn the mission over to the secular clergy, and the lands would be divided up among the adult male Christian Indians. This practice had already proved successful and profitable for Spain in other parts of the Americas.

Spanish governor Gaspar de Portola joined Serra as military leader of the Alta California expedition. The **presidio** and mission of San Diego de Alcala was established in July 1769. Soon after the founding of San Diego, Gaspar de Portola and some of his soldiers headed north to seek a site at Monterey Bay. However, Portola's party failed to recognize Monterey Bay and passed it, continuing north to what Padre Juan Crespi later described as "a protected bay large enough to hold all the ships of Europe." The Spanish named the area San Francisco, after Saint Francis of Assisi, the founder and patron saint of the Franciscan order. On the return journey, Portola's party found Monterey Bay, but because they were short of supplies and many of the soldiers were ill, the Portola expedition continued south, returning to San Diego on January 24, 1770.

Plans were immediately made to return to Monterey with the supplies necessary to establish the mission and presidio. By mid April 1770 two expeditions headed north, the first, headed by Serra, sailed up the California coast aboard the *San Antonio*. The second, led by Portola, traveled by land. Both arrived at Monterey in late May and began to scout for a good place to build the second mission and presidio in California. They chose a site on the southern tip of Monterey Bay, and on June 3, 1770, Junipero Serra blessed the land and celebrated mass there. The mission was dedicated to Italian cardinal San Carlos Borromeo (Saint Charles Borromeo, 1538–84). Workers began building a log stockade and simple thatched-roofed **adobe** buildings to serve as temporary chapel, warehouses, and sleeping quarters for the priests and soldiers until permanent structures could be constructed.

Padre Serra quickly realized that the mission's original site was unsuitable because it was too far away from water and useful

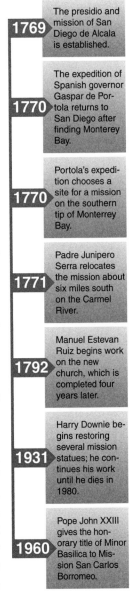

1769 The presidio and mission of San Diego de Alcala is established.

1770 The expedition of Spanish governor Gaspar de Portola returns to San Diego after finding Monterey Bay.

1770 Portola's expedition chooses a site for a mission on the southern tip of Monterrey Bay.

1771 Padre Junipero Serra relocates the mission about six miles south on the Carmel River.

1792 Manuel Estevan Ruiz begins work on the new church, which is completed four years later.

1931 Harry Downie begins restoring several mission statues; he continues his work until he dies in 1980.

1960 Pope John XXIII gives the honorary title of Minor Basilica to Mission San Carlos Borromeo.

presidio: a fortified place or military post.

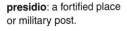

adobe: sun-dried brick.

The main church at San Carlos Borromeo mission in Carmel, California.

farmland. Serra had also come to believe that the Spanish soldiers were not good role models for the newly converted Indians, and he wanted to separate the Indians from the military presidio. In June 1771, Serra relocated the mission about six miles south on the Carmel River. The mission would now be known as San Carlos Borromeo de Carmelo del Rio. No time was wasted; the site was blessed and construction on the first adobe buildings began. They were similar to those at the original Monterey site. The new San Carlos Borromeo mission had plenty of good land for farming and for grazing livestock. Sandstone, as well as redwood, elm, and pine trees, was also abundant in the area and provided building material.

A crude temporary structure served as a place of worship for more than twenty years, until the mission's second president, Padre Fermin Lasuen, ordered construction of a permanent stone church. In 1792 master stonemason Manuel Estevan Ruiz began work on the new church, which was completed four years later. The church's towers and domes exhibit the influence of Spain's Moorish architecture. Official reports of the time describe the church as "built of cut stone with a tile roof, and presenting a harmonious and beautiful appearance."

The new church was surrounded by a quadrangle compound, lined with adobe buildings that served as workshops and living quarters for the priests. Outside the quadrangle were dormitories for the mission Indians, as well as barracks for a small group of soldiers stationed at San Carlos to protect the mission. Gardens and orchards were established south of the mission compound. At its peak, about six hundred Native Americans were under the protection of the San Carlos mission, although only a small number of the Christianized Indians actually lived at the mission at any given time.

San Carlos Borromeo mission became the official Franciscan headquarters in Alta California during the administrations of padres Serra and Lasuen. The Spanish governor resided at the nearby presidio of Monterey, from which location he could communicate quickly with the Franciscans. The Mexican government began **secularization** of the California mission in 1833, and San Carlos Borromeo de Carmelo del Rio was one of the first missions to be effected. When the Spanish-Mexican population began to attend religious services at the presidio chapel and the Indians abandoned the mission, signs of neglect appeared. By 1841 the mission was in ruins. The mission's roof tiles, timbers, cut stone, and adobe bricks were stolen for construction of other buildings. What wasn't taken was now exposed to the elements of nature, and in little time the once grand quadrangle became a pile of melted adobe bricks. The stonework of the church façade, bell towers, and domes remained essentially intact, but the roof and parts of the upper walls deteriorated.

secularization: the change from religious to civil ownership or use.

It was not until 1884, the centennial of the death of Padre Junipero Serra, that any real attempt at restoration occurred. Repairs were made to the stone walls and a new wood shingle roof was placed on the church. No attempt was made at that time to restore any of the outlying buildings. In August 1931 Harry Downie, a young Irish-American cabinetmaker born in San Francisco, traveled to Monterey to restore several of the mission's statues. Downie planned to stay only two weeks, but continued his restoration work at Carmel until he died in 1980. He eventually took charge of every aspect of the mission's restoration. In order to re-create the mission's original appearance, Downie studied mission documents, historic drawings, photographs, and buildings he had seen during travels to Spain and Mexico. He built a reputation for not only the aesthetic quality of his work but also for its historical accuracy. Harry Downie passed his knowledge and expertise on to his young intern Richard Joseph Menn, who continues to restore and preserve California's Spanish mission heritage at Carmel's San Carlos Borromeo mission.

In 1960 Pope John XXIII gave the honorary title of Minor Basilica to Mission San Carlos Borromeo de Carmelo del Rio. Pope John Paul II visited the mission in 1987. The San Carlos Borromeo mission continues to function as a working parish and school. It is visited each year by thousands of tourists, as well as pilgrims who come to pray at the tomb of Blessed Junipero to the mission Serra. ◆

Spanish Cabildo

New Orleans, Lousiana

The Cabildo, built by the Spanish in the late 1700s in what is now the heart of New Orleans's French Quarter, may not be as famous as the Louisiana Purchase, which was signed on its second floor in December 1803, but one need only look at the noble Spanish-style structure to sense that this is historic ground. The three-story building, completed in 1799, is one of the cornerstones of Jackson Square, the center of the French Quarter. As you face St. Louis Cathedral, the Cabildo sits on the left side, and on the right of the cathedral is the presbytère, the Cabildo's twin (begun 1795, completed 1813).

The first Cabildo burned in the great fire of 1788.

The Cabildo and the presbytère are both part of the Louisiana State Museum complex and contain a wealth of archives, paintings, costumes, artifacts, curiosities (including a death mask of Napoleon Bonaparte), and elaborate displays of the history of this state that was a colonial territory of France and Spain for about a hundred years before it became part of the United States. France had founded the city of La Nouvelle-Orléans in 1718, and laid out a street plan in 1722—roughly the 120 square blocks that are now called the French Quarter. On part of the ground now occupied by the Cabildo, the French built a corps de garde, or police station, beginning in 1723 and completed in 1725. According to the city plan, the parish church would be in the center, and on the other side would be a presbytère, or a residence for the priests. The three buildings in a row faced the river; between this early municipal complex and the river was an open square known as the Place d'Armes, or military drill field. A prison and criminal courtroom were constructed between the corps de garde and the church (built 1724–27). The city was growing, and the original corps de garde was crumbling, so a new, larger police station was built in 1751.

After Spain took control of Louisiana, the second Spanish governor, Don Alexandro O'Reilly (an Irishman in the service of Spain), ordered the construction of a new town hall and in 1769 signed a contract for its construction on the site of the French corps de garde. The Spanish assembly, called the Cabildo, met in the new town hall (then called the Casa Capitular, or Council House) for the first time on September 7, 1770. Eventually, the building came to be called by the name of the Spanish legislative assembly that met there.

The first Cabildo burned in the great fire of 1788. Its successor also burned in a second fire that ravaged the city in 1794. Construction of the new capitol house began in 1795 and was completed four years later. The wide, sturdy building is constructed of stuccoed brick, with nine wide arches, originally a flat roof, and is graced by French wrought-iron balconies and attractively proportioned cornices, pilasters, and pediment. The French-style mansard roof, added in 1847, with its nine dormer windows and the cupola on top, may at first appear incongruous to architects familiar with the "Hispano-Moresque" style, but in the century and a half since its addition (matched by the mansard roof of the presbytère, also added in 1847), it has become so much a part of the Cabildo and the look of Jackson Square that most people assume the roof has always looked as it does today.

The Cabildo was built with funds provided by Don Andrés Almonester y Roxas (1725–98), a Spanish nobleman who generously contributed also to the construction of the cathedral, where he lies buried, and to the presbytère. The look and feel of Jackson Square would be entirely different without the contributions of Don Andrés and his daughter, Micaela, the baroness de Pontalba. She built the two great apartment buildings that face each other across Jackson Square, known as the Pontalba apartments, the United States' oldest apartment complex originally built as apartments (some older structures have since been subdivided into apartments).

The most significant historical event that took place in the Cabildo was the signing of the Louisiana Purchase in 1803. The

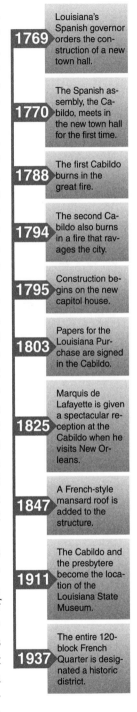

1769 Louisiana's Spanish governor orders the construction of a new town hall.

1770 The Spanish assembly, the Cabildo, meets in the new town hall for the first time.

1788 The first Cabildo burns in the great fire.

1794 The second Cabildo also burns in a fire that ravages the city.

1795 Construction begins on the new capitol house.

1803 Papers for the Louisiana Purchase are signed in the Cabildo.

1825 Marquis de Lafayette is given a spectacular reception at the Cabildo when he visits New Orleans.

1847 A French-style mansard roof is added to the structure.

1911 The Cabildo and the presbytere become the location of the Louisiana State Museum.

1937 The entire 120-block French Quarter is designated a historic district.

The Spanish colonial Cabildo in New Orleans, Louisiana.

agreement between France and the United States was signed in the Sala Capitular, a large room on the second floor (on the side opposite the cathedral, overlooking Jackson Square and St. Peter Street), now called the Louisiana Transfer Room. The Louisiana Purchase grew out of President Thomas Jefferson's determination to gain control of the city of New Orleans—or, at the very least, unrestricted use of its port. Jefferson wrote in 1802, "There is one single spot, the possessor of which is our natural and habitual enemy. . . . Every eye in the U.S. is now fixed on this affair of Louisiana." In 1801 word spread of an agreement between Spain and France that gave back the territory to France, which set off alarms in the U.S. government because Napoleonic France was an aggressive power, and the United States wanted no limits to its westward expansion. Jefferson wrote to Robert Livingston, the minister to France, "The day that France takes possession of New Orleans . . . we must marry ourselves to the British fleet and nation." The Pinckney Treaty of 1795 that had given Americans the right of deposit (to use the port) at New Orleans was temporarily retracted by the Spanish. This, too, alarmed the Americans. Jefferson instructed Livingston to attempt to purchase the "Isle of Orleans" (New Orleans) and West Florida from France, and appointed James Monroe to serve with Livingston. Congress appropriated $2 million for the ministers to bargain with.

It was the United States' good fortune that France was losing interest in retaining the territory, in part because Napoleon was nearing a war with Britain, and he did not want his forces spread too thin. On April 11, 1803, the French foreign minister Charles Maurice de Talleyrand surprised Livingston by asking how much the United States would pay for all of the Louisiana Territory.

Spanish explorers were the first Europeans to discover the Mississippi (Alonso Alvarez de Pineda in 1519, and Hernando de Soto in 1541), but it was not till a hundred years later that French Jesuit missionaries came down the Mississippi from the north and claimed the region for France. In 1682 the French explorer Sieur de La Salle descended to the mouth of the Mississippi and claimed on behalf of King Louis IX all "the seas, harbors, ports, bays, adjacent straits, and all the nations, people, provinces, cities, towns, villages, mines, minerals, fisheries, streams and rivers comprised" of the vaguely defined area he named, in honor of the king, Louisiana.

Except for the city of New Orleans, founded in 1718 by Jean-Baptiste Le Moyne, Sieur de Bienville, France never colonized the Mississippi River valley with anything like the commitment with which England settled the Atlantic coast. Facing the loss of the region to the British as a result of defeat in the Seven Years' War (1756–63), France ceded Louisiana to Spain. The American Revolutionary War ended with Britain's defeat in 1783, and Spain's control of the Louisiana territory was soon threatened when the independence of the thirteen colonies unleashed a flood of Americans into the Ohio and Mississippi river valleys. Friction with Spain was eased in 1795 by Pinckney's Treaty, which guaranteed Americans navigation rights on the Mississippi and the right to deposit goods for export at New Orleans.

In 1801 rumors that Spain had transferred Louisiana back to France provoked near-panic in the United States. Americans had expected that Spain would eventually lose its hold on the territory, but the idea of France as a close neighbor and an obstacle to westward expansion was intolerable. Then, suspension of the right of deposit at New Orleans threatened to cut off a substantial

"I know that the acquisition of Louisiana had been disapproved by some from a candid apprehension that the enlargement of our territory would endanger its union. But who can limit the extent to which the federative principle may operate effectively?"

Thomas Jefferson, second inaugural address, 1805

National Trust for Historic Preservation

New Orleans, Louisiana, and many other American cities boast historic buildings that have deteriorated and stand in grave need of preservation. The National Trust for Historic Preservation plays a key role in saving such buildings by providing technical advice, advocacy, seed money, and other financial assistance for repair and maintenance of buildings of importance to the nation's history and culture. Chartered by Congress in 1949 as a private, nonprofit organization, the trust fights to save historic buildings and the neighborhoods and landscapes they anchor. So far, the organization has acquired twenty historic properties that it maintains as museums, including Decatur House, its Washington, D.C., headquarters.

To continue to carry out its goal of preserving the historical and cultural foundations of the nation, the trust established its Main Street program in 1980. The program has involved more than 800 communities in forty-five states, which have invested nearly $3 billion in historic business districts. As a result, there have been 21,000 building rehabilitations, and the creation of more than 50,000 jobs and nearly 15,000 new businesses. The trust's budget comes principally from private sources, including dues from 250,000 members, corporate and foundation grants, endowment income, and merchandise sales. Congress contributes about one-fifth of the trust's income in the form of matching grants through the United States Department of the Interior.

portion of the nation's trade. Congressional war hawks called for the territory to be taken by force, though President Jefferson preferred to try diplomacy first. He dispatched Robert Livingston of New York and, later, James Monroe of Virginia to Paris to negotiate the purchase of New Orleans and Florida west of the Perdido River from France for no more than nine million dollars.

An uprising in the French sugar colony of Santo Domingo by an army of black slaves led by Toussaint L'Ouverture changed Napoleon's mind about trying to extend his colonial holdings in the Western Hemisphere. This revolt, combined with the rising tensions between France and Great Britain, led to Napoleon's decision to rid himself of all of Louisiana in order to consolidate his forces.

On April 30, 1803, Livingston, Monroe, and the French finance minister, the Marquis de Barbé-Marbois, initialed agreements transferring all of the Louisiana territory to the United States in exchange for $11.25 million. In addition, the United States assumed $3.75 million in claims of its citizens against France. Even though they were going "over budget" and beyond the instructions they had been given, Livingston and Monroe did not hesitate in agreeing to the purchase, for they knew that this was not an opportunity to be missed.

Yet the deal did not clearly define the exact dimensions of the territory. The treaty stipulated the boundary as "the same extent . . . that it had when France possessed it" before 1763—that is, before France turned it over to Spain. In what may have been an attempt to create future problems for the United States, French minister Talleyrand remained purposely evasive about the region's limits. When Livingston and Monroe attempted to pin him down to specifics, Talleyrand replied, "I can give you no direction. You have made a noble bargain for yourselves, and I suppose you will make the most of it."

For approximately three cents per acre, out of the Louisiana Purchase eventually emerged all or part of thirteen states: the states of Louisiana, Arkansas, Iowa, Missouri, Nebraska, North Dakota, South Dakota, and Oklahoma; and parts of Kansas, Minnesota, Colorado, Montana, and Wyoming.

When the Revolutionary War hero the Marquis de Lafayette visited New Orleans in 1825, he was given a spectacular reception at the Cabildo. Other prominent visitors to the building have included Henry Clay, Sarah Bernhardt, Mark Twain, Grand Duke Alexis of Russia, and William McKinley, Theodore Roosevelt, and William Howard Taft. The entire French Quarter (120 blocks) was designated a historic district in 1937, and this status has protected the old city from new developments that might disfigure or destroy its old European character. The Cabildo and the presbytère have housed the Louisiana State Museum since 1911. The museum was recently renovated, and visitors today can view the impressive collection of documents, portraits, costumes, furniture, and historical artifacts in well-marked displays. The significant contributions to Louisiana and Mississippi Valley history by women, African Americans, and Native Americans are highlighted in a way that earlier exhibits tended to overlook or take for granted. ◆

> Livingston and Monroe did not hesitate in agreeing to the purchase, for they knew this was not an opportunity to be missed.

Statue of Liberty

NEW YORK HARBOR

The Statue of Liberty in New York harbor is the most famous and beloved symbol of freedom in the world, and with more than two million visitors every year, it is one of America's most frequently visited national monuments. The image of "Lady Liberty" has been used to sell all manner of goods and services and every imaginable souvenir, from miniature replicas and postcards to T-shirts and headpieces. On the more sincere and idealistic side, a likeness of the statue appeared briefly in Tiananmen Square in Beijing, China, in the short-lived students' democracy movement of 1989. All around the world, the majestic and somewhat mysterious face of Miss Liberty has become inseparable from the idea and the promise of America. Americans have the people of France to thank for this national treasure, for it was they who paid for its construction in the 1870s and '80s as a gift of friendship between nations.

The idea for the statue arose at a dinner party at the chateau outside Paris of Édouard-Rene Lefebvre de Laboulaye (1811–83), a French journalist and politician, and a professor of political history at the Sorbonne. Laboulaye was a great admirer of the United States, in particular of how the young nation had so quickly risen from a loose confederation of **agrarian** colonies to prominence among the nations of the world, and how effectively the American government put into practice many of the ideals of liberty and equality that lay behind the French Revolution (1789). After dinner one evening in the spring of 1865, Laboulaye asked his dinner guests whether the bonds of friendship can last between nations. Many argued that it was unthinkable among the nations of the Old World, but Laboulaye insisted that France and the United States had a special relationship, and that something ought to be done to celebrate and commemorate that strong bond. France had contributed to the colonists' war effort against Britain in the American Revolution, and the new nation across the Atlantic was putting into action many of the best ideas in French political philosophy. Laboulaye was particularly impressed with the United States' balance of liberty and stability, even after a catastrophic civil war.

For most of the guests, this was just an after-dinner conversation. But one, a young Alsatian sculptor named Frédéric-Auguste Bartholdi (1834–1904), a former student of Laboulaye, was excited by the idea of some kind of tribute to Franco-American friendship. He told his professor that he would pursue the idea. Laboulaye was pleased, and supplied Bartholdi with letters of introduction to President Ulysses S. Grant, Henry Wadsworth Longfellow, and other prominent Americans.

Bartholdi first visited the United States in June 1871. As his New York–bound ship sailed through the Verrazano Narrows,

agrarian: of agriculture or farmers.

"We will not forget that liberty here made her home; nor shall her chosen altar be neglected."
President Grover Cleveland, 1886

his first sight was of Bedloes Island (then the site of Fort Wood, constructed as a defense in the War of 1812), and he knew instantly that this island was the perfect spot for the statue he dreamed of building. He could see how travelers to the great city would gaze with admiration at a magnificent statue rising out of the waters to welcome them. Bartholdi was thinking of the Colossus of Rhodes, one of the legendary seven wonders of the ancient world, a giant statue (by some accounts 100 feet tall) of the sun god Helios that had towered over the port of Rhodes in ancient Greece around 280 B.C.E., until it was toppled by an earthquake. (The ancient Greek historian Herodotus used the word *kolossos* in describing certain giant statues in Egyptian temples; Bartholdi was thinking, too, of ancient Egyptian colossi.) On this visit and on a later trip to the United States, he managed to generate interest in the scheme, and it was agreed that if the French would make the statue, the Americans would provide the base and pedestal to put it on.

The Statue of Liberty in New York Harbor.

The sculptor was commissioned to design a colossus, with the projected completion date of 1876, the centenary of the Declaration of Independence. Laboulaye, Bartholdi, and others founded a Union Française-Américain (Franco-American Union) and raised about 600,000 French francs (about $400,000 in U.S. dollars at the time) for the statue's construction; money was raised through public fees, a lottery, and admission fees for various entertainments.

Bartholdi and his assistants began constructing the statue in sections in his Paris studio. Alexandre-Gustave Eiffel, who later designed the Eiffel Tower, was responsible for constructing the iron **pylon** and skeletal framework under the sheets of copper "skin." The American public got an early view of the statue—or part of it—when its torchbearing arm was displayed at the 1876 Philadelphia Centennial Exhibition.

pylon: a tall, supporting structure.

The U.S. fund-raising efforts, however—which included benefit performances, auctions, art exhibitions, and prize

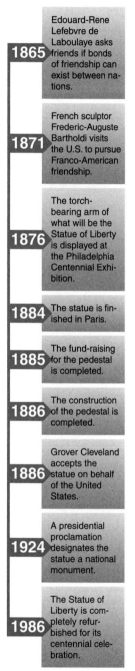

1865 Edouard-Rene Lefebvre de Laboulaye asks friends if bonds of friendship can exist between nations.

1871 French sculptor Frederic-Auguste Bartholdi visits the U.S. to pursue Franco-American friendship.

1876 The torch-bearing arm of what will be the Statue of Liberty is displayed at the Philadelphia Centennial Exhibition.

1884 The statue is finished in Paris.

1885 The fund-raising for the pedestal is completed.

1886 The construction of the pedestal is completed.

1886 Grover Cleveland accepts the statue on behalf of the United States.

1924 A presidential proclamation designates the statue a national monument.

1986 The Statue of Liberty is completely refurbished for its centennial celebration.

fights—did not generate much money at first. Prominent citizens of Boston and Philadelphia notified the French that if the fine city of New York could not bring itself to raise the needed money, they could, and would. Finally, exasperated by the disappointing show of American spirit, the publisher Joseph Pulitzer (a Hungarian-born immigrant) chastised the apathetic public in his newspaper *The World*. Pulitzer, after whom the renowned prize is named, criticized both the wealthy who had not been more generous and the middle classes who were apparently waiting for the rich to do all the giving. Shamed by Pulitzer's appeals, New Yorkers and other Americans reached deeper into their pockets, and eventually about $250,000 was raised to provide a solid foundation for the colossus.

The statue, formally named *Liberté éclairant le monde*, or *Liberty Enlightening the World*, was finished in Paris in July 1884, shipped in 350 pieces packed into 214 crates, and arrived in New York harbor in June 1885 onboard the frigate *Isère*. The fund-raising for the pedestal was only completed in August 1885, and the construction of the pedestal was finished in April 1886. It took four months to assemble the statue on its granite pedestal inside the star-shaped walls of Fort Wood.

A sonnet called "The New Colossus" by American poet Emma Lazarus (1849–87) was inscribed on a plaque on a wall of the statue's pedestal in 1903. The poem's well-known final lines read:

> Give me your tired, your poor,
> Your huddled masses yearning to breathe free,
> The wretched refuse of your teeming shore,
> Send these, the homeless, tempest-tossed to me:
> I lift my lamp beside the golden door.

Lazarus's poem has helped link the statue with her neighbor, the Ellis Island Immigration Station, through which more than twelve million immigrants passed before entering the United States between 1890 and 1954.

In addition to the classical grandeur of the colossus, robed like a Roman goddess, the statue's physical dimensions are impressive. The statue itself stands 151 feet tall, and the pedestal is 154 feet high; thus, from the pedestal's base to the tip of the torch is a height of 305 feet. Miss Liberty's head, from the tip of her chin to her cranium, is 17 feet 3 inches high, and 10 feet across; and her right arm is 42 feet long and 12 feet thick. The tablet she holds (inscribed in Roman numerals *July IV, MDCCLXXVI*

[July 4, 1776]) is 13 feet 7 inches high and two feet thick. There are twenty-five windows in her crown, one for each of the gemstones found in the world, and the crown's seven rays represent the seven seas and continents of the world.

President Grover Cleveland accepted the statue on behalf of the United States and dedicated it at a public ceremony attended by thousands on October 28, 1886. "We will not forget that Liberty has here made her home," said the president, "nor shall her chosen altar be neglected." The statue was cared for by the United States Lighthouse Board from its dedication until 1901, when it was turned over to the War Department. On October 15, 1924, a presidential proclamation designated Fort Wood and the statue as a national monument. Care and administration for the monument was turned over to the National Park Service in 1933, and on September 8, 1937, the jurisdiction was enlarged to include all of Bedloe's Island (until then the monument's boundary had been set at the edge of the fort). The name of the island was changed in 1956 from Bedloe's to Liberty Island, and on May 11, 1965, President Lyndon Johnson signed an order transferring Ellis Island to the National Park Service and uniting it with the Statue of Liberty National Monument. The two monuments together receive about four and a half million visitors every year.

The statue was completely refurbished for her centennial celebration in 1986, helped by a national drive for contributions led by automobile executive Lee Iacocca, chairman of the Statue of Liberty–Ellis Island Foundation and a proud descendant of Ellis Island immigrants. For two years a team of French and American craftsmen worked on the statue inside and out, repairing popped rivets in the 2.5-mm-thick copper "skin," replacing the corroded iron ribs with stainless steel, and reinforcing the arm, which had been installed incorrectly in 1886. French metal crafters replaced the old flame with a gold-plated copper flame lit by reflection, as Bartholdi had originally conceived it.

Liberty Island, like Ellis Island, is reached by ferryboats departing from Battery Park in lower Manhattan and from Liberty State Park in New Jersey. At the Statue of Liberty, energetic visitors can climb 354 steps (22 stories) to the statue's crown, though people with health problems are advised not to try it. On busy days in summer, the wait in line can take three hours; lines are shorter if you arrive early in the morning, or come in the off season. The highest level accessible by elevator is to the

Prominent citizens of Boston and Philadelphia notified the French that if New York could not bring itself to raise the needed money, they could, and would.

observation level at the top of the pedestal (154 feet). The elevator will also take you to the museum exhibits, which include the statue's history and the evolution of its significance, from its inception as a gift from the people of France to the people of the United States to an international symbol of political freedom. National Park Service rangers are available to give tours and answer questions. ◆

Stone Mountain Memorial

STONE MOUNTAIN, GEORGIA

Images of Confederate heroes Robert E. Lee, Stonewall Jackson, and Jefferson Davis are etched across the northern face of Stone Mountain sixteen miles east of Atlanta, Georgia. Begun by the sculptor of Mount Rushmore, the massive carving of the two principal generals and the president of the Confederate States of America (1861–65) took about sixty years to complete and is the largest **bas-relief** sculpture in the world, carved into the world's largest mass of exposed granite. Today Stone Mountain is the centerpiece of a 3,200-acre park visited by about four million people annually.

From a distance Stone Mountain looks like a massive gray egg half buried in a green plateau; it rises 825 feet (the top is 1,683 feet above sea level). The granite mountain was formed about 300 million years ago when tremendous subterranean pressures caused molten rock to push upward to the earth's surface. The molten rock cooled over a period of about 100 million years, and formed compact, uniform crystals. A two-mile-thick overlay of earth once covered the hardened granite, but over the next 200 million years the ground eroded and left the mountain that is visible today. Covering 583 acres above ground, the dome-shaped rock is the highest point of an enormous subterranean mass of granite that underlies half of Georgia and part of North Carolina.

While granite is the earth's most common igneous (heat-formed) rock, geologists have found that the granite of Stone Mountain is of an uncommon variety, a mixture of feldspar, mica, and quartz, very dense in texture and closely grained. Granite from Stone Mountain, quarried since the mid 1840s, has been used in buildings around the world, including the

bas-relief: structure in which figures are carved in a flat surface so that they project a little from the background.

"I can anticipate no greater calamity for the nation than the dissolution of the Union."

Robert E. Lee

United States Capitol building, the Imperial Hotel in Tokyo, the University of Havana, Cuba, and the locks of the Panama Canal.

Archaeologists have found evidence of primitive settlements around Stone Mountain in pieces of soapstone bowls and dishes possibly made five thousand years ago. Creek Indians farmed around the mountain, and traded with early Spanish, British, and French explorers. The first recorded sighting of the mountain by a European was by the Spanish captain Juan Pardo in 1567, on a mission to set up forts in the New World. Pardo described the great rock as a "Crystal Mountain." He and his men believed the quartz mountain was made of diamonds and rubies, but their hopes of digging for treasure were discouraged by attacks from the Creeks.

Historians and geologists have long been intrigued by two mysterious formations (or creations) that were "cleared away" by quarrymen in the 1800s. Early settlers described a rock formation that they called the "Devil's Cross Roads": two crevices about two hundred feet long, one running north–south and the other east–west, with an enormous rock at the intersection. The second curiosity was a wall of loose stones that encircled the top of the mountain, discovered by the Reverend Francis R. Goulding in 1822 and described in his book *Sapelo*. The circular wall has never been fully explained, but archaeologists and historians suspect it was used in Indian ceremonies.

Not long after the Civil War, particularly from 1895 to 1915, southern towns and cities erected statues and other memorials to honor the defenders of the Confederacy. Many statues in town squares and cemeteries honored the common soldiers, and many monuments were raised to commemorate the generals, particularly Robert E. Lee, the commander in chief of the Army of Northern Virginia, and Thomas J. "Stonewall" Jackson, the brilliant lieutenant general whose untimely death by friendly fire in 1863 was a crippling blow to the South. Among the most renowned statues of Lee are those at Washington and Lee University in Lexington, Virginia, along Monument Avenue in Richmond, Virginia, and at Lee Circle in New Orleans. Richmond's Monument Avenue also displays statues of Stonewall Jackson and President Jefferson Davis, among others.

The carving on the north face of Stone Mountain was originally the idea of Mrs. C. Helen Plane, a charter member of the United Daughters of the Confederacy (UDC), and a journalist named John Graves. Mrs. Plane's idea was for a colossal carved

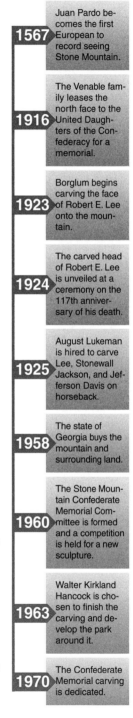

1567 Juan Pardo becomes the first European to record seeing Stone Mountain.

1916 The Venable family leases the north face to the United Daughters of the Confederacy for a memorial.

1923 Borglum begins carving the face of Robert E. Lee onto the mountain.

1924 The carved head of Robert E. Lee is unveiled at a ceremony on the 117th anniversary of his death.

1925 August Lukeman is hired to carve Lee, Stonewall Jackson, and Jefferson Davis on horseback.

1958 The state of Georgia buys the mountain and surrounding land.

1960 The Stone Mountain Confederate Memorial Committee is formed and a competition is held for a new sculpture.

1963 Walter Kirkland Hancock is chosen to finish the carving and develop the park around it.

1970 The Confederate Memorial carving is dedicated.

The images of Confederate heroes Jefferson Davis, Robert E. Lee, and Stonewall Jackson are carved into the side of Stone Mountain in Georgia.

memorial on one of the south's grandest vistas, whose north face offered a sheer cliff of about 800 feet. The mountain had been owned since 1887 by the Venable family; in 1916 the Venables leased the north face of the mountain to the UDC for twelve years, during which time a suitable memorial could surely be completed.

The sculptor Solon Borglum had carved a statue of Confederate general John B. Gordon for placement in Atlanta, and in 1915 Mrs. Plane and the Stone Mountain Monumental Association commissioned his brother, Gutzon Borglum, as the carving consultant after hearing high praises for his recent head of Abraham Lincoln. Gutzon Borglum's vision of how the monument should look exceeded even the grand hopes of Plane and Graves. He dismissed their idea for a portrait of Robert E. Lee as little more than "a stamp on a barn door," and proposed instead a monumental **frieze** that would feature colossal sculptures of seven central figures—most prominently Lee, Jackson, and Davis—accompanied by artillery and infantry, "an army of thousands."

frieze: a horizontal band decorated with ornaments.

Such plans are easier to sketch than pay for; funding problems and the United States' entry into the Great War (World War I) in 1917 distracted Borglum's initial planning efforts, and he was not able to resume work until 1922. Actual carving began on June 18, 1923, as Borglum was lowered by ropes down the face of the mountain in a boatswain's chair. With dynamite, the carving team blasted away large chunks from the north face of the mountain, and Borglum was able to complete the head of Lee in time for a ceremonial unveiling before a crowd of about 20,000 on January 19, 1924, the 117th anniversary of Lee's birth.

The next year, Borglum and the Monumental Association quarreled over money and artistic control. When the association fired him, he destroyed all his models (though other accounts say he took the models and sketches with him). Borglum went on to find greater fame as the sculptor of Mount Rushmore in South Dakota, while the Stone Mountain Monumental Association was left to find a new sculptor.

Augustus Lukeman was hired in 1925 and worked diligently for three years on a carving of Lee, Jackson, and Davis on horseback, grinding away at the granite with **pneumatic** drills. Borglum's head of Lee had been chiseled away to clean the slate for a fresh start. By 1928, the original deadline, only the new head of Lee was complete, and funds were exhausted. The Venable family did not renew the lease, and the sculpture was left at a standstill for thirty-six years. (The delay might not have lasted so long, but for the stock market crash of October 1929 that led to the Great Depression through most of the 1930s, and then the great disruptions of World War II in the first half of the 1940s.)

pneumatic: worked by compressed air.

The state of Georgia purchased the mountain and surrounding land in 1958 with the intention of developing Stone Mountain as a tourist attraction, and the Georgia General Assembly created the Stone Mountain Memorial Association. The Stone Mountain Confederate Memorial Committee was formed in 1960, and a competition was held for a new sculpture. The Memorial Association took the recommendations of the advisory committee and in 1963 chose Walter Kirkland Hancock of Gloucester, Massachusetts, to complete the carving and develop the park around it. George Weiblin was in charge of completing the sculpture. Work resumed the following year, and was helped along by a new technique that used thermo-jet torches to carve away at the granite. A marine veteran named Roy Faulkner was the chief carver, and with the thermo-jet torches he was able to remove tons of stone per day. The crew worked for eight years, sometimes amid seventy-mile-an-hour winds, and their improved equipment allowed them to carve with impressive detail on the figures' eyebrows, belt buckles,

"It is well that war is so terrible—we should grow too fond of it."

Robert E. Lee, 1862

and strands of hair. The sculpture is much larger than it appears from a distance, and the depths of the relief carving allowed workers to climb inside a horse's mouth to escape sudden rain showers.

The Confederate Memorial carving was dedicated on May 9, 1970, though finishing touches were added through 1972, sixty years after Mrs. Plane and John Graves first discussed the idea. Today the monument stands as an impressive achievement that will probably last for millennia. The carving is 400 feet off the ground, measures 90 by 190 feet in a frame 360 feet square, and is recessed 42 feet into the mountain. Lee's horse, Traveler, stretches across 145 feet—nearly the height of the Statue of Liberty from toe to torch. Lee, Davis, and Jackson are all mounted, facing east. Lee is the central figure, and projects farthest out from the mountain, with Davis in front and Jackson behind Lee, at about the same level of relief. All three hold their hats over their hearts.

> *"Neither current events nor history shows that the majority rules, or ever did rule."*
> Jefferson Davis, 1864

In addition to the famous sculpture, Stone Mountain Park offers a skylift to the summit, rides on a railroad around the mountain, a zoo, and hiking, tennis, swimming, and boating. On summer nights crowds gather to watch the laser light show on the north face of the mountain, a colorful extravaganza choreographed to music, splashed on the one-million-square-foot "natural screen." Stone Mountain has developed into a general theme park that seems to have little connection with the Confederate Memorial—so much so that one might suspect that the park is trying to call attention to everything but the Civil War—yet it is in keeping with Atlanta's enterprising, commercial spirit. One can easily imagine that hundreds and thousands of years from now, long after the theme park has been dismantled or rusted away, the three horsemen will still be galloping toward the rising sun, and new generations will ponder who they were and what they did. ◆

Sutter's Mill

COLOMA, CALIFORNIA

The great California landowner John Sutter and his trusted builder James Marshall were simply making a new sawmill at Coloma near the American River when

Marshall happened upon specks of gold in the water one January morning in 1848. With that discovery they triggered what has been called the greatest mass movement of people since the Crusades. The gold rush made thousands of prospectors rich beyond all imagining, but brought only disappointment and hardship to Sutter and Marshall. Sutter's Fort, the first European settlement in California's Central Valley, is located in what has since become downtown Sacramento; Sutter's Mill is about an hour's drive northeast. Each site is a state historic park with museums and period replicas of the fort and sawmill.

The first non-Indian to settle in the California interior, John Sutter (originally Johann August Suter), was born to Swiss parents in Kandern, Germany, near Switzerland, in 1803. He fled to America in 1834, leaving behind debts, a wife, and five children, and after roundabout travels he arrived in San Francisco Bay in 1839. He became a Mexican citizen in 1841—California was still part of Mexico at the time—and received a grant of 48,000 acres in the Sacramento Valley from Governor Alvarado. On this land, at the confluence of the Sacramento and American rivers, he founded Nueva Helvetia (New Switzerland). Fur traders and trappers had been through the region since 1827, if not earlier, but Sutter was the first European to settle here on any large scale. His labor force of Indians built a **citadel** known as Sutter's Fort, with walls two and a half feet thick and fifteen to eighteen feet high.

Overland emigrants came to New Helvetia, and Sutter employed them in his shops and fields and helped them establish their own farms. In 1846 a substantial number of Americans had settled in the vicinity of New Helvetia. Sutter became famous for his hospitality and assistance to struggling settlers; in 1847 he sent rescuers to the aid of the Donner Party, who were starving and trapped by winter snows in the Sierra Nevada. John Sutter professed loyalty to the Mexican goverment, but the Americans resented Mexican rule and rebelled at the time of the United States–Mexican War. Sutter eventually joined the American cause, and his fort became a center of American military operations during the conflict.

After the war Sutter's agricultural empire needed lumber for its new construction projects. He asked James Wilson Marshall, a skilled carpenter, originally from New Jersey, who had worked for him for many years, to find a suitable place for a sawmill. Marshall selected a site at Coloma by the American River, where there was a stand of large pine trees for lumber and river

"My sawmill is finished and I have made a discovery of a gold mine . . . which is extraordinarily rich."
John Sutter, letter to Mariano Vallejo, February 10, 1848

citadel: a fortress; stronghold.

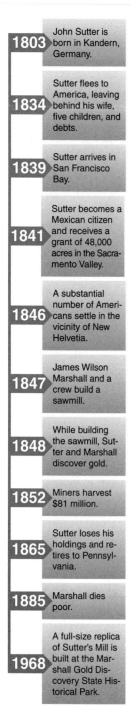

1803 John Sutter is born in Kandern, Germany.

1834 Sutter flees to America, leaving behind his wife, five children, and debts.

1839 Sutter arrives in San Francisco Bay.

1841 Sutter becomes a Mexican citizen and receives a grant of 48,000 acres in the Sacramento Valley.

1846 A substantial number of Americans settle in the vicinity of New Helvetia.

1847 James Wilson Marshall and a crew build a sawmill.

1848 While building the sawmill, Sutter and Marshall discover gold.

1852 Miners harvest $81 million.

1865 Sutter loses his holdings and retires to Pennsylvania.

1885 Marshall dies poor.

1968 A full-size replica of Sutter's Mill is built at the Marshall Gold Discovery State Historical Park.

water for power. (Coloma was called Culloomah or Cullumah by the Indian tribe of that name.) The sawmill was a joint venture between Sutter and Marshall; Sutter provided the capital, and Marshall oversaw the mill's construction.

In September 1847 Marshall and a crew of about a dozen began construction, and the mill was ready by year's end. But there was a problem. The sawmill was operated by water flowing through a diversion channel from the American River. In keeping with standard mill construction, a low dam had been built across the river to raise the water level and send part of the water through a diversion channel, known as a millrace; this water would drive the mill wheel and power the machinery. The lower part of the diversion channel, called the tailrace, was to carry the water back to rejoin the river. The problem was that the tailrace had been dug too shallow, so the water backed up and the wheel would not turn. It was necessary to dig the tailrace channel deeper, all the way down to the bedrock. The mill workers and some Cullumah Indians moved boulders and dirt to deepen the tailrace.

On the morning of January 24, 1848, Marshall was inspecting the tailrace when he saw a shining speck of some kind of mineral in the water. He scooped it up—it was about the size of a pea—tested its hardness with his fingernail, and rushed to find the others. "Boys, by God, I believe I have found a gold mine." The other workers were skeptical, and tested the metal's authenticity by pounding it, boiling it in lye, and heating it; the mineral passed all the tests. Marshall decided he must tell Sutter of his find.

Sutter, too, tested the metal, consulted his encyclopedia, and again the substance did indeed appear to be gold. But Sutter needed his lumber, and wanted the mill to start operating, so he and Marshall decided to keep the discovery a secret until the mill was completed and in operation. They were interested in the gold, but within reason, for they had no idea how extensive the deposits might be, and, after all, gold had been discovered in California before, and those finds had been relatively small and were quickly exhausted.

Word of Marshall's find leaked, however. Sutter himself mentioned the discovery, and the word spread to Sam Brannan, one of his partners who owned a general store at the fort. Brannan went to the mill to see for himself and was given a bit of gold. He went to San Francisco in early May and walked through the streets showing a chunk of gold in a bottle of qui-

A reconstruction of Sutter's Mill at Marshall Gold Discovery State Historical Park in Coloma, California.

nine, and shouting, "Gold, gold, gold, from the American River!" Many had heard rumors of a gold discovery, but Brannan's demonstration convinced doubters. By June 1 San Francisco was said to be half empty. "The blacksmith dropped his hammer," wrote Walter Colton, the alcalde (mayor) of Monterey at the time, "the carpenter his plane, the mason his trowel, the farmer his sickle, the baker his loaf, and the **tapster** his bottle. All were off for the mines, some on horses, some on carts, and some on crutches . . . ." The *WPA Guide to California*, written by the Federal Writers' Project in the 1930s, reports that by June 1848 "scarcely a male remained in Monterey, San Francisco, San Jose, or Santa Cruz. Soldiers deserted, and so did the detachments sent to capture them. . . . Fields of wheat went unharvested, homes and shops were abandoned, newspapers suspended publication, and city officials closed their desks." Families, too, were abandoned, in great numbers.

tapster: a bartender.

The California gold rush was the first of a series of mining rushes that spread across the west in the second half of the 1800s. In its economic, social, political, and environmental consequences, the gold rush was the most significant national event between the Louisiana Purchase and the Civil War. And, coming about a decade before that traumatic conflict, the gold discoveries also vastly enriched the United States Treasury and strengthened the Union's ability to sustain a prolonged war.

News of the gold discoveries generated immigrations of a fever pitch like the world had never seen before. California's non-Indian population jumped from 14,000 in 1848 to about 100,000 at the close of 1849, and then to a quarter of a million by the end of 1852. Within the first decade, more than 500,000 "forty-niners" came to California in search of the fabled fields of gold. The newcomers included Americans from every state and territory; representatives of every occupation, social class, and ethnic group, including slaves and free persons of color; and eventually foreign-born immigrants from Europe, Latin America, and, after 1852, from Asia. Mining was concentrated along the mother lode on the western slope of the Sierra Nevada, a belt about 120 miles long and two miles wide, from Coloma in the north to central Mariposa County in the south. Of the gold-producing areas, Nevada County was the richest. Among the major strikes were those at Feather River, Coloma, and in the Columbia diggings.

Across the mining region, the forty-niners harvested $10 million in 1848, $41 million in 1850, and $81 million in 1852. The total returns from the gold fields exceeded $300 million in the first six years. Production slowly declined thereafter to about $20 million annually by 1865 and remained at that level for the rest of the 1800s. From the time of the discovery to the end of the century, some 125 million ounces of gold were mined, worth some $50 billion in today's dollars. The economic impact spread from the mining camps to the burgeoning towns of Sacramento, Stockton, and San Francisco, and from California to the east coast and even to the financial capitals of Europe. The United States became a major gold-producing nation for the first time, and the new wealth powered the nation's rise in international influence.

The returns for individual miners reflected the rising numbers of forty-niners: from $20 a day in 1848 and $16 in 1849, the yield gradually fell to $5 in 1853, held at that level until the late 1850s, and then sank to $3 per day. Miners had to pay inflated prices for food, tools, transportation, and access to water.

Mining began with a pick, pan, and shovel in the placers. The rocker (or cradle) and long tom had become standard equipment by 1849, soon followed by the sluice. Miners also began using mercury to amalgamate with gold dust. By late 1849 and early 1850, miners had organized into larger companies for damming rivers and hydraulic mining; by 1851 vein or lode mining using stamp mills was established. Opportunities for individuals in washing gravel had ended by the mid-1850s, as the exhausted waterways had been dug over many times.

The gold rush brought about communities that were almost entirely male. Miners dressed alike, pursued similar strategies in work and recreation, and maintained a powerful sense of loyalty to their own small mining company. Each man asked few questions and guarded his privacy. Living conditions were generally temporary, and the forty-niners often took turns at domestic chores. At informal meetings in the camps and bars, miners drew up regulations for registering claims, adjudicating disputes, and ensuring the preservation of order. Those charged with violations were tried by juries of their peers, and sentences were carried out immediately. It was a society largely without formal institutions, such as law and courts, churches, and schools. And yet, according to the *WPA Guide*, "the mining camps, in distinction to the cities, stand as one of the world's best examples of men's spontaneous ability to govern themselves. With no formal legal setup, the miners, extremely diverse in background and nationality, established a society with a high degree of justice and democracy—particularly in the early years. Later, when 'loose fish' and 'bad whites' came to California in increasing numbers, crime became more difficult to control, both in the camps and in the feeder-town, San Francisco."

The tens of thousands of miners generated the need for a wide range of goods and services, and many, such as Levi Strauss, made their fortunes not directly from gold digging but from supplying the miners. Large numbers of people came to California to sell to (and prey on) the miners: merchants who sold food, clothing, and whiskey and exchanged gold dust; workers and owners of freight services and stagecoaches; professionals, from doctors and lawyers to newspaper publishers; skilled tradesmen, especially carpenters, builders, and sawmill operators; and, soon, "providers of entertainment," particularly saloon keepers and gamblers. While these groups were as temporary as the mining communities they served, they often ended up with most of the gold.

The discovery of gold should have made Sutter and Marshall rich, but the miners who rushed to the region overran Sutter's land, stole his livestock, and took advantage of his hospitality and gullibility. Sutter had always operated on the margins of financial ruin, and he could not keep up with the dizzying speed of the gold rush. In 1865 he finally lost what remained of his vast California holdings and retired to Pennsylvania. Until

> The California gold rush was the most significant national event between the Louisiana Purchase and the Civil War.

he died, in 1880, Sutter unsuccessfully petitioned the federal government to pay him for the losses he suffered during the war with Mexico and the gold rush.

James Marshall's claims to mining rights on the sawmill land were denied, obstructed, and swindled away, and armed guards were posted to keep him out of the mines. Marshall was never able to earn much of a living off the gold he discovered, though in deference to public sympathy, the California legislature voted in 1872 to appropriate $200 a month for two years for Marshall, though in the next session the legislators reduced the stipend by half. James Marshall died desperately poor on August 10, 1885, and was buried on a hill in Coloma overlooking the spot where he saw the first glimpse of the gold that for centuries explorers had known was somewhere to be found in the New World.

> **The miners who rushed to the region overran Sutter's land, stole his livestock, and took advantage of his hospitality and gullibility.**

Today Sutter and Marshall are commemorated in the state parks at Sacramento and Coloma. Sutter's Fort has been restored to its appearance in 1847, the year before Marshall's discovery. The park staff offers Demonstration days and Living History days when visitors can learn about blacksmithing, weaving, baking, and militia skills. The fort is across the street from the California State Indian Museum, where visitors can inquire about the Cullumah Indians who lived here before the Europeans.

At the Marshall Gold Discovery State Historic Park in Coloma, the Gold Discovery Museum has exhibits of gold-rush era mining equipment and horse-drawn vehicles. One of the favorite attractions is the full-size replica of Sutter's Mill, built in 1968. (The original mill, like much of Sutter and Marshall's property, was vandalized and finally abandoned, and it disappeared in floods in the 1850s.) Near the mill, visitors can try their hand at panning for gold. They say the gold veins all gave out many years ago, but you never know. ◆

Teapot Dome Oil Reserve

Teapot Dome is a 9,481-acre government-owned oil field near Midwest, Wyoming. The name Teapot Dome, which comes from a teapot-shaped rock formation near the field, became associated with one of the most extensive and damaging political scandals in United States history. At the center of the scandal, which rocked the administration of President Warren G. Harding, was the control and use of naval oil reserves at Teapot Dome, Wyoming, and Elk Hills, California.

The search for and production of petroleum became a major concern in the United States as the use of automobiles became widespread. In 1920 about eight million automobiles were registered in the United States. Nine years later that number had nearly tripled to twenty-three million. By 1910 the U.S. government realized that oil was a crucial resource both for citizens and for the armed forces. The U.S. Congress authorized the government to take over two large oil fields in California to be held in reserve for the U.S. Navy. In 1915 President Woodrow Wilson authorized the addition of Teapot Dome, called Naval Oil Reserve Number Three. Teapot Dome was named for a large rock rising from the land that resembled a teapot. The oil in the three reserves was to be kept in their natural reservoirs, or domes, in case it was needed by the navy in the future.

However, some business people suggested that the oil fields should not lay unused, and they clamored to make use of them. After some governmental squabbling, the responsibility for the reserves was placed in the care of the secretary of the navy, Josephus Daniels, in 1920. The congressional bill authorizing the

> "When one surveys the world about him after the great storm, noting the marks of destruction and yet rejoicing in the ruggedness of the things which withstood it, if he is an American he breathes the clarified atmosphere with a strange mingling of regret and new hope."
> Warren G. Harding, inaugural address, March 4, 1921

365

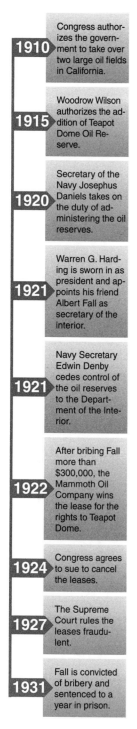

1910 Congress authorizes the government to take over two large oil fields in California.

1915 Woodrow Wilson authorizes the addition of Teapot Dome Oil Reserve.

1920 Secretary of the Navy Josephus Daniels takes on the duty of administering the oil reserves.

1921 Warren G. Harding is sworn in as president and appoints his friend Albert Fall as secretary of the interior.

1921 Navy Secretary Edwin Denby cedes control of the oil reserves to the Department of the Interior.

1922 After bribing Fall more than $300,000, the Mammoth Oil Company wins the lease for the rights to Teapot Dome.

1924 Congress agrees to sue to cancel the leases.

1927 The Supreme Court rules the leases fraudulent.

1931 Fall is convicted of bribery and sentenced to a year in prison.

move instructed him to "conserve, develop, use, and operate," the three oil reserves in the best interest of the navy and of national defense.

In March 1941 Warren G. Harding was sworn in as the twenty-ninth American president. As he filled key positions in his administration, he appointed his friend Albert B. Fall, a rancher and Republican senator from New Mexico, as secretary of the interior. Fall urged the president to transfer control of the oil reserves from the Navy Department to the Department of the Interior. The new secretary of the navy, Edwin Denby, did so in the fall of 1921, despite some criticism from Congress.

In the spring of 1922 Fall secretly arranged for two firms to lease the rights to these fields. The first was the Teapot Dome field, which was granted to Harry F. Sinclair's Mammoth Oil Company on April 7, 1922. Edward Laurence Doheny, president of Pan-American Petroleum Company and a long-time friend of Fall, got the rights to the Elk Hills and Buena Vista Hills reserves in California. At the time the leases were signed, Doheny gave Fall a $100,000 secured, interest-free loan, and Sinclair gave Fall more than $300,000 in government bonds and cash.

The "gifts and loans" Fall accepted were an illegal bribe. However, nobody knew about Fall's new wealth except for the neighbors of Fall's ranch near Three Rivers, New Mexico, where he suddenly purchased more land, acquired more cattle, and paid off old debts. The second illegal aspect of the oil leases was the secrecy under which the contracts were signed. Normally, government contracts must be open for bidding so that the government can get the best deal for taxpayers. By conducting the contract in secret, Fall excluded any other bidders.

As rumors of the secret leases circulated in Washington during the spring of 1923, President Harding began to worry about the state of his loosely run administration. The rumors are believed to have been a source of stress leading to his sudden death on August 2, 1923. After Harding's death, the Senate Public Lands Committee, led by Senator Thomas J. Walsh of Montana, launched an investigation that revealed the bribes given to Fall by Doheny and Sinclair. On February 8, 1924, in a joint resolution from the House and Senate, the Congress agreed to sue to cancel the leases. In 1927 the Supreme Court ruled the leases fraudulent and the transfer of the oil reserves from the Navy Department to the department of the interior illegal.

In the aftermath, Fall, Doheny, and Sinclair were tried for conspiracy to defraud the government but were acquitted. Sinclair spent six and a half months in jail for contempt of the Senate and jury tampering, and Fall paid a large fine and spent a year in prison after being convicted for bribery in 1931. Neither Denby nor Harding was implicated in the case. The scandal became the symbol for the corruption of the Harding administration, also tainted by fraudulent transactions in the Veterans Administration and Justice Department and by the president's extramarital affairs with Nan Britton and Carrie Phillips. Moreover, the Teapot Dome scandal seemed to reflect what many saw as the decay in the country's morals during the excesses of the Prohibition era. The impact of the scandal on the Republican party's national dominance during the 1920s, however, was minimal.

Teapot Rock in Wyoming from which the oil field takes its name.

The term "Teapot Dome" became synonymous with scandal and political corruption in the American vocabulary. During the 1924 New York gubernatorial campaign between Al Smith and Colonel Theodore Roosevelt Jr., Eleanor Roosevelt used the scandal against her cousin. In her vigorous efforts to support Smith, she followed "Ted" Roosevelt around the state in a car with a teapot mounted on top, unfairly implying that, as assistant secretary of the navy under Harding, he had been involved in the scandal. Straitlaced Calvin Coolidge, who had been Harding's vice president, was elected in his own right in 1924, and given his demeanor, was not tainted by the story that dominated the headlines for much of the campaign year.

The first reported production from Teapot Dome was in October 1922, but the field was shut down in December 1927 as a result of the court ruling. The field was turned back over to the navy in January 1928, but production did not resume until 1976 when, in the aftermath of the Arab oil embargo, Congress directed the reserve oil fields to be produced commercially at maximum rates. The government's share of revenues from the sale of crude oil, natural gas, and natural gas liquids from all of the Naval Petroleum Reserves totaled about $490 million in 1992. Teapot Dome's total production during 1992 averaged

2,300 barrels per day, with revenues from the oil and liquid products sales totaling $18 million.

Teapot Dome is located near Midwest, Wyoming, a small town of about 500 people forty miles north of Casper. It was an oil boomtown, thriving in the 1920s and 1930s from the rich Salt Creek oil field, which also brought Casper prosperity. But the oil boom went bust in Midwest by the 1960s, leaving the town with a deteriorated water system. The state spent millions of dollars building a water pipeline from Casper to Midwest to save the town, though some argued it was a waste of money.

The Salt Creek Museum, in Midwest, houses exhibits and artifacts covering the history of Salt Creek and Teapot Dome oilfields from 1889 to the present. The museum also holds a large circulating collection of Midwest Refining Company books dating from 1920 to 1930, which describe operations in Salt Creek oil field. ◆

Tippecanoe Battlefield

BATTLEGROUND, INDIANA

Tippecanoe Battlefield in Battleground, Indiana, is a historically significant landscape that has been designated a National Historic Landmark. Visitors walking the

Tippecanoe Battlefield in Battleground, Indiana.

battlefield will discover a serene, beautifully wooded area that was the site of a fierce battle between the forces of the United States and the Prophetstown Confederacy. The Tippecanoe Battlefield has been preserved so all may remember and learn from the conflict that took place on November 7, 1811.

In the early 1700s the Woodland Indians lived a traditional lifestyle based on horticulture, hunting, and gathering, but they had become dependent on the products of American industry, such as cotton, metal pots, metal projectile points and tomahawks, gunpowder, lead, and muskets. Living in tribes with close-knit kinship ties, the Indian people made decisions based on a general consensus. Peer pressure was a powerful tool for maintaining social order since tribal affiliation was important for individual identity.

After the American Revolutionary War ended in 1781, the Woodland people had been forced to change at an accelerating pace. The policy of the new United States of America was designed to promote American expansion and diminish the Indian people's land holdings. Westward migration across the Appalachian Mountains brought pioneer settlements into traditional

A monument in memory of the soldiers who died during the Battle of Tippecanoe.

Indian territories. In this increasingly tense situation, the Indian people became political players and pawns in the early history of the United States. British agents implied that the Indian people owned the western lands and encouraged Indian resistance to American settlements. The American government viewed the western lands as source of money. Furthermore, the U.S. government argued that the Indian people had no claim to the land. At the same time pioneer lifestyles influenced Native

American farming techniques and food preparation, while pioneer settlements reduced available hunting grounds. In addition to losing valuable land, the Indian people were increasingly subject to disease, alcoholism, and social disintegration. The Woodland Indian lifestyle was unraveling.

Woodland tribes reacted differently to these pressing problems. Some Shawnee and Delaware choose acculturation. They adopted the white man's lifestyle by learning farming practices, living in log cabins, and keeping domesticated livestock. But other Shawnee, Miami, and Kickapoo refused to give up the traditional ways, resisting acculturation. These resisters wanted to maintain a traditional lifestyle and refused "to walk the white man's road."

Two Shawnee brothers, Tecumseh and Prophet, were charismatic leaders in the Indian resistance to American settlement in the Indiana territory. An outstanding orator, Tecumseh imagined a strong Pan-Indian Confederacy, uniting all the tribes under a common goal. Tecumseh's future vision was based on a unique idea. He believed in the common ownership of all Indian lands, an idea alien to the traditional tribal perspective, in which each tribe had its own territory. At the same time, Prophet preached a return to the old ways, rooting his ideology in traditional tribal values. Prophet condemned the American technology, encouraging his followers to start the fires in the old ways, abstain from alcohol, respect their elders, and return to using the food and implements of their ancestors.

Many native people heard these hopeful messages. In the last week of April 1808, Tecumseh, Prophet, and their followers arrived at the site of a new village. Situated at the confluence of the Wabash and Tippecanoe rivers in north central Indiana, Prophetstown was a religious mecca and the capital of Tecumseh's Pan-Indian Confederacy. Bark wigwams spread over the river bottom and stretched up over the bluff to the grassy prairie. The Indian people also constructed three public buildings, making space for anticipated visitors. Prophetstown emerged out of an idea. Representing a symbolic boundary line between settlers and Indian people, Prophetstown beckoned the Woodland Indians with a vision illuminated by the traditional lifestyle. Prophetstown, a true historical intersection, offers a glimpse of an **archetypal** last stand.

William Henry Harrison had been the governor of the Indiana territory since 1801. He and many pioneers believed it was America's manifest destiny to populate all of North America

1781 The Woodland Indians are forced to change at an accelerating pace.

1808 Tecumseh, Prophet, and their followers arrive at the site of a new village.

1811 Indian warriors invade the military camp at the battlefield of Tippecanoe.

1836 John Tipton buys the battlefield and deeds it to the state of Indiana.

1873 An iron fence is erected around the battlefield.

1892 The Tippecanoe Battlefield Monument Association spearheads the funding and construction of several monuments.

1908 Hundreds gather for the 97th anniversary of the Battle of Tippecanoe.

archetypal: a perfect example; model.

"Tippecanoe and Tyler Too!"

"Tippecanoe and Tyler Too!" was the Whig party political slogan used for presidential candidate William Henry Harrison and vice-presidential candidate John Tyler in the 1840 national election. The Whig party chose the slogan to stir up and excite voters about Harrison as president. Because Harrison was already a national hero for his role in the Battle of Tippecanoe, the Whig party effectively used the slogan to beat incumbent Martin Van Buren, Harrison's Democratic opponent.

The Whig convention, assembled at Harrisburg, Pennsylvania, in December, 1839, nominated General William Henry Harrison of Indiana for president and John Tyler of Virginia for vice president. The Whig party was historically divided on many issues and had yet to win a national election. The only bond uniting the various groups under the Whig banner during the election of 1840 was a determination to defeat the Democrats. The Whig party used "Tippecanoe and Tyler Too" as well as other slogans like "Hard Cider and Log Cabin" to appeal to the common, everyday person. The party painted a picture of Harrison as a hero, a simple frontiersman, and a common man to sway voters and present a contrast to Van Buren's luxurious life in the Executive Mansion. The election of 1840 was unique because the Whigs focused their campaign on winning votes from everyday people whereas other presidential candidates made a habit of ignoring them.

Although the causes for Van Buren's defeat included the financial Panic of 1837 and the unpopular Seminole War, the campaign methods used by the Whigs in 1840 were a large part of Harrison's success. Harrison won the election, beating Van Buren by an overwhelming margin. The election was the first national victory for the Whig party.

from the Atlantic to the Pacific oceans. The United States government, prompted by letters from William Henry Harrison, was concerned with the ideas and strength emanating from Prophetstown. William Henry Harrison said this about Tecumseh: "He is one of those uncommon geniuses, which spring up occasionally to produce revolutions and overturn the established order of things."

In September of 1811, taking advantage of Tecumseh's absence from Prophetstown, William Henry Harrison organized an army of about 1,000 men and marched north from Vincennes, Indiana, the capital of the Indiana territory. The regiment arrived at the battlefield site on November 6, 1811. Harrison aimed to disperse the Native Americans living at Prophetstown and to disrupt the goals of the Pan-Indian Confederacy.

Prophet was duly concerned with the U.S. military presence only one and a half miles from his village. Confederacy warriors prepared to engage the U.S. Army. Choosing not to wait for reinforcements, Prophet disregarded Tecumseh's order of restraint and patience.

Indian warriors invaded the military camp on the rainy morning of November 7, 1811. John Tipton, a soldier, recorded a personal version of the Battle of Tippecanoe. Tipton wrote:

> Thirsday the 7 agreeable to their Promise Last night we ware answered by the firring of guns and the Shawnies Brakeng into our tents a blood Combat Took Plaice at Precisely 15 minutes Before five in the morning which Lasted 2 hours and 20 minuts of a Continewel firing while maney times mixd among the indians so that we Could not tell them indians and our men apart they kept up a firing on three sides of us took our tent from the gueard fire our men fought brave and By the timely help of Capt Cook with a Companey of infantry We maid a Charge and Drove them out of our timber across the Prairie our Losst in killed and wounded was 179 and their graiter than ours among the Dead was our Capt Spier Spencer and first Lieut Mcmahan and Capt Berrey that had Been attatchd to our Compney and 5 more killd Dead and 15 wounded after the indians gave ground we Buried our Dead among the kentucians was killd mayj Davis badly wounded and a number of others in all killd and wounded was 179 but no company suffered like ours we then held an Election for officers I was elected Capt. (John Tipton Papers, vol. 1, 1809–27)

Initially, it appeared that the Indian Confederacy would determine the outcome of the battle. But after two hours and twenty minutes of intense fighting, the U.S. military held the ground and the Indian warriors retreated. During the battle, Prophet stationed himself near a marshy prairie on a small hill near Prophetstown, across from Harrison's camp. The American forces numbered 1,000 men and 188 were killed or wounded. The Indian warriors numbered about 600 to 700 men and 70 to 80 were killed or wounded. On November 8 the U.S. military invaded a deserted Prophetstown and burned it to the ground.

The Battle of Tippecanoe had consequences. Prophet lost his power base and moved to Kansas. Tecumseh's plan of a strong Pan-Indian Confederacy was dashed. He believed it was his destiny to always fight against the U.S. government. He joined with the British, fighting in the War of 1812. Harrison parlayed the Battle of Tippecanoe into a political rallying point, "Tippecanoe and Tyler Too!" He was elected the ninth president and died after a month in office. Pioneers continued westward expansion, pushing Indian people farther west.

In commemoration of the battle, thirteen counties in Indiana have been named after officers and volunteers from the

The American government viewed the western lands as a source of money and argued that the Indian people had no claim to the land.

Battle of Tippecanoe. John Tipton purchased the sixteen-acre battlefield and deeded it to the state of Indiana on November 7, 1836, the twentieth-fifth anniversary of the battle. An iron fence, erected in 1873, surrounds the battlefield to this day. Beginning in 1892, the Tippecanoe Battlefield Monument Association spearheaded the funding and construction of an **obelisk**, commemorating the battle, and smaller monuments, each marking where an officer fell. On November 7, 1908, the ninety-seventh anniversary, many people gathered at the battlefield to hear patriotic speeches and participate in memorializing the Battle of Tippecanoe.

obelisk: a tall, slender, four-sided stone pillar with a pyramidal top.

The Tippecanoe County Historical Association operates the Tippecanoe Battlefield Museum and the Tippecanoe County Parks and Recreation Department maintains the 102-acre Tippecanoe Battlefield Park. The Tippecanoe Battlefield Museum contains informative exhibits on the Battle of Tippecanoe. Artifact displays reflect the military and Woodland Indian lifestyles. A fiber-optic map with a ten-minute narrative illustrates and explains the movement of troops on November 7, 1811. The museum exhibits aim to weave a story, encouraging visitors to draw their own conclusions about the Battle of Tippecanoe. ◆

Trinity Church

NEWPORT, RHODE ISLAND

Trinity Church in Newport, Rhode Island, is one of the best known and most beautiful colonial churches in America. Built in 1726, the simple, elegant structure became the **prototype** for churches built throughout New England in the next century.

prototype: a model; perfect example of a particular type.

The story of the Rhode Island Colony and the founding of Trinity Church is essentially a story of a quest for religious freedom and has its roots in the earlier establishment of the Massachusetts Bay Colony, in 1620. That was when the first of the religiously motivated emigrants arrived from England, landing at Plymouth Rock.

The Puritans were a sect unwelcome in England in the early seventeenth century, and their migration to the New World was encouraged as a way to remove what was perceived as their disruptive presence. They were dissenters from the Anglicanism that prevailed in the home country, and were vocal in demanding church reform, particularly with regard to what they considered to be excessive ceremony and a too-rigid hierarchy. These elements of the state-sanctioned religion struck the Puritan faction as smacking of "popery"—Catholicism—the faith for which much blood had been shed during the years of religious **schism** and contention especially during the contest between Queen Mary and Queen Elizabeth. Adopting a more literal approach to scripture than prevailed within **orthodox** Anglicanism, many were motivated to make the dangerous trip to the new lands across the Atlantic, where they hoped to establish a church that would be more pure and more faithful to the teachings of the Bible.

Trinity Church in Newport, Rhode Island.

schism: a division in a church as the result of differences of opinion or doctrine.

orthodox: conforming to the usual beliefs of a religion.

Over the course of the decade following the founding of Plymouth Colony, many such dissenting Puritans came to the conclusion that they, too, must leave England behind in order to remain true to their religious convictions. By the end of the decade, the Great Migration—a veritable mass exodus of Puritans—set sail for what had now become known as the Massachusetts Bay Colony. Among these voyagers was one Roger Williams, who was, at twenty-seven years old, one of the youngest ministers to make the trip. He came with a reputation for eloquent oratory and erudition already well established, and was immediately offered the position of pastor for the church in Boston.

While every Puritan who came to the Massachusetts Bay Colony was agreed in opposition to certain of the practices and procedures of the Anglican church they had left behind, not all Puritans were agreed as to how this opposition should be expressed. In Williams's Boston congregation, the majority viewpoint was that disagreement with certain Anglican practices did not necessitate a complete break with the mother church. These were known as "Non-Separating" Puritans—they considered themselves to be good Anglicans who simply wished to strip away the excessive ceremony and **hierarchical** structure

hierarchical: of a system of church government arranged in order of graded ranks.

that they felt compromised their underlying faith. But Roger Williams was a Puritan of the other sort—a "Separating" Puritan who held that anything short of a complete severance of ties with the Anglican church was unacceptable.

Roger Williams, who had sailed to the Americas to escape what he felt to be religious oppression in England, now found that his mode of belief remained in conflict with the prevailing establishment. Among other controversies, he disagreed with the right of civil authorities to assume jurisdiction over transgressions of church law, and these positions quickly earned for him a reputation as a radical and a troublemaker. The colonial administration soon recognized in Williams a potential threat— his contentious views could easily alienate the crown's support of the American settlement and jeopardize the very existence of the colony.

Seeing that there was little tolerance for his views, Williams soon left Boston, hoping to take up a ministry in Salem. This community was more amenable to his Separatist beliefs, but it feared estrangement from the Boston settlement and declined to take him on. He ultimately found a position with the church in Plymouth Plantation, but even in that openly Separatist community he stood out as an extremist. After a time, he traveled back to Salem and, for a brief while, took over the church there, but the General Court of Massachusetts could not turn a blind eye to his teachings and banished him from the Massachusetts Bay Colony in its entirety late in 1635. The condition of Williams's banishment required that he be returned to England, but this was not acceptable to the sternly **dogmatic** Separatist minister. Instead, he chose to flee, heading south into the wilderness.

With the help of members of the Narragansett tribe, Williams was able to make it through the difficult winter of 1636. Eventually he settled down to farm and trade, and called his new home "Providence." As his only neighbors were the indigenous people of the area, he set himself the task of learning their language, drawing on the intimate relationships he had established while wandering in exile during the previous winter. Once he was established in his new home, however, other religious outcasts sought him out. Soon his private settlement became a community of nonconformist religious thinkers, and Williams himself devised its charter to reflect a complete separation of the functions of church and state. His community welcomed all those whom the Massachusetts Bay Colony to the

"Congress shall make no law respecting an establishment of religion, or prohibiting the free exercise thereof; or abridging the freedom of speech, or of the press; or the right of the people peaceably to assemble, and to petition the Government for a redress of grievances."
Amendment 1, the Bill of Rights, 1788

dogmatic: stating an opinion in an authoritative manner.

National Register of Historic Places

In November 1968 Newport's Trinity Church was added to the National Register of Historic Places. The National Register is an official list of notable properties in the United States that have been determined to be worthy of preserving. These places include districts, sites, buildings, structures, or objects that are important in American history, architecture, archeology, engineering, or culture. The National Register contains more than 70,000 listings. These properties have been nominated by governments, organizations, and individuals because they are significant to the nation or to a particular state or community. All historic areas in the national park system and nearly 2,300 national historic landmarks are included.

The National Historic Preservation Act of 1966 created the National Register to help public and private groups that seek to protect America's historic and archeological resources. The U.S. Department of the Interior administers the National Register through the National Park Service. National Register properties must meet a set of standards that determines their value in the history and heritage of the United States. They must be associated with events that have made a significant contribution to history or be associated with the lives of significant people. Some sites are chosen because they represent certain types, periods, or methods of construction. Some represent the work of a master or possess high artistic values. Some sites are important for their valuable information about history or prehistory. Owners of sites on the National Register can be eligible for federal tax benefits and may qualify for federal assistance for historic preservation when such money is available.

north refused to accept: Catholics, Jews, Quakers, and other dissenting Protestant sects.

Within a few short years, other communities grew up in the area, settled by people who shared Williams's nonconformist views. Among the earliest of these was Newport, which was established in 1639. In 1644 the population of the region had grown so dramatically that Williams was determined to get the recognition of the British parliament for his young colony. It was duly granted, uniting Providence, Newport, Portsmouth, and Warwick into a single entity, the Providence Plantations. When Williams sought a royal charter from King Charles III in 1663, this too was given, with the terms of the charter explicitly guaranteeing religious liberty to all who lived within the colony.

Roger Williams began his settlement with strong, friendly relations with the local Indians. Indeed, his very survival through the first winter of his stay in the region depended on the good will of the Narragansetts, who ceded some of their land to him. Philosophically, Williams was a firm believer in

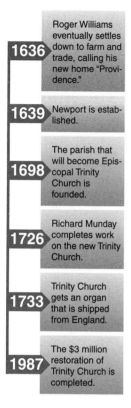

1636 — Roger Williams eventually settles down to farm and trade, calling his new home "Providence."

1639 — Newport is established.

1698 — The parish that will become Episcopal Trinity Church is founded.

1726 — Richard Munday completes work on the new Trinity Church.

1733 — Trinity Church gets an organ that is shipped from England.

1987 — The $3 million restoration of Trinity Church is completed.

dealing fairly with his indigenous neighbors, but as the Massachusetts and Rhode Island settlements increased in size, those relations became strained. By the 1670s they had broken down irreparably, and a leader—called "King Philip" by the colonists—arose to incite rebellion. The ensuing war, named for the Narragansett chief who led it, lasted only a year—from 1675 to 1676—but when it was over, the colonists no longer needed to concern themselves with their indigenous neighbors.

In Newport, the settlement was enjoying significant growth, and by the late 1690s the churchmen of the community felt it was time to build a church that reflected their prosperity. The parish that would become Episcopal Trinity Church was therefore founded in 1698. The congregation quickly outgrew its first small church, and decided to commission a larger one. Newport carpenter Richard Munday was hired to build it. Munday admired the work of English architect Christopher Wren (who designed Saint Paul's Cathedral in London), and built Trinity Church to reflect Wren's style. The new church was completed in 1726, and has been in continual use since then. Its most prominent feature is a graceful 150-foot pointed spire. Brass chandeliers installed in 1728 still hang from its ceiling, and a distinctive three-tiered pulpit still adorns its alter. The church also boasts a remarkable collection of communion silver. The church organ was shipped from England in 1733. Composer George Frideric Handel is said to have tested the organ before Bishop George Berkeley, the eminent British clergyman and moral philosopher, sent it to Newport.

Not long after Trinity Church was built, George Washington himself stepped in to attend a service (he sat in pew 81). More recently, the Archbishop of Canterbury visited in 1976. In the 1980s the church was deemed in need of repair, and the rehabilitation, completed in 1987 at a cost of three million dollars, restored all the original features of the structure. ◆

Tuskegee Institute

Tuskegee, Alabama

The Tuskegee Normal and Industrial Institute, founded in Tuskegee, Alabama, was the first institution of higher learning dedicated to the education of African

Americans. Still in operation today, the institute was designated a National Historic Site in 1974.

Two important figures in the history of American education and invention are inextricably linked to Tuskegee Institute: Booker T. Washington, founder and pioneer in education for African Americans, and George Washington Carver, one of the most prolific inventors in American history. While they are honored at the Tuskegee Institute site, each also has a historical site dedicated to his memory. The Booker T. Washington National Monument is located on the plantation where he was born, in Hardy, Virginia. The George Washington Carver National Monument is located in Diamond, Missouri, where he was born into slavery and where he lived for the first decade of his life.

Without Booker T. Washington, there would be no Tuskegee Institute. But the conditions of his birth gave no early hint of the influential and controversial leader he would grow up to become. When he was born, to a slave woman named Jane, who was a cook on a tobacco plantation in Hale's Ford, Virginia, on April 5, 1856, he was given only the name of Booker. His father may have been a white man, but his identity is unknown. Like most slave children, Booker and his siblings were put to work at a very young age, and received no schooling.

The end of the Civil War and the Emancipation Proclamation (1865) did not bring ease for most slaves, and young Booker's family faced grinding poverty. They moved to Malden, West Virginia, with Washington Ferguson, whom Booker's mother had married while still a slave. Ferguson alone could not earn enough to support the family, so it was necessary that nine-year-old Booker find work to help out. He took jobs in the local salt furnace and later in the coal mines, but all the while he dreamed of going to school and getting an education. Sadly, family circumstances made that impossible—he could only attend classes sporadically, when his job left him a little free time. It was during one of these periods, when Booker was about ten years old, that he was asked by a teacher for his "full" name and he adopted the surname Washington (he added a middle name, Taliaferro, many years later).

At the age of sixteen, Booker Washington finally got his chance for formal education. He learned of the Normal and Agricultural Institute, in Hampton, Virginia—a school that had been founded in 1869 by General Samuel Chapman Armstrong. The institute's mission was to train black elementary

"Almost from the first Tuskegee has kept in mind— and this I think should be the policy of all industrial schools— fitting students for occupations which would be open to them in their home communities."

Booker T. Washington, 1903

1856 Booker T. Washington is born on a tobacco plantation in Hale's Ford, Virginia.

1872 Washington enrolls in the Normal and Agricultural Institute.

1875 Despite having to work as a school janitor, Washington graduates in only three years.

1881 Washington gets approval from the Alabama state legislature to establish Tuskegee Normal and Industrial Institute.

1888 George Washington Carver becomes the first black student at Simpson College in Indianola, Iowa.

1896 Carver joins the Tuskegee faculty.

1905 Carver issues a bulletin on cultivation methods of peanuts.

1938 Tuskegee Institute establishes the George Washington Carver Museum.

1974 Tuskegee Institute is designated a National Historic Site.

1985 Tuskegee Institute becomes Tuskegee University.

school teachers. Booker combined his own savings and the financial help of black residents in the community and managed to enroll full time at the Institute in 1872.

General Armstrong firmly believed that the development of thrift and industry and a strong moral character were essential to the education for African Americans, and he imposed this philosophy on his institute and on its students. Booker T. Washington would adopt this same philosophy as the cornerstone of his own approach to education in later years, combining it with the belief that education was the key to achieving equality for black people in the United States.

School did not bring Booker respite from hard work—he had to make the lengthy trek to and from school each day, and he had to take a job as school janitor in order to defray his educational expenses. Nonetheless, his dedication and his perseverance were such that he completed his course of study in three years, graduating in 1875. But, Booker's commitment to education went far beyond securing for himself the advantages that literacy and learning could provide—he wanted to extend those advantages to all African Americans who were excluded from the opportunities that he firmly believed education would bring.

With this firm conviction and with diploma in hand, Booker went home to Malden to take a post as teacher in the local school. Soon, however, General Armstrong invited him back to join the faculty of his alma mater. A few years later he was nominated by General Armstrong to found a new institute being planned for Tuskegee, Alabama. In 1881, after receiving the approval of the Alabama state legislature, Booker moved to the proposed site and set to work to create the Tuskegee Normal and Industrial Institute, mandated to serve as a training school for African-American teachers.

With little by way of funding from the state, the early years of the school were difficult. A local church donated a shack, and this served as the institute's first classroom. Washington tirelessly canvassed for support throughout the black communities in the region and eventually raised enough money to purchase land—an old plantation—and the materials needed to raise buildings to house classrooms and offices. But finances were always tight, and so the first students to enroll in the Normal School were also its builders—even the bricks from which the buildings are constructed were formed on the school property by the students themselves. From these difficult beginnings, however, the school quickly grew in size and in reputation.

A laboratory at Tuskegee Institute, c. 1902.

In these early years of the institute's history, Washington was applauded by blacks and whites alike. His philosophy, strongly influenced by the policies of his old mentor, General Armstrong of the Hampton Institute, was that self-help, hard work, and frugality were the essential attributes of an educated black. And his insistence upon economic self-sufficiency as a necessary precursor to true independence and equality led him to emphasize vocational training rather than a grounding in the liberal arts. These positions would soon earn him the hostility of other African-American leaders, such as W. E. B. Du Bois.

But all that was yet to come. In the year after founding the Institute, Washington married his hometown sweetheart, Fannie N. Smith of Malden, Virginia. She died just two years later, in childbirth. Washington later married Olivia A. Davidson, who joined her husband wholeheartedly in his crusade to make Tuskegee a topflight educational institution. Her particular gift was for fund-raising, and she worked tirelessly to keep contributions coming in to support the school. After her death, Washington married a third time, to Margaret James Murray, who similarly dedicated herself to supporting her husband in his work at the Institute.

In 1896, just fifteen years after the Institute's first brickwork was mortared into place, George Washington Carver joined the school—now rechristened Tuskegee Institute. Like Washington, Carver had been born to slavery on a plantation in Diamond, Missouri, sometime between the years 1861 and 1864, while the Civil War still raged.

Unlike Washington, Carver had the opportunity to go to school, although his education was interrupted several times. He got his first schooling in Neosho, Missouri, in 1877. He was an extraordinarily gifted student, and he soon surpassed his teachers at Neosho, so he moved to Fort Scott, Kansas, to find work and to continue his education. But he fled Fort Scott after witnessing a lynching, and in 1879 he settled for a time in Olathe, Kansas. There he worked odd jobs and once again enrolled in school, but he moved once again, to Minneapolis, Kansas, in 1880.

"By the side of industrial training should always go mental and moral training, but the pushing of mere abstract knowledge into the head means little. We want more than the mere performance of mental gymnastics. Our knowledge must be harnessed to the things of real life."

Booker T. Washington, 1903

In Minneapolis, Carver finally attained his high school diploma in 1884 and applied by mail to a Presbyterian-church-run college in Highland, Kansas. He was accepted for enrollment, but was turned away when he arrived on campus because the school would not accept black students. He temporarily gave up on his dream of a college education, and tried his hand at homesteading in western Kansas. But he could not stay away from learning for long, and in 1888 he once again applied to college, this time to the Methodist-run Simpson College, in Indianola, Iowa. He was accepted there and became the first black student in the history of the school.

On the strength of a recommendation from his art teacher, Carver transferred to the Iowa Agricultural College, which housed the nations finest agricultural experimental station. His work so impressed his faculty that, once he had received his bachelor's degree in agricultural science in 1894, he was invited to stay on to earn his master's degree, which was granted in 1896. He taught there as well, but stayed less than a year before accepting Booker T. Washington's invitation to join the faculty at the Tuskegee Institute.

Carver's affiliation with Tuskegee Institute would last for the remainder of his life, but his tenure there was not always comfortable. He considered himself a researcher and inventor rather than an educator, and he lacked the administrative and political skills to make his relations with the rest of the faculty run smoothly. Nonetheless it was at the Tuskegee Experiment Station, which he headed, that his many contributions to agricultural science were accomplished.

Carver's first research was focused on developing better farming methods and crops that would help southern farmers improve their productivity and reduce their reliance on "king cotton," the dominant crop of the region. He introduced the idea of crop rotation as a means of allowing the soil to regain its nutrients over time, and he taught local farmers food preservation techniques such as curing, pickling, and canning.

But perhaps Carver's most famous contribution to agricultural sciences was his work with the peanut. The soils of the south were largely exhausted after years of cotton farming, and he was looking for a suitable replacement crop that would restore the damaged soil. Peanuts, which were unknown as a farm product in the south at the time, were extremely useful because they helped restore nitrogen to depleted soil, and in 1905 he issued a bulletin that explained their value and taught the proper methods to cultivate them. He ultimately developed more than a hundred food uses for the peanut, and he discovered 187 peanut by-products, that ranged from food and food additives to ink, drugs, and fodder for livestock. Because of his influence, by 1940 the peanut had become the south's second most important cash crop.

Booker T. Washington died in 1915, having dedicated his life to the institute he founded. With his death, George Washington Carver became the unofficial spokesman for the school and took to the lecture circuit and fundraising trail. He earned the support of Henry Ford and Thomas Edison, who backed his research into the use of chemicals to enhance farming productivity. Like Washington, Carver enjoyed a national reputation as a spokesman for African-American concerns and had the ear of presidents Franklin Roosevelt and Calvin Coolidge. Carver died, from complications arising from anemia, in 1943. His estate established the George Washington Carver Research Foundation, which still provides support for African-American students wishing to pursue studies in botany, chemistry, and agronomy.

In 1938 Tuskegee Institute honored Carver by establishing the George Washington Carver Museum on the campus. The museum has been enlarged through the years, and is now part of

"On such a foundation as this will grow habits of thrift, a love of work, economy, ownership of property, bank accounts. Out of it in the future will grow practical education, professional education, positions of public responsibility. Out of it will grow moral and religious strength."
Booker T. Washington, 1903

the Tuskegee Institute National Historic Site, maintained by the National Park Service. The museum houses Carver's scientific notes, his desk and laboratory equipment, and numerous displays on his research. Some of Carver's paintings and needlework are also on display. The Tuskegee Institute National Historic Site also includes Booker T. Washington's home, the Oaks, which was built during the 1890s.

The Tuskegee Institute became Tuskegee University in 1985. From humble origins, the university now enrolls about 4,000 students and includes a College of Arts and Sciences, and schools of Agriculture and Home Economics, Business, Education, Engineering and Architecture, Nursing and Allied Health, and Veterinary Medicine. Tuskegee University employs approximately 1,000 personnel and comprises over 4,500 acres of land and more than 155 buildings and structures. ◆

USS *Arizona* Memorial

The graceful white arc of the USS *Arizona* Memorial floats above the remains of the submerged battleship USS *Arizona*, which sank during the Japanese air raid on Pearl Harbor, Hawaii, on December 7, 1941. The Japanese attack on the U.S. Pacific Fleet propelled the United States into World War II. On America's first day in a war that would continue for four more years, more than 2,400 Americans died; their average age was twenty-three. The trauma of this sudden loss of life had strong political repercussions. It changed the minds of many Americans who had been philosophically opposed to entering the war, which by 1941, already gripped most of Europe and threatened Asia.

The devastating attack convinced nonsupporters and those assuming a neutral stance that America was resolutely and justifiably involved in World War II. Particularly potent to the transformation of public opinion was a simple photograph of the USS *Arizona*, taken shortly after the bombing and emblazoned on the front pages of newspapers across the land. The photo revealed the devastation of the once proud and powerful battleship—tilted, half-submerged, and engulfed in flames. That image became one of the most reproduced scenes of the war. And the cry "Remember Pearl Harbor," first used by a small newspaper in Oregon, quickly became a national slogan. Thus, the destruction of the *Arizona* became a symbol for America's war effort, inspiring large and small acts of courage, sacrifice, and heroism.

From Japan's point of view, the attack was the culmination of nearly a decade of protests from the United States against

"Yesterday, December 7, 1941— a date which will live in infamy— the United States of America was suddenly and deliberately attacked by naval and air forces of the Empire of Japan."

President Franklin D. Roosevelt, address to Congress, December 8, 1941

The USS *Arizona* in flames after being hit by a Japanese bomb on December 7, 1941.

Japan's armed offense against China. These protests had begun a decade earlier when a group of Japanese extremists first invaded the province of Manchuria in northeastern China in 1931. The future independence of China and the other countries of southeast Asia were overtly threatened by Japan's military aggression. Although the United States condemned Japan for these military infractions, the United States was hesitant to respond with military force. Many Americans were not convinced that the problems in Europe and Asia were any of their concern. Even fewer people thought we should send American soldiers and sailors for what seemed to be "foreign" causes. To mediate between this domestic uncertainty and foreign pleas for help, the United States pressured Japan's compliance with economic **sanctions**, diplomatic negotiations, and a slow buildup of the U.S. Pacific Fleet in Hawaii.

sanction: a coercive action, such as a boycott, taken by one nation against another to enforce demands.

embargo: a prohibition of trade in a particular line of goods.

The Japanese empire, however, viewed these pressures—especially an **embargo** on their oil supplies—as direct threats to their national security. To counter this threat, and to continue their expansion in Asia, a Japanese admiral, Isoruko Yamamoto, conceived a daring plan—immobilize the Pacific Fleet before it reached its full strength. Since America's economic and industrial resources were significantly larger than Japan's, only a quick and decisive victory, one that rendered the fleet unusable, could provide Japan with the military advantage.

As a military strategy, it was both sophisticated and bold. A week before the attack, the Japanese sent thirty-three warships, including six aircraft carriers, toward the Hawaiian Islands, specifically Oahu, which housed Pearl Harbor. They followed a route far north of the normal shipping lanes to avoid detection and reached their launching position, 230 miles from Oahu, in the early morning of December 7. Five midget submarines had been launched the previous night and were already lurking in the harbor, waiting for the coded signals "To, To, To" and "Tora, Tora, Tora" that would indicate the fight had begun and that the element of surprise had been maintained. Those signals came shortly before 8:00 A.M.

While Japan prepared for attack, on Battleship Row in Pearl Harbor where 130 vessels were moored closely together, a serene Sunday morning had begun to settle over the Pacific Fleet. Since there had been no overt threat from Japan, the military watches were being minimally run. The evening before the attack, there had been a competition between the military bands that had been widely attended. Sailors and marines had stayed up late to enjoy the music and root for their favorites.

Before 7 A.M. the radar station on the north point of the islands picked up signals that a large flight of planes was approaching. They reported it to Command Headquarters, but were told it was probably a group of B-17s or some aircraft from the fleet's own carriers. Shortly before that sighting, the USS *Ward* spotted a midget submarine outside the entrance to Pearl Harbor and fired on it. These warning signs—obvious in hindsight—were at the time not considered significant cause for alarm.

Just minutes later, a 1,760-pound bomb pierced through the USS *Arizona*'s deck, penetrating deep into its innards, and exploding near a forward magazine, which held much of the ship's **munitions**. Nearly all of the almost two thousand crewmembers were killed instantly and men standing on ships near the *Arizona* were blown off their decks by the sheer force of the explosion. In less than nine minutes the ship sank with her crew. In the U.S. Navy's recorded history, there has never been a ship that has taken so many of its crew down with her.

The attack on Pearl Harbor came in two waves of air strikes, nearly an hour apart, and all other military sites on the islands—airfields, army barracks, supply stations, and docks—were also bombed, significantly reducing the United States ability to retaliate. When the strikes and retaliations were over and

"The attack yesterday on the Hawaiian Islands has caused severe damage to American naval and military forces. I regret to tell you that very many American lives have been lost. In addition, American ships have been reported torpedoed on the high seas between San Francisco and Honolulu."
President Franklin D. Roosevelt, address to Congress, December 8, 1941

munitions: war supplies and weapons.

The USS *Arizona* Memorial at Pearl Harbor, Hawaii.

the damages tolled, the United States had sustained significant losses: 164 aircraft lost with nearly as many damaged; twelve ships either sunken or beached, with another nine damaged. Despite such catastrophic damage, Japan failed to achieve its goal of permanently crippling the Pacific Fleet. Rather it had enraged a sleeping giant.

The next evening, a calm but forceful U.S. president Franklin Delano Roosevelt delivered a brief war speech to Congress and the American people in a clear, controlled voice. "Yesterday, December 7, 1941—a date which will live in infamy—the United States was suddenly and deliberately attacked by naval and air forces of the Empire of Japan." That opening statement became one of the best known phrases spoken by an American president. With the United States now ardently involved in World War II, the first business was one of salvaging the Pacific Fleet. In the largest maritime salvage operation ever attempted, damaged ships and planes were quickly repaired, guns and ammunition were removed from sunken ships and mounted on seabound vessels, and anything usable was recycled. In the end, an incredible eighteen of the twenty-one vessels returned to the war effort.

Fiftieth Anniversary of Pearl Harbor

On December 7, 1991, ceremonies were held to commemorate the fiftieth anniversary of the bombing of Pearl Harbor naval base in Hawaii and the United States entry into World War II. United States president George Bush, along with 2,000 veterans who survived the Japanese attack, hailed the 1,177 Americans who died aboard the USS *Arizona* on the "date which will live in infamy." A navy pilot who had enlisted after Pearl Harbor, Bush avowed that fifty years later he held "no rancor in my heart toward Germany or Japan." He praised Japan's recent acknowledgment of "responsibility" for starting the Pacific War. Scholarly conferences, including one at Hofstra University, also remembered Pearl Harbor in the United States. There were no commemorative events in Japan.

In the weeks immediately following the sinking of the *Arizona*, about 900 of the victims were removed from the hulking mass of metal. Family and community members made pleas to recover the rest of bodies for formal burial, but medical teams advised against this, explaining that between the explosion and the sustained submersion, the human forms would not be recognizable. Following that advice and a long-standing navy tradition that sailors who die at sea be buried at sea, 1,177 crewmembers remain entombed in the battleship, resting in the shallow waters of Pearl Harbor. The ship was officially decommissioned in 1942.

The fact that Pearl Harbor is a watery grave for hundreds of sailors and marines immediately marked it as a sacred, revered place. During the war, ships would render a full salute as they passed by the wreckage and in 1950 the traditional military practice of colors—the raising and lowering of the American flag—was initiated on the remaining stub of the *Arizona* masthead. Although the *Arizona* had been indelibly memorialized in the minds of the nation, an official memorial was authorized in 1958.

In 1962 the present USS *Arizona* Memorial was ceremoniously opened to the public on Memorial Day. Alfred Preis, the architect who designed the memorial, explains, "The structure sags in the center but stands strong and vigorous at the ends, express[ing] initial defeat and ultimate victory. . . . The overall effect is one of serenity." Preis says he deliberately omitted any explicit overtones of sadness in order to allow each viewer to form his or her own emotional response.

1931 Japanese extremists invade the province of Manchuria in northeastern China.

1941 The Japanese Army attacks Pearl Harbor; the USS *Arizona* sinks during the air raid.

1942 The USS *Arizona* is officially decommissioned.

1958 The U.S. government authorizes an official memorial for the USS *Arizona* crew.

1962 The USS *Arizona* Memorial opens to the public.

In 1950 the traditional military practice of colors—the raising and lowering of the American flag—was initiated on the remaining stub of the *Arizona* masthead.

A tour of the USS *Arizona* Memorial begins at the waterfront center where visitors view a short film describing the events and fallout of December 7, 1941. The film, which contains many still photos of the World War II era, sets the stage for what is often a moving reminder for those old enough to remember the events, and a powerful history lesson for others who, whether they have considered it or not, live in a world profoundly effected by that war. Visitors are then ferried by navy shuttle boats to the sunken vessel; they disembark on the memorial itself. The 134-foot structure spans the midsection of the sunken battleship, but does not touch it. It consists of three distinct sections: an entryway, a central area for viewing the battleship and military ceremonies, and, last, a shrine room where the names of those killed on the USS *Arizona* are engraved. The long lists of engraved names, reaching from ceiling to floor on stately marble walls, spur some visitors to lay flower bouquets and leis in front of the shrine. Others respectfully toss wreaths in the water over the ship's gun turrets and the outline of the superstructure. Over a million people, a good portion of them Japanese citizens, visit the memorial each year. A museum and visitor center on the waterfront encourage educational projects and feature "The Remembrance Exhibit" listing the names of the other U.S. military personnel who died during the Pearl Harbor attack but were not aboard the USS *Arizona*.

As a sustained tribute to all the military personnel killed in the Pearl Harbor attack, the American flag has remained attached to the severed mainmast of the battleship and is still raised each morning and lowered each evening in a formal military colors ceremony. ◆

Valley Forge

PENNSYLVANIA

T he winter of 1777–78 at Valley Forge was a supreme test for the Continental Army under George Washington. No battles were fought there, but during the months of their encampment at the site more than two thousand American soldiers died from disease and exposure to cold. From this crucible of suffering, however, a fighting force emerged with new confidence and pride in themselves, their leaders, and their country. Today, Valley Forge has been preserved as a National Historical Park commemorating the sacrifices made during the American Revolution for the cause of independence.

When George Washington brought his Continental Army to Valley Forge on December 19, 1777, his ragged, hungry, poorly equipped men were exhausted from their unsuccessful attempt to prevent the British forces from occupying Philadelphia. British troops led by Sir William Howe had entered the patriot capital in late September, after Howe skillfully outmaneuvered Washington's army at the Battle of Brandywine. The failure of Washington's surprise attack on the British in the Battle of Germantown on October 4 dashed American hopes of quickly regaining the city, the seat of the Second Continental Congress. Members of the congressional government were forced to flee to York, Pennsylvania.

With the onset of winter, active military campaigning came to a halt, and Washington sought quarters for his army of some twelve thousand men. Valley Forge, named for a nearby iron foundry on Valley Creek, was chosen for its location, eighteen miles northwest of Philadelphia. The area was close enough to

"For some days past, there has been little less than a famine in camp."
George Washington, February 16, 1778

391

Revolutionary War-era cannons, guarded by a soldier at Valley Forge, Pennsylvania.

the British occupying forces to limit their raiding and foraging parties in Pennsylvania, but far enough away to prevent the threat of a surprise British attack. Bordered on the north by the Schuylkill River, the site consisted of farmland sloping up to the hills named Mount Joy and Mount Misery.

The ground was already covered with snow when the men arrived in December, and within days the Schuylkill River was frozen over. At first the men lived in canvas tents, which provided no protection from the cold. Washington then set them to building two thousand huts of sticks, logs, and mud plaster. These dirt-floored, rough-hewn huts still did not provide adequate shelter against freezing temperatures and strong winds, especially for men suffering from a lack of food and warm clothing. Dr. Albigence Waldo, a surgeon serving at Valley Forge, wrote in his diary, "Poor food—hard lodging—cold weather—nasty clothes—nasty cookery . . . why are we sent here to starve and freeze?"

Clothing and feeding the army was a problem throughout the Revolutionary War. Homespun textiles could not entirely make up for the shortages caused by the interruption of shipments of woolen goods from England. Transportation difficulties hampered the food supply. Congressional neglect, poor ad-

Reconstructed officers' quarters at Valley Forge.

ministration, and lack of funds also contributed to insufficient and inferior food and uniforms.

At Valley Forge the army faced dire shortages of supplies of every kind. At one point Washington reported nearly 4,000 of his men unfit for duty because of their lack of clothing. Long marches had worn out the soldiers' shoes, and blankets were scarce. The army ration of food consisted of a pound and a half of flour or bread per day; dried beef, salt fish, or bacon; and sometimes peas or beans. At times the men went for days without meat or even bread. Weakened by hunger and cold, some two thousand men died from infectious diseases that swept through the camp. Congress ignored Washington's calls for assistance. He wrote that he feared the army would be forced to "disperse in order to obtain subsistence in the best manner they can."

Some officers feared that driven to desperation, the men might **mutiny**. Brigadier General James Varnum wrote to General Nathanael Greene, whom he and Washington considered one of the most able commanders in the army, "The situation of the camp is such that in all human probability the Army must soon dissolve. Many of the troops are destitute of meat, . . . and the horses are dying for want of forage."

mutiny: rebellion of soldiers or sailors against their officers.

> *"To see the men without clothes to cover their nakedness, without blankets to lie upon, without shoes . . . without a house or hut to cover them until those could be built, and submitting without a murmur, is a proof of patience and obedience which, in my opinion, can scarcely be paralleled."*
> George Washington at Valley Forge, April 21, 1778

The men did not mutiny, however, and there were remarkably few desertions. George Washington's strong and compassionate leadership kept the army together. In the early days of the winter, Washington lived in a tent, among his men, and shared their hardships. When he later made his headquarters in a modest stone house nearby, he continued to demonstrate his dedication to the well-being of his men, winning their loyalty and their love.

Other officers played an important role in keeping up the morale of the army. The young French nobleman the Marquis de Lafayette, who had bought a ship to come to America and join Washington's army in 1777, also shared the misery of Valley Forge. His devotion to Washington and to the cause of liberty endeared him to his fellow officers and men.

Conditions began to improve at Valley Forge when Washington appointed Nathanael Greene as quartermaster general, in charge of supplying the army with food and clothing. An ex-Quaker from Rhode Island, General Greene had helped prevent a rout among the American troops when they were outmaneuvered by the British in the Battle of Brandywine. He now put his immense energy and determination to procuring supplies for the men at Valley Forge. By spring, the army and its reinforcements of men were well clothed and fed.

The Continental Army did not only lack food and clothing when it arrived at Valley Forge. It also lacked much of the military training needed for consistent success on the battlefield. Washington found the man to remedy this deficiency in Friedrich Wilhelm von Steuben, a former staff officer in the Prussian army of Frederick the Great. Von Steuben arrived at Valley Forge from France on February 13, 1778, with a letter of introduction from Benjamin Franklin. Washington asked him to take on the duties of acting inspector general. It was von Steuben's task to develop and carry out an effective training program.

mercenary: a soldier hired to serve in a foreign army.

Von Steuben understood that American soldiers were different from hired **mercenaries**. Americans were independent men, he said, who wouldn't take orders unless they knew the reasons for them. Von Steuben broke with tradition to work directly with the men. Although he was an officer, he performed the functions of a drill sergeant, personally training a model company of 100 men. All day his voice was heard in camp, shouting commands in broken English. Soon companies, regiments, then brigades moved briskly through their exercises of marching and maneuvering, loading muskets with precision, and skillfully charging with their **bayonets**.

bayonet: a detachable blade on the end of a rifle for hand-to-hand fighting.

While the Continental Army endured the hardships—and hard work—at Valley Forge, the British spent a pleasant winter in Philadelphia, where they were entertained by families loyal to England. In early May the British officers organized a farewell celebration for their popular commander, Sir William Howe, who was returning to England. The lavish festivities, for which the officers contributed the immense sum of four thousand pounds, included a **regatta**, a ball, and a tournament. Dressed as medieval knights, the British officers jousted with lances for the favor of the ladies, local Pennsylvania girls decked out in Turkish costumes.

General Washington's quarters at Valley Forge.

regatta: a boat race.

The Continental Army was also celebrating during the first week of May. News had arrived from France of an alliance that guaranteed military aid to the Americans. Washington gave von Steuben the honor of organizing Alliance Day activities on May 6, 1778, to display the military training of the soldiers. The whole army passed in review as cannons boomed in salute. Thousands of muskets were fired in the ceremonial "feu de joie" (fire of joy), a running fire that passed up and down the double ranks of infantrymen.

Five weeks later the British left Philadelphia, led by their new commander, Sir Henry Clinton. The following day a well-trained, well-equipped Continental Army set off after them and

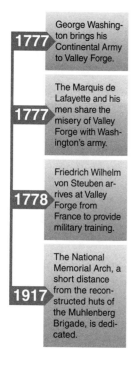

1777 George Washington brings his Continental Army to Valley Forge.

1777 The Marquis de Lafayette and his men share the misery of Valley Forge with Washington's army.

1778 Friedrich Wilhelm von Steuben arrives at Valley Forge from France to provide military training.

1917 The National Memorial Arch, a short distance from the reconstructed huts of the Muhlenberg Brigade, is dedicated.

successfully engaged the British troops at the Battle of Monmouth in New Jersey. Washington, with von Steuben's help, had created a skilled fighting force out of a ragtag band of patriot volunteers. From the suffering at Valley Forge, the Continental Army emerged with renewed spirit and determination. The Americans could now proceed with their struggle for independence.

Today the encampment at Valley Forge is preserved as a National Historical Park. A modern Visitor's Center near the park entrance displays a wide variety of artifacts from the winter of 1777–78, among them Washington's sleeping marquee. Visitors can drive through the park on a road that follows in places the perimeter of the Grand Parade, the drill ground where von Steuben trained the Continental Army. The road also passes the field fortifications that made up the outer line defenses to the south and the inner line defenses on the slopes of Mount Joy.

Washington's headquarters, a four-room stone house that belonged to gristmill owner Isaac Potts, stands near the Schuylkill River, in the northwestern corner of the camp. Reconstructions of the huts that housed the 150 men assigned to guard Washington may be visited nearby. General James Varnum's quarters, a stone house overlooking the Grand Parade, is also open to the public. Houses that quartered other members of the high command—Lord Stirling, Henry Knox, Lafayette, and William Maxwell—are closed but can be seen from the roads and trails.

At the reconstructed huts of the Muhlenberg Brigade, guides in period uniforms demonstrate the way of life of the soldiers who guarded the outer line of defense. A short distance from the huts is the National Memorial Arch, dedicated in 1917, which bears George Washington's words "Naked and starving as they are, we cannot enough admire the incomparable patience and fidelity of the soldiery." ◆

Vanderbilt Mansion

HYDE PARK, NEW YORK

The Vanderbilt Mansion National Historic Site, at Hyde Park, New York, was built in 1899 by Frederick Vanderbilt. It is an impressive example of the palatial estates of

The façade of Vanderbilt Mansion in Hyde Park, New York.

the Gilded Age, a period of American history between the Civil War and World War I. The Gilded Age was an amazing period of economic, social, and artistic change in American society. Believing themselves to be the heirs to a great Western tradition, the Americans who made their fortunes from industry during this period built grand palaces in New York City, in Newport, Rhode Island, and in the Hudson River Valley.

More than any other family, the descendents of Cornelius Vanderbilt personified the elite of the Gilded Age. In the 1890s approximately 90 percent of the wealth in the United States was controlled by 10 percent of the population. Unhampered by income tax, the wealthy at the turn of the century lived an

The entrance hall of
Vanderbilt Mansion.

**More than any
other family, the
descendents of
Cornelius Van-
derbilt personi-
fied the elite of
the Gilded Age.**

extraordinary life of spending and building. Their primary
legacy is the mansions that they left behind.

Frederick William Vanderbilt was the grandson of "Commodore" Cornelius Vanderbilt, shipping tycoon and founder of
the New York Central Railroad. The Commodore left his $100
million dollar fortune to his oldest son, William Henry Vanderbilt. William H. Vanderbilt doubled the family fortune and died
the richest man in America in 1885. He divided his fortune between his eight children, endowing them great wealth. This
generation represented the true rich of the Gilded Age and
lived a lavish lifestyle almost beyond our imagination.

In 1895 Frederick Vanderbilt, the youngest son of William
H. Vanderbilt, and his wife, Louisa, purchased Hyde Park, a 600-
acre estate in the Hudson River Valley. Frederick had noticed
the estate as he was yachting up the Hudson River. Hyde Park,
designed by André Parmentier in the mid-nineteenth century,
was one of the finest landscapes in America, featuring gorgeous
river views, century-old trees, and a meandering creek. It become just one of the grand estates of the Frederick Vanderbilts,

who also owned mansions in Newport, Bar Harbor, the Adirondacks, and on Fifth Avenue in New York City.

The architectural firm of McKim, Meade and White demolished the previous house on the estate and built the Greek Revival mansion that still exists today. It was designed to imitate an ancestral home of a noble European family. The 50,000-square-foot mansion has fifty rooms on four levels. A light Indiana limestone façade covers a modern steel and concrete structure. During the Vanderbilts' time, all of the utilities were up to date, included central heating, modern plumbing, and electric power. The mansion was finished by 1899 and the Vanderbilts threw their first house party on May 12, 1899. It took seven hundred laborers two years to build and the total cost of constructing and furnishing the mansion is estimated to have been $2,250,000. An absolute fortune in today's dollars.

The centerpiece of the mansion is an oval-shaped grand reception hall built as a focal point for the reception rooms on the first floor. On either side of the huge reception hall are the formal dining room and the drawing room. Designed by Stanford White, these rooms are furnished with antiques purchased by White in London, Paris, Florence, Rome, and Venice. The dining room, with its elaborate carved wooden ceiling, is thirty by fifty feet. Its floor is covered by a valuable 300-year-old oriental rug. The enormous dining room table can seat thirty people. Louisa Vanderbilt always insisted that the china, serving ware, and tablecloth be changed to exactly match the color of the flowers on the table. In the south wing of the mansion, the drawing room features a Steinway grand piano decorated with gold leaf and portraits of notable composers. A French salon, just off of the Reception Hall, is decorated in 22-karat gold leaf.

A grand staircase leads up to the second floor of the mansion where an oval-shaped gallery with a **balustrade** looks down on the first floor Reception Hall. The skylight above was added in 1906 when architect Whitney Warren opened the ceiling of the reception hall to add light and space to the center of the mansion. Several formal guestrooms open from the hall. At the south end of the second floor, just above the first floor drawing room, are the master bedrooms. Frederick Vanderbilt's room is dark and masculine with carved woodwork and dark reds. Among the wealthy upper class of the time it was common for husbands and wives to maintain separate bedrooms. Louisa Vanderbilt's room, adjoining Frederick's, is a reproduction of a French queen's bedroom of the Louis XV period. The **canopied**

"Conspicuous consumption of valuable goods is a means of reputability to the gentleman of leisure."
Thorstein Veblen, *Conspicuous Consumption*, 1902

balustrade: a railing held up by small posts.

canopy: a drapery hanging above a bed.

Louisa Vanderbilt's
bedroom.

bed is surrounded by an elaborate rail. The third floor features
five more guestrooms as well as servants' quarters.

The Vanderbilts lived at Hyde Park in the spring, fall, and
occasionally at Christmas. They, like most of the wealthy elite
of this period, maintained a Fifth Avenue townhouse in New
York City where they lived from the middle of November
through the end of January. March and April were usually spent
at the Vanderbilts' Palm Beach home where the Vanderbilts
and their guests spent time indulging in their favorite pastime,
yachting. After spending the spring at Hyde Park, the couple
would move the household to Newport, Rhode Island, the
Adirondacks, or Bar Harbor, Maine. Part of the summer was
usually spent in Europe on their yacht.

Childless, the Vanderbilts lived in a world of grand balls and
country house parties. Guests invited to the Vanderbilt mansion for a weekend in the country were accommodated in lavish
guestrooms, each furnished with reproductions of eighteenth-
century antiques. Additional guests were housed in the nearby
pavilion, built to provide for the comfort of Vanderbilt's gentleman friends.

The Vanderbilt mansion at Hyde Park was considered modest by Vanderbilt standards. It was called "Uncle Freddie's cottage" by the other, more ostentatious members of his family, most notably his brothers. Cornelius Vanderbilt II built the Breakers, an Italian Renaissance-style palazzo in Newport, Rhode Island. The seventy-room mansion was designed by Richard Morris Hunt, a famous architect of the time. William K. Vanderbilt and his wife, Alva, built Marble House, also in Newport. Biltmore, the home of George Washington Vanderbilt near Asheville, North Carolina, also by Hunt, features a 125,000-acre estate designed by Frederick Law Olmsted. With 250 rooms, thirty-four bedrooms, and forty-three bathrooms, Biltmore is the largest privately owned home in the United States.

Publicity-shy Frederick Vanderbilt avoided the limelight of his notorious brothers and sisters. He and his wife gave generously to children's charities. After his wife's death in 1926, Vanderbilt sold his other homes and lived at Hyde Park until his death in 1938 at the age of eighty-two. The era of the Gilded Age has vanished, along with most of the family fortunes of the time. We are left with historic sites, like the Vanderbilt Mansion, that stand as symbols of a bygone era, monuments to the limitless wealth and opulent lifestyles. ◆

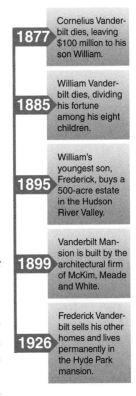

1877 Cornelius Vanderbilt dies, leaving $100 million to his son William.

1885 William Vanderbilt dies, dividing his fortune among his eight children.

1895 William's youngest son, Frederick, buys a 500-acre estate in the Hudson River Valley.

1899 Vanderbilt Mansion is built by the architectural firm of McKim, Meade and White.

1926 Frederick Vanderbilt sells his other homes and lives permanently in the Hyde Park mansion.

Vietnam Veterans Memorial

WASHINGTON, D.C.

The Vietnam Veterans Memorial, the most visited National Park Service site in Washington, D.C., was erected in 1982, nine years after America officially ended its involvement in the Vietnam War. Known by most people as "the Wall," the memorial is a V-shaped, ground-embedded granite sculpture that bears the names of the 58,214 American military personnel killed or declared missing in the war.

The memorial is unique among U.S. monuments in that it was built to honor Americans who gave their lives for their country, but it makes no political statement about the validity of the United States' twelve-year involvement in the twenty-one-year conflict in southeast Asia. The memorial was intended to serve as a testament to the sacrifice of American military personnel during one of the country's least popular wars. The national organization that decided on how veterans of the Vietnam War would be memorialized to their fellow citizens also hoped to create a public venue for reconciliation between, on the one side, veterans and their families, and on the other a country that had by and large turned either indifferent or hostile to those who participated in the conflict.

Congress authorized the Vietnam Veterans Memorial in 1980, stating that it would be located prominently on the National Mall on two acres at the western end of Constitution Gardens. The Vietnam Veterans Memorial Fund, the nonprofit organization authorized by Congress in 1979 to oversee the memorial's design, decided on these criteria for the monument: (1) that it possess a reflective and contemplative character; (2) that it harmonize with its surroundings, especially the neighboring national memorials; (3) that it contain the names of all who died or remain missing; and (4) that it make no political statement about the war.

"South Vietnam is fighting for its life against a brutal campaign of terror and armed attack inspired, directed, supplied, and controlled by the Communist regime in Hanoi." State Department White Paper on Vietnam, February 27, 1965

Following a contest involving 1,421 entries, a jury appointed by the Vietnam Veterans Memorial Fund selected the design of Maya Ying Lin of Athens, Ohio, then a twenty-one-year-old architecture student at Yale University. Lin's design called for two walls of polished black granite, each some 246 feet (75 meters) in length, that would cite chronologically by date of casualty the name of every U.S. serviceman and -woman killed or declared missing in the war. To integrate this objective with the landscape, Lin specified that the memorial "appear as a rift in the earth," with the ground sloping "gently downward and the low walls emerging on either side, growing out of the earth." Lin conceived her design as creating a park within a park—a quiet, protected place unto itself, yet one harmonious with the overall plan of Constitution Gardens—and this objective she achieved to great effect. As visitors descend a walkway that runs along each wall of the memorial, they can see on the polished stone surface reflections of both themselves and the surrounding gardens.

The walls intersect at a 125-degree angle, with one segment pointing to the Washington Monument and the other to the Lincoln Memorial, thus bringing the memorial into the nation's historical context. The names are inscribed continuously in rows that can be easily read by most people. The list begins at the vertex of the walls, below the date of the first casualty, and continues to the end of the east wall. The list resumes at the tip

The Vietnam Veterans Memorial in Washington, D.C.

of the west wall, ending at the vertex, above the date of the last death. The meeting of the beginning and ending of personal sacrifice serves to symbolize a major epoch in American history.

In her design, Lin sought to convey the somber reckoning of so many lives lost. "These names," she has said, "seemingly infinite in number, convey the sense of overwhelming numbers, while unifying these individuals into a whole." Originally the memorial bore 57,939 names; by Veterans Day 1998 that number had increased to 58,214.

While the United States has been involved in a number of armed interventions worldwide since it withdrew from Vietnam in 1973, the war created an ongoing debate about the right of the United States to intervene in the affairs of other nations. It also raised the ethical issue of whether America has the right to risk the lives of its citizens to help resolve another country's conflicts. Along with the more than 58,000 military personnel who died in Vietnam, over 300,000 American soldiers were wounded, half of them seriously. No reliable accounting has ever been made of the number of U.S civilians (government agents, religious missionaries, Red Cross nurses) who were killed throughout southeast Asia.

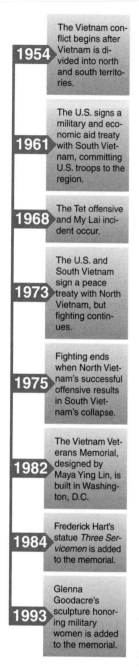

1954 The Vietnam conflict begins after Vietnam is divided into north and south territories.

1961 The U.S. signs a military and economic aid treaty with South Vietnam, committing U.S. troops to the region.

1968 The Tet offensive and My Lai incident occur.

1973 The U.S. and South Vietnam sign a peace treaty with North Vietnam, but fighting continues.

1975 Fighting ends when North Vietnam's successful offensive results in South Vietnam's collapse.

1982 The Vietnam Veterans Memorial, designed by Maya Ying Lin, is built in Washington, D.C.

1984 Frederick Hart's statue *Three Servicemen* is added to the memorial.

1993 Glenna Goodacre's sculpture honoring military women is added to the memorial.

The conflict we know as the Vietnam War began shortly after Vietnam was divided into north and south territories in 1954 and soon escalated into a civil war that was fought primarily in the south. The South Vietnamese forces were aided by the United States, and the guerrilla forces in the south (initially known as the Vietcong) were aided by communist North Vietnam. United States participation began in 1961, when America signed a military and economic aid treaty with South Vietnam that committed U.S. troops to the region and established a U.S. military command. The United States believed that if all of Vietnam fell under communist rule, communism would spread throughout southeast Asia and beyond. President John F. Kennedy and, after his assassination, President Lyndon B. Johnson felt they had to take a forceful stance on Vietnam so that other communist countries would not think that the United States lacked resolve.

America's involvement in the fighting increased dramatically in 1964, after the North Vietnamese attacked two U.S. destroyers in the Tonkin Gulf. When Congress passed the Gulf of Tonkin Resolution, it effectively handed over war-making powers to President Johnson until "peace and security" had returned to Vietnam. President Johnson steadily escalated U.S. bombing of North Vietnam. In 1965 the United States began air raids on North Vietnam and communist-controlled areas in the south. By 1966 190,000 American troops were stationed in South Vietnam. During this period of heightened U.S. intervention, North Vietnam was receiving armaments and technical assistance from the Soviet Union and other communist countries.

The Tet Offensive of January 1968, sparked by an attack on South Vietnamese and American positions during the celebration of the Vietnamese New Year, Tet, lasted into the fall of 1968. During this time, the North Vietnamese and the political organization of the Vietcong, the National Liberation Front (NLF), suffered acute losses. A critical event during the Tet Offensive occurred in March 1968, when a U.S. army division killed 500 unarmed civilians, mostly women and children, in a hamlet called My Lai. Public dissatisfaction with the war grew in the United States as the 1960s drew to a close. The length of the war, the number of U.S. casualties, and the exposure of U.S. involvement in war crimes such as the My Lai massacre helped to turn many Americans against the effort.

Despite the mounting antiwar sentiment, the U.S. military, under President Richard M. Nixon, continued heavy saturation bombing of the north, even as peace talks between the combatants were being held in Paris. The number of U.S. troops in southeast Asia was declining from its peak of 550,000 in 1969, and it was increasingly evident that massive U.S. military aid and relentless heavy bombing were not able to deter the NLF and North Vietnamese forces. A peace treaty was finally signed on January 27, 1973, by the United States, South Vietnam, North Vietnam, and the NLF. Fighting nonetheless continued until 1975, when North Vietnam's successful offensive resulted in South Vietnam's collapse and the unification of Vietnam by the North. The war devastated much of southeast Asia: approximately three to four million Vietnamese on both sides were killed, in addition to another 1.5 to 2 million Laotians and Cambodians who were drawn into the war.

Early protests against the war were organized around questions about the morality of U.S. military involvement in Vietnam. Polls conducted midway through 1969 showed that half of all Americans felt that the war was "morally indefensible," while 60 percent admitted that it was a mistake. On October 15, 1969, citizens across the United States participated in the Moratorium, the largest one-day demonstration against the war. Millions of people stayed home from work to mark their opposition to the war; college and high school students demonstrated on hundreds of campuses. In Vietnam troops wore black armbands in honor of the home-front protest. The participation of Vietnam veterans in protests against the war gave greater impetus to the antiwar movement.

The Vietnam War changed the American public's idea of what it meant to be a "good soldier." The first U.S. combat troops to arrive in Vietnam were mainly volunteers; the escalating war, however, required more draftees. In 1965 about 20,000 men per month were inducted into the military, most of them into the army; by 1968 about 40,000 men were drafted each month to meet the demand for increased troop levels. The **conscript** army was largely composed of teenagers—the average U.S. soldier being nineteen years old. The conscripted were mostly from the poorer sections of American society; they did not have access to the exemptions that were available to their more privileged fellow citizens. The draft laws effectively enabled many upper- and middle-class eighteen-year-olds to avoid

"At the intersection of these walls, on the right side, is carved the date of the first death. It is followed by the names of those who died in the war, in chronological order. These names continue on this wall appearing to recede into the earth at the wall's end. The names resume on the left wall as the wall emerges from the earth, continuing back to the origin where the date of the last death is carved."

Maya Lin, memorial design submission, 1980

conscripted: drafted into military service.

military service. All these factors contributed to an unprecedented low morale among U.S. troops in southeast Asia.

After returning from the war, many Vietnam veterans suffered from post-traumatic stress disorder, which is characterized by persistent emotional problems such as anxiety and depression. Throughout the 1970s and 1980s, unemployment and rates of prison incarceration for Vietnam veterans, especially among those who saw heavy combat, were significantly higher than in the general population. Clearly, the veterans of this war endured emotional duress long after the fighting ended.

Attitudes toward the war among Vietnam veterans are as diverse as the American population itself. Consequently, for some veterans, the Vietnam Veterans Memorial was at first a source of controversy because it does not glorify the military but invites somber reflection. The Asian ancestry of designer Maya Lin was also an issue for a number of veterans. Rather than allow the memorial to the veterans of a controversial war to itself become divisive and controversial, however, Congress decided to erect another memorial. Thus Frederick Hart's bronze statue *Three Servicemen*, depicting one white, one black, and one Hispanic American soldier, was added to the overall design in 1984. In 1993 Glenna Goodacre's bronze sculpture depicting three women cradling a wounded soldier was also added to commemorate the service of the 11,000 military nurses who treated soldiers in Vietnam.

Despite all of the controversies it has created, the Vietnam Veterans Memorial has become a site of pilgrimage for veterans and civilians alike. For many Americans, the memorial is a poignant reminder of how, by confronting the troubling and often painful aspects of our past, we can become more caring and responsible citizens. ◆

> The Vietnam Veterans Memorial was at first a source of controversy because it does not glorify the military but invites somber reflection.

Washington Monument

Today, the Washington Monument is one of America's most renowned sites, but this great white obelisk got off to a slow and rocky start. The idea for the monument began shortly after the American Revolution, when in 1783 the Continental Congress proposed honoring the country's first president, George Washington, with some type of monument during his lifetime. Then, a group of citizens founded the Washington National Monument Society to raise private funds to build a monument. The original plans for the Washington, D.C., federal district had called for a large **equestrian** statue of the president, but that project was abandoned.

Congress was slow to act on the proposals for a monument to honor George Washington, and officially authorized the construction of a monument only in 1833. In 1836 the government sponsored a competition for the best design. The winning architect, Robert Mills, conceived of the monument as a great **obelisk** surrounded by a **colonnade** at its base, with a colossal statue of Washington and other sculptures of America's Founding Fathers. The Washington National Monument Society raised $87,000 by asking institutions, businesses, and individual American citizens to contribute up to $1. Despite this sum—very impressive considering the era—financial constraints eventually forced the abandonment of all but the central obelisk in Mills's design.

The cornerstone—a giant block of marble—was laid on July 4, 1848, complete with a time capsule containing statistics about the nation, American coins, newspapers, governmental reports, and information about George Washington and his

equestrian: rider on horseback.

obelisk: a tall, slender, four-sided stone pillar.

colonnade: a series of columns supporting a roof or series of arches.

407

family. Future presidents Abraham Lincoln, James Buchanan, and Andrew Johnson stood among the 29,000 people who attended the inaugural event.

In 1854 construction on the monument came to a halt as public interest waned, private donations stopped, and the events surrounding the Civil War began to unfold. Political turmoil within the Washington National Monument Society also contributed to the stall, as members of an enigmatic political group known as the Know-Nothing Party gained control of the society. The stunted, unfinished monument stood at about 156 feet for nearly twenty-five years. Finally, during the nation's centennial celebration of 1876, the Grant administration urged the Washington Monument Society to donate the half-finished monument to the American people, and authorized Congress to appropriate public funding to complete it. The Army Corps of Engineers resumed construction with a more simplified design in 1878, under the direction of Lieutenant Colonel Thomas Casey. In 1884–85 the engineers topped the obelisk with a nine-inch-high pyramid made of cast aluminum. When President Chester Arthur officially opened its doors to the public in 1888, the monument's price tag had escalated to $1,181,710.

Today's visitors can easily see where the break in construction occurred. A visible change in the type of marble used about one-third the way up the obelisk marks the stalled and restarted building campaigns. When construction was reinitiated in 1878, the Massachusetts quarry that had provided the original marble had been emptied. The builders turned to a Maryland quarry with similar marble, but the difference in the two types of marble is notable. The Washington Monument stands 555 feet tall and counts 897 steps, making it one of the tallest masonry structures in the world. The base of the monument measures 55 feet, 1 1/2 inches wide, while the top of the shaft measures 34 feet, 5 1/2 inches wide. The width of the walls ranges from 15 feet at the base to 18 inches at the summit. The structure was constructed with 36,000 bricks faced with a layer of granite, then covered with marble. It weighs over 90,000 tons. Today, an elevator ferries visitors to a landing 500 feet above ground for spectacular views of the nation's capital. The elevator was part of the original plan, but until 1901 it was operated by steam hoist.

The obelisk is a time-honored symbol that was used in honorary contexts in ancient Egypt and in the Greek and Roman

"His was the singular destiny and merit of leading the armies of his country successfully through an arduous war for the establishment of its independence, of conducting its councils through the birth of a government, new in its forms and principles, until it settled down into a quiet and orderly train."

Thomas Jefferson, describing Washington, 1814

periods. It reflects a taste for neoclassical art that prevailed at the time of the original design competition in the 1830s. In fact, Mills's original design even called for a statue of Washington in a classical toga driving a battle chariot, an idea that was scrapped along with the projected colonnade. Rather, today the monument is encircled by fifty aluminum flagpoles bearing American flags representing each American state.

The Washington Monument honors the memory and legacy of America's first president. Congressman Henry Lee described George Washington as "First in war, first in peace, and first in the hearts of his countrymen." This statement sums up the multifaceted career of the man who went from being a gentleman farmer on his vast estate at Mount Vernon to a military officer, statesman, and America's first president.

The Washington Monument in Washington, D.C.

Washington had served in the French and Indian War, but his real test on the battlefield came when he took command of the newly formed Continental Army in 1775. Having successfully led his small, untrained troops to victory against their British oppressors, Washington quickly became a symbol of the triumphant Revolution and American independence. However, his influence did not stop there. After the Revolution, he oversaw the drafting of the Articles of the Confederation and the American Constitution. He was unanimously elected as the country's first president in 1789. Washington is partly credited for laying the political, legal, and philosophical groundwork for the new American nation, principles that endure today.

The interior stairwell of the Washington Monument bears witness to the scope of Washington's influence. It is lined with 192 memorial stones donated by all fifty states as well as representatives of foreign governments, organizations, and individuals. In the **rotunda** on the ground floor, a bronze replica of a sculpture by the French artist Jean-Antoine Houdon depicts George Washington in an active stance. Annually on Washington's birthday, patriotic groups lay wreaths and make commemorative speeches to honor the memory and spirit of the first president.

rotunda: a round room or building with a dome.

Since its dedication, the Washington Monument has been the site of countless public celebrations, meetings, demonstrations, rallies, and protests. One of the largest of these, held on July 4, 1945, was a rally to sell more than $1,250,000 in government savings bonds to finance the war effort. More than a dozen anti-Vietnam War protests were launched on the grounds of the Washington Monument between 1967 and 1973.

The Washington Monument is located in the heart of Washington, D.C.'s National Mall, a green park teeming with national monuments and memorials. It has been under care of the National Park Service since 1933. The monument draws more than a million visitors annually. ◆

Watergate Complex

WASHINGTON, D.C.

"I would say only that if some of my judgments were wrong, and some were wrong, they were made in what I believed at the time to be in the best interest of the nation."
Richard Nixon, resignation speech, August 8, 1974

The Watergate is a complex of six large buildings that includes a luxurious hotel, expensive apartments, and two office buildings in Washington, D.C. Set near the Potomac River and located about a mile from the White House and about two miles from the United States Capitol, the Watergate has accommodated many famous and important people. But its lasting fame results from the role it played in one of the most damaging high-level scandals in American history. Watergate, as the scandal came to be known, led to the first resignation of a U.S. president.

The Watergate's semicircular shape with its patterned rows of balconies made it a stylish, futuristic building in the early 1970s. Residents enjoy majestic views of the river, and from high balconies eastward views encompass the capital city's greatest sites. The Watergate's closeness to the heart of the city and to the heart of the nation's government made the Watergate a very desirable place to live and work in the late 1960s and early 1970s. Many wealthy and powerful politicians, many of them Republicans including top people in the administration of President Richard Nixon, lived at the Watergate in those years. Someone nicknamed the Watergate the "Republican Bastille," after 1,000 war protestors targeted high officials at the Water-

gate in a 1970 action. In spite of the Republican presence, Democrats also took advantage of the Watergate's excellent location. During the campaign for the 1972 presidential elections, the Democratic National Committee (DNC) rented the entire sixth floor of a Watergate office building to serve as its national headquarters.

The Watergate complex in Washington, D.C.

The DNC headquarters became the site of the opening act of a drama of political scheming, power relationships, and ruthless ambition. That story began with low criminal activity. In the dark early hours of June 17, a young security guard found something amiss at the Watergate office building. A door leading to the garage had been taped to keep it from locking. He phoned police, who sent three officers over. Carefully scouting through various offices, the men suddenly came upon five burglars in DNC offices. The men surrendered to police peacefully and were taken to jail. Oddly, the men possessed telephone-tapping microphones, burglary tools, cameras, and walkie-talkies. It seemed the burglars intended to spy on the Democrats.

The burglary made barely a ripple in busy Washington, D.C., but two eager young reporters were assigned the story at the

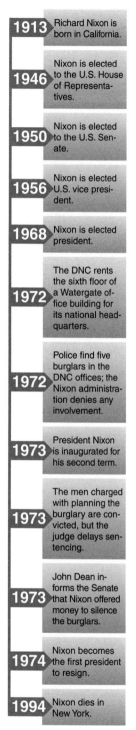

1913 Richard Nixon is born in California.

1946 Nixon is elected to the U.S. House of Representatives.

1950 Nixon is elected to the U.S. Senate.

1956 Nixon is elected U.S. vice president.

1968 Nixon is elected president.

1972 The DNC rents the sixth floor of a Watergate office building for its national headquarters.

1972 Police find five burglars in the DNC offices; the Nixon administration denies any involvement.

1973 President Nixon is inaugurated for his second term.

1973 The men charged with planning the burglary are convicted, but the judge delays sentencing.

1973 John Dean informs the Senate that Nixon offered money to silence the burglars.

1974 Nixon becomes the first president to resign.

1994 Nixon dies in New York.

Washington Post. Carl Bernstein and Bob Woodward, who became famous for their dogged journalism, pursued the first clues that suggested the burglars had high connections. One of the men, James W. McCord Jr., a former agent of the Central Intelligence Agency, was the security chief for Nixon's Committee to Reelect the President (CRP). Nixon, who had served as president since 1969, was seeking reelection in 1972. The head of CRP was Nixon's former attorney general, John N. Mitchell, who had quit that post to direct Nixon's campaign for reelection.

The day after the break-in, Mitchell issued a statement denying any involvement by Nixon's people. He was lying. Not only were Nixon's aides involved in the break-in, but Nixon also knew about it soon after it happened. In the drama that unfolded, Nixon first denied knowledge of the break-in, then denied his efforts to cover up any knowledge. It would take two years of painstaking investigation by journalists, lawyers, judges, and legislators to uncover all of the plots and subplots of Nixon's actions and those of his loyal followers.

On June 22, days after the break-in, Nixon denied any involvement. Soon after, Mitchell quietly resigned as Nixon's reelection manager. Nixon won the Republican nomination at the August convention, and by the November 7 elections, few Americans understood much about the Watergate scandal. Nixon was able to defeat his opponent, Democratic candidate George McGovern, by the biggest landslide of any Republican presidential candidate in history up to that time.

But soon after Nixon's joyful inauguration on January 20, 1973, Watergate resurfaced. The trial of the five burglars—plus two men charged with planning the burglary, E. Howard Hunt and G. Gordon Liddy—took place from January 8 to 30. The men were convicted, but the judge, John Sirica, delayed sentencing. Sirica expressed concern that the defendants would not tell why they had broken into the DNC headquarters, and he hoped they would reveal their motives in order to receive a lighter sentence. On February 7, the U.S. Senate voted to create a committee to investigate charges of corruption by the Republican party in the 1972 election. It was called the Senate Select Committee on Presidential Campaign Activities, and it began public hearings on May 17.

Meanwhile, on March 23, McCord admitted to Sirica that he had lied under oath and that, in fact, high-level politicians had ordered the burglary. Sirica sentenced all the defendants to prison. Senate committee members, meanwhile, learned from

---

Scandal–*gate*

Since the Watergate scandal, the third syllable of the word Watergate has entered modern English as a suffix that indicates political scandal involving corruption or illegal acts within powerful circles. A scandal called "Koreagate" developed in the mid 1970s following reports of South Korean efforts to influence U.S. government policy and of U.S. congressmen who profited from the efforts. President Jimmy Carter was faced with "Billygate" when his younger brother, Billy, became a paid agent of the Libyan government. President Ronald Reagan and Vice President George Bush became embroiled in "Contragate," also called "Iran-Contragate," after officials in the Reagan White House sold arms to Iran to secure the release of American hostages, then used the profits to aid the contra rebels fighting in Nicaragua. When Bush became president, he had to deal with "Iraqgate" after reports surfaced that agencies in the executive department had knowingly permitted the Atlanta branch of Italy's Banco Nationale del Lavoro to issue $5 billion in illegal loans to Iraq shortly before the Persian Gulf War. In the 1990s a scandal dubbed "Chinagate" broke out when President Bill Clinton and Democratic party leaders were accused of accepting campaign contributions from Chinese officials and businessmen. The suffix came in handy when numerous other scandals emerged during Clinton's tenure and were referred to variously as "Monicagate," "Filegate," " Travelgate," " Troopergate," and "Whitewatergate."

McCord that two top Nixon aides were involved in the scandal, John Dean, Special Counsel to the President, and Jeb Magruder, second in charge of CRP. When the committee summoned Dean and Magruder to testify, the White House became alarmed. To save himself, Nixon fired John Dean and asked three of his top advisors to resign. The men who resigned were Assistant to the President for Domestic Affairs John Erlichman, Chief of Staff H. R. Haldeman, and Attorney General Richard Kleindienst. On May 18 Nixon's new attorney general, Elliot Richardson, appointed a special prosecutor, Archibald Cox, to conduct a full-scale investigation of the Watergate break-in. Nixon hoped these moves would convince the public of his innocence in the Watergate incident.

But Nixon was not out of the woods. In late June and early July two bombshells dropped. From June 25 to 29 Dean testified before the Senate committee, opening with a 245-page statement that shocked the nation. Dean told of a long-standing pattern of devious and illegal policies under Nixon, of which the break-in at Democratic headquarters was just one small part. Dean also told the packed hearing room when Nixon had

"Always give your best, never get discouraged, never be petty; always remember, others may hate you, but those who hate you don't win unless you hate them, and then you destroy yourself.

Richard Nixon,
farewell speech,
August 9, 1974

subpoena: to order that specified records or documents be brought to a court.

"My conscience tells me clearly and certainly that I cannot prolong the bad dreams that continue to reopen a chapter that is closed. My conscience tells me that only I, as President, have the constitutional power to firmly shut and seal this book."

Gerald Ford, announcing Nixon's pardon, September 8, 1974

learned and what he knew about the cover-up of the Watergate burglary, including Nixon's offer of money to silence the burglars. Dean said Haldeman and Erlichman had acted as middlemen for the president.

A few weeks after Dean's testimony, Alexander Butterfield, a former aide to Haldeman, dropped another bomb. He told the staff of the committee that the president's offices at the White House were equipped with recording devices that had taped every conversation since 1971. The committee quickly moved to **subpoena** the tapes, making their demand on July 23, 1973. Nixon refused to hand them over. Politicians on both sides began suggesting that Nixon be impeached, and finally Nixon released some of the tapes. One of the tapes had an eighteen-minute gap that experts said was an erased portion. The committee demanded sixty-four more tapes. Instead, on April 30, 1974, Nixon turned over 1,308 typed pages that his personal secretary, Rose Mary Woods, had transcribed from the tapes. But that was not acceptable to the special prosecutor, who asked the Supreme Court to intervene. On July 24, 1974, the Court ruled 8–0 in *United States* v. *Nixon* that the president must turn over the tapes.

Before Nixon released the tapes, the House Judiciary Committee voted to impeach him. The House charged Nixon with obstructing justice, abusing the powers of the presidency, and defying the demands of Congress. When Nixon realized that his support among members of Congress was nil, he decided to resign.

On the evening of August 8, 1974, Nixon appeared on national television to tell the American people that he was leaving office. He said, "I regret deeply any injuries that may have been done in the course of the events that led to this decision. I would say only that if some of my judgments were wrong, and some were wrong, they were made in what I believed at the time to be in the best interest of the nation." Observers noted that Nixon did not admit he was guilty of any crime. The next day, Gerald R. Ford was sworn in as president. In a month, on September 8, Ford pardoned Nixon for any federal crimes that he might have committed while in office. Many Americans reacted angrily to Ford's move, feeling that Nixon deserved to be punished for his crimes and for subjecting the nation to a two-year nightmare. But Ford decided that a long trial to determine Nixon's guilt would only prolong the nation's turmoil.

Many well-connected and famous people have lived at the expensive Watergate complex, including some who were either directly or indirectly involved in the Watergate scandal. Rose Mary Woods and John N. Mitchell both lived at the Watergate. Former Republican senator Bob Dole and his wife, Elizabeth, also maintained a residence at the Watergate. The Watergate hotel-apartment complex became famous for scandal again in 1998 as the Washington home of Monica Lewinsky, whose romance with President Bill Clinton while she was a White House intern became part of a sexual harassment lawsuit against Clinton brought by another woman. ◆

Weedpatch Camp

ARVIN, CALIFORNIA

T he federal Farm Security Administration managed Weedpatch Camp and similar installations in California starting in the mid 1930s. It provided shelter and other basic assistance to refugees from the Dust Bowl in the southwestern Great Plains. The camps' inhabitants, widely known as Okies, had come to California to find work as agricultural laborers.

The Dust Bowl, a natural and social disaster, resulted from poor management of the land and extreme drought conditions in southeastern Colorado, northeastern New Mexico, southwestern Kansas, and the Oklahoma and Texas panhandles. Before World War I, farmers in the region engaged primarily in raising livestock. But when the war came, rising grain prices led farmers to plow up some one million acres of grassland and grow wheat. A major drought began in the early 1930s. Without the grasses that had once anchored the land and conserved water in their roots, the topsoil was vulnerable to severe winds. Windstorms created "dust blizzards" that obscured the sun and piled the soil into high drifts lying against homes and barns and covering roads, fences, and farm equipment. Some 150,000 square miles were affected.

Under the supervision of the U.S. Soil Conservation Service, grasses and trees were planted and farmers were taught various techniques to restore the soil. These included leaving land fallow, contour plowing, and terracing to help the soil store water. Methods for reducing the soil's vulnerability to wind were also taught. By 1941 the land had been restored.

From 1935 through 1940 the Dust Bowl had driven over one million people out of the region.

Before then, however, the Dust Bowl had driven over one million people out of the region, mostly during the years from 1935 through 1940. They left in family groups, virtually destitute except for what they could carry. Hundred of thousands of them headed for California; they had heard that agricultural work was available there. The Okies overwhelmed the state. The problem was not just their large overall numbers, but the fact that they were concentrated primarily in rural areas such as the Sacramento Valley and, farther south, the San Joaquin Valley. The population of most counties in the San Joaquin Valley, for example, grew by over 30 percent from 1935 to 1937.

In these sparsely settled areas the Okies proved a financial burden. The migrants' children swelled the school population. Expenditures for county health services grew, and not only because the Okies were **indigent**. A poorly educated group often without knowledge of modern disease-prevention strategies like good nutrition, they were especially prone to disease. Furthermore, the newest migrants settled in squalid "ditch bank camps" alongside roads, rivers, and canals. These settlements were filthy and unsanitary to a degree journalists found hard to describe. Typhoid and smallpox epidemics broke out, and tuberculosis, malaria, and pneumonia were common. These conditions threatened not only the Okies, but the rest of the population.

Previous agricultural workers, mostly Mexican and Filipino, had not caused such problems. They came to California as individuals, not families, lived in housing provided by the agricultural growers that was at least somewhat better than the ditch settlements, and stayed only for the growing season. Therefore, most native Californians came to resent the Okies for the new burdens they were imposing. In addition to anger, the Okies were also the objects of ridicule. Just the fact they were poorly paid agricultural laborers put them at the bottom of the social scale. But the Okies' distinct accents and different social habits made them even more likely targets of abuse. So did their appearance: they wore ragged clothing and often were skinny because of malnourishment. The racist attitudes that native Californians had previously directed at the Mexican and Filipino workers were inherited by the Okies, who although white came to be regarded by many as an inferior, degraded subcategory of humanity. Native Californians kept them out of mainstream social institutions. Some migrants were subjected to violence both by individuals and police. Attempts were made to stop them from entering the state.

indigent: poor.

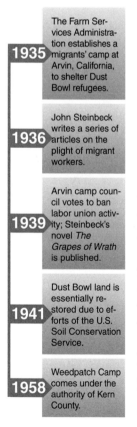

1935 The Farm Services Administration establishes a migrants' camp at Arvin, California, to shelter Dust Bowl refugees.

1936 John Steinbeck writes a series of articles on the plight of migrant workers.

1939 Arvin camp council votes to ban labor union activity; Steinbeck's novel *The Grapes of Wrath* is published.

1941 Dust Bowl land is essentially restored due to efforts of the U.S. Soil Conservation Service.

1958 Weedpatch Camp comes under the authority of Kern County.

Thanks to World War II, the Okies were able to escape their plight as a subordinated caste. Beginning in 1941 they began flocking away from the fields and toward the defense plants springing up in the state's urban areas. Earning good pay, they and their children quickly assimilated into the California mainstream and lost their separate identity.

In the meantime, though, the federal government succeeded in giving thousands of Okies—albeit a small proportion of them—a haven of physically decent living conditions where they were treated with respect. In 1935 the Farm Security Administration began constructing a string of camps for the migrants in California's rural areas, each run by a manager. The shelter, consisting of tin housing and wooden platforms for tents, was rudimentary but clean. Sanitary facilities were provided. Nurses were stationed there to provide elementary health care and education. Social activities such as dances, amateur theater, and recreational activities were organized.

Many of the managers were graduate students at the University of California. Most were liberals and some were socialists, so they generally sympathized with the plight of the Okies. Most of them allowed, and some even encouraged, union organizers to enter the camps. (Outside the camps, the organizers were often beaten and jailed.) Under the managers' guidance, a type of limited democratic self-government was set up. Each camp had a constitution. All residents over twenty-one elected a community council to make rules about the general welfare; management of the community fund to which everyone contributed; and regulation of the camps' common property. The council elected a community court to try individuals accused of disobeying camp rules and settle disputes between campers.

But the managers, who constituted the executive branch of the camp governments, could and often did overrule the other two branches. The better managers did it by persuasion rather than command, but everyone knew where the real power lay. So after the first year or two after a camp opened, the number of campers voting for the community council declined sharply.

In addition to turning away from the limited democracy offered them, the Okies resisted attempts by the managers to modernize their way of life. For example, some of the migrants belonged to faith-healing religious sects. Managers saw these groups as a roadblock to the acceptance of modern medicine, but their disapproval did little to change the migrants' religious

The racist attitude that Californians had previously directed at the Mexican and Filipino workers was inherited by the Okies.

beliefs. The Okies were also highly individualistic. They believed in making their own way and disliked group activities. Therefore they were inclined to oppose not only union organizing activities but even the community social activities of the camps.

Insofar as the camps were meant to "reform" the Okies and assimilate them into modern society, they were not highly successful. But they did provide a clean, healthy, and safe place for many Okies in the midst of a sea of hostility and squalor.

In 1935 the Farm Security Administration began to prepare a migrants' camp at Arvin, Kern County, in the San Joaquin Valley. It was officially called the Arvin Federal Camp but was commonly referred to as the Government Camp, or Weedpatch Camp after a small settlement nearby. The Works Progress Administration built the camp's community hall, for church gatherings and social events, post office, and library. Tin houses and wooden tent platforms were erected. Bath and laundry facilities were available. In 1936 some 300 migrants were in the camp, paying one dollar a week to stay there.

In 1935 the Farm Security Administration began constructing a string of camps for migrants in California's rural areas.

Following the policy of most camps, the manager of Weedpatch Camp tried to create a friendly and open environment, in contrast to repressive conditions outside. In 1936 journalist John Steinbeck, best known as the author the famous novel *The Grapes of Wrath* (1939) about the Okies, wrote a series of articles about their plight in the *San Francisco News*. Shortly after they appeared, the camp manager distributed the articles among the camp residents. He allowed union organizers into the camp; in fact, for a time the camp newspaper, the *Tow and Sack,* was edited by an organizer for the United Cannery, Agriculture, Packing, and Allied Workers of America. Yet many Weedpatch residents opposed the union. In April 1939 the Arvin camp council voted to ban union literature from the bulletin board and prohibit the holding of union meetings in public. During a cotton workers strike the following autumn, Weedpatch was one of seven camps used as unofficial union headquarters. The strike, however, failed. At Weedpatch Camp, as elsewhere, the Okies resisted collective activity.

Again like the other Dust Bowl migrants, the Arvin residents also resisted attempts to change their beliefs. In 1936 the manager reported on his unsuccessful efforts to combat a secret faith-healing sect in the camp. He wrote to his superiors that whenever he heard what sounded "very much like a dog on a distant hill baying a mournful ritual at the full moon," he knew that a faith-healing service was being held for a sick person. But since he could never catch the faith healers in action, he decided that they must station lookouts.

In 1958 Weedpatch Camp came under the authority of Kern County. Now known as the Sunset Labor Camp, it houses migrant workers from April to December. The original tin and tent housing has been replaced by wooden frame buildings. The community hall, post office, and library still stand as they were in the 1930s, except that a roof has been placed over the original shingles of the community hall to prevent interior decay. But the three buildings are now vacant and fenced in and have suffered deterioration. The Kern County Housing Authority plans to restore them as nearly as possible to their original condition.

Aside from these buildings, images of the original Weedpatch Camp are also available on film; some of the footage for *The Grapes of Wrath* (1940), the movie version of Steinbeck's novel, directed by John Ford, was filmed at Weedpatch. The Okies in general have become a celebrated part of American popular culture thanks to Steinbeck and Ford, the folk songs of Woody Guthrie, and the photographs of Dorothea Lange. ◆

John Steinbeck, author of the book *The Grapes of Wrath,* wrote a series of articles about the Okies' plight in the *San Francisco News.*

Wesleyan Chapel

SENECA FALLS, NEW YORK

The Wesleyan Chapel lies in the Women's Rights National Historical Park in Seneca Falls, New York. The chapel was the site of the First Women's Rights Convention in 1848. The United States Congress authorized the establishment of the park in 1980 to commemorate American women's struggle for equal rights. In the late twentieth century, it has become difficult to imagine the conditions that drove those women to declare so firmly that it was time for women to be treated as equals. They simply asked for the right to retain their own wages, the right to a higher education, the right to own property, and the right to vote.

The rise of individual rights brought on by the French and American revolutions in the late 1770s helped pave the way for early feminists. In addition, in the mid 1850s the women's movement gained momentum from the abolitionist movement.

The protected remains of Wesleyan Chapel, site of the 1848 women's rights convention, in Seneca Falls, New York.

Many women saw a link between the enslavement of blacks by whites and the domination of women by men. In the early 1800s women were not allowed the freedoms that men enjoyed by law. Women could not vote, hold elective office, or earn their own living. If married, they could not make legal contracts, divorce an abusive husband, or gain custody of their children.

In 1840 Lucretia Coffin Mott, a Quaker minister and abolitionist, traveled to London, England, with her husband, James Mott, as delegate to the World's Anti-Slavery Convention. Elizabeth Cady Stanton, a Seneca Falls housewife and mother of three sons, also attended the convention with her husband, delegate Henry Stanton. After discussing it at length, conventioneers decided not to allow women delegates to participate. Lucretia Mott and Elizabeth Cady Stanton instead were seated behind a curtain in a gallery. The two women met, talked, and decided to hold a meeting to discuss the rights of women after they returned to the United States.

Back in New York, Mott, Stanton, and Mott's sister, Martha Coffin Wright, gathered a small group of Quaker and abolitionist women and planned a convention in Seneca Falls for July of

1848. That July 14, the *Seneca County Courier* published the following announcement:

WOMAN'S RIGHTS CONVENTION!

A Convention to discuss the social, civil and religious condition and rights of woman will be held in the Wesleyan Chapel, at Seneca Falls, N.Y., on Wednesday and Thursday, the 19th and 20th of July . . . . During the first day the meeting will be exclusively for women, who are earnestly invited to attend. The public generally are invited to be present on the second day, when Lucretia Mott of Philadelphia, and others, ladies and gentlemen, will address the convention.

Up to 300 gathered at the chapel, where they held discussions on how best to achieve the goal of women's rights. They agreed that their primary aim should be to obtain the vote for women. They voted to ratify the "Declaration of Sentiments," written by Stanton. She modeled it after the Declaration of Independence, with such wording as "We hold these truths to be self-evident; that all men and women are created equal; that they are endowed by their Creator with certain inalienable rights; that among these are life, liberty, and the pursuit of happiness . . . ."

The document continued with the radical "Whenever any form of Government becomes destructive of these ends, it is the right of those who suffer from it to refuse allegiance to it, and to insist upon the institution of a new government . . . ." It went on "Prudence, indeed, will dictate that governments long established should not be changed for light and transient causes . . . . But when a long train of abuses [oppresses people], it is the duty [of the oppressed] to throw off such government and to . . . demand the equal station to which they are entitled."

The document continues with a list of "repeated injuries" by man toward woman through history. He never permitted her to vote; he compelled her to submit to laws that she had not formed; he denied her all property rights, including her own earned wages; he has made husbands her master; he has framed divorce laws based on the "false supposition of the supremacy of man, and giving all power into his hands."

The list went on. Even though women were deprived of rights when married, single women had to pay taxes to support a government that barely recognized them. Furthermore, the list alleged that man "has monopolized nearly all the profitable employments," and "He closes against her all the avenues to wealth and distinction, which he considers most honorable to

> *"We hold these truths to be self-evident; that all men and women are created equal; that they are endowed by their Creator with certain inalienable rights; that among these are life, liberty, and the pursuit of happiness; that to secure these rights governments are instituted, deriving their just powers from the consent of the governed."*
> Declaration of Sentiments, adopted at the Seneca Falls Women's Rights Convention, 1848

Elizabeth Cady Stanton house.

himself . . . . He has denied her the facilities for obtaining a thorough education—all colleges being closed against her." Men also, the document declared, denied women access to anything more than subordinate positions in the church.

Ultimately, man has "endeavored, in every way that he could to destroy [woman's] confidence in her own powers, to lessen her self-respect, and to make her willing to lead a dependent and abject life." The last paragraph of the document stated intentions to carry the message far and wide—through the press, in the **pulpit**, and by petitioning state and national legislatures. Sixty-eight women and thirty-two men signed the Declaration of Sentiments. Of the people who signed the document, many would continue playing significant roles in the women's rights and other movements. Among these was Frederick Douglass, an escaped slave who became a legendary abolitionist, orator, and writer.

Only two early published accounts of the Seneca Falls Convention exist. The *North Star*, a newspaper run by Frederick

pulpit: a raised platform from which a person of the clergy preaches in a church.

Douglass in nearby Rochester, printed a "Report of the Woman's Rights Convention" soon afterward. The second appeared thirty years later in the *National Citizen and Ballot Box*, as a draft of *A History of Woman Suffrage*, edited by Elizabeth Cady Stanton, Matilda Joslyn Gage, and Susan B. Anthony, a great leader among suffragists.

In spite of its high-minded goals, the Seneca Falls convention merely started what was to become a seventy-two-year struggle for American women to obtain the right to vote. Although many prominent Americans supported the women's movement, many others treated female activists with ridicule and scorn. Many women began meeting to work for their rights, but some suffragists were subjected to physical violence and had their meetings disrupted by thugs. In 1866 Stanton and Anthony formed the American Equal Rights Association, an organization for white and black women and men dedicated to the goal of universal suffrage.

In 1868 the Fourteenth Amendment to the U.S. Constitution prohibited states from denying Constitutional rights to any of its citizens. However, the Amendment defined "citizens" and "voters" as "male." Disagreements over the Fourteenth and the proposed Fifteenth Amendments, which would give black men the vote, split the women's movement in 1869. Stanton and Anthony formed the somewhat radical National Woman Suffrage Association (NWSA). A well-known feminist-abolitionist couple, Lucy Stone and her husband, Henry Blackwell, along with author and reformer Julia Ward Howe, organized the more conservative American Woman Suffrage Association (AWSA).

The NWSA refused to work for ratification of the Fifteenth Amendment, arguing instead for an amendment that would give everyone—including women—the vote. This caused Frederick Douglass to break with Stanton and Anthony. Blacks did obtain the vote in 1870, but it was not until 1878 that a Woman Suffrage Amendment was first introduced in the U.S. Congress. It did not pass, but through the late 1800s and early 1900s, a number of states, mainly in the west, gave women the right to vote. In 1890 the AWSA and the NWSA joined forces to become the National American Woman Suffrage Association (NAWSA).

In 1913 Alice Paul and Lucy Burns organized a group that later became the National Women's Party. Members of the party held hunger strikes, picketed the White House, and engaged in other forms of civil disobedience to promote their

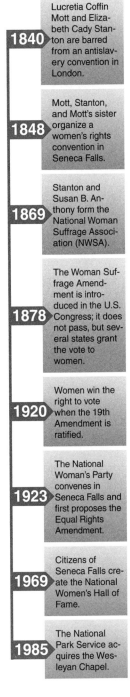

1840 Lucretia Coffin Mott and Elizabeth Cady Stanton are barred from an antislavery convention in London.

1848 Mott, Stanton, and Mott's sister organize a women's rights convention in Seneca Falls.

1869 Stanton and Susan B. Anthony form the National Woman Suffrage Association (NWSA).

1878 The Woman Suffrage Amendment is introduced in the U.S. Congress; it does not pass, but several states grant the vote to women.

1920 Women win the right to vote when the 19th Amendment is ratified.

1923 The National Woman's Party convenes in Seneca Falls and first proposes the Equal Rights Amendment.

1969 Citizens of Seneca Falls create the National Women's Hall of Fame.

1985 The National Park Service acquires the Wesleyan Chapel.

M'Clintock House, in Waterloo, New York, where the "Declaration of Sentiments" was drafted.

cause. Finally, on August 18, 1920, women won the right to vote when the Nineteenth Amendment was ratified.

After it achieved its victory, the NAWSA dissolved, but members later formed the League of Women Voters, a group that has remained strong into the beginning of the twenty-first century. In 1923, the National Woman's Party first proposed the Equal Rights Amendment to eliminate discrimination on the basis of gender. It has never been ratified.

Visitors to the Women's Rights National Historical Park can learn about the women's movement as they tour the nearly three-acre area owned by the National Park Service and an additional three acres of nonfederal land in Seneca Falls and nearby Waterloo, New York. In addition to the Wesleyan Chapel, visitors can see the Stanton home, the M'Clintock House where the Declaration of Sentiments was written, and an Education and Cultural Center housing the Suffrage Press Printshop.

Before the NPS acquired the Wesleyan Chapel in 1985, it had been an opera hall, movie theater, an automobile dealership, and a laundromat. The National Endowment for the Arts sponsored a competition for a design to restore the building to its original state. However, there were no images portraying the chapel as it looked in 1848, so a design was chosen that best highlighted the original portions.

Between the Wesleyan Chapel and a Visitors Center lies Declaration Park. Visitors from all over the world come here to read the Declaration of Sentiments. The full text of the Declaration is set into a water wall, which provides a peaceful spot for contemplation. In addition to the Water Wall, Declaration Park provides an amphitheater for public performances. Across the street from the Wesleyan Chapel, lies the Elizabeth Cady Stanton Park, dedicated in 1980.

The First Presbyterian Church in Seneca Falls became the site for a convention of the National Women's Party in 1923, the seventy-fifth anniversary of the 1848 convention. At that event, the Women's Party adopted the Equal Rights Amendment, drafted by Alice Paul. In 1969, citizens of Seneca Falls created their own National Women's Hall of Fame, to honor the contribution of American women in the village where so much history had begun. The hall is home to exhibits, artifacts of historical interest, a research library, and an office.

In 1998 many people throughout the United States celebrated the 150th anniversary of the Women's Rights Convention of 1848. A reported 15,000 Americans traveled to Seneca Falls in July to commemorate the anniversary. Visitors were reminded of how far women progressed in 150 years toward gaining political freedom, influence, and power. Participants in the commemoration expressed a commitment to work for future goals such as equal participation of women in politics and business, equal pay for equal work, an end to violence and harassment, and policy changes to help family caregivers. ◆

White Bird Canyon

CENTRAL IDAHO

O n June 17, 1877, near the confluence of the Snake and Salmon rivers in central Idaho, the Wallowa band of the Nez Percé tribe met the United States military at White Bird Canyon. The battle they fought there marked the beginning of what became later known as the Nez Percé Wars. On that day, the Wallowa band, consisting of only 200 warriors and well over five hundred women and children, routed a far superior force, killing thirty-four soldiers and losing none. Over the next five months, the Nez Percé would somehow manage to outmaneuver and elude more than 2,000 U.S. soldiers in a retreat extending more than 1,500 miles. Before they were finally defeated, their flight would capture the attention of the entire nation, and the eloquence of one of their leaders, Chief Joseph, would forever stand as a symbol of Native American dignity in the face of tragedy and despair.

Nez Percé, French, means *pierced nose*, and this name was given by early French explorers to the bands of Indians they found living in the plateau country of what is now northeast Oregon, southwest Washington, and central Idaho. The name was applied mistakenly, though, for these people who called themselves *Nee-Me-Poo* did not pierce their noses. They were a hunting and fishing people who lived in moveable tepees and

> Chief Joseph would forever stand as a symbol of Native American dignity.

Nez Percé Hinmaton-Yalakit, better known as Chief Joseph, during the 1870s.

large, permanent multifamily lodges, often along the banks of the region's major rivers. Bands of the Nez Percé lived in distinct villages at various distances from one another, depending on the availability of resources, especially salmon.

The Nez Percé first encountered whites in September of 1805, when the Lewis and Clark expedition stumbled down out of the Bitterroot Range, desperately exhausted and cold from their journey over the mountains. The Nez Percé fed and sheltered the expedition, and then helped them find their way to the Pacific. Lewis and Clark promised the Nez Percé that from then on the white man would always be their friend.

The Wallowa band of the Nez Percé lived in the mountains and valleys of what is today northeastern Oregon. In 1855 a

Wallowa chief known as Joseph the Elder helped establish a treaty between the federal government and the Nez Percé, and this treaty guaranteed the Nez Percé rights to their traditional homelands. This treaty would not last long. In 1860 gold was discovered in the region. The gold rush that would devastate Native American tribes all over the west would be no different for the Nez Percé. In 1863 the federal government "renegotiated" the earlier treaty, appropriating nearly six million acres, leaving the Nez Percé with less than one tenth of their traditional homeland.

Many Nez Percé chiefs refused to sign this treaty, and Joseph the Elder was among them. In 1838 Joseph the Elder had been baptized at a Nez Percé mission in Lapwai, Idaho, and since the time of Lewis and Clark, he and his people had always prided themselves on their good relations with whites. But now Joseph the Elder renounced his Christianity, burned his Bible, and destroyed his American flag. His oldest son, who succeeded him as chief, vowed that their homelands would never be sold to the white man. Chief Joseph, whose Nee-Me-Poo name *Hinmaton-Yalakit* means Thunder Rolling from the Mountains, would keep this promise. Over the next ten years, other Nez Percé bands reluctantly moved onto the Lapwai reservation in Idaho, converted to Christianity, adopted the white man's style of dress, and took up farming. But the Wallowa remained where they had always been.

But in 1877 this all changed. The U.S. military, under the command of General Oliver Howard, arrived in the Wallowa Valley to enforce the treaty of 1863. General Howard, prior to his military days, had been a mathematics professor in New England, and he later distinguished himself in the Civil War. He had also championed black suffrage after the war and helped to found Howard University, a school for emancipated blacks in Washington, D.C. Howard was sympathetic to the rights of the Nez Percé, and he offered to purchase their homeland. Their land, however, was not negotiable and his offer was rejected. And so Howard would follow his orders. If the Nez Percé did not relocate to Idaho, a cavalry attack would soon follow.

Unwilling to shed blood, Chief Joseph capitulated, and in early June, he led his people on their journey to the reservation in Idaho. But soon after they crossed the Snake River, several Wallowa warriors, out for retribution, killed four settlers, and in the two days that followed other warriors joined them, killing fourteen or fifteen more whites. Knowing that General Howard

1805 The Nez Percé Indians first encounter whites when the Lewis and Clark expedition arrives.

1855 Chief Joseph helps establish a treaty guaranteeing the Nez Percé rights to their traditional homelands.

1860 The discovery of gold in the region devastates Native American tribes.

1863 The federal government renegotiates the earlier treaty, leaving the Nez Percé with less than one tenth of their land.

1877 The U.S. military, under the command of Oliver Howard, arrives to enforce the treaty of 1863.

1877 Chief Joseph formally surrenders to Howard.

1885 The Nez Percé are finally allowed to return to the Pacific northwest.

1990 By this time, only 4,113 Native Americans claim to be descendants of the Nez Percé tribe.

would respond to the killings with force, they abandoned their Lapwai destination and fled to White Bird Canyon. Like Crazy Horse and Sitting Bull and their bands of Sioux, like Geronimo and the Apache, from then on Chief Joseph and his people would be relentlessly pursued by the U.S. Army until forced to surrender.

The battle at White Bird Canyon was the first of four major battles and seventeen engagements in the Nez Percé's flight east and north toward Canada. They next met the U.S. Army on the banks of the Clearwater River, not far from where the Nez Percé had sheltered Lewis and Clark more than seventy years before. The band was later surprised at Big Hole in southwest Montana, when between sixty and ninety Nez Percé were killed before they were able to regroup and escape south back into Idaho.

During this time, the exploits of the Nez Percé had touched upon the national consciousness, as press reports to the east told of how their warriors neither scalped nor defiled in any way their enemies' dead. Reports told of the Nez Percé's humane treatment of prisoners, and of how they bought supplies from traders rather than stealing them. While true, these portrayals perhaps better characterize the assumptions of whites than they do the ethics of the Nez Percé.

Another popular historical assumption surrounding the Nez Percé has to do with their leadership and military tactics. By many accounts, Chief Joseph not only led his people bravely into battle, but was also responsible for the Nez Percé's deft out-maneuvering of U.S. troops. Indeed, the eastern press of the day referred to Chief Joseph as the "red Napoleon." While this is the stuff of myth and legend, it is not entirely accurate. Chief Joseph was one of many Nez Percé leaders. His younger brother, Olikut, and another leader, Looking Glass, were the bands' principal military strategists and battlefield commanders, skillfully employing rear guards, skirmish lines, and field fortifications. Chief Joseph's primary responsibility was to guard the camp, their elders, and their women and children.

The Nez Percé's hope as they fled was to meet up with Crow bands to the northeast, and together, hold off the military and escape into Canada, where they would join Lakota Sioux chief Sitting Bull and his band. But the Nez Percé soon learned that both Crow and Bannock Indian scouts were assisting the U.S. military in their pursuit, and so this hope was dashed. The Nez Percé retreated across the Yellowstone Plateau (which had five

Unwilling to shed blood, Chief Joseph surrendered and led his people on their journey to the reservation in Idaho.

years earlier been named the first U.S. National Park), and they once again reentered Montana. After crossing the Missouri River, they stopped to rest along the Snake Creek in the shadow of the Bear Paw Mountains. They knew Howard to be two days march behind them, and they rested before pushing on to the less than forty miles to Canada and safety. What they did not know was that General Nelson Miles and his army had for days been approaching from the east, and in late September, at dawn, his army surprised the Nez Percé. The Nez Percé fought bravely and eventually repelled Miles's troops, but in the surprise attack, the military was able to drive off the Nez Percé's horses, and so a swift escape was impossible. The army dug in for a siege, and the weather turned bitterly cold.

Over the next five days, as many as 150 Nez Percé escaped into Canada, including Chief Joseph's twelve-year-old daughter—though, at the time, he did not know she was safe. But Howard's army had since arrived from the south, and defeat was inevitable. On October 5, 1877, Chief Joseph rode out to meet General Howard and to formally surrender. He was heard to have said this:

> I am tired of fighting. Our chiefs are all killed. Looking Glass is dead. . . . The old men are all dead. It is cold, and we have no blankets. The little children are freezing to death. My people, some of them, have run away to the hills, and have no food. No one knows where they are. . . . I want to have time to look for my children, and see how many of them I can find. Maybe I shall find them among the dead. Hear me, my chiefs! I am tired. My heart is sick and sad. From where the sun now stands I will fight no more forever.

Both General Miles and Howard promised Chief Joseph that his people would be allowed to return to the reservation at Lapwai, but this treaty, like innumerable others, was not kept, and the Nez Percé were shipped by train first to Kansas, and then to Indian Territory, in what is now Oklahoma, more than two thousand miles from their homeland. In the first year alone, sixty-eight Nez Percé died there of epidemic diseases brought on by unsanitary conditions and malnutrition. Not until 1885 were the Nez Percé allowed to return to the Pacific northwest. But they were not allowed to go to Lapwai, and they were not allowed to go to the Wallowa Valley. Chief Joseph would never see his home again. He died while sitting in front of his campfire on the Colville Reservation in Washington. By 1990 only 4,113 Native Americans claimed to be descendants of the Nez Percé tribe.

The Nez Percé's hope, as they fled, was to meet up with Crow bands to the northeast and together, hold off the military and escape into Canada.

Today, the National Park Service maintains thirty-eight separate sites in the four states of Oregon, Idaho, Washington, and Montana, to commemorate the battles and participants in the Nez Percé War. The Nez Percé National Historical Park, which contains the battlefields at both White Bird Canyon and Big Hole, hosts interpretive talks, films, and self-guiding trails. ◆

The White House

T he mansion at 1600 Pennsylvania Avenue in Washington, D.C., has been the president's official residence since 1800. The White House, besides being home to the president of the United States and his family, also contains offices, various state rooms, parlors, private suites, and of course, the Oval Office.

The Founding Fathers started from scratch in planning a capital for a new nation that had just won its independence. George Washington and Thomas Jefferson, both Virginians, greatly influenced the decision to locate the new federal city on the shores of the Potomac River. During the last decade of the eighteenth century, Washington, along with planner Pierre Charles L'Enfant, scouted sites for an appropriate presidential residence. They chose an eighteen-acre site on a hill overlooking the river. On an axis with the U.S. Capitol, the Jefferson Memorial, and the Washington Monument, today the White House in part makes for the dramatic vistas that characterize Washington, D.C. Although George Washington oversaw the construction, he never lived there. John Adams, the second president of the United States, was the first to live in the White House, beginning in November 1800.

> *"I pray Heaven to bestow the best of Blessings on this House and all that shall hereafter inhabit it. May none but honest and wise Men ever rule under this roof."*
>
> John Adams, in a letter to his wife, November 1, 1800

The Irish architect James Hoban won $500 in a contest for the design of the new state residence. His competition included a design by Thomas Jefferson, who entered the contest using the mysterious pseudonym "AZ." Hoban's design for the neoclassical mansion, with its towering columns and stark white sandstone façade, is thought to have been modeled on the residence of the duke of Leiner in Dublin, Ireland.

Work began on the building on October 13, 1792, exactly 300 years after Columbus had arrived in the New World. Eight

years later, when John and Abigail Adams moved in, construction on the elegant mansion was not yet complete, and Mrs. Adams complained that "neither the chief staircase nor the outer steps were completed, so the family had to enter the house by temporary wooden stairs and a platform." There was no running water, and White House staff lugged in water from a spring in Franklin Park, five blocks away.

The White House, residence of the president of the United States, in Washington, D.C.

During a raid on Washington, D.C., British troops set fire to the White House on August 24, 1814. The inside was nearly gutted, but a two-hour rainstorm helped save the building's exterior. First Lady Dolley Madison managed to salvage a few of the building's treasures, most notably the Declaration of Independence and a portrait of George Washington by the artist Gilbert Stuart. It took three years to rebuild the house, and the architect Hoban returned to complete the work. Running water was piped into the house in 1833, and electricity was installed in 1889–93.

A major 1902 renovation under Theodore Roosevelt included adding bathrooms, as well as constructing the West Wing so that residential quarters could be confined to the upper floors, entirely separate from state offices. In 1927, under Calvin Coolidge, a third story was added. A large, historic building like

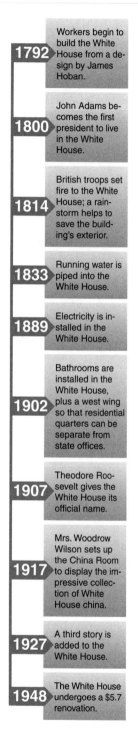

1792 — Workers begin to build the White House from a design by James Hoban.

1800 — John Adams becomes the first president to live in the White House.

1814 — British troops set fire to the White House; a rainstorm helps to save the building's exterior.

1833 — Running water is piped into the White House.

1889 — Electricity is installed in the White House.

1902 — Bathrooms are installed in the White House, plus a west wing so that residential quarters can be separate from state offices.

1907 — Theodore Roosevelt gives the White House its official name.

1917 — Mrs. Woodrow Wilson sets up the China Room to display the impressive collection of White House china.

1927 — A third story is added to the White House.

1948 — The White House undergoes a $5.7 renovation.

the White House requires constant maintenance. By 1948 the White House was so deteriorated that some suggested it needed to be demolished rather than restored. It underwent a $5.7 million renovation, requiring the Truman family to spend most of the president's second term at Blair House, a government-owned residence across the street. The renovation included reinforcing Hoban's original exterior walls with a steel frame.

Currently the White House has 132 rooms. Most of the public rooms and offices occupy the first floor, while the residential quarters for the president and his family take up the second and third floors. Below ground, facilities and maintenance workers keep the house in good working order. President Roosevelt employed fifty people in the White House. Today, a staff of nearly 2,000 works in offices in the East and West Wings.

The function of individual rooms has changed with different administrations. What is now the State Dining Room served as a drawing room, office, and Cabinet Room for past presidents. A formal parlor now known as the Diplomatic Reception Room once provided a location for the White House's boiler and furnace. The Blue Room, now a reception area, served as the south entrance hall under President Adams.

Rooms in the White House have been redecorated often to reflect the changing tastes of the times as well as those of individual families. The Committee for the Preservation of the White House oversees renovation and refurbishing plans for the White House, but the First Lady is usually actively involved in the projects. First Lady Jacqueline Kennedy had an enduring influence on the decoration of the White House, as she sought to refurbish the state rooms with authentic furnishings and fabrics reflecting different periods in American history. Subsequent first ladies have tended to respect Mrs. Kennedy's choices; Nancy Reagan completed some of Mrs. Kennedy's original plans that were never executed.

Among the public rooms on the ground floor, formal receptions and press conferences usually take place in the East Room. The Library is furnished with late Federal-style furniture of Duncan Phyfe, and houses a collection of books and presidential papers. The Diplomatic Reception Room opens from the South Grounds of the White House, so that it is easily accessible for guests arriving at the White House. Currently it is furnished with Federal-style furniture, including a panoramic wallpaper printed in 1834 called "Views of North America," with vistas of Niagara Falls, West Point, and Boston Harbor.

Dolley Madison

Dolley Payne Todd Madison, the wife of U.S. president James Madison, lived in the White House from 1809 until 1817. During her long tenure as First Lady, Dolley Madison became famous for her hospitality. After her husband's inauguration, Dolley Madison's charm and popularity proved an asset for the shy, retiring president. She curried favor with legislators' wives by making social visits to all who came to the capital, thus serving as a kind of national Welcome Wagon. Exceptionally egalitarian in her parties, she opened the President's House on Wednesday evenings to almost anyone inclined to call. Although she did not intervene in partisan disputes, she used her social skills to promote her husband's popularity, and historians have generally judged her an asset to him, particularly in his 1812 reelection campaign.

With the help of architect Benjamin Latrobe, Dolley Madison turned the White House into a showplace. She furnished the State Dining Room and the suite of rooms on the south side of the first, or public, floor, later known as the Red, Green, and Blue Rooms. When the British troops attacked Washington in August 1814, Dolley Madison arranged for the most treasured possessions in the house, including the Gilbert Stuart portrait of George Washington that Congress had purchased in 1800, to be removed from the mansion and stored in a safe place.

Other public rooms are designated by the color that currently dominates its decorative scheme: the Red Room, the Green Room, and the Blue Room. The Red Room functions as a state reception room, but has served as a drawing room, **antechamber**, and small dining room for past presidents. Redecorated to its current state during the Kennedy administration, the Red Room is furnished with American Empire-style furniture of 1810 to 1830. The Green Room was refurbished in 1971, but incorporated many of the choices made by Mrs. Kennedy. It is furnished using furniture of the Federal period. The Blue Room, an elegant oval-shaped space, serves as a formal reception room with French Empire-style furniture.

antechamber: a small room leading into a larger room.

Formal dinners take place in the State Dining Room, which seats up to 140 guests and is the largest room in the White House. During their 1902 renovations, the architects McKim, Mead & White enlarged the State Dining Room and remodeled the interior architectural details to resemble late-eighteenth-century English houses. A portrait of Abraham Lincoln tops the mantle piece, along with an inscription quoting a letter that John Adams wrote on his second night in the White House: "I pray to Heaven to Bestow the Best Blessings on THIS

HOUSE and on All that shall hereafter Inhabit it. May none but honest and Wise Men ever rule this roof." The China Room was set up in 1917 by Mrs. Woodrow Wilson to house the impressive assortment of White House china, a collection that has grown under nearly every administration.

The White House boasts an important collection of nearly 450 works of art, which, like the state rooms, reflects the changing tastes of the house's inhabitants. Many First Families have donated portraits of themselves, First Ladies, or presidential predecessors to the White House collection. First Lady Edith Roosevelt established a gallery of portraits of First Ladies on the ground floor. Family members of Zachary Taylor, Martin van Buren, and Abraham Lincoln all donated portraits of the respective presidents. The Kennedy family donated a painting by Claude Monet to the White House collection. Many of the collection's sculptures and paintings, however, have been donated by the American people.

"I never forget that I live in a house owned by all the American people and that I have been given their trust."

Franklin D. Roosevelt, 1938

Reflecting on his residence in Washington, President Franklin Delano Roosevelt remarked that "I will never forget that I live in a house owned by all the American people." In fact, the White House is the only private residence of a head of state that is open to the public, free of charge. Money for the White House's upkeep, renovations, and daily operations has always been allotted by Congress, and the White House welcomes the public into various state rooms of the building. Currently, nearly 6,000 people visit the White House daily.

For many First Families, living privately in a public monument presents challenges. Calvin Coolidge had to discontinue his longtime practice of sitting on the front porch after dinner when he moved into the White House, as he drew crowds of curious onlookers. Staff watched in dismay when the five children of Theodore Roosevelt brought pet cats, dogs, a badger, a bear, raccoons, guinea pigs, snakes, and a pony to live in the White House. Since the 1960s presidential families have faced the challenge of carrying out their inherently public roles while at the same time limiting intense media scrutiny of their private lives during their residence in the White House.

Before 1907, when President Theodore Roosevelt gave the White House its official name, it was known as the President's Palace, the President's House, and the Executive Mansion. Until the Civil War, it was the largest residence in the United States. ◆

Whitman Mission

The Whitman Mission National Historic Site lies seven miles west of Walla Walla, Washington, and commemorates the mission of Marcus and Narcissa Whitman. The mission became an important way station in the early days of the Oregon Trail. The Whitmans spent eleven years working at their station, but their efforts to introduce the Cayuse Indians to evangelical Christianity and American culture contributed to the disintegration of the native way of life and to tribal division. The deep cultural differences and a measles epidemic led to violence in 1847, when Cayuse Indians murdered the Whitmans and eleven other whites. While the massacre resulted in the termination of their organization's work in Oregon, it also helped elevate the Whitmans to the status of Protestant martyrs during the nineteenth century.

Narcissa Whitman, born in 1808, and Marcus Whitman, born in 1802, were members of the first missionary group sent to the Oregon Country by the American Board of Commissioners for Foreign Missions (ABCFM). Born in Prattsburg, New York, Narcissa Prentiss grew up in a comfortable middle-class, rural household. She attended local schools and Franklin and Auburn academies before teaching school herself. She experienced a religious conversion at the age of eleven and joined the Presbyterian church. Active in the religious revivals of the Second Great Awakening, she dreamed of a missionary life. As a single woman, however, her chances of being accepted for missionary work were slight.

Like other missionary candidates, Marcus Whitman needed a wife, and when he proposed marriage to Narcissa, whom he probably knew only slightly, she promptly agreed. Marcus had come to his vocation only with difficulty. Born in Rushville, New York, he spent much of his childhood living with relatives and attending school in Massachusetts, where he experienced conversion. Returning to New York at the age of eighteen, he worked in his stepfather's tannery and shoe shop and taught school. He decided to pursue a medical career and practiced in Pennsylvania, Canada, and rural New York. Gradually, he concluded that he should become a medical missionary.

"The Indians are anxious about the consequence of settlers among them, but I hope there will be no acts of violence on either hand. An evil affair at the Falls of the Willamette, resulted in the death of two white men killed and one Indian. But all is now quiet."

Marcus Whitman, letter to his parents, May 27, 1843

The Whitman graves near Walla Walla, Washington.

evangelical: relating to Protestant churches that emphasize salvation by faith.

In 1835 Marcus set out with the Reverend Samuel Parker on his exploratory trip for the ABCFM. While Parker continued west to ascertain the readiness of the western Indians for Christianity, Marcus returned home. Convinced that the overland trip was possible even for women, he gathered a missionary party that included his new wife, Henry Harmon, Eliza Hart Spalding, and William Gray. Narcissa and Eliza became the first Anglo women to cross the Rocky Mountains in 1836 on what was to become the Oregon Trail. The group traveled over the Blue Mountains with guide John McLeod, a fur trader for the Hudson's Bay Company. While the Whitmans enjoyed the rivers and greenery of the Grand Ronde Valley and the Blue Mountains of what is now Oregon, the terrain proved challenging. Narcissa's diary for August 29, 1836, contains this entry: "Before noon we began to descend one of the most terrible mountains for steepness and length I have yet seen. It was like winding stairs in its descent and in some places almost perpendicular. . . . We had no sooner gained the foot of this mountain, when another more steep and dreadful was before us."

The group arrived in Oregon in the fall of 1836. The Whitmans settled in the eastern part of the Oregon Country among the Cayuse Indians, a small tribe culturally similar to the Nez Percé. Although Narcissa was taken aback by some of the realities of Indian life and disapproved of Indian culture, she and Marcus were initially optimistic about the possibility of converting the Cayuse Indians to both **evangelical** Christianity and a settled American way of life. However, despite the willingness of the Indians to adopt some facets of white religion and life, the Whitmans gradually became disillusioned with missionary work. The Indians had their own religion, and during eleven years the Whitmans made no Cayuse converts. Teaching Indians that without conversion they were doomed to hell increased tribal hostility and division. The Whitmans confronted many threatening situations, characteristic of the Cayuses' displeasure with the missionaries.

Eventually the Whitmans retreated from their missionary goals. While Narcissa devoted herself to her large family of adopted children and to religious work with white emigrants, Marcus busied himself with his medical practice. Both gave assistance to overland emigrants who stopped at the mission. As emigrants began moving westward in the 1840s, Whitman Mission became an important station on the Oregon Trail. Historians have acclaimed the Whitmans contribution to the opening of the northwest. Although their initial route across the Blue Mountains did not become the Oregon Trail, they proved that women and families could make the trip to the Oregon Country. American settlement changed the Oregon Country from an open land to a land of farms and pastures. This had a profound impact on both the United States as a nation and on the Indians who lived there, as they had been a nomadic people.

The Whitmans experienced difficulties with other members of the ABCFM mission, and these problems almost resulted in the closing of their mission. Relations between the missionaries improved somewhat, but that did not save their endeavor as a whole. A combination of factors led the Indians to attack the mission in 1847. A measles epidemic had shattered their trust in the missionaries' promise of well-being, and with increasing white emigration to Oregon, there came a growing realization on the part of the Cayuse of the implications of the Whitmans and other whites living in the area. Their murder of the Whitmans and others, however, did them only harm. In the 1860s the government forced the Cayuse tribe onto the Umatilla Reservation with members of the Walla Walla and Umatilla tribes.

With the Whitmans' deaths, the ABCFM closed down its Oregon missions. The Whitmans, however, became missionary heroes, a reputation that survived into the twentieth century. A reevaluation in the 1980s and 1990s of American missionary work among Native Americans has prompted new interpretations of the Whitman mission. Although early historians assumed that the Whitmans were heroic martyrs to Christian service, later historians have been more critical of the missionaries and more sensitive to the perspectives of the Cayuse Indians. The mission was authorized as the Whitman National Monument June 29, 1936, then changed to Whitman Mission National Historic Site January 1, 1963. The site is now a unit of the U.S. National Park System.

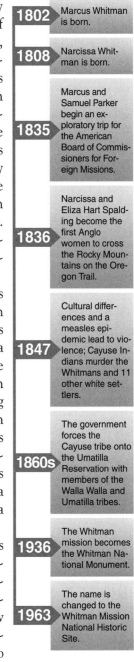

1802 Marcus Whitman is born.

1808 Narcissa Whitman is born.

1835 Marcus and Samuel Parker begin an exploratory trip for the American Board of Commissioners for Foreign Missions.

1836 Narcissa and Eliza Hart Spalding become the first Anglo women to cross the Rocky Mountains on the Oregon Trail.

1847 Cultural differences and a measles epidemic lead to violence; Cayuse Indians murder the Whitmans and 11 other white settlers.

1860s The government forces the Cayuse tribe onto the Umatilla Reservation with members of the Walla Walla and Umatilla tribes.

1936 The Whitman mission becomes the Whitman National Monument.

1963 The name is changed to the Whitman Mission National Historic Site.

The park preserves the site of the Whitmans' buildings and Mill Pond, a short segment of the Oregon Trail, and the grave where the victims are buried. Although the original buildings did not survive the years, their locations are outlined on the grounds and outdoor exhibits provide an idea of how the mission must have looked. Native grasses give visitors a sense of how the area looked in the 1840s. The Visitor Center museum features a slide program and exhibits covering the Whitman missionaries, the Cayuse Indians, and the Oregon Trail. Spanish, Japanese, French, and German language trail guides are available, and texts of the slide program and trailside recordings are available for sight or hearing impaired. Visitors also can walk the 0.7-mile trail, which provides a history of the site through numerous exhibits and the original building foundations. ◆

Wounded Knee

SOUTHWESTERN SOUTH DAKOTA

The Plains Indian Ghost Dance religion was a fundamentally peaceful movement, but it took on militant overtones among the Teton Sioux.

In the southwest corner of South Dakota, on the Pine Ridge Indian Reservation, lies the tiny town of Wounded Knee. The town is several miles from the site of the 1890 Battle of Wounded Knee, also called the Wounded Knee Massacre, which was the last major armed conflict between Sioux Indians and the United States Army. The town rose to national prominence again in 1973, when armed members of the American Indian Movement (AIM) occupied Wounded Knee and demanded the return of lands taken from their tribes.

The massacre at Wounded Knee was the final blow to Native Americans after decades of warfare waged against them by the American government. During the 1880s the Plains Indian Ghost Dance religion, which grew from the Indians' hopes of triumphing over their conquerors, spread through many reservations. A fundamentally peaceful movement, it nevertheless took on militant overtones among the Teton Sioux. The Ghost Dance phenomenon frightened white authorities. Pine Ridge Reservation agent Daniel F. Royer telegraphed Washington, D.C., in November 1890: "Indians are dancing in the snow and are wild and crazy. We need protection and we need it now." On November 20, 1890, cavalry and infantry reinforcements arrived at Pine Ridge and at the Rosebud Reservation. When the

soldiers arrived, some 3,000 Indians had gathered on a plateau
called the Stronghold at the northwest corner of Pine Ridge.

Brigadier General John R. Brooke, commander of the Pine
Ridge area, sent emissaries to negotiate with the militants but to
no avail. Brooke's commanding officer, General Nelson Apple-
ton Miles, decided to deal with the Ghost Dance situation himself and transferred his headquarters to Rapid City, South
Dakota. In the meantime, Sitting Bull, the most influential of
all Sioux leaders, began promoting the Ghost Dance doctrine at
the Standing Rock Reservation. The agent in charge there,
James McLaughlin, decided to arrest Sitting Bull. The operation went terribly wrong, and, on December 15, 1890, the arrest
escalated out of control and Sitting Bull was killed.

It was in this explosive atmosphere that Miles moved to arrest another Ghost Dance leader, Big Foot, chief of the Min-
neconjou Sioux, who lived on the Cheyenne River. What Miles
did not know was that Big Foot, concluding that the Ghost
Dance religion offered nothing but desperation and futility, had
personally given it up. Miles was also unaware that Chief Red
Cloud, a Pine Ridge leader friendly to the whites, had invited Big
Foot to come to the reservation in order to use his influence to

dragnet: an organized system for apprehending people who are wanted by the authorities.

persuade the Stronghold party to surrender. The only information Miles had was that—with a reservation uprising in the offing and Sitting Bull martyred—Big Foot was headed for the Stronghold. Miles broadcast a **dragnet** across the prairie and Badlands to intercept all Minneconjous and, in particular, Big Foot.

On December 28, 1890, a squadron of the 7th Cavalry located Big Foot (who was extremely ill with pneumonia) and about 350 Minneconjous camped near a stream called Wounded Knee Creek. That night more troops arrived. By morning 500 soldiers under Colonel James W. Forsyth had surrounded Big Foot's camp. Positioning four Hotchkiss guns—small cannons, capable of rapid fire—on the surrounding hills, Forsyth ordered his men to disarm the Indians and take them to the railroad in order to "remove them from the zone of military operations." Despite tensions, it was seen at a routine operation, and the soldiers entered the camp to search for guns.

Enraged by the intrusion, medicine man Yellow Bird began dancing wildly, urging his people to resist. Yellow Bird reminded them all that they wore ghost shirts, which would protect them against white men's bullets. Next, Black Coyote, whom another Indian described as "a crazy man, a young man of very bad influence and in fact nobody," defiantly raised his Winchester rifle above his head as the troopers moved about collecting weapons. He protested that the rifle had cost him dearly, that it was his, and that nobody was going to take it from him. The soldiers responded by crowding him, shoving him, and then spinning him around.

At this point, a rifle discharged. It may have been Black Coyote's. It may have been deliberate. It may have been accidental. In any case, both sides now opened fire—although few of the Indians were armed. Hand-to-hand combat ensued, after which the Indians broke away and began to flee. The Hotchkiss guns opened fire—almost a shell a second—at men, women, and children.

Within less than an hour, Big Foot and 153 other Minneconjous were dead. But so many others staggered, limped, or crawled away that it was never determined precisely how many finally died. Most likely, 300 of the 350 who had been camped at Wounded Knee Creek perished. Casualties among the Seventh Cavalry were twenty-five killed and thirty-nine wounded, mostly from stray Hotchkiss rounds.

Wounded Knee, which the army called a battle and the public immediately dubbed a massacre, promoted the union of

1890 The Sioux Indians and the United States Army fight in the Battle of Wounded Knee.

1891 The Sioux Indians formally surrender to the U.S. Army.

1970 Historian Dee Brown's book *Bury My Heart at Wounded Knee* is published.

1973 Armed AIM activists seize the village at Wounded Knee.

1975 Gunfire breaks out between AIM members and FBI agents, leaving three people dead.

so-called hostile and previously friendly Sioux factions. These warriors came together in a December 30 ambush of the 7th Cavalry near the Pine Ridge Agency. Elements of the 9th Cavalry came to the rescue, and General Miles subsequently marshaled 3,500 troops around the Sioux, who had assembled fifteen miles north of the Pine Ridge Agency along White Clay Creek. Dealing from a position of strength, Miles gradually closed in the circle of troops around the Indians, all the while urging their surrender and pledging good treatment.

Miles succeeded, for it had become clear even to the most resolute among the Sioux leaders that their cause was lost. The union among the Sioux was short-lived, and a formal surrender on January 15, 1891, effectively brought to an end not only the series of conflicts that the U.S. Army called the Indian Wars, but some four centuries of warfare between whites and Indians in North America. Miles condemned the cavalry's actions at Wounded Knee, relieved Forsyth of command, and ordered a court of inquiry. To the commanding general's consternation, the inquiry excused the 7th Cavalry's colonel, and over Miles's protests, Forsyth was reinstated to his command.

But Wounded Knee was not forgotten. In 1970 the popular western historian Dee Brown incorporated it into the title of his best-selling critical history of white-Indian relations, *Bury My Heart at Wounded Knee: An Indian History of the American West.*

On February 28, 1973, activists in the American Indian Movement (AIM) drew the attention of the nation and the world to Wounded Knee when 200 armed Indians seized the village. The activists were challenging local tribal leadership, and they demanded the return of lands that had been taken from them in violation of treaties signed with the American government. They demanded a U.S. Senate investigation of Native American problems. The government sent federal law enforcement officers to the site, and exchanges of gunfire occurred. Two Native Americans died and several people on both sides received injuries. After a siege of seventy-one days, the protesters surrendered. Over 300 people were arrested. The government promised that negotiations concerning the protestors' grievances would be considered, but no significant progress took place on that issue.

In June 1975 AIM members and the tribal government on the Pine Ridge Indian Reservation still disputed AIM's charges that the leadership was corrupt and insensitive to tribal traditions. The tribal leaders said AIM was trying to replace them.

> In 1973 AIM activists drew the attention of the world to Wounded Knee when 200 armed Indians seized the village.

Agents of the Federal Bureau of Investigation (FBI) came to subdue rising tensions. On June 26, in an isolated section of the reservation, gunfire erupted between AIM members and FBI agents. The shootout left two FBI agents and one AIM member dead. Leonard Peltier, a Chippewa Sioux from North Dakota and a leader of AIM, was later arrested and sentenced to two life terms in prison. Political activists have continued to argue his innocence and seek his release. Peltier has been the subject of books, articles, and documentary films. He was also nominated for a Nobel Peace Prize. Some people believe Peltier is a political prisoner, as he remains at Leavenworth penitentiary. Several appeals and requests for a new trial have been turned down, and the U.S. Supreme Court twice has refused to hear his case.

Wounded Knee remains a vital symbol to many Native Americans. Sioux people especially commemorate the event of the massacre with ceremonies and prayers. Families visit the cemetery where Big Foot's people were buried in a mass grave. Today, a solitary stone monument stands on the mass gravesite. The Indian community, the National Park Service, and the state of South Dakota worked in the 1990s to create a national memorial park to honor the victims of the Wounded Knee massacre, but the project progressed slowly. ◆

Yorktown

T he decisive fighting that won independence for the thirteen colonies during the American Revolutionary War occurred at the small Virginia village of Yorktown, located on the high western shore near the mouth of the York River. It was there that General George Washington, in alliance with French naval and ground troops, laid siege to British forces led by General (and Lord) Charles Cornwallis. The standoff and brief battle that took place at Yorktown from September 28 to October 19, 1781, virtually concluded military operations in the Revolution and eventually guaranteed independence to the United States.

Before colonists from Europe settled the area in 1631, the land around Yorktown was occupied by Kiskiack Indians, who called the York River the Pamunkey. The area along York River where the town now stands was **patented** by Nicholas Marteau (or Martiau), a Walloon, soon after his first appearance in Virginia in 1621. York County, then called Charles River County (the name was changed in 1640) was one of the eight original counties of Virginia, set up in 1634. In 1691 Benjamin Reade, a grandson of Marteau, sold the county fifty acres of his ancestral tract, on which a port was to be located, for 10,000 pounds of tobacco. The town thus founded quickly became the county seat, and after 1680, when a port was authorized by the Virginia General Assembly, Yorktown became a busy shipping center. The first **customhouse** in America was built in Yorktown in 1706.

In the final months of the Revolutionary War, General Cornwallis selected Yorktown not only for the evacuation of his troops but also in response to a request from the Royal Navy to

patented: exclusively licensed by an individual.

customhouse: a building where taxes are paid and ships are cleared for entering or leaving.

443

The October 1781 surrender at Yorktown, Virginia, as depicted by American painter John Trumbell.

find a snug harbor in the lower Chesapeake Bay. The Revolutionary War was entering its seventh year, a seemingly endless struggle, and the British admiralty wanted a base for small men-of-war and gunboats that could stifle American traffic on the bay and its tributaries, thereby forcing American military traffic westward and onto rising hills. Before the war the tremendous convenience of abundant waterways had retarded the development of roads. Those roads that did exist tended to be overland links between two rivers. Thus, aggressive patrolling of the Chesapeake waterways by the British would have seriously curtailed the American war effort. It was therefore ironic that Cornwallis dug in at Yorktown and was not rescued by his navy when American and French forces entrapped him.

The Yorktown campaign was sired by the frustrations Cornwallis experienced in his 1780–81 southern campaign while fighting northward through Georgia and the Carolinas. Unable to defeat the skillful American general Nathanael Greene, Cornwallis looked for greater success in Virginia, where 4,200 men had been sent from New York by the British commander in chief, General Henry Clinton. Commanded by General William Phillips and **turncoat** Benedict Arnold, the British were carefully watched by 1,500 Americans under Marie Joseph du Motier, Marquis de Lafayette.

turncoat: a traitor.

Cannons line an
American battery at
Yorktown.

On his own initiative, subsequently approved by London, Cornwallis marched from Wilmington, North Carolina, with the still-fit 1,500 veterans of his southern venture. Reaching Petersburg, Virginia, on May 20, 1781, he took command of troops demoralized by the death of Phillips on May 13. Dismissing Arnold and inspirited by more fresh troops from New York, giving him 7,200 men altogether, Cornwallis moved against Lafayette's slender force, standing only a hard day's march away at Richmond. Lafayette adeptly disengaged, retreating toward oncoming general Anthony Wayne and 1,000 Pennsylvania Continentals; Wayne and Lafayette met on June 10 near the Rapidan River as General Friedrich Wilhelm von Steuben approached with 450 recruits. The increase of Lafayette's forces to 3,200 men sapped the offensive spirit of Cornwallis, who swerved toward the James River and was followed by an emboldened Lafayette. At Jamestown a skirmish checked Lafayette on July 6 with a loss of 137 to the British 75.

Meanwhile, Clinton, with 16,700 men at New York, the main bastion of the king's power, thought himself menaced by the moves of General George Washington's 8,500 troops, augmented by 4,756 French regulars commanded by Jean Baptiste

The Moore House, site of the surrender negotiations at Yorktown.

de Rochambeau. By repeated orders Clinton told Cornwallis to hasten 3,000 troops by sea to New York. Since this relief action required embarkation, Cornwallis began looking for a harbor suitable for a naval station. Rejecting Portsmouth and Old Point Comfort (both in Virginia) as indefensible against land attack, Cornwallis on July 26 selected Yorktown and then quickly commenced earthworks to hold Lafayette's 4,760 men at bay until the British fleet could arrive. Cornwallis mustered 7,315 soldiers and 840 sailors.

With the French fleet of Francois Joseph de Grasse and some regiments in the West Indies available, the allies could strike either the major British concentration at New York or the minor one at Yorktown. The latter was selected for complex reasons. On August 21 Washington detached twelve of his battalions under General William Heath to watch Clinton and then slipped away with Rochambeau so adroitly that the allied army was two weeks gone and south of Philadelphia before Clinton realized it. After touching Chesapeake Bay's Head of Elk and Annapolis, the allies were assisted by light vessels from de Grasse in concentrating with Lafayette to start a formal siege of Yorktown on September 28. The French portion, bolstered by three regiments from their Caribbean garrison plus some marines from their fleet, put in line 7,800 regulars. Washington had 5,640 Continentals and 3,200 Virginia militia. The allied total was about 17,000.

Early in September, de Grasse and his fleet had won what became a vast strategic victory in the Battle of the Virginia Capes. Unmenaced by the British fleet, Washington and Rochambeau husbanded men by careful, time-consuming siege-work. After opening the first parallel—a protective earthwork conforming to the twists in the British outer defense line—on October 6, the allies made their way inward to within 300 yards of the British earthworks by October 11. The second parallel was close enough for a charge. A night attack led by Colonel Alexander Hamilton on October 14 pushed in the British left that had been strongly set above the York River.

Unless the British fleet could intervene, the end was inevitable. Cornwallis, erroneously thinking himself abandoned, opened surrender negotiations on October 17. Two days later (October 19) the British troops at Yorktown formally surrendered. Within a week, Clinton, with 7,150 troops and twenty-five ships of the line, reached the entrance to the Chesapeake Bay. Learning of the surrender, he took the relief force back to New York.

Small though the actual numbers were that the British lost at Yorktown, the disaster was an echo of Saratoga, the first time that an entire British field army had ever capitulated. The repetition of this humiliation gave the king's loyal opposition in Parliament final, persuasive argument for acknowledging American independence. Although nearly two years would lapse before the signing of the Definitive Treaty of Peace, the campaign and victory at Yorktown ended all major combat.

Yorktown's prosperity as a port was destroyed by the Revolutionary War. Strategically located, the town was besieged by Union general George B. McClellan during the Peninsular Campaign of the Civil War, in 1862, and evacuated by the Confederates. In the twentieth century Yorktown's original prosperity revived somewhat through nearby naval establishments and tourism.

Today, Yorktown is part of the Colonial National Historical Park, which also comprises nearby Jamestown, the first permanent English settlement in North America. The two sites are connected by the scenic twenty-three-mile Colonial Parkway. Visitors to Yorktown can see original and reconstructed eighteenth- and nineteenth-century earthworks, the field where the

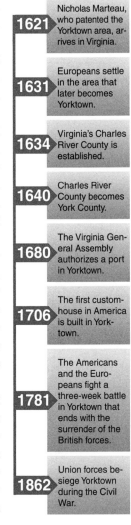

1621 Nicholas Marteau, who patented the Yorktown area, arrives in Virginia.

1631 Europeans settle in the area that later becomes Yorktown.

1634 Virginia's Charles River County is established.

1640 Charles River County becomes York County.

1680 The Virginia General Assembly authorizes a port in Yorktown.

1706 The first customhouse in America is built in Yorktown.

1781 The Americans and the Europeans fight a three-week battle in Yorktown that ends with the surrender of the British forces.

1862 Union forces besiege Yorktown during the Civil War.

British surrendered, original eighteenth-century buildings including the Moore House and Nelson House, the York Victory Monument, the French Memorial (which commemorates the American-French alliance that helped with the decisive battle), and the Yorktown National Cemetery (a Civil War cemetery). The Colonial National Historic Park also includes the Yorktown Battlefield Museum, which offers displays about the history of the Revolutionary War and the Yorktown siege and battle. ◆

Suggested Reading

Books and Web Sites Describing Monuments and Historic Places in General

Books

Ayer, Eleanor H. *Our National Monuments*. Millbrook Press, 1992.

Brownstone, David M. *Historic Places of Early America*. Athenaeum, 1989.

Butcher, Devereux. *Exploring Our National Parks and Monuments*. 9th ed. Roberts Rinehart, 1995.

Kochmann, Rachel M. *Presidents' Birthplaces, Homes and Burial Sites*. 13th ed. Osage Publications, 1999.

Lewis, Michael. *National Geographic Guide to America's Historic Places*. National Geographic Society, 1996.

MacNeice, Jill. *A Guide to National Monuments and Historic Sites*. Prentice Hall, 1990.

Stone, Tanya Lee. *America's Top 10 National Monuments*. Blackbirch, 1998.

Zinsser, William Knowlton. *American Places: A Writer's Pilgrimage to 15 of This Country's Most Visited and Cherished Sites*. HarperCollins, 1992.

Web Sites

American Battle Monuments Commission. http://www.abmc.gov/abmc3.htm
Web site of federal commission that operates and maintains 27 memorials, monuments, and markers.

Maps of National Historic and Military Parks, Memorials, and Battlefields:
http://www.lib.utexas.edu/Libs/PCL/Map_collection/National_parks/historic_parks.html

Maps of United States National Parks and Monuments:
http://www.lib.utexas.edu/Libs/PCL/Map_collection/National_parks/National_parks.html
Two comprehensive sites of online maps, produced by the U.S. National Park Service and placed online by the University of Texas at Austin.

National Geographic Online.
http://www.nationalgeographic.com/archives.html
http://www.nationalgeographic.com/search.html
Index and text of articles from the magazine and special online features.

National Historic Landmarks.
http://www.cr.nps.gov/nhl/
Links by state to individual national historic landmarks.

National Park Service.
http://www.nps.gov/parks.html
Links to individual national parks and monuments.

Books, Articles, and Web Sites for Specific Monuments and Historic Places

The Alamo

Davis, William C. *Three Roads to the Alamo: The Lives and Fortunes of David Crockett, James Bowie, and William Barret Travis.* HarperCollins, 1998.

Jacobs, William Jay. *War with Mexico.* Millbrook Press, 1993.

Livermore, Abiel Abbot. *The War with Mexico Reviewed (The Chicano Heritage).* Ayer Company, 1976.

Nofi, Albert A. *The Alamo and the Texas War of Independence: Heroes, Myths, and History.* Da Capo Press, 1994.

Banks, Suzy. "Texas Fun in Fiesta Town." *National Geographic Traveler,* January/February 1999.

The Alamo. http://thealamo.org/

Alfred P. Murrah Federal Building

Forever Changed: Remembering Oklahoma City, Apr. 19, 1995. Prometheus Books, 1998.

Serrano, Richard A. *One of Ours: Timothy McVeigh and the Oklahoma City Bombing.* W. W. Norton, 1998.

Sherrow, Victoria. *The Oklahoma City Bombing: Terror in the Heartland.* Enslow Publishers, 1998.

"Bombing Memorial to Feature Empty Chairs." *New York Times,* July 2, 1997.

Thomas, Jo. "A Task Unfinished: Planning an Oklahoma City Memorial." *New York Times,* April 6, 1996.

Oklahoma City National Memorial Foundation. http://connections.oklahoman.net/memorial/

Amoskeag Mills

Hareven, Tamara K. *Amoskeag: Life and Work in an American Factory-City.* Pantheon Books, 1978.

Kulik, Gary, et al., eds. *The New England Mill Village.* MIT Press, 1982.

Samson, Gary. *A World Within a World: Manchester, the Mills and the Immigrant Experience.* Arcadia, 1995.

Manchester and Amoskeag: The Industrial Revolution in New Hampshire. http://www.nhptv.org/kn/itv/ournhma.sht

Angel Island Immigration Station

Chetin, Helen. *Angel Island Prisoner, 1922.* New Seed Press, 1982 (fiction).

Lai, Him Mark, et al. *Island: Poetry and History of Chinese Immigrants on Angel Island, 1910–1940.* University of Washington Press, reprint 1991.

Prior, Katherine. *The History of Emigration from China and Southeast Asia.* Franklin Watts, 1997.

Angel Island. http://angelisland.org/index.html

Appomattox Court House

Catton, Bruce. *A Stillness at Appomattox*. Doubleday, 1953.

Gallagher, Gary W., and A. Wilson Greene. *National Geographic Guide to the Civil War: National Battlefield Parks*. National Geographic Society, 1992.

Marrin, Albert. *Unconditional Surrender: U. S. Grant and the Civil War*. Maxwell Macmillan, 1994.

The Road to Appomattox: A Sourcebook on the Civil War. Millbrook Press, 1993.

Wheeler, Richard. *Witness to Appomattox*. Harper & Row, 1989.

Appomattox Court House National Historical Park. http://www.nps.gov/apco/

Arlington National Cemetery

Ashabranner, Brent K. *A Grateful Nation: The Story of Arlington National Cemetery*. Putnam, 1990.

Peters, James Edward. *Arlington National Cemetery, Shrine to America's Heroes*. Woodbine House, 1988.

Reef, Catherine. *Arlington National Cemetery*. Maxwell Macmillan, 1991.

Stein, Richard Conrad. *Arlington National Cemetery*. Children's Press, 1996.

Bruns, Roger A. "Known But to God." *American History*, November/December 1996 (Tomb of the Unknown Soldiers).

Arlington National Cemetery Web Site (unofficial). http://www.arlingtoncemetery.com/

Belle of Louisville *Steamboat*

Gandy, Joan W., ed. *The Mississippi Steamboat Era in Historic Photographs*. Dover Publications, 1989.

Harness, Cheryl. *Mark Twain and the Queens of the Mississippi*. Simon & Schuster Books for Young Readers, 1998.

Petersen, William J. *Steamboating on the Upper Mississippi*. Dover Publications, 1996.

Belle of Louisville. http://www.belleoflouisville.org

Belle of Louisville (National Historic Landmark Study). http://www.cr.nps.gov/maritime/nhl/belle.htm

Benjamin Franklin National Memorial

Aliki. *The Many Lives of Benjamin Franklin*. Simon & Schuster Books for Young Readers, 1988.

Franklin, Benjamin. *Autobiography and Other Writings*. Penguin USA, 1986.

Jennings, Francis. *Benjamin Franklin, Politician*. W. W. Norton, 1996.

Van Doren, Carl. *Benjamin Franklin*. Penguin USA, reprint 1991.

Wright, Esmond. *Franklin of Philadelphia*. Harvard University Press, reprint 1988.

Benjamin Franklin National Memorial. http://sln.fi.edu/tfi/exhibits/memorial.html

The Bering Land Bridge

Dixon, E. James. *Quest for the Origins of the First Americans*. University of New Mexico, 1993.

Schurke, Paul. *Bering Bridge: The Soviet-American Expedition from Siberia to Alaska*. Pfeifer-Hamilton, 1989.

West, Frederick Hadleigh. *American Beginnings: The Prehistory and Palaeoecology of Beringia*. University of Chicago Press, 1996.

Elias, Scott, and Robert Anderson. "Bridge to the Past." *Science*, April 1997.

Fountain, Henry. "Fossil Dates Land Bridge." *New York Times*, February 9, 1999.

Bering Land Bridge National Preserve. http://www.nps.gov/bela/

Camp David

Carter, Jimmy. *Keeping Faith: Memoirs of a President*. University of Arkansas Press, 1995.

Kochmann, Rachel M. *Presidents' Birthplaces, Homes and Burial Sites*. 13th ed. Osage Publications, 1999.

Nelson, W. Dale. *The President Is at Camp David*. Syracuse University Press, 1995.

Thurman, James Skip. "President's Retreat: Camp David Is Place to Get Away From It All." *Christian Science Monitor*, March 16, 1998.

Castillo de San Marcos

Ashabranner, Brent K. *A Strange and Distant Shore: Indians of the Great Plains in Exile*. Cobblehill Books/Dutton, 1996.

Deagan, Kathleen A., ed. *America's Ancient City: Spanish St. Augustine 1565–1763*. Garland, 1991.

Manucy, Albert. *Sixteenth-Century St. Augustine: The People and Their Homes*. University Press of Florida, 1997.

Wade, Linda. *Saint Augustine: America's Oldest City*. Rourke Book Company, 1991.

Castillo de San Marcos National Monument. http://www.nps.gov/casa/

Charles W. Morgan *Whaling Ship*

Baldwin, Robert F. *New England Whaler*. Lerner Publications, 1996.

Dow, George Francis. *Whale Ships and Whaling: A Pictorial History*. Dover Publications, 1985.

Haley, Nelson Cole. *Whale Hunt: The Narrative of a Voyage by Nelson Cole Haley, Harpooner in the Ship Charles W. Morgan, 1849–1853*. 3d ed. Mystic Seaport Museum Publications, 1990.

McNeese, Tim. *Clippers and Whaling Ships*. Maxwell Macmillan, 1993.

Stackpole, Edouard A. *The Charles W. Morgan: The Last Wooden Whaleship*. Meredith Press, 1967.

On Board the Morgan: America's Last Wooden Whaler (videorecording). Mystic Seaport Film-Video Services, 1992.

"Whaleboat Exhibit at Chubb's Wharf." *Mystic Seaport.* http://www.mysticseaport.org/visiting/exhibits/ships.boats/whaleboat.html

Cumberland Gap

Arnow, Harriette Simpson. *Flowering of the Cumberland.* University of Nebraska Press, reprint 1996 (original ed. Macmillan, 1963).

Arnow, Harriette Simpson. *Seedtime on the Cumberland.* University of Nebraska Press, reprint 1995 (original ed. Macmillan, 1960).

McCague, James. *The Cumberland.* Holt, Rinehart and Winston, 1973.

Cleaver, Joanne. "Off the Beaten Path: These Undiscovered National Parks Offer Wide-open Spaces, Not Traffic Jams." *Parents Magazine,* April 1997.

Cumberland Gap National Historical Park. http://www.nps.gov/cuga/

Daniel Freeman Homestead

Cather, Willa. *My Antonia.* Bantam Classics, reprint 1994.

Layton, Stanford J. *To No Privileged Class.* Signature Books, 1988.

Stein, R. Conrad. *The Story of the Homestead Act.* Children's Press, 1978.

Wade, Mary Dodson. *Homesteading on the Plains: Daily Life in the Land of Laura Ingalls Wilder.* Millbrook Press, 1997.

"Rediscovering Nebraska's Rich Pioneer Heritage." *Midwest Living,* April 1995.

Homestead National Monument of America. http://www.nps.gov/home/

Dealey Plaza

Bishop, Jim. *The Day Kennedy Was Shot.* Crown Publishers, 1983.

Manchester, William Raymond. *The Death of a President.* Galahad Books, 1996.

Sneed, Larry A. *No More Silence: An Oral History of the Assassination of President Kennedy.* Three Forks Press, 1998.

Warren Commission Report: Report of President's Commission on the Assassination of President John F. Kennedy. St. Martin's Press, 1992.

Conspiracy Theories. http://www.4conspiracytheories.com/jfk.shtml (Links to Web sites on the assassination).

The President John F. Kennedy Assassination Records Collection (National Archives and Records Administration). http://www.nara.gov/research/jfk/jfk.html

Sixth Floor Museum at Dealey Plaza. http://www.jfk.org/

Dinosaur Ridge

Arnold, Caroline. *Dinosaur Mountain: Graveyard of the Past.* Clarion Books, 1989 (juvenile).

Hagood, Allen. *Dinosaur: The Story Behind the Scenery.* KC Publications, 1990.

Petersen, David. *Dinosaur National Monument.* Children's Press, 1995.

Stegner, Wallace, ed. *This Is Dinosaur: Echo Park Country and Its Magic Rivers.* Roberts Rinehart, 1985.

Dinosaur National Monument. http://www.nps.gov/dino/

Donner Pass

Hill, William E. *The Oregon Trail: Yesterday and Today.* Caxton Press, 1987.

Murphy, Virginia Reed. *Across the Plains in the Donner Party.* Linnet Books, 1996 (personal narrative).

Stefoff, Rebecca. *The Oregon Trail in American History.* Enslow Publishers, 1997.

Stewart, George Rippey. *Ordeal by Hunger: The Story of the Donner Party.* Houghton Mifflin, 1992.

"The Donner Party." *American Experience.* http://www.pbs.org/wgbh/pages/amex/donner /route2hell2.html

Truckee-Donner Historical Society. http://tahoenet.com/tdhs/

Edison Laboratories

Baldwin, Neil. *Edison: Inventing the Century.* Hyperion, 1995.

Cousins, Margaret. *The Story of Thomas Alva Edison.* Random House, 1997.

Hutchings, David W. *Edison at Work: The Thomas A. Edison Laboratory.* Hastings House, 1969.

Israel, Paul. *Edison: A Life of Invention.* John Wiley, 1998.

Pretzer, William S., ed. *Working at Inventing: Thomas Edison and the Menlo Park Experience.* Edison Institute, 1990.

Edison National Historic Site. http://www.nps.gov/edis/

Effigy Mounds

1491, America Before Columbus. National Geographic Society, 1991.

Keller, Robert H. *American Indians and National Parks.* University of Arizona Press, 1998.

Fenster, Julie. "Iowa's Earth Sculptures." *New York Times,* November 14, 1993.

Effigy Mounds National Monument. http://www.nps.gov/efmo/

Indian Mounds. http://www.library.wisc.edu/etext/WIReader/Galleries/First.html

El Morro Fortress

Carrion, Arturo Morales. *Puerto Rico: A Political and Cultural History.* W. W. Norton, 1984.

The Forts of Old San Juan. National Park Service, 1996.

Manucy, Albert C. *Puerto Rico and the Forts of Old San Juan.* Devin-Adair, 1974.

Wilson, Patricia L. *Old San Juan, El Morro, San Cristobal.* American World Geographic Publications, 1995.

San Juan National Historic Site (Castillo de San Felipe del Morro). http://www.nps.gov/saju/morro.html

Ellis Island

Coan, Peter M. *Ellis Island Interviews: In Their Own Words*. Facts on File, 1997.

Hine, Lewis, et al. *Ellis Island: Echoes from a Nation's Past*. Aperture, reprint 1991 (photographs).

Jacobs, William Jay. *Ellis Island: New Hope in a New Land*. Athenaeum, 1990.

Yans-McLaughlin, Virginia. *Ellis Island and the Peopling of America*. New Press, 1997.

Hall, Alice J. "New Life for Ellis Island," *National Geographic*, September 1990.

Lutyk, Carol B. "America's National Monuments: 41 of History's Best." *National Geographic Traveler*, January/February 1996.

Statue of Liberty National Monument and Ellis Island. http://www.nps.gov/stli/

Ethan Allen Homestead

Allen, Ethan, et al. *Ethan Allen and His Kin: Correspondence, 1772–1819*. University Press of New England, 1998.

Bellesiles, Michael A. *Revolutionary Outlaws: Ethan Allen and the Struggle for Independence on the Early American Frontier*. University Press of Virginia, 1995.

Hahn, Michael T. *Ethan Allen: A Life of Adventure*. New England Press, 1994.

Jellison, Charles Albert. *Ethan Allen: Frontier Rebel*. Syracuse University Press, reprint 1983.

Ethan Allen Homestead Trust. http://www.ethanallen.together.com/

Ford's Theatre

Bak, Richard. *The Day Lincoln Was Shot: An Illustrated Chronicle*. Taylor, 1998.

Bishop, Jim. *The Day Lincoln Was Shot*. Crown Publishers, 1984.

Clark, Champ. *The Assassination: Death of the President*. Time-Life Books, 1987 (Civil War series).

Kent, Zachary. *The Story of Ford's Theatre and the Death of Lincoln*. Children's Press, 1987.

Ethier, Eric. "Ford's Theatre National Historic Site." *American History*, August 1998.

Ford's Theatre National Historic Site. http://www.nps.gov/foth/

Fort Clatsop

Ambrose, Stephen E. *Lewis and Clark: Voyage of Discovery*. National Geographic Society, 1998.

Ambrose, Stephen E. *Undaunted Courage: Meriwether Lewis, Thomas Jefferson, and the Opening of the American West*. Simon & Schuster, 1997.

Clark, William. *Off the Map: The Journals of Lewis and Clark*. Walker and Company, 1993.

Dattilio, Daniel J. *Fort Clatsop: The Story Behind the Scenery*. KC Publications, 1986.

Duncan, Dayton. *Lewis and Clark: An Illustrated History*. Alfred A. Knopf, 1997.

Fort Clatsop National Memorial. http://www.nps.gov/focl/

Lewis and Clark National Historic Trail. http://www.nps.gov/lecl/

Lewis and Clark Online Base Camp. http://www.nationalgeographic.com/lewisclark/

Fort Delaware

Hesseltine, William B., ed. *Civil War Prisons*. Kent State University Press, 1997.

Speer, Lonnie R. *Portals to Hell: The Military Prisons of the Civil War*. Stackpole Books, 1997.

Wade, Linda R. *Prison Camps of the Civil War*. Abdo, 1999.

Fort Delaware State Park. http://www.destateparks.com/fdsp.htm

Fort Laramie

Hafen, Leroy. *Fort Laramie and the Pageant of the West, 1834–1890*. University of Nebraska Press, 1984.

Hedren, Paul L. *Fort Laramie and the Great Sioux War*. University of Oklahoma Press, reprint 1998.

Legg, John. *Treaty at Fort Laramie*. St. Martin's Press, 1994.

Nadeau, Remi A. *Fort Laramie and the Sioux*. Crest, 1997.

Fort Laramie National Historic Site. http://www.nps.gov/fola/

Fort Larned

Lavender, David Sievert. *The Santa Fe Trail*. Holiday House, 1995.

Oliva, Elo E. *Fort Larned: Guardian of the Santa Fe Trail*. Kansas State Historical Society, 1982.

Russell, Marion Sloan. *Land of Enchantment: Memoirs of Marion Russell Along the Santa Fe Trail*. University of New Mexico Press, 1984.

Simmons, Marc. *Following the Santa Fe Trail: A Guide for Modern Travelers*. 2d ed. Ancient City Press, 1986.

Fort Larned National Historic Site. http://www.nps.gov/fols/

Fort Mandan

Ambrose, Stephen E. *Lewis and Clark: Voyage of Discovery*. National Geographic Society, 1998.

Ambrose, Stephen E. *Undaunted Courage: Meriwether Lewis, Thomas Jefferson, and the Opening of the American West*. Simon & Schuster, 1997.

Clark, William. *Off the Map: The Journals of Lewis and Clark*. Walker and Company, 1993.

Duncan, Dayton. *Lewis and Clark: An Illustrated History*. Alfred A. Knopf, 1997.

Lewis and Clark National Historic Trail. http://www.nps.gov/lecl/

Lewis and Clark Online Base Camp. http://www.nationalgeographic.com/lewisclark/

Fort McHenry

Heidler, Jeanne T., ed. *Encyclopedia of the War of 1812*. Abo-Clio, 1997.

Kroll, Steven. *By the Dawn's Early Light: The Story of the Star Spangled Banner*. Scholastic, 1993.

Lord, Walter. *The Dawn's Early Light*. Johns Hopkins University Press, reprint 1994.

Roosevelt, Theodore. *The Naval War of 1812*. Modern Library, reprint 1999.

Whitcraft, Melissa. *Francis Scott Key*. Franklin Watts, 1994.

Fort McHenry National Monument and Historic Shrine. http://www.nps.gov/fomc/

Fort Raleigh

Durant, David N. *Raleigh's Lost Colony*. Athenaeum, 1981.

Hume, Ivor Noel. *The Virginia Adventure: Roanoke to James Towne; An Archaeological and Historical Odyssey*. Alfred A. Knopf, 1994.

Kupperman, Karen Ordahl. *Roanoke: The Abandoned Colony*. Rowman and Littlefield, reprint 1991.

Quinn, David Beers. *The Roanoke Voyages, 1584–1590*. Dover Publications, 1991.

Quinn, David Beers. *Set Fair for Roanoke: Voyages and Colonies 1584–1606*. University of North Carolina Press, 1985.

Fort Raleigh National Historic Site. http://www.nps.gov/fora/

Fort Sumter

Gallagher, Gary W., and A. Wilson Greene. *National Geographic Guide to the Civil War: National Battlefield Parks*. National Geographic Society, 1992.

Hendrickson, Robert. *Sumter, the First Day of the Civil War*. Dell, 1991.

January, Brendan. *Fort Sumter*. Children's Press, 1998.

Swanberg, W. A. *First Blood: The Story of Fort Sumter*. Meridian, 1992.

Wheeler, Richard. *A Rising Thunder: From Lincoln's Election to the Battle of Bull Run: An Eyewitness History*. HarperCollins, 1994.

Fort Sumter National Monument. http://www.nps.gov/fosu/

Franklin Delano Roosevelt Memorial

Goodwin, Doris Kearns. *No Ordinary Time: Franklin and Eleanor Roosevelt*. Simon & Schuster, 1995.

Halprin, Lawrence. *The Franklin Delano Roosevelt Memorial*. Chronicle Books, 1997.

Peduzzi, Kelli. *Shaping a President: Sculpting for the Roosevelt Memorial*. Millbrook Press, 1997.

Clines, Francis X. "In F.D.R. Memorial, an Era's Emotion Is Revived." *New York Times*, May 2, 1997.

Gabor, Andrea. "Even Our Most Loved Monuments Had a Trial by Fire." *Smithsonian*, May 1997.

"New Roosevelt Sculpture to Include a Wheelchair." *New York Times*, July 2, 1998.

Franklin Delano Roosevelt Memorial. http://www.nps.gov/fdrm/

Gateway Arch

Doherty, Craig A. *The Gateway Arch*. Blackbirch Press, 1995.

Mehrkoff, W. Arthur. *The Gateway Arch: Fact and Symbol*. Bowling Green State University, 1992.

Stone, Tanya Lee. *America's Top 10 Construction Wonders*. Blackbirch Press, 1998.

Lowry, Beverly. "St. Louis, the City Under the Arch." *New York Times Magazine*, September 14, 1997.

"The Arch Turns 25." *Southern Living*, November 1990.

Jefferson National Expansion Memorial. http://www.nps.gov/jeff/

Gettysburg Battlefield

Catton, Bruce. *Gettysburg: The Final Fury*. Doubleday, reissue 1990.

Foote, Shelby. *Stars in Their Courses: The Gettysburg Campaign, June–July 1863*. Modern Library, reprint 1994.

Gallagher, Gary W., and A. Wilson Greene. *National Geographic Guide to the Civil War: National Battlefield Parks*. National Geographic Society, 1992.

McDonald, Joanna. *The Faces of Gettysburg: Photographs from the Gettysburg National Military Park Library*. Stackpole Books, 1998.

Miers, Earl Schenck, and Richard A. Brown, eds. *Gettysburg*. M. E. Sharpe, 1996 (eyewitness accounts).

Stackpole, Edward J. *The Battle of Gettysburg: A Guided Tour*. Updated and revised ed. Stackpole Books, 1998.

Gettysburg National Military Park. http://www.nps.gov/gett/

Golden Spike National Historic Site

Hollingsworth, J. B. *The History of American Railroads*. Exeter Books, 1983.

Jensen, Oliver Ormerod. *The American Heritage History of Railroads in America*. American Heritage, 1981.

Mayer, Lynn Rhodes, and Kenneth E. Vose, eds. *Makin' Tracks: The Story of the Transcontinental Railroad in the Pictures and Words of the Men Who Were There*. Praeger, 1975.

Rails Across America: The Story of American Railroads. Smithmark Publishers, 1993.

Stover, John F. *American Railroads*. 2d ed. University of Chicago Press, 1998.

Golden Spike National Historic Site. http://www.nps.gov/gosp/

Harpers Ferry

Cox, Clinton. *Fiery Vision: The Life and Death of John Brown*. Scholastic Trade, 1997.

Du Bois, W. E. B. *John Brown: A Biography*. M. E. Sharpe, 1997.

Gallagher, Gary W., and A. Wilson Greene. *National Geographic Guide to the Civil War: National Battlefield Parks*. National Geographic Society, 1992.

Renehan, Edward J. *The Secret Six: The True Tale of the Men Who Conspired with John Brown*. University of South Carolina Press, reprint 1997.

Scott, John Anthony. *John Brown of Harpers Ferry*. Facts on File, 1988.

Harpers Ferry National Historical Park. http://www.nps.gov/hafe/

Haymarket Square

Adelman, William. *Haymarket Revisited.* 2d ed. Charles H. Kerr, 1976.

Avrich, Paul. *The Haymarket Tragedy.* Princeton University Press, 1984.

Foner, Philip Sheldon. *Autobiographies of the Haymarket Martyrs.* Pathfinder Press, 1978.

Glenn, Robert W. *The Haymarket Affair.* Greenwood Press, 1993.

Roediger, David R., and Franklin Rosemont. *Haymarket Scrapbook.* Charles H. Kerr, 1986.

"1886: Haymarket Tragedy." *Chicago Public Library Special Collections.* http://cpl.lib.uic.edu/004chicago/disasters/haymarket.html

Hearst Castle

Carlson, Oliver. *Hearst, Lord of San Simeon.* Greenwood Press (reprint of 1936 ed.).

Davies, Marion. *The Times We Had: Life with William Randolph Hearst.* Ballantine Books, 1977.

Hearst, Patricia. *Murder at San Simeon.* Pocket Books, 1998.

Leon, Vicki. *Hearst Castle Photo Tour Guide.* Blake Publishing, 1983.

Murray, Ken. *The Golden Days of San Simeon.* Doubleday, 1971.

Swanberg, W. A. *Citizen Hearst: A Biography of William Randolph Hearst.* Collier Books, 1986.

Hearst Castle. http://www.hearstcastle.org/

Highland Park Ford Plant

Bryan. Ford R. *Henry's Attic: Some Fascinating Gifts to Henry Ford and His Museum.* Wayne State University Press, 1996.

Burlingame, Roger. *Henry Ford.* Quadrangle/The New York Times Books, 1970.

Ford, Henry. *My Life and Work.* Ayer, 1996.

Lacey, Robert. *Ford, the Men and the Machine.* Ballantine Books, 1987.

Sinclair, Upton. *The Flivver King: A Story of Ford-America.* Charles H. Kerr, 1984.

"Highland Park Ford Plant." *National Historic Landmarks in Michigan.* http://www.sos.state.mi.us/history/preserve/phissite/highland.html

Hoover Dam

Doherty, Craig A., et al., eds. *Hoover Dam.* Blackbirch Marketing, 1995.

Maxon, James C. *Lake Mead–Hoover Dam.* KC Publications, 1980.

Stevens, Joseph E. *Hoover Dam: An American Adventure.* University of Oklahoma Press, reprint 1990.

DiChristina, Mariette. "The Hoover Dam." *Popular Science,* April 1998.

The Official Web Site for Hoover Dam. http://www.hooverdam.com/

Independence Hall

Bishop, Jim. *The Birth of the United States*. Morrow, 1976.

Ferris, Robert G., and Robert E. Morris. *Signers of the Declaration of Independence*. Interpretive Publications, reprint 1982.

Hawke, David Freeman. *Honorable Treason: The Declaration of Independence and the Men Who Signed It*. Viking Press, 1976.

Maier, Pauline. *American Scripture: Making the Declaration of Independence*. Vintage Books, 1998.

Schleifer, Jay. *Our Declaration of Independence*. Millbrook Press, 1992.

Independence National Historical Park. http://www.nps.gov/inde/

Iolani Palace

Daws, Gavan. *Shoal of Time: A History of the Hawaiian Islands*. Macmillan, 1968; University of Hawaii Press, reissue 1989.

Guzzetti, Paula. *Liliuokalani, the Last Hawaiian Queen*. Benchmark Books, 1997.

Seiden, Allan. *Hawai'i, the Royal Legacy*. Mutual Publishing, 1992.

The Friends of Iolani Palace. http://alaike.lcc.hawaii.edu/OpenStudio/Iolani/

Iolani Palace—Kingdom of Hawai'i. http://hawaii-nation.org/palace.html

Jamestown

Bridenbaugh, Carl. *Jamestown, 1544–1699*. Oxford University Press, 1980.

Hayes, Kevin J. *Captain John Smith: A Reference Guide*. G.K. Hall, 1991.

Hume, Ivor Noel. *The Virginia Adventure: Roanoke to James Towne; An Archaeological and Historical Odyssey*. Alfred A. Knopf, 1994.

Sakurai, Gail. *The Jamestown Colony*. Children's Press, 1997.

Colonial National Historical Park. http://www.nps.gov/colo/

Jamestown Rediscovery Archaeological Project. http://www.apva.org/

Jefferson Memorial

Ambrose, Stephen E. *Undaunted Courage: Meriwether Lewis, Thomas Jefferson, and the Opening of the American West*. Simon & Schuster, 1997.

Boorstin, Daniel J. *The Lost World of Thomas Jefferson*. Revised ed. University of Chicago Press, 1993.

Cunningham, Noble E. *In Pursuit of Reason: The Life of Thomas Jefferson*. Ballantine Books, 1988.

Ellis, Joseph J. *American Sphinx: The Character of Thomas Jefferson*. Alfred A. Knopf, 1997.

Jefferson, Thomas. *The Life and Selected Writings of Thomas Jefferson*. Modern Library, reprint 1996.

Gabor, Andrea. "Even Our Most Loved Monuments Had a Trial by Fire." *Smithsonian*, May 1997.

Thomas Jefferson Memorial. http://www.nps.gov/thje/

John F. Kennedy Space Center

Benson, Charles D., and William Barnaby. *Moonport: A History of Apollo Launch Facilities and Full Operations.* NASA, 1978.

Bondar, Barbara, and Roberta Bondar. *On the Shuttle: Eight Days in Space.* Owl Communications, 1993.

Campbell, Peter A. *Launch Day.* Millbrook Press, 1995.

Gaffney, Timothy R. *Kennedy Space Center.* Children's Press, 1987.

Gold, Susan Dudley. *The Kennedy Space Center: Gateway to Space.* Maxwell Macmillan, 1992.

Joels, Kerry Mark. *The Space Shuttle Operator's Manual.* Ballantine Books, 1988.

Kennedy Space Center. http://www.ksc.nasa.gov/

Kettle Moraine

Bennett, Matthew R., and Neil F. Glasser. *Glacial Geology: Ice Sheets and Landforms.* John Wiley, 1996.

Erickson, Jon. *Glacial Geology: How Ice Shapes the Land.* Facts on File, 1996.

Ferguson, Sue A. *Glaciers of North America: A Field Guide.* Fulcrum, 1992.

Driving America's Dairyland: Kettle Moraine and Lake Michigan. http://www.gorp.com/gorp/publishers/falcon/drv_wisc.htm

Kitty Hawk

Crouch, Tom D. *The Bishop's Boys: A Life of Wilbur and Orville Wright.* W. W. Norton, 1989.

Howard, Fred. *Wilbur and Orville: A Biography of the Wright Brothers.* Alfred A. Knopf, 1987.

Sobol, Donald J. *Wright Brothers at Kitty Hawk.* Scholastic Paperbacks, reissue 1989.

Wescott, Lynanne. *Wind and Sand: The Story of the Wright Brothers at Kitty Hawk.* Abrams, 1983.

Wright Brothers National Memorial. http://www.nps.gov/wrbr/

Korean War Veterans Memorial

Blair, Clay. *The Forgotten War: America in Korea, 1950–1953.* Anchor Books, 1989.

Hooker, Richard. *MASH.* Morrow, 1997.

Knox, Donald. *The Korean War.* Harcourt Brace Jovanovich, 1985.

Leckie, Robert. *Conflict: The History of the Korean War, 1950–53.* Da Capo Press, 1996.

Sandler, Stanley, ed. *The Korean War: An Encyclopedia.* Garland, 1995.

Korean War Veterans Memorial. http://www.nps.gov/kwvm/

Lexington Green

Kent, Deborah. *Lexington and Concord.* Children's Press, 1998.

Nordstrom, Judy. *Concord and Lexington.* Dillon Press, 1993.

Tourtellot, Arthur B. *Lexington and Concord*. W. W. Norton, 1963.

Battle of Lexington and Concord.
http://www.wpi.edu/Academics/Depts/MilSci/BTSI/lexcon/lexcon.html

Minute Man National Historical Park. http://www.nps.gov/htdocs4/mima/brvc/
http://www.nps.gov/mima/

Lincoln Memorial

Donald, David Herbert. *Lincoln*. Simon & Schuster, 1995.

Freedman, Russell. *Lincoln: A Photobiography*. Clarion Books, 1987.

Goldstein, Ernest. *The Statue of Abraham Lincoln: A Masterpiece by Daniel Chester French*. Lerner Publications, 1997.

Kent, Deborah. *The Lincoln Memorial*. Children's Press, 1996.

McPherson, James M. *Abraham Lincoln and the Second American Revolution*. Oxford University Press, reprint 1992.

Oates, Stephen B. *With Malice Toward None: A Life of Abraham Lincoln*. Harper Perennial, reprint 1994.

Lincoln Memorial. http://www.nps.gov/linc/

Little Bighorn Battlefield

Reynolds, Quentin James. *Custer's Last Stand*. Random House, 1987.

Rice, Earle. *The Battle of the Little Bighorn*. Lucent Books, 1998.

Taylor, William O. *With Custer on the Little Bighorn: A Newly Discovered First-Person Account*. Viking, 1996.

Viola, Herman J. *It Is a Good Day to Die: Indian Eyewitnesses Tell the Story of the Battle of the Little Bighorn*. Crown, 1998.

Welch, James. *Killing Custer: The Battle of the Little Bighorn and the Fate of the Plains Indians*. W. W. Norton, 1994.

Lutyk, Carol B. "America's National Monuments: 41 of History's Best." *National Geographic Traveler*, January/February 1996.

Little Bighorn Battlefield National Monument. http://www.nps.gov/libi/

Little Rock Central High School

Beals, Melba. *Warriors Don't Cry: A Searing Memoir of the Battle to Integrate Little Rock's Central High*. Pocket Books, 1994.

Hampton, Henry. *Voices of Freedom: An Oral History of the Civil Rights Movement from the 1950s Through the 1980s*. Bantam Books, 1991.

Lucas, Eileen. *Cracking the Wall: The Struggles of the Little Rock Nine*. Carolrhoda Books, 1997.

O'Neill, Laurie. *Little Rock: The Desegregation of Central High*. Millbrook Press, 1994.

Williams, Juan. *Eyes on the Prize*. Penguin USA, 1988.

"President Clinton Signs Bill Designating Little Rock Central High School a National Historic Site." *1998 White House Education Press Releases and Statements.* http://www.ed.gov/PressReleases/11-1998/wh-1106.html

Lorraine Motel

Bennett, Lerone. *What Manner of Man: A Biography of Martin Luther King, Jr.* 8th rev. ed. Johnson Publishing, 1992.

Branch, Taylor. *Pillar of Fire: America in the King Years, 1963–65.* Simon & Schuster, 1998.

Hampton, Henry. *Voices of Freedom: An Oral History of the Civil Rights Movement from the 1950s Through the 1980s.* Bantam Books, 1991.

King, Martin Luther, Jr. *The Autobiography of Martin Luther King, Jr.* Warner Books, 1998.

Oates, Stephen B. *Let the Trumpet Sound: A Life of Martin Luther King, Jr.* Harper Perennial, 1994.

Williams, Juan. *Eyes on the Prize.* Penguin USA, 1988.

National Civil Rights Museum. http://www.midsouth.rr.com/civilrights/

Los Alamos National Laboratory

Fermi, Rachel. *Picturing the Bomb: Photographs from the Secret World of the Manhattan Project.* Abrams, 1995.

Juggk, Robert. *Brighter Than a Thousand Suns: A Personal History of the Atomic Scientists.* Harcourt Brace Jovanovich, 1970.

Rosenthal, Debra. *At the Heart of the Bomb: The Dangerous Allure of Weapons Work.* Addison-Wesley, 1990.

Shroyer, Jo Ann. *Secret Mesa: Inside Los Alamos National Laboratory.* John Wiley, 1998.

Stoff, Michael B., et al., eds. *The Manhattan Project: A Documentary Introduction to the Atomic Age.* McGraw-Hill, 1991.

Rissen, James. "U.S. Inquires Why Suspect at Atom Lab Kept Access." *New York Times,* April 23, 1999.

Los Alamos National Laboratory. http://www.lanl.gov/worldview/

Manzanar War Relocation Center

Armor, John, and Peter Wright. *Manzanar.* Times Books, 1988.

Houston, Jeanne Wakatsuki. *Farewell to Manzanar.* Bantam Starfire, reissue 1983.

Smith, Page. *Democracy on Trial: The Japanese-American Evacuation and Relocation in World War II.* Simon & Schuster, 1995.

Tateishi, John. *And Justice for All: An Oral History of the Japanese American Detention Camps.* Random House, 1984.

Unrau, Harlan D. *Manzanar National Historic Site, California: The Evacuation and Relocation of Persons of Japanese Ancestry During World War II.* National Park Service, 1996.

Manzanar National Historic Site. http://www.nps.gov/manz/

Mayo Clinic

Nourse, Alan Edward. *Inside the Mayo Clinic*. McGraw-Hill, 1979.

Alperovitz, Gar. "Medicine With a Heart." *Technology Review*, April 1993.

Armour, Lawrence A. "Me and the Mayo." *Fortune*, July 21, 1997.

Napoli, Lisa. "Hospitals Reaching New Patients Online." *New York Times*, May 11, 1999.

Roach, Mary. "Physical Evidence." *Vogue*, March 1993.

Mayo Clinic. http://www.mayo.edu/

Melrose Estate

Alford, Terry. *Prince Among Slaves*. Oxford University Press, reprint 1986 (a Mississippi slave's biography).

Blassingame, John W. *The Slave Community: Plantation Life in the Antebellum South*. Oxford University Press, 1979.

Stone, Lynn M. *Plantations*. Rourke, 1993.

Wayne, Michael. *The Reshaping of Plantation Society: The Natchez District, 1860–1880*. Louisiana State University Press, 1983.

Wiencek, Henry. *Plantations of the Old South*. Oxmoor House, 1988.

Natchez National Historical Park. http://www.nps.gov/natc/

Mesa Verde

Ferguson, William M. *The Anasazi of Mesa Verde and the Four Corners*. University Press of Colorado, 1996.

Martell, Hazel Mary. *Native Americans and Mesa Verde*. Dillon Press, 1993.

Martin, Linda. *Mesa Verde: The Story Behind the Scenery*. KC Publications, 1993.

Thybony, Scott. *Canyon Country Parklands: Treasures of the Great Plateau*. National Geographic Society, 1993.

Banks, Joan. "Mystery of the Cliff Dwellers." *National Geographic World*, February 1998.

Mesa Verde National Park. http://www.nps.gov/meve/

Monticello

Adams, William Howard. *Jefferson's Monticello*. Abbeville Press, reissue 1988.

Ellis, Joseph J. *American Sphinx: The Character of Thomas Jefferson*. Alfred A. Knopf, 1997.

Lautman, Robert C. *Thomas Jefferson's Monticello: A Photographic Portrait*. Monacelli Press, 1997.

McLaughlin, Jack. *Jefferson and Monticello: The Biography of a Builder*. Henry Holt, reprint 1990.

Stein, Susan R. *The Worlds of Thomas Jefferson at Monticello*. Abrams, 1993.

Begley, Esther, and Sharon Pan. "Jefferson's DNA Trail." *Newsweek*, November 9, 1988.

Monticello: The Home of Thomas Jefferson. http://www.monticello.org/

Mount Rushmore

Curlee, Lynn. *Rushmore*. Scholastic Press, 1999.

Santella, Andrew. *Mount Rushmore*. Children's Press, 1999.

St. George, Judith. *The Mount Rushmore Story*. Putnam, 1985.

Smith, Rex Alan. *The Carving of Mount Rushmore*. Abbeville Press, 1985.

Preston, Lydia. "Rushmore's 50th Birthday." *National Geographic Traveler*, September/October 1991.

Mount Rushmore National Memorial. http://www.nps.gov/moru/

Mount Vernon

Dalzell, Robert F. *George Washington's Mount Vernon: At Home in Revolutionary America*. Oxford University Press, 1998.

Flexner, James Thomas. *Washington: The Indispensable Man*. Little, Brown, 1994.

Garrett, Wendell, ed. *George Washington's Mount Vernon*. Monacelli Press, 1999.

Breene, T. H. "Finding Washington at Home: At Mount Vernon, Reflections of an Elusive Man." *New York Times Magazine*, May 16, 1993.

Zinsser, William. "An American Icon." *National Geographic Traveler*, July/August 1992.

George Washington's Mount Vernon. http://www.mountvernon.org/

O.K. Corral

Barra, Allen. *Inventing Wyatt Earp: His Life and Many Legends*. Carroll and Graf, 1998.

The Gunfighters, Time-Life Books, reissue 1997.

Marks, Paula Mitchell. *And Die in the West: The Story of the O.K. Corral Gunfight*. Morrow, 1989.

Peterson, Roger S. "Wyatt Earp: Man Versus Myth." *American History*, August 1994.

OK Corral. http://www.ok-corral.com/

Plymouth Rock

Bradford, William. *Of Plymouth Plantation, 1620–1647*. Modern Library, 1981.

Reece, Colleen L. *The Mayflower Adventure*. Chelsea House, 1998.

Roop, Connie, ed. *Pilgrim Voices: Our First Year in the New World*. Walker and Company, 1998.

Schmidt, Gary D. *William Bradford: Plymouth's Faithful Pilgrim*. William B. Eerdmans Publishing, 1998.

Seelye, John D. *Memory's Nation: The Place of Plymouth Rock*. University of North Carolina Press, 1998.

Plymouth (MA) Official Tourguide. http://pilgrims.net/plymouth/

Pony Express Stables

Bensen, Joe. *The Traveler's Guide to the Pony Express Trail.* Falcon Publishing, 1995.

DiCerto, Joseph. *The Pony Express, Hoofbeats in the Wilderness.* Franklin Watts, 1989.

Van der Linde, Laurel. *The Pony Express.* New Discovery/Maxwell Macmillan, 1993.

Ellis, Jerry. "Reliving a Dusty Western Legend; From Missouri to California, Walking and Riding the 2,000 Hard Miles of the Pony Express." *New York Times,* June 19, 1994.

Findley, Rowe. "The Pony Express." *National Geographic,* July 1980.

Pony Express National Historic Trail. http://www.nps.gov/poex/

Portland Head Lighthouse

Grant, John, and Ray Jones. *Legendary Lighthouses.* Globe Pequot Press, 1998.

Holland, Francis Ross. *America's Lighthouses: An Illustrated History.* Dover Publications, reissue 1989.

Thompson, Courtney. *Maine Lighthouses: A Pictorial Guide.* CatNap Publications, 1998.

Portland Head Light. http://www.portlandheadlight.com/

Rankin House

Bial, Raymond. *The Underground Railroad.* Houghton Mifflin, 1995.

Blockson, Charles L. *The Underground Railroad.* Berkley, 1989.

Buckmaster, Henrietta. *Let My People Go: The Story of the Underground Railroad and the Growth of the Abolition Movement.* University of South Carolina Press, 1992.

Chadwick, Bruce. *Traveling the Underground Railroad: A Visitor's Guide to More Than 300 Sites.* Carol Publishing Group, 1999.

Hamilton, Virginia. *Many Thousand Gone: African Americans from Slavery to Freedom.* Alfred A. Knopf, 1995.

Rankin House. http://www.ohiohistory.org/places/rankin/

Rhea County Courthouse

Blake, Arthur. *The Scopes Trial: Defending the Right to Teach.* Millbrook Press, 1994.

Larson, Edward J. *Summer for the Gods: The Scopes Trial and America's Continuing Debate over Science and Religion.* Basic Books, 1997.

Lawrence, Jerome. *Inherit the Wind.* Bantam Books, reissue 1982.

Nardo, Don. *The Scopes Trial.* Lucent Books, 1997.

Applebome, Peter. "70 Years After Scopes Trial, Creation Debate Lives." *New York Times,* March 10, 1996.

Rhea County, Tennessee Attractions. http://www.rheacounty.com/attractions.html

Russell Cave

McNulty, Deirdre. "Discovery Among the Ruins." *National Parks,* September/October 1984.

"Russell Cave, Haven of Early Man." *Southern Living,* September 1980.

Russell Cave National Monument. http://www.nps.gov/ruca/

Salem Witch Trials Memorial

Conde, Maryse. *I, Tituba, Black Witch of Salem.* Ballantine Books, 1994.

Kallen, Stuart A. *The Salem Witch Trials.* Lucent Books, 1999.

Rinaldi, Ann. *A Break with Charity: A Story About the Salem Witch Trials.* Harcourt Brace Jovanovich, 1992.

Shapiro, Laura. "The Lesson of Salem." *Newsweek,* August 31, 1992.

Watson, Bruce. "Salem's Dark Hour: Did the Devil Make Them Do It?" *Smithsonian,* April 1992.

Salem Witch Trials Memorial. http://www.salemweb.com/memorial/stones1.htm

San Carlos Borromeo Mission

Abbink, Emily. *Missions of the Monterey Bay Area.* Lerner Publications, 1996.

Dolan, Sean. *Junipero Serra.* Chelsea House, 1991.

Kennedy, Roger G. *Mission: The History and Architecture of the Missions of North America.* Houghton Mifflin, 1993.

Levick, Melba. *The Missions of California.* Chronicle Books, 1998.

Heavens, Alan J. "California Missions Are Still Active, as Well as Links to Colonial Past." *Knight-Ridder/Tribune News Service,* April 20, 1998.

Mission San Carlos Borromeo. http://www.carmelmission.org/

Spanish Cabildo

Din, Gilbert C. *The New Orleans Cabildo: Colonial Louisiana's First City Government, 1769–1803.* Louisiana State University Press, 1996.

Wall, Bennett H., ed. *Louisiana: A History.* 3d ed. Harlan Davidson, 1997.

"History in Ashes." *Time,* May 23, 1988.

Cabildo Online Exhibit. http://www.crt.state.la.us/crt/museum/cabildo/cabildo.htm

Statue of Liberty

Burchard, S. H. *The Statue of Liberty: Birth to Rebirth.* Harcourt Brace Jovanovich, 1985.

Coerr, Eleanor. *Lady with a Torch: How the Statue of Liberty Was Born.* Harper & Row, 1986.

Mercer, Charles E. *Statue of Liberty.* Updated centennial ed. Putnam, 1985.

Shapiro, Mary J. *How They Built the Statue of Liberty.* Random House, 1985.

Hall, Alice J. "Liberty Lifts Her Lamp Once More." *National Geographic,* July 1986.

Lutyk, Carol B. "America's National Monuments: 41 of History's Best." *National Geographic Traveler,* January/February 1996.

Statue of Liberty National Monument and Ellis Island. http://www.nps.gov/stli/

Stone Mountain Memorial

Freeman, David B. *Carved in Stone: The History of Stone Mountain*. Mercer University Press, 1997.

Morse, Minna. "The Changing Face of Stone Mountain." *Smithsonian*, January 1999.

Starling, Kelly. "Stone Mountain Mayor: Black Leads Former Klan Stronghold." *Ebony*, October 1998.

Warner, Gary A. "At Georgia's Stone Mountain, Southerners of All Stripes Make Peace With the Past." *Knight-Ridder/Tribune News Service*, July 13, 1998.

Stone Mountain Park. http://www.stonemountainpark.org/

Sutter's Mill

Ito, Tom. *The California Gold Rush*. Lucent Books, 1998.

Kelly, Leslie A. *Traveling California's Gold Rush Country*. Falcon Press, 1997.

Ketchum, Liza. *The Gold Rush*. Little Brown, 1996.

Van Steenwyk, Elizabeth. *The California Gold Rush: West with the Forty-Niners*. Franklin Watts, 1991.

"Gold Fever." *The American Experience*. http://www.pbs.org/wgbh/pages/amex/gold/

Marshall Gold Discovery State Historic Park. http://www.windjammer.net/users/isg/coloma/

Teapot Dome Oil Reserve

Davis, Margaret L. *Dark Side of Fortune: Triumph and Scandal in the Life of Oil Tycoon Edward L. Doheny*. University of California Press, 1998.

Frederick, Richard G. *Warren G. Harding*. Greenwood Publishing Group, 1992.

Mee, Charles L. *The Ohio Gang: The World of Warren G. Harding*. M. Evans, 1983.

Stratton, David H. *Tempest Over Teapot Dome: The Story of Albert B. Fall*. University of Oklahoma Press, 1998.

Brooke, James. "Site of Earlier Scandal Frets Over Faded Luster." *New York Times*, September 18, 1998.

Tippecanoe Battlefield

Dowd, Gregory Evans. *A Spirited Resistance: The North American Indian Struggle for Unity, 1745–1815*. Johns Hopkins University Press, 1992.

Keenan, Jerry. *Encyclopedia of American Indian Wars 1492–1890*. Abo-Clio, 1997.

Mason, Philip Parker, ed. *After Tippecanoe*. Greenwood Publishing, 1973.

Peterson, Norma Lois. *The Presidencies of William Henry Harrison and John Tyler*. University Press of Kansas, 1989.

Tippecanoe Battlefield. http://www.tcha.mus.in.us/battle.htm

Trinity Church

Daniels, Bruce Colin. *Dissent and Conformity on Narragansett Bay: The Colonial Rhode Island Town*. Wesleyan University Press/Harper & Row, 1984.

Fradin, Dennis Brindell. *The Rhode Island Colony*. Children's Press, 1989.

Turbeville, Deborah. *Deborah Turbeville's Newport Remembered: A Photographic Portrait of a Gilded Past*. Abrams, 1994.

"Paint Helps to Rescue Part of Newport's Past." *New York Times*, August 30, 1987.

Trinity Church.
http://www.ritourism.com/Pic%20Newport%20Trinity%20Church.htm

Tuskegee Institute

Neyland, James. *George Washington Carver*. Holloway House, 1996.

Washington, Booker T. *Up From Slavery*. W. W. Norton, 1995.

Washington, Booker T. *Working with the Hands*. Ayer, 1970.

Wellman, Sam. *George Washington Carver: Inventor and Naturalist*. Chelsea House, 1999.

Stuart, Reginald. "Tuskegee Institute Going Strong at 100." *New York Times*, April 13, 1981.

Tuskegee Institute National Historic Site. http://www.nps.gov/tuin

USS Arizona Memorial

Cohen, Stan B. *East Wind Rain: A Pictorial History of the Pearl Harbor Attack*. Pictorial Histories Publications, 1981.

Prange, Gordon William. *At Dawn We Slept: The Untold Story of Pearl Harbor*. Viking Press, reprint 1991.

Slackman, Michael. *Remembering Pearl Harbor: The Story of the USS Arizona Memorial*. 3d ed. Arizona Memorial Museum Association, 1987.

Stein, R. Conrad. *The USS Arizona*. Children's Press, 1992.

Zinsser, William. "At Pearl Harbor There Are New Ways to Remember." *Smithsonian*, December 1991.

USS Arizona Memorial. http://www.nps.gov/usar/

Valley Forge

Jackson, John W. *Valley Forge: Pinnacle of Courage*. Thomas Publications, 1996.

Stein, R. Conrad. *Valley Forge*. Children's Press, 1994.

Treese, Lorett. *Valley Forge: Making and Remaking a National Symbol*. Pennsylvania State University Press, 1995.

Morrow, Lance. "Valley Forge: Crucible of Independence." *National Geographic Traveler*, July/August 1994.

Valley Forge National Historical Park. http://www.nps.gov/vafo/

Vanderbilt Mansion

Auchincloss, Louis. *The Vanderbilt Era: Profiles of a Gilded Age*, Scribners, 1990.

Formean, John, and Robbe Pierce Stimson, *The Vanderbilts and the Gilded Age: Architectural Aspirations, 1879–1901*. St. Martin's Press, 1991.

Hoyt, Edwin P. *The Vanderbilts and their Fortunes*, Doubleday, 1982.

King, Robert B., and Charles O. McClean, *The Vanderbilt Homes*. Rizzoli Press, 1989.

Stasz, Clarice, *The Vanderbilt Women: Dynasty of Wealth, Glamour, and Tragedy*. St. Martin's Press, 1991.

Vanderbilt, Arthur T., II, *Fortune's Children: The Fall of the House of Vanderbilt*. William Morrow, 1989.

Vanderbilt Mansion National Historic Site: http://www.nps.gov/vama/

The Newport Mansions: http://www.newportmansions.org/

Biltmore: http//:www.biltmore.com/ (The North Carolina mansion of George W. Vanderbilt).

Vietnam Veterans Memorial

Ashabranner, Brent K. *Always to Remember: The Story of the Vietnam Veterans Memorial*. Putnam, 1989.

Donnelly, Judy. *A Wall of Names: The Story of the Vietnam Veterans Memorial*. Random House, 1991.

Palmer, Laura. *Shrapnel in the Heart: Letters and Remembrances from the Vietnam Veterans Memorial*. Random House, 1987.

Scruggs, Jan C. *To Heal a Nation: The Vietnam Veterans Memorial*. Harper & Row, 1986.

"A New Memorial Honors Women Vietnam Vets." *National Geographic*, December 1993.

"The Wall's Mistaken Men." *Time*, November 23, 1987 (men still alive named on the Wall).

Vietnam Veterans Memorial. http://www.nps.gov/vive/

The Virtual Wall. http://www.thevirtualwall.org/

Washington Monument

Doherty, Craig A. *The Washington Monument*. Blackbirch Press, 1995.

Flexner, James Thomas. *Washington: The Indispensable Man*. Little Brown, 1994.

Freidel, Frank Burt. *George Washington: Man and Monument*. 3d ed. Washington National Monument Association, 1988.

Gabor, Andrea. "Even Our Most Loved Monuments Had a Trial By Fire." *Smithsonian*, May 1997.

Kernan, Michael. "Renovating Washington's Monument, Designer-Style." *Smithsonian*, June 1999.

Washington Monument. http://www.nps.gov/wamo/

Watergate Complex

Bernstein, Carl, and Bob Woodward. *All the President's Men*. Simon & Schuster, 1994.

Drew, Elizabeth. *Washington Journal: The Events of 1973–1974*. Macmillan, 1984.

Sirica, John J. *To Set the Record Straight: The Break-in, the Tapes, the Conspirators, the Pardon*. New American Library, 1980.

Dunham, Kemba. "Celebrating the Night That Made Woodward and Bernstein Famous." *Wall Street Journal*, June 16, 1977.

Schwarz, Frederic D. "The Watergate Bursts." *American Heritage*, February/March 1998.

Watergate 25. http://www.washingtonpost.com/wp-srv/national/longterm/watergate/front.htm (*Washington Post* 25th anniversary archive of scandal's history).

Weedpatch Camp

Guthrie, Woody. *Bound for Glory*. New American Library, 1983.

Stanley, Jerry. *Children of the Dust Bowl: The True Story of the School at Weedpatch Camp*. Crown Publishers, 1992.

Steinbeck, John. *The Grapes of Wrath*. Penguin, 1992.

Colvin, Richard. "Dust Bowl Legacy." *Los Angeles Times Magazine*, March 26, 1989.

"Dust Bowl." *National Geographic*, September 1984.

Weedpatch Camp (Arvin Federal Government Camp). http://www.netxn.com/~weedpatch/

Wesleyan Chapel

Davis, Lucile. *Elizabeth Cady Stanton: A Photo-illustrated Biography*. Bridgestone Books, 1998.

DuBois, Ellen Carol, ed. The *Elizabeth Cady Stanton–Susan B. Anthony Reader: Correspondence, Writings, Speeches*. Revised ed. Northeastern University Press, 1992.

Gurko, Miriam. *The Ladies of Seneca Falls: The Birth of the Women's Rights Movement*. Schocken Books, 1976.

Clines, Francis X. "Tracking Origins of the Women's Movement in the Suffragists' Footsteps." *New York Times*, November 18, 1994.

Gross, Jane. "A Place in the History of Women; Seneca Falls Marks 150th Anniversary of Rights Convention." *New York Times*, July 17, 1998.

Women's Rights National Historical Park. http://www.nps.gov/wori/

White Bird Canyon

Beal, Merrill D. *"I Will Fight No More Forever": Chief Joseph and the Nez Percé War*. Ballantine Books, 1971.

Joseph, Nez Percé Chief. *That All People May Be One People, Send Rain to Wash the Face of the Earth*. Mountain Meadow Press, 1995.

Keenan, Jerry. *Encyclopedia of American Indian Wars 1492–1890*. Abo-Clio, 1997.

Yates, Diana. *Chief Joseph: Thunder Rolling Down the Mountains*. Ward Hill Press, 1992.

"Fight No More Forever." *The West* (Episode Six). http://www.pbs.org/weta/thewest/

Nez Percé National Historical Park. http://www.nps.gov/nepe/

The White House

Caroli, Betty Boyd. *Inside the White House: America's Most Famous Home*. Riverhead Books, 1999.

Friedel, Frank, and William Pencak, eds. *The White House: The First Two Hundred Years*. Northeastern University Press, 1994.

Kessler, Ronald. *Inside the White House: The Hidden Lives of the Modern Presidents and the Secrets of the World's Most Powerful Institution*. Pocket Books, 1995.

Seale, William. *The President's House: A History*. Abrams, 1992.

Oxford, Edward. "The White House." *American History Illustrated*, September/October 1992.

White House. http://www.nps.gov/whho/

Whitman Mission

Jeffrey, Julie Roy. *Converting the West: A Biography of Narcissa Whitman*. University of Oklahoma Press, 1991.

Keenan, Jerry. *Encyclopedia of American Indian Wars 1492–1890*. Abo-Clio, 1997.

Kennedy, Roger G. *Mission: The History and Architecture of the Missions of North America*. Houghton Mifflin, 1993.

Sabin, Lewis. *Narcissa Whitman, Brave Pioneer*. Troll Communications, 1982.

Whitman Mission National Historic Site. http://www.nps.gov/whmi/

Wounded Knee

Brown, Dee. *Bury My Heart at Wounded Knee: An Indian History of the American West*. Henry Holt, reprint 1991.

Flood, Renee Sansom. *Lost Bird of Wounded Knee: Spirit of the Lakota*. Da Capo Press, 1998.

Keenan, Jerry. *Encyclopedia of American Indian Wars 1492–1890*. Abo-Clio, 1997.

"A Century After a Massacre, a New Peace Pipe in Dakota." *New York Times*, February 3, 1990.

Smith, Gene. "Lost Bird: The Infant Survivor of Wounded Knee Spent Her Life in Desperate Pursuit of a Heritage That Always Eluded Her." *American Heritage*, April 1996.

Cankpe Opi Wounded Knee Home Page. http://www.dickshovel.com/WKmasscre.html (tribal-approved materials)

"One Sky Above Us." The West (Episode Eight). http://www.pbs.org/weta/thewest/

Yorktown

Ferrie, Richard. *The World Turned Upside Down: George Washington and the Battle of Yorktown*. Holiday House, 1999.

Kent, Zachary. *The Story of the Surrender at Yorktown*. Children's Press, 1994.

Morrissey, Brendan. *Yorktown 1781: The World Turned Upside Down*. Stackpole Books, 1997.

"Colonial: A Whole Lot of Legacy." *Newsweek*, May 18, 1998.

Snow, Richard F. "Yorktown." *American Heritage*, September/October 1989.

Colonial National Historical Park. http://www.nps.gov/colo/

Glossary

abolitionism (ăb′ə-lĭ sh′ə-nĭ z′əm) (also **abolitionist**)   Most commonly used to refer to the political or philosophical policy supporting the abolition of slavery in the southern states prior to the Civil War.

acclaim (ə-klām′)   To praise enthusiastically, usually with applause and in a public setting.

accolade (ăk′ə-lād′, -läd′)   A special acknowledgement or expression of approval.

acoustical (ə-kōō′stĭ -kəl)   A musical term that refers to an instrument that does not use an electrical source to amplify or modify the sound that is created. The term also refers to the science of sound and hearing.

acre (ā′kər)   A unit of measure equaling 4,840 square feet, most often used to measure land and the ocean floor.

activism (ăk′tə-vĭ z′əm) (also **activist**) In political terms, the philosophy or practice of assertive action.

adobe (ə-dō′bē)   A type of architecture in which the building material consists of sun-dried clay and straw that are formed into bricks. This style of structure is most common in Spain, Mexico, and the southwestern United States.

aegis (ē′jĭs)   Sponsorship or patronage. Also used to refer to a kind of protection offered by a more powerful person, or business or political entity.

aeronautics (âr′ə-nô′tĭks)   The science or study that deals with the operation of aircraft.

aesthetic (ĕs-thĕt′ĭk)   A term used to describe the science and appreciation of beauty and the fine arts.

affirmative action (ə-fûr′mə-tĭ v ăk′shən)   The collective term for government policies in the United States intended to promote opportunities for minorities by setting specific goals or quotas. Affirmative action favors minorities in hiring, promotion, college admissions, and government contracts to offset the effects of past discrimination against a group. The term was first used by President Lyndon B. Johnson in 1965, and the first federal policies designed to guarantee minority hiring were implemented by President Richard Nixon in 1969.

affluent (ăf′lōō-ənt, ə -flōō′-)   A term that refers to someone who has a generous supply of money, property, or possessions.

agrarian (ə-grâr′ē -ən)   A sociological term used to refer to cultures or economies that are based on or derive their primary economic means from uses of the land, such as farming.

agriculture (ăg′rĭ-kŭl′chər)   A general term for different aspects of the study and industry of managing the growth of plants and livestock for human use, also referred to as "farming." In modern times the agriculture industry has come to include a variety of different disciplines and sciences, all with the efficient production of food as their primary purpose.

allegory (ăl′ĭ-gôr′ē, -g ōr′ē)   A style of drama, fiction, or art in which specific elements or characters are used to represent abstract principles, ideas, or powers.

altruism (ăl′trōō-ĭ z′əm)   Selflessness, or concern for the welfare of others without thought of personal gain.

anarchy (ăn′ər-kē) (also **anarchist**)   A state of political disorder and confusion, with unclear or no political authority.

anecdote (ăn′ĭk-dōt′)   A short story or allegory, often in the form of personal experience or recollection, that relates to the conversation or matter at hand.

annexation (ə-něk-sā′shən)   The process of adding on to or joining various elements into a larger single unit.

antebellum (ăn′tē-bĕl′əm)   From the Latin for "before the war," a term used primarily to refer to the southern United States in the period before the Civil War.

anthropology (ăn′thrə-pŏl′ə-jē)   The science or study of the origins, development, culture, cultural institutions, and behavior of human beings.

antiquity (ăn-tĭk′wĭ-tē)   Of or referring to ancient times. The term is most often used to refer to historical periods before the Middle Ages.

antisepsis (ăn′tĭ -sĕ p′sĭ s)   A medical term in which the prevention of infection is achieved through the destruction of the microorganisms that cause disease.

apprentice (ə-prĕn′tĭs)   One who studies or learns a trade or skill under the supervision of a recognized or accredited master.

appropriation (ə-prō′prē-ā′shən)   A set amount of public funds set aside for a specific cause or purpose.

archaeology (är′kē-ŏl′ə-jē) (also **archeologist**)   The science and study of past human life and culture by means of recovered artifacts and other material evidence.

architecture (är′kĭ -tĕ k′chər)   A term used to describe the method and style in which a building is designed and constructed.

archive (är′kīv′)   The process of storing items such as documents and records for the purpose of future reference or historical interest.

archetype (är′kĭ-tīp′)   A prototype, or original model, on which other things are based, or an ideal example of a type.

arid (ăr′ĭd)   A type of climate characterized by an extreme lack of moisture or insufficient rainfall, to the point where trees and other woody forms of vegetation cannot be supported.

aristocracy (ăr′ĭ-stŏk′rə-sē) (also **aristocrat**)   From the Greek words *aristos*, meaning "best," and *kratos*, meaning "power," a term used either for a form of government ruled by an elite class or group, or to refer to the members of such a group.

armada (är-mä′də, -m ā′-)   A Spanish term used to describe a fleet of battleships.

armistice (är′mĭ-stĭs)   A truce or other temporary stop in fighting by the mutual agreement of the warring parties.

armory (är′mə-rē)   A building used by the military to store firearms and equipment.

arsenal (är′sə-nəl) A place for the storage or manufacture of weapons. The term is also used to refer to the weapons themselves.

artifact (är′tə-făkt′) An object produced or shaped by human beings. The term most often refers to archeological specimens that provide insight into the lives of earlier civilizations. In the same sense, it may also refer to an object specifically associated with a particular person or place, although not necessarily ancient.

artillery (är-til′ə-rē) A term used to describe large caliber weapons as a whole, including guns, missile launchers, and cannons.

artisan (är′tĭ-zən, -s ən) A skilled laborer or craftsperson.

assimilation (ə-sĭm′ə-lā′shən) A sociological term referring to the process by which individuals or groups are brought and absorbed into a new and dominant culture.

asteroid (ăs′tə-roid′) A small celestial body in orbit around the sun. Asteroids are irregular in shape, have an eccentric orbit, and vary in size from a few kilometers to substantial planetoids.

atrocities (ə-trŏs′ĭ -tē z) Specifically, acts of vicious cruelty, often used to refer to the killing of unarmed people or other depraved acts.

auspices (ô′spĭ-sĭz, -s ēz′) A term used to describe a sign that predicts a future event; an omen. The term can also refer to protection or support that is provided to a person or institution.

autonomy (ô-tŏn′ə-mē) From the Greek word *autonomos*, meaning self-ruling, autonomy is a lack of control by others, or self-governing.

autopsy (ô′tŏp′sē, ô ′təp-) A medical procedure performed by examining a dead body to assist in determining the cause of death.

axiom (ăk′sē-əm) A universally recognized truth, rule, or principle.

Aztec (ăz′těk′) A Native American tribe that created one of the world's great civilizations and empires in central and southern Mexico from the 14th to 16th centuries. The Aztec built great cities and developed complex and advanced social structures, and their capital, Tenochtitlan, located where the modern Mexico City now stands, was possibly the largest city in the world. The Aztec empire was conquered by the Spanish in 1519.

bacteriology (băk-tîr′ē-ŏl′ə-jē) (also **bacteriologist**) A scientific term used to describe the study of bacteria and their effects on living organisms and agriculture.

ballad (băl′əd) In folk music, a type of song in the form of a narrative poem, comprised of simple stanzas and often a recurring refrain, and the music that accompanies it. The term also refers to a type of pop song, often slow and romantic.

ballistic (bə-lĭ s′tĭ k) The scientific study of projectiles, their motion and effects, specifically relating to firearms.

bar (bär) A legal term used to describe the profession of law or attorneys that are considered to be part of a group.

barracks (băr′əks) Housing facilities provided for military personnel on a military base.

barter (bär′tər) A system of trade in which services are exchanged for goods or other services in lieu of money.

basilica (bə-sĭl′ĭ-kə) A Christian religious structure, or church building, designed after an ancient Roman style, with a central nave, a semicircular apse, two or four aisles, a narthex, and a clerestory.

bas-relief (bä-rĭ-lēf′) An artistic form in which the images or forms are raised or projected in relation to the surface of the background. It is most common in sculpture or carving, but the effect is used in painting to add the illusion and appearance of depth.

bastion (băs′chən, -t ē-ən) A stronghold or place of strength. Also used to refer to the projecting part of a fort or castle.

behemoth (bĭ-hē′məth, b ē′ə-məth) A biblical term used to describe a large animal, often thought to be a hippopotamus. In modern usage, the term refers to something huge in size.

berth (bûrth) A term used to describe the space in which a ship maneuvers while in the water.

bipedal (bī-pĕd′l) A term used to describe an animal with two feet.

blockade (blŏ-kād′) The entrapment of an area by hostile troops of ships in an effort to prevent an area's citizens from traveling or exchanging goods and services.

blockhouse (blŏk′hous′) A type of fortress constructed of concrete blocks by the military with openings only to allow for defensive firing.

bluff (blŭf) An area of land that drops off in a steep manner, similar to a cliff.

boardinghouse (bôr′dĭng-hous) A type of housing in which the guests are provided with both lodging and meals.

botany (bŏt′n-ē) The scientific study of plants.

boycott (boi′kŏt′) A form of protest in which a person or group refuses to buy products from or support companies, individuals, nations, or other groups with which they disagree. The intent of a boycott is to bring about or force change. It is used as a tool or weapon in labor disputes, by consumers, and in international affairs.

brigade (brĭ-gād′) An army unit made up of a varying number of battalions, along with their supporting units and services.

bulwark (bo͞ol′wərk, -wôrk ′, b ŭl′-) A term often used to refer to something or someone serving as a source of strength, or a safeguard.

Bureau of Reclamation Originally called the Reclamation Service, an agency of the U.S. federal government created by the Reclamation Act, signed in 1902 by President Theodore Roosevelt. Its purpose was to stimulate the settlement of 16 western states by improving the arid and sparsely populated land through irrigation. It has since grown to include such projects as flood control, preservation of fish and wildlife, the construction of dams, and providing electricity and water for millions of people.

bureaucracy (byo͞o-rŏk′rə-sē) A general term for the employees and administrative structure of a company or organization, characterized by a specific hierarchy of authority or responsibility.

cabal (kə-bāl′) A group of people whose purpose is to plot and conspire against an enemy.

camber (kăm′bər) A term used to describe something that has an arched surface, such as a ship's deck, a road, or a ski run. The term also refers to automobile manufacturing, in which the wheels are set in a way that they are closer together at the bottom part of the axle than at the top.

campaign (kăm-pān′) A series of military operations enacted to achieve a large-scale objective, or distinct phase, during a war.

canal (kə-năl′) A man-made waterway, usually connecting two bodies of water, created for the passage of ship traffic. In some places, most famously Venice, Italy, canals are used for travel within the city.

cannibalism (kăn′ə-bəl ĭz′əm) The practice of eating the flesh of the same species, most often used to refer to humans eating human flesh.

cannon (kăn′ən) A large firearm, usually mounted on a ship, that projects large iron balls. In zoological terms, the word refers to the portion of an animal's leg below the knee and above the hoof that contains the cannon bone.

canyon (kăn′yən) A topographic feature, usually a narrow chasm or gorge with steep, sheer cliff walls, created by the action of running water.

capitalism (kăp′ĭ-tl-ĭz′əm) The overall term for the economic system in which individuals and companies produce and exchange goods and services through a network of prices and markets within a free market, that is, without government control or intervention.

carcass (kär′kəs) A dead body, most often that of an animal that was killed for food.

carnivorous (kär-nĭ v′ər-əs) A term used to describe animals that only eat the flesh of another animal.

casualty (kăzh′ōō-əl-tē) A victim of an accident, most often resulting in the loss of life.

cathedral (kə-thē′drəl) A large church, usually the main church within a diocese.

cavalcade (kăv′əl-kād′, k ăv′əl-kād′) A parade or procession consisting of riders on horseback or horse-drawn carriages.

cavalier (kăv′ə-lîr′) A knight or chivalrous man, often acting as an escort to a woman attending a social event. The term is also used to describe behavior that is arrogant or carefree.

cavalry (kăv′əl-rē) Historically, a military division or unit mounted on horses. In modern usage, the term is used to refer to any highly mobile unit using any variety of vehicular transport.

chandlery (chănd′lə-rē) A place where candles are made. The term may also be used to refer to a retail shop specializing in the manufacture and sale of candles.

chapel (chăp′əl) A small church or place of worship, often located in a hospital or prison.

charisma (kə-rĭz′mə) (also **charismatic**) An indefinable personal quality sometimes found in leaders that inspires devotion and enthusiasm in others.

chemistry (kĕ m′ĭ -strē) A scientific term referring to the study of the composition, structure, properties, and reactions of a specific matter or substance.

cholera (kŏl'ər-ə) An infectious disease of the small intestine that is caused by bacteria. Symptoms include diarrhea, vomiting, muscle cramps, and a depletion of electrolytes.

cistern (sĭs'tərn) Most commonly used to refer to a large receptacle or basin used to catch and hold rainwater.

civil rights (sĭv'əl rīts) The rights belonging to an individual by virtue of citizenship in the United States. The fundamental basis of civil rights is freedom and the privileges guaranteed by the 13th and 14th Amendments to the U.S. Constitution. These privileges include civil liberties, due process, equal protection of the laws, and freedom from discrimination.

clergy (klûr'jē) A term used to describe those who have the authority to act on behalf of the church, including priests, ministers, and rabbis.

clergyman (klûr'jē-mən) A person who is a recognized member of the clergy, or ordained ministry, of a religion.

cliff dwelling A type of housing, most often found in the southwestern United States, consisting of homes constructed from adobe or rock, positioned on the side of a cliff or carved from the cliff face.

cobblestone (kŏb'əl-stōn') A type of road surface consisting of round rocks.

colonialism (kə-lō'nē-ə-lĭz'əm) A political philosophy or policy by which a governing nation maintains control over its foreign colonies. The term is also used to refer to an attitude in which a citizen of the ruling country may view citizens of a subject nation with a certain disdain or sense of superiority.

columbarium (kŏl'əm-bâr'ē -əm) A vault or tomb designed with niches in the walls to house urns filled with ashes of the dead.

comet (kŏm'ĭt) A celestial object consisting of a solid body in a highly eccentric orbit, which when it approaches the point of its orbit closest to the sun often develops a characteristic "tail" that points away from the sun.

commissary (kŏm'ĭ-sĕr'ē) A grocery store or market exclusively for use by military personnel and their families.

communism (kŏm'yə-nĭz'əm) A political theory and model for a government system in which all resources, businesses, and means of production are jointly owned by all members of the community. Modern communist theory is based in large part on the work of Karl Marx (1818–83) and Friedrich Engels (1820–95) as set forth in their book *The Communist Manifesto*. The term "Marxism" is sometimes used to refer to the political theories underlying certain modern communist states such as the former Soviet Union and Cuba.

condominium (kŏn'də-mĭn'ē-əm) A type of apartment or townhouse in which the unit is owned by the resident, while the common areas are shared by all residents of the complex. The term also refers to territory ruled and owned jointly by two or more nations.

convent (kŏn'vənt, -vĕnt') A building or group of buildings designed to house nuns.

cornice (kôr′nĭs)   An architectural term used to describe a decorative piece of molding that is positioned at the top of a wall or building to serve as a finishing cap or crown.

cortege (kôr-tĕzh′)   A group of attendants who serve an aristocrat, monarch, or member of the nobility. The term is also used to describe the attendants of a funeral or ceremonial procession.

cottage industry   A business or industry operated out of the home where all merchandise is manufactured or assembled on the premises.

courtier (kôr′tē-ər, -ty ər, k ōr′-)   A member of a group of attendants at a monarch's court. A courtier may be a figure of minor nobility, or a member of the gentry.

court-martial (kôrt′mär′shəl, kōrt′-)   A court composed of military personnel where military crimes and offenses are tried.

cowcatcher (kou′kăch′ər, -kĕch′-)   The metal frame or grille attached to the front of a train engine designed to clear objects from the track.

cremation (krĭ-mā′shən)   The process of incinerating bodies as an alternative to traditional burial.

crop rotation   An agricultural term used to describe the process of planting a different crop every few years in an effort to keep the soil fertile.

crusade (krōō-sād′)   Originally referring to any of the military expeditions undertaken by the Christian leaders of Europe in the Middle Ages to recover the Holy Land from the Muslims, now commonly used to describe an organized, passionate campaign or movement for a specific cause. Its use is often meant to imply religious or spiritual overtones.

cryogenics (krī′ə-jĕn′ĭks)   A scientific term that refers to the study of low temperatures and their effects on the environment and body.

cult (kŭlt)   A religious or other type of spiritualist sect that is considered extremist or radical.

culvert (kŭl′vərt)   A submerged sewer or drain that runs under a roadway, embankment, or other structure.

cupola (kyōō′pə-lə)   An architectural term used to describe a low, domed ceiling.

cyst (sĭ st)   A sac containing fluid, found in the body, that is often the result of an infection.

damask (dăm′əsk)   A type of fabric made from cotton, wool, linen, or silk, that is characterized by bold, rich patterns.

decree (dĭ-krē′)   An order or statement from a recognized authority that has the force of law.

delta (dĕl′tə)   The fourth letter of the Greek alphabet. In geophysical terms, the triangular alluvial deposit found at the mouth of a river.

demagoguery (dĕm′ə-gô′gə-rē, -gŏg′ə)   The practice of speech or rhetoric delivered by a leader who gains power through the use of emotional appeals to the populace.

Democrat (dĕm′ə-krăt′)   A member of a political party of the United States, or a general term used to describe someone who is an advocate of the political system of democracy.

denim (dĕ n′ĭ m)   A type of coarse cloth made of cotton that is used to make jeans, overalls, and rugged uniforms.

desegregation (dē-sĕg′rĭ-gā′ shən) The opposite of segregation, which separates one group from another, desegregation refers to the end of the separation. Most often used in reference to the civil rights struggles of the 1960s, which sought to end the forced segregation of blacks and whites.

destroyer (dĭ-stroi′ər) A small warship armed with guns, torpedoes, or missiles designed to maneuver easily through tight areas.

dictator (dĭk′tā′tər, d ĭk-tā′-) Originally the title of a magistrate in ancient Rome, appointed by the Senate in times of emergency, in modern times the term has come to refer to an individual who assumes sole and often absolute power over a country.

distillery (dĭ -stĭ l′ə-rē) An establishment in which alcoholic beverages are made and manufactured.

doctrine (dŏk′trĭ n) The collective term for the body of principles, or beliefs, accepted by a religious, political, or philosophic group.

Doric column A term used to describe a column characterized by the earliest and simplest Greek architecture.

duke (do͞ok, dyo͞ok) Traditionally, a term used to describe a nobleman of Great Britain with a hereditary link to the royal family who owns land bestowed by the monarch.

dynasty (dī ′nə-stē) A succession of rulers from the same family or group that maintains power over a period of years and generations. Most often used to refer to political leaders.

dysentery (dĭs′ən-tĕr′ē) An inflammatory disorder of the lower intestinal tract, usually caused by a bacterial or parasitic infection and resulting in pain, fever, and severe diarrhea, often accompanied by the passage of blood and mucus.

earthwork (ûrth′wûrk′) An embankment or bulwark made of earth. The term is most often used to refer to a type of fortification.

ecosystem (ĕk′ō-sĭs′təm, ē ′kō-) An ecological term referring to an area or community in which all elements of the environment work in balance.

effigy (ĕf′ə-jē) A symbolic portrayal or depiction, often in the form of a crude figure or image, used to represent a hated figure or group.

egalitarian (ĭ-găl′ĭ-târ′ē-ən) The affirmation of or one who affirms political, economic, and social equality for all people.

emancipation (ĭ -măn′sə-pā′shən) Literally meaning to free from bondage, oppression, or restraint, most often used to refer to freedom from slavery, as in the Emancipation Proclamation.

Emancipation Proclamation Proclamation issued by U.S. president Abraham Lincoln on January 1, 1863, effectively ending slavery in the United States. Although excluding some slaves in areas of the Confederacy held by Union armies, the Emancipation Proclamation was a radical change in governmental policy, and was instrumental in leading to the enactment of the 13th Amendment to the Constitution in 1865, by which slavery was wholly abolished.

embargo (ĕm-bär′gō) The government prohibition of certain or all trade with another nation.

emigrate (ĕm′ĭ-grāt′) To move from one land or nation and settle in another.

émigré (ĕm′ĭ-grā′) A person who has left or been forced to leave his or her native country, often for political reasons.

epicenter (ĕp′ĭ-sĕn′tər) The point at which an earthquake makes contact with the earth's surface.

epicure (ĕp′ĭ-kyŏor′) (also **epicurean**) Someone who is devoted to the refined taste of food and its preparation, and wine.

epigram (ĕp′ĭ-grăm′) A short poem based on a single clever or witty thought or subject.

epoch (ĕp′ək, ē′pŏk′) A non-chronologically specific unit for measuring or describing a historical period or a geological time, defined by the characteristics of the period rather than a specific time frame. The term is also used to refer directly to the event considered to be the beginning of the period.

equatorial (ē′kwə-tôr′ē-əl) A term referring to anything relating to the equator of the earth.

era (îr′ə, ĕr′ə) A term used to describe a chronological span of time in which a specific event, person, or circumstance acts as a common theme.

estate (ĭ-stāt′) A large area of property, usually containing a residence.

estuary (ĕs′chŏo-ĕr′ē) The portion of a river where the current is met by the tide.

ethnicity (ĕth-nĭs′ĭ-tē) A sociological classification referring to a person's ethnic character, background, or affiliation.

eulogy (yŏo′lə-jē) A speech or written tribute to and in praise of someone who has died.

evangelism (ĭ-văn′jə-lĭz′əm) The preaching or spreading of a religion, as with missionary work. The term is often used to refer to a type of minister who attempts to bring conversion to large masses of people, and carries connotations of showmanship and personality.

evolution (ĕv′ə-lŏo′shən, ē′və-) Change over the course of time; specifically, the change in the nature and characteristics of living things through natural processes and selection for survival traits.

excavate (ĕk′skə-vāt′) The process of digging or hollowing out. The term is often used to refer to an ancient burial site or civilization in search of human remains, tools, or jewels to provide information about the society.

exoskeleton (ĕk′sō-skĕl′ĭ-tn) The hard outer shell of a crustaceous animal, such as a lobster or an insect.

expansionism (ĭk-spăn′shə-nĭz′əm) In political policy or action, the practice of expanding a nation's physical or economic boundaries.

expatriate (ĕk-spā′trē-āt′) A person who has left his or her native country, usually through banishment or exile, to live in another country.

extinct (ĭk-stĭngkt′) (also **extinction**) A term used to describe a species of animal or plant that is no longer in existence. Extinction describes the process such a species undergoes before becoming extinct.

extraterrestrial (ĕk′strə-tə-rĕs′trē-əl) A term used to describe an event or living organism that is not native to the earth, originating in the atmosphere or outside the earth's surface.

façade (fə-säd′)   An architectural term referring to the face or outer layer of a structure. The term can also be used to describe someone or something that appears different from the outside than on the inside.

famine (făm′ĭn)   A term used to describe a widespread food shortage and starvation.

flannel (flăn′əl)   A soft woven fabric most often made of cotton or wool.

flax (flăks)   A type of plant that produces seeds used to make linseed oil. The stems of the plant are used to make a fine gauge textile fabric.

folklore (fōk′lôr′, -lōr′)   A term used to describe myths and legends that are believed by a society, traditionally passed down through storytelling.

foreclosure (fôr-klō′zhər, fōr-)   The process of redeeming a loan, such as a mortgage, especially when payments have not been made.

forensic (fə-rĕn′sĭk, -zĭk)   Evidence relating to a crime that is proved valid to be used in a court of law.

fortification (fôr′tə-fĭ-kā′shən)   The process of strengthening and securing a structure, often by the military, in an attempt to keep out enemy forces.

fossil (fŏs′əl)   An archaeological term referring to bone or other matter that has been preserved under the earth's surface and has turned to stone with time.

foundation (foun-dā′shən)   The founding or establishing of an institution, or an endowed institution created by a wealthy individual or company, most often with the purpose of providing charitable services or public works.

Founding Fathers   The name given to the group of men, including George Washington, Thomas Jefferson, and Benjamin Franklin, who were instrumental in the creation of the United States. As a group, the Founding Fathers wrote and ratified most of the important documents of the United States, including the Declaration of Independence, the Constitution, and the Bill of Rights. Many, including Washington, Jefferson, and James Madison, went on to serve as presidents, and their work formed the basis of most of the American governmental policies that remain to this day.

Franciscan (frăn-sĭs′kən)   A religious order founded by Saint Francis of Assisi in 1209 C.E. The Franciscans were a mendicant order, meaning that they were dependent on alms, or begging, for support, and were forbidden to own property.

fraternity (frə-tûr′nĭ-tē)   Members of a society or group that are connected by a common bond, belief, or interest.

frontier (frŭn-tîr′)   A term often used to describe the end of civilized land, or the area just beyond it. In American history, the frontier represented the boundary of western expansion.

gallstone (gôl′stōn′)   A small, stone-like mass formed by cholesterol, calcium salts, and bile pigments that becomes lodged in the gallbladder.

garrison (găr′ĭ-sən)   A military post. The term may also be used to refer to the troops or other military personnel assigned to the post.

genealogy (jē′nē-ŏl′ə-jē, - ăl′-, j ĕn′ē-) (also **genealogical**) The record or account of the descent of a person, family, or group from a specific ancestor or group of ancestors.

genetics (jə-nĕt′ĭks) A branch of biology that deals with the heredity and variation of organisms.

gentry (jĕ n′trē) The upper or ruling class of a society. One of the foremost connotations in common usage was to imply certain rights and privileges associated with the ownership of land.

genus (jē′nəs) A biological term referring to a classification of organisms from the same species that are related through similar characteristics, yet remain different enough so that they are not of the same family.

geography (jē-ŏg′rə-fē) The scientific study of the earth's surface.

geology (jē-ŏl′ə-jē) The scientific study of the origin, history, and structure of the earth.

glacier (glā′shər) A large body of ice moving slowly down a slope or valley or spreading outward on a land surface.

gout (gout) A medical condition characterized by an inflammation of the joints, especially of the feet and hands, and arthritic symptoms. As a result of these symptoms, the level of uric acid in the blood becomes elevated and may result in a deformity of the joints.

grade (grād) The degree of slope or inclination of a road, path, or other surface. The term is also used to refer to a gradual degree of inclination, as in a railroad grade.

Great Depression (grāt dĭ -prĕ sh′ən) The worst and longest economic collapse in modern industrial society, the Great Depression in the United States began in late 1929 and lasted through the early 1940s, spreading to most of the world's other industrial countries.

guerrilla (gə-rĭ l′ə) From the Spanish word *guerra*, meaning war, a term used to refer to a soldier who is a member of a small, irregular military force that operates in small bands in hostile or occupied territory, harassing and working to undermine and disrupt the enemy. "Guerrilla warfare" refers to an organized campaign along these lines.

guild (gĭld) A term used to describe a group of people with a similar interest or skill.

habitat (hăb′ĭ-tăt′) The environment in which a creature or species makes its home. In a broad sense, a habitat includes not only the physical characteristics of an area, but the entire ecological community.

hegemony (hĭ-jĕm′ə-nē, hĕj′ə-mō′nē) The predominant influence of one state over another.

herbivorous (hûr-bĭ v′ər-əs, ûr-) A term used to describe animals that only eat plants and vegetation.

heresy (hĕr′ĭ-sē) An opinion or belief based in religion. Most often heresy refers to the denials of the Roman Catholic church by a follower or believer.

hierarchy (hī ′ə-rär′kē) Most often used to refer to the structure of authority in a group or organization, ranked by authority or ability.

homesteader (hōm′stĕd′ ər) An early settler in the midwestern United States who made a living as a farmer.

horsepower (hôrs′pou′ər) A unit of measuring power most often used to measure the strength and speed of an engine. One unit of horsepower is equal to 33,000 foot-pounds per minute or 745.7 watts.

humanitarian (hyo͞o-măn′ĭ -târ′ē -ən) Someone who is devoted to the promotion of the well-being of humans.

hunter-gatherer (hŭn′tər-gath′ər-ər) A term used to describe a primitive society that obtains its food through hunting animals and gathering vegetation from the area.

hydroelectric power (hī′drō-ĭ -lĕk′trĭk pou′ər) (also **hydropower**) The process of producing electricity through the use of water as a means of converting energy.

hypothesis (hī-pŏth′ĭ-sĭs) A theory or belief developed as an explanation for a set of circumstances or events. A hypothesis is usually supported by proven facts to be taken as truth.

hysteria (hĭ-stĕr′ē-ə, -stîr′-) A medical condition characterized by anxiety, amnesia, hallucinations, or a state of panic that is triggered by a mental imbalance rather than an organic cause.

idealism (ī-dē′ə-lĭz′əm) The philosophy or practice of envisioning things in an ideal form. The term is often used to describe the subject of a piece of artwork or literature.

ideology (ī′dē-ŏl′ə-jē, ĭ d′ē-) The collective term for the body of ideas and principles reflecting the social needs and aspirations of an individual, group, or culture.

idiom (ĭd′ē-əm) A literary term used to describe a word or expression that is peculiar to itself grammatically, or has no individual meaning.

igneous (ĭg′nē-əs) A term used to describe something relating to fire. In geology, the term refers to rock created from a molten substance such as lava.

immigration (ĭm′ĭ-grā′ shən) The process of entering and settling into a country or region that is not one's native land.

imperialism (ĭ m-pîr′ē -ə-lĭ z′əm) The policy and practice by which a powerful nation extends and maintains economic and political control over weaker countries.

indigenous (ĭn-dĭj′ə-nəs) A term used to describe people, animals, or plant life that is native to a specific area or environment.

indigo (ĭn′dĭ-gō′) A type of shrub or plant that produces purple or red flowers that are used to make a blue dye for fabric.

indolent (ĭn′də-lənt) A term used to describe someone who is lethargic, lazy, or refrains from exerting him- or herself.

industrialism (ĭn-dŭs′trē-ə-lĭz′əm) An economic and social system based on the development of large-scale industries and their productions. Other characteristics include mass production of inexpensive goods and the concentration of employment in urban factories.

infamy (ĭn′fə-mē) An event or reputation that is characterized by a negative connotation or criminal act.

infantry (ĭ n′fən-trē) Combat troops trained to fight on foot.

infirmity (ĭn-fûr′mĭ-tē) An ailment of the body, often characterized by weakness, frailty, or old age.

infrastructure (ĭn′frə-strŭk′chər)   The founding belief on which a society or organization is formed. The term also refers to the facilities and services that are necessary for a modern society to function, including schools, transportation, water, power, and a government.

integration (ĭn′tĭ-grā′shən)   The incorporation of diverse ethnic or social groups into a unified society. The term is most often used to refer to the process of racial integration, by which black Americans and other ethnic minorities are afforded the same rights, status, and opportunities as whites. True integration implies that an individual's ability to enjoy any benefits of society are not denied or restricted by reason of race, religion, or national origin.

inter (ĭn-tûr′)   To bury someone in a tomb or grave.

internment (ĭn-tûrn′mənt)   The process of interring or confining someone. The term is often used to describe the process of retaining prisoners during a war.

intervention (ĭn′tər-vě n′shən)   The process of coming between two opposing sides.

irrigate (ĭr′ĭ-gāt′)   The process of supplying water through pipes to a crop or field to provide ample water for growth.

isolationism (ī′sə-lā′shə-nĭ z′əm) (also **isolationist**)   A political policy or philosophy that advocates the belief that a nation's interests are best served by avoiding alliance or excessive contact with other nations.

itinerary (ī-tĭn′ə-rěr′ē, ĭ -tĭn′-)   A plan outlining a trip or journey.

keelboat   A riverboat with a keel or central beam, but without sails, that is used to carry freight.

kiln (kĭ ln, k ĭ l)   A large brick-lined oven used for drying wood, clay, or grain. A kiln is most often used in the firing of ceramics to provide strength and a glazed finish.

landfill (lănd′fĭl′)   The process of transforming solid waste into material that is used to fill in an area and bring it up to the same height as the surrounding land.

lift (lĭft)   A term pertaining to the science of aeronautics in which the force of gravity is counterbalanced by the design of the wings, tail, and airfoil allowing the plane to "lift" into the air.

lime (līm)   Also called quicklime, a compound of calcium oxide in any of various forms or degrees determined by water content and percentage of constituent elements.

loyalist (loi′ə-lĭ st)   One who maintains political loyalty to the government or sovereign during a time of revolt.

magnate (măg′nāt′)   A powerful or influential person. The term is often used to refer to business or industry leaders.

malaria (mə-lâr′ē-ə)   A disease caused by the bite of a female anopheles mosquito. The illness creates an infection of the red blood cells with symptoms including fever, chills, and sweating.

mandate (măn′dāt′)   A law or command administered by a civil authority or ruler.

manifesto (măn′ə-fě s′tō)   A public statement or proclamation in which the beliefs and policies of a monarch or government are delivered.

maritime (măr′ĭ-tīm′) A term used to describe objects relating to marine life or the sea.

martyr (mär′tər) Generally used to refer to a person who dies rather than renounce his or her religious principles, or one who makes great sacrifices for a cause.

mason (mā′sən) A term used to describe someone who works with stone and brick as a building material.

masonry (mā′sən-rē) The art or trade of a mason.

massacre (măs′ə-kər) The act of killing a large number of human beings indiscriminately and cruelly.

maternal (mə-tûr′nəl) A term referring to characteristics most often associated with a mother or motherhood.

matinee (măt′n-ā′) An artistic performance, such as a play or movie, that is shown during the afternoon.

matrilineal (măt′rə-lĭn′ē-əl) A sociological term referring to a society whose descendants follow a maternal ancestral line.

memorabilia (mĕm′ər-ə-bĭl′ē-ə, -bĭl′yə) Objects considered of monetary or sentimental value because of their association with certain historical or past events.

mentor (mĕn′tôr′, -t ər) A teacher or counselor whose trust and wisdom are conveyed to the student.

mercantile (mûr′kən-tē l′, -t ī l′, -t ĭ l) From the Italian *mercante*, meaning merchant, anything involved in or relating to merchants, mercantilism, or trade.

mesa (mā′sə) From the Spanish word meaning "table," a broad, flat-topped geographical feature with one or more steep sides. Mesas are common in the southwestern United States.

metallurgy (mĕt′l-ûr′jē) The study or science of metals, metal mining, the extraction of metallic ores, alloys, and the creation or manufacture of objects made of metal.

metaphor (mĕt′ə-fôr′, -f ər) A phrase or figure of speech in which one word or phrase is used to designate something else in order to invoke a specific comparison.

methodology (mĕth′ə-dŏl′ə-jē) A term used to indicate a formal structure or body of practices and procedures used in a particular discipline.

migration (mī -grā′shən) The act of moving from one place to another as a group.

militia (mə-lĭ sh′ə) (also **militiamen**) The term used to describe an army made up of ordinary citizens rather than professional or career soldiers. A militia would be intended to function as a reserve or contingent force, available to be called on in case of emergency.

minimum wage A base rate, established by the federal government, that determines the least amount a worker of a certain age in most industries must be paid for an hour of work.

minority (mə-nôr′ĭ-tē, -n ŏr′-, m ī-) A racial, religious, political, national, or other group regarded as different from the larger group of which it is part.

mission (mĭ sh′ən) A religious group sent to a foreign country or frontier territory to establish the structure of the church and provide teaching and human services to the native population. The term is also often used to refer to the buildings built to house church services, functions, or clergy.

missionary (mĭsh′ə-nĕr′ē) A member of a particular religious organization whose tradition is to "witness" by word and deed to the beliefs of his or her religion, so that others may come to know and understand it.

monarchist (mŏn′ər-kĭ st) Someone who believes in and advocates the principles of the monarchy.

monarchy (mŏn′ər-kē , -är ′-) (also **monarch**) A form of government in which the leader rules by hereditary right, or the nation that is governed. Monarchs include such rulers as kings, emperors, and czars.

monastery (mŏn′ə-stĕr′ē) A religious house, consisting of living quarters and places of worship, and often associated with some means of provender, such as a farm. The residence of monks.

monk (mŭngk) A Christian brother, living in a monastery, following a life devoted to rituals and disciplines defined by his "order."

moratorium (môr′ə-tôr′ē-əm, -t ôr′-, m ŏr′-) A formal or contracted period of delay, or the suspension of an obligation or ongoing event.

mortar (môr′tər) The two most common usages refer to a type of portable cannon used to fire shells at short range and low velocities, and to a bonding material used in construction and surfacing. Modern mortar usually consists of cement mixed with sand and water, and is most commonly used to bind together stone- or brickwork.

mural (myo͞or′əl) A type of painting or art form, often very large in size, that is applied directly to a wall or other building surface.

musket (mŭs′kĭ t) An early type of firearm, a shoulder gun considered a precursor of the modern rifle, common from the late 16th century through the 18th century.

mutiny (myo͞ot′n-ē) An open rebellion against authority. It is most often used to refer to military personnel turning against a superior officer.

mysticism (mĭs′tĭ-sĭz′əm) A belief in or consciousness of a transcendent or higher reality, such as God or spirits.

NAACP An acronym for the National Association for the Advancement of Colored People, an organization founded in 1909 to protect the rights and improve the living and working conditions of black Americans.

nascent (nās′ənt, n ĭ′sənt) Something that is developing or coming into existence, emerging but not yet fully developed or realized.

nationalism (năsh′ə-nə-lĭ z′əm) The devotion to the beliefs and interests of a specific nation.

New Deal The collective name given to a large-scale program of domestic government policies enacted under President Franklin D. Roosevelt, especially those intended to counteract the effects of the Great Depression between 1933 and 1938.

nomadic (also **nomad** [nō′măd′]) A term used to describe someone who is a member of a group of people who have no fixed home and move according to the seasons from place to place in search of food, water, and grazing land.

odometer (ō-dŏm′ĭ -tər)   An instrument used to measure distance traveled. It is most commonly found in automobiles and other motor vehicles.

opportunism   (ŏp′ər-tōō′nĭ zm)   The practice or trait of taking advantage of opportunities that present themselves, sometimes without regard for principles or consequences, in order to achieve a specific end.

oratory (ôr′ə-tôr′ē) (also **orator**)   The art of speaking or speechmaking, especially speeches designed to influence the judgments or feelings of those listening. Oratory is often characterized by effective and effusive use of language, and the term implies a certain memorable quality attributed to the speech or speaker.

ordnance (ôrd′nəns)   A term used to refer to weaponry and other military materiel. The term also refers to the branch of a military organization that deals with weaponry, the maintenance of weapons, and weapon supply.

orthodoxy (ôr′thə-dŏk′sē)   An accepted or established doctrine or creed, and the adherence to it. The term "orthodox" is also often used to refer to the most conservative or traditional element, especially of a religion.

paleontology (pā′lē-ŏn-tŏl′ə-jē) (also **paleontologist**)   The science or study of life and life forms that existed in prehistoric times, most often via the fossils of extinct plants and animals.

palisade (păl′ĭ -sād′)   Most often used to refer to a geological or topological feature consisting of a line of steep cliffs, most often along the path of a river. The term may also be used to describe a type of fortification consisting of spikes or pointed sticks in a circular, defensive formation.

pantheon (păn′thē-ŏn′, - ən)   A circular temple in Rome, completed in 27 B.C.E., that was dedicated to all the gods.

paradigm (păr′ə-dīm′, -d ĭm′)   An example or incident that serves as a pattern or model for all that follows.

parapet (păr′ə-pĭt, -p ĕt′)   A protective or decorative low wall surrounding the edges of a raised structure such as a balcony or deck.

parliament (pär′lə-mənt)   In some countries, a branch of government, similar to the U.S. Congress, that is responsible for enacting laws, levying taxes, and serving as the highest court of appeal.

patriarchal   (pă′trē-är′kəl)   A type of social system in which the father is the head of the household, and ancestry is determined through the paternal, or father's line.

patrician (pə-trĭsh′ən)   A person of refined upbringing, manners, and tastes. In some societies, the term also refers to a member of the aristocracy or ruling class.

patrilineal (păt′rə-lĭn′ē-əl) (also **paternal** [pə-tûr′nəl])   The determination or account of ancestry or lineage through the father's line.

patrimony (păt′rə-mō′nē)   An inheritance from a father or other ancestor.

patriotic (pā′trē-ŏt′ĭk)   A term used to describe someone who expresses love and devotion to one's country.

patron (pā′trən)   Someone who supports, protects, or champions an institution, event, or cause.

patronage (pā′trə-nĭ j, p ăt′rə-) The support of a cause by means of financial assistance.

pavilion (pə-vĭ l′yən) A light, often temporary and ornamental structure, commonly used for exhibits at a show or fair.

payload (pā′lōd′) A term commonly used to refer to the portion of a load or shipment containing revenue or profit producing goods. It may also indicate the most important or most vital portion of the cargo.

pediment (pĕd′ə-mənt) An architectural feature or element, as in a wide, slightly pitched gable surrounding the façade of a building.

peninsula (pə-nĭ n′syə-lə, -s ə-lə) A piece of land projecting into a body of water, surrounded by water on three sides, and connected to the mainland by a narrow strip of land called an isthmus.

pension (pĕn′shən) A sum of money paid regularly as a retirement benefit or as patronage for service.

philanthropy (fĭ-lăn′thrə-pē) In business, a term used to describe the ongoing practice or philosophy, usually of an individual, of giving to or establishing charitable or humanistic causes or foundations.

physics (fĭz′ĭks) The study or science of matter and energy.

pilaster (pĭ-lăs′tər) In architecture and design, a decorative rectangular column with a capital and base set into a wall.

pilgrim (pĭl′grəm) A person who travels to or visits a place of spiritual or political importance to seek refuge or insight.

pilgrimage (pĭ l′grə-mĭ j) The voyage taken by a pilgrim to a site of spiritual or political importance. Most often used to refer to a religious journey.

pioneer (pī ′ə-nîr′) The first to discover, found, or settle a particular land or scientific discovery. Widely used to refer to the early settlers of the American west.

pirogue (pĭ-rōg′) A type of ship or canoe made from a hollowed-out tree trunk.

plantation (plăn-tā′shən) A term originating in colonial times, a plantation is a settlement or piece of land used to grow crops and that houses the workers who tend the crops. The land was independently owned and self-contained, often housing the owner of the land as well.

polarize (pō′lə-rīz′) From the physics term indicating an opposite or opposing alignment, a term meaning to divide or separate into two contrasting or opposed positions.

poliomyelitis (pō′lē-ō-mī′ə-lī′tĭs) An infectious viral disease, affecting mostly children, that affects the motor neurons of the spinal cord and brainstem and can cause paralysis, deformity, and muscular atrophy.

polygraph (pŏl′ē-grăf′) An instrument that uses biosensors to track and record changes in involuntary physical processes such as heartbeat and respiration. Also called a lie detector, it is often used by law enforcement officials or employers to give an indication of truthfulness.

portal (pôr′tl, p ōr′-) A doorway, entrance, or gate.

portico (pôr′tĭ-kō′, p ōr′-) In architecture, a porch or covered walkway with a roof supported by columns. A portico is often used leading up to the entrance of a building.

postmortem   (pōst-môr′təm)   Something that is done or that occurs after death. The term is most commonly used to refer to the medical examination that attempts to determine the cause of death in criminal investigations.

poverty   (pŏv′ər-tē)   An economic condition in which people lack the income to obtain the minimal levels of such essentials as food, clothing, medical services, and housing necessary to maintain an adequate standard of living. In a strict sense, the "poverty line" is defined as those households earning a certain percentage below the average family income. In the United States, the group that currently makes up the largest portion of the population living in poverty is single mothers, who account for roughly one-third of all poor people in this country.

prairie   (prâr′ē)   An extensive area of grasslands. The term is most often associated with the rolling, mostly treeless plains of the American west.

promulgate   (prŏm′əl-gāt′, prō-mŭl′gāt′)   To make known through a public declaration or official announcement.

protégé   (prō′tə-zhā′, pr ō′tə-zhā′)   A person who is provided for, and trained in, a specific career by an influential person within that field.

prototype   (prō′tə-tī p′)   An original model or concept, on which future versions are based.

pueblo   (pwĕ b′lō)   A Spanish word meaning town or village (and also nation or people), the term is most often used to describe a village characterized by multilevel, terraced adobe structures, surrounding a central area. It derives from the name Pueblo, used by the Spanish to refer to any of some 25 Native American peoples who were originally associated with this type of architecture.

purview   (pûr′vyoo′)   A term used to refer to the extent or range of something, such as authority, competence, or responsibility. The use of the term implies limits, either purposely imposed or restricted by outside factors.

quota   (kwō′tə)   In legal or political terms, a predetermined number or percentage of a business's new hires that must be members of a minority.

racist   (also **racism** [rā′sĭ z′əm])   Describing the belief that a racial or ethnic group is inferior due to its race or nationality.

radiocarbon dating   Also called carbon dating, a method of determining the age of a geological, archeological, or fossil record by measuring the amount of the element carbon 14 it contains. Carbon 14 is a slightly radioactive element with a half-life of 5,780 years, meaning that in that period of time, half of the nuclei in the sample will have undergone radioactive decay.

ration   (răsh′ən, r ā′shən)   A set or established portion, or a percentage of a whole divided by the number of shares. The term is commonly used to refer to the meal allotted to military personnel.

reformist   A person with the political intent of bringing about change or reform.

registrar   (rĕj′ĭ-strär′, r ĕj′ĭ-strär′)   A person charged with the keeping and organization of official records. The term is often used to refer to the office or officer at a university responsible for keeping track of students, attendance, and academic performance.

rehabilitation   The process of restoring something to usefulness, or to its former condition.

repatriation (rē -pā′trē -ā′shən)   The process of returning someone to his or her native country.

replica (rĕp′lĭ-kə)   A highly accurate reproduction or copy, often intended to duplicate the appearance of an original in great detail, but on a smaller scale.

Republican (rĭ-pŭb′lĭ-kən)   A member of a political party of the United States, or one who advocates a republican form of government.

reservation (rĕz′ər-vā′shən)   Land set aside by a government that provides a place for a specific group of people to live. This land is "reserved" for them to use. Most often used to refer to the areas used for the forced relocation of Native Americans during the settlement of the American west.

restitution (rĕs′tĭ -too′shən, -ty oo′-)   The restoration of lost or stolen things to their rightful owner, or the compensation for things lost, stolen, or destroyed. Use of the term implies things wrongly taken or destroyed, as in war.

restoration (rĕs′tə-rā′shən)   The reconstruction or restoring of something that has been destroyed or badly damaged. The term is commonly used to refer to the rebuilding of the southern United States after the Civil War.

rhetoric (rĕt′ər-ĭk)   The study or art of the use of language and persuasion.

rocket (rŏk′ĭt)   A type of vehicle used for launching other vehicles, satellites, or other payloads from the surface of the earth into earth orbit or space. The term is also used to refer to the device used to carry a missile or warhead, often in atmospheric flights or trajectories.

rotunda (rō-tŭn′də)   An architectural term for a circular building, most often possessing a dome. The term may also refer to a circular room. A rotunda is most often characteristic of a civil or memorial building or architecture, and the term implies a certain majesty or formality.

rustic (rŭs′tĭk)   A characteristic distinguished by elements of rural life, motifs, or people. Use of the term implies a certain quaint or antiquated style.

rye (rī)   A cereal grass or grain. Rye is widely used for making flour, a distinctive type of whisky, and for livestock feed.

Sabbath (săb′əth)   The first day of the week, Sunday, observed as the day of rest and worship by most Christians. The seventh day of the week, observed from Friday evening to Saturday evening as a day of rest and worship by Jews.

sandstone (sănd′stōn′)   In geology, a type of sedimentary rock or stone comprised of deposited and compressed sand, held together by a natural adhesive or cement, such as silicate.

schooner (skoo′nər)   A type of sailing vessel possessing at least two masts: a foremast and a mainmast.

scourge (skûrj)   Someone or something associated with widespread devastation or terror. The term is often used, as with *bane,* to refer to something seen as or believed to be an instrument of punishment, affliction, or terror specific to a given situation, nation, or people.

secede (sĭ-sēd′) To formally withdraw from a union, association, or alliance.

secession (sĭ-sĕsh′ən) The process of withdrawing from a union or branch. The term is most famously associated with the withdrawal of the southern states from the United States, causing the Civil War.

secessionist (sĭ-sĕsh′ə-nĭst) Most often used to refer to a person or to the political or philosophical belief that supported the right of the southern United States to secede from the Union.

sect (sĕkt) A smaller, distinct unit, sometimes separated from a larger group or denomination by variations in common beliefs.

secular (sĕk′yə-lər) A term referring to an approach that does not relate to religious or spiritual views.

sediment (sĕd′ə-mənt) The material or trace solids that settle to the bottom of a volume of liquid. Most often, the term is used to refer to the small particles of soil or organic material that are carried along with the flow of water, as in a river, and either settle gradually to the bottom or are deposited into an alluvial basin.

sedimentary (sĕ d′ə-mĕ n′tə-rē , -m ĕn′trē) In geology, a type of layered rock formed from the accumulated deposit of sediments.

segregation (sĕg′rĭ-gā′shən) To be separated, usually through force, from the mainstream for reasons of race or creed. The term is most often used to refer to the forced separation of blacks and whites, most notable in the southern United States.

seminary (sĕ m′ə-nĕ r′ē) The name most often associated with a school or university for the teaching and training of members of the clergy. The term may also refer to a school of higher education, usually private, and most often exclusively for girls.

separatist (sĕp′ər-ə-tĭst) One who secedes or advocates separation, especially from an established church.

shale (shāl) A type of fissile, or layered, rock, similar to sandstone or siltstone, comprised of multiple, often thin layers of fine-grained sediments.

sharecropper (shâr′krŏp′ər) A person who is placed in a position of servitude by which he or she provides labor for the landowner in return for a share of the profits of the merchandise, usually an agricultural crop. The landowner not only provides the land to be tended, but also the equipment, animals and seed, and housing to the sharecropper.

shrine (shrīn) Originally used to refer to a receptacle containing sacred relics, a term generally meaning a structure or building erected as a tribute to or resting place for the relics or remains of a respected or venerated person. Use of the word most often implies a certain religious or otherwise sacred association.

siege (sēj) A military blockade of an area, intended to bring about surrender.

siltstone (sĭ lt′stōn′) A sedimentary type of rock, similar to sandstone but comprised of consolidated silt.

silversmith (sĭl′vər-smĭth′)   An artist or craftsman who works in silver, making or repairing objects or works of art.

sit-in (sĭt-ĭn)   A nonviolent protest during which the protesters literally sit as a means of reaching their goal. By the protesters physically being in place, the normal process of events is interrupted, therefore creating the obstacle that in turn gets results.

smallpox (smôl′pŏks′)   An acute, highly infectious, often fatal disease caused by a virus. The disease is characterized by high fever and aches with subsequent widespread eruption of pimples that blister, produce pus, and form pockmarks.

sod (sŏd)   A section or mat of tightly interwoven grasses, held together by matted roots. Sod was often used as a roofing material.

sovereign (sŏv′ər-ĭn, sŏv′rĭn)   Someone who exercises supreme authority over a nation or governmental unit, often a king, queen, or other ruler.

sovereignty (sŏv′ər-ĭn-tē, sŏv′rĭn-)   A supreme political power free from external control.

species (spē′shēz, -sēz)   In biology, a basic classification of life forms within genus (a group of species with similar characteristics) and subgenus (a further refining classification) levels, made up of different but related organisms capable of interbreeding.

stagecoach (stāj′kōch′)   A form of long-range, horse-drawn transportation, common in the era before railroads and automobiles, that followed a regular route and schedule. The name derives from the effect of scheduled stoppages, dividing the ex-

tended trip into discrete legs, or stages.

statesman (stāts′mən)   A person who is knowledgeable in the principles of government.

status quo (stă′təs kwō)   A Latin term used to refer to the state of affairs as it exists, or the present situation.

steward (stoo′ərd, styoo′-)   The person charged with managing the affairs of estates of a wealthy person or monarch. The term is commonly used to refer to anyone who temporarily takes charge of important affairs in the absence of the usual leader.

stockade (stŏ-kād′)   A fort or other type of defensive fortification, comprised of wood posts or timbers positioned upright and driven into the ground for stability.

stranglehold (strāng′gəl-hōld′)   Literally an illegal wrestling hold intended to exert pressure on the throat of an opponent and choke off his air supply, the term is commonly used to refer to a powerful influence or hold by an outside force that restricts progress or mobility.

strata (stră′tə)   Various layers or divisions. The term is most often used in geology to refer to the various layers of sedimentary rock.

strike (strīk)   An organized work stoppage carried out by a group of employees, usually as a tactic to enforce demands or to protest unfair labor conditions. Strikes are most frequently conducted by workers organized into trade unions, and are often used as a bargaining tool during contract negotiations.

stucco (stŭk′ō)   In building, an external finish composed of cement, sand,

and lime. It is usually applied while wet, and adds a rough, variable texture. The term is also used to refer to a finer interior finish, often used for ornamental devices.

summit (sŭm′ĭt) The top or highest point. The term is also used to refer to a high-level meeting, most often between heads of state.

supercomputer (sōō′pər-kəm-pyōō′tər) A extremely powerful mainframe computer, generally defined as among the fastest and largest of any given era of computational power.

telemedicine A technology by which distant physicians may observe and participate in an operation through the use of a closed-circuit television connection. It was used in the treatment of King Hussein of Jordan, to transmit images to doctors at the Mayo Clinic in the United States.

tenement (tĕn′ə-mənt) A structure intended for human habitation. The term is most often associated with rundown urban apartment buildings with extremely low maintenance standards.

terminus (tûr′mə-nəs) The end or end point. The term is often used in regard to public transportation, especially rail lines.

theology (thē-ŏl′ə-jē) The science or study of the nature and person of God and religion though beliefs and truths.

tiller (tĭl′ər) A nautical term for the device or lever used to steer or turn a boat.

tinderbox (tĭn′dər-bŏks′) A portable means of storage, usually in the form of a box, used for carrying tinder (wood), or the means to start fires.

tipi (tē′pē) A variant of the word teepee, a portable dwelling usually made of cured animal skin, much like a tent, used by certain Native American peoples.

topographical (tə-pŏg′rə-fĭ-kəl) (also **topography**) A term used to describe the graphic presentation of the surface features of a place or region as depicted on a map.

tramway (trăm′wā′) In mining, the track or rail on which the transportation system runs. The term may also refer to a streetcar line or the cables in a cable car system.

travesty (trăv′ĭ-stē) A parody or other highly exaggerated or debased imitation. The term implies feelings of an extreme degree and may indicate a certain repulsion or offensiveness.

trestle (trĕs′əl) A type of foundational support made up of a horizontal beam supported by two pairs of divergent legs.

Underground Railroad A network of antislavery northerners that illegally helped black southern slaves escape slavery and reach safety in free states and Canada. The refugees traveled from "station" to "station" (usually farms), aided by a "conductor" who helped them find safe places to hide during their journey.

union (yōōn′yən) Also called a craft or trade union, an organization or association of workers established to improve or protect their working conditions.

usurper (yōō-sûrp′r) A term used to describe someone who takes power by force, without legal authority.

viceroy (vīs′roi′) The political leader of a vassal or colonial country or province, who rules as a representative of the sovereign.

vigil (vĭj′əl)   A watch or guard held during what would normally be considered sleeping hours. The term implies a certain formality or devotion, and may refer to a ritual or ceremonial watching or observance on the eve of a holy day or festival.

villa (vĭl′ə)   An Italian word derived from the Latin, a term used to refer to a substantial country house or estate owned by a wealthy person.

wetland (wĕt′lănd′)   A geographical feature or habitat, a low-lying area saturated with moisture such as a marsh or swamp.

Whig   One of the two dominant political parties in power in the United States from the mid-1830s to the mid-1850s. The Whig party was opposed to the Jacksonian Democrats, associated mainly with manufacturing, commercial, and financial interests. The Whigs were replaced by the Republicans in 1854.

yellow fever   An infectious disease most often found in tropical climes. Yellow fever is a viral illness carried by mosquitoes, and is characterized by fever, jaundice, and vomiting.

zoology   The branch of biology concerned with the classification, properties, and vital phenomena of animals.

Photo Credits

Alamo (page 2): Archive Photos
Alfred P. Murrah Federal Building (page 7): CORBIS/Bettmann
Amoskeag Mills (page 11): CORBIS/G. E. Kidder Smith
Angel Island Immigration Station (page 15): CORBIS/Philip Gould
Appomattox Court House (page 21): Archive Photos
Arlington National Cemetery (page 24): National Archives
Arlington National Cemetery (page 25): CORBIS/Catherine Karnow
Arlington National Cemetery (page 27): CORBIS/James P. Blair
Belle of Louisville Steamboat (page 30): CORBIS/Paul Almasy
Benjamin Franklin National Memorial (page 35): National Archives
Benjamin Franklin National Memorial (page 37): CORBIS/Bettmann
Bering Land Bridge (pages 39, 40, 41, 42): National Park Service/Western Arctic National
    Parklands
Camp David (page 46): CORBIS
Castillo de San Marcos (page 51): CORBIS/Bettmann
Castillo de San Marcos (page 53): National Park Service/Castillo de San Marcos and Fort
    Matanzas National Monuments
Charles W. Morgan Whaling Ship (page 56): CORBIS/Schenectady Museum; Hall of Electrical
    History Foundation
Cumberland Gap (page 60): Lambert/Archive Photos
Daniel Freeman Homestead (pages 66, 68): National Park Service/Homestead National
    Monument of America
Dealey Plaza (page 72): CORBIS/Charles E. Rotkin
Dinosaur Ridge (pages 77, 79): Courtesy of Friends of Dinosaur Ridge
Edison Laboratories (pages 88, 89, 90, 91): National Park Service/Edison National Historic Site
Effigy Mounds (pages 93, 94, 96): National Park Service/Effigy Mounds National Monument
El Morro Fortress (page 99): CORBIS/Charles O'Rear
Ellis Island (pages 104, 106): National Park Service, 1990
Ethan Allen Homestead (page 110): National Archives
Ethan Allen Homestead (page 112): Harry Wicks/Ethan Allen Homestead Trust
Ford's Theatre (page 114): CORBIS
Ford's Theatre (pages 116, 118): National Archives
Fort Clatsop (pages 120, 122, 124): National Park Service/Fort Clatsop National Memorial
Fort Delaware (page 126): CORBIS/Kevin Fleming
Fort Laramie (page 130): National Archives
Fort Larned (page 133): National Park Service/Fort Larned National Historic Site
Fort Mandan (page 137): Courtesy of North Dakota Lewis and Clark Bicentennial Foundation,
    Washburn, ND
Fort McHenry (pages 142, 144, 146): National Park Service/Fort McHenry National Monument
    and Historic Shrine
Fort Sumter (page 151): National Archives
Franklin Delano Roosevelt Memorial (page 155): Archive Photos/Joseph Sohm; ChromoSohm Inc.

Gateway Arch (page 160): Lambert/Archive Photos
Gettysburg Battlefield (page 163): National Archives
Gettysburg Battlefield (page 164): Archive Photos
Harpers Ferry (page 172): National Archives
Haymarket Square (page 177): CORBIS/Hulton-Deutsch Collection
Hearst Castle (pages 182, 183, 184, 185): Courtesy of Hearst San Simeon State Historical
    Monument
Highland Park Ford Plant (page 188): CORBIS/Bettmann
Hoover Dam (pages 192, 194): U.S. Department of the Interior, Bureau of Reclamation
Independence Hall (page 198): Archive Photos
Iolani Palace (page 202): CORBIS/Douglas Peebles
Jamestown (page 208): National Park Service/Colonial National Historical Park
Jefferson Memorial (page 213): Archive Photos
John F. Kennedy Space Center (page 218): Lambert/Archive Photos
Kettle Moraine (page 223): Bob Queen/Wisconsin Department of Natural Resources
Kettle Moraine (page 225): Courtesy of Fond Du Lac CVB
Kitty Hawk (page 227): CORBIS
Kitty Hawk (page 229): Archive Photos
Korean War Veterans Memorial (page 233): CORBIS/James P. Blair
Lexington Green (page 238): CORBIS/Lee Snider
Lincoln Memorial (page 242): Russell Thompson/Archive Photos
Little Bighorn Battlefield (pages 246, 247, 248): National Archives
Little Bighorn Battlefield (page 249): CORBIS/Kevin R. Morris
Little Rock Central High School (page 251): CORBIS/Bettmann
Lorraine Motel (page 256): CORBIS/Kevin Fleming
Lorraine Motel (page 257): Courtesy of the National Civil Rights Museum, Memphis, Tennessee
Los Alamos National Laboratory (page 260): CORBIS/Wolfgang Kaehler
Manzanar War Relocation Center (page 266): CORBIS
Manzanar War Relocation Center (page 267): National Archives
Manzanar War Relocation Center (page 268): CORBIS/Phil Schermeister
Mayo Clinic (page 272): CORBIS/Bettmann
Melrose Estate (page 276): CORBIS/Bettmann
Mesa Verde (page 282): Archive Photos
Monticello (page 288): American Stock/Archive Photos
Mount Rushmore (page 291): Lambert/Archive Photos
Mount Vernon (page 296): CORBIS/Bettmann/James P. Blair
O.K. Corral (pages 300, 301): CORBIS/Bettmann
Plymouth Rock (page 306): CORBIS/Buddy Mays
Pony Express Stables (page 313): Courtesy of the Pony Express Museum, St. Joseph, Missouri
Portland Head Lighthouse (page 317): CORBIS/Peter Finger
Rankin House (page 320): CORBIS/Layne Kennedy
Rhea County Courthouse (page 327): CORBIS/Bettmann
Russell Cave (page 332): CORBIS/David Muench
Salem Witch Trials Memorial (page 336): CORBIS/Lee Snider
San Carlos Borromeo Mission (page 342): CORBIS/G. E. Kidder Smith
Spanish Cabildo (page 346): Archive Photos
Statue of Liberty (page 351): CORBIS/Gail Mooney
Stone Mountain Memorial (page 356): CORBIS/Kevin Fleming
Sutter's Mill (page 361): Courtesy of Marshall Gold Discovery State Historic Park, Coloma, CA

Teapot Dome Oil Reserve (page 367): CORBIS/Bettmann

Tippecanoe Battlefield (pages 369, 370): Courtesy of Tippecanoe County Historical Association

Trinity Church (page 375): CORBIS/G. E. Kidder Smith

Tuskegee Institute (page 381): CORBIS/Bettmann

USS *Arizona* Memorial (page 386): National Archives

USS *Arizona* Memorial (page 388): Archive Photos

Valley Forge (pages 392, 393, 395): National Park Service/Valley Forge National Historical Park

Vanderbilt Mansion (pages 397, 398, 400): National Park Service/Vanderbilt Mansion National Historic Site

Vietnam Veterans Memorial (page 403): Dan Coleman/Archive Photos

Washington Monument (page 409): Archive Photos

Watergate Complex (page 411): Archive Photos

Wesleyan Chapel (pages 420, 422, 424): National Park Service/Women's Rights National Historical Park

White Bird Canyon (page 426): National Archives

White House (page 431): Archive Photos

Whitman Mission (page 436): CORBIS/Dave G. Houser

Wounded Knee (page 439): CORBIS/Bettmann

Yorktown (page 444): National Archives

Yorktown (pages 445, 446): National Park Service/Colonial National Historical Park

Article Sources

The following authors contributed articles to Macmillan Profiles: *Monuments and Historic Places of America*.

Alamo	Patrick Butler and Irene Quintanilla/Mark LaFlaur
Alfred P. Murrah Federal Building	Mary Carvlin
Amoskeag Mills	Michael Levine
Angel Island Immigration Station	Mark LaFlaur
Appomattox Court House	Nancy Gratton
Arlington National Cemetery	Laura Morelli
Belle of Louisville Steamboat	Mark LaFlaur
Benjamin Franklin National Memorial	John Jones
Bering Land Bridge	Greg Martin
Camp David	Mary Carvlin
Castillo de San Marcos	Colbey Emmerson
Charles W. Morgan Whaling Ship	John Jones
Cumberland Gap	Nancy Gratton
Daniel Freeman Homestead	Nancy Gratton
Dealey Plaza	Mary Carvlin
Dinosaur Ridge	Greg Martin
Donner Pass	Fred L. Koestler/Mark LaFlaur
Edison Laboratories	John Jones
Effigy Mounds	Greg Martin
El Morro Fortress	Nancy Gratton
Ellis Island	Mark LaFlaur
Ethan Allen Homestead	Farar Elliot
Ford's Theatre	Bruce Hopkins
Fort Clatsop	Cindy Orlando
Fort Delaware	John Jones
Fort Laramie	Paul L. Hedron
Fort Larned	Nancy Gratton
Fort Mandan	Thomas William Dunlay
Fort McHenry	Nancy Gratton
Fort Sumter	Colbey Emmerson
Franklin Delano Roosevelt Memorial	Michael Levine
Gateway Arch	John Jones
Gettysburg Battlefield	Colbey Emmerson
Golden Spike National Historic Site	Bruce Powell
Harpers Ferry	Michael Levine
Haymarket Square	Michael Levine
Hearst Castle	Ben Proctor/John Blades
Highland Park Ford Plant	Michael Levine
Hoover Dam	Candace Floyd/Mary Carvlin

501

Independence Hall	Laura Morelli
Iolani Palace	Nancy Gratton
Jefferson Memorial	Doris Eder
John F. Kennedy Space Center	Cheryl Slean
Kettle Moraine	Greg Martin
Kitty Hawk	Colbey Emmerson
Korean War Veterans Memorial	Barbara Sutton
Lexington Green	Barbara Morrow
Lincoln Memorial	Bruce Hopkins
Little Bighorn Battlefield	Robert M. Utley/Mary Carvlin
Little Rock Central High School	Michael Levine
Lorraine Motel	Michael Levine
Los Alamos National Laboratory	Cheryl Slean
Manzanar War Relocation Center	Kevin Allen Leonard/Mark LaFlaur
Mayo Clinic	Mary Carvlin
Melrose Estate	Mark LaFlaur
Mesa Verde	Greg Martin
Monticello	Doris Eder
Mount Rushmore	Laura Morelli
Mount Vernon	Laura Morelli
O.K. Corral	Mary Carvlin
Pony Express Stables	Nancy Gratton
Portland Head Lighthouse	John Jones
Rankin House	Lisa Simon
Rhea County Courthouse	Mary Carvlin
Russell Cave	Mark LaFlaur
San Carlos Borromeo Mission	Thom Davis
Spanish Cabildo	Mark LaFlaur
Statue of Liberty	Mark LaFlaur
Stone Mountain Memorial	Mark LaFlaur
Sutter's Mill	Mark LaFlaur
Teapot Dome Oil Reserve	Patrick Butler/Mary Carvlin
Tippecanoe Battlefield	Cindy Bedell
Trinity Church	John Jones
Tuskegee Institute	John Jones
USS *Arizona* Memorial	Lisa Simon
Valley Forge	Barbara Morrow
Vanderbilt Mansion	Jill Lectka
Vietnam Veterans Memorial	Barbara Sutton
Washington Monument	Laura Morelli
Watergate Complex	Mary Carvlin
Weedpatch Camp	Michael Levine
Wesleyan Chapel	Mary Carvlin
White Bird Canyon	Greg Martin
White House	Laura Morelli
Whitman Mission	Julie Roy Jeffrey/Mary Carvlin
Wounded Knee	Alan Axelrod/Mary Carvlin
Yorktown	Andrew Gottlieb

Index

A

Abolitionists, 171–172, 319–324
Adams, Abigail, 431
Adams, John, 36, 199, 430, 431
Adams, Samuel, 199, 237, 239
African-American monuments. *See also* Civil rights monuments
   Rankin House, 319–324
   Tuskegee Institute, 378–384
Agassiz, Louis, 223
Agricultural Adjustments Acts of 1933 and 1938, 156
Alamo, The, 1–5
Alfred P. Murrah Federal Building, 5–9
Allen, Ethan, 108–112
Allison, Samuel, 262
Altgeld, John P., 180
American Civil Liberties Union (ACLU), 326
American Equal Rights Association, 423
American Federation of Labor, 176–177
American Indian Movement (AIM), 441–442
American Revolution monuments. *See also* Civil War monuments; Military monuments; War monuments
   Battle of Yorktown, 443–448
   Benjaming Franklin National Memorial, 34–37
   Fort McHenry, 141–146
   Independence Hall, 197–201
   Jefferson Memorial, 211–215
   Lexington Green, 237–241
   Valley Forge, 391–396
   Yorktown, 443–448
American west monuments
   The Alamo, 1–5

Daniel Freeman Homestead, 65–71
   Fort Clatsop, 119–125
   Gateway Arch, 159–162
   Golden Spike National Historic Site, 165–169
   Hoover Dam, 191–196
   O.K. Corral, 299–303
   Pony Express Stables, 310–314
   Sutter's Mill, 358–364
   Whitman Mission, 435–438
American Woman Suffrage Association (AWSA), 423
Amoskeag Mills, 10–14
Anasazi, 281–286
Anderson, Marian, 245
Angel Island Immigration Station, 14–19
Antarctic Ice Sheet, 226
Anthony, Susan B., 423
Apollo program, 219–220
Appomattox Court House, 19–23
Archer, James J., 128
Arlington House, 242
Arlington National Cemetery, 23–28, 242
Armstrong, Neil, 219
Armstrong, Samuel Chapman, 379–380
Arnold, Benedict, 109, 444
Arnold, Samuel, 115
Arthur, Chester, 408
Arvin Federal Camp, 415–419
Ashland, James N., 90
Asian immigration, 17–19
Assembly line, 189–190
Astoria, Oregon, 123
Atzerodt, George, 115
Autopsies, 272
Avalon. See Belle of Louisville
Ayala, Juan Manuel de, 15–16
Aylsworth, Jonas, 91

B

Babbitt, Bruce, 14
Bacher, Robert, 262
Bacon, Henry, 242, 243
Bacon's rebellion, 211
Badlands, The (South Dakota), 293
Ball, Thomas, 243
Banking Act of 1933, 156
Bartholdi, Frédéric-Auguste, 350–351
Bateaus, 30–31
Battle of the Bulge Memorial, 26
Beauregard, Pierre Gustave Toutant, 151, 152
Becknell, William, 134–135
Beecher, Henry Ward, 322
Begin, Menachem, 48
Bell, John, 117
Belle of Louisville (steamboat), 29–33
Benjamin Franklin National Memorial, 34–37
Benteen, Frederick W., 247–249
Bering, Vitus, 38
Bering Land Bridge, 37–43
Bering Land Bridge National Preserve, 43
Bernstein, Carl, 412
Bethe, Hans, 261, 262
Big Foot (chief), 439–440
Biltmore (Asheville, North Carolina), 401
Black, Hugo, 26
Blackwell, Henry, 423
Blassie, Michael J., 28
Bloch, Felix, 261
Blossom, Virgil, 252
Boone, Daniel, 60, 61–62
Boon Island, Maine, 316
Boon Island Lighthouse, 318
Booth, John Wilkes, 22, 113–115, 116

Borglum, Gutzon, 291–294, 356–357

Boston Tea Party, 237–238

Boulder Dam. *See* Hoover Dam

Bowie, James, 1, 3

Bradford, William, 308

Branch Davidian religious group, 8, 9

Brandywine, Battle of, 391

Brannan, Sam, 360–361

Braun, Wernher von, 218

Breakers, The (Newport, Rhode Island), 401

Breckinridge, John C., 117

Brennan, William J., 26

Brocius, "Curly" Bill, 302

Brown, Dee, 441

Brown, George Scratchley, 25

Brown, John, 171–176

Brown v. Board of Education of Topeka, Kansas (1954), 251

Bryan, William Jennings, 183, 290, 326–329

Buchanan, James, 150, 171, 408

Buckner, Simon B., 22

Burger, Warren, 26

Burns, Lucy, 423

Bush, George, 49, 270

Butler Act, 326, 327

Butterfield, Alexander, 414

C

Cabildo, the, 344–349

Cabrilho, João, 15

Cahokia, 95

California

  Chinese immigration to, 17–19

  gold rush of 1848, 354–358

Calliopes, 31

Callon, Mr. and Mrs. John, 280

Camp David, 45–50

Camp David Accords, 48–49

Canizares, Don José de, 16

Cape Neddick Lighthouse, 316, 318

Carpetbaggers, 22

Carter, Jimmy, 48

Cartwright, Samuel, 10

Carver, George Washington, 379, 382–384

Castillo de San Marcos, 50–54

Catoctin Mountain Park, 50

CCC. *See* Civilian Conservation Corps (CCC)

Central, Virginia, 19–23

Central Pacific Railroad, 166–167

Chaffee, Roger, 26

Challenger disaster, 220

Chanute, Octave, 228

Charbonneau, Toussaint, 121, 138

Charles III (king of Spain), 99–100, 340

Charles W. Morgan (whaling ship), 54–58

Chestnutt, Jacob Joseph, 26

Chimney Rock, 368

Chinese Exclusion Act of 1882, 18, 266

Christy, Robert, 263

Chrysler Corporation, 190

Churchill, Winston S., 46–47

Civilian Conservation Corps (CCC), 45, 156

Civil Rights Act of 1964, 257–258

Civil rights legislation, 156

Civil rights monuments. *See also* African-American monuments

  Little Rock Central High School, 250–254

  Lorraine Motel, 255–259

  Rankin House, 319–324

Civil War monuments. *See also* Military monuments; War monuments

  Appomattox Court House, 19–23

  Arlington National Cemetery, 23–28

  Ford's Theatre, 113–119

  Fort McHenry, 141–146

  Fort Sumter, 150–153

  Gettysburg Battlefield, 162–165

  Harpers Ferry, 171–176

  Lincoln Memorial, 241–245

  Stone Mountain Memorial, 354–358

Claiborne, William (Billy), 299

Clanton, Joseph Isaac (Ike), 299, 301

Clanton, William (Billy), 299

Clark, Jim, 257

Clark, William, 119–124, 136–141

Classic Natchez (Delahanty and Martin), 278

Clatsop people, 121

Cleveland, Grover, 101, 205, 353

Clinton, Bill, 9, 49, 254, 324, 415

Clinton, Sir Henry, 395, 444–446

Cody, William "Buffalo Bill," 312–313

Colonial monuments

  Benjaming Franklin National Memorial, 34–37

  Castillo San Marcos, 50–54

  Ethan Allen Homestead, 108–112

  Fort Raleigh, 147–150

  Jamestown, 207–211

  Plymouth Rock, 305–310

  Salem Witch Trials Memorial, 335–340

  San Carlos Borromeo Mission, 340–344

  Trinity Church, 374–378

Colorado River, 192

Concord, Battle of, 240

Condon, Edward, 262

Confederate Memorial, 354–358

Connally, John B., 72

Connor, Eugene "Bull," 256, 259

Constitution of the United States

  Fifteenth Amendment, 423

  Fourteenth Amendment, 423

Continental glaciation, theory of, 223

Continental shelves, 39

Cook, James, 203

Cook, Marlo, 33

Coolidge, Calvin, 292, 367, 431, 434

Cornwallis, Lord Charles, 443–446

Coronado, Don Francesco Vasques de, 133

Corps of Discovery, 62, 136–141, 159. *See also* Lewis and Clark expedition
Cotton gin, 10, 277
Courthouse Rock, 368
Cox, Archibald, 413
Cox, James, 154
Crawford, J., 151
Crazy Horse (chief), 246, 428
Creationists, 329–330
Crockett, David (Davy), 3
Crook, George, 21, 25, 247
Cuba, 100–101
Cumberland Gap, 58–63
Cumberland Gap National Park, 59
Cunningham Falls State Park, 50
Custer, George Armstrong, 246, 247–249
Custer National Cemetery, 250
Custer's Last Stand. *See* Little Bighorn, Battle of
Custis, George Washington Parke, 24
Custis, Mary Anna Randolph, 24, 25, 28

D

Daley, Richard J., 258
Daniel Freeman Homestead, 65–71
Dare, Virginia, 149
Darrow, Clarence Seward, 326–329
Darwin, Charles, 325
Daughters of the American Revolution, 245
Daughters of the Republic of Texas, 5
Davids, Tice, 321
Davies, Marion, 186
Davis, Elizabeth and George Malin, 279–280
Davis, Isaac, 240
Davis, Jefferson, 151, 152, 354, 355, 358
Dawes, William, 239
Dealey Plaza, 71–76
Dean, John, 413–414
Deane, Silas, 37

Declaration of Independence (United States), 36–37, 240
Declaration of Sentiments (women's rights), 421, 424
Delehanty, Randolph, 278
Delta Queen, 33
Desegregation, 250–254
Desert Land Act of 1877, 70
Dickson, William Kennedy Laurie, 92
Dinosaur Ride, 76–81
Dinosaurs, 77–78
Disasters, monuments to
    Alfred P. Murrah Federal Building, 5–9
    Dealey Plaza, 71–76
    Donner Pass, 81–85
    Pan American Bombing Memorial, 26
    Space Shuttle Challenger Memorial, 26–27
Dixie Highway, 62
Dole, Bob and Elizabeth, 415
Dole, Sanford, 205
Donner Memorial State Park, 81
Donner Party, 81–85
Donner Pass, 81–85
Doran, John, 331
Douglas, Stephen A., 117
Douglas, William, 26
Douglass, Frederick, 422–423
Downie, Harry, 343–344
Drake, Sir Francis, 15, 147–148
Draper, Ira, 10
Dred Scott v. *Sanford* (1857), 171
Driscoll, Clara, 4–5
Drumlins, 224–225
Du Bois, William Edward Burghrdt, 381
Dust Bowl, 415–416

E

Earp, Morgan, 299–302
Earp, Virgil, 299–302
Earp, Wyatt, 299–302
Edison, Thomas Alva, 87–92
Edison Laboratories, 87–92
Effigy Mounds, 92–97
Effigy Mounds National Monument, 94, 97

Eggers, Otto R., 212, 213
Eiffel, Alexandre-Gustave, 351
1812, War of, 141–145
Einstein, Albert, 261
Eisele, Donn, 26
Eisenhower, David, 47
Eisenhower, Dwight David
    and Camp David, 47
    and Korean War, 235
    and Little Rock Central High School, 251, 253
    and NASA, 218
Elizabeth I (queen of England and Ireland), 147, 207, 209
Ellis Island, 102–107
El Morro Fortress, 98–102
Emerson, Ralph Waldo, 240
Emigrants' Guide to Oregon and California (Hastings), 81
Emigrant Trail Museum, 85
End moraines, 224
Engle, George, 179
Equal Rights Amendment, 424
Erlichman, John, 413
Erratics, 224
Eskimo Indians, 43
Ethan Allen Homestead, 108–112
Evans, Rudolph, 214
Evolution, theory of, 325–326

F

Factory system, 10
Fair Labor Standards Act of 1938, 156
Fall, Albert B., 366
Farm Security Administration, 415, 417, 418
Faubus, Orval, 250, 252–254
Federal Emergency Relief Act of 1933, 155–156
Federation of Organized Trades and Labor Unions, 176–177
Feminist monuments, and Wesleyan Chapel, 419–425
Fermi, Enrico, 262
Fielden, Samuel, 179, 180
Fifteenth Amendment (United States), 423

First Continental Congress, 199, 238
Fischer, Adolph, 179
Fitch, John, 31
Flying shuttle, 10
Footprints, fossil, 80
Ford, Gerald, 48, 270
Ford, Henry, 187–190
Ford Motor Company, 187–191
Ford's Theatre, 113–119
Forsyth, John, 151
Fort Abanico, 100
Fort Boone, 61
Fort Clatsop, 119–125, 140
Fort Delaware, 125–129
Fort El Canuelo, 100
Fortier, Michael, 9
Fort John. *See* Fort Laramie
Fort Laramie, 129–132
Fort Laramie Treaty of 1868, 131
Fort Larned, 132–136
Fort McHenry, 141–147
Fort Mandan, 136–141
Fort Marion, 54. *See also* Castillo de San Marcos
Fort Matanzas, 51
Fort McDowell (Angel Island, California), 16–17
Fort Mose, 51–52
Fort Raleigh, 147–150
Fort Sumter, 150–153
Fort Ticonderoga, 109
Fort Whetstone. *See* Fort McHenry
Fossil footprints, 80
Foster, John G., 128–129
Fourteenth Amendment (United States), 423
Fowler, Jacob, 135
Franklin, Benjamin, 34–37, 199, 394
Franklin Delano Roosevelt Memorial, 154–158
Franklin Institute Science Museum, 34
Fraser, James Earle, 34
Freedman's Village, 24–25
Freeman, Daniel, 65–66
Freeman School, 65
French, Daniel Chester, 31, 243–244
Fugitive Slave Act, 171–172, 320, 322

Fulton, Robert, 31
Fundamentalist Christians, 325–326

G

Gage, Matilda Joslyn, 423
Gage, Thomas, 238
Gandhi, Mohandas Karmchand, 255
Garrison, William Lloyd, 324
Gary, Joseph E., 179
Gateway Arch, 159–162
Gemini program, 219
General Motors, 190
George Greenman & Co., 58
Germantown, Battle of, 391
Geronimo, 25, 428
Gettysburg Address, 165, 245
Gettysburg Battlefield, 162–165
Ghent, Treaty of, 146
Ghost Dance religion, 438–439
Gibbon, John Oliver, 247–249
Gibson, John Michael, 26
Gilbert, Sir Humphrey, 147
Gilded Age, 396–397
Glaciers, 222–226
Glenmont, 92
Glenn, Hugh, 135
Glenn, John H., 219
Goat Island Lighthouse, 316–317
Golden Spike National Historic Site, 165–169
Goodacre, Glenna, 406
Gorbachev, Mikhail, 49
Gordon, John, 20
Gore, Al, 5
Gorsage, J. Herod, 33
Graham, Edith, 273
Grant, Ulysses Simpson, 19, 22, 113, 249
Grapes of Wrath, The (Steinbeck), 419
Graves, John, 355
Great Bear Mound, 94
Great Depression monuments, and Weedpatch Camp, 415–419
Great Sioux War of 1876–1877, 131

Greeley, Horace, 67
Green, Ernest, 253
Greene, Nathanael, 393, 394, 444
Green Mountain Boys, 109–110
Grenet, Hugo, 4
Grissom, Virgil (Gus), 219
Ground moraines, 224
Groves, Leslie, 261, 263
Guadalupe Hidalgo, Treaty of, 4
Guthrie, Woody, 419

H

Haldeman, H. R., 413
Hamilton, Alexander, 199, 447
Hancock, John, 239
Handel, George Frideric, 378
Harding, Warren G., 244, 365, 366, 367
Hargreaves, James, 10
Harpers Ferry, 171–176
Harriot, Thomas, 148–149
Harris, Lillian, 26
Harrison, Burton H., 128
Harrison, William Henry, 371–372
Hart, Frederick, 406
Haslam, "Pony Bob," 312
Hastings, Lansford Warren, 81
Hayes, Rutherford B., 23
Haymarket Square, 176–181
Hays, Brooks, 252, 254
Hearst, William Randolph, 182
Hearst Castle, 181–186
Heisenberg, Werner, 260
Hemings, Sally, 289–290
Henderson, Richard, 60–61
Henry, Patrick, 199
Herold, David, 114–115
Hi-Catoctin, Camp, 45–46
Higgins, Daniel P., 212, 213
Higgins, Marguerite, 26
Highland Park Ford Plant, 187–191
Historic houses
   Hearst Castle, 181–186
   Iolani Palace, 201–206
   Melrose Estate, 275–280
   Monticello, 286–290
   Mount Vernon, 295–298

Rankin House, 319–324
Vanderbilt Mansion, 396–401
The White House, 430–434
Historic Shrine, 146
History of Plymouth (Thatcher),
305–306
Hoban, James, 430
Holliday, John Henry (Doc),
299–302
Homestead Act, 65, 67–68, 71
Homestead National Monu-
ment, 66
Honest Creek Treaty, 131
Hoover, Herbert, 155
Hoover Dam, 191–196
Hopkins, Juliet, 26
Hopper, Grace Murray, 26
Howard, Oliver, 427, 429
Howe, Julia Ward, 423
Howe, Sir William, 391, 395
Hughes, Charles Evans, 183
Hughes, Sarah T., 73
Hunt, E. Howard, 412
Hunt, Richard Morris, 401
Hussein I (king of Jordan), 274

I

Iacocca, Lee, 353
Ice Age, 38–40, 222–223
Ickes, Harold, 245
Idlewild. See *Belle of Louisville*
Illinois Labor History
Society, 181
Immigration, early American
policy of, 102–107
Immigration Act of 1924, 266
Immigration monuments
Angel Island Immigration
Station, 14–19
Ellis Island, 102–107
Statue of Liberty, 349–354
Independence Hall, 197–201
Indian monuments. *See* Native
American monuments
Indian Wars, 441
Individual rights, 419–420
Industrial monuments
Amoskeag Mills, 10–14
Highland Park Ford Plant,
187–191
Industrial Revolution, 10

Integration, 252–254
Interlobate moraines, 224
International Space Station
(ISS), 221
Iolani Palace, 201–206
Issei, 266
Iwo Jima Memorial, 27
IWPA (International Working
People's Association),
177–178

J

Jackson, Andrew, 145
Jackson, Thomas J. "Stonewall,"
354, 355, 358
Jail Rock, 368
James, Daniel "Chappie," Jr., 25
James, Jesse, 314
James I (king of Scotland and
England), 208, 211
Jamestown, Virginia, 207–211
Japan, and attack on Pearl Har-
bor, 385–387
Jefferson, Thomas, 36
and Declaration of Indepen-
dence, 240
and founding of Washington,
D.C., 430
and Lewis and Clark expedi-
tion, 119–120, 136–137
and Louisiana Purchase,
161–162, 346
and Monticello, 286–290
and Mount Rushmore,
291, 293
and USS *Chesapeake* inci-
dent, 143
Jefferson Memorial, 211–215
Jefferson National Expansion
Memorial, 159
Jesse James house (St. Joseph,
Missouri), 314
John F. Kennedy Space Center
(KSC), 217–221
John Paul II, Pope, 344
Johnson, Andrew, 22, 115, 408
Johnson, Lady Bird, 48
Johnson, Lyndon B.
and Camp David, 48
and designation of Ellis Island as part of Statue of

Liberty National Monu-
ment, 107, 353
and Kennedy assassination,
72–73
and Vietnam War, 404
Johnson, William, 280
Johnston, Joseph, 20, 22
John XXIII, Pope, 344
Jones, Thomas Hudson, 28
Joseph (chief), 425–429
Joseph the Elder (chief), 427
Judah, Theodore, 166

K

Kaahumanu (queen of
Hawaii), 203
Kahn, Albert, 189
Kalakaua (king of Hawaii),
201–204
Kamehameha I (king of
Hawaii), 202–203
Kamehameha II (king of
Hawaii), 203
Kansas-Nebraska Act,
171–172
Kay, John, 10
Keelboats, 31
Keetley, Jack, 312
Kelly, George and Ethel, 280
Kennedy, John F.
assassination, 71–74
burial at Arlington National
Cemetery, 26
and Camp David, 47
designated Russell Cave as
monument, 330, 331
and Vietnam War, 404
Kentucky, 111
Kentucky Derby, 33
Kettle Moraine, 222–226
Kettles, 224
Key, Francis Scott, 144
Kill Devil Hills (North Car-
olina), 226, 228,
230–231
Kimball, Fiske, 212
Kim Il Sung, 233
King, Martin Luther, Jr., 245,
255–259, 410
Kitty Hawk (North Carolina),
150, 226–231

Kivas, 283, 286
Kleindienst, Richard, 413
Knights of Labor, 176
Knox, Frank, 266
Konopinski, Emil, 261
Korea, North, 232–235
Korea, South, 232–235
Korean War Veterans Memorial, 231–236
Koresh, David, 8
Kosciuszko, Thaddeus, 214
Krushchev, Nikita S., 47
Ku Klux Klan, 22

L

Labor monuments, and Haymarket Square, 176–181
Labor movement, and Haymarket Square riot, 176–181
Laboulaye, Édouard-Rene Lefebvre de, 350
Lafayette, Marquis de, 394, 444–445
Land run of 1893, 70–71
Lange, Dorothea, 419
Langley, Samuel, 227
La Salle, Sieur de, 347
Laurentide Ice Sheet, 223
Lazarus, Emma, 352
League of Women Voters, 424
Leale, Charles A., 114
Lee, Arthur, 37
Lee, Custis, 25
Lee, Fitzhugh, 20
Lee, Robert E., 113, 242
  and Appomattox Court House, 19–23
  and Arlington National Cemetery, 24–25, 28
  and Battle of Gettysburg, 163–164
  and John Brown attack at Harpers Ferry, 174–175
  and Stone Mountain Memorial, 354–355, 358
Lend-Lease, 156–157
L'Enfant, Pierre Charles, 430
Lenz, Mike, 8
Levy, Jefferson M., 290
Levy, Uriah P., 290
Lewinsky, Monica, 415

Lewis, Meriwether, 119–124, 136–141
Lewis and Clark expedition. *See also* Corps of Discovery
  at Fort Clatsop, 119–124
  Nez Percé and, 426
Lexington, Battle of, 237, 240, 241
Lexington Green, 237–241
Liberty Bell, 197–198
Liddy, G. Gordon, 412
Light bulb, invention of, 90
Lighthouses, 314–318
Liliuokalani (queen of Hawaii), 202, 204
Lin, Maya Ying, 402
Lincoln, Abraham, 22, 23, 26, 200, 408
  Ford's Theatre and, 113–119
  Gettysburg Address and, 165
  Homestead Act and, 67
  meeting with Harriet Beecher Stowe, 324
  Mount Rushmore and, 291, 293
Lincoln, Mary Todd, 113, 116, 118
Lincoln, Robert Todd, 244
Lincoln Memorial, 241–245
Lingg, Louis, 179, 180
Lister, Sir Joseph, 272
Little Bighorn, Battle of, 246–250
Little Bighorn Battlefield National Monument, 246–250
Little Rock Central High School, 250–254
Livingston, Robert R., 161, 162, 348
Long Barrack Museum, 5
Longfellow, Henry Wadsorth, 239
Lorraine Motel, 255–259
Los Alamos national laboratory, 259–264
Lost Colony. *See* Fort Raleigh
Louis, Joe, 26
Louisiana Purchase, 159–162, 346
Louisville, Kentucky, 29–33
Lowell, Massachusetts, 11
Lukeman, Augustus, 357

M

Maars, 43
McAddo, William Gibbs, 26
MacArthur, Douglas, 233–234
McAuliffe, Christa, 27
McClellan, George B., 117, 183
McCord, James W., Jr., 412–413
McGee, Anita, 26
McGovern, George, 412
McHenry, James, 141
McKinley, William, 101
McLaury, Robert Finley (Frank), 299, 301
McLaury, Thomas Clarke, 299
McLean, Wilmer and Virginia, 19, 22
McMurran, John Thompson and Mary Louisa, 277–279
McMurran, Mary Elizabeth, 279
McVeigh, Timothy, 9
Madison, Dolley, 431, 433
Madison, James, 199, 433
Magruder, Jeb, 413
Maine lighthouses, 314–318
Malcolmson, Andrew Y., 187
Manchester, New Hampshire Amoskeag Mills, 10–14
Manhattan Project, 259–263
Manley, John, 262
Mann, Woodrow, 252
Manzanar War Relocation Center, 265–271
Marble House (Newport, Rhode Island), 401
Marine Corp War Memorial, 27
Marine Historical Association, 55, 58
Marion, Francis, 54
Marshall, James, 358–360, 364
Marshall, John, 198
Marshall Gold Discovery State Historic Park, 364
Martin, Laurence, 8
Martin, Van Jones, 278
Marvin, Lee, 26
Massachusetts Bay Company, 309
Massasoit (chief of the Wampanoag), 308–309
Mather, Cotton, 336
Mayflower, 307

Mayflower Compact, 308
Mayo, Charles Horace, 271–274
Mayo, William James, 271–274
Mayo, William Worrall, 271–275
Mayo Clinic, 271–275
McMillan, 262
Meade, George G., 163
Mechanical loom, 19
Meigs, Montgomery C., 24
Melrose Estate, 275–280
Melville, Herman, 57
Memorial Institute for the Prevention of Terrorism, 7
Menn, Richard Joseph, 344
Mesa Verde, 281–286
Mesa Verde National Park, 285
Mesozoic era, 77–79
Mexican-American War, 4
Meyer, E. A., 33
Midwest, Wyoming, 368
Migrants' camps, 415–419
Miles, General Nelson, 429, 439–441
Military monuments. *See also* War monuments
    Castillo de San Marcos, 50–54
    El Morro Fortress, 98–102
    Fort Delaware, 125–129
    Fort Laramie, 129–132
    Fort Larned, 132–136
    Fort Mandan, 136–141
    Fort McHenry, 141–146
    Fort Sumter, 150–153
    Tippecanoe Battlefield, 369–374
Mill girls, 11
Mills, Robert, 407, 408
Mission San Antonio de Valero, 1
Mississippian civilizations, 93
Missouri Compromise of 1820, 171
Misty Mount, Camp, 45
Mitchell, John N., 412, 415
Miwok Indians, 15
M'Murtrie, Henry, 31
Moby-Dick (Melville), 57
Model A automobile, 191
Model T automobile, 187–191
Monroe, James, 161, 162, 348

Montgomery Bus Boycott, 255, 258
Monticello, 286–290
Moraines, 224
Morgan, Julia, 185
Moton, Robert, 244
Mott, Lucretia Coffin, 420
Mound Builders, 93–97
Mount Rushmore, 290–294
Mount Vernon, 295–298
Mudd, Samuel, 114, 115
My Lai massacre, 404
Mystic Seaport, Connecticut, 57–58

N

NAACP (National Association for the Advancement of Colored People), 252
    and *Brown v. Board of Education of Topeka, Kansas,* 251
    and Eleanor Roosevelt, 156
Narragansett Indians, 377–378
NASA (National Aeronautics and Space Administration), 217–221
Natchez, Mississippi, 275–277
Natchez National Historical Park, 275, 280
National Historic Preservation Act of 1966, 377
National Industrial Relations Act of 1933, 156
National Labor Relations Act of 1935, 156
National Origins Act of 1924, 107
National Park Service, 284
National Register of Historic Places, 377
National Research Council, 75
National Road, 62
National Trust for Historic Preservation, 348
National Underground Railroad Network to Freedom Act, 324
National Woman Suffrage Association (NWSA), 423

National Women's Hall of Fame, 425
National Women's Party, 423–424
Native American monuments
    Effigy Mounds, 92–97
    Little Bighorn Battlefield, 246–250
    Mesa Verde, 281–286
    White Bird Canyon, 425–430
    Wounded Knee, 438–442
Native Americans
    early presence of, 40–43
    Eskimo Indians, 43
    Narragansett Indians, 377–378
    Nez Percé tribe, 425–430
    Sacagawea, 128, 138, 139
    Sitting Bull, 246
    Woodland Indians, 369–371
Natural monuments
    Bering Land Bridge, 38–43
    Cumberland Gap, 58–63
    Dinosaur Ridge, 76–81
    Kettle Moraine, 222–226
    Russell Cave, 330–334
Neebe, Oscar, 179, 180
New Deal, 155–156
New Orleans, Battle of, 145
Newport, Christopher, 209
New St. Louis and Calhoun Packet Company, 33
Nez Percé National Historical Park, 430
Nez Percé tribe, 425–430
Nez Percé Wars, 425
Nichols, Terry, 9
Nineteenth Amendment to the U.S. Constitution, 424
Nisei, 266
Nixon, Richard M.
    and Camp David, 48
    and Vietnam War, 405
    and Watergate complex, 410, 412, 414
Nubble Island, Maine, 316

O

Obelisks, 408–409

O'Daly, Thomas, 98, 100
Oglethorpe, James Edward, 52
O.K. Corral (Tombstone, Arizona), 299–303
Okies, 416–418
Oklahoma City bombing, 5–9
Oklahoma City National Memorial, 9
Oklahoma City National Memorial Act, 9
Oklahoma City National Memorial Foundation, 6–7
Oklahoma City National Memorial Trust, 9
O'Laughlin, Michael, 115
Olson, Culbert L., 266
Onassis, Jacqueline Kennedy, 26, 71–73, 432
Onate, Don Juan de, 133–134
On the Origin of the Species By Means of Natural Selection (Darwin), 325
Oppenheimer, J. Robert, 259–262
Ord, Edward, 22
Oregon Trail, 368
O'Reilly, Alejandro, 98, 99
Ornithopods, 80
Osio, Antonio Maria, 16
Oswald, Lee Harvey, 74
Ott, John, 92

P

Paleontology, 77
Palmer-Epard cabin, 66
Pan American Bombing Memorial, 26
Paris, Treaty of, 102
Parker, John, 237, 239
Parks, Rosa, 255
Parsons, Albert, 178, 179
Pasteur, Louis, 272
Patee House (St. Joseph, Missouri), 314
Paul, Alice, 423, 424
Pea Patch Island, 125
Pearl Harbor, Hawaii, 385–390
Peltier, Leonard, 442
Peralta, Don Pedro de, 134
Petersen, William, 114

Philadelphia, Pennsylvania
Benjamin Franklin National Memorial, 34–37
Phillips, William, 444
Phonograph, invention of, 90–91
Pickens, Francis W., 151
Pickett, George E., 20, 164
Pickett's Charge, 164–165
Pierce, Franklin, 171
Pike, Zebulon, 134
Pikes Peak Stables, 310, 313
Pilgrim Memorial State Park, 310
Pilgrims, 305–310
Pinckney Treaty of 1795, 346–347
Pineda, Alonso Alvarez de, 347
Pirogues, 30
Plane, C. Helen, 355–356
Plessy v. *Ferguson* (1896), 251
Plymouth Colony, 305–310
Plymouth Rock, 305–310
Pony Express, 310–314
Pony Express Stables, 310–314
Pope, Franklin L., 90
Pope, John Russel, 212–213, 243
Portland, Maine, 314–315
Portland Head Lighthouse, 314–315
Portolá, Gaspar de, 15
Portsmouth, New Hampshire, 315
Powell, Lewis (Paine), 115
Preis, Alfred, 389
Presbytère, 344, 349
Presidential monuments
Camp David, 45–50
Dealy Plaza, 71–78
Ford's Theatre, 113–119
Franklin Delano Roosevelt Memorial, 154–158
Jefferson Memorial, 211–215
Lincoln Memorial, 241–245
Monticello, 286–290
Mount Rushmore, 290–294
Mount Vernon, 295–298
Washington Monument, 407–410
Process in Flying Machines (Chanute), 228
Project Mercury, 219

Prophet, 371–373
Prophetstown, Indiana, 371–372
Public Works Administration (WPA), 156
Pueblo people, 286
Puerto Rico, 100–102
Pulitzer, Joseph, 183, 352
Puritans, 374–375
Putnam, Israel, 238

Q

Quota Laws of 1921, 107

R

Railroads, 165–169
Railroad travel, 32
Rainey, Barbara, 26
Raleigh, Sir Walter, 147–148, 207
Rankin, John, 320, 322–323
Ranking House, 319–324
Rathbone, Henry Reed, 113
Ray, James Earl, 258
Reagan, Nancy, 432
Reagan, Ronald, 49
Ream, Vinnie, 26, 243
Recessional moraines, 224
Reclamation Act, 191–192
Reno, Janet, 8
Reno, Marcus A., 247–249
Reptiles, Age of, 77–79
Resettlement Administration, 156
Revere, Paul, 237, 238–239
Rhea County courthouse, 325–330
Rhee, Syngman, 233
Richardson, Elliot, 413
Ridgway, Matthew B., 234
Ridley, Oscar, 331
Ringo, John Peter, 302
Ring spinning, 10
Riverboats, 29–33
Roanoke Island, 147, 207–208, 305
Roanoke Island Historical Association, 149–150

Robinson, Doane, 291–292
Rochambeau, Jean Baptiste de, 445–447
Roman, A. B., 151
Roosevelt, Eleanor, 154, 156, 158, 245, 367
Roosevelt, Franklin Delano, 71, 261, 434
 and Camp David, 45–47
 and Executive Order 9066, 267
 and Jefferson Memorial, 212–213
Roosevelt, Theodore, Jr., 191, 291, 293, 367, 431, 434
Rumsey, James, 31
Russell, Thomas, 331
Russell Cave, 330–334
Rustin, Bayard, 255

S

Saarinen, Eero, 159
Sacagawea, 121, 138, 139
Sadat, Anwar, 48
Saint Augustine, Florida, 50–54
Salem Witch Trials Memorial, 335–340
San Buenaventura Olivares, Antonio de, 1
San Carlos Borromeo Mission, 340–344
San Cristobal, Castle of, 100
San Francisco Bay, California, 14–19
San Il de Fonso, Treaty of, 161
San Juan National Historic Site, 98
Santa Anna, Antonio López de, 1, 3–4
Sante Fe Trail, 132–135
Saturn/Apollo program, 219–220
Scandals, 413
Scandals
 Teapot Dome Oil Reserve, 365–368
 Watergate complex, 410–415
Schwab, Michael, 179, 180
Scientific and technology monuments
 Edison Laboratories, 87–92

Hoover Dam, 191–196
John F. Kennedy Space Center, 217–221
Kitty Hawk, 222–226
Los Alamos National Laboratory, 259–264
Mayo Clinic, 271–275
Rhea County Courthouse, 325–330
Tuskegee Institute, 378–384
Scopes, John T., 326, 329
Scopes Monkey Trial, 325–330
Scopes Trial Museum, 330
Second Continental Congress, 199, 240
Self-acting temple, 10
Seneca Falls Convention. *See* Women's Rights Convention (1848)
Serber, Robert, 262
Serpent Mound, 94
Serra, Padre Junipero, 340–343
Seward, William Henry, 115, 151
Shepherd, Alan B., 219
Sheridan, Philip H., 20–21
Sherman, Roger, 199
Sherman, William Tecumseh, 19–20, 22, 129
Shivers, Allen, 252
Shreve, Henry Miller, 31–32
Shuttle program, 220–221
Sickles, Daniel, 26
Sioux War of 1876, 246
Sirica, John, 412
Sitting Bull (chief), 246, 428, 439
Sixth Floor Museum, 71, 75
Skylab program, 220
Slater, Samuel, 10
Slavery, 319–320
Slidell, John, 4
Smith, Al, 367
Smith, Edmund Kirby, 22
Smith, John, 208–210
Social Security Act of 1935, 156
Soto, Hernando de, 97, 347
Southern Christian Leadership Conference, 256
Space Shuttle Challenger Memorial, 26–27
Space Transportation System (STS), 220

Spain, 98–101
Spangler, Edman, 115
Spanish-American War, 101–102, 183
Speedwell, 307
Spies, August, 178, 179, 181
Spinning jenny, 10
Squanto, 308
Stamp Act, 36
Stanton, Edwin M., 118–119, 244
Stanton, Elizabeth Cady, 420, 421, 422, 423
Statue of Liberty, 102, 349–354
Steamboats, 29–33
Steinbeck, John, 418, 419
Steuben, Friedrich Wilhelm von, 394, 395–396, 445
Stone, Lucy, 423
Stone Mountain Memorial, 354–358
Stowe, Harriet Beecher, 322, 323–324
Strauss, Levi, 363
Striations, 224
Student Nonviolent Coordinating Committee (SNCC), 256
Suez Canal, 168
Sunset Labor Camp, 419. *See also* Weedpatch Camp
Superposition, Law of, 77
Surgery, 272
Sutter, John, 358–360, 363–364
Sutter's Fort, 359, 364
Sutter's Mill, 358–364

T

Taft, Charles S., 114
Taft, William Howard, 26, 244
Taylor, Frederick, 190
Taylor, Richard, 22
Teapot Dome Oil Reserve, 365–368
Teapot Rock, 367–368
Technology monuments. *See* Scientific and technology monuments
Tecumseh, 371–373

Telegraph, 89
Teller, Edward, 261, 262
Terminal moraines, 224
Terry, Alfred Howe, 247–249
Tet Offensive, 404
Texas monuments, and the
    Alamo, 1–5
Texas Revolution, 2–5
Textile industry, emergence of,
    in United States, 10–11
Thatcher, James, 305–306
Thatcher, Margaret, 49
Therapods, 80
Thomas, Cyrus, 97
Thomas Jefferson Memorial,
    211–215
Thorp, John, 10
Three Servicemen statue, 406
Thurston, Lorrin, 204, 205
Tilden, Samuel J., 22
Till, 224
Timber Culture Act of 1873, 70
Time-and-motion studies, 190
Tippecanoe Battlefield,
    368–374
Tipton, John, 373–374
Tocqueville, Alexis de, 32
Tolman, Richard, 261
Tomb of the Unknowns, 27–28
Tombstone, Arizona, 299,
    302–303
Tombstone Courthouse State
    Historic Park, 303
Tonkin Resolution, Gulf of, 404
Trace fossils, 76, 80
Transportation monuments
    Belle of Louisville steamboat,
        29–33
    Charles W. Morgan whaling
        ship, 54–58
    Golden Spike National His-
        toric Site, 165–169
    Highland Park Ford Plant,
        187–191
    Kitty Hawk, 222–226
    Pony Express Stables,
        310–314
    Portland Head Lighthouse,
        314–318
Transylvania Company, 61
Travis, William Barret, 1, 3
Trinity Church (Newport,
    Rhode Island), 374–378

Tri-State Ferry Company,
    32–33
Truman, Harry S, 47,
    233–234, 432
Truth, Sojourner, 324
Tubman, Harriet, 324
Tuskegee Institute, 378–384
Twain, Mark, 29
Tyler, John, 4, 372

U

Uncle Tom's Cabin
    (Stowe), 322
Underground Railroad,
    319–324
Union Pacific Railroad,
    166–167
United States
    Chinese immigration to,
        17–19
    emergence of textile industry
        in, 10–11
U.S. Constitution, 199–200
USS *Arizona* Memorial,
    385–390
USS *Chesapeake*, 143
USS *Maine*, 101

V

Valley Forge, 391–396
Van Buren, Martin, 372
Vanderbilt, Cornelius, II, 401
Vanderbilt, Frederick William,
    396, 398–399, 401
Vanderbilt, George Washing-
    ton, 401
Vanderbilt, William K., 401
Vanderbilt Mansion, 396–401
Van Fleet, James, 234
Van Vleck, John, 261
Vargas, Don Diego de, 134
Varnum, General James, 393
Vermont, 111
Vertical integration, 190
Vietnam Veterans Memorial,
    401–406
Vietnam War, 404–406
Virginia Capes, Battle
    of the, 447

Virginia Company of London,
    208–210, 305, 306
Virginia House of Burgesses,
    207, 210
Voting Rights Act of 1965,
    257–258

W

Waco siege, 8
Waldo, Albigence, 392
Walker, Elroy P., 152
Walker, Thomas, 58–59
"Wall, the." *See* Vietnam Veter-
    ans Memorial
Wall of History (the Alamo), 5
War monuments. *See also* Mili-
    tary monuments
    Arlington National Ceme-
        tery, 23–28
    Korean War Veterans Memo-
        rial, 231–236
    USS *Arizona* Memorial,
        385–390
    Valley Forge, 391–396
    Vietnam Veterans Memorial,
        401–406
War Relocation Authority
    (WRA), 268
Warren, Earl, 74, 266
Warren, Whitney, 399
Warren Commission, 74
Washington, Booker T.,
    379–383
Washington, George, 28
    appointed commander in
        chief of Continental
        Army, 240
    and First Continental Con-
        gress, 199
    and location of Washington
        D.C., 430
    and Mount Rushmore, 291,
        293, 294
    and Mount Vernon,
        295–298, 314, 378
    at Valley Forge, 391–396
    at Yorktown, 443–447
Washington Monument,
    407–410
Washington-on-the-Brazos con-
    vention, 2

Watergate complex, 410–415
Watie, Stand, 22
Wayne, General Anthony, 445
Weedpatch Camp, 415–419
Weinman, A. A., 214
Weiss, Alexander, 19
Wesleyan Chapel, 419–425
West Memphis Packet Company, 32
Westwart Expansion, Museum of, 159
Whaling Enshrined, Inc., 55
Whaling industry, 54–58
Whig party, 372
White, John, 148–149
White, Stanford, 399
White Bird Canyon, 425–430
White House, 430–434
Whitman, Narcissa and Marcus, 435–437
Whitman Mission, 435–438
Whitney, Eli, 10, 277
Wiesel, Elie, 340
Wilderness Road, 62
Wilkes, Charles, 26
Wilkinson, James, 134
William Johnson House, 280
Williams, Roger, 375–378

Williamsburg, Virginia, 211
Wilson, Woodrow, 154, 184, 284, 365
Windrim, John T., 34
Winthrop, John, 309
Wisconsinan glacial period, 40, 222–223
Witch-hunting, 335–340
Women in Military Service for America Memorial, 27
Women's movement, 419–425
Women's Rights Convention (1848), 419, 421
Women's rights monuments, and Wesleyan Chapel, 419–425
Women's Rights National Historical Park, 419, 424–425
Woodland Indians, 369–371
Woods, John, 331
Woods, Rose Mary, 414, 415
Woodward, Bob, 412
Works Progress Administration (WPA), 45, 156
World War II monuments
Manzanar War Relocation Center, 265–271
Wounded Knee, 438–442

WPA. *See* Works Progress Administration (WPA)
Wren, Christopher, 378
Wrentmore, Ernest, 25
Wright, Frank Lloyd, 212
Wright, Martha Coffin, 420
Wright, Orville, 150, 226, 227–231
Wright, Wilbur, 150, 227–231
Wright Brothers National Memorial, 227

Y

Yamamoto, Isoruko, 386
Yellow journalism, 183
Yorktown, Battle of, 443–447
Yorktown, Virginia, 443–448

Z

Zapruder, Abraham, 75
Zavala, Adina de, 4–5
Zavala, Lorenzo de, 4